BRUCE CATTON
THE COMING FURY

"Catton has a rare felicity for entertaining the buffs while enticing the tyro. A clear, clean writer, he is also a gentle one: few villains appear in his books—only humans, tossed by events. . . ."   —*Time Magazine*

"No historian writing in America today equals Catton in his sense of timing, his use of essential minor details, his ability to ensure reader participation. . . . This is history at its best."
                    —*The Kirkus Reviews*

". . . a wonderful book that should be required reading. . . . Catton writes history with the vigor, flair, grace and charm of fiction. He takes no liberties with facts, but he does not miss the picturesque incident, the telling speech, the heroic action. History the Catton way is history the very finest way."   —*The Detroit News*

Books by Bruce Catton

Published by POCKET BOOKS

Bruce Catton

THE COMING FURY

PUBLISHED BY POCKET BOOKS NEW YORK

**POCKET BOOKS, a Simon & Schuster division of
GULF & WESTERN CORPORATION
1230 Avenue of the Americas, New York, N.Y. 10020**

Copyright © 1961 by Bruce Catton

Published by arrangement with Doubleday & Company, Inc.

All rights reserved, including the right to reproduce
this book or portions thereof in any form whatsoever.
For information address Doubleday & Company, Inc.,
245 Park Avenue, New York, N.Y. 10017

ISBN: 0-671-82445-7

First Pocket Books printing, April, 1967

20 19 18 17 16 15 14 13 12 11 10

Trademarks registered in the United States and other countries.

Printed in the U.S.A.

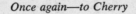

Once again—to Cherry

Foreword

THE CENTENNIAL HISTORY OF THE CIVIL WAR by Bruce Catton is a project begun in 1955 by Doubleday & Company, Inc., in conjunction with *The New York Times*. As originally planned, this is a three-volume work constituting a modern history, based on the fullest as well as the most recent research. The three volumes, which are entitled THE COMING FURY, TERRIBLE SWIFT SWORD, and NEVER CALL RETREAT, may be read and understood separately.

In the foreword of Volume One of the original publication of the work, Mr. Catton wrote of Mr. E. B. Long: "As Director of Research for this project he has made a more substantial contribution than it is possible to acknowledge properly." Mr. Catton also noted the "able assistance given by that indefatigable and charming person, Mrs. Barbara Long."

Contents

List of Maps
and Graphs

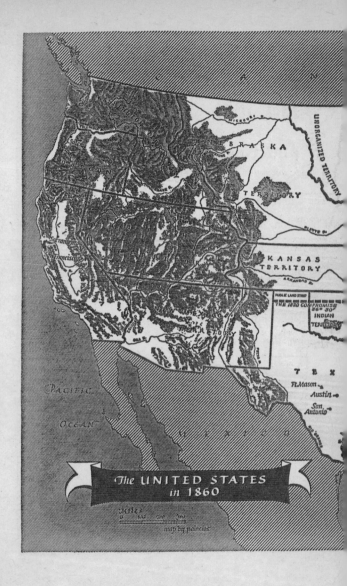

The UNITED STATES
in 1860

Miles
0   100   200   300

map by palacios

The Centennial History of the Civil War

VOLUME ONE

THE COMING FURY

CHAPTER ONE

Springtime of Decision

1. The City by the Sea

MR. YANCEY could usually be found at the Charleston Hotel, where the anti-Douglas forces were gathering, and a Northerner who went around to have a look at him reported that he was unexpectedly quiet and mild-mannered: as bland and as smooth as Fernando Wood, the silky Democratic boss from New York City, but radiating a general air of sincerity that Wood never had. No one, seeing Yancey in a room full of politicians, would pick him out as the one most likely to pull the cotton states into a revolution. He was compact and muscular, "with a square-built head and face, and an eye full of expression," a famous orator who scorned the usual tricks of oratory and spoke in an easy conversational style; he was said to have in his system a full three-hour speech against the Illinois Senator Stephen A. Douglas, to be unloaded at the proper time, and the Northern observer reflected uneasily that although Douglas probably had most of the votes at this convention, the opposition might be a little ahead in brains.[1]

William Lowndes Yancey was worth anybody's study. The Democratic party was convening in Charleston, South Carolina, in late April of 1860, to nominate a candidate for the presidency, and the future of the country perhaps depended on the way the convention acted. The delegates might look for a safe middle ground, and (finding what they sought) work out some sort of compromise that would avert a split in party and nation; or they might listen to the extremists, scorn the middle ground, and commit all of America to a dramatic leap into the dark. Yancey, who was called the Prince of Fire-Eaters, was ready for such a leap. This convention would indulge in no compromise if he could help it.

There was no secret about what Yancey wanted. More than

1

a decade earlier he had denounced "the foul spell of party which binds and divides and distracts the South," and had proclaimed the hope that someone would eventually break it—a task to which he was now devoting himself. He had asked his fellow Southerners whether "we have any hope of righting ourselves and doing justice to ourselves in the Union"; answering his question in the negative, he had said that he would work with those who did hope in the belief that eventually they would discover that nothing but secession would do.[2]

There was nobody quite like Yancey, and yet he was somehow typical: one of the men tossed up by the tormented decade of the 1850s (John Brown was another) who could help to bring catastrophe on but who could not do anything more than that. The mildness of his manner was deceptive; he had once had a great fight with his wife's uncle, and, in self-defense, had killed the man (a thing which proper Charlestonians still remembered), and while in Congress he had fought a famous although bloodless duel with a fellow Southerner. In his youth he had briefly brushed elbows with the crusading anti-slavery spirit which he now hated above all other things. Born in Georgia in 1814, he had been taken north while still a child when his widowed mother married a Presbyterian minister and moved to Troy, New York; and in this stepfather's church, in 1826, Charles Grandison Finney had preached at the beginning of the great revivalist campaign which was to spread abolitionism like a virulent infection (as Yancey would have said) all across the Middle West. Close friends of the stepfather, too, were such anti-slavery men as Theodore Weld and Lewis Tappan. None of this touched Yancey, however. He moved south, fell under the spell of John C. Calhoun, entered law, politics, and planter society (he married a rich planter's daughter), and in the mid-1840s entered Congress, where his first speech was an impassioned denial that Calhoun wanted or worked for disunion and an independent Southern Confederacy. What he disavowed for Calhoun, however, he presently accepted for himself; a great orator in a land that loved to listen to speeches, he eventually found in slave-state extremism a base to which his oratory could be solidly anchored. Over the years he had developed into the most fluent and persuasive of fire-eaters.[3]

Now he was busy among the delegates who were arriving for the convention. A disturbing sign, if any of Senator Douglas's men had noticed it, was the presence in the same hotel of Senator John Slidell, of Louisiana, who one day would make a famous trip to France; a hard-working, resolute man with thinning white hair over a cherry-red face, one who apparently enjoyed good health and good living; accepted here as spokesman and chief hatchet man for the administration of President James Buchanan, very busy among delegates from the deep South. It was whispered that Slidell ran the President—Buchanan, it was told, was "as wax in his fingers"—and though Buchanan had explicitly refused to seek or even to accept a renomination, he was deeply determined that the nomination should not go to Senator Douglas.[4]

Until the convention actually opened, the combinations and hazards and deeply laid schemes would be only partly visible. Yet during the last days before the convention opened—the chairman was to call the delegates to order on April 23—there hung in the air a sense that events here might not go according to routine. The mere fact that the delegates were meeting in Charleston, rather than in some other city, seemed to make a difference, and as the steamboats came up the harbor to the water front, the delegates from Northern states lined the rails to look about them with eager curiosity. For a generation, Charleston had been a symbol; now it was reality, seen for the first time, its horizons lost in the blue haze of wooded lowlands that enclosed the broad sparkling bay.

At first glance it looked familiar enough, a quiet American city of 40,000 people spread out on a flat peninsula between two rivers to face the sea, its slim white church spires seeming all the taller because land and houses all lay so close to the water level. Yet there was a strangeness here, as if Charleston were a stage set designed to remind outlanders that along this coast which had been stained by so much history, life had found a pattern unlike that which the rest of America knew. The shops seemed unexpectedly quaint, almost foreign, there were long rows of dwellings where delicate iron filigree of gateway and railing was outlined against pastel plasterwork, and there were mansions whose long piazzas with slim white pillars looked inward toward shaded courtyards, as if the people who owned and controlled this land proposed to remain aloof. There were palmettos in the streets, unfamiliar blossoms topped the garden walls and gleamed in the half-hidden lawns, and in the park along the Battery the twisted live oaks were dripping with Spanish moss. On the wharves there were crowds of wide-eyed colored folk, kept in order by "ferocious-looking policemen, mounted on rickety nags, wearing huge spurs, swords and old-fashioned pistols." The coaches and omnibuses that clattered down to the docks moved with a negligent, leisurely haste.

Early arrivals had time to make brief explorations, and most of them, no doubt, would have agreed with the Northerner who wrote that he was impressed by Charleston's "singular beauties." The most charming spot was the Battery, where upper-class folk rode disdainfully by in their carriages, and where one could see the town houses of wealthy planters, with columned streets going past toward the business center. Seaward there was Castle Pinckney on its low island, with Fort Sumter lying beyond at the gateway to the sea—Fort Sumter, an unfinished reality now, not yet an earth-moving abstraction, with a few workmen unhurriedly putting together bricks and stones in deep casemates; a place no one needed to give a second glance. Parts of Charleston looked almost French, for there was a strong Huguenot tradition here; other parts might have come straight from Georgian England, and like the English, the people of Charleston chose to follow certain picturesque customs from the old days. When an official proclamation was to be made, for instance, the sheriff in uniform and cocked hat would ride slowly down the street in an open carriage, with fife and drum to play him along and announce his magnificence, and he would stop at street corners to arise and read the proclamation at the top of his voice. Drums beat retreat at night and reveille in the morning to warn Negroes that they must be off the street during the hours of darkness unless their owners had provided them with tickets of leave.

This last point was of special interest to the men from the North. As Democrats, they were friendly to slavery (or at least they were willing to get along with it), but they rarely saw anything of it at first hand, and they knew very little about it, and one of the things an early arrival could do was see for himself what Negroes living in bondage were actually like.

The yoke seemed to be rather light in these parts. A newspaper correspondent from New York felt it his duty to attend services in a Negro church. Politely patronizing, he noted the strange folk who made up the congregation, the white-haired old men, the women in their turbans, the gay colors in all of the clothing, not overlooking "the flashily-dressed, coquettish-looking younger women"; and he was so moved by the singing that when the minister lined out the first words of a hymn—"Blow ye the trumpet, blow"—he confessed that he and all the other visitors joined in with enthusiasm, so that "if we didn't blow that trumpet then no trumpet was ever blown." He reported that many Northern visitors went to near-by plantations, where they poked about in the slave quarters, admired the white teeth of the girls and the tumbling and crawling of wide-eyed infants, and absorbed such impressions as twenty minutes would give them of the peculiar institution on its own ground. Their impressions were not unfavorable: "The darkies, so far as I have seen, both house servants and field hands, seem greatly attached to their masters and are apparently contented and happy." He added cautiously: "Whether that is anything in favor of the system or not is a question."[5]

Most of the delegates had already formed their opinions about the system. It was not properly a subject for debate here, because the Democratic party (whose orators liked to refer to it as the One and Indivisible Democracy) was supposed to be a unit on the question. The unity was partly a matter of tradition; in this party, and in this party alone, men of the North and men of the South could find a common rallying ground, not too greatly vexed by the rising agitation of the slavery issue. Partly, too, the unity came from external pressure, applied chiefly by the new Republican party of the North. The Republicans were hostile to slavery, and this spring they seemed very likely to nominate Senator William H. Seward, of New York, who had spoken darkly of an irrepressible conflict and whose election, if it should come to pass, might readily bring that conflict into being. The Democracy's task here was to name someone who could win the election over Black Republicans or any other divisive forces, and the man who had most of the votes was the one for whom Yancey and Slidell were digging a cunning pit—Senator Stephen A. Douglas, of Illinois.

Senator Douglas was a man about whom no one could be indifferent. He was either a remorseless scheming politician or a hero defending the eternal truth, the appraisal depending partly on the observer's point of view and partly on what Douglas himself was up to at the moment. As a scheming politician he had opened the door for the great tempest in Kansas and now he was standing in the wind's path, defying the storm and those who had made it; a man who could miscalculate disastrously but who would not under pressure run away from what he had done. Very few men either hated or admired him just a little. A passionate man himself, he evoked passion in others, in his friends and in his enemies.

In a party dominated by Southerners, he spoke for the muscular new Northwest—roughly, the area later generations would call the Middle West. A maker of odds would have considered him a likely winner. He was obviously the front runner, and while his managers had to find some way to push his majority up to the two-thirds mark, he did not seem to be opposed by anyone except a handful of favorite sons and the task should not be too hard. Douglas was not here himself, but his people had set up headquarters in Hibernian Hall, a block and a half from Institute Hall, where the convention would be held, and the place was packed and alive. There were scores of cots, so that no Douglas delegate need lack a place to sleep; there was an abundance of whisky on tap; and any visitor who lounged in and looked receptive was apt to find someone pressing a campaign biography of the Senator into his hand. The bubbling confidence of the Douglas leaders seemed to be justified.[6]

Yet there were disquieting omens. Of all the cities in America, the Democrats had chosen for this 1860 convention the one in which the climate for Senator Douglas's candidacy would be the least favorable. The city itself was not so much in active opposition as living on the edge of a different world; it simply was not a place where the great Northwest could find its proper voice. Douglas himself had declared, somewhat brashly, in the heat of debate, that this Northwest, the limitless new land above the rivers and beyond the mountains, would yet "be able to speak the law to this nation and to execute the law as spoken"; but was Charleston the place for it?

Although the Northwest did not yet know quite what it

would say, if indeed it should try to speak and execute any law, the one certainty was that if it found its voice it would speak for change—for adjustment to the irresistible pressures that were pulling America through the middle of the nineteenth century. This adjustment would come as a matter of course in the Northwest, where all things were fluid, but it would look like utter destruction in Charleston. Charleston was the past incarnate, the city that had forced time to stand still, carefully preserving a cherished way of life which had a fragile and immutable pattern, and it would listen to no demand for change. And although Charleston stood apart, it did not stand alone. Whatever there was in all the South which had to resist the pressures of the outside world would form its ranks here, vigilant to beat down anything that even looked like a concession to the demand for change. It would take an extreme position because no other position was left to it. The institution of chattel slavery on which it was based was broad but extremely delicate, and to touch it at all could cause the collapse of everything that rested on it. Hence it was forbidden even to admit that it might some day be necessary to touch it. On this point Douglas was dangerously unsound: his Freeport doctrine, which held that no conceivable safeguard of Federal laws could protect slavery in a territory where the people themselves wanted no slavery, was open and unforgivable heresy.[7]

So there were men in this convention who would fight Douglas without paying any heed to the cost of the fight, and they had the advantage which any completely determined minority has in a meeting where the majority would like to have harmony. They were ready to go to extremes. They would accept harmony if they could get it on their own terms, but otherwise they were perfectly ready to accept discord. Northern delegates who were coming in by train began to meet these men before they even reached Charleston.

Murat Halstead, the perceptive editor of the Cincinnati *Commercial,* was one who discovered the omens, and he warned his Ohio readers that a strong wind was blowing. From Atlanta he sent an account of a conversation in a day coach. A Georgia delegate, convention-bound, had announced loudly that Senator Douglas just would not do. If nominated, Douglas would probably get the delegate's vote, but it would be cast with great reluctance; the delegate knew of but one other man in his district who would vote for this man from Illinois. Another Georgian, present as an observer—he had been beaten in his own race for delegate—disagreed: Douglas men were as thick as blackberries in his part of the state, and if Douglas got the nomination he would carry Georgia by 20,000—"there will be such a war whoop as never was heard in the land." When someone protested that Douglas's famous doctrine of popular sovereignty was no better than rank abolitionism, this supporter said that he himself "went the whole of it," and he was backed by a delegate from Kentucky. But the delegate from Georgia said that the nominee must be someone who could unite the party, not a man who was obnoxious to a whole section: not, to be specific, Stephen A. Douglas, who had recently stood side by side with the Black Republicans themselves.

The Democracy unquestionably needed unity, but the unity might be hard to get. Halstead's train paused one evening at a station stop in Georgia to let the passengers get out for dinner, and at table two Mississippians broke out a bottle of whisky, passed it around, and offered a toast "to the health of the nominee." Did this, asked a man from Indiana (no doubt bristling a little), include Senator Douglas? Mississippi replied that it did not: Douglas was simply not in the running, and because he could not possibly be the nominee an offer to toast the nominee's health could not apply to him. Indiana thought this unfair, and said that if Douglas won the nomination he ought to have the support of a united party: delegates could not in honor go to the convention and then bolt the nominee if they did not like him. As an afterthought, the Northerner asked why Indiana did not have as much right to criticize Mississippi's Senator Jefferson Davis as Mississippi had to criticize Senator Douglas. One of the Mississippians retorted that the reason was simple: "Davis was a patriot and Douglas was a traitor, d——d little better than Seward— that was the difference." Indiana protested that Douglas and the Northern Democrats had been fighting the South's battles, but this helped not at all. The South, said a Mississippian, could fight her own battles and protect her own rights, and if she could not do this in the Union, she would do it outside of the Union. Halstead wrote that other delegates at the table shook their heads and muttered that the party was in for stormy times.[8]

So ran the talk on the trains. Reaching Charleston, many of the Douglas men tended to be quieter; the Little Giant had his enemies here, and there was no sense in stirring them up with loose talk. As convention time drew nearer, it seemed that the Douglas people were making headway. Three nights before the convention would open, the correspondent of the Richmond *Dispatch* was writing that "Douglas is hourly becoming less objectionable," and was explaining that personal antagonisms were subsiding and that the success of the party was the main object. The friends of Douglas, he said, were quietly meeting Southern delegates as they arrived and were trying to convince them that nothing but the nomination of Douglas would counter-balance the anticipated nomination of Seward at Chicago. As a clincher, there was the statement: Douglas was the only Democrat who could possibly win the fall election.[9]

It was a good argument, with men who thought victory in November important. There were 303 electoral votes, and a man who could get 152 of them would be the next President. If the party held its unity, the Democratic nominee should get 120 votes in the South and along the border; as of April 23 it seemed highly probable that Douglas could pick up the thirty-two additional votes in the North or in the Northwest no matter what the Republicans might do. No other Democrat could conceivably do as well. It was an open-and-shut case.

But the argument was worse than useless with men who wanted something else a great deal more than they wanted a Democratic victory in the fall, and although such men were in a small minority, they were working in Charleston with vast energy and singleness of purpose. These men, the all-out fire-eating secessionists, believed that they could get what they wanted if the party lost the election. Beyond the wrangling over platform and candidate they could see a completely new nation, an independent South embodying the most soaring dreams of the cotton empire, zealously preserving the peculiar institution and the complex values that rested on it. A beating in November might bring this to pass. Most Southerners were not yet ready to embrace secession, much as the business had been talked about in the past ten years, but the profound shock of a Black Republican victory would almost certainly make them ready. Such men as Yancey, who wanted to see this shock applied, refused even to talk about concessions or party unity.

Yet until the convention actually opened, none of this would come to a head and it was possible to accept this meeting in Charleston as just another political convention. On the surface that was what it looked like. Hotel lobbies had the aspect that hotel lobbies always have during political conventions. There were bands, striking up appropriate tunes at odd moments, and there were impromptu orators to address anyone who would listen. Most of the 4000 visitors, it was reported, hardly went to bed at all, which was not surprising, since the bedrooms were so crowded and the nights were so noisy, and there was a good deal of drunken rowdyism— most of it, as a Northerner admitted, contributed by "roughs from New York," whose delegation, led by smooth Fernando Wood, seemed prepared to be all things to all men, with special reference to the men who could offer the best deal. Everywhere there were the perennial political types, moving with dignity about the lobbies, lounging against veranda pillars and railings, being vocal and visible. There were men who seemed to have spent so much time in the public eye that merely being looked at had put its mark on them; there were cold-eyed operators who looked like professional gamblers, and there were stout, perspiring men in glossy black, wearing fine linen and stovepipe hats, carrying gold-headed canes, eternally busy with portentous whispered conversations with other men who looked exactly like them.[10]

Among those who could be seen in the lobbies were certain Northerners of whom the South would see much more, in the years just ahead. There was John Logan, of Illinois, with his thick, black hair and his piercing black eyes, his back against a veranda pillar, meditatively chewing tobacco; and there was another man from Illinois, John A. McClernand, with his bristly beard and his hawk-beaked face, watching the crowd and toying absently with his watch chain. Not least of the group was Benjamin Butler, of Massachusetts, bald-headed and cock-eyed, "with the little brown mustache under his sharp crooked nose"—Ben Butler, who could never forget the demands made by his soaring ambition, or the concessions that might have to be made to it, an unpredictable man who was known now as a firm friend of the South. Two years earlier Jefferson Davis had made a Fourth of July speech in the North, expressing love for the Union and deriding the chance that secessionists could do any lasting harm; Butler had liked the speech, and he was here as a fervent supporter of the Senator from Mississippi.

. . . Editor Halstead believed more and more strongly that the current was beginning to run the wrong way, as far as Senator Douglas's hopes were concerned. The Douglas men were confident, insisting that "the universal world is for the Little Giant," but there seemed to be no iron in them: Halstead felt that these Northwesterners were "not so stiff in their backs nor so strong in the faith" as the hard-core Southerners who wanted Douglas beaten. An Alabama delegate, doubtless strongly infected by Yancey-ism, explained the case to him. There was going to be a showdown; once and for all the South would find out whether Northern Democrats would stand squarely with the South on true Constitutional principles. Both platform and candidate would have to be explicit; "there must be no Douglas dodges—no double constructions —no janus-faced lying resolutions—no double-tongued and doubly damned trifling with the people." Of all Northern Democrats, said the Alabaman, Douglas was the most obnoxious to Southerners. His nomination would be an insult which the South would repay by defeating him in the election, no matter what it might cost.

The truth of the matter was that the American political system, which can survive almost any storm because of its admirable flexibility, was in 1860 breaking down because it had been allowed to become rigid. Senator Douglas's offense was that he had relied on the flexibility after it had ceased to exist. Finding America facing a sectional issue too hot to handle, he had proposed a subtle adjustment. Accept the obvious (he had said, in effect), admit that the people can always nullify an unpopular law by refusing to permit it to be enforced, and then give the territories, in respect to slavery, any law you choose; in the end the people will have things as they want them, in the meantime you will have the legislation you want, and, all in all, much argument and bitter feeling will be avoided. . . . It was the politician's recourse, one of the things that make democracy work; avert a crisis long enough and it often becomes manageable. The trouble now was that men increasingly wanted to meet the crisis, to have a final showdown no matter what it might cost.[11]

The situation had grown intolerable. What the delegates did at Charleston would be done in a hot twilight where nothing could be seen clearly and in which action of any sort might seem better than a continuation of the unendurable present. They acted under the shadow of things done earlier, at other places—in Congress, in Kansas, at Harper's Ferry— and they were ceasing to be free agents. A storm was rising, and there were leaders who proposed to meet it with stiff backs.

2. *"The Impending Crisis"*

IF THE Democratic convention was meeting in an irrational atmosphere, the reason is clear. During the last few years events themselves had been irrational; politics in America could no longer be wholly sane. Here and there, like flickers of angry light before a thunderstorm, there had been bursts of violence, and although political debate continued, the nearness of violence—the reality of it, the mounting threat that it would monstrously grow and drown out all voices— made the debaters shout more loudly and appeal more directly to emotions that made reasonable debate impossible. Men put special meaning on words and phrases, so that what sounded good to one sounded evil to another, and certain slogans took on their own significance and became portentous, streaming in the heated air like banners against the sunset; and even the voices that called for moderation became immoderate. American politicians in 1860 could do almost anything on earth except sit down and take a reasoned and dispassionate view of their situation.

Four months before the Charleston convention opened, the House of Representatives at Washington had tried to elect a speaker—a routine task, done every two years since the birth of the Republic, done ordinarily without jarring the foundations of the nation. Its furious inability to do this until it had exhausted itself by long weeks of argument, all legislative activities at a standstill, members coming armed to the sessions of an assembly intended for reasonable debate, was a clear sign that the democratic process had all but collapsed. It was both a symptom of trouble and a cause of more trouble. The fact that the row over the speakership seemed at last to center on the question of whether certain members had or had not read and admired a comparatively little-known book was the crowning touch of irrationality.

The first session of the Thirty-sixth Congress met in Washington on December 5, 1859, three days after John Brown had been hanged at Charlestown, Virginia—a fact not without influence on the proceedings of the House. The new Congress contained, on the House side, 109 Republicans and 101 Democrats, 13 of the Democrats being "anti-Lecompton" men, Northerners who had followed Senator Douglas in revolt against the Buchanan administration. There were also twenty-six members of the dying American party, the Know-Nothings, and, vestigial survival of a vanished era, one lone Whig. No party had a majority.[1] Even under the best of conditions there was bound to be a good deal of jockeying and in-fighting before a speaker could be named.

Conditions in the fall of 1859 were not of the best and they rapidly got a good deal worse. The first ballot showed the Democrats lining up behind Thomas S. Bocock of Virginia, with the Republicans backing John Sherman, of Ohio. Galusha Grow, of Pennsylvania, received forty-three votes and then withdrew, more than a score of ballots were listed as "scattering," and no one was elected. But before a second ballot could be cast, Representative J. B. Clark, of Missouri, came down into the well of the House with a resolution for members to consider . . . "resolved, that the doctrine and sentiments of a certain book, called 'The Impending Crisis of the South—How to Meet It,' purporting to have been written by one Hinton Helper, are insurrectionary and hostile to the domestic peace and tranquility of the country, and that no member of this House who has endorsed or recommended it or the Compend from it is fit to be Speaker of this House."[2]

That did it. The book was everything Mr. Clark said it was: in fact, it was a poor book written by a man notably lacking in balance. But from the time the Missouri Congressman dropped his resolution into the hopper, the House of Representatives became completely impotent. It could not elect a speaker, it could not get itself organized, it could not even vote the pay which its members needed so badly, until it had worn itself out in hot discussion of a book which, taken by itself, was hardly even of minor importance. The row to

which it gave birth settled nothing whatever. It simply registered (in terms that would be ratified in blood, a short time
thereafter) the appalling height the American political fever
had reached. The irrational had become wholly logical.

Hinton Rowan Helper was one more of those baffling people whose sole function, historically, seems to be to make
other men angry. He was a rarity, not to say a freak: a born-
and-bred Southerner who had become a violent lone-wolf
abolitionist, and who either advocated or at least appeared
to be advocating a Southern uprising against the planter
aristocracy. He believed that many things were wrong with
the South, he had assembled a great many figures (some of
them badly jumbled) to prove his point, and he argued that
all of these defects were the result of the slave system. Of
the slaveholders themselves, he suggested—"as a befitting
confession of their crimes and misdemeanors, and as a reasonable expiation for the countless evils which they have inflicted on society"—that they do penance for a season in
sackcloth, after the Biblical manner, and then go and hang
themselves. Curiously enough, it was no sympathy for the
Negro that led Helper into this frame of mind: few Americans have ever put down in print a more passionate hymn
to race hatred, and if Helper hated slavery, one reason obviously was that he began by hating the slave. Before disap-
pearing from the scene, Helper was to indulge in much cloudy
rhetoric in which the extermination of the black race would
appear as a positive good, and in which Negroes would be
likened to "hyenas, jackals, wolves, skunks, rats, snakes,
scorpions, spiders," and "other noxious creatures."[3]

Clearly enough, Helper was an incendiary with lighted
matches, the inflammatory nature of his work lying in the
fact that, as a Southerner, he fought slavery because it was
bad for white Southerners rather than for the slaves themselves. But his *The Impending Crisis,* published in 1857, had
not been widely read, and in the South—the only place
where it could be expected to do any harm—it had hardly
been read at all. Not until spring of 1859 did the book begin
to emerge as a national irritant. Then, taking thought for the
coming election, certain Republican leaders concluded that
this book could be made the basis for a fine campaign document. Francis P. Blair, head man of the famous Blair family,
an old-line Democrat who had drifted into the new party's

ranks, would prepare a pamphlet—a digest, or "compend," of the original—and money would be raised so that 100,000 copies of the pamphlet might be placed where they would do the most good.

Concerning which the best that can be said is that it looked like a good idea at the time. Helper had spoken what sounded like good Republican doctrine. He had complained, as a Southerner, that "we have no foreign trade, no princely merchants, nor respectable artists," and that "we contribute nothing to the literature, polite arts and inventions of the age"—the cause of all of which, of course, was slavery. He had found the Southerner dependent on the Northern manufacturer from birth to death; as a child, the Southerner was "swaddled in Northern muslin," and at the far end of life, he was "borne to the grave in a Northern carriage, entombed with a Northern spade and memorized with a Northern slab." All of this, he asserted, had brought Southerners "under reproach in the eyes of all civilized and enlightened nations," and there was only one remedy for it: "The first and most sacred duty of every Southerner who has the honor and the interest of his country at heart is to declare himself an unqualified and uncompromising abolitionist."[4]

This was saying bluntly what most Republicans believed, and since it was written by a man who came from North Carolina, every good Republican was bound to feel that it was a gift from the gods—as perhaps it would have been if American politics could still be played by the old rules, under which it was always advisable to shoot irritating darts into the opposition's hide. Sales of *The Impending Crisis* went up as the Republicans talked about their plan, Mr. Helper found it advisable to move out of the South and take up residence quietly in New York, and spokesmen for the cotton South discovered that there was on earth one book more detestable than *Uncle Tom's Cabin*.

When Clark, the Congressman, urged the House to resolve that anyone who had endorsed the Helper book was unfit to be speaker, he was not taking a wild shot in the dark. Sixty-eight Republican members of the House had so endorsed it, and they included just about every Republican who could conceivably be a candidate for the speakership; included, as a matter of fact, John Sherman himself, who found himself called on to explain the inexplicable.

Sherman did his best. Gaining the floor, he recited the deal with Mr. Blair, and said that Blair had told him, after an exchange of letters with Helper, that "the obnoxious matter in the original publication" would be eliminated; it was because of this assurance, said Sherman, that eminent Republicans had given their endorsement to the scheme. As for his own part: "I do not recollect signing the paper referred to, but I presume, from my name appearing in the printed list, that I did sign it. I therefore make no excuse of any kind. I never read Mr. Helper's book, or the compendium founded upon it. I have never seen a copy of either. . . . I never addressed to any Member such language as I have heard today. I never desire such language to be addressed to me if I can avoid it."[5]

Since the House had not formally organized, and was presided over by a confused and ineffective clerk, there was no rule to keep members from discussing an extraneous resolution at a time when they were supposed to be balloting on the speakership. The kind of language which John Sherman deplored grew worse and worse. Congressman Clark had asked: "Do gentlemen expect that they can distribute incendiary books, give incendiary advice, advise rebellion, advise non-intercourse in all relations of life, spread such works broadcast over the country, and not be taken to task for it?"[6] As one Southerner after another rose to speak on this point, Sherman learned that no man in politics ever gets very far by explaining that he lent his name without knowing precisely what the borrower intended to do with it.

Representative Shelton F. Leake, of Virginia, demanded whether he was asked to consent to the election of an official "who, while I am here in the discharge of my public duties, is stimulating my Negroes at home to apply the torch to my dwelling and the knife to the throats of my wife and helpless children." Sherman, who confessed afterward that he had never dreamed the Helper book would kick up such an uproar, replied that he would repeat once more—having said it, on the floor of the House, five times before—that "I am opposed to any interference by the people of the free States with the relations of master and slave in the slave states"; but another Virginian retorted hotly: "They do not mean to interfere with slavery in the states, and yet when a band of assassins violate the sacred soil of my native state, we hear not one word of denunciation from you." He was followed by Lucius Q. C. Lamar, of Mississippi, who cried that when the spirit of the Constitution was no longer observed on the floor of the House, "I war upon your government: I am against it." Republican William Kellogg, of Illinois, got the floor to assert that slavery was "a moral, social and political wrong" which he would resist to the end; the shorthand reporter noted that this was greeted by a mixture of applause and hisses, and there was a great deal of shouting and threatening which did not get taken down. At one point Kellogg was recorded as demanding: "Does the gentleman call me a spaniel coward?" and the clerk who was trying to preside over all of this, being called on to order the sergeant-at-arms to restore quiet, confessed that he did not know if that functionary were in the House or if he himself had the authority to give him orders in any case.[7]

It went on, for week after week, all business at a standstill; nothing mattered, apparently, except the single issue of slavery, and the men who spoke so hotly on this issue were not so much trying to persuade one another as to give vent to their own pent-up emotions. In the end—on January 30, 1860—John Sherman concluded that he had had enough. He withdrew his candidacy, and after a series of involved deals the House, on February 1, managed to elect a speaker—William Pennington, of New Jersey, a Republican, recently a Whig, chosen by a majority of one vote. At various places in the North, ardent Republicans celebrated, firing cannon and making jubilant speeches, as if some sort of victory had been won; and if the House had in fact discharged the unendurable emotional tension that possessed it, so that it could now get down to business and give the nation orderly government, a celebration would have been in order.[8] But nothing had been settled. One stalemate had been ended, but the greater stalemate remained: the undigestible lump of slavery remained, and this one effort to cope with it had been a noisy and spectacular failure. Only the extremists had gained anything.

The political system clearly was being strained beyond its limit. The attempt to name a speaker had hinged, for week after week, on the question of one undistinguished book; and this question, in turn, had been discussed in the lurid, distorting light that came down from Harper's Ferry. John

Brown had underlined Helper's confused message; his abortive uprising, quenched in blood and leading him to a scaffold, gave the whole business its cutting edge. The violence that smoldered just below the surface on the floor of the House had been terribly real at Harper's Ferry, and it was not for a moment out of any man's mind. Congressman McClernand, of Illinois, a devout Douglas Democrat, wrote to a friend that "our country for the first time is in serious danger of Civil Commotions," adding that unless conservative patriotism somehow triumphed in the coming presidential election "the result must be disastrous." The situation now was made to order for the extremists. Southerners who loved the Union and wanted it preserved were being driven into the camp of the fire-eaters. Their uneasy fears about the dire things that might happen if the slave system were tampered with seemed to have been confirmed, and they were drifting to the point where they would permit no one to touch the system in any way. The Democratic party was their party, and nothing mattered now but to retain a firm control over it. If the party was wrecked thereby, that could not be helped.

On the day after the speaker election, Senator Jefferson Davis, of Mississippi, arose in the Senate to present a series of resolutions on the slavery question. These began by reasserting the state-sovereignty doctrines of John C. Calhoun, declared that it was the Senate's duty "to resist all attempts to discriminate either in relation to person or property" in the territories, and then flatly stated that there was no power anywhere to limit slavery in the territories. Congress could not do it; its solemn duty was to protect slavery there. Residents of a territory could not do it; they could outlaw slavery only when their territory was admitted to the Union as a state. Meanwhile, all acts of Northern individuals or states which interfered with the return of fugitive slaves were asserted to be "hostile in character, subversive of the Constitution and revolutionary in their effect." A little later, Davis modified the resolutions slightly, but the meaning remained unchanged.[9] In effect, he had presented a straight slave code as a principle for Senatorial adoption.

That the Senate would actually adopt any such code was highly improbable, as Davis knew. The real target was the approaching convention of the Democratic party. If the policy set forth in these resolutions could be made to stick as official party doctrine—and the Senate Democratic caucus, in March, endorsed it—Douglas would be in an impossible position, for he could never defend this code in the Northwest and he obviously would never try to do so. Davis was not one of the fire-eaters, and men like Yancey considered him unsound, and when in mid-May he was still arguing for his resolutions, Davis spoke optimistically about the prospects of the Federal Union: "I have great confidence in the strength of the Union. Every now and then I hear that it is about to tumble to pieces, that somebody is going to introduce a new plank into the platform and if he does the Union must tumble down. . . . I come to the conclusion that the Union is strong and safe —strong in its power, as well as in the affections of the people." And yet, fighting to assure Southern control over the party, he had given Yancey and the other extremists a solid platform.[10]

Douglas was in the middle, and he quickly recognized the fact. Declaring that it was "the path of duty and wisdom to stand by the doctrine of non-intervention," he asked bitterly why these resolutions should be offered in the Senate. "There is no necessity for legislation; no grievances to be remedied; no evil to be avoided; no action is necessary; and yet the peace of the country, the integrity of the Democratic party, is to be threatened by abstract resolutions, when there is confessedly no necessity for action."[11]

Douglas was under dual pressures, from the sectionalists of North and South alike. The gist of the Davis resolutions was simply an assertion that the slavery issue was untouchable; in the frenzy built up by the John Brown raid, the South was likely to agree with deep determination. But the untouchable had to be touched, for there were determined men in the North who felt quite as deeply about it as any Southerner. The John Brown episode had stirred profound passions in the North as well as in the South. The institution of slavery had one maddening quality: it ennobled its opponents. John Brown was a brutal murderer if there ever was one, and yet to many thousands he had become a martyr, made a martyr by the character of the thing he attacked. Unbalanced to the verge of outright madness, he had touched a profound moral issue, an issue that ran so deep that he took on a strange and moving dignity when he stood upon the scaffold. If what he had done made adoption of a slave code seem essential in the South, it also made acceptance of such a code unthinkable in the North.

Before the month of February ended, Douglas came under Northern fire. It came from a Republican, rather than from a Northern Democrat, but it illustrated perfectly the size of the obstacle he would meet if he campaigned in the Northwest on anything like the Davis resolutions; and it was delivered by his old opponent in the 1858 Senatorial campaign, Abraham Lincoln, of Illinois, who went on to New York on February 27 to make a speech before a substantial audience at the Cooper Institute.

Lincoln was not quite a national figure at this time. His long debate with Douglas in 1858 for the Illinois Senatorial seat had drawn attention, and he had maneuvered Douglas into frank statement of that Freeport doctrine which slavery leaders found so vicious, but he was still comparatively a minor figure in the Republican party. He was being brought to New York by Republicans who opposed Seward and thought that this effective speaker might offset Seward's predominant strength in the party, and he came with some nervousness, fearing that he might be a little too Western, too countrified, for a New York audience; but he got a cordial reception, and he immediately aimed his guns at Douglas and at the whole pro-slavery position. He made it clear that although Douglas might seem hostile to slavery in the South, there were Northerners who considered him altogether too friendly to it; for slavery was "an evil not to be extended, but to be tolerated and protected only because of and so far as its actual presence among us makes that toleration and protection a necessity."

This was the inadmissible point. Lincoln spoke for men who were willing to agree that the institution was not to be touched—not *now;* but they insisted that it must be recognized as a wrong which must be contained in such a way that it could some day die a natural death. Looking beyond his immediate audience to the men of the South, Lincoln put his finger on the problem to which American politics could not find the solution: "The question recurs, what will satisfy them? Simply this: We must not only let them alone, but we must somehow convince them that we do let them alone. This, we know by experience, is no easy task."[12]

Two days after Lincoln spoke, Senator Seward arose in the Senate to contribute his own bit. He was untidy, carelessly slouchy, hoarse of voice, a man described by Editor Halstead as "a jay bird with a sparrow hawk's bill"; and the South hated him for having spoken of an irrepressible conflict. He was disowning the irrepressible conflict now, speaking hopefully of the Union as something that would endure despite temporary storms, but his voice brought no healing. If the Union were to be assailed, he said, the assault could come only from the Democratic party, for the threat of disunion was made, if not in that party's name, at least in its behalf, and he spoke of the existing turmoil as of something that arose because "a great policy fastened upon the country through its doubts and fears, confirmed by its habits, and strengthened by personal interests and ambitions, is to be relaxed and changed."[13] Saying this, Seward came mortally close to touching the untouchable; at the very least he was going opposite to the spirit of the Davis resolutions, and he offered no help at all to Lincoln's despairing complaint: "We must somehow convince them that we do let them alone."

These men were moderates—Lincoln and Davis, Seward and Douglas. Each man had a love for the Union, an awareness of the mysterious force that operates as a sort of continental destiny. But in this winter when the lines were growing taut, each man was reaching a position from which he could not retreat and on which he would not compromise.

Davis believed that the North must willingly adapt itself to the fact of slavery. Slavery existed and it had to be accepted; it should not be agitated as a moral issue by people remote from it. When Northerners interfered with slavery, they interfered with the well-being and hopes of the whole Southern community, and the very attempt to contain and limit slavery, looking as it did toward its eventual demise, *was* interference despite all disclaimers. People in the North must make the necessary adjustments to something which, after all, was a purely Southern concern.

Lincoln and Seward had come to an opposite position. They saw slavery as an evil affecting the entire country, and although they were willing to accept its present existence as a hard fact, they refused to admit that it must be extended into the indefinite future. They could stomach even the fugitive slave laws if—and only if—they could be sure that some day no such laws would be necessary. Like Davis, they were being driven into sectionalism, and were leaders in a purely sectional party, because slavery itself was sectional.

Douglas was the most flexible of the group. He was perfectly willing to tolerate slavery as long as his toleration did not require him to do intolerable things. Slavery could be voted up or down in the territories, as far as he was concerned, so long as it was at least disposed of by the people directly concerned; he wanted it to cease to be a constant irritant, and he hoped that the country could get on with its other business. Standing in the middle, he stood also in storm center, and sometimes it seemed as if everybody was fighting him.

Thus the moderates, as immoderate winds gathered: the forces that drove them being the same as those that blew in on the delegates at Charleston. With the moderates the will to work out some sort of solution survived; with lesser men the will to hate and to hurt grew strong. Symptomatic of this was the action, in this same session of a divided Congress, a short echo ahead of the Charleston convention, of Congressman Owen Lovejoy, of Illinois, who stood up on April 5 to address his fellow legislators.

Lovejoy had been through the mill. He had seen his older brother, Elijah, preacher of abolition, killed by a mob in Alton, Illinois, more than twenty years earlier, and kneeling by his body had vowed "never to forsake the cause"; he had been a minister and an anti-slavery agitator, and in 1856 had been elected to Congress, a die-hard Free-Soil Republican who bore scars from his long fight against slavery. He spoke now as too many others were speaking—out of complete conviction that his own cause was reasonable and right and that men who opposed him were willfully wrong in the head; spoke not so much to convince as to castigate, to discharge anger that could no longer be contained. Breathing upon the tempest, he made it blow all the harder.

Slavery, he declared, was the sum of all villainies, worse than robbery, worse than piracy, worse than polygamy: "It has the violence of robbery, the blood and cruelty of piracy, it has the offensive and brutal lusts of polygamy, all combined and concentrated in itself." If heaven were run on slaveholding principles, Jehovah would be a Juggernaut "rolling the huge wheels of his omnipotence, axle-deep, amid the

crushed and mangled and bleeding bodies of human beings."
As he spoke, waving his arms, his fists clenched, Lovejoy
stalked over to the Democratic side of the House to speak
into the faces of his opponents, and Virginia's Roger Pryor
came out to meet him, shouting that it was bad enough to
have to listen to such talk "but he shall not, sir, come upon
this side of the House, shaking his fist in our faces." A Republican from Wisconsin, John Potter, cried that Democrats
were just as offensive when they made speeches, and got
into such a wrangle with Pryor that he was challenged to
fight a duel. (He accepted, specifying that they must fight
with bowie knives; Pryor's second replied that these were
outside the code, and in the end there was no duel.) Thirty
or forty Congressmen gathered about the speaker, some to
heckle Lovejoy, others to demand that people stay on their
own side of the House; all to no effect whatever. Congressman William Barksdale, of Mississippi, grated out: "Order
that black-hearted scoundrel and nigger-stealing thief to take
his seat and this side of the House will do it"—and, after
contributing some spirited columns to the *Congressional
Globe*, Lovejoy came to a close and the uproar died down.[14]

A Congress in this mood was not likely to do anything
very constructive in the way of passing legislation; yet the
House did manage, early in March, to pass a homestead bill
that would grant Western land, free, to any adult American
who cared to settle and make a farm—a thing greatly desired by the free-state North, solidly opposed by the South.
Strangely, the thing was not debated at length, although
it offered a more fundamental threat to the future of slavery
than anything the most ranting abolitionist could say in or
out of Congress. With little talk it was sent on to the Senate,
where at last it was amended out of all likeness to the
original. Eventually, considering that he would thereby strike
a blow at Douglas, President Buchanan vetoed it.[15]

Yet although the whole Congressional session had been
filled with talk of secession and war—and, by its mad un-
balance, had given the nation a certain push in that direction—most men did not seem to think that war would ever
occur. There came before the House, in this session, a
naval appropriation bill, and on motion of John Sherman
the estimate for repairs and re-equipment was sliced by a
million dollars. Lovejoy, of all people, agreed with him,

asserting: "I am tired of appropriating money for the army and navy when, absolutely, they are of no use whatever . . . I want to strike a blow at this whole naval expenditure and let the navy go out of existence."[16]

So the appropriation was reduced, and the navy's ability to put its warships in order was limited; one result being that U.S.S. *Merrimack,* in the Norfolk Navy Yard for engine overhaul, lay unrepaired at her dock . . . to emerge, two years after Lovejoy's speech, as the terrifying ironclad C.S.S. *Virginia.*

3. Star after Star

IT HAD been unseasonably hot and dry in Charleston through most of April, but a cool rain drifted in just before the Democratic convention was called to order, at noon on April 23, and Institute Hall was fairly comfortable when the delegates crowded in to find their places. The big auditorium had a level floor, with long rows of plain wooden chairs bolted together; above there was a gallery in which, by agreement, a third of the seats had been reserved for the ladies of Charleston. Making his way to the press section, where reporters were ready with piles of paper, pencils sharpened at both ends, and a messenger to rush copy off to the telegraph office, Editor Halstead took a leisurely look about him and noted disapprovingly that there was "a good deal of gaudy and uncouth ornamentation" about the hall, with inexpert frescoing over the stage. It quickly developed, also, that the acoustics were very bad, largely because loaded wagons and drays were constantly rattling along over the cobblestoned street just outside, creating a powerful racket. The invocation, delivered by "a fine, fat old clergyman" from the deep South, was totally inaudible, at least to earthly listeners, and the authorities hastily arranged to have loads of sawdust dumped in the roadway to deaden the noise.[1]

On this first day there was not, actually, a great deal for anyone to listen to. There was a spirited wrangle over appointment of a committee on credentials and organization, with a certain amount of oratory to which the delegates paid a minimum of attention, but the real struggle was not quite ready to boil over from committee and caucus rooms to the floor of the convention. Floor manager for the Douglas forces was broad-shouldered, harsh-voiced W. A. Richardson, of Quincy, Illinois, dominating his following and his section of the hall by the force of his strong personality. He had joined in the row over organization, making a brief speech on the matter, but for the moment his real responsibilities would be met off the floor. With him as lieutenant was an Illinoisan with the pleasing nickname of "For God's Sake Linder"—a title acquired a few years earlier when Douglas, in the heat of some state political fight, had wired him "For God's Sake Linder come down here I need help." Bustling, sweating, with rumpled linen, Linder was very busy, looking somehow like the sort of man to whom one would say "For God's sake."[2] At the end of the day, when the convention adjourned for the night, nothing in particular had taken place.

Things happened off the stage, however, that evening, that would be of lasting importance, and the next morning Halstead detected a feeling that "the convention is destined to explode in a grand row." This row did not immediately develop; indeed, as the second day's session began, the Douglas floor managers won a victory that might be decisive. By majority vote, the convention agreed that unless a state convention, instructing its delegation, had provided otherwise, delegates need not be bound by the unit rule. It was believed that this would free as many as forty pro-Douglas delegates from the control of certain delegations where a majority was anti-Douglas; Manager Richardson had gained something here, for Douglas now would almost certainly get a majority of the votes when the balloting started, and that in itself would give powerful impetus to his attempt to get the necessary two thirds. If this convention went by the ordinary rules of politics, Senator Douglas was well on his way.[3]

Behind the stage, however, it was becoming clear that this convention was not going to go by the ordinary rules of politics. It would go by its own rules, and these might well take it where no American political convention had ever gone before. Late at night after the opening session had adjourned, the delegates representing the cotton states caucused, and they agreed to follow the lead of the Alabama delegation in respect to the adoption of a party platform: and the Alabama delegation, on this specific issue, rested in the firm hand of William L. Yancey and would go where he took it.

Alabama's Democratic convention had met in January, and there Yancey had put through a resolution that said much the same thing, in briefer scope, as the resolutions Jefferson Davis brought up in the Senate a little later: in effect, it was an iron-tight restatement of the demand for a slave code in regard to the territories. This, the state convention ordered, was to be submitted to the Charleston convention, and Alabama's delegates were instructed to withdraw if the Charleston convention should refuse to adopt it. Now, taking counsel together, the delegations from Georgia, Florida, Louisiana, Texas, Arkansas, and Mississippi had agreed to go where Alabama went; and Alabama obviously was going all the way out of the convention unless the convention adopted the platform Alabama wanted.

Here was a decisive victory for the extremists: a victory, actually, if it could have been recognized as such, for the men who were already contemplating the final step of secession from the Federal Union. They were the people who had thought their way through this question of breaking the Democratic party in halves, and they knew, even though others might not, what the final consequences of this pledge to leave the convention could be. Long before the convention, Yancey had been very explicit about it. "All my aims and objects," he had written, "are to cast before the people of the South as great a mass of wrongs committed on them, injuries and insults that have been done, as I possibly can. One thing will catch our eye here and determine our hearts; another thing elsewhere; all, united, may yet produce spirit enough to lead us forward, to call forth a Lexington, to fight a Bunker's Hill, to drive the foe from the city of our rights." To Yancey it seemed that "the Union has already been dissolved": what remained at Washington was indeed a government, but "not the Union which the Constitution made," and he wanted to war upon it.[4]

Another who saw things this way was Robert Barnwell Rhett, the publisher of the Charleston *Mercury*. In the preceding October his paper had printed a program for South Carolina and by extension for the cotton states generally. In susbstance, this demanded a straight slave code in the party platform and acceptance of it by the party candidate, and urged that if the convention refused to grant this, the Southern delegates should withdraw and put forward their own candidate. If, all of this being done, the candidate should fail of election, the next legislature should recall the state's members from Congress and invite the co-operation of other Southern states on matters affecting the common safety.[5] Rhett was unmistakably calling for secession if either the convention or the campaign turned out to be unsatisfactory; the pledges made by cotton-state delegates in their midnight conference almost certainly meant that either the convention or the campaign, if not both together, would be unsatisfactory to a marked degree.

For what the cotton states were demanding was the one thing the Democracy of the Northwest could never concede. A few months earlier, speaking from the Senate floor, Douglas had said flatly: "I tell you, gentlemen of the South, in all candor, I do not believe a Democratic candidate can ever carry any one Democratic state of the North on the platform that it is the duty of the Federal government to force the people of a territory to have slavery if they do not want it."[6] Here Douglas was drawing the line. The whole effort of his managers just now was devoted to an effort to get the convention to side-step the big issue—to use the soft pedal, to adopt some sort of platform which would somehow satisfy the South without alienating the North. Ordinarily, this is the sort of thing a political convention does without taking a second thought, but at Charleston it was exactly what could not be done. The caucus of the cotton-state delegates was a clear warning that the bitter differences of opinion which lay underneath all of these words would have to be handled out in the open.

. . . clear warning, as well, that Douglas's prospects were not as good as they looked. President Buchanan's friends were making gleeful note of this, and on April 26 one of them wrote to the President that Douglas "is utterly lost," adding that the South would as soon vote for Seward as for Douglas . . . "the hostility to him in the South is even more intense than I expected." Another delegate reported to the President that "the feeling of the South to Douglas is of implacable hostility and his nomination would produce an alienation."

Formulation of the all-important platform was entrusted to a committee, which wrestled with its responsibility off stage while the convention installed its permanent chairman, dignified Caleb Cushing, of Massachusetts. Cushing reminded the delegates that they had convened "in the exercise of the highest functions of a free people, to participate, to aid in the selection of the future rulers of the Republic." They were present, of course, as representatives of the Democratic party, which had its own special mission—"to reconcile popular freedom with constituted order, to maintain the sacred reserved rights of the sovereign states, to stand, in a word, the perpetual sentinels on the outposts of the Constitution." Great applause interrupted Mr. Cushing when he mentioned the rights of the sovereign states; applause joined in even by the Douglas delegates, who considered Cushing no friend of their candidate and who had not wanted him as chairman. He went on to denounce the new Republican party, without naming it, as the creature of men who promoted "a traitorous sectional conspiracy of one-half the states of the Union against the other half," and he called on his listeners to accept for the Democratic party the noble duty of striking down and conquering "those who, impelled by the stupid and half-insane spirit of faction and fanaticism, would hurry our land on to revolution and to civil war." Having heard him through, the convention went on to other matters. It entertained and then rejected a motion to reconsider its vote on the unit rule; it handled various contested-delegation arguments, giving the Douglas people further victories to talk about by seating certain pro-Douglas factions; it referred to the platform committee innumerable resolutions which were brought forward . . . and, like men waiting for an imminent explosion, it teetered on the edges of its chairs until the platform committee should deliver itself of the material on which the convention would either divide or unite, once and for all.[7]

On April 27, the fifth day of the convention's labors, the committee brought in its reports. Significantly, there were three of these—a majority anti-Douglas report, a minority pro-Douglas report, and (infinitely fitting, in view of the unfathomed future) a one-man report submitted by Benjamin Butler, of Massachusetts.

The reports perfectly illustrate the way in which, at an hour of high crisis, men can wrangle over words. No medieval theologians could spin out doctrinal points with more emphasis on the necessity for finding the precise, salvation-encompassing phrase or clause than men of action who are about to disagree can devote to the selection of the exact sentences upon which their disagreement is to be based. This extreme concern over comparatively minor points of verbiage is an infallible sign that there is going to be a row. If men are going to go together, they will ride on almost any words, but if they are going to break apart, the words seem to be of very great significance.

All three of the reports went back to what any contemplative party man in 1860 must have considered the Democracy's golden age, the year 1856, when the convention met at Cincinnati and without difficulty put together a platform that satisfied everybody. All three reports proposed that this Charleston convention begin by readopting, as its own, the Cincinnati platform of 1856. That platform contained a broad, rather undemanding statement of the party's position on slavery. After asserting that Congress could not legally interfere with slavery in the several states (a point acceptable to practically everyone except the most unrestrained of abolitionists) and denouncing those who disagreed as trouble-makers, it went on to endorse the compromise of 1850 and to uphold, "as embodying the only sound and safe solution of the slavery question," the doctrine of popular sovereignty as set forth in the Kansas-Nebraska Act. It held that the Democracy, as the party of the Union, must defend the rights of the states, thereby strengthening the Union itself, and it called for adherence to principles "which are broad enough and strong enough to embrace and uphold the Union as it was, the Union as it is, and the Union as it shall be, in the full expansion of the energies and capacity of this great and progressive people."

To persuade the delegates to say all of this over again was no problem. The trouble came in the effort to determine what, if anything, should be added to it.

Ben Butler, coming forth as a minority of one and speaking for moderation and the avoidance of controversy, proposed that the convention adopt the Cincinnati platform and stop there. If what had been said in 1856 meant different things to men of 1860, let each individual Democrat be his own interpreter.

The report of the pro-Douglas group asserted that "Democratic principles are unchangeable in their nature when applied to the same subject matters," and demanded that the Cincinnati platform be adopted with an all-important rider which, in effect, would say that the vexatious problems centering about slavery in the territories were really judicial in their character and hence should be left to the Supreme Court for determination. It added, almost as an afterthought, that there ought to be a railroad to California, that Cuba should be annexed, and that Northern attempts to nullify the fugitive slave laws were deplorable.

The majority report differed from this, materially, in just one paragraph—half a dozen lines of type hard and uncompromising enough to split the party. In place of the Northwesterners' pious hope that the slavery-in-the-territories matter could be left to the Supreme Court (which was simply the formulation of an agreement not to fight about it within the party), the majority report contained a statement that could be read just one way:

"Resolved, that the Democracy of the United States hold these cardinal principles on the subject of slavery in the Territories; First, that Congress has no power to abolish slavery in the Territories. Second, that the Territorial Legislature has no power to abolish slavery in any Territory, nor to prohibit the introduction of slaves therein, nor any power to exclude slavery therefrom, nor any right to destroy or impair the right of property in slaves by any legislation whatever."[8]

Here was the Yancey program, spelled out, the policy on which Douglas had warned that no Democrat could hope to carry a single Northern state; the declaration of principles whose adoption seven cotton-state delegations had solemnly declared vital to their continued presence in the convention.

. . . It looks simpler now than it did then. As practical politicians, many of the Douglas men were willing to see a certain amount of defection by Southern delegates—it would make it that much easier to get a two-thirds majority and nominate Douglas. There were Southern delegates who knew

perfectly well that a split party would give the advantage to
the Republicans, but who believed that the candidate of
Yankee sectionalism could never get a majority in the electoral college and that the election would as a result be
thrown into Congress, where the Democracy had enough
votes to protect itself. And there were many men on both
sides who did not see their way clearly but who bent before pressure, or simply followed the crowd for lack of any
real guiding star. It may have been very hard, on April 27,
1860, to see that a bitter-end fight on the slavery issue in
this convention would be one ounce more than party or
nation could carry without breaking.

Platform reports were presented some time after eleven in
the morning. A soaking rain came up, and the ladies of
Charleston, present in the galleries by the hundred, had
brought no umbrellas, nor were carriages waiting for them
outside. There was nothing for it but to go dinnerless during
the noon recess, huddling dispirited in the galleries to protect new dresses and bonnets. The atmosphere in the hall
grew damp and chilly; yet after the recess there was revival,
for Mr. Yancey arose to speak to the convention and he
took the galleries with him.

Yancey addressed himself directly to the Douglas Democrats of the North and Northwest, speaking bluntly, making
a positive advantage out of the fact that the cotton-state
Democrats were in a minority. Reviewing the tale of the
Democracy's defeats in Northern states on the slavery issue,
he asserted that these came because Northern Democrats
tried to adjust themselves to anti-slavery sentiments. That
could not be done, and there was but one ground for the
Democracy to take—that slavery was right. Neither he himself nor the Alabama delegation for which he spoke wanted
a break-up of the Union, but someone had to make it clear
to the Democrats of the North that the Union would be dissolved unless constitutional principles triumphed at the polls.
(Constitutional principles, as no one needed to explain,
were clearly set forth in the majority paragraph dealing
with slavery in the territories.)

Like it or not, no delegate could misunderstand Yancey's
meaning. He was a pleasant, smiling man, who spoke easily,
with ingratiating good humor; and he talked today with a
quiet dignity, as if he saw in the near future dark perils

which no man who did not stand with him could detect. He dropped his fatal, quietly eloquent sentences into the hushed convention hall with deadly precision.

"Ours is the property invaded," he said. "Ours are the institutions which are at stake; ours is the peace that is to be destroyed; ours is the property that is to be destroyed; ours is the honor at stake—the honor of children, the honor of families, the lives, perhaps, of all—all of which rests upon what your course may ultimately make a great heaving volcano of passion and crime, if you are enabled to consummate your designs. Bear with us then, if we stand sternly here upon what is yet that dormant volcano, and say we yield no position here until we are convinced we are wrong."[9]

Perhaps the split had already come, and all that could be done now was to formalize it; perhaps the talk about dormant volcanoes and the destruction of families must sound, to the majority—must perhaps really be, to an extent—nothing more than the familiar business of a politician prophesying doom unless his party or his piece of the party can prevail. Yancey was displaying the baleful ghost of John Brown, arguing that slave uprisings and the massacre of innocent families were apt to follow any concession to the moderates in this convention; and among those who considered this rather far-fetched was George A. Pugh, of Ohio, a Douglas Democrat who promptly rose to make reply. With heavy irony, Pugh remarked that an honest Southerner had at last spoken and that the truth about the South's demands was finally on the record. Like Yancey, Pugh reviewed the party's troubles in the Northern states—the real root of the difficulty, he said, was that the Northern Democrats had worn themselves out defending Southern interests—and he declared that the Northern Democrats like himself were now being ordered to hide their faces and eat dirt.

"Gentlemen of the South," said Pugh, "you mistake us—you mistake us—we will not do it."

Whereupon there was vast uproar. All over the floor, delegates were on their feet, waving their arms, yelling furiously for recognition—"screaming like panthers," Editor Halstead wrote, "and gesticulating like monkeys." Caleb Cushing, supposedly presiding over this scene, was helpless, one problem being that in the encompassing racket he could not make out a single word anyone was saying. In desperation, at last, he singled out a delegate from Missouri, who had leaped upon a table and was bellowing something incomprehensible, shaking his head passionately, waving his long red hair. This man, Cushing discerned, was moving adjournment: he recognized him, put the question, and after several minutes of general shouting and surging about on the floor, Cushing announced that the convention had adjourned until morning, and brought down his gavel with hard finality. Out into the cold rain went the delegates, each man earnestly questioning the man nearest him as if no one were quite sure what had been done this day.[10]

Morning of Saturday, April 28, brought no improvement. The weather remained cold and wet, and no man had yet found a fresh light. By a one-vote margin, the convention voted to recommit the various resolutions to the platform committee, and in the afternoon slightly modified reports were brought back. There was a deal of parliamentary sparring, as the Douglas men tried to force adoption of their platform (feeling that they had the votes, if the question could be brought before the house) while their opponents tried to stave off a vote, making endless speeches, bringing in motions to adjourn, motions to lay the whole business on the table, motions involving personal privilege; and at last, not long before midnight, the convention adjourned with nothing accomplished. Next day was Sunday; only technically a day of rest, for although the convention would not reconvene until Monday, the politicking in hotel lobbies, illventilated bedrooms, and party committee rooms went on without a break. It was the day when everybody promised everything. The Buchanan administration was exerting all the power of patronage to keep anti-Douglas delegates in line, and the Douglas men had offered (by one estimate) approximately ten times as many offices as they would be able to give if Douglas should become President. The crowd became thinner, as men who had come just to see the show went back home, and the pressure on hotel lobbies and on barrooms was diminished. One result of this, not foreseen by the Douglas people, was that the convention galleries would increasingly be crowded by Charlestonians, who would stiffen wavering Southern delegates by cheering every anti-Douglas development. In the headquarters of the Ohio and Kentucky delegations it was noted that the supply of whisky was exhausted. Some of the party faithful, gloomily considering that the party had already taken all the steps necessary for a complete wreck, went about muttering that the next President would be named at Chicago—would, in other words, be a Republican.[11]

Monday morning came, April 30, the day of the big showdown, the delegates entering the hall "with a curious mixture of despair of accomplishing anything and hope that something will turn up." The weather was pleasant, after a weekend of blustery rain and wind, and the crowd was charged with nervous expectancy. Despite the general exodus of out-of-town visitors the galleries were more densely packed than ever. With a minimum of delay the convention permanently shelved the Ben Butler report; then, grappling with the crucial problem, it voted by 165 to 138 to adopt the minority resolution in place of the majority report. The Douglas platform, in other words, was formally accepted and the Northwest had won its great victory. It remained to be seen what the victory would be worth.

It quickly became evident that it might not be worth very much. Having substituted the minority report for that of the majority, the convention settled down to vote on the separate planks. First of all, the 1856 Cincinnati platform was reaffirmed. Then stocky Richardson, the Douglas floor manager, moved for harmony by offering to forget all about the controversial plank referring the ins and outs of popular sovereignty to the Supreme Court. This appeased no one; and as the crowd in the galleries sat tensely silent, the cotton-state delegations, one after another, announced their withdrawal. It was done quietly. A writer for the Richmond *Dispatch* recalled that "there was no swagger, no bluster. There were no threats, no denunciations. The language employed by the representatives of these seven independent sovereignties was as dignified as it was feeling, and as courteous as it was either. As one followed another in quick succession, one could see the entire crowd quiver as under a heavy blow. Every man seemed to look anxiously at his neighbor as if inquiring what is going to happen next. Down many a manly cheek did I see flow tears of heartfelt sorrow."[12]

Sorrow there may have been; among the Douglas contingent there was unquestionably dismay. They would have welcomed a small eruption, as a thing that would clear the air, rally Democratic sentiment in the North, and make it easier to get a two-thirds majority in the fight for nomination; but it began to be clear that they had got a very large eruption indeed, which could easily make the nomination either unattainable or worthless, and a haunting sense that the split in the party could be prelude to a split in the Union itself began to torment the men from the Northwest. Delegate R. T. Merrick, of Illinois, arose to inquire, plaintively: "I find, sir, star after star madly shooting from the great Democratic galaxy. Why is it, and what is to come of it? Does it presage that, hereafter, star after star will shoot from the galaxy of the Republic, and the American Union become a fragment, and a parcel of sectional republics?"

Consoling answer there was none. Delegate Charles Russell, of Virginia, announced that if a break-up was indeed at hand, Virginia would go with the rest of the South. Virginia had seen John Brown and his violence, the appeal for a servile uprising, gunfire and death in a peaceful market town; Virginia today stood amid her sister states "in garments red with the blood of her children slain in the first outbreak of the 'irrepressible conflict.' " Gaining eloquence as he continued, Delegate Russell looked mournfully to the uncertain future: "Not when her children fell at midnight beneath the weapon of the assassin was her heart penetrated with so profound a grief as that which will wring it when she is obliged to choose between a separate destiny with the South and her common destiny with the entire Republic." Amid all of this, Editor Halstead looked at Yancey and found him "smiling as a bridegroom." Things were going as Yancey wanted them to go.

The day ended so. The Douglas people had their platform, plus a split convention and the prospect that there would presently be two national Democratic parties.

That night there was a Fourth of July air in Charleston. The moon came out, to silver the live oaks and their Spanish moss and to gleam from the fronts of the fine old houses, and the Southern delegates who had left the convention met in St. Andrews' Hall. A band was playing, and in the street people were cheering for Yancey. Yancey appeared, declaring that the delegates who had seceded would now form the "constitutional Democratic convention," with the others making do as well as they could as a rump convention. The South, he cried, must stand as a unit; perhaps, even now, "the pen of the historian was nibbed to write the story of a new revolution."[13]

4. *"The Party Is Split Forever"*

WHAT WAS left of the Democratic convention did its best to pick up the pieces. It had lost fifty delegates, along with all chance for unity and most of its prospects for victory in the presidential election, and three days were enough to show that it could not do much with what remained. Officially, it had adopted a platform and could now proceed to the nomination of a candidate, and the Douglas leaders approached this task with some hope; since the most violent of the Senator's enemies had seceded, surely it would be simple for him to rally two thirds of those who remained? This, it developed, would not be enough. Caleb Cushing, presiding, ruled that whoever was nominated must get two thirds, not of the delegates in the hall, but of the total originally accredited to the convention, and this ruling stuck. The Southern delegates who yet remained would walk out if the convention overruled the chairman on this point, and they got a good deal of support from anti-Douglas elements in a number of Northern delegations, including that of New York. To nominate, then, the convention must give some candidate more than 200 votes, and it quickly became apparent that this was not going to be possible.

The session of May 1 began hopefully enough, with Cushing half invisible behind a huge bouquet of red roses and with a good clergyman offering a pious prayer for harmony. There were speeches. Twenty-six of Georgia's delegates had left the premises, and one Georgian who remained, Delegate Solomon Cohen, of Savannah, addressed the convention with impassioned pathos: "I will stay here until the last feather be placed upon the back of the camel—I will stay until crushed and broken in spirit, humiliated by feeling and knowing that I have no longer a voice in the counsels of the Democracy of the Union—feeling that the Southern states are as a mere cipher in your estimation—that all her rights are trampled under-foot; and I say here that I shall then be found shoulder to shoulder with him who is foremost in this contest." This, although vague, was considered somehow ominous. A South Carolina delegate, B. F. Perry—oddly enough, an early benefactor and teacher of Yancey—arose to identify himself as "an old-fashioned Union Democrat," announcing: "I love the South, and it is because I love her, and would guard her against evils which no one can foresee or foretell, that I am a Union man and a follower of Washington's faith and creed . . . I came here not to sow the seeds of dissension in our Democratic ranks but to do all that I could to harmonize the discordant materials of our party."[1]

The discordant materials were beyond ready fusion. After the unsuccessful attempt to upset Cushing's ruling about what a two-thirds majority really meant, the convention got down to the business of placing names in nomination. Nominating speeches were brief, and late in the afternoon, when it was time for the first roll call, the convention had six names before it—Douglas, of Illinois; James Guthrie, of Kentucky; Daniel S. Dickinson, of New York; R. M. T. Hunter, of Virginia; Joe Lane, of Oregon; and Andrew Johnson, of Tennessee. When Douglas's name was presented, the Northwestern men raised a brief cheer, but it seemed to lack body, and the gallery maintained a cold silence.

The first ballot told the story. There were 253 votes in the hall, and to win, someone would need to get 202 of them, which obviously was out of the question. Douglas got 145½ on the first ballot, and even his most hopeful followers realized that he would never rise much above this level. The Northwest was sullen and silent, and when Richardson stood up to announce the vote of Illinois, he looked and acted like a man attending a funeral—which, in a way, was the case. Eleven more ballots were taken before the day's session ended, and Douglas could pick up only 5 additional votes, for a top strength of 150½. As the delegates left the hall, Halstead felt that wounds had been inflicted that could not be healed. "I hear it stated here a hundred times a day, by the most orthodox Democrats and rampant Southerners, 'William H. Seward will be the next President of the United States,' " he wrote. "And I have heard this remark several times from South Carolinians: 'I'll be damned if I don't believe Seward will make a good president.' The fact is, there is a large class to whom the idea of Douglas is absolutely more offensive than Seward."

If the Southerners were growing more set in their anger against Douglas, the wrath of the Northwesterners was rising, also. It was a wrath against the party and against the Southerners who had exercised a veto power in the party, and Halstead heard Northern delegates mutter that they would "go home and join the black Republicans." He added: "I never heard Abolitionists talk more uncharitably and rancorously of the people of the South than the Douglas men here. . . . Their exasperation and bitterness toward the South that has insisted upon such a gross repudiation of the only ground upon which they could stand in the North, can hardly be described. . . . They say they do not care a d——n where the South goes, or what becomes of her."[2]

To make things even more vexing, this was no longer the only convention in town. On May 1, while the convention was dolefully haggling over rules, placing names in nomination and balloting so fruitlessly, the die-hard Southerners who had seceded from it held an organization meeting in Military Hall and denominated themselves the real Democratic convention; the majority group which they had deserted was, as Yancey contemptuously insisted, the "rump convention." The new convention appointed a platform committee and selected as its chairman a Buchanan administration stalwart, Senator James Bayard, of Delaware, and on Tuesday morning, May 2, when the original convention resumed its attempt to make a nomination, the opposition drew itself together in the Charleston Theater and got down to business. The ladies of Charleston had concluded that this was the real attraction, and they filled the galleries, leaving those at Institute Hall half empty; and on the stage, calling the convention to order, was courtly Senator Bayard—romantic in his name and ancestry, brightly dressed, wearing long brown curls parted in the middle. Behind him was a stage backdrop which, without political significance, depicted the Palace of the Borgias.

The platform committee reported promptly, recommending readoption of the by now shopworn Cincinnati platform of 1856, with a postscript which defined that platform's meaning in unmistakable terms. The postscript explained that neither Congress nor a territorial legislature could impair any citizen's rights to his property in a territory, and stipulated that it was the Federal government's duty to protect such rights with all its power. Only when a territory became a state could slavery therein be outlawed. This platform was unanimously adopted and the delegates then sat back to see what the "rump convention" was going to do—the idea being that the new convention would either nominate its own candidate or, in case Douglas should be beaten by someone acceptable to the cotton states, endorse the nomination made at Institute Hall.[3]

At Institute Hall nobody was getting anywhere. A brass band that came down with the Massachusetts delegation got into the gallery and played several national airs, after which Delegate Flournoy, of Arkansas, proposed three cheers for the Union, which were given; but when the balloting was resumed, it went just about as it had gone the day before. On the twenty-third ballot, Douglas got a total of 152½, a majority of the original convention strength of 303, if that made any difference—but he could rise no higher, and after fifty-seven ballots, in which Ben Butler voted at least fifty times for Jefferson Davis, the day's session was ended with Douglas one vote weaker than he had been at his ineffective peak. And on the morning of Wednesday, May 3, throwing in their hands, the delegates agreed to vote no more but to adjourn and to reconvene in Baltimore in June. Caleb Cushing spoke a brief swan song, assuring everyone that he had tried hard "in the midst of circumstances always arduous and in some respects of peculiar embarrassment" to behave as an impartial chairman should. Then, announcing that the convention would meet again on June 18, he brought down his gavel and the delegates scurried back to their hotels to pack up and look for the quickest way out of town.

This left the opposition convention with nothing in particular to do; left it, actually, slightly at a loss. Whatever Yancey and Rhett may have hoped, the dominant idea with most of the delegates who had walked out on the original convention had been the expectation that Douglas would eventually withdraw (whether voluntarily, for the good of the party, or in frank recognition of defeat) and that an acceptable compromise candidate would then be named. It had been supposed, also, that the act of withdrawal and the organization of a separate convention would help to bring all of this to pass; then the cotton-state delegates would return to the convention and a reunited party could get on with the presidential campaign, with a candidate who would interpret whatever the platform happened to say in a manner acceptable to everybody.

Now none of this had happened, and those who had withdrawn were as nonplussed as the Douglas men themselves, who had thought that Douglas could be nominated promptly once the die-hards had left the hall. Nobody, apparently (unless it was Yancey himself), had calculated accurately. The secessionist convention could do no more now than agree to meet again, in Richmond on June 11, and then adjourn. The galleries were emptied; Charleston no longer had a convention.[4]

The delegates were not the only ones who failed to see what the split in the party would finally mean. Editorializing on the matter, the Republican New York *Times* mused that a great step forward had been taken; political power now would pass to the North, which henceforth would be united just as the South had been united. Enthusiastically, the *Times* editorial writer continued: "The Democratic party is the last of the great national organizations to yield to the 'irrepressible conflict' which slavery and freedom have been waging for control of the Federal government. . . . The Northern section of the party has asserted its power, and with new and unlooked-for firmness has maintained its position. If it stands still in its present attitude, the sectional contest is over."[5]

In Richmond, the *Dispatch* professed the hope that "the apparent split is more superficial than radical," and that the Democratic party was not yet sectionalized. The real fight, the *Dispatch* felt, had been over a man, not over a platform: "After all, the public have not much faith in any platforms, except such as Gov. Wise constructed for John Brown and those other distinguished members of the Republican party who called a Convention and nominated a ticket in Virginia last fall."[6]

Actually, this man whose platform the *Dispatch* editorialist commended so warmly had seen the trouble coming long before he ever saw John Brown. Henry A. Wise, governor of Virginia from 1856 through 1860, had indeed seen to it that the John Brown uprising was stamped out (this with the help of Robert E. Lee and a handful of United States Marines) and that Brown and co-workers were properly hanged. But back in 1858 he had anticipated what was going to happen in Charleston in 1860, and he had not liked it very much. Tall, lean, lantern-jawed, and outspoken, Governor Wise was a strong pro-slavery man who still believed that the South should fight for its rights within the Union, and in 1858 he had taken a pessimistic look into the future. Writing then to a friend, he had warned that the South contained "an organized, active and dangerous faction" which hoped to disrupt the Union and wanted to create a United South rather than a united Nation. This faction, Wise wrote, wanted in 1860 the nomination of an extremist "for no other purpose than to have it defeated by a line of sections. They desire defeat for no other end than to make a pretext for the clamor of dissolution."[7]

The clamor of dissolution was going on now and it would become stronger, but the extremists were not really in control. Thoughtful Southerners of stature, like Jefferson Davis, did not want the party split made permanent. This could mean only a rise in Republican power and destruction of the South's traditional control of the Democratic party—along, perhaps, with blood and battle smoke and hundreds of thousands of deaths—and the clamor of dissolution was not attractive. There would be a breathing spell now, and much might happen. Conceivably, the Douglas people could win new Southern delegates who would approach Baltimore with less stiffness in the back; conceivably, on the other hand, Douglas himself might be driven off stage so that the party could reunite behind someone less troublesome. Neither possibility was in the least likely, but almost anything was possible; there would be much electioneering and maneuvering in the Congressional districts back home, especially in the South, and there would also be a great to-do in Congress. Possibly something could be done here that would destroy this Northwesterner and permit all good Democrats to get together? Whatever the odds, the thing would be tried.

The handiest instrument that was available was embodied in the Davis resolutions regarding a Southern-rights code, which had been introduced in the Senate in February, had been endorsed by the Democratic caucus there, and now awaited final disposition. These would be brought up now and driven through to formal endorsement by the Senate, and May 7—four days after the collapse at Charleston—was the day appointed for it.

The Senate galleries were full, and the people who filled them had something to look at. Into the Senate chamber came Senator Douglas—"a queer little man, canine head and duck legs"—who went stumping down to his chair amid moderate applause. He had been through the mill lately, this Senator, and he was not well. (He would die, within little more than a year, a passionate spirit exhausting an inadequate body.) He got to his seat, twisted himself down in it, and put his feet on his desk, his mouth closed in a thin, bitter line. Fidgety, he clasped his hands, lolled in his chair, rubbed his nose, and waited to see what was going to happen.

Next came the man whose long shadow had affected so much that happened at Charleston—Senator Seward, of New York. Seward was in a good mood. As things then stood, he was very likely to be the Republican nominee and the next President, and he knew it. He was also, underneath everything else, a ham actor, and he played up to the limelight that was on him today. He stalked about the Republican side of the Senate chamber, his coat tails adrift behind him, found his seat, took a prodigious pinch of snuff, flourished a yellow silk handkerchief across his beaklike nose, and talked with a studied lack of self-consciousness to Republican die-hards like Ohio's Senator Salmon P. Chase, who had all of the dignity and the ostentatious integrity which Seward seemed to lack. Seward cracked a joke, flourished the great handkerchief again, and all in all acted the part of a presidential candidate who is aware that things are going his way.

A third man, now: Jefferson Davis, tall and slim and haggard, coming into the chamber to the sound of muted rustlings in the galleries, going to his desk and depositing documents there with thin, bloodless hands, sitting down as if ineffably weary.[8] The Vice-President called the Senate to order and recognized the Senator from Mississippi. Senator Davis rose to speak.

Davis had something to say. The revolution that hardly anyone really wanted was coming closer and he did not like the sound of it; as a reasonable man, he would urge his opponents to be reasonable enough to see things as he saw them. Through his words there came, not only the Southerners' unappeasable opposition to Douglas, but the defiant challenge of a whole section which, if it did not consciously want disunion, would endure continued union only on its own terms.

There had been agitation (Davis told the Senate) for a generation and more, aimed at Southern institutions. This agitation had recently reached the point of revolution and civil war. "It was only last fall that an open act of treason was committed by men who were sustained by arms and money raised by extensive combinations among the non-slaveholding states to carry treasonable war against the state of Virginia." It was time to go back to the spirit of the founding fathers, who had made a compact with one another, and to ask soberly what should be done to save the country. The people of the North were threatened by nobody. Their institutions were not under attack and their rights were not invaded, and by now they had a majority in the representative districts and in the electoral college. Yet they were aggressive, hostile to the institutions of the South. What should be done?

"The power of resistance," said Senator Davis, "consists, in no small degree, in meeting the enemy at the outer gate. I can speak for myself—having no right to speak for others—and do say that if I belonged to a party organized on the basis of making war on any section or interest in the United States, if I know myself, I would instantly quit it. We of the South have made no war upon the North. We have asked no discrimination in our favor. We claim but to have the Constitution fairly and equally administered."9

Firmly entrenched at the outer gate, Senator Davis would await the assault, which at the moment was verbal. He was fighting over words. If it could be said plainly, flatly, and irrevocably that the United States government must under no circumstances interfere with slavery, all might be well, but the drift of the times, unhappily, was against it. The desperate intransigence of Southern leaders in this spring of 1860 carried an anxiety that their cause might be doomed no matter what anyone said. The intricate, fragile, and cherished society based on slavery could not endure very much longer, simply because the day in which it might live was coming to a close and nobody could stave off the sunset. Senator Davis would try, stalking into the shadows with infinite integrity and fixity of vision, and the immediate target of his wrath would go down too, entering the shadows a little ahead of him—a man who might, if fate had not touched him so hard, have found a way past the barriers.

Douglas listened while Davis spoke, and in due time he made reply, but for the moment the passion had gone out of him. He knew that the intended effect of the Davis resolutions was to state a policy for the Democracy which he could not accept. He was under fire from two directions, and there was very little that he could say. He had remarked, at Freeport, under prodding by Abraham Lincoln, that the Federal government could not possibly make slavery live in a place where the people did not want slavery, and he had done no more than state an obvious fact: the people can always nullify an unpopular law if they feel like it, and there is no power on earth that can stop them. But it was precisely this fact which the slave-state leaders could not accept, and as the man who had compelled them to gaze upon the abhorrent fact, Douglas was their enemy. In addition, he was involved in an old-fashioned political feud in which no one would give quarter or ask it. He had broken with the Buchanan administration on the question of the admission of Kansas as a state, and the administration would destroy him if it could. It could, and destroying him it would destroy much more; but his destruction was all important because if it could not be accomplished, Southern control of the party and the Federal government must come to an end.

In the winter of 1858 President Buchanan had urged Congress to admit Kansas as a state, the admission being based on a proposed constitution framed in a convention at the Kansas town of Lecompton. The Lecompton convention had been rigged, and the constitution itself was rigged; when the territorial voters were asked to pass on it, they had not been given a choice between slavery and no slavery. They could vote, if they chose, for the Lecompton constitution, which flatly stated the right of slave owners to continue to hold their slaves but forbade the importation of any more slaves, or they could vote for the same constitution with a proviso that the slave trade would be continued; could vote, in short, for limited slavery or for unlimited slavery, but could not vote for no slavery. Free-state people in Kansas had boycotted the plebiscite, considering the whole business an arrant fraud; but Buchanan, under vast pressure from Southern leaders and hoping as well that the troublesome Kansas problem could at last be solved if the Lecompton constitution were adopted, had put on the heat. Douglas had fought him, the Lecompton constitution had died like the fading leaves of autumn, a subsequent vote had shown that free-state residents of Kansas far outnumbered the slave-state people, and Kansas was still a territory and a living vexatious problem. It was here that Douglas had sinned. He was out of line not only on a matter of doctrine but also on a crucial question of workaday politics, and he was going to be punished for it.

Douglas had been extremely clear in his attitude on what ought to be done with the Lecompton constitution. In the Senate he had expressed himself unmistakably: "If Kansas wants a slave-state constitution she has a right to it; if she wants a free-state constitution she has a right to it. It is none of my business which way the slavery clause is decided. I care not whether it is voted down or voted up. . . . I care not how that vote may stand. . . . I stand on the great principle of popular sovereignty, which declares the right of all people to be left perfectly free to form and regulate their domestic institutions in their own way. I will follow that principle wherever its logical consequences may take me, and I will endeavor to defend it against assault from all quarters."[10]

The right of the people to form and regulate their institutions will always be accepted by anyone who believes that the people will form and regulate things in his own particular way; but an American in that hour who declared that he did not care what the people did so long as they were allowed to do it was committing heresy against the zealots on both sides. Douglas now was detested equally, as a man devoid of principle, by the abolitionists and by the slave-state leaders.

The Davis resolutions passed the Senate on May 24. They were ineffective, except that their passage indicated that the coming Democratic meeting in Baltimore would almost certainly go the way of the one at Charleston. Nothing could be compromised, after all; in this spring of 1860 the country's most terrible problem was simply the fact that the will to compromise had gone out of so many people. Preparing for their meeting in Chicago, the Republicans gazed about joyously, with wild surmise; and little Alexander Stephens, of Georgia, considered the future and concluded that the nation was heading straight into unmeasured trouble.

Stephens was a wisp of a man, half an invalid, weighing no more than 100 pounds, shrill but movingly eloquent, a man who had been given one of the most haunting nicknames ever worn by an American politician: "The Little Pale Star from Georgia." A former Whig, he had served in Congress and had known Lincoln there; the two had been drawn to one another, possibly because each man in his innermost brooding took a deeply tragic view of human existence. Stephens had supported Virginia's R. M. T. Hunter for the nomination at Charleston, but when the split came he swung to Douglas. The strictest of strict constructionists on the states' rights issue, he nevertheless believed that Southerners could fight for their just dues in the Union better than out of it. As the Democratic split grew wider, Stephens remarked that the men who were working for secession were driven by envy, hate, jealousy, spite—"these made war in heaven, which made devils of angels, and the same passions will make devils of men. The secession movement was instigated by nothing but bad passions. Patriotism, in my opinion, had no more to do with it than love of God had with the other revolt."[11]

Not long after the deadlock at Charleston a friend asked Stephens: "What do you think of matters now?"

"Think of them?" repeated Stephens. "Why, that men will be cutting one another's throats in a little while. In less than twelve months we shall be in a war, and that the bloodiest in history."

The friend suggested that things might be patched up at Baltimore, but Stephens insisted there was no chance of it: "The party is split forever. The only hope was at Charleston."

"But why," asked the friend, "must we have civil war, even if the Republican candidate be elected?"

"Because," said Stephens, "there are not virtue and patriotism and sense enough left in the country to avoid it. Mark me, when I repeat that in less than twelve months we shall be in the midst of a bloody war. What is to become of us then God only knows. The Union will certainly be disrupted; and what will make it so disastrous is the way in which it will be done."[12]

5. The Crowd at the Wigwam

THE DEMOCRATS had met and they would fruitlessly meet again, their division beyond healing; and meanwhile the Republicans were going to Chicago. They were going noisily, impatiently, like men who see the promised land not far ahead, and Editor Halstead observed that on the trains there was a good deal more drinking of whisky than there had been on any of the trains going to Charleston.[1] The great Northwest was about to have its day, and it was not going to be quiet or restrained about it.

Halfway between Charleston and Chicago, in point of time, there was an unexpected development which arrested the attention briefly. On May 9 a number of aging politicians and distinguished-citizen types, who liked the look of things little better than Alexander Stephens did, met in Baltimore and, calling themselves the Constitutional Union Convention, nominated John Bell, of Tennessee, as their candidate for President. Mr. Bell could not conceivably be elected. He stood for moderation and the middle road in a country that just now was not listening to moderates, and the professional political operators were not with him. But he would win a certain number of votes just the same; he might even divide the Northern vote to such an extent that the election finally would be thrown into the House of Representatives. In the horse-trading that would result from this, anything at all might happen.

John Bell was an old-time leader of the Tennessee Whigs. In his sixties, a former Congressman, former Secretary of War, and present member of the Senate, he was a slaveholder who deplored strife, detested the Lecompton constitution, and believed that reasonable men could yet find a way out of their difficulties. A few years earlier he had supported the Know-Nothings, and he was popular all along the border; the new Constitutional Union party was made up of remnants of the moribund Whig party and of the short-lived Know-Nothing party. Without especially meaning to, he stood now as an obstacle in the path of Senator Seward.

The Constitutional Union Convention had been a scratch affair, with representatives from twenty-four states. It had met in a former church, which was decorated with flags, an American eagle, and a large portrait of George Washington, and it tried valiantly to provide a voice for the people who had not yet given up hope. Presiding officer was Senator John J. Crittenden, of Kentucky. Crittenden was ancient, a veteran of the War of 1812, an old supporter of Henry Clay; he had held many state and national offices and he would spend his final years in a fight to keep the Union from dissolving. The convention applauded him, as indeed it applauded all other speakers; no one said anything very controversial, and every mention of the flag, the Constitution, the Union, and the founding fathers drew long cheers. It was almost as if the delegates were making noise in order to drown out the tramp of marching feet, off stage.

This convention denounced most political-party platforms as frauds, and adopted one of its own which was commendably brief and unassailable: it declared simply for the Constitution, the Union, and enforcement of the laws. Then, having nominated Mr. Bell, and having named the distinguished orator, Edward Everett, of Massachusetts, for Vice-President, it adjourned. It had not so much as mentioned slavery in the territories or the fugitive slave laws, and even John Brown had been referred to only twice, in passing. This was mostly a convention of old men, past their time but trying stoutly to work things out so that young men would not have to die in the years just ahead, and it represented a good deal of strength in the border states, where slavery existed on a softer basis than in the cotton South, and where men could occasionally argue about it without wanting to destroy one another. Actually, this convention was all but openly seeking an election that would be settled in Congress (where compromise might yet prevail), and Northern politicians noted that it would inevitably get many votes from members of the dying Know-Nothing party, who expressed their own deep fear of the advance of the nineteenth century by opposing the foreign-born and the Catholic rather than by running a temperature over slavery. This group could win no election itself, but it might keep other people from winning. Its existence would affect what was going to happen in Chicago.[2]

So would Chicago itself. Despite the enthusiasm it had displayed, Charleston had been somewhat dignified and aloof, and Chicago never dreamed of being either of those things.

The mere fact that the convention was being held here was evidence that western America had blown off the lid. As a city, Chicago was hardly a quarter-century old. Ten years ago it had been a raw frontier town of fewer than 30,000 inhabitants; it had more than 100,000 now, and although it remained raw, it was expansive, vibrant, explosively aware that to be the central city of the Northwest was somehow to be at the very hub of America. Just as the atmosphere of Charleston had had its influence on what the Democrats did there, so Chicago's own atmosphere would shape what the Republicans would do. The party was new and the city was new, and each was growing too fast, and was too enthusiastic about its own growth to worry very much about restraint or dignified behavior.

The delegates would meet in a specially built auditorium—a sprawling two-story affair of lumber known as the Wigwam, measuring 180 feet along one side and 100 feet along the other. It had not been in existence when April began, but it was there now, built in six weeks at surprisingly moderate cost, with the area for the delegates laid out like an enormous stage, a series of spaces for spectators rising upward all about it, a gallery running around three sides. Nobody really knew how many people could be jammed into the place; estimates ranged from 6000 to more than double that number. Pillars were decorated with tinder-dry evergreen boughs, red, white, and blue streamers ran everywhere, and the hall was brilliantly lighted by flaring gas jets; all in all, the Wigwam must have been one of the most dangerous fire traps ever built in America. For the first time, the press gallery was provided with on-the-spot telegraph instruments. Never before had so many reporters tried to cover a convention: the press gallery, big as it was, did not have nearly enough room. More than 900 reporters applied for seats in a space designed to hold sixty.[3]

It was believed that the convention had brought in 25,000 visitors. Chicago contained forty-two hotels, and all of them seemed to be jammed; one observer with a taste for odd statistics learned, or at least estimated, that fully 130 people, unable to rent better resting places, were sleeping on tables in the various hotel billiard rooms. On the Monday and Tuesday just before the opening day of May 16, there were incessant parades along Michigan Avenue, as special trains deposited state delegations and cheering crowds of the curious and the hangers-on. Battalions of Wide-Awakes, the party's new marching clubs, flourishing torches and banners, tramped to and from the lake-front depot while brass bands played and enthusiastic Chicagoans set off rockets from the tops of buildings. Just as at Charleston, the henchmen who came along with the New York delegation struck the host city as rather uncouth; one dazed witness wrote that "they can drink more whiskey, swear as loud and long, sing as bad songs and get up and howl as ferociously as any crowd of Democrats you ever heard."[4] Before the convention ended, it would develop that Chicago could produce enthusiasts quite as noisy.

One thing was clear to everybody: Senator Seward was the man to beat. He was the country's best-known Republican, the man with more delegates than anyone else had, and his campaign manager, wily Thurlow Weed, of Albany, knew all of the devious ways of politics and wanted, more than he had ever wanted anything in the world, to see Seward become President. Weed was installed in a suite at the Richmond House, holding day-long receptions for delegates who dropped in, or were brought in, to be cultivated, his aides busy everywhere. They were a mixture, these Weed-Seward headquarters men; among them were sluggers like Tom Hyer, the professional pugilist, solid men of commerce, such as Moses H. Grinnell, men of letters, like George W. Curtis—all of them, whatever they were doing, wearing an air of bright confidence. (One wag went so far as to pin a Seward badge, gaudy with the candidate's name and likeness, on the back of Horace Greeley, the distinguished New York editor who wanted Seward beaten as poignantly as Weed wanted him nominated.) Their confidence was reasonable. The convention would cast 465 votes, and a simple majority, 233, would bring the nomination. Seward would certainly get close to 175 on the first ballot, and it seemed likely that the momentum of enthusiasm (aided by loud noises from the galleries) could send him on to victory.[5]

The trouble with being the man to beat is that everybody else tries to beat you. This was especially true at Chicago, where all men knew that with reasonable luck this convention would name the next President; the awareness of approaching victory pressed men here just as forebodings of defeat had pressed men at Charleston. The man who attached himself to the winner could expect to be rewarded. The party faithful wanted to listen to The Word, but as necessitous human beings they were also intensely concerned with the eventual division of the loaves and fishes. There was an especial point to this because the party itself was so new; it had never distributed national patronage before, and it was developing an immense appetite for it. Furthermore, this appetite was concentrated in the Northern section of the country, which meant that the chosen candidate's capacity to win votes could have an equally narrow focus. Only five of the fifteen slave states—Delaware, Maryland, Virginia, Kentucky, and Missouri—were represented here. The Democrats had painstakingly examined each candidate's record to see whether his orthodoxy could meet every test; the Republicans were examining records to find the man who could most surely carry the North and thus win a majority in the electoral college. Nobody was going to take anything for granted.

Senator Seward's position was weaker than either he or Weed realized, and there were in Chicago men who had diagnosed its weaknesses and were working, literally without sleep, to exploit them. The most effective of these were buzzing in and out of a set of rooms at the Tremont Hotel, where a fat down-state lawyer, Judge David Davis, had set up headquarters for Abraham Lincoln.

Davis had known Lincoln ever since the old circuit-riding days, and when Long John Wentworth, the Republican mayor of Chicago, advised Lincoln that "you ought to have a feller to run you like Seward has Weed," Lincoln had chosen Davis. Never noted as a trial lawyer, and almost wholly lacking in the ability to make a good stump speech, Davis was a thorough man, a hard worker, careful about details, a good organizer and behind-the-scenes executive, and he was about to demonstrate that his political instincts were alert and sensitive. He had gathered together an able group of co-workers. Among them were such men as Leonard Swett, of Bloomington, State Auditor Jesse Dubois, Judge Stephen Logan, who used to be Lincoln's law partner, Norman Judd, the railroad lawyer and political leader who had arranged the Lincoln-Douglas debates, hard-fisted Ward Lamon, of Springfield, and the two canny editors of the Chicago *Tribune,* Charles Ray and Joseph Medill. Their first job now was to survey the field and see what this race was really like.[6]

Aside from Seward, the principal candidates were Governor Salmon P. Chase, of Ohio, Judge Edward Bates, of St. Louis, Simon Cameron, of Pennsylvania, and of course Lincoln himself. Chase was a famous anti-slavery leader: a little too much so, perhaps, for a new party that was going to have to draw some support from the Northern Democrats. Chase had lofty hopes, and yet he was not quite making a campaign of it; he was merely standing off stage, full of dignity and rectitude, willing to receive whatever might be given to him, but not equipped with the guides and beaters needed by a man who hoped to penetrate a jungle like this one at the Wigwam. Bates had the important backing of the famous Blair family and he came from a border state, which was in his favor. If the convention should try to placate the South (which was somewhat unlikely), Bates would be a very likely choice. He had, however, presided over the national convention of the Know-Nothings in 1856 and he would be a loser in any state where the German or other foreign-born vote was essential. Cameron was a typical political boss who could hardly hope to carry anything except his own state of Pennsylvania.

Then there was Lincoln, and Davis and his aides were hard at work reminding people of him. Mayor Wentworth had warned Lincoln to "look out for *prominence*." The convention would eventually realize, Wentworth said, that a really prominent candidate could not be chosen; then the man who had avoided prominence would have his chance.[7] Now the Lincoln managers were trying as hard as they could to keep their man out of the limelight and at the same time set men thinking about him; he was a dark horse and for the moment he must stay dark, but he must never become so dark as to be lost to view. The job called for expert handling.

Expert handling it was getting. The immediate problem was to line up as many second-choice votes as possible, to cultivate friendships everywhere, and to get accurate, hour-by-hour knowledge of the shifting political currents among the delegates. Nothing could be done, of course, with a delegation like that of New York, where Weed had everything under control, but if there was the slightest doubt as to where a state's votes would finally land, Davis had one or more aides attached, full time, to that state's delegation.

This involved some intensely practical considerations. If

an important politician led his delegation to a candidate and so made that candidate a winner, he would expect to be rewarded for it, in the essential currency of politics—jobs, patronage, a say in the inner councils. Before this convention week began, Dr. Charles Ray, senior editor of the Chicago *Tribune*, had written a "profoundly private" letter to Lincoln pointing out that "you need a few trusty friends here to say words for you that may be necessary to be said," and urging that the principal managers at Chicago be properly empowered. "A pledge or two," Ray reminded him, "may be necessary when the pinch comes." Lincoln, who had been around politics long enough to know what can happen to a candidate who puts himself unrestrictedly in the hands of his managers, refused to take this bait, writing in return: "Make no contracts that will bind me." Davis and his co-workers would have to do the best they could with promises of their own. They felt their prospects were good, and on May 15 Davis telegraphed Lincoln that "nothing will beat us but old fogy politicians the heart of the delegates are with us."[8]

Down-to-earth problems were not overlooked. The men of the 1860s lived in what are now assumed to be innocent years, but they knew as much as anyone needs to know about the creation and manipulation of mass enthusiasm, and with the primitive means at their disposal they got excellent results. It became evident, for instance, that in the immense pro-Seward entourage that had come on from New York there were hundreds of men who had been brought to Chicago simply because they could yell very loudly. Properly spotted about the Wigwam under orders to stand up and cheer whenever Seward's name was mentioned, these might make uncertain delegates believe that enthusiasm for Seward was sweeping the convention, and the Seward band wagon might thus begin to roll irresistibly. Lincoln needed his own shouters, and the headquarters group at the Tremont Hotel saw to it that he got them.

As Congressman Isaac Arnold remembered afterward: "There was then living in Chicago a man whose voice could drown the roar of Lake Michigan in its wildest fury; nay, it was said that his shout could be heard, on a calm day, across that lake." And there was another man, who lived down on the Illinois River, whose remarkable voice had equal range and carrying qualities; he unfortunately was a Democrat, but he seems to have been malleable and he was asked to take the first train to Chicago. These two, then, the man from Chicago and the down-state Democrat, were told to bring together a group of huskies and take station on opposite sides of the Wigwam. When a key member of the Illinois delegation should take out his handkerchief, each man was to yell as hard as he could, his huskies yelling with him, and the yelling was to continue until the handkerchief vanished. As a matter of pride, Illinois would not let its favorite son be out-shouted.[9]

The convention would generate its own intensity. Vast as the Wigwam was, it could hold but a fraction of the crowd that wanted to get in. Long before the main gates were thrown open, at noon on Wednesday, May 16, the galleries were filled to capacity—3000 persons. The rule here was that only gentlemen accompanied by ladies could be admitted, and ladies were greatly in demand; schoolgirls, it was said, were paid twenty-five cents apiece to help male spectators get by the gatemen, and Halstead reported that certain women of the town plied a brisk if honest business along the same line. One hopeful man found an Indian woman who, at a sidewalk stand, was selling moccasins or some such artifacts to the visitors, and tried to escort her in—failing, when an official lacking in gallantry ruled that she was no lady. . . . When the three 20-foot doors giving access to the convention floor were opened, a dense crush of men came powering into the hall—delegates, alternates, and newspapermen mixed with spectators.[10]

In the various delegations were men whose names were now or soon would be nationally famous. Thaddeus Stevens went limping to his place with the Pennsylvanians, and Gideon Welles, his wig a poor match for his voluminous whiskers, led the delegation from Connecticut. John A. Andrew, who would be war governor of his state, led the Massachusetts delegation, and the Wisconsin group was headed by the tense, black-bearded German, Carl Schurz; the immense Davis lounged at ease under the Illinois standard, and William Evarts, a lawyer and orator of national reputation, took his seat as chairman of the New York contingent, expecting to see the nomination go to Seward without delay once the balloting began.

There would be no balloting, however, for two days, and

this opening session was an anti-climax. The convention got itself organized, named committees, listened to an anti-slavery speech by the David Wilmot whose famous proviso had touched off so much trouble in Congress after the Mexican War, installed George Ashmun, of Massachusetts, as its president, listened to more oratory, and then adjourned early, one reason for adjournment being the fact that the Chicago Board of Trade, with four steamboats at the water front, was offering all hands a short excursion on Lake Michigan. Some delegates and visitors accepted this invitation. Others returned to the Wigwam to watch an exhibition drill by a corps of Zouaves; and the rest strolled about, visited bars, gathered in hotel rooms for argument, for song, for cards, or for private drinking, and in general disposed of the evening in the way traditional at political conventions.[11] The air of pent-up excitement increased, and on Thursday—the day when the convention would hear the report of its platform committee —it began to break loose.

The Seward contingent met that morning in front of Richmond House and paraded straight to the Wigwam, all of the men wearing huge badges, a uniformed band in front blaring away at a popular air—"Oh Isn't He a Darling?" Inside the hall, the immense crowd greeted the report of the platform committee wtih wild shouts, interrupting at almost every paragraph to cheer the statement of the party's creed.

The platform had been drawn up so as to please all Republicans, and it met this desire precisely. It began by asserting that conditions in America made the Republican party a necessity, and it went on to endorse the Declaration of Independence, with especial reference to the part about all men being created equal. It demanded preservation of the Constitution, the rights of the several states and the Federal Union, drawing attention to the fact that all of the recent talk about disunion had been uttered by Democrats, whose incendiary language was briskly denounced as "an avowal of contemplated treason." The Buchanan administration and the Lecompton constitution were condemned, and "the new dogma" that the Constitution automatically carried slavery into the territories was held unsound, "revolutionary in its tendency and subversive of the peace and harmony of the country." The normal condition of people in the territories was held to be one of freedom, the authority of Congress to make slavery legal in a territory was denied, and the admission of Kansas as a free state was demanded.

Then, after assailing extravagance in government, the platform advocated a protective tariff, called for a homestead act, denounced the Know-Nothing demand for restriction on the citizenship rights of naturalized immigrants, called for Federal aid for internal improvements, and commended the projected railroad to the Pacific Coast. It concluded by inviting the co-operation of all citizens who agreed with the importance of these "distinctive principles and views."

There was something here for everyone except Southerners —for anti-slavery people, for the foreign-born, for the Eastern manufacturers, for the developing Northwest—and the platform was adopted with a great burst of cheers. Delegates and spectators sprang to their feet, waved their hats, and yelled, the ladies in the gallery fluttered their handkerchiefs and clapped their hands, and Halstead reported that "such a spectacle as was presented for some minutes has never before been witnessed at a convention." He felt, too, that all of this jubilation carried a powerful element of enthusiasm for Seward, and as the crowds poured out into the streets, he wrote that "there is something almost irresistible here in the prestige of his fame."[12]

Seward that Thursday evening was within reaching distance of the nomination, and if balloting could have begun then, he would probably have attained his goal. When the uproar that followed adoption of the platform died down slightly, some Seward delegate arose to move that the convention proceed to the nomination of a candidate, and if this had been done, Seward almost certainly would have got what he wanted. Unfortunately, the convention secretary was compelled to announce that the tally sheets were not quite ready. They would arrive in a few minutes; would the delegates wait?

At that moment the delegates were prepared to do anything but wait. The mood to shout, to parade about, to slap backs, and to rejoice in the prospect of victory was too strong, and the convention adjourned for the evening. The nomination would be made Friday, and the Seward managers were unworried. There would be a great deal of caucusing and pleading during the evening, but the New Yorkers' lines looked firm. At Richmond House headquarters an immense quantity of champagne was opened and consumed, brass bands tramped all over town with Seward banners in the breeze, serenading state delegations that might still be uncommitted . . . and at the Tremont Hotel the determined men from Illinois settled down for a night of very hard work.[13]

6. Railsplitter

WHEN THE convention opened, David Davis weighed very nearly 300 pounds. He had hardly had half a dozen hours of sleep in three days, he was mussed and rumpled, and beyond question he had worked off some of that surplus flesh. On this Thursday evening he telegraphed Lincoln that he was "nearly dead from fatigue," and when the convention ended he would be all but completely exhausted;[1] he believed, however, that the convention was going to go the way he wanted it to go if proper steps were taken, and he and the rest of the Lincoln high command went to work the moment the Thursday afternoon session adjourned to see what they could do.

They would work from the fact that the Seward front was not really as solid as it looked, even though most of the political experts in Chicago were about ready, this evening, to concede Seward's nomination. To win the election the Republicans must carry at least three of the four states which were listed as doubtful—New Jersey, Illinois, Indiana, and Pennsylvania. Despite the wild jubilation that followed adoption of the platform, the party could lose those states if it followed the wrong candidate. Illinois illustrated the problem perfectly. As was the case in most other Northern states, the Republican party in Illinois contained a number of diverse factions. There were the outright abolitionists, and the Free-Soilers who had a more conservative bent; there were former Know-Nothings who distrusted foreigners, and German-born voters who were repelled by Know-Nothingism; there were former Democrats and there were old-line Whigs to whom all former Democrats were suspect; and of all the candidates, only Lincoln had managed to avoid arousing the enmity of one or more of these groups. If the delegates from such states as Indiana, New Jersey, and Pennsylvania could be shown that Lincoln could please all factions in their states and that Seward could not, Seward could be stopped.

A point of immense importance here was the fact that both Pennsylvania and Indiana, through a quirk in state laws, would hold their state elections in October, a month ahead of the national election. Other things being equal, their voters would line up in these state elections just about as they would in the national election. If the national ticket could not produce internal harmony, the Republicans in Indiana and Pennsylvania would lose in the October balloting and hence would lose in November as well—and, in addition, would provide the party with a deadly psychological handicap all across the North. It was essential, therefore, for the Wigwam to produce a candidate who could win in Indiana and Pennsylvania, and the principal Republican politicians in those two states did not believe Seward could do it. The job facing the group at the Tremont suite was to demonstrate that Lincoln could.

Seward was paying the price which, as Wentworth had said, was apt to be exacted of the man who was too prominent. In his famous remark about the irrepressible conflict, he had, as a matter of fact, said nothing that Lincoln himself had not said when he asserted that a house divided against itself could not stand, but somehow it had made more people angry. He had coupled it with vague, damaging talk about a "higher law" than the Constitution; also—and in some ways this was the biggest handicap of all—he was totally unacceptable to the suspicious Know-Nothings, because he had, as governor of New York, years ago, urged the support of Catholic parochial schools with public funds. Both Indiana and Pennsylvania contained many voters strongly tinged with the Know-Nothing prejudice. Like the Free-Soil moderates who felt that Seward's statements on slavery had been a bit extreme, they might not follow the Republicans if Seward carried the banner. There was, indeed, grave danger that dismaying numbers of them would vote for John Bell, running on the Constitutional Union ticket; if that happened, states which the Republicans ought to carry might wind up in the Democratic column.

The pivotal state of Indiana was already pretty well in line for Lincoln. Key man here was Caleb Smith, a former Whig who had been friendly with Lincoln when Lincoln was in Congress, prominent enough in Indiana Republican ranks to believe that he ought to be named to the cabinet if a Republican won the election. Davis had talked to him carefully and persuasively—indeed, the whole Indiana delegation had been most carefully cultivated—and Smith and the delegation had been won over. It would be asserted afterward that, in flat disregard of Lincoln's order that no binding pledges be made in his name, Davis had promised Smith the cabinet appointment. This may be an overstatement, but in any case Smith had agreed to second Lincoln's nomination from the floor, and the Indiana delegation was prepared to vote for Lincoln on the first ballot.[2] The job now was to win Pennsylvania, plus such other delegations as might feel that Seward was an unsafe candidate.

So on that Thursday evening there was a meeting at Davis's suite, and if the hoary tradition of a smoke-filled room was not born there, it at least took on a good deal of growth. The Lincoln men had been working hard in Pennsylvania and in New Jersey—another delegation that was uneasy about Seward—and delegates from Illinois, Indiana, Pennsylvania, and New Jersey were convening now to take stock of the situation. On Judd's suggestion, a subcommittee composed of three men from each state was formed, with the hope that it could agree on a candidate, and this group met for five hours and more.

Somewhere around ten o'clock that night the door to Davis's suite opened and the pink, cherubic face of Horace Greeley, fringed with silky hair and whiskers, peered blandly in. As a determined foe of Seward, Greeley realized that the fate of the stop-Seward movement depended on what was being done right here, and as a good reporter he wanted to know what was going on. Had they, he inquired, agreed upon a candidate? Told that they had not agreed, he withdrew. Shortly afterward he sent to his New York *Tribune* a story that began: "My conclusion, from all that I can gather tonight, is that the opposition to Gov. Seward cannot concentrate on any candidate and that he will be nominated." Editor Halstead, who was also keeping in touch, sent a similar dispatch to his Cincinnati *Commercial*. He explained later that at midnight on Thursday every man in Chicago believed that Seward was in, and the champagne party at Seward headquarters took on the aspects of a victory celebration.[3]

But the caucus in the Tremont Hotel was not over. After

Greeley left, someone suggested that it was time to see just how many votes each candidate could count on. Davis was very well informed on this point and he produced his own tabulation, which showed that Lincoln had far more votes than any other candidate except Seward. The men from New Jersey and Pennsylvania thereupon agreed that they would call their own delegations into caucus and recommend support of Lincoln on the second ballot. Later that evening the New Jersey crowd swung into line. Pennsylvania would act the following morning, just before the convention was called to order.

What was working for Lincoln here was the old matter of availability. The delegates from these important states were against Seward because they did not think they could carry their states with him, and of the other candidates only Lincoln seemed to lack Seward's handicaps. Judge Bates, satisfactory on so many points, was fatally handicapped now by his former activity in the Know-Nothing party: desperately needing the votes of the foreign-born, the Republicans could hardly hope to get them with Bates. Chase was branded as an extremist; a good many Douglas Democrats would vote Republican this fall if they were appealed to properly, but they could not in any circumstances be won by Chase, whose abolitionist tendencies were pronounced and unmistakable. That left Lincoln. He had avoided the pitfall that awaits the man who is too prominent.[4]

The thing was not yet done, however. Next morning—Friday, May 18, with the opening of the session very near—Davis and Swett had a caller: Judge Joseph Casey, of Harrisburg, who was empowered to speak for the ambitious Pennsylvania boss, Simon Cameron. Cameron, said Casey, wanted to make a deal. He would swing the Pennsylvania vote to Lincoln, provided he could be sure that he would become Secretary of the Treasury in the new cabinet, and provided also that he could have complete disposal of all Federal patronage in his state.

This was a lot to ask, and Davis and Swett fenced for a time. Cameron was not widely admired. He was the archetype of the political boss: anything goes, so long as you hold on to the throttle of the machine. He had enemies in his own state, among them brisk Andrew Curtin, who was going to be the next governor, and the Philadelphia publisher Alex-

ander K. McClure, but for the moment Cameron had the
Pennsylvania delegation in his pocket, and a candidate who
wanted that delegation's votes had to deal with him. No one
supposed that he really ought to be Secretary of the Treasury,
and the notion that any state boss should at this moment be
given complete control of patronage in his state was outlandish, but the Pennsylvania delegation today was probably going to vote the way Cameron told it to, and Davis and Swett
were under the gun.

The accepted version is that they surrendered and promised (in Lincoln's name, although Lincoln had told them to
do nothing of the kind) that Cameron would be paid off as
he wished. A wire was sent to Lincoln, and his answer came
back: "I authorize no bargains and will be bound by none."
But the managers had victory within their purchase. Davis
is supposed to have said: "Lincoln ain't here and don't know
what we have to meet, so we will go ahead as if we hadn't
heard from him and he must ratify it." To Joseph Medill, of
the Chicago *Tribune,* Davis is alleged to have said that he
got the Pennsylvanians "by paying their price." It may not
have been that simple. A century later Davis's biographer,
Willard King, after an exhaustive study, concluded that the
bargain was not made. Davis and Swett, he believed, said
only that Pennsylvania certainly was entitled to a place in
the cabinet and that they personally would recommend Cameron; when Casey refused to accept this, they added that
they would get every member of the Illinois delegation to
endorse Cameron's claim. They agreed, also, that Cameron
would, on their word, have access to Lincoln immediately
after the election. With this, Casey finally was content.[5]

However it was done, it was done. When delegates and
spectators elbowed their way into the Wigwam, the Pennsylvania delegation was committed to vote for Lincoln on the
second ballot.

There had been other things to do. On this day when the
names would be formally placed in nomination and the votes
would be counted, the pressure of the galleries would be extremely important. There were many delegates outside of the
wavering Indiana, Pennsylvania, and New Jersey groups who
were ready to desert Seward and go with a winner if they
saw the actual victory taking shape before their eyes and
within sound of their ears. Vermont and Virginia would

break away with suitable incentive, and even Chase's Ohio delegation contained men who knew Chase could not win and were looking for a place to light. Persuasive men from Illinois would work on all such groups. Also, certain political realists would make certain that the Wigwam was as full as possible of men who would cheer for Lincoln whenever the occasion offered.

The Seward people this morning were as confident as they had been the night before. More than a thousand leather-lunged rooters from New York were ready to make a cheering section, and these were marshaled in front of the Richmond Hotel with a brass band to play them down to the convention. It took time to get these people assembled, and the march was not brisk—and when the procession reached the Wigwam, every empty seat (aside from the section reserved for accredited delegates) was occupied by a man from Illinois, ready to yell his head off for the home-state favorite. The Seward rooters were frozen out. It was rumored afterward that Davis's cohorts had had a print shop run off fake admission tickets, although this apparently had not been necessary; but whether outright fakery was employed or not, the galleries and aisles were crammed almost to suffocation with Lincoln men. The gallery at Charleston had helped to kill Douglas; now Seward would be killed with the help of the gallery at Chicago.[6]

When the Friday session opened, there was not in the Wigwam room for one more man, and thousands of people, some of them doubtless cursing vigorously, jammed the streets outside. In the hall there was a tense hush; then the roll was called, and the states put their candidates in nomination. The modern custom of thirty-minute nominating and seconding speeches did not then prevail, fortunately for the tempers of all concerned, and the nominations were made quickly. Evarts put in Seward's name, Judd offered Lincoln's, Francis P. Blair nominated Bates, and others put up Chase, Cameron, and such outside contenders as Justice John McLean, of Ohio, and William L. Dayton, of New Jersey. Most of the applause, it was noticed, came for the names of Seward and Lincoln; and when Caleb Smith, of Indiana, rose to second Lincoln's nomination, and Austin Blair, of Michigan, seconded Seward, Halstead wrote that "the shouting was absolutely frantic," so that some delegates stopped their ears in pain, and hundreds of hats, tossed toward the ceiling by enthusiastic delegates, filled the air like a swarm of hornets. The loudest shouting, Halstead said, came for Lincoln: "Imagine all the hogs ever slaughtered in Cincinnati giving their death squeals together, a score of big steam whistles going . . . and you can conceive something of the same nature." Henry S. Lane, of Indiana, who was going to run for governor this fall and wanted to be on a winning ticket, stood on a table, swinging hat and cane, touching off an uproar of yelling and foot-stamping that made the wooden auditorium quake. After a time quiet was restored, and the balloting began.[7]

The first ballot showed clearly that the Seward men had underestimated Lincoln's strength. Seward led, as had been expected, with 173½ votes, but Lincoln polled 102, Bates had 48, and Cameron had 50½; the votes of these three, plus anticipated defections which were sure to come on later ballots, might well be enough to stop Seward, and sharp cries of "Call the roll!" demanded a second vote.

On the second ballot the trend was clear. Seward lost votes in New England, and Pennsylvania swung obediently away from Cameron into the Lincoln column. In all, Lincoln picked up 79 votes while Seward was gaining only 11; the tabulation showed Seward with 184½, Lincoln with 181, and the rest nowhere. The band wagon was rolling at last, and the convention began to understand that those delegates who had gone to bed at all the night before had done so under a mistaken assumption. Seward was not going to make it.

The third ballot did it. Seward lost a few votes, in New England and in Ohio, and when the roll call was ended, Seward had dropped to 180 and Lincoln had gone to 231½, just one and one-half votes away from victory. No candidate ever got that close to the top without going the rest of the way, and before a fourth roll call could be ordered (while state delegations were furiously canvassing their memberships), Delegate D. K. Cartter, of Ohio, got to his feet and won the attention of the chair. Cartter was a big man with a shock of bristling black hair, afflicted by an unfortunate impediment in his speech, but the impediment did not matter now. The crowd collectively held its breath, while he forced out the words: "I rise (eh) Mr. Chairman (eh) to announce the change of four votes of Ohio from Mr. Chase to Mr. Lin-

coln." There was a brief pause, and then an enormous yell
went up, while chairmen of other delegations fought for a
chance to put their own change of heart on the record.

On the roof there was a man who had been put there to
fire off a salute from waiting small-bore cannon once a
nomination had been made. He heard the wild racket coming up from below and thrust his head through a skylight,
gesturing madly to get someone to tell him what had happened. Some functionary, tally sheet in hand, saw him and
shouted: "Fire the salute—Old Abe is nominated!" and the
guns promptly went off, whereon the mob outside took up
the shouting. The noise from outside stimulated the hoarse
crowd within to new endeavors, and the racket became so
intense that the banging of the cannon overhead could not be
heard. Wisps of powder smoke drifted down into the auditorium, and a woman in the gallery wrote that although
everybody seemed to be joining in the cheering, "I think
everyone was half joyful and half frightened"; some of the
yelling seemed to come from men who wanted to reassure
themselves that what they had just done would really be for
the country's good.

State chairmen continued to shout for recognition so that
their timely switch to the winner could be properly recorded.
Someone brought in an immense picture of Lincoln and began to tack it up over the rostrum. Delegates began grabbing
state standards and started a jubilant procession up and down
the crowded aisles. The stunned New York delegates refused
to let their own standard be carried in this parade. A newspaperman saw Thurlow Weed, overcome by the supreme
disappointment of his life, pressing his finger tips against his
eyelids to keep from weeping. After a time, however, the
spokesman for the dejected New York delegation, orator
Evarts, got to the platform and, standing on a table, expressed his grief at the convention's failure to nominate Seward and with tears running down his cheeks moved that the
nomination be made unanimous. Somehow the convention
managed to pass this motion, whereupon there was adjournment for supper and the exhausted delegates headed for their
hotels—the Seward men stumping along, all downcast, in
glum silence, the Westerners trying to carry on with their jollification. Some of these had gone into such an emotional
state that although they had not tasted liquor they lurched

and staggered like drunken men. At the dining room in the Tremont Hotel, an awry-eyed celebrant announced loudly that "Abe Lincoln has no money and no bullies, but he has the people by the ——," and when a waiter thrust a menu under his nose, he shoved it aside with a scornful: "Go to the devil—what do I want to eat for? Abe Lincoln is nominated, G—— d—— it, and I'm going to live on Liberty." Then he grabbed the menu and said he would take "a great deal of everything."[8]

He had pretty well expressed Chicago's mood. An unvarnished Westerner was going to be the next President, and for tonight everybody would take a great deal of everything. Down the streets went disorganized processions, with much whooping and cavorting. From nowhere men appeared carrying fence rails—whether authentic relics of the nominee's rail-splitting youth or run-of-the-mill rails split by someone else made no difference—and these were carried and displayed and brandished, hour after hour. Cannon on top of the Tremont Hotel fired a 100-gun salute, the offices of the Chicago *Tribune* were gaily illuminated, and unheard-of quantities of whisky were consumed. At the Briggs House, where the Cameron people had their headquarters, hundreds of Pennsylvanians presented "a scene of indescribable joy and excitement." (As the group that had set the band wagon rolling, the Pennsylvania Republicans could count on abundant rewards when the new administration took office.) They would build rail pens, they declared, in every school yard in Pennsylvania, and they sent a telegram to Decatur, Illinois, where there was alleged to be a fence made of rails split by Lincoln in 1830. This fence the Pennsylvanians wanted to buy, *en bloc*. Other groups also wanted to buy those rails, and Decatur did a brisk business while the supply lasted.[9]

The convention somehow finished its business that evening, while Chicago celebrated. For Vice-President it nominated Hannibal Hamlin, of Maine—another choice reflecting the professional politicians' profound concern over making the proper appeal to all elements in this elated but fundamentally disharmonious party. There was powerful sentiment among the delegates for Cassius Clay, of Kentucky. He received more than 100 votes on the first ballot, and might easily have been nominated by acclamation—at one point half of the people in the Wigwam seemed to be chanting "Clay! Clay! Clay!" But the professionals got things in hand. Clay was an out-and-out radical on the slavery issue, he came from west of the Alleghenies, and, like Lincoln, he was a former Whig. Hamlin, a good friend of Séward, was a moderate, an Easterner, and a former Democrat—and, altogether, he would give the ticket better balance. Hamlin it was, on the second ballot. Then, after naming a committee to go to Springfield and formally tell Lincoln that he was the candidate, the convention adjourned.

Cassius Clay was in Chicago at this time, and he was wholeheartedly glad that Lincoln had been nominated, but he did not want any illusions about what was probably going to come of this convention's work. A Kansas Republican recalled afterward how he and some friends, on the night before the nominations were made, went to a meeting of border-state delegates and met Clay. Clay was impressive—huge, powerful, fearless, as became one who had preached emancipation for years in a slave state, defying his enemies to silence him. (He was a distinguished knife fighter, which probably helped him in that career.) At this meeting he warned the Kansans: "Gentlemen, we are on the brink of a great civil war."

They had probably heard that before, Clay continued, but as a Southerner he wanted them to know that if the North elected a candidate on the platform the Republicans had just adopted, the South would fight. He was not going to run away from that war, but it gave him a deep anxiety about the kind of man the party might nominate. "You must give us a leader at this time who will inspire our confidence and our courage. We must have such a leader or we are lost." Then, impressively: "We want you to name Abraham Lincoln. He was born among us and we believe he understands us."[10] Like Clay and like Jefferson Davis, Lincoln had been born in Kentucky.

But Clay's somber warning was not on anybody's mind tonight. A good part of the Northwest, apparently, was taking Lincoln's nomination as a great victory, and as the night trains carried out-of-town visitors and delegates off to their homes, every trackside village put on its own celebration— people shouting, tar barrels ablaze, drums being beaten, firearms banging, and more fence rails in evidence. On the train that carried Halstead and other Ohioans toward Cincinnati, the Lincoln enthusiasts were simply too groggy to respond to these evidences of enthusiasm. Halstead wrote in amazement: "I never before saw a company of persons so prostrated by continued excitement."11

CHAPTER TWO

Down a Steep Place

1. Division at Baltimore

ROBERT E. LEE, of Virginia, lieutenant colonel in the 2nd United States Cavalry, a colonel by brevet and acting commander of the Department of Texas, took a preoccupied look at political matters in this haunted summer of 1860 and wrote down his thoughts in a letter to his friend, Major Earl Van Dorn.

"The papers," he wrote, "will give you the news of the Baltimore convention. If Judge Douglas would now withdraw & join himself & party to aid in the election of Breckinridge, he might retrieve himself before the country & Lincoln be defeated. Politicians I fear are too selfish to become martyrs."[1]

It was not a summer for martyrs and the withdrawal would not take place, and whether it would have changed things very much is open to question anyway. Politics had lost its flexibility, and the loss reflected grass-roots sentiment. Too many leaders had dug in for a last-ditch stand—whether for high principle, for practical political profit, or for a blend of both—and although it was increasingly clear that the result was likely to be disastrous, everybody felt that the necessary concessions ought to be made by someone else; it was always the other side that was stiff-necked and obstinate.[2] The politicians who were driving on toward a shattering climax were supported by plain citizens whose response seemed to be almost automatic. Lee's attitude was a case in point. He had as little of the fire-eating extremist in him as any man in America, but he was a man of his time, of his class, and of his section—and the cotton-state extremists were somehow speaking for him. Instinctively he was aligning himself with them; oppressed by the obvious drift of things, he could say no more than that it was up to Douglas to master self-interest and to retire from the struggle.

As Colonel Lee suspected, there were too many candidates for the presidency, but the problem was not so much their number as the sharp divisive forces that insisted on bringing them forward.

The Republicans had named Mr. Lincoln, and the Constitutional Union party had named Mr. Bell. Now the one and indivisible Democracy had broken into halves. Its Northern wing, insisting that it was the National Democratic party, had nominated Senator Douglas, and its Southern wing, bearing the name of the Constitutional Democratic party, had nominated John C. Breckinridge, currently the Vice-President of the United States; and so now there were four tickets, each supported by men who felt that they were following the only possible path to salvation. A Republican victory was almost certain, and the Democrats, who had the most to lose from such a victory, were blindly and with a fated stubbornness doing everything they could to bring that victory to pass.

Senator Douglas, as a matter of fact, had been prepared to withdraw. He had even written a message of withdrawal, confiding slightly different versions of it to two of his party's leaders for issuance in case such a step would prevent a break in the party, but it had not been issued. Baltimore had simply put the seal on what had been begun at Charleston. Northern sectionalism, finding its voice in the unrestrained jubilation of the Republican ceremony at the Wigwam, had its counterpart in a Southern sectionalism which would hold to the letter of its own restrictive law though the heavens fell. The story of 1860 is the story of a great nation, marching to the wild music of bands, with flaring torches and with banners and with enthusiastic shouts, moving down a steep place into the sea.

According to schedule the Democratic convention reconvened in Baltimore on June 18. Caleb Cushing, profoundly dignified in blue coat with brass buttons, bearing something of the air of a latter-day Daniel Webster, was again in the chair as delegates and spectators filed into the Front Street Theater, and the tension that had pervaded the air at Charleston seemed greater than ever. Right at the outset Mr. Cushing had a problem. After the adjournment at Charleston, conventions in certain Southern states had named new delegations, friendly to Douglas, to replace the ones that had walked out in April, and these were present in Baltimore—along with the delegations they were supposed to replace. Which groups were legally entitled to seats? What the convention would finally do depended in large part on the decision that would be made on this point, and the chairman was under immense pressure. The men from the Northwest were confident, almost arrogant. They would nominate the Little Giant at any cost, and they would begin by making certain that the new Southern delegates were accepted, and they insisted on this so strenuously that the first day's session was one long wrangle. Cushing ruled that all delegates who were on the roll when the Charleston convention adjourned were still delegates as far as he was concerned; the chairman, he held, had no power to rule on conflicting credentials. The matter was passed to a credentials committee for determination, and there was much uproar on the floor, with hissing and cat-calling from the crowded galleries.[3]

It would take the credentials committee three days to wrestle with this problem, and until the wrestling ended, the convention could do nothing but wait, its collective temperature rising hour by hour. Douglas men paraded the streets with brass bands, pausing when the spirit moved them to listen to stump speeches; Southern die-hards, in turn, had a way of gathering in front of the Gilmore House, where Yancey was staying, for stump speeches of their own; and nothing that was said or done at any of these meetings served to promote harmony. At the Douglas meetings, held often enough on the steps of the home of the eminent Reverdy Johnson, former Senator, former Attorney General, and a leader of the "moderates" on the slavery question, orators shouted that devotion to Douglas was the only true test of Democratic fidelity. At the Gilmore House, in turn, the Douglas men were denounced as abolitionists in disguise, and Yancey cried that these Douglas leaders were selfish men who, ostrich-like, "buried their heads in the sands of squatter sovereignty" and thereby exposed their anti-slavery posteriors. On the fringes of these meetings there were often a number of fist fights.[4]

The unyielding temper of the anti-Douglas group had been

hardened by events in Richmond a week earlier. At Richmond the Southern delegates who had walked out at Charleston had reconvened, asserting their claim to represent the true Democratic faith and, after oratory, agreeing in effect to wait and see what happened at Baltimore; but the keynote speeches at Richmond left no doubt that this wing of the party was in for a fight to the finish. Lieutenant Governor F. R. Lubbock, of Texas, who called the Richmond meeting to order, spoke for all hands when he declared that they had met "to carry out our principles whatever may be the result," and he drew loud applause when he asserted: "If we cannot succeed in sustaining those principles we must create—no, we will not 'create' a new Democratic party, but we will simply declare ourselves the true Democratic party, and we will unfurl our banner and go to the country upon true Democratic principles." John Erwin, of Alabama, who succeeded him as permanent chairman of this impermanent convention, insisted that "we must yield nothing, whether we remain here or whether we go elsewhere." Whatever happened, the South must insist on its rights, and "the serpent of squatter sovereignty must be strangled."[5]

On June 21, fourth day of the Baltimore convention, the credentials committee had finished its labor. The Front Street Theater was jammed when the delegates were called to order, and proceedings were delayed when a section of the floor gave way, sending delegates in a wild scramble for safety, a sudden panic which might have led to serious trouble but fortunately did not. After an hour's recess, during which proper repairs were made, the session got under way and the committee offered two reports—a majority report, which held that new delegations from Alabama, Louisiana, and Arkansas should be seated, with a compromise by which the Georgia delegation would be equally divided between seceders and newcomers; and a minority report emphasizing states' rights and demanding the seating of the original Charleston delegations. The majority report, of course, was strictly pro-Douglas. If the convention accepted it, Douglas's nomination was certain; almost equally certain, by now, was the fact that such action would cause the Southern extremists to walk out of this convention just as they had walked out at Charleston. The convention would have to decide; but further adjournment became necessary when the big New York delegation asked for time in which to make up its mind—a step which discouraged the Douglas people, who believed the New Yorkers had already committed themselves to the Douglas cause.[6]

So the business went over to the next day, Friday, June 22, and at seven o'clock that evening there came the show-down. The theater was packed, as before, and there was a strange silence as the roll was called. Everyone realized that by now the Democracy had crowded itself into a corner; no matter how this vote went, the party was going to divide, and the division would almost inevitably mean the election of Abraham Lincoln in November. But until the vote was recorded, something might happen; and just now, suddenly, a rumor went the rounds—a rumor that Senator Douglas had offered to withdraw his name in the interests of harmony.

The rumor, as it happened, was perfectly true. Douglas had given one of those letters of withdrawal to his floor manager, Richardson, of Illinois, but Mr. Richardson was keeping the letter in his pocket and was saying nothing about it. Suspecting, perhaps, that this was what Richardson would do, Douglas had also written to Dean Richmond, one of the leaders of the New York Democracy, and this letter, dated June 22, read as follows:

"The steadiness with which New York has sustained me will justify a word of counsel. The safety of the cause is the paramount duty of every Democrat. The unity of the party and the maintenance of its principles inviolate are more important than the election or defeat of any individual. If my enemies are determined to divide and destroy the Democratic party, and perhaps the country, rather than see me elected, and if the unity of the party can be preserved and its ascendancy perpetuated by dropping my name and uniting upon some other reliable non-intervention and Union-loving Democrat, I beseech you, in consultation with our friends, to pursue that course which will save the party and the country without regard to my individual interest. I mean all this letter implies. Consult freely and act boldly for the right."

This dispatch was not exactly an olive branch. With its firm insistence on non-intervention—that is, non-intervention by the Federal government in the matter of slavery in the territories—and on Union-loving Democrats, it by no means constituted a surrender to the Southern group. At most, it would simply remove one controversial figure from the party fight; the fiight itself, if Douglas's letter were taken at face value, would continue. But for whatever the letter might be worth, Dean Richmond had it. Like Richardson, he kept it securely pocketed.

The convention proceeded to adopt the majority report, and defeated a series of parliamentary maneuvers looking toward a reconsideration. The Douglas men had won; their delegates were officially seated; now the Senator from Illinois could be nominated.

He could not, however, be nominated by a united convention. Someone moved that the convention now ballot on candidates, but Chairman Cushing, refusing to recognize the motion, gave the floor to Delegate Charles W. Russell, of Virginia, who arose to make an announcement:

"I understand that the action of this convention upon the various questions arising out of the reports from the committee on credentials has become final, complete and irrevocable. And it has become my duty now, by direction of a large majority of the delegation from Virginia, respectfully to inform this body that it is inconsistent with their convictions of duty to participate longer in its deliberations."

The Civil War came out of the words of many men, spoken under intense pressure and out of the depths of deep conviction and overpowering emotions. In part it came out of the quiet, mannered announcement of Delegate Russell. One more moment of decision had passed, not to be called back. . . .

When Mr. Russell finished, there was a throbbing wave of confused sound—cheers, hisses, angry cries for "Order!", a moving and a shifting of delegates and spectators. Caleb Cushing ordered the galleries cleared, made no attempt to enforce the order, waited for the tumult to subside. (The galleries were applauding Mr. Russell: whatever the convention itself might do, most of the spectators this night seemed to be much against the Senator from Illinois.) Then, after some minutes of turmoil, most of the Virginia delegates got up and left the hall. They were followed by men from Carolina and from Tennessee. The delegation from Kentucky retired to caucus. A number of Maryland delegates withdrew, to be followed by scattered groups from a few Northern states and by a substantial bloc from the Pacific Coast, where the party was largely dominated by pro-Southerners. Essentially, the walkout meant that the deep South had formalized the decision made earlier at Charleston: it would not go along with Douglas under any circumstances.

Not all of the Southerners left the hall, and those who remained were plainly uneasy. Delegate T. B. Flournoy, of Arkansas, protested that he was a thick-and-thin slavery man who would "apply the torch to the magazine and blow it to atoms" before he would submit to wrong; yet he did not think a wrong was being done here, and he firmly believed that "in the doctrine of non-intervention and popular sovereignty are enough to protect the interest of the South." And S. H. Moffat, of Virginia, cried passionately: "In the name of common sense, have we not enough of higher law, revolutionary, abolitionist scoundrels in the North to fight without fighting our friends?"

The delegates applauded fervently, but nothing was changed. The factions of the Democracy were going to fight their friends, the atmosphere having become so filled with distorting heat waves that friends and enemies had begun to look terribly alike. Late in the evening, unable to proceed further without rest, the convention adjourned until morning. There were the usual mass meetings that night, but the spirit had gone out of them. All men could see that they had crossed a divide, and Editor Halstead, doggedly covering his fourth convention in three months, reported that "the private cursing was not loud but deep."[7]

Having lost its anti-Douglas cotton-state delegations, the convention discovered on the following morning that it was also losing its chairman. Caleb Cushing announced that inasmuch as delegations from a majority of the states had withdrawn, either wholly or in part, he felt that it was his duty to resign. His speech was greeted with cheers—the Douglas crowd cheering because they were happy to see Cushing leave (they had considered him anti-Douglas, from the start), and the galleries cheering to show that they approved his course. David Tod, of Ohio, took Cushing's place, and tried to call the roll of states so that nominations could be made. But there was continuing uproar, with more speeches to be made, or at least to be attempted. One of these came from Ben Butler, who announced that he himself was quitting this convention, partly because there had been a partial withdrawal of a majority of the states and partly because "I will not sit in a convention where the African slave trade, which is piracy by the laws of my country, is approvingly advocated." Butler stalked out, followed by part of the Massachusetts delegation. Then Pierre Soulé, of Louisiana, obtained the floor.

Soulé was a member of the new pro-Douglas delegation from Louisiana, seated by the convention's action in adopting the majority report of the committee on credentials. He was dark, intense, unmistakably French in manner and in accent, and he arose to denounce "the conspiracy which has been brooding for months past" to defeat Senator Douglas; a conspiracy, he said (with obvious reference to the activities of the Buchanan administration leaders), which had been devised by "political fossils so much incrusted in office that there is hardly any power that can extract them." He was bitter about the men who were so determined to defeat Douglas, and he spoke of them with scorn: "Instead of bringing a candidate to oppose him; instead of creating before the people issues upon which the choice of the nation could be enlightened; instead of principles discussed, what have we seen? An unrelenting war against the individual presumed to be the favorite of the nation—a war waged by an army of unprincipled and unscrupulous politicians, leagued with a power which could not be exerted on their side without disgracing itself and disgracing the nation."[8]

Heartened, presumably, by the thought that there were still Douglas supporters in the South, the convention at last got down to the business of making a nomination. Since the die-hard anti-Douglas men had all departed, this was easy. On the first ballot, Douglas got 173 of 190½ votes cast, and on a second ballot he received 181½ out of 194½; and then the convention unanimously adopted a motion stating that inasmuch as Douglas had received two thirds of all the votes, he should be declared the nominee. Mild cheering and more speeches followed; and in the evening, after naming Senator Benjamin Fitzpatrick, of Alabama, as its choice for Vice-President, the convention sat back to listen to Richardson, of Illinois.

Senator Douglas, said Richardson, would accept the nomination. But he had been prepared, "for the harmony of the party, for the success of the party, for the preservation of the government always and at all times," to withdraw his name. Then Richardson read the letter which he had had in his pocket during the recent in-fighting.

Douglas's letter to Richardson said what his letter to Richmond had said, in somewhat sharper language. Douglas began by reiterating his doctrine of non-intervention and went on: "While I can never sacrifice the principle, even to attain the Presidency, I will cheerfully and joyfully sacrifice myself to maintain the principle. If, therefore, you and my other friends, who have stood by me with such heroic firmness at Charleston and Baltimore, shall be of the opinion that the principle can be preserved and the unity and ascendancy of the Democratic party maintained and the country saved from the perils of Northern abolitionism and Southern disunion by withdrawing my name and uniting upon some other non-intervention and Union loving Democrat, I beseech you to pursue that course."

Richardson put the letter back in his pocket and added his own final word of defiance to his foes in the deep South:

"I have borne this letter with me for three days, but those gentlemen who have seceded from this convention placed it out of my power to use it. And the responsibility, therefore, is on them. . . . We in the North have one sectional party to fight, and intend to whip them. You have an equally sectional party to fight in the South, and we expect you to whip them."[9]

Then the convention adjourned, its labor accomplished for good or for ill. (One last chore remained. Senator Fitzpatrick, named for the vice-presidency, felt himself unable to accept, and the Democratic National Committee a few days later named Herschel V. Johnson, of Georgia, in his place.)

But the show was not over. Like Charleston, Baltimore on this final day had two conventions. While the original convention was nominating Douglas, the anti-Douglas men convened in the hall of the Maryland Institute. They considered themselves the real Democratic convention, and they were in high good spirits. The Baltimore *Sun* remarked that there were no arguments and no fights: "All restraint of feeling had disappeared," and it was easy to recognize "the perfect restoration of that geniality of intercourse which is alone the earnest diagonal of a harmonious result." Caleb

Cushing, greeted with applause, was installed as chairman, and when he called the roll of the states, it became apparent that this was largely a Southern convention.

Sixteen delegates were present from Massachusetts, two from New York, one from Vermont, and one from Iowa; the border states were all represented, and there were delegations from California and from Oregon. No other Northern states were represented, but the cotton states were out in force—except for South Carolina: clinging rigidly to principle, the South Carolina delegation was still in Richmond, watching from afar, prepared to endorse what was done here if all went as it should. The reporter from the *Sun* remarked that he had never before seen the Southern leaders looking so happy. Yancey sat at his ease and "glowed with satisfaction," and even Georgia's redoubtable Senator Robert Toombs, usually so grim of visage, showed a face "for once lit up with good cheer." The general atmosphere, the *Sun* man believed, was "a feeling of sectional pride and loyalty to the Southern leaders that is superior to convictions of either principle or expediency."

It did not take this harmonious convention long to do what it had convened to do. A platform was speedily put together and adopted, bluntly asserting the sharp pro-slavery principles that had been fought for so hard at Charleston, commending the projected acquisition of Cuba and endorsing the plan for a railroad from some point on the Mississippi River to some point on the Pacific Coast. Then John C. Breckinridge was placed in nomination; he won a two-thirds majority on the first ballot, and was given the nomination unanimously, and Joseph Lane, of Oregon, was named for the vice-presidency. (These nominations were warmly approved by the Richmond convention.) And then, before final adjournment, the convention listened to Yancey.

Yancey was jubilant. What he had worked for over the years was now coming to pass, and it was his time to crow. "The storm clouds of faction have drifted away," he said, "and the sunlight of principle, under the Constitution, and of the Union under the Constitution, shines brightly upon the national Democracy." The party, the Constitution, and the Union itself were safe: and yet he himself was no worshiper at the shrine of the Union. "I am no Union shrieker. I meet great questions fairly, on their own merits.

I do not try to drown the judgment of the people shrieking for the Union. I am neither for the Union nor against the Union—neither for disunion nor against disunion. I urge or oppose measures upon the ground of their constitutionality and wisdom or the reverse."[10]

Yancey went on at length, reaching at last the point of anti-climax; spectators in the gallery began to leave, Chairman Cushing fidgeted visibly in his chair, and this speech was the last one. The convention adjourned . . . and the country had two Democratic parties and two Democratic candidates. Editor Halstead reflected that the real trouble lay in the convention system, which was no better than "a system of swindling." The Douglas men, he felt, had come to Baltimore blinded by their own enthusiasm: "They did not know the power and desperation of the South, and were foolish enough to believe the opposition to them in that quarter would quietly subside. They were, however, met in a spirit more intolerant than their own."[11]

2. The Great Commitment

IF THE leaders could speak for the people, the South had committed itself. It would not permit Stephen A. Douglas to become President, even though the price of beating him might be the election of a Black Republican. Such an election, since it would be manifestly intolerable, would be proper ground for dissolution of the Federal Union; but the dissolution would come, not to avoid an immediate threat to the stability of Southern society, but as an alternative preferable to the tacit admission that the institution which Southern society lived by might some day have to undergo change. At Charleston and at Baltimore the South had taken its stand. It would remain the South, separate and unalterable. He who could not subscribe to that fact would be an enemy.

The motives that compel men to act are sometimes as confusing as the things that grow out of the completed actions. When the Southern delegates walked proudly out of the Democratic conventions they drew armies after them, and put the touch of fire on quaintly named places which no one then knew anything about—Chickamauga Creek,

Stone's River, the tidewater barrens at Cold Harbor, and the drowsy market town of Gettysburg, to name but a few. But why they did this and why it had to come out as it did are questions that no one then could have answered and that remain riddles to this day.[1] In part, what was done and what came of it depended on what other men would do in response —it took two sides, after all, to bring about a Sumter bombardment, a battle of Antietam, or a rough-neck march from Atlanta to the sea. But a certain part of it came out of a refusal to admit that the nineteenth century was not going to end as it had begun. For a great number of reasons the American South was fated to try to stay just as it was in a time when everything men lived by was changing from top to bottom. This was the commitment that had been made and that would be paid for. Why?

Men's motives (to repeat) are mixed and obscure, and none of the many separate decisions which brought war to America in 1861 is wholly explicable. It is quite possible that the choice which was made at these conventions in 1860 came at least in part out of a general, unreasoned resentment against immigration and the immigrant.

In the middle of the nineteenth century, Americans both North and South could see that something cherished and familiar was being lost. Looking back only a few years, it was easy to see a society where (if the glaze of years could be trusted) everyone thought, spoke, and acted more or less alike, living harmoniously by a common tradition. That society, in retrospect, seemed to have been singularly uncomplicated and unworried—a loose amalgam of small cities, quiet towns, and peaceful farms, slow in movement, lacking railroads and telegraph lines and owning no factories of consequence, simple and self-sustaining, owing the outside world no more than casual acknowledgment—a society stirred by perfectionist impulses, perhaps, but nevertheless living to itself alone.

But this fragment of the golden age was growing dimmer as years passed. Revolutionary change was taking place everywhere, or was visibly ready to take place, and people who liked things as they had been found the change abhorrent.[2] Furthermore, it seemed possible that newcomers were at least partly responsible for the change. People whose background touched neither Jamestown nor Plymouth Rock were arriving by the thousands—Germans, Irish, French, Italians, men of new tongues and new creeds and new folk ways, cut adrift from Europe by famine, by revolution, or by simple restless hope, crossing the ocean to make this new land their own. It was easy to feel that they were corrupting the old America. So there was a sudden flare-up of bitter nativist feeling. A whole political party dedicated to curbing the immigrant arose, elected Congressmen and governors, even aspired (without success) to take control of the Federal government; the American, or Know-Nothing, party, which stained generations of American life with the indelible hue of its own intolerant yearning for a simple age. As a political movement it did not live long. A country where every citizen was the descendant of immigrants could not for very long ascribe to the immigrant all of the disturbing problems that were coming as the inevitable consequence of the Industrial Revolution. So Know-Nothingism died, even though its lingering existence was one reason why Mr. Seward was not blessed with the Republican nomination at Chicago; but the mere fact that it had risen so quickly and spread so widely testified to a changing nation's profound unease in the presence of change.

To fear change meant to fear the alien—the man who looked and talked and acted differently, and who therefore was probably dangerous. And of all the groups whose migration to America had caused strain, the largest of all, and the one whose presence seemed to be the most disturbing, was one racially homogenous bloc which, to men of that day, seemed to be entirely beyond assimilation. Its members had been coming in for the better part of two centuries. When they arrived they did not fan out across the land, dispersing and mingling and losing clear-cut identity among people already stamped with Americanism, as most immigrants did. These, instead, settled in large groups, congregating in some states until they actually constituted a majority of the population, going to other states hardly at all, clinging with pathetic tenacity to their own customs and folk ways. Of all the immigrant groups these were the most distinctive—in language, in appearance, in culture— and although they were among the most peaceful, easygoing, and uncomplaining people the world has ever seen, their mere presence frightened native Americans almost beyond endurance. Because this was so, the navy patrolled the seas to see that no more of these people took ship for America, and in the states where they settled there were strict laws, rigidly enforced, for their control.

These people, of course, were the Negroes, who had come from Africa—mostly from the enormous, ill-omened bight of Benin, the Slave Coast, from the steaming concentration camps which had been set up for them on those pestilential shores as depots of embarkation. That they had emigrated from their native lands through no desire of their own made no difference; they had come from beyond the seas and now they were here, and a bewildered country that was inclined to give all immigrants some of the blame for its unresolved problems had become so exasperated by the mere presence of these Africans that in 1860 it could discuss its present difficulties and its future way out of them only in terms of this one specific group.

The long voyage across the sea to America lies embedded in the subconscious memory of every American. It was a hard trip even under the best of conditions, and many people died trying to achieve it, but it was made more tolerable by the unvoiced promise that lay at the end. After it was made, its hardships and dangers faded slowly out of sight because those who came were volunteers led on by hope, and there was something in the New World to justify that hope after the trip had ended. But for the Negro it had been different. The trip itself was worse—fearfully, unspeakably worse—and what came after it was very little better than the trip itself. The institution of slavery had become comparatively benign, to be sure, but it was still slavery: a vast system of forced labor that sustained the economy of half a continent, offering to those who labored no prospect whatever for a better life. To the Negro, hope was denied. There was only survival, bought at the price of surrendering human dignity. The Negro had to remain what he was and as he was, his mere presence a mocking denial of the nation's basic belief in freedom and the advancement of the human spirit. He was the one man in America who could not be allowed a share in America's meaning.

Since he was not allowed to talk, the Negro did not complain much about this, but the business was disturbing to other people because it was obvious that slavery was morally wrong and everyone knew that things morally wrong could not endure; nor could they bring enduring good fortune to anyone. It was supposed, half a century or more before this darkening year of 1860, that in the fullness of time slavery would wither away in the natural course of things as an evil outgrown. But the business did not work out that way. The America which had seemed as pastoral as Eden was becoming a very different sort of place, and the conditions under which slavery existed grew extremely complex; and presently the very forces that made slavery more and more of an anachronism worked powerfully to keep it alive. Modern industrialism, taking shape beyond the seas but touching America as well, exerted a pressure beneath which the Southern states of America were all but helpless. These states could produce enormous quantities of cotton. Using slave labor they could produce it very cheaply, and in steadily increasing volume; and because they could do this they had to do it, for their land had become the base for an industrial process that was entirely outside of their control. By the middle of the nineteenth century, America had reached a point at which it could discard slavery only at an incalculable cost.

A profound change was taking place in the world. Because of such unconsidered factors as the invention of the steam engine, the development of semi-automatic machinery, the growth of world-wide systems of cheap transportation and finance, and the opening of limitless markets that had never existed before, the existence of the industrial nation became possible. It was possible, that is, for a busy nation to sustain itself by selling, to a market beyond its own borders, goods made from raw materials which it did not produce. To a certain extent what was happening in America now—what was putting the 1860 election outside of political rationality—was simply a reflection of this fact.

By singular circumstance, the great cotton-spinning industry of England, paralleled somewhat by a similar industry in France and by an American counterpart to the east of the Connecticut River, was the first great industry to develop in this way. The British textile manufacturers were showing what could happen when centralized production relying on distant sources of supply had a world market to exploit, and this was something altogether new under the sun.[3] The nations of the earth would no longer be entirely self-sustaining; in a backhanded and wholly misunderstood way, men all about the world would become members of one another, not because they wanted to, but because the world itself was changing. The black field hand in the Yazoo Delta and the rich planter who owned him, the mill hand in Manchester and the ultimate consumer in Berlin, Capetown and Baghdad were tied together now, made subtly interdependent in a way no one was ready to understand.

This had two immediate effects as far as American slavery was concerned; effects which went in precisely opposite directions.

Human slavery, obsolescent for generations, was now being made wholly obsolete, especially if it existed in a nation which itself was beginning to be industrialized. America had a more prodigious industrial potential just then than any other nation. It contained an almost limitless supply of industry's raw materals, from cotton and lumber to coal and iron ore; it also offered the world's richest market; and of all countries it was the one that was most certain to see the greatest development of the Industrial Revolution. This development was visibly taking place. Less and less were men producing in their own homes the things they needed for working and living. Homemade manufactures, as the census people called them—farm implements, textiles, bits of furniture and household equipment, home-cured meats, the innumerable products of plantation workshop and frontier farm—declined all through the decade of the 1850s, dropping from more than $27,000,000 in 1850 to slightly over $24,000,000 in 1860. This happened despite a huge growth in population and a sharp expansion in Southern plantations and the development of new frontiers in the West.[4] A nation which was just beginning to exploit its own immense agricultural potential was at the same time expanding its factory system.

The day of the semi-independent handcraftsman was swiftly coming to a close. Iron and textile industries grew ever larger, an imperfect but constantly improving national railroad network was coming into being, manufactured goods were being finished for export as well as for domestic consumption, and the intricate mass-production processes of modern manufacturing were well in hand. (To make even as uncomplicated an instrument as a muzzle-loading Springfield rifle, more than 100 different automatic power tools were being used.)[5] The new industrial state was coming into being at an accelerating rate, and in such a state chattel slavery could not live.

Most of this development was taking place in the Northern states. The South remained pastoral, producing raw materials for the outside world and relying on the outside world for an increasing portion of its finished goods. Yet the South was directly, inescapably involved in the wave of industrialization, as much responsible for it as the manufacturers of Manchester or the shipping magnates of New York and Liverpool. The vast cotton fields of the Gulf states were the base for the great world textile industry. The mills of England and France were built on them. The entire Southern area whose ways were being made more and more out of date by the economic revolution that was taking place was itself an integral factor in the growth and progress of that revolution.

This put the South in an extremely difficult position. It was contributing to the very process that was certain to transform its own society. Not without a prodigious wrench, unendurably expensive in dollars, almost unthinkable in its effect on social organization and on cherished habits of thought, could the South do away with the slave system on which its production of raw materials was based. Each upward surge in the industrial advance made slavery more and more central to the Southern economy—and, at the same time, increased the odds against slavery's continued existence. The Southern planters who so jubilantly proclaimed that cotton was king would have had to admit, if pressed, that the king was a very hard master. The domain of King Cotton had to sink further and further into a colonial status.[6] It was committed to industrial progress for other lands but not for itself. It was a complex society dependent on modern processes in manufacture, in transportation, and in finance, and yet these had to be controlled elsewhere because colonialism had no place for them. What the rest of the nation wanted very much—protection for industry and for industry's markets, expansion of the free-farm system, internal improvements fostered by the central government, all of the things that would speed up the incomprehensible developments that were under way—these the South wanted not at all. But its opposition to these things had to take the form of opposition to any attack on slavery itself. Confronting the most complex problems, Southerners were compelled to discuss them in terms of their effect on the one peculiar institution.

Yet in its instinctive and violent defense of this institution the South was not so much defending an old culture, as it supposed itself to be doing, as fighting against the odds for a share in a new one. As cotton prices went on up and new western lands came into production, new men could enter the magical planter class and, entering it, could make money. The very symbol of a man's chance to get on in life became the possibility that he could acquire new land and more slaves. When men like Yancey insisted that anything that menaced slavery menaced all the South, they were talking to the hard new men who were on the make as well as to the old aristocrats lounging at their ease on the storied verandas of Charleston.

The argument over slavery thus pointed in several directions at once, and the abolitionist who declared that slavery was morally wrong was not contributing much because he was ignoring all of the complexities that made the case so difficult. Yet the business might conceivably have been settled, by argument and negotiation among men of good will, if slavery had not included one element that could not be discussed rationally.

For the tragedy of the Negro, and of the America to which he had been compelled to come as a valuable but undesirable immigrant, was that his detention in servitude involved emotions deeper than the pit and blacker than midnight, convulsive stirrings in the nerve system that went beyond anything with which men of that day could cope intellectually. Beyond everything else, slavery was a race problem. It was *the* race problem, demanding attention at a time when Americans of the blood prided themselves on their inborn superiority to people who showed even minor differences in accent, in pigmentation, or in cultural background. No one was ready to face up to this problem.

As long as slavery existed the problem did not have to be faced. Slavery did not solve the race problem, but it plowed around it. As a slave the Negro might be a strain on the conscience, but he was not really a bother, and those who thought he should not be a slave could spend their time happily denouncing his masters rather than reflecting on the limitless implications of the concept of the universal brotherhood of man. Enslaved, the Negro was under control and so was the race problem. But if he should be freed, en masse, all across America, he would have to be dealt with as a human being, and a nation whose declaration of independence began by asserting that all men were created equal would have to make up its mind whether those words were to be taken seriously.

This was what almost nobody was prepared to do. Even many of the Northerners who were most anxious to free the Negro were ready to agree that he ought to be deported as soon as he lost his chains. Lincoln himself felt this way, and with others who felt as he did he had urged that some sort of resettlement scheme be devised. Let the Negro be planted in Central America, in Africa, or perhaps in the dim lands on the far side of the misty mountains of the moon—anywhere at all, so long as it was not in America. Even slavery's enemies had some small part in keeping slavery alive.

The Southerner was perfectly clear on this point, and he would close ranks in defense of slavery instinctively, even though he might privately be of two minds about the institution's morality or cash value. His determination to keep his a white man's country did not necessarily imply personal feeling against the man who had to remain a slave. The master actually liked the slave better than did the man who owned no slaves. Frederick Law Olmsted, the Northerner whose journey through the slave states confirmed him in his abolitionist views, noted with amazement that "when the Negro is definitely a slave, it would seem that the alleged antipathy of the white race to associate with him is lost."[7] With the enormous gulf between owner and owned fixed by law and enforced by all the power of the state, there could be a sort of toleration, even a fondness, which did the slave little good but which at least served to gloss over the innate ugliness of the system itself.

That ugliness, so clearly visible to Northerners who did not have to rub elbows with the institution, was also visible in the South. Orations and sermons and pamphlets might extol slavery as a positive good, but there was an underlying uneasiness about it. An outsider like Olmsted might deplore the

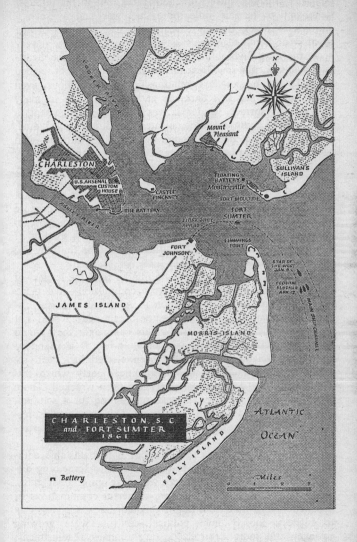

COOPER RIVER

CHARLESTON

U.S. ARSENAL
CUSTOM
HOUSE

ASHLEY RIVER

CASTLE
PINCKNEY

THE BATTERY

Mount
Pleasant

FLOATING
BATTERY
Moultrieville

SULLIVAN'S
ISLAND

FORT MOULTRIE

FORT
SUMTER

FIRST SHOT
APR.12

FORT
JOHNSON

CUMMINGS
POINT

STAR OF
THE WEST
JAN.9

FEDERAL
FLOTILLA
APR.12

JAMES ISLAND

MORRIS ISLAND

MAIN SHIP CHANNEL

CHARLESTON, S.C.
and FORT SUMTER
1861

ATLANTIC

OCEAN

FOLLY ISLAND

◼ Battery

Miles
0   1   2   3

debasing effect of slavery on both races, but in his bitterest denunciations he said little more than was said by such a woman as Mary Boykin Chesnut, mistress of one of the greatest of South Carolina's slave empires, who saw slavery from the most favorable of all vantage points and was heartsick over what she saw. Beneath the easy intimacy that seemed to make the master-slave relationship so harmonious, even so rewarding, she saw darkness and horrors. The intimacy was on the surface. Under it was a great estrangement, a total lack of communication, a latent hostility which would, and at times did, break through the varnished surface, with violence and murder.[8] Slavery rested finally on the ability to use unmeasured force, and every slave and master knew it. What happened in San Domingo might conceivably happen on the Yazoo Delta or in the South Carolina rice fields, and John Brown had been so frightening precisely because no one could be entirely certain that his monstrous dream was impossible of attainment. Beneath the easy solidity of Southern life there was a haunting realization that the ice was very thin.

So the leaders of the South—no blinder than the leaders of the North, but driven by a sharper compulsion—had made the most disastrous miscalculation in American political history. The fearfully explosive issues of the day would not be brought nearer a solution by this campaign; they would only be intensified. The one candidate who, as a friend of the South, might possibly have been elected had been rejected out of hand; the national political party which traditionally served Southern interests had been wrecked. There would be no great debate. Instead of hunting for a solution, the politicians had worked for a crisis. This they would presently get, and when they got it they would find it a catastrophe.

America just then was in a state of highly unstable equilibrium. Everything seemed to be turning into something different. A simple pastoral society was developing great cities, a network of mines and factories, powerful combinations of production and trade and finance. Smallness was giving way to bigness, loosely held political controls were growing stronger and more centralized, revolutionary readjustments in almost every aspect of national life were beginning to take place. The Industrial Revolution was under way and it could

not be stopped; responsible men could do no more than appraise what was happening and work out some means to
minimize the shock. But the responsible men had refused to
do anything of the kind. No adjustments would be made.
The collision would be head-on, and the shock would be
cataclysmic. The campaign of 1860 was little more than an
open invitation to revolution.

3. By Torchlight

IT WAS like no campaign ever waged before—except possibly
the log-cabin-and-hard-cider monstrosity of 1840. There was
a great confusion of voices, but what men said did not seem
to matter very much. North and South, the people were going to vote by their emotions, and the nervous unease that
lay across all sections of the country drove men to sudden
displays of wild enthusiasm, as if in the flare of torches and
the excitement of moving parades some reassurance about
the future might be found. The country moved blindly on
toward an election that would bring none of its problems to
a solution. Its political machinery was being loaded with
more than it could carry, and after the votes were cast and
counted, something was bound to break.

The Democrats were prisoners of their own division, and
the initiative lay with the Republicans, who would exercise
it with a peculiar mixture of canny forethought and energetic
irresponsibility. The anticipation of victory would be controlling. The tide was going their way, and they would run no
risk of reversing it; as far as they could, they would make
the voter feel that he must move with it.

The sense of movement was quite literal, and it seemed
to be contagious, drawing people with it, driving an insistent
new pulse beat through the blood stream. Mid-summer twilight, in city after city all through the Middle West, saw
the strangest of parades—smoky torches flaring in the thick-
ening dark, thousands of men tramping out a disturbing
rhythm as they moved down the streets to the sound of military bands, with their own impassioned shouting stirring the
senses of the crowds that lined the sidewalks to watch. America was beginning to march, and the marching was more readily started than stopped; this campaign, whose outcome

would leave the nation so aroused and desperate that it would create great armies and start them off for unimaginable goals, was ominously hinting at what was to come.

The marching was done by the Wide-Awakes, faintly military organizations of young Republican enthusiasts whose formation was simply a revival of an old device for generating political enthusiasm. The business first came to view in the winter of 1860, when Abraham Lincoln went to New England to speak after his performance at New York's Cooper Institute. In Hartford he was met by a formation of a few dozen of the faithful, togged out in oil-cloth capes and bearing torches, and they marched behind a band to escort him from his hotel to the place where he was to speak. The performance seemed effective, and after the Wigwam convention had made its nominations and the party leaders began to get the campaign under way, the idea was picked up and expanded.[1]

Before long there were many Wide-Awake clubs, parading at party rallies, parading sometimes simply for the sake of parading, putting thousands of men in line, conveying an increasing feeling that this new party carried immense popular support. A Chicago newspaper remarked that a stranger, seeing the Wide-Awakes for the first time, "is strongly impressed with the peculiar spectacle they present," and it commended the precision of the rudimentary drill which the marchers had practiced. Lincoln was the Railsplitter—a fact of no apparent significance, but somehow a fine talking point—and so the marchers took to carrying long rails, each with a swinging lamp at the top, or an American flag bearing the names of the Republican nominees. "The uniform of the privates," said the Chicago paper, "is a black enamelled circular cape, quite full and of good length, and a glazed military fatigue cap with a brass or silver eagle in front. Some companies are uniformed with blue, red, drab and gray silver caps and capes and relieve the monotony of the darker uniforms. The captains and non-commissioned officers are distinguished by an Inverness overcoat, with black cape and undress military caps . . . The measured tread, steady front and unbroken lines speak of strict attention to drill, and the effective manner in which the various bodies are managed by their officers shows conclusively that men of military experience control their movements."[2]

This came to its brightest flowering on August 8, in a great ceremony at Springfield, Illinois, where there was to be a grand "ratification meeting" to endorse, underline, and celebrate the nomination of Lincoln. Into Springfield came the Wide-Awakes from, apparently, all parts of Illinois. The young men in oil-cloth capes got off trains by the scores and hundreds, came trundling in from near-by towns by wagons, or made the hike on foot, camping by the roadside at night, presenting the appearance (as the stoutly Republican Illinois *State Journal* remarked) of "a veritable political earthquake." Springfield was all bannered and beflagged, and the *State Journal* reporter, confessing that "we have no adequate words to describe what our eyes beheld," asserted that the country had never seen a larger or more magnificent political demonstration. With much effort and confusion, parade marshals importantly vocal, company commanders barking orders, teamsters cursing their mounted floats into line, the parade began to move by mid-morning. At the head of the procession a wagon carried an immense ball, with the placard: "The Republican ball is in motion." (Another banner proclaimed, in handy doggerel: "The people mourn insulted laws, And curse Steve Douglas as the cause.") It was followed by a score or more of Wide-Awake companies, each with its own band, all the bands playing at once to produce a marvelous discord and an unceasing thump of bass drums; and there were floats, delegations of true believers from neighboring towns and counties, each delegation riding in wagons. The men who had devised the floats had let themselves go; one float, harking back to the wild campaign of old Tippecanoe's day, mounted a log cabin with a stout pioneer splitting rails in front of it; another, a huge dray hauled by twenty-three yoke of oxen, had a whole gang of railsplitters at work; on still another wagon a small steam engine worked a power loom which was visibly producing yards and yards of jeans cloth, which a tailor immediately fabricated into a pair of pants for the fortunate nominee, while a banner overhead proclaimed the party's devotion to "Protection to Home Industry." There were speakers' stands all over town, and at times a dozen orators were in action simultaneously.

Lincoln himself appeared at last, riding in a carriage, and the cheering crowd dragged him forth and carried him on sweating shoulder tops to one of the platforms, depositing him there and demanding lustily that he make a speech—a thing which for a full ten minutes he was unable to do because the jostling audience would not stop yelling. When comparative quiet was obtained, Lincoln's words were few: "It has been my purpose, since I have been placed in my present position, to make no speeches . . . I appear upon the ground here at this time only for the purpose of affording myself the best opportunity of seeing you and enabling you to see me. . . . You will kindly let me be silent." Then he managed to get away, riding from the scene on horseback. That evening there were torchlight parades, and fireworks, and the *State Journal* felt that it was "a magnificent display . . . the streets were all ablaze with light and enthusiasm."[3]

The significant word, here and elsewhere, was "enthusiasm." Party leaders had discovered that in Lincoln they had a man they could shout about, and they would offer the electorate fence rails, brass bands, torchlight hurrahs, and the incessant tramp of marching feet. In Cincinnati a campaign newspaper —named, inevitably, *The Railsplitter*—was produced for thirteen issues, bearing in its logotype an unrecognizable woodcut of Lincoln with the words "An Honest Man's the Noblest Work of God." Like most of the rest of the campaign documents the party got out that year, this sheet rarely quoted Lincoln. It devoted most of its space to unceasing attacks on Douglas, suggesting in one issue that Douglas was a Catholic and asserting that while in Europe he had visited the Pope. Its approach to the slavery issue was as down to earth as a village watering trough, and as devoid of reasoned argument: "The Democracy are pretty much bankrupted for arguments but they have one last resource when everything else fails—everlasting 'nigger equality.' Of course there will be no 'nigger equality' where there are no 'niggers,' and as the Republican party proposes to save the Territories for free white men, while the Democracy leave a way open for their introduction, it is difficult to see how the slang phrase here quoted applies to any other party than themselves."[4]

As a matter of course there were campaign songs. One of these, set to the tune of the "Star Spangled Banner," began: "Lo! See the bright scroll of the Future unfold! Broad farms and fair cities shall crown our devotion." Another one, sung to the tune of "Old Uncle Ned," aimed derision at Douglas:

Dere was a little man, and his name was Stevy Dug,
To de White House he longed for to go:
But he hadn't any votes through de whole of de Souf
In de place where de votes ought to grow.[5]

The campaign was moving, and there could be no doubt
about it; the unresolved question was where it might be moving to, and for this no one had an answer. To be sure, it was
moving toward victory, but the trouble was that the victory
in November would start more than it would finish, and
there did not seem to be in the width and breadth of America
anyone, North or South, who cared to look beyond victory.
The campaign would go by torchlight, with moving feet
drumming out a pulse beat on cobblestones and on dusty
main streets; there would be music and bright slogans and
songs and cheers and intensive jubilation, America would go
along with it, it would be demonstrated that the Northwest
at last could name a President—but what would happen after
all of this was ratified was a mystery, and if what was being
done was good, it was not, unfortunately, quite good enough.

Nobody would say anything that might make trouble: that
was understood. And Mr. Lincoln, who was moodily reflecting on all of the promises his managers had made on those
hot nights in Chicago, would play it straight. He would stand
on the record, which was as clear as any politician's record
need be; the trouble was that the record was incomplete, and
now there was no way to extend it. Lincoln had been nominated by men who (having many subsidiary matters on their
minds) at least knew where he stood on such problems as
slavery in the territories, the homestead act, protection for in-
fant industries, and so on; but nobody knew where anybody
stood on the grim, explosive questions which the country
might have to face once the election had been completed.
Would the election of a Republican cause all or part of the
South to secede from the Union? If one or many states seceded, what should the Federal government do about it? Was
there any way by which the people of the United States could
be induced to pause and take thought and see whether the
issues which divided them might somehow be disposed of
without the necessity for killing anybody? On such questions
as these (which, in the summer of 1860, were the only questions that really mattered), a silence as of the grave settled

down on the country where gay young men in varnished capes paraded under flags with what they supposed to be proper military precision; on that other part of the country where other men, not yet uniformed, were buying muskets and laying plans and stiffening themselves for an impending shock, and resolving to give not an inch to the unspeakable aggression which was being committed by men who did not think slavery an immutable benefit.

Many people, in this summer, were writing to Lincoln, trying to find out what he thought and proposed to do about the dangerous points that were at issue; and for these Lincoln's secretariat prepared a form letter, which was signed by the right subordinates and sent out by wholesale to the Northerners who had embarrassing questions to ask. It went like this:

"Your letter to Mr. Lincoln, of ——, and by which you seek to obtain his opinion on certain political points, has been received by him. He has received others of a similar character; but he also has a greater number of the exactly opposite character. The latter class beseech him to write nothing whatever upon any point of political doctrine. They say his positions were well known when he was nominated, and that he must not now embarrass the canvass by undertaking to shift or modify them. He regrets that he cannot oblige all, but you perceive that it is impossible for him to do so."[6]

This letter was sent out to earnest seekers after light. John G. Nicolay, the earnest young man who was Lincoln's secretary, noted that a caller had urged that Lincoln say something to reassure the Southerners who were sincerely alarmed by the course of the Republican campaign. To this, Lincoln remarked curtly that "there are no such men"; and he went on to explain that this was simply "the trick by which the South breaks down every honest man." He would go to Washington, if he tried to reassure all alarmed Southerners, "as powerless as a block of buckeye wood"; honest men could look at the Republican platform and at what Lincoln had already said, and find therein everything that he could say now. Musing with his young secretary, Lincoln spoke his mind: "Let us be practical—there are many general terms afloat such as 'conservatism'—'enforcement of the irrepressible conflict at the point of the bayonet'—'hostility to the South,' and so forth—all of which mean nothing without definition. What then could I say to allay their fears, if they will not define what particular act or acts they fear from me or my friends?" The candidate felt that he owed something to the men who, feeling that he stood for something, had entrusted him with the candidacy: "If I shall begin to yield to these threats, if I begin dallying with them, the men who have elected me, if I shall be elected, would give me up before my inauguration—and the South, seeing it, would deliberately kick me out. . . . If I should be elected the first duty to the country would be to stand by the men who elected me."[7]

Sound as the word of gospel, indisputably—bearing, however, no word of wisdom for guidance through the hard days that might come after the electoral votes had been cast and tabulated. The Wide-Awakes marched and the bands played and the candidate was very cautious; and as the summer weeks wore away, men in the South, caught up by some reverse reflex from the emotion that was moving across the North, began to see Lincoln as the sign and symbol of what they dreaded most. In South Carolina the Charleston *Mercury* remarked that the hated Seward had, after all, been rejected at Chicago because "he was disposed to temporize the South," and lacked the iron to move on for subjugation. Lincoln, the *Mercury* believed, was different; he had "the decision of character and the earnestness" needed to beat down the South's resistance to oppression, and all things considered, he was "the beau ideal of a relentless, dogged free-soil border ruffian . . . a vulgar mobocrat and a Southern hater in political opinions." In Richmond, the *Enquirer* began to see Lincoln as "an illiterate partisan . . . possessed only of his inveterate hatred of slavery and his openly avowed predilections of Negro equality"; he surpassed Seward "in the bitterness of his prejudices and in the insanity of his fanaticism," and his election would mean "Negro equality."[8] If Lincoln considered that it was useless for him to try to talk sense to the Southern leaders who were whipping up hatred for him, there were Southern voices that would confirm him in his belief.

Seward himself, as a matter of fact, was talking as gently as any cooing dove, this summer. He had adjusted himself with difficulty to the idea that he was not going to be President, to the astounding fact that his party had actually nominated this gawky frontiersman from Illinois in place of himself; and for a time it had seemed that he might sulk in his tent, revenging himself, by inaction, on the misguided majority. But although the adjustment was hard, Seward had made it, and now he was taking the stump—in Michigan, in Iowa, in Illinois, in Wisconsin, all through the impassioned West—and as he pleaded for a solid Republican vote he minimized the dangers that might lie ahead.

Looking toward the angry men of the South, Seward was saying: "I can hear their disputes, their fretful controversies, their threats that if their own separate interests are not gratified and consulted by the Federal government they will separate from this Union—will secede from it, will dissolve it; and while I hear on their busy sidewalks these clamorous contentions I am able to say: 'Peace, be still. These subjects of contention and dispute that so irritate and anger and provoke you are but ephemeral and temporary. These institutions which you so much desire to conserve, and for which you think you would sacrifice the welfare of the people of this continent, are almost as ephemeral as yourselves.' "

Seward refused to worry—at least to worry in public—and he assured an audience at St. Paul, in a speech which was reprinted in pamphlet form and distributed in every Northern state: "The man is born today who will live to see the American Union, the American people—the whole of them—coming into the harmonious understanding that this is the land of the free men—for the free men—that it is the land for the white man; and that whatever elements there are to disturb its present peace or irritate the passions of its possessors will in the end—and that end will come before long—pass away, without capacity in any way to disturb the harmony of, or endanger, this great Union."[9]

These were fine words, and Seward would repeat them. Speaking in New York a little later, he had words of jaunty confidence: "For ten, aye twenty years, these threats have been renewed in the same language and in the same form, about the first day of November every four years, when it happened to come before the day of the presidential election. I do not doubt but that these Southern statesmen and politicians think they are going to dissolve the Union, but I think they are going to do no such thing."[10]

Chanting these assurances, Seward doubtless spoke for

most of the men who were listening to him. Yet there was an uneasy doubt under everything—as uneasy as the doubt of slavery's own eternal rightness which disturbed the subconscious minds of men in the South—and it centered about that grim question: If the Republicans win this election, will the Southern states leave the Union? As Seward said, the threat had been made before. It had lost its force in the North, like the alarming cry of "Wolf!" too often repeated. As a nation of poker players the Americans knew what to do with a bluff when they met one; the trouble now was that no one could be entirely certain that this was a bluff, and the consequences that might come if it were called and turned out to be no bluff were staggering to think about. The result was that nobody talked about them. Seward went about the country voicing his vibrant belief that all of this was talk and nothing more, and Lincoln stayed in Springfield (dusty smoke from the torchlight parade still hanging in the air to cloud men's vision: ominously like powder smoke and the mist of dreadful combat, if anyone had thought about it) and had the secretariat send out form letters, on the logical ground that no one could honestly believe that he meant enmity toward the South; and Stephen A. Douglas, pausing in Chicago in the midst of a furious campaign which he knew he could not win, remarked soberly; "I believe this country is in more danger now than at any other moment since I have known anything of public life."[11]

The Republican campaign was enormously effective. It moved, it had hot life in it, it caught men up and pulled them along, and the Wide-Awakes went down the sultry streets with torchlight to lead them on, bands playing, men yelling, stump speakers orating from every available soap box, with the marchers flourishing fence rails and displaying log cabins and flaunting banners to proclaim the overriding honesty of the chosen man; and no one stopped to ask: Do these men to the South of us really mean what they are saying, and if they do mean it, what are we prepared to do? There was an undertone of violence in this election. Preparations were being made in the cotton belt, and in the North the men who supported Lincoln were, as if by deep instinct, forming vaguely military marching groups, dressing in gaudy uniforms and parading to military music, troopers enlisted to defend they did not quite know what. The campaign might, on surface appearance, be blowing off steam, but it was actually building up an uncontainable pressure. The country as a whole wanted no irrepressible conflict between the sections, but the claims of sectionalism had become too strong to be ignored. The South had one sectional party and the North had another, and as far as anyone could see, it would probably be a case where the devil would take the hindmost, or perhaps everyone together in a hand basket.

The campaign, in short, was unreal. Posing as the most cynical of realists, the politicians had retained cynicism but had lost realism, and now they were entangled with something they could not handle. Parades and loud noises were taking the place of reasoned discussion. The slanting plain that led down to the sea was growing steeper and steeper, and the rush was moving faster and faster. In the North, men could listen to military music and to the unbroken thud of the feet of marching men; in the South, they could listen to the extremists. Edmund Ruffin was writing to Yancey, saying that a Republican victory was obviously coming and that it would be "a clear and unmistakable indication of future & fixed domination of the Northern section & its abolition policy over the Southern states & their institutions, & the beginning of a sure & speedy progress to the extermination of Negro slavery & the consequent utter ruin of the prosperity of the South." The only possible answer to this, he wrote, must be secession. In his diary, Ruffin wrote that his sons hoped that Lincoln would be defeated but that he did not. "I most earnestly & anxiously desire Lincoln to be elected—because I have hope that at least one State, S.C., will secede, & that others will follow—& even if otherwise, I wish the question tested & settled now. If there is a general submission now, there never will be future maintenance of our rights—& the end of Negro slavery may be considered as settled. I can think of little else than this momentous crisis of our institutions & our fate."[12]

Few men were as realistic or as outspoken as Edmund Ruffin. There were even times when it seemed as if the proslavery and anti-slavery parties were repeating the same ugly words. Yancey himself got into New York, in the middle of this campaign, and he made a lighthearted, taunting speech which was strangely like the thoughts which that Cincinnati campaign newspaper, *The Railsplitter,* had given to the North a few weeks earlier.

Slavery, said Yancey, was an institution necessary to the prosperity of the South and to that of the North as well; and, furthermore, it was nothing any Northerner need worry about. "It is an institution, too, that doesn't harm you, for we don't let our niggers run about to injure anybody; we keep them; they never steal from you; they don't trouble you with that peculiar stench which is very good in the nose of the Southern man but intolerable in the nose of a Northerner." Yet the North might elect Lincoln, who would "build up an abolitionist party in every Southern state," and Yancey warned that this would not be borne: "With the election of a black Republican, all the South would be menaced. Emissaries will percolate between master and slave as water between the crevices of the rocks underground. . . . The keystone of the arch of the Union is already crumbling. A more weighty question was never before you. One freighted with the fate of societies and of nationalities is on your mind."[13]

4. *Little Giant*

PERHAPS Senator Douglas had been both too clever and too outspoken. He was a tough little man who knew all of the political tricks, and he was also a hard-boiled realist, and in these capacities he had devised a Kansas-Nebraska act with popular sovereignty for an antidote, and the nation was not quite ready for it. He had unintentionally compelled the North to contemplate an arrogant slave power which would inflict its peculiar institution on the harsh western plains, as if everything beyond the Missouri could be brought under the confines of a law that seemed to fit the Tombigbee and the Yazoo. To the South, at the same time, he had given foreknowledge of an unendurable truth—that slavery would die unless the outside world dropped all other concerns to prop it up, which was obviously impossible. Because he had done these things he could not become President of the United States; the North derided him for liking slavery too much, and the deep South hated him because he liked it too little. Perhaps the truth was that the issue of slavery had become, as men's emotions then stood, both intolerable and insoluble.

Douglas had tried to reduce the issue to something that could be disposed of in the ordinary give-and-take of politics, to present America's destiny as something that did not have to lie under the control of extremists. The conflicting moralities of men profoundly in earnest would prevent it. The showdown might have shattering impact, but it would have to come.

It was worst in the South. There Douglas was a symbol. Lincoln might be the black-visaged enemy who threatened to upset everything the South lived by—namely, the notion that a chosen people might live by the unremitting toil of an inferior race fated to hew wood and draw water—but Douglas had come to look like the apostate, the turncoat, the former friend who appeared on the other side when the pinch came. Douglas was the more menacing because he bore no ill-will. In his position, in this summer of 1860, the slavery system could read its own sentence of ultimate death. To get away from him, the men who had Southern sentiment in their control had determined that the choice would be between the Black Republicans and disunion.[1]

As the hot weeks passed, following the great conventions, the choice began to be clearer. A political maneuver designed to force concessions was running into the knowledge that the forced concessions would not be made; and the alternative was to break away altogether, to try against impossible odds to erect a self-contained nation that would base itself on an outworn foundation. In sheer self-defense the people who had chosen this gambit were asking whether what they were going to do would mean war and destruction. Since no other candidate was readily available, they would ask it most directly of Senator Douglas himself.

For Douglas, of all the candidates, was the one who was trying to make a real campaign. The swing around the circle was new at that time. A man nominated for the presidency usually stayed at home, letting what he was speak for him, reflecting quietly that a politician's first duty was to get elected, and although his supporters might go to almost any log-cabin-and-hard-cider excess, the candidate himself was supposed to act as if he did not really know what they were doing. Douglas would not follow this pattern. He was intense, dynamic, a man who was burning himself out, a crafty politician lifting himself in this final year of his life above the craft of politics; he would campaign across all the South, openly bidding for votes, arguing his case in person from any stump that was available. He came to Norfolk, Virginia, late in August, to speak from the steps of the City Hall, and he was blunt without qualification.

"I desire no man to vote for me," he said, "unless he hopes and desires the Union maintained and preserved intact by the faithful execution of every act, every line and every letter of the written Constitution which our fathers bequeathed to us." Sectional parties, whether they were born in the North or in the South, were "the great evil and curse of this country," and it was time for men who loved the unbroken country to see whether they could not find some common principle on which they could stand and defeat both Northern and Southern agitators. Someone in the audience called out to ask whether, if Lincoln should be elected, secession would not be justified. Douglas met this without flinching.

"To this I emphatically answer 'No,'" he said. "The election of a man to the presidency by the American people, in conformity with the Constitution of the United States, would not justify any attempt at dissolving this glorious confederacy."

There was another question. Suppose the cotton states, on the election of Lincoln, should secede from the Union without waiting for some overt act against their constitutional rights: where would Senator Douglas then stand in respect to the act of Southern secession? His reply was uncompromising: "It is the duty of the President of the United States, and of all others in authority under him, to enforce the laws of the United States passed by Congress and as the courts expound them: and I, as in duty bound by my oath of fidelity to the Constitution, would do all in my power to aid the government of the United States in maintaining the supremacy of the laws against all resistance to them, come from whatever quarter it might."[2]

A man asking Southerners to vote for him in the summer of 1860 had to have courage to say that. Saying it, Douglas raised a storm; and when protest was made, he demanded that the same questions be asked of John C. Breckinridge. (One oddity of the campaign was the fact that in the North Douglas was running against Lincoln, and in the South he was running against Breckinridge; and the Lincoln managers, although they aimed most of their shots at Douglas, were sometimes worried much more about the vote John Bell might get.)

Not long after he had spoken in Norfolk, Douglas was at Raleigh, North Carolina, and there he was even more explicit about what the Constitution meant to him and the way in which he would enforce it. Speaking for the men of the Northwest, he declared that since they had so great a stake in the Union, the men who felt as he felt were determined to maintain it, and that they knew but one way to do this—to enforce the Constitution rigidly, line by line and clause by clause, precisely as it had come down from the founding fathers, without stopping to ask whether Southern fire-eaters or Northern abolitionists liked it or not.

So far, so good; in the political jargon of that day, to speak for strict enforcement of the Constitution was simply to say that the Constitutional guarantee of slavery must be respected. But Douglas went on to insist that the Constitution also provided for the integrity of the Federal Union, and he wanted all men to know that he considered this guarantee as good as the other. "I am in favor," he said, "of executing in good faith every clause and provision of the Constitution and of protecting every right under it—and then hanging every man who takes up arms against it." While the audience was digesting this assertion, Douglas went on to drive the point home. He would use force and the extreme rigor of law against disunionists:

"Yes, my friends, I would hang every man higher than Haman who would attempt by force to resist the execution of any provision of the Constitution which our fathers made and bequeathed to us."[3]

Nobody else was talking that way. Secession was being threatened openly, but most politicians were either deploring the hard feelings which brought such talk to the surface, or were refusing to take the talk seriously, or were ignoring it altogether. John Bell stood for the Union and the Constitution, without any elaboration of the steps which such a belief might entail. Typical of his support was the plea put forward by the Cincinnati *Daily Times,* which plaintively asked "Why Should We Quarrel?" and lamented that brothers were ceasing to be brothers. "Why seek to meddle with that which concerns us not?" inquired the *Times.* "Why not return to

the happy days when we were homogeneous, and undivided
in sentiment from Maine to Georgia?" The Republicans were
not offering much more. Lincoln was letting his record speak
for itself, refusing to elaborate on it lest designing men twist
his words out of shape, and Seward was blandly insisting
that this talk of secession was no more than empty talk. A
party organ like the Pittsburgh *Gazette* held that the talk
was deplorable, but it refused to be alarmed: "As to the
threats of Revolution so freely indulged in, we do not care
whether they are sham or in earnest. We believe them to
be mere bravado—empty gasconading, intended merely to
alarm, but that is no matter. They are equally disgraceful
whether made for political effect or otherwise; and the people of the North will be false to their rights if they fail to rebuke them." The implication, of course, was that the people
of the North ought to administer such rebuke by voting the
straight Republican ticket.[4]

Breckinridge was being most careful of all. He touched on
the subject once, in a speech at a big political barbecue in
Lexington, Kentucky, where he said that he would "proudly
challenge the bitterest enemy I may have on earth to point
out an act, to disclose an utterance, to reveal a thought of
mine hostile to the Constitution and the Union of the States."
He went on to assert that Lincoln, who represented "the
most obnoxious principles at issue in this canvass," was advancing unconstitutional ideas, "and if the Republican party
should undertake to carry them out they will destroy the
Union." He then hastened back to safer ground with a ringing peroration: "Conscious that my foot is planted on the
rock of the Constitution, surrounded and sustained by friends
I love and cherish, holding principles that have been in every
form endorsed by my native commonwealth, with a spirit
erect and unbroken I defy all calumny and calmly await the
triumph of the truth."[5]

Breckinridge might defy calumny with all of his vigor, but
he was still going to get the votes of all Southerners who
actively hoped for a break-up of the Union. He would get,
as well, most of the votes of the numerous Southerners who,
not actively desiring disunion, would still prefer it to life
under a Black Republican President. Like Lincoln, he would
let the fermenting times themselves work for him. Only

Douglas, with his talk of building a gallows higher than Haman's, would speak out.

So the campaign moved on toward its climax. A brief flurry of panic touched Republican headquarters in Springfield as the first election tests drew near. It was all-important for the Republicans to carry Pennsylvania and Indiana for their state tickets at the state elections in October. What with factional fights, and the chance that the still powerful Know-Nothing element would go against the Republicans, it looked for a time as if these state elections might be lost, and Judge Davis made a hurried trip to Harrisburg to consult with Simon Cameron, the lanky party boss to whom so much had been promised so rashly at Chicago. Davis found Cameron "a genial, pleasant and kind-hearted man," the geniality all the warmer because Cameron examined certain notes expounding Lincoln's position on the tariff and found them "abundantly satisfactory." Republican victory in Pennsylvania, said Cameron, was certain. Davis got further reassurance farther east, returned to Indiana and found party leaders uneasy, saw to it that campaign funds were raised, and believed that the danger had been averted. Until the votes were counted, however, Judge Davis would worry, and a week before the election he wrote to his wife that if Pennsylvania and Indiana went against the Republicans, "I shall consider the idea that the people are capable of self-government a heresy."

Either his worries were groundless or his desperate fence-mending was effective. Pennsylvania went Republican in October by more than 30,000, and the Republican ticket won in Indiana by nearly 10,000. Judge Davis was trying a case in Clinton, Illinois, when the good news reached him, and his judicial decorum collapsed under the strain: Lincoln's friend Ward Lamon wrote that the judge kicked over the clerk's desk, "turned a double somersault and adjourned court until after the presidential election." To intimates, Davis confided that he believed Douglas "is sorry he didn't die when he was little." Lamon probably exaggerated slightly, but Davis's excitement was understandable: the victories in the state elections unquestionably meant that Lincoln was going to win in November.[6]

Nowhere was this more clearly visible than in the South. Ruffin drafted a letter to Yancey remarking that there was but one remedy for the impending calamity—"secession of some (if all are not then ready) of the Southern states from the Union with the Northern, which has been changed from the former bond of fraternal love, & of mutual defence & support, to a yoke & manacles on the South." The Charleston *Mercury,* Rhett's organ, published a doleful editorial on "The Terrors of Submission," asserting that the inauguration of Lincoln and Hamlin would reduce the value of all Southern slaves by $100 each, and going on to declare: "If the South once submits to the rule of abolitionists by the General Government, there is, probably, an end of all peaceful separation of the Union. We can only escape the ruin they meditate for the South by war." The *Mercury* added that "the ruin of the South, by the emancipation of her slaves, is not like the ruin of any other people. It is not a mere loss of liberty . . . but it is the loss of liberty, property, home, country—everything that makes life worth having."[7]

Not all were as outspoken. The New Orleans *Daily True Delta* noted sadly that "the South is now rapidly drifting into the fatal embrace of her most implacable enemies," and felt that "the insanity or malignancy" of the South's most prominent leaders had led Dixie off into a constricting box: the South was now estranged, not just from the North (which did not really matter), but from the Northwest, and the result was likely to be deadly. But there was no help for it. On October 16 the Mississippi *Free Trader* printed a letter from Jefferson Davis, sounding the tocsin with dignified reserve: "Confronted by a common foe, the South should, by the instinct of self-preservation, be united. . . . The recent declarations of the candidate and leaders of the Black Republican party . . . must suffice to convince many who have formerly doubted the purpose to attack the institution of slavery in the states. The undying opposition to slavery in the United States means war upon it where it is, not where it is not" [that is, the Republicans did not simply oppose slavery in the territories: they opposed slavery in the slave states, and they would not stop until they had obliterated it], "and the time is at hand when the great battle is to be fought between the defenders of the constitutional government and the votaries of mob rule, fanaticism and anarchy."[8]

Davis saw how things were drifting. It was dawning on him that it did not really matter who got the votes in the

South—Breckinridge, Douglas, or Bell; the Republican party was going to win the election, and if these votaries of mob rule were to be stopped, something would have to be done very quickly. Davis suggested that all three candidates who were opposing Lincoln should withdraw; let the opposition center on one man, and the menacing Republican might yet be beaten. But who would withdraw? It came down, apparently, to Douglas, and he would not withdraw; after all, he was the only one of the three who had the remotest chance of winning a straight two-man contest . . . and the Wide-Awakes marched down the dusty streets with smoking flares and with incessant music and cheers, the tide was moving and no one could stop it, and Douglas himself, the one man who might have kept the Republicans from victory, was in the fight to the finish, holding up, for any who had eyes to see, the monstrous vision of a high gallows for traitors. . . . It was too late.

The governor of South Carolina at that time was William H. Gist, a dedicated man and, like so many of that kind, somewhat strait-laced; one-time president of the Methodist State Sunday School convention, a lawyer and a planter, one who believed there should be restrictions on the manufacture and sale of strong drink; a stout South Carolina patriot and a man with an eye to see things and a heart to act on what the eye saw. Even before the Indiana and Pennsylvania elections, he could see that Abraham Lincoln was going to win the election, and on October 5 he wrote letters to the governors of the cotton states urging "that there may be concert of action, which is so essential to success." South Carolina, said Governor Gist, would call a state convention as soon as Lincoln's election was official. If any other state would secede, South Carolina would follow; if no other state would take the lead, South Carolina would go it alone—provided that there was some reason to think that other states would fall in line. And so: "If you decide to call a convention upon the election of a majority of electors favorable to Lincoln, I desire to know the day you propose for the meeting, that we may call our convention to meet the same day, if possible."[9]

The Republicans had had a gaudy float going down the streets of Springfield with a big banner announcing that the ball was in motion. Now a Southern ball was in motion, rolling slowly, even wobbling unsteadily on its axis, but nevertheless moving; started on its way by this letter of Governor Gist's, which was delivered to the various governors by a South Carolina militia officer with the completely suitable name of States' Rights Gist. States' Rights Gist would become a Confederate general and would die in action at Franklin, Tennessee; when he set out on his fateful mission he had just four years to live.

The governors were by no means unrestrained in their enthusiasm when they wrote their replies. As political veterans they could not get very far ahead of local sentiment, and local sentiment had not yet hardened. Governor John W. Ellis, of North Carolina, wrote that the people of his state simply had not made up their minds what to do in case Lincoln should be elected: "Some favor submission, some resistance, and others would await the course of events that might follow." They probably would not think a Republican victory, in itself, proper cause for leaving the Union, although they would never support "the monstrous doctrine of coercion." From Louisiana came similar words. Governor Thomas O. Moore would need more than "the deplorable event" of a Republican victory to make him advise secession, and he believed most people in Louisiana felt the same way. He did think that Louisiana should meet with other slave states to "endeavor to effect a complete harmony of action," but he feared this harmony would be hard to get. To be sure, if the Federal government tried coercion, the case would be different; meanwhile, Louisiana was totally unprepared "for any warlike measures," and her arsenals were empty.

Mississippi was a different case. Governor John J. Pettus felt that his people would do anything in their power to keep the state "from passing under the Black Republican yoke," but Mississippi could not go it alone. He would call a special session of the legislature as soon as it was known that Lincoln had won the election, and he believed Mississippi would ask a council of the slave states; if such a council advised secession, Mississippi would probably go along. In Georgia, Governor Joseph E. Brown believed that a convention of the people, meeting sometime between election day and March 4, would determine the state's course of action. In his opinion the people would "wait for an overt act" rather than vote to go out of the Union, regardless of what other states might do, simply because Lincoln was elected. Still, "events not yet foreseen" might lead to more immediate action. Governor Andrew B. Moore, of Alabama, favored consultation among cotton-state executives. He did not think Alabama would secede alone, but "if two or more states will cooperate with her she will secede with them; or if South Carolina or any other Southern State should go out alone and the Federal Government should attempt to use force against her, Alabama will immediately rally to her rescue." Governor M. S. Perry, of Florida, felt that Florida could not take the lead in secession, "but will most assuredly cooperate with or follow the lead of any single Cotton State which may secede." A state convention would be called as soon as Lincoln's election became a fact; meanwhile, "if there is sufficient manliness at the South to strike, for our rights, honor and safety, in God's name let it be done before the inauguration of Lincoln."[10]

Presumably these men knew how the people in their states were thinking, and it is clear that even in the heart of the cotton belt a majority was not yet ready to secede and would not consider Lincoln's election adequate reason for secession. But the majority by now was at the mercy of events. It had been brought—by fear, by suspicion, and by anger—to a point just one step short of the final act; the smallest accident, the most casual misstep by some politician in Washington, might compel it to take that last step. Nor would it be necessary for the majority in all of the Southern states to be won over. The sense of regional solidarity had immense power, and where one state led, other states might well follow.

One state would lead. On October 12 Governor Gist, as a matter of routine, called the legislature of South Carolina into special session to name the state's presidential electors. This was necessary, since of all of the states only South Carolina did not call the people to the polls in presidential elections; the legislature decided where the state's electoral vote would go. But when he summoned the legislature, Governor Gist announced that it might well be called on, in addition, to take some action "for the safety and protection of the State," and when it met to perform its quadrennial duty, on November 5, he recommended that it remain in session until the nation had cast and counted its ballots. If the nation elected Lincoln, the legislature would be advised to sum-

mon a state convention, and it was correctly taken for granted
that such a convention would have no reason for existence
except to pass an ordinance of secession.

The drift was not universally visible, even in the South.
The confused campaign would go on to its fateful confused
climax, and one of the most momentous votes in American
history would be cast by a nation that had no way to know
what it was doing when it voted. No candidate had declared
for secession; both Douglas and Bell had called for national
unity, and Breckinridge had proudly challenged anyone to
show that he had ever said or even thought anything hostile
to the Union; and by surface appearances the attempt to
make a Republican victory the signal for a general exodus
of the cotton states had failed to win substantial popular support. Even Yancey, in his mocking address in New York, had
talked like a man who was prepared to fight for slavery within the Union. Yet the campaign had completely failed to do
what a political campaign is supposed to do—bring the nation to full awareness and earnest discussion of its most crucial issues and lead to a verdict that would put those issues
on the way toward settlement. There had been nothing even
resembling an attempt by reasonable men to analyze a baffling problem and see what could be done about it. Only
Douglas had tried to make a debate of it, and by election
night he knew that his struggle had failed. The election would
be a shock which could benefit no one but the extremists on
both sides.

Election day was November 6. Douglas was in Mobile,
Alabama, and he got the returns in the office of his friend
John Forsyth, proprietor of the Mobile *Register*. By the middle of the evening it was clear that Lincoln had won. Forsyth
drew up an editorial prepared for the next day's issue, urging
Alabama to call a state convention to consider what ought to
be done, and he and Douglas argued about the matter. Forsyth felt that Union men in the state could beat the drift
toward secession only by accepting the plan for such a convention and then winning control of it; Douglas urged that
if the Union men could not keep such a convention from
being called, they had no chance to control it when it was
held. Forsyth was insistent, however, and the copy went to
the printer's to be published, and Douglas trudged off to his

hotel. To his secretary, Douglas seemed "more hopeless than I had ever seen him before."[11]

5. Verdict of the People

ABRAHAM LINCOLN spent November 6 in the governor's office in the state capitol building at Springfield, leaving the place in mid-afternoon long enough to walk to a polling booth and cast his own ballot, then coming back to chat casually with friends—waiting, with no one knows how much of suspense, hope, and anxiety, to see what the people had decided. As the afternoon passed, the tension rose. By evening the office was jammed; a larger crowd filled the chamber of the House of Representatives and a still greater crowd stood in the street outside. The first returns came in at seven o'clock—a dispatch showing that the Republican vote in near-by Decatur was larger than it had been in 1856. A few more local returns came in during the next hour, whetting the appetite but proving nothing much, and at last the waiting became unendurable. Lincoln and a few others walked over to the telegraph office to get the returns as they came off the wire.

Now the pace became faster. Illinois had gone Republican —although Lincoln, rather disturbingly, had failed to carry his own county; there were still plenty of Douglas men in central Illinois—and then it became known that Indiana had been won. By ten o'clock it was clear that the Northwest was going Republican; then, a surer omen of final victory, came word that Pennsylvania was in line, with Allegheny county carried by 10,000 and a clear majority in Philadelphia. Now if New York would follow Pennsylvania, Lincoln could consider himself elected.

Near the telegraph office was an ice-cream parlor, taken over for the evening by a group of Republican women, and to the telegraph office came a delegation to ask if Mr. Lincoln and his friends would not step over and have a little refreshment. By now there was no need to keep hanging over the telegraph instrument—the crowds in the street had begun to yell and sing and fire guns in the air, and Secretary Nicolay noted that the mob in the House of Representatives chamber was "shouting, yelling, singing, dancing and indulging in all sorts of demonstrations of happiness." Lincoln went to the ice-cream parlor, where a long table was spread with coffee, sandwiches, cake, oysters, and the like, and as he came in, a chorus of feminine voices greeted him for the first time with the proudest salutation an American can hear: "How do you do, Mr. President?" Lincoln sat down, and the crowd began to sing:

> Ain't you glad you joined the Republicans—
> Joined the Republicans—
> Joined the Republicans—
> Ain't you glad you joined the Republicans
> Down in Illinois?

Then, while this homespun jollification was going on, word came in that New York State had gone Republican and that victory was certain, and there were cheers and back-slappings and a general milling-about and happy confusion. Lincoln, who seemed to be the least elated man in the room, excused himself at last and went home to give the news to his wife and to try to get some sleep.[1] The rest of Springfield kept on celebrating (except for the silent people who had gathered at Democratic headquarters), and the cheering and banging went on until dawn. Nicolay wrote that he himself managed to get to bed at four in the morning, but that there was so much noise outside even at that hour that he could not sleep.

Springfield celebrated from provincial pride, from joy that the Northwest had at last sent one of its sons to the White House, perhaps too from a feeling that a period of great strain had ended and that something which had perplexed and disturbed men for a long time had finally been put on the road to settlement. But the strange thing about this election was that the Republican victory was celebrated in the deep South as well—the deep South, where no single man had voted for Abraham Lincoln, where his name and party label did not even appear on the ballot. Charleston was as jubilant and as excited as Springfield, and there were as many flags and black-powder salutes along the Battery as in front of the Illinois state house. Here too there was a feeling of release from tension. Whatever the future might conceal, one pressure at least had been discharged. This Republican triumph, by its very completeness, was so intolerable that men would behave in a new way. There would be a new nation, it would be born in South Carolina, and it would begin to take shape at once.

So the day after the election was an informal holiday in Charleston. Business was neglected, and men crowded around the bulletin boards to cheer at each new confirmation of Lincoln's election. A palmetto flag was hoisted in front of the office of the *Mercury,* which editorialized gaily: "The tea has been thrown overboard, the revolution of 1860 has been initiated." A Boston steamer in the harbor (one of its owners was the Caleb Cushing who had presided with such dignity when the Democrats tried in vain to have a harmonious convention) saluted the flag of South Carolina with fifteen guns, and the foreman of a grand jury in the Federal court at Charleston informed the judge that the jury had no presentments to make—as a creature of United States authority it considered its function at an end in Charleston. The judge agreed, remarking: "So far as I am concerned the Temple of Justice raised under the Constitution of the United States is now closed. If it shall never again be opened I thank God that its doors have been closed before its altar has been desecrated with sacrifices to tyranny." That night there were fireworks and illuminations, and within a few days the state's two United States Senators, James Chesnut, Jr., and James H. Hammond, sent in their resignations. Simultaneously the legislature called a convention of the people to meet on December 17 to consider the state's relations with the Northern states and with the government of the United States; a tall liberty pole was raised, cannon saluted the palmetto flag, and bands played the *"Marseillaise."*

Elsewhere in the deep South there was parading and cheering, although the tone was not quite so deep and sure as in Charleston. Men began to wear blue cockades, emblem of resistant liberty ever since the old Nullification days, in their hats, and in many places semi-military marching groups called "Minute Men," "Sons of the South," and so on recruited members. In Alabama, where a convention similar to South Carolina's had been called, candidates for convention seats began to campaign, with oratory and with patriotic appeals. The Mississippi legislature was called into special session, and in Georgia—after some debate—the legislature agreed that

delegates to a state convention should be elected shortly after
the beginning of the new year. The process which South
Carolina's governor had initiated just before the election was
beginning to work.[2]

Yet there may have been less of a swing and a sweep to
this than appears on the surface. To most men the situation
still was not entirely clear. The election returns themselves,
if anyone bothered to analyze them, did not show even the
deepest South speaking with a united voice. Breckinridge, the
supposed candidate of the secessionists, had indeed carried
eleven states, but he had lost such powerful slave states as
Virginia, Tennessee, Kentucky, and Missouri, and the vote
for the stoutly Unionist Bell-Everett ticket all through the
South had been significantly large. Douglas had carried no
slave state except Missouri, but in the popular vote his total
was second only to Lincoln's, and if a good part of his vote
came from Northern states, the Breckinridge vote was not
exclusively Southern, either; approximately a quarter of all
the votes cast for Breckinridge were cast in the North. So
far there was no mandate for secession or any other kind
of immediate action.

But there was still deep confusion and bewilderment, and
in such times men of intense singleness of purpose can often
drive through to their chosen goal and compel their fellows
to trail along after them. The Southern men who, in November of 1860, proposed secession and the creation of a new
nation had the advantage of knowing precisely what they
wanted and of standing for immediate, emotion-releasing action. Those who counseled delay and full exploration of the
possibilities of compromise were using the kind of talk that
should have been (but was not) voiced in the presidential
campaign; now it came too late, it had no force in it, and
state and regional patriotism were generating a pressure that
made it sound empty.

Alexander Stephens unintentionally proved the point. He
had been a Douglas man, and he had seen profound trouble
coming as far back as the previous spring, and now he tried
to persuade the Georgia legislature that it was not yet time
for direct action. He was not very persuasive. "My object,"
he told the legislators, "is not to stir up strife but to allay it;
not to appeal to your passions, but to your reason." The
election of Lincoln he liked no better than the next man, but

it was not by itself sufficient reason for fracturing the Constitution: "Do not let *us* break it because, forsooth, he *may*. If he does, then is the time to strike." But although Stephens hoped the Union might be preserved, he would go where Georgia went, bowing to the will of the people: "Their cause is my cause, and their destiny is my destiny."[3]

No broken dike, crumbling before a powerful flood, was ever repaired with that kind of talk. The men at Milledgeville, Georgia's capital, applauded, for they loved frail little Stephens, but to all intents and purposes they did not hear him. Singularly enough, his voice struck a spark only in the Northern state capital of Springfield, where Lincoln read a newspaper account of what Stephens had said and wrote to ask if Stephens could forward a revised copy. This Stephens could not do, since he had nothing except the reporter's notes, which he thought were substantially accurate; and he wrote sadly to Lincoln: "The country is certainly in great peril, and no man ever had heavier or greater responsibilities than you have in the present momentous crisis."

There had always been a shadowy bond of liking and understanding between Stephens and Lincoln, and now Lincoln spoke his troubled mind in a letter marked "for your eye only." He saw both the peril and the responsibility, but he did not quite understand what was troubling the South so violently or what he himself ought to do about it. Neither directly nor indirectly would he, as President, interfere with slavery in the Southern states, and the South during the next four years would be in no more danger in that respect than it was in the days of George Washington.

"I suppose, though, this does not meet the case," Lincoln went on. "You think slavery is *right*, and ought to be extended; while we think it is *wrong* and ought to be restricted. That I suppose is the rub. It certainly is the only substantial difference between us."

It was difference enough. Stephens replied that neither Lincoln's election nor fears of the new administration's immediate actions really caused the trouble; the problem was that Lincoln's election and eventual inauguration would "put the institutions of nearly half the states under the ban of public opinion and national condemnation. This, upon general principles, is quite enough of itself to arouse a spirit not only of general indignation but of revolt on the part of the proscribed." Stephens hoped that Lincoln could find something to say that would calm men's minds; finally, he would remind this faraway friend from Illinois that "conciliation and harmony, in my judgment, can never be established by force. Nor can the Union under the Constitution be maintained by force."[4]

This thought was bothering Lincoln profoundly, in the days when he tried to adjust himself to the knowledge that he was going to be the next President of the United States. Nicolay noted that on November 15 Lincoln was considering how the government should try to maintain the Union. To "two gentlemen" who were with him, Lincoln spoke his mind: "My own impression is, at present (leaving myself room to modify the opinion, if upon a further investigation I should see fit to do so) that this government possesses both the authority and the power to maintain its own integrity. That however is not the ugly point of the matter. The ugly part is the necessity of keeping the government together by force, as ours should be a government of fraternity."[5]

For a few weeks the question of what the Federal government ought to do if one or more states announced that they had left the Union would be an academic matter, evoking opinions very different from the ones that would be wrenched out of men when the physical break actually came. The New York *Tribune*'s Horace Greeley, who had done about as much as any one man to give the slaveholding Southerners the idea that a Republican victory would be fatal to their cause, was writing now that the Union should not be maintained by force: "If the Cotton States shall become satisfied that they can do better out of the Union than in it, we insist on letting them go in peace. . . . Whenever a considerable section of our Union shall deliberately resolve to go out, we shall resist all coercive measures designed to keep it in. We hope never to live in a republic whereof one section is pinned to the residue by bayonets."[6]

One of the tragic facts about the year 1860 was that the Northern men who worked so hard to elect an anti-slavery ticket understood hardly at all, beforehand, what their victory would mean; but they recognized its probable effect very clearly, once the election had taken place. No single cotton-state convention had met, no legislature had voted for disunion, no concrete, tangible evidence of approaching seces-

sion which might not have been discerned earlier had come
to the surface at this time; but the election was hardly a week
behind them when such men as Lincoln and Greeley (and,
with them, many other thoughtful Northerners) were facing
the fact that these slave-state men were very likely to go out
of the Union at once without waiting for any overt act.
What had been dismissed earlier as "gasconade" and the
meaningless vaporings of contentious hotheads was accepted
now for what it so obviously was—the plain statement of a
clear intent. And although in years to come many Northerners would feel that there had been a devious conspiracy to
create a new cotton-state empire on the merest pretext, it is
probable that Lincoln in his musings had said it as well as
need be: men of the North and South simply had different
notions about slavery.

The peculiar institution, even as it existed in the deepest
heart of the cotton belt, was exceedingly fragile. It could
endure only in a section that was of one mind about it,
about its value, its rightness, its essential place in a community where all men's interests were as one. The new Republican administration in Washington might indeed, as Lincoln said, lack either the power or the desire to reach into
this region and interfere, but the Southerners who now demanded secession as a matter of self-preservation were entirely right on the one important point—the mere existence
of a Federal administration hostile to slavery spelled eventual
doom for the institution even though the doom might be
delayed for a great many years. The South's monolithic unity
on the matter would be broken, slowly but certainly. In the
border states the institution already showed signs of wither-
ing on the vine. Sooner or later, the Southern white man who
owned no slaves (and he was very much in the majority)
would come to see that what was good for the slaveholder
was not necessarily good for him . . . and that would be the
beginning of an inevitable end.

So a sound instinct moved the men who refused to let secession wait until the new administration had committed
some openly hostile act. The votes to make an anti-slavery
man President existed, at last, and they had been cast, and
the fact that the Republicans had not been able to win a
majority in either house of Congress made little difference.
A turning point had been reached, and if the preservation of

slavery topped all other concerns in importance, then the only thing to do was to leave the Union as quickly as might be.

Among those who saw this was Jefferson Davis, who had hoped that the deep South might be able to remain in the Union on its own terms, and who was meditating at his Mississippi home on the meaning of Lincoln's election. To R. B. Rhett, Jr., a few days after this election, Davis wrote a veiled letter, confessing that he doubted the strength of secession sentiment in some states as of that particular moment. If a convention of the slave states were called, he believed, the proposition to secede from the Union would probably fail. At the same time, there did exist a powerful community of interest among the cotton-planting states—that booming area of factory farms where cotton mass-produced by slaves was so immensely profitable—and sooner or later these states were certain to get together; united, they would be perfectly capable of defending their own interests. The newer cotton states doubtless would be slow to act, although in the end they would be bound to follow the older states, and Davis had believed all along that they should be brought into co-operation before the leadership concluded to ask "for a popular decision upon a new policy and relation to the nations of the earth." Nevertheless, Davis felt that if South Carolina should resolve to secede before that sort of co-operation could be attained—going out independently, leaving even such states as Georgia and Alabama and Louisiana in the Union, without any assurance that they would follow—in that case "there appears to me to be no advantage in waiting until the government has passed into hostile hands and men have become familiarized to that injurious and offensive perversion of the general government from the ends for which it was established."[7]

Although the leaders in South Carolina had pretty well determined on their course before this letter from Davis came in, what Davis said and the fact that he said it at all had much meaning. Stephens had shown that even a devoted Unionist would in the end go along with his state; now Davis was showing that a conservative and a constitutionalist would go along with the fire-eaters, if need be.

In the face of all of this, what was a President-elect to do? Lincoln himself did not know. It seemed to him (while office-hunters swarmed about him like blow flies, crowding the little

room in the state house almost to suffocation, leaving him
scant time for deep thoughts about statecraft) that his best
course was to keep quiet. Alexander Stephens had urged that
the right word from Lincoln just now "could indeed be like
'apples of gold in pictures of silver,'" but the right word was
very hard to find and in any case there were many men ready
to twist it out of shape even if it could be said. The young
newspaper correspondent Henry Villard, observing things in
the Illinois state house, was shocked by Lincoln's appearance,
thinking the man showed unbearable strain: "Always cadaver-
ous, his aspect is now almost ghastly. His position is wearing
him terribly." It did not seem to Villard that Lincoln had
enough firmness for the position he was entering: "The times
demand a Jackson."[8] Yet Douglas had spoken in Jacksonian
terms, at Norfolk and at Raleigh, and after he had spoken,
the South had gone along with Breckinridge; possibly the
situation had passed the point where it could be set straight
by the Jackson touch.

It may be that the mounting pressure for offices, the increasing evidence that there were many among the multitudes
who wanted a political victory to bring tangible political rewards, made it hard for the man in Springfield to tell the
difference between revolutionary fervor and a simple political
maneuver. Donn Piatt, a Cincinnati journalist, interviewed
Lincoln before November was over, found him not cynical
but at least profoundly skeptical, one who with easy good
humor took a low view of human nature and believed nothing until he actually saw it. "This low estimate of humanity,"
wrote Piatt, "blinded him to the South. He could not understand that men would get up in their wrath and fight for an
idea. He considered the movement South as a sort of political game of bluff, gotten up by politicians and meant sole-
ly to frighten the North. He believed that when the leaders
saw their efforts in that direction were unavailing the tumult
would subside." A little later, seeing Lincoln in Chicago,
Piatt told him that the Southern people were deeply in earnest and said that he was doubtful whether Lincoln could be
inaugurated at Washington. Lincoln laughed at him and said
that the fall in the price of pork at Cincinnati had affected
Piatt's judgment; and when Piatt retorted that in ninety days
the land would be white with the tents of soldiers, Lincoln remarked that "we won't jump that ditch until we come to it."

After a pause, Lincoln added: "I must run the machine as I find it."[9]

It is probable that in talking with Piatt, Lincoln did not give a full glimpse of his own thinking—and, indeed, Piatt confessed that he had gathered many of his impressions from what Mrs. Lincoln said rather than from anything Lincoln himself told him. Lincoln probably did begin by suspecting that the elaborate talk about secession was largely a bluff, meant to win concessions: and up to a certain point that had actually been the case—one of the controlling factors in the whole crisis was that an attempt to put on the political heat had got out of hand. But by the end of November, Lincoln was beginning to be aware of the real state of things. He would not have written to Alec Stephens as he had done if his attitude had been what Piatt thought it was, and he was clearly doing much more soul-searching about the government's ability to defend its own integrity than he would have been doing if he supposed the Southern leaders were bluffing.

Nobody was bluffing. The time for that had passed. What was done now and hereafter must be done in earnest, according to the best light a man could find. The trouble was that the lights were all imperfect. The election had clarified nothing. It simply meant that a nation which had spent a long generation arguing about slavery had grown tired of talk and wanted to see something done—without specifying what that something might be.

6. Despotism of the Sword

WINFIELD SCOTT was commanding general of the Army of the United States, an officer of higher rank (a lieutenant general by brevet) and more distinction than any American since George Washington. He had immense pride and he considered that his responsibilities were those not merely of a soldier but of an elder statesman, and in a time of crisis he would not hesitate to give gratuitous advice to the government which employed him. Even before Lincoln's election he was worrying about the drift of things, and at the end of October it seemed to him that he should tell the President and the country how the Union might be preserved. He put

his views down on paper, sent the result to President James
Buchanan, gave a copy to Secretary of War John B. Floyd—
who, as the general's immediate superior, had not asked him
to do anything of the kind—and saw to it that the document
was circulated elsewhere.

Scott's letter was ponderous, confused, not far short of
fantastic: yet it did help to compel men to face up to the
unlimited potentialities which this strange campaign had developed. Quite correctly, Scott believed that secession was at
hand. A Bell and Everett man himself, he did not think that
Lincoln's impending victory (he dated his letter October 29)
really threatened "any unconstitutional violence of breach
of law," but trouble obviously was coming. He proceeded.

"From a knowledge of our Southern population it is my
solemn conviction that there is some danger of an early act
of rashness preliminary to secession, viz, the seizure of some
or all of the following posts: Forts Jackson and St. Philip,
on the Mississippi, below New Orleans, both without garrisons; Fort Morgan, below Mobile, without a garrison; Forts
Pickens and McKee [McRee], Pensacola Harbor, with an insufficient garrison for one; Fort Pulaski, below Savannah,
without a garrison; Forts Moultrie and Sumter, Charleston
harbor, the former with an insufficient garrison, the latter
without any; and Fort Monroe, Hampton Roads, without a
sufficient garrison. In my opinion all these works should be
immediately so garrisoned as to make any attempt to take
any one of them, by surprise or coup de main, ridiculous.
With the army faithful to its allegiance, and the navy probably
equally so, and with a Federal Executive, for the next twelve
months, of firmness and moderation, which the country has
a right to expect—moderation being an element of power
not less than firmness—there is good reason to hope that the
danger of secession may be made to pass away without one
conflict of arms, one execution or one arrest for treason. In
the meantime it is suggested that exports might be left perfectly free—and to avoid conflicts all duties on imports be
collected outside of the cities, in forts or ships of war."

As the perplexed Buchanan remarked, "these were themes
entirely foreign to a military report, and equally foreign from
the official duties of the Commanding General." But this was
not all. If the Union fell apart, Scott wrote, "there would be
no hope of reuniting the fragments except by the laceration

and despotism of the sword." Roaming far afield, he even suggested that it might be well to divide the nation into four separate confederacies—roughly, Northeast, Southeast, Northwest, and Southwest—the effect of which, he apparently believed, would be to isolate the cotton belt and make its conquest simpler. To Floyd, Scott sent a covering note urging that the commanders of such forts as were garrisoned be warned to be on their toes. He pointed out that the army had a total of five companies—one each at Boston, New York, Pittsburgh, Augusta, and Baton Rouge—which might be used for reinforcements.[1]

This did not strike the harassed President as especially helpful. As he remarked later, to try to garrison eight forts with five companies would have been an open confession of weakness, an invitation to secession rather than a preventative. Indeed, the entire United States Army at that moment numbered hardly more than 16,000 officers and men, and these were scattered all over the continental United States, guarding the frontiers, protecting emigrant trains, overawing contumacious Indians, and in general trying to do a very large job with inadequate means. Three years earlier, thinking only of frontiers and Indians and not dreaming that ornamental forts in drowsy harbors needed anything more than caretakers, Buchanan had urged Congress to add five new regiments to the army's strength, but Congress had refused to do this and appropriations for the army had been going down—from $25,000,000 in 1858, high for the decade, to a little more than $16,000,000 for 1860. In plain fact, the United States was all but disarmed. It possessed 198 companies of regulars, and it had 183 of these on the frontier or in the empty West.

General Emory Upton, analyzing this situation some years later, pointed out that to suppress Indians and guard inhabitants and emigrant trains in all the region west of the Mississippi, there was one soldier for every 120 square miles; to do whatever might be necessary in all the rest of the country there was one soldier for every 1200 square miles. Theoretically, the militia of course could be called on, and theoretically it could bring three million men to the colors, but in actual fact the militia "did not merit the name of a military force," since it was destitute of instruction and training and very nearly destitute of equipment. The states could, to be sure,

draw their quotas of arms from the War Department, but
during the fifties the War Department was equipping the
regulars with new weapons, and what was available for the
states consisted very largely of material that was nearly obsolete. In any case, many of the states neglected to draw the
weapons they might have had.

The War Department itself slumbered in an easy placidity
befitting this state of affairs. Its eight dominant bureaus were
bound up in red tape and made practically senile by sheer
age; of the officers who commanded these bureaus, all but
one had been in service since the War of 1812, and several
had held their posts for decades, happily contributing to the
lethargic routine which slowed all activities down to a crawl.
There were great leather-bound ledgers into which incoming
letters were methodically copied; there were some scores of
clerks, whose chief qualification for their jobs was that they
wrote a fine legible hand. During 1860 Congress had be-
stirred itself slightly in regard to the army. It had increased
the enlisted man's ration of sugar and coffee, it had set up
a commission to look into the course of instruction and system of discipline at West Point, and the Senate had ordered
its Committee on Military Affairs (whose chairman was Jefferson Davis) to determine whether expenditures on the army
might not further be reduced without detriment to the public
service. As matters stood in the fall of 1860, the country
could do almost anything with its army except fight with it.
The obvious explanation for all of this was that nobody had
supposed that it would have to fight at all.[2]

Now General Scott was speaking up, demanding that empty forts be provided with garrisons, and President Buchanan
felt that this request was illogical and impractical, which is
not to be wondered at—especially in view of the fact that
Buchanan was not a man who was easily brought to affirma-
tive action under any circumstances. As a matter of fact,
there is more to be said on Buchanan's side than usually gets
said, or listened to. He was a Doughface, as men used words
then, a Northerner with Southern sympathies, and his cabinet
was of very little help to him. His administration had been
able to do nothing of any consequence except keep Stephen
Douglas from being the presidential candidate of a united
Democracy, and now it had to face the most outlandish
domestic crisis in American history. The general of the armies

was stepping far out of his proper sphere to give unwanted advice on high policy, and the worst of this was that with his uncertain vision the old soldier had seen one thing with great clarity—there was probably going to be a big fight, and something ought to be done to get ready for it.

This was a time when most men were purblind. The tragedy of the leaders of the North had been that they could not see that a Republican victory would almost automatically mean secession of one or many of the states of the deep South; and the tragedy of the Southerners was that they were not able to see that secession would finally mean war. Neither side believed that the other side was deeply in earnest, and neither side was prepared to face the consequences of its own acts. Now the consequences were beginning to take shape, and the aged general saw what was coming and demanded that his government be prepared to fight. It was all dreadfully upsetting.

The whole point of the Buchanan cabinet was that, like the President himself, it was qualified to do nothing of any consequence with great dignity. Now the heat was on, and there was going to be some sort of action, even if the best action the administration could devise might be to let things drift on toward catastrophe. Few presidents ever faced a harder task than Buchanan now faced.

Lewis Cass, of Michigan, very old and very dignified and very stuffy, was Secretary of State, and Howell Cobb, of Georgia, who was not in the least aged or stuffy, was Secretary of the Treasury. John B. Floyd, of Virginia, was Secretary of War; a bumbling incompetent who had permitted much corruption without (as would finally appear) being personally touched by very much of it, the man who held top command over an army that was about to do things not specified in the tables of organization. Isaac Toucey, of Connecticut, an amiable nonentity, was Secretary of the Navy (which was quite as crippled by declining appropriations as was the Army) and the forceful Jacob Thompson, of Mississippi, was Secretary of the Interior. Joseph Holt, of Kentucky, sour and limited but strongly pro-Union, was Postmaster General, and the Unionist Jeremiah Black, of Pennsylvania, was Attorney General. Cobb and Thompson and Floyd were devout Southerners, Toucey was either neutral or a cipher, and the rest were run-of-the-mill Northerners, some of them devoted, some of them less so. These were Buchanan's closest advisers.

If Buchanan had been a man of original force, this would not have mattered so much, but he was nothing of the kind. He was 69, and he was torn by two deep emotions—a strong, automatic sympathy for the South, and an equally potent love for the unbroken Union of the States: a situation that left him feeling that to secede was illegal and that to prevent secession by force was equally illegal. The cabinet members on whom he most relied were Cobb and Thompson, and both men came from states that obviously were about to leave the Union. The cabinet could not possibly agree on anything of importance, and Buchanan was a man who could not act without the counsel of his cabinet; and now he was facing a problem without precedent in American history, the general of the armies was calling for action that would undoubtedly precipitate a crisis, and it was also time to compose the annual message to Congress—a lame-duck Congress, chosen two years earlier, when no one supposed that either the executive or the legislative branch would have to deal with a general disruption of the government.

On November 7, the day after election, Buchanan wrote an anxious note to Floyd. He had been told that armed South Carolinians had assaulted and taken the forts at Charleston; would the Secretary of War please visit him at once? The Secretary did so, assured the President that the rumor was false, and agreed that the signs were all bad: disunion apparently was on the way, Floyd wrote, but Buchanan's emotions "repelled the convictions of his mind." Two days later there was a cabinet meeting to consider the annual message to Congress, and at this meeting, as Floyd remembered it, Buchanan asked for advice regarding an idea he had developed. He admitted that he was "compelled to notice the alarming condition of the country," and he proposed calling a general convention of all of the states to provide some means for compromising the disputes between extremists of the North and the South. The cabinet hemmed and hawed and said nothing very definite. There was another meeting on the following day, November 10, at which Buchanan presented his proposal in the form of a draft that might either go into his annual message to Congress or be presented to the country in the form of a presidential proclamation. The paper was supported by an opinion from Attorney General Black, which in effect asserted the Federal government's legal power to maintain the Union by force if necessary.

The cabinet promptly divided on sectional lines. The Northerners praised Buchanan's proposal—Floyd wrote that it "met with extravagant commendation" from Black, Cass, Holt and Toucey—and the Southerners expressed grave doubts, objecting in particular to the statement that the government possessed and could use the power of coercion. Both Cobb and Thompson felt that the President was urging "submission to Lincoln's election," and Floyd wrote that Buchanan failed to understand "the temper of the Southern people" and was adopting an improper stand in respect to the use of force. Floyd added: "I do not see what good can come of the paper, as prepared, and I do see how much mischief may flow from it."[3]

In the face of this split, Buchanan temporized, which was unfortunate. It was not yet too late to handle the developing crisis. Formal action for secession had not been taken anywhere, and there was still a strong nucleus of Unionist sentiment in the South, as evidenced by the substantial vote that had been cast for Bell and for Douglas. A forthright move by the executive to encourage this Unionist sentiment and to bring all of the states together in an attempt to settle the growing argument by negotiation and compromise might have made a vast difference. Buchanan could not take the lead. He told Attorney General Black that he had a "desire to stand between the factions . . . with my hand on the head of each counselling peace," but a more decisive step was called for. If he proposed to lead the country away from secession, his first step must be to get rid of the secessionists in his own cabinet, and this was beyond him. He asked Black to give him a second, more moderate opinion, exploring in detail the government's legal capacities in the situation, and the plan for a convention of the states began to drift out of sight.[4]

Black was a stalwart Union man, but now the fire went out of him. In effect, he seemed now to say that the government had the legal power to prevent secession but that it could not legally use this power. "Your right to take such measures as may seem to be necessary for the protection of the public property is very clear ... you may employ such parts of the land and naval forces as you may judge necessary for the purpose of causing the laws to be duly executed." But these powers were purely defensive; with its armed forces the government could do no more than what might be done by an ordinary civil posse, called out to suppress combinations that were obstructing the execution of the laws. Suppose the judges and other civil authorities in the areas where obstruction was taking place were themselves on the side of the obstructionists, so that there were no courts to issue judicial process and no ministerial officers to execute it? "In that event troops would certainly be out of place and their use wholly illegal." If they were sent to aid courts and marshals, there must be courts and marshals to aid, and if such were lacking—as they obviously would be in a state that had seceded—"the laws cannot be executed in any event, no matter what may be the strength which the government has at its command."

If a state announced that it was leaving the Union, Black continued, it might be exercising a right guaranteed under the Constitution or it might be engaging in a revolutionary movement, but whether it was acting legally or illegally made no difference; "it is certain that you have not in either case the authority to recognize her independence or to absolve her from her Federal obligations." Whether Congress had the right to make war against one or more states was something for Congress to determine, but "if Congress shall break up the present Union by unconstitutionally putting strife and enmity and armed hostility between different sections of the country, instead of the domestic tranquility which the Constitution was meant to insure, will not all the States be absolved from their Federal obligations?" And so, in conclusion: "If this view of the subject be correct, as I think it is, then the Union must utterly perish at the moment when Congress shall arm one part of the people against another for any purpose beyond that of merely protecting the General Government in the exercise of its proper constitutional functions."[5]

Here was a charter for inaction which the baffled Buchanan for the time being could do nothing but follow religiously. And at this point, with the proposed convention of the states receding forever into the shadows, a significant new turn was given the whole sectional argument. Up to this moment slavery itself, in one way or another, was what men were arguing about, and the argument had brought up the question of secession. Now, with secession about to take place, the big question was the legal right of a state to secede, which was something very different; for now the question came down from the level at which only the impassioned extremists would be willing to fight about it and got into an area where it touched the deep emotions of millions of men, North and South alike. A state's right to make its own laws respecting slavery was unquestioned even by the radical Republicans, and the rights of the several states in regard to slavery in the territories were abstractions. But the question of a state's right to leave the Union entirely, and the linked question of the central government's right to prevent this by force—here was something infinitely broader, something that went to the very heart of the democratic experiment. Without entirely realizing it, the President and cabinet, in these days following the election, were witnessing the development of a situation that could easily lead to war. What old General Scott had so ponderously spoken of as "the laceration and despotism of the sword" had drawn perilously close.

If all of this was not clearly seen by the country at large, it was beginning to be very clearly felt. South Carolina had not yet seceded, but no one had the least doubt that she would presently do so, and that other cotton states were very likely to follow, and South Carolina officials were working to lay in a supply of arms—if there was going to be any coercion, this state would be prepared to meet it. While the cabinet was considering the President's plan for a convention, Thomas L. Drayton, of South Carolina, was in Washington negotiating with Secretary Floyd for the purchase of surplus army muskets. He could, he wrote to Governor Gist, buy 10,000 old smooth bores, flint locks altered to percussion, and although these were rather out of date they were at least lethal weapons, and the quartermaster-general of the army, Joseph E. Johnston, who was also president of the Ordnance Board, has assured him that "for our purposes" they were perfectly acceptable. They could be shipped from the arsenal at Watervliet, New York, and Drayton urged that the deal be put through without delay: "The cabinet may break up at any moment on differences of opinion with the President as to the right of secession—and a new Secretary of War might stop the muskets going south, if not already on the way when he comes into office." A South Carolina militia officer, Roswell S. Ripley, who was shopping for guns in Philadelphia, wrote that his state would probably have to buy in Europe if it wanted first-rate weapons, and he believed the state could not be fully prepared until February; in view of which fact he urged that no overt act be taken until Lincoln had been inaugurated. "Let her take her position & act March 4th & until that time she cannot be interfered with—other states will do the same thing & Mr. Lincoln will walk into a house gutted of its best furniture."[6]

As South Carolina proceeded with the election of delegates for the convention that would pass the ordinance of secession, her leaders were kept posted on the drift of affairs in Washington. The key figure was a cheerful little man from Charleston, William Henry Trescot, a lawyer and a planter who had written books on diplomacy and who was now Assistant Secretary of State; a sincere patriot but also a man who could see the fun in things—Mrs. Chesnut, who liked him, called him "a man without indignation." Trescot was reporting now on the cabinet's activities. On November 17 he wrote, "I have no idea that any intention to use coercive measures is entertained," and shortly after this he wrote to Drayton that it could be taken for granted, as long as Cobb and Thompson remained in the cabinet, that "no action has been taken which seriously affects the position of any Southern State." He himself would know as soon as any decision was reached, and "upon such knowledge I will act as I ought."[7] Meanwhile, everything awaited the convening of Congress.

Congress convened on December 3. No Southern members had resigned except for Senators Chesnut and Hammond, of South Carolina; all the rest were present to look out for their states' interests in what might be a history-making session. It was possible that some compromise might be worked out, but the chances were dim. Everybody seemed to hope that there could be peace, but most of the cotton-state men were deeply committed to secession by now and their opposite numbers, the Republicans, were equally committed to a resolute containment of slavery, and unless one group or the other gave ground, the chances for peace were not good. Perhaps the President would have something to suggest.

The President's annual message, delivered on December 4, pleased practically nobody, and reflected accurately the state of distressed indecision which Mr. Buchanan had brought out of the long cabinet meetings. He began by denouncing Northern abolitionists, urging them to let the sovereign states of the South manage their own domestic institutions in their own way, and he balanced this by remarking that the mere "election of any one of our fellow-citizens to the office of President does not of itself afford just cause for dissolving the Union." He believed that secession was nothing less than revolution—justifiable, possibly, but nevertheless revolution. It was a time for calmness and deliberation; the slavery question, like everything else, would have its day, but if the excitement about it caused the Union to dissolve, "the evil may then become irreparable." As to coercion: "Our Union rests upon public opinion and can never be cemented by the blood of its citizens shed in a civil war. If it cannot live in the affections of its people it must one day perish. Congress possesses many means of preserving it by conciliation but the sword was not placed in their hands to preserve it by force."

By way of making a concrete proposal, Buchanan suggested that Congress might submit "an explanatory amendment" to the Constitution on the subject of slavery. Such an amendment might expressly recognize the right of property in slaves in states where slavery existed, might state the duty of protecting this right in the territories, and might stress the right of a master to have a fugitive slave speedily restored to him. With this, which did no more than restate the very issues over which the country was dividing, the President had said his say.[8]

There was something here to irritate everyone and to encourage no one. Facing both ways, Buchanan had been able to see nothing but the difficulties. Obviously, his administration through the months that remained to it would mark time, trying to avoid collisions and hoping for the best. The next step was going to be up to South Carolina.

CHAPTER THREE

The Long Farewell

1. The Union Is Dissolved

BEYOND ANY question, almost all of the people in the United States in 1860 wanted to remain at peace. Wanting this, they kept drifting toward war, and as they drifted, the power to make the final, irrevocable decision—the ability to say or to leave unsaid the words that would start the guns firing—got farther and farther out of their hands. This meant that 600,000 young men who otherwise might have lived were going to die, but it seemed that there was no help for it.

It seemed so because the powers that could have been used were not used. In the spring every piece of the intricate machinery by which a democracy can make its solemn choice was available—party conventions, speeches and petitions and debates, a national-election campaign, finally a vote on candidates and parties; yet by mid-November all of this had gone by and nothing had been settled. So then the focus narrowed to the White House and the national Capitol; what was said and done there might still determine whether the crisis could be solved or must be brought to the point of explosion.

Somehow this did not work, either; from the noblest of motives, all of the public servants involved seemed to shy away from the crucial point. So now it came down, in December, to an even more constricted field; specifically, to the state convention of South Carolina, which brought 170 men together to say what was going to happen next. These 170, elderly and slightly tired by the standards of that day but nevertheless good men and true, had been chosen by the voters of South Carolina to say whether the Union

THE UNION IS DISSOLVED

of states would endure or dissolve. (The focus would become even narrower in the weeks just ahead, so very narrow
that when the explosion finally came it would seem a thing
foreordained, brought on by nobody in particular; but even
in December it was too narrow for comfort.) The people
had lost control over their own destiny. One trouble was
that they had passed beyond the stage of reason and wanted
only an act. The act would quickly be forthcoming.

Pursuant to instructions from the general assembly of
South Carolina, delegates chosen by the several electoral
districts of the state came together in the state capital, Columbia, on December 17, seated themselves in the Baptist
Church, and permitted themselves to be called to order.
President of the convention was a state patriot and militia
officer, D. F. Jamison, who addressed his compatriots with
much eloquence.

In the auditorium before him were the state's best men—
clergymen and railroad presidents, manufacturers and planters and merchants, present and former United States Senators, including the noted secessionist R. Barnwell Rhett, not
to mention Robert W. Barnwell, William F. DeSaussure,
and James Chesnut, Jr., and five former governors, one of
them being the W. H. Gist who had just been replaced in the
gubernatorial chair by Francis W. Pickens. Most of these
and the lesser delegates had come here to vote for secession,
but they were faintly nervous about it. They wanted it done
peacefully, and they hoped everything would come out all
right; still, they had no love for the old Union, they were
not prepared to compromise, and they had a deep sense
of their historic responsibilities. They would lead their
state out into what might be a starless dark, and they had
the kind of courage that keeps forlorn hopes alive beyond
rational expectation, but they believed that the rest of the
South would follow them and they clung to the hope that
whatever they did would have a peaceful aftermath. President Jamison rose to talk to them.

Jamison mentioned a point that was familiar to all: the
elections that had created this convention had shown that
South Carolina was determined to get out of the Union as
quickly as might be. There were, however, two dangers—
"overtures from without, and precipitation within." He did
not believe that any overtures from men in the North would

have any effect. "As there is no common bond of sympathy or interest between the North and the South, all efforts to preserve this Union will be not only fruitless but fatal to the less numerous section"; but there might be trouble, arising from "too great impatience on the part of our people to precipitate the issue, in not waiting until they can strike with the authority of law." With proper caution but with iron hearts, therefore, the people of South Carolina must go forward, trusting in the revolutionary motto of Danton (who, after all, did come to the guillotine, although this was not mentioned): "To dare! and again to dare! and without end to dare!"[1]

The speech was applauded, and it was clear that the delegates had met not to debate secession but to accomplish it. Unanimously, the convention voted to instruct a select committee to prepare a proper resolution separating the palmetto state from the rest of the American Union. Then, smallpox being prevalent in Columbia, the convention voted to reconvene in Charleston, and adjourned.[2]

The delegates reached Charleston early in the afternoon of December 18, and there was a fifteen-gun salute at the railroad station and a big parade. The Marion Artillery Company, on no more than two and one-half hours' notice, assembled to fire the salute and do the honors, and a battalion of State Cadets stood in line at the railroad station to meet the delegates. With shouldered arms, the cadets escorted President Jamison to his carriage, and infantry and artillery together marched down to the Mills House, where the chief dignitaries would be quartered. An outlander, reporting these events for the New York *Times,* said that most of the adult males in Charleston were members of one or another of the numerous military organizations; all in all, he wrote, the state could put 33,000 armed men in uniform (about twice as many men as were enlisted in all of the United States Army), and he asserted that these men had taken guns and uniforms for no purpose but to resist, if need be, the power of the Federal government.[3]

Meeting in Institute Hall amid the shadows of the Democratic convention of the past spring, the convention appointed committees, referred sundry motions and resolutions to them, received commissions sent to observe and report by the governors of Alabama and Mississippi, and agreed to hold subsequent meetings in St. Andrews' Hall. Two days passed thus, then, on December 20, the convention sat back to hear the report from the Committee to Prepare an Ordinance of Secession, Mr. John A. Inglis.

The report was brief and to the point. It was a resolution that read as follows:

"We, the people of the State of South Carolina, in Convention assembled, do declare and ordain, and it is hereby declared and ordained, that the Ordinance adopted by us in Convention of the twenty-third day of May, in the year of our Lord one thousand seven hundred and eighty-eight, whereby the Constitution of the United States was ratified, and also all Acts and parts of Acts, of the General Assembly of this State, ratifying amendments of the said Constitution, are hereby repealed; and that the union now subsisting between South Carolina and other States, under the name of 'The United States of America,' is hereby dissolved."

There was no debate. The motion was put to a vote and was carried, 169 to 0. The delegates then voted to meet again that evening for formal signing of the ordinance and for a general celebration, to which the governor, members of the legislature, and sundry other dignitaries were invited. Then, at one o'clock, the convention adjourned for the afternoon, and as these new founding fathers came out into the streets, bells were ringing, bold-faced placards were being circulated, cannon were being fired, and parades were in movement. By its own declaration South Carolina was now an independent nation, and Charleston was in a mood to celebrate.[4]

South Carolina was a state (or a nation) of complete individualists, and one of these—frail, aging, picturesque, and outspoken—refused to go along with the rejoicing. James Louis Petigru, an old-time Whig, a leading lawyer for thirty years and an old-fashioned Federalist of the Alexander Hamilton school, seems to have been the one outspoken Union man in Charleston, and he did not care who knew how he felt. Stalking down Broad Street just after the convention had adjourned, he heard all of the bells ringing and, meeting a friend in front of the city hall, asked dryly: "Where's the fire?" There was no fire, the friend replied; the bells were ringing to announce the city's joy at the passage of the ordinance of secession. Old Petigru turned on him.

"I tell you there is a fire," he snapped. "They have this day set a blazing torch to the temple of constitutional liberty and, please God, we shall have no more peace forever." Then he turned and walked away. (He had told a friend, some days before this, that the Constitution was only two months older than he himself was; he expected now to outlive it.)[5]

Petigru was one individualist: a very different one was Edmund Ruffin, old and wispy, with white hair that came down to his shoulders—the most dedicated and appealing of all the men who had worked so hard for secession. He had spent himself, for years, not merely to make the Southland independent, but to make it fully fit for independence. He had waged an effective one-man campaign to restore the declining fertility of the Southern earth, teaching his fellow planters how to keep their lands from wearing out, doing all that one man could do to make his beloved region strong enough to stand on its own feet. He had tried, with some success, to blend scientific farming with the institution of slavery, and the South owed him a deeper debt than it owed to any other secessionist. He could celebrate, if any man could, with a clear conscience, and he went that evening to the convention hall—known then and thereafter as Secession Hall—to watch while the delegates signed the fateful ordinance. Some hours later he described the business in his diary:

"The signing occupied more than two hours, during which time there was nothing to entertain the spectators except their enthusiasm & joy. Yet no one was weary, & none left. Demonstrations of approbation in clapping & cheers were frequent—& when all the signatures had been affixed, & the President holding up the parchment proclaimed South Carolina to be a free and independent country, the cheers of the whole assembly continued for some minutes, while every man waved or threw up his hat, & every lady waved her handkerchief. The convention then adjourned, & the meeting separated. In the streets there had been going on other popular demonstrations of joy, from early in the afternoon. Some military companies paraded, salutes were fired, & as night came on bonfires, made of barrels of rosin, were lighted in the principal streets, rockets discharged, & innumerable crackers fired by the boys. As I now write, after 10 P.M.,

I hear the distant sounds of rejoicing, with the music of a military band, as if there was no thought of ceasing."[6]

Midway between outspoken Petigru and dedicated Ruffin in his emotional response to this outpouring of high spirits was one frustrated Yankee—Caleb Cushing, the Massachusetts Democrat who had presided over assorted conventions during the spring months. He was here now as an envoy sent by President Buchanan, bearing a letter from the President to Governor Pickens; a sober man entrusted with an impossible mission. The President wrote that "from common notoriety" he gathered that South Carolina was considering secession. Feeling it his duty "to exert all the means in my power to avert so dread a catastrophe," he hoped that Cushing would be able to persuade the governor and delegates to reconsider or at least to delay their projected action.

This of course was useless. No one in South Carolina cared to hear such talk at this late day, Governor Pickens perhaps least of all. A lawyer and planter who had both inherited and married money, Pickens had embraced the cause of immediate secession only lately, but he had all the fire of a new convert. Beginning his term as governor just before this convention opened, he made it clear in his inaugural address that the "overt act" for which secession was supposed to wait had already been committed—by the Northern people, at the ballot box. Now he told Cushing that as governor he could not even reply to the President's letter; there was no hope to preserve the Union, and South Carolina would go ahead as planned. Preserving the amenities, he politely invited Cushing to witness the evening's ceremonies connected with the signing.[7]

A mile from Secession Hall a militia regiment, the First South Carolina rifles, was in camp. A messenger galloped to the camp and the men were paraded, to listen to a reading of the ordinance and to cheer loudly. Newspapers were on the streets within fifteen minutes, and a Federal army officer from Fort Moultrie, looking on, felt that "the whole heart of the people had spoken." The New York *Times* reporter suspected that some people had private doubts: "There is a lingering apprehension of anarchy which startles men in the home of their families . . . I am convinced that many a family is now experiencing the darkest forebodings." Later, however, this reporter had to admit that everybody seemed happy, and he told how thousands of people joined in a parade that moved all through the downtown section, with music, banners, and transparencies: "The city was alive with pleasurable excitement."[8]

But parades and fireworks and a general mingling in the streets could not go on forever, and on Saturday, December 22, the convention met again to consider what had to be done next. It had created a new nation, and for at least a time it would have to fill some of the functions of a revolutionary government, because many things must be done before independence could be a working reality. There were technicalities to consider. Over the years, the Congress at Washington had passed many laws; with the Union dissolved, were these laws still in force in South Carolina, and if they were not, how could confusion and anarchy be prevented? There were more material problems, as well, which must be considered without delay. In Charleston there were certain forts, built and maintained by United States authority. These were Fort Moultrie, lying amid the sand dunes and the summer cottages near the sea front on Sullivan's Island, garrisoned by a handful of regulars; Castle Pinckney, a small masonry work on a mud flat not far from the Battery, held by one caretaking sergeant; Fort Johnson, a largely abandoned group of buildings on James Island facing the harbor, untenanted, of little apparent military value; and Fort Sumter, out at the entrance to the harbor, still unfinished, completely unoccupied except for the workmen who were taken out there by boat every morning and brought back to town every evening. By their mere existence, these forts demanded immediate attention.

The forts, the convention believed, by right belonged to South Carolina; three commissioners, accordingly, must be sent to Washington at once to negotiate for their transfer, along with the transfer of lighthouses, arsenals, and other bits of real and personal property in South Carolina to which the government at Washington still held title.[9]

The forts would be taken over in due time. Meanwhile it was important to make the people of the United States understand the justice and logic behind secession; important, especially, to impress this on the attention of the people of the cotton belt, and to invite them to bring their states into a new Southern nation whose creation had begun with South Carolina's action in Secession Hall on December 20.

Two documents were produced by December 24. The first was gravely headed "Declaration of the Immediate Causes which Induce and Justify the Secession of South Carolina from the Federal Union." It went on to assert that the benefits the Federal Constitution had been drawn up to secure had been defeated by the actions of the free states of the North: "Those States have assumed the right of deciding upon the propriety of our domestic institutions; and have denied the rights of property established in fifteen of the States and recognized by the Constitution; they have denounced as sinful the institution of Slavery; they have permitted the open establishment among them of societies, whose avowed object is to disturb the peace and to eloign the property of the citizens of other States." This had been going on for a full quarter-century, and now a sectional party avowedly hostile to the South was about to take possession of the government. "The guaranties of the Constitution will then no longer exist; the equal rights of the States will be lost. The slave-holding States will no longer have the power of self-government, or self-protection, and the Federal Government will have become their enemy." Therefore, the people of South Carolina, "appealing to the Supreme Judge of the world for the rectitude of our intentions," had, in a word, seceded.

The other document was an address "to the People of the Slave-holding States of the United States," and it was somewhat more pointed. It recited that the government of the United States had become a despotism, said that the Constitution was but an experiment that had failed—"the whole Constitution, by the constructions of the Northern people, has been absorbed by its preamble"—and came to a ringing peroration:

"Citizens of the Slave-holding States of the United States! Circumstances beyond our control have placed us in the van of the great controversy between the Northern and Southern States. We would have preferred that other States should have assumed the position we now occupy. . . . You have loved the Union, in whose service your great statesmen have labored and your great soldiers have fought and conquered—not for the material benefits it conferred,

but with the faith of a generous and devoted chivalry. You
have long lingered in hope over the shattered remains of a
broken Constitution. Compromise after compromise, formed
by your concessions, has been trampled under foot by your
Northern confederates. All fraternity of feeling between the
North and the South is lost, or has been converted into
hate; and we, of the South, are at last driven together by
the stern destiny which controls the existence of nations. . . .
All we demand of other peoples is to be left alone, to
work out our own high destinies. United together, we must
be the most independent as we are the most important
of the nations of the world. United together, and we require
no other instrument to conquer peace than our beneficent
productions. United together and we must be a great, free
and prosperous people, whose renown must spread through
the civilized world, and pass down, we trust, to the remotest age. We ask you to join us in forming a Confederacy
of Slave-holding States."[10]

The statement was forthright and revealing, touched with
simple eloquence, expressing deep determination. Yet somehow it was not quite the sort of manifesto which men compose when they know they are going to have to make desperate war. It was written in the light of the faith that King
Cotton was irresistible, and it hinted strongly at the belief
that no one would be insane enough to take up arms against
a united band of cotton states visibly in earnest. Implicit
in all that was said and done was the conviction that the
rest of the South would follow where South Carolina led,
provided the leadership was vigorous and unhesitating. Ten
days before the vote on the ordinance, the case had been
expressed perfectly by South Carolina's Congressman, William Porcher Miles, who urged speedy action because of the
effect on the other slave states. Secessionists in the other
states, he wrote, "tell us that any delay, under any pretext
will demoralize them at home—while it will answer no possible good purpose. . . . We must move instantly or we injure our friends."[11] The immediate target was not so much
the North as the remainder of the South.

The first reports from the deep South were good. The
news from Charleston brought crowds into the streets at
New Orleans; there were parades, bands again played the
"Marseillaise," a bust of John C. Calhoun was crowned with

a blue cockade, and the press noted "a general demonstration of joy." In Mobile there was a big parade, followed by the firing of a 100-gun salute; at Montgomery there was a similar salute, which was duplicated at Pensacola and at Wilmington. In Memphis a mass meeting commended the secessionists, and even in Virginia, which tended to be a little more reserved, there were demonstrations. A lofty "secession pole" bearing a palmetto flag was hoisted at Petersburg—to be cut down, during the night, by parties undetected—and there were flags and salutes at Norfolk and Portsmouth.[12]

But the response in the border states was less encouraging. Kentucky, where the new legislature would have a Unionist majority, was obviously going to wait and see, and the situation in Missouri seemed no brighter. The governor of Maryland, Thomas B. Hicks, was an avowed Unionist, and the first attempt to bring Maryland into the secessionist bloc met with failure. At the instigation of the Mississippi legislature, the Mississippi governor had appointed one A. H. Handy a commissioner to enlist Maryland's support, and Hicks flatly rebuffed the man. Maryland, wrote Governor Hicks, although identified with the Southern states "in feeling and by the institutions and habits which prevail among us," was above all things devoted to the Union; not until actual events had clearly shown that the rights guaranteed by the Constitution could not be obtained would Maryland have anything to do with an attempt to disrupt the Union.

Addressing a public meeting in Baltimore, Handy indicated that the movement for secession might be a deep political maneuver rather than an outright effort to set up a new nation.

"Secession," he said, "is not intended to break up the present union but to perpetuate it. We do not propose to go out by way of breaking up or destroying the Union as our fathers gave it to us, but we go out for the purpose of getting further guarantees and security for our rights. . . . Our plan is for the Southern states to withdraw from the Union, for the present, to allow amendments to the Constitution to be made, guaranteeing our just rights; and if the Northern States will not make those amendments, by which these rights shall be secured to us, then we must secure them the best way we can. This question of slavery must be settled now or never."[13]

It was a game for high stakes, and no one could be sure just how the cards were going to fall. If Mr. Handy spoke for the secessionist leaders as a group—which, in view of the fact that they included some of the most self-assured individualists ever born in America, may be somewhat doubtful—the gamble was very delicate indeed. The people whose votes had made Lincoln President-elect may not have known precisely what they were doing when they voted for him, but it was obvious that they had been deeply moved by *something,* and to assume that a declaration of cotton-belt independence would quickly cause them to give up that something and make liberal concessions was to make a very long gamble. The significant clause in Mr. Handy's remarks was still his assertion that if the South could not win her rights by negotiation, "then we must secure them the best way we can."

Unhappiest man in America just now was almost certainly President James Buchanan. On that portentous twentieth of December, the President had attended a wedding in the home of friends, in Washington, and early in the evening he had blandly assured his hostess that his health and spirits were of the best. "I have never enjoyed better health nor a more tranquil spirit," he said. "I have not lost an hour's sleep nor a single meal." A little later that evening, with Buchanan sitting in the drawing room while most of the other guests were strolling about looking at the wedding presents, there were noises and bustlings at the front door. Buchanan glanced over his shoulder, and then (strangely echoing old Mr. Petigru's remark, made that same evening) he asked his hostess: "Madam, do you suppose the house is on fire? I hear an unusual commotion in the hall." The hostess went to the door and encountered Congressman Lawrence Keitt, of South Carolina, who bore a telegram and an air of great excitement; the telegram informed him that his state had just voted to secede, and he was shaking it in the air and crying "Thank God! Thank God!"

The hostess bore this news to the President. Later on, she remembered the response she got. "He looked at me, stunned, for a moment. Falling back and grasping the arms of his chair, he whispered: 'Madam, might I beg you to have my carriage called?' "[14] The carriage came, and Buchanan rode off to the White House. The crisis he had hoped to avoid was at last upon him . . . and upon the country.

2. *A Delegation of Authority*

THE FORTS at Charleston had begun to draw attention to
themselves early in November. They drew attention, or attention was thrust upon them; it can be said either way, and it
makes no difference, since it was the mere fact that the forts
existed at all that was so stirring and so perilous. They were
wholly inert little plots of ground surrounded by masonry,
either obsolescent or unfinished, made to drowse under the
Southern sun, looking seaward. Yet time had moved over
them, transforming everything, so that the most prosaic of
objects or actions—even the fact that little pyramids of
freshly tarred cannon balls were stacked in the rear of the
gun carriages, even the matter of having a sentry walking
post atop a parapet, or of hoisting a familiar flag every morning and hauling it down at sunset—these had suddenly started
to cast fearful shadows. They symbolized an unbearable aggression against the safety of a state which, trying to become
a nation, bristled with immense pride and a certain unsure
arrogance.

Commanding these forts when November began was Colonel John L. Gardner, Massachusetts-born, old and near the
end of his career; he was a veteran of the War of 1812 and
he felt that the Charleston garrison ought to be increased.
The War Department had suggested that the arms might be
issued to the civilians who were employed on the completion
of Fort Sumter so that they could be used as a species of
militia, but Colonel Gardner felt that these men were bad
security risks. Some of them were foreign-born and many of
them were Southerners, possibly not to be trusted on Federal
property with guns in their hands. Still, it would be comfort-
ing to have the weapons, and Colonel Gardner undertook to
get them—and, in the process, set off a minor storm that
blew him all the way out of the army.

The weapons were stored in a Federal arsenal that occupied a neatly kept four acres of grounds within the Charleston city limits. An officer bearing the cumbersome title of
Military Storekeeper of Ordnance, F. C. Humphreys, with
fourteen enlisted men, had charge of this place and its con-
tents, which included 22,000 stands of arms, a good deal of

heavy ordnance, and substantial quantities of ammunition
and other military stores. Colonel Gardner wanted the small-
arms ammunition and certain of the weapons moved to Fort
Moultrie, where he could quickly lay his hands on them in
case of need, but when he sent an officer ashore with a boat
to make the transfer, on November 7, an angry crowd collected on the wharf and refused to let anything be shipped.¹
Storekeeper Humphreys was not molested, and the arsenal
remained intact, but six weeks before secession Charleston
was refusing to let the Federal garrison increase its supply
of arms, and it was complaining bitterly to Washington because the attempt had been made.

Captain Fitz John Porter, of the adjutant general's office,
went to Charleston a day or so after this to inspect and report. He found Fort Moultrie, the only active military post
in the harbor, manned by Companies E and H of the First
Artillery, along with the regimental band, for a total strength
of ten officers and sixty-four men. Of the men, deducting
musicians, sick men, and those under arrest for various military misdemeanors, there were thirty-six available for regular
duty. Enlisted men and non-coms seemed intelligent and industrious, as such things went in the army in those days, and
the officers appeared to be sober and on their toes. But Fort
Moultrie itself was in rather poor shape.

Its walls enclosed less than two acres of ground. Its barracks, officers' quarters, hospital, storehouses, everything indeed except the actual fortifications, were of wood, easily
burned; along the sea front the winds had drifted sand nearly
up to the top of the walls, so that any venturesome child
could wander into the place without difficulty. A little farther
away there were sand hills covered with scrubby undergrowth,
so situated that a regiment of riflemen could sweep the fort's
parapets with fire from protected positions. Fort Moultrie
was old-fashioned, even in 1860. It had no casemates to give
guns and gunners proper protection, and all of its armament
was mounted "en barbette"—out in the open, with nothing
but a low parapet to provide shelter from hostile fire. In addition, there were a good many houses and summer cottages
to interfere with defensive fire, and on top of everything else
Fort Moultrie had been laid out so that most of its guns
would bear on a single point in the channel leading from the
open sea to the harbor. The fort had no guns controlling the

approach from the rear, which was precisely the point from which an attack now was most likely to come. The place contained fifty-five guns of all calibers, including ten 8-inch Columbiads, and there were altogether too many of these guns for two under-strength companies of artillery to handle.

All in all, Captain Porter felt that the garrison ought to be increased, if that could be done without stirring up trouble. He mentioned "the inflammable and impulsive state of the public mind" in Charleston, and indicated that the commanding officer at the fort would need to show much prudence and good judgment "in all transactions which may bear upon the relations of the Federal Government to the State of South Carolina and of the Army to our citizens."[2]

The administration in Washington already knew that the public mind in Charleston was inflammable and impulsive, and the row stirred up by Colonel Gardner's attempt to get small arms and ammunition did not make him look like a man of prudence and good judgment; and, besides, he was Yankee-born, and the people of Charleston were vexed with him; so on November 15 Major Robert Anderson was named as his replacement, and Colonel Gardner was transferred away to stand by for orders that never came.

Anderson was a lean, graying veteran, clean-shaven, noted both for an excellent combat record (he had won brevets for gallantry in the Black Hawk and Mexican wars and had been wounded at Molino Del Rey) and for a mildly bookish quality, which was somewhat rare among army officers at that time. He had translated French texts on artillery and these were used as manuals of instruction, he had served with credit on various War Department boards, and he was known as an industrious and energetic officer. It seemed important, too, that he was a Southerner. Of Virginian ancestry, he had been born in Kentucky, and was married to a woman from Georgia. His principles were considered proslavery, and some of the officers at Fort Sumter told each other that this was why Secretary Floyd had chosen him.

Floyd seems, at his interview with Anderson, to have given the man little more than a quick fill-in on the background of the situation, along with orders to send back a report as soon as possible. Anderson went to Charleston, Colonel Gardner departed, and Anderson got down to business. He had no way of knowing it, but the Charleston forts were to be the

effective bounds for all the remainder of his career. He
would live until 1871, but everything of importance that he
had to do, everything of real meaning to himself and to the
nation, would be done here, at Moultrie and at Sumter, in
the next five months.[3]

Anderson quickly realized that Fort Moultrie could be
taken at any time. There were, indeed, funds available to put
it in better condition; acting long before anyone had thought
it would make any particular difference, Congress had voted
money for repairs here, as well as for the slow completion of
Fort Sumter, and it would be possible at least to get the sand
shoveled away from the walls so that (as Captain Abner
Doubleday, of the garrison, remarked) stray cattle would be
kept from blundering into the place. But even when all had
been done that could be done, there just were not enough
soldiers present to make a good defense. In anything like a
siege, the skeleton force would be spread so thin that the
simple job of manning the works would quickly exhaust it.[4]

Fort Sumter was different. It was unfinished, and its guns
were not yet mounted—although those in the lower tier
would be, within three weeks, and the accommodations for
the men were finished—but it had been built on a shoal out
in the harbor, with deep water all around it, and even a small
garrison there could hold out against any sudden rush by
state militia. Fort Sumter, wrote Major Anderson on November 23, ought to be occupied. Castle Pinckney also should
be manned, and there should be more men in Fort Moultrie;
"the clouds are threatening and the storm may break upon us
at any moment," and there was no time to spare. Yet it
would be risky. "I firmly believe," the major wrote, "that as
soon as the people of South Carolina learn that I have demanded reinforcements, and that they have been ordered,
they will occupy Castle Pinckney and attack this fort." If
the reinforcements were sent, they had best reach the harbor
before anyone in Charleston knew that they were on the
way. If this could be done, Major Anderson felt that South
Carolina would not try to take the forts by force but would
rely on diplomacy; but if the forts remained weak, "she will,
unless these works are surrendered on their first demand,
most assuredly immediately attack us."[5]

It was dangerous to be weak, and dangerous to be strong,
and a few days later Anderson sent another dispatch from

his quarters in Fort Moultrie. "There appears," he wrote, "to be a romantic desire urging the South Carolinians to *have possession* of this work . . . I am inclined to think that if I had been here before the commencement of expenditures on this work, and supposed that the garrison would not be increased, I should have advised its withdrawal, with the exception of small guard, and its removal to Fort Sumter, which so perfectly commands the harbor and this fort."[6]

The major's next report, written on December 1, was even gloomier. Officers who had visited the city reported that the people were determined to allow neither reinforcements nor extra supplies to be landed. It was clear that "anything which indicates a determination on the part of the General Government to act with an unusual degree of vigor in putting these works in a better state of defense will be regarded as an act of aggression" and would undoubtedly cause an attack on Fort Moultrie. The government, Major Anderson warned, must decide very quickly what it proposed to do about the forts since South Carolina had seceded. If it was going to surrender the forts on demand, Major Anderson needed to be informed and told what course to pursue; if it was not going to give up the forts, it had better send reinforcements at once, or at least station some men of war in the harbor. Either course, the major admitted, might cause some of the other Southern states to join South Carolina in secession. Meanwhile, for his own part, "I shall go steadily on, preparing for the worst, trusting hopefully in the God of Battles to guard and guide me in my course."[7]

Major Anderson's advice was pointed but unwelcome. The President was under intense pressure, and nearly a fortnight before the South Carolina convention voted to secede he had agreed to an informal truce, concerning which there would be hard words and bad feeling a little later. By the beginning of December, the people of South Carolina had persuaded themselves that the forts were destined to come into their possession as soon as secession was voted; this being the case, it was only fair to preserve the status quo, by agreement, until secession should become effective, and on December 8 most of the state's Congressional delegation went to see Buchanan about it. They worked out with him a slightly vague agreement that at least for the present Major Anderson would neither be attacked nor reinforced, and Buchanan was given a letter dated December 9 setting forth this agreement as the South Carolina Congressmen understood it. The letter read as follows:

"In compliance with our statement to you yesterday, we now express to you our strong convictions that neither the constituted authorities nor any body of the people of the State of South Carolina will either attack or molest the U. S. Forts in the harbor of Charleston previously to the action of the convention, and we hope & believe not until an offer has been made through an accredited Representative to negotiate for an amicable arrangement of all matters between the State and the Federal government, provided that no reinforcements shall be sent into those Forts & their relative military status remains as at present."

The letter was signed by J. W. McQueen, William Porcher Miles, M. L. Bonham, W. W. Boyce, and Lawrence M. Keitt.

Buchanan said afterward that he objected to the word "provided," since it might imply an agreement which he would never make; and this, he said, was understood by everyone present. A member of the delegation, however, had a different version. Someone, he said, asked Buchanan: "Suppose you should hereafter change your policy for any reason, what then? That would put us, who are willing to use our personal interest to prevent any attack upon the forts before commissioners are sent on to Washington, in rather an embarrassing position." To this, Buchanan was said to have replied: "Then I would first return you this paper." The delegation left the White House feeling that the President was wavering but that he was bound in honor not to make any change in the situation then existing in Charleston harbor. The President, for his part, considered himself actually pledged to nothing once a vote to secede had been taken.[8]

To Major Anderson, meanwhile, had gone nothing much better than the expression of a pious wish that everything would turn out all right. From the adjutant general of the army, on December 1, came a message saying that the Secretary of War hoped all of the major's actions would "be such as to be free from the charge of initiating a collision." If attacked, Major Anderson would of course defend himself as best he could. Meanwhile, "the increase of the force under your command, however much to be desired, would, the

Secretary thinks . . . but add to that excitement and might lead to serious results."[9]

Major Anderson had at least been told that he could defend himself if someone started shooting at him, but he felt that the instructions were inadequate. He reminded the War Department that Fort Sumter was empty, except for the workmen, so that a boatload of militia could occupy it any time. The South Carolina authorities, he added, were apparently beginning to think more and more about Sumter, and less about Moultrie, which was intelligent of them; once they had Fort Sumter, with its guns mounted and a proper garrison on hand, they would have perfect control of Charleston harbor, Washington could send in neither warships nor supply ships, and the garrison of Fort Moultrie could be driven out with great ease.

That Anderson needed better guidance was clear, even in the War Department, and at the end of the first week in December, Secretary Floyd summoned an austere and methodical officer from the adjutant general's staff, Major Don Carlos Buell, and gave him a special mission of some delicacy. Buell was to go to Charleston and give to Major Anderson certain instructions, which the Secretary would now transmit verbally; they would amount to a broad explanation of general policy, rather than explicit orders, and much would be left to Major Anderson's discretion—and, presumably, to the intelligence and fidelity with which Major Buell recited Secretary Floyd's remarks. The Secretary would put nothing in writing.

Off to Charleston went Major Buell. He talked with Major Anderson, made his own appraisal of the situation, and finally concluded to do what the Secretary of War had refrained from doing—put the orders down in writing. To the best of his ability (and Major Buell was a painfully conscientious man) he drew up for Major Anderson's benefit a memorandum of the verbal message which he had been given.

Dated December 11, this document began by reciting the administration's desire to avoid a violent collision with the people of South Carolina. Major Anderson was not, "without evident and immediate necessity," to do anything that even looked hostile. At the same time, he was to hold possession of the forts "and if attacked you are to defend yourself to the last extremity." The major did not, to be sure, have enough men to occupy more than one of the forts, but an attack or an attempt to occupy any of them he would take as an act of hostility, whereupon he could put his command into whichever fort he considered most defensible. Furthermore: "You are also authorized to take similar steps whenever you have tangible evidence of a design to proceed to a hostile act."

When Buell wrote this out, he had become convinced that unless the government acted, Fort Sumter would very soon be seized, whether with or without the order of the state authorities, and the feeling unquestionably influenced him in his interpretation of the Secretary's instructions. When he gave the memorandum to Anderson he said: "This is all I am authorized to say to you, but my personal advice is, that you do not allow the opportunity to escape you." He made some further suggestions, "all looking to the contemplated transfer of his command," and then went back to Washington, bearing a copy of the paper he had written. After reporting to the Secretary, he gave it to the chief clerk of the War Department for deposit in the department's files.[10] Whether Floyd himself actually read the copy is a question; if he did, he quickly forgot about it, and he was behaving with uncommon fogginess these days.

President Buchanan, however, did see it, and one sentence bothered him. Major Anderson had been told that in case he was attacked he was to "defend himself to the last extremity," and it seemed to James Buchanan that this was going beyond common sense. At the President's instance, a letter over Floyd's signature was sent to Anderson. The major was not to sacrifice his own life or the lives of his men in a hopeless fight; if he was obviously overpowered, he could bow to necessity and make the best terms possible—this would be the course of a brave and honorable officer, "and you will be fully justified in such action." Additionally, the part of Buell's memorandum which told Anderson he could occupy any fort he chose if he had reason to believe that he was going to be attacked was mildly qualified by the addition of the word "defensive" in the description of the steps that were permitted him.[11]

Whether anyone realized it or not, the administration had

at last taken a positive step. Until now Major Anderson had been told nothing except that he could defend himself if attacked. Now he was given full authority to move from Fort Moultrie to Fort Sumter—not merely if he was attacked, but whenever he had tangible evidence "of a design to proceed to a hostile act." Inasmuch as tangible evidence of such a design lay all over Charleston as thick as a winter's fog, Anderson had in substance been told he could go over to Sumter whenever he thought best. What effect such a move might have on the hypersensitive spirits of the South Carolina authorities—who considered, mistakenly or otherwise, that they had the President's word of honor that no such step would be taken unless they were first consulted about it— was left entirely up to the imagination of anyone who chanced to think about it. Major Anderson had his government's written permission to take, on his own initiative, a step that might set off all the guns.

It appears that Major Anderson himself did not immediately understand how broad his instructions had become. A few days after Major Buell left him, Anderson wrote to a Northern friend saying that he did wish the government would send him clearer orders. Why would not Washington tell him to abandon Fort Moultrie if he had to? "I would rather not be kept here to 'Surrender' when a demand is made for the Fort. I don't like the name of 'having surrendered.' No one has been, or could have been, authorized to give a pledge of what this state will do."[12]

Although he would presently see that the responsibility which had been given to him was almost fantastically heavy for one aging major of artillery to bear unaided, Major Anderson would not grow entirely discouraged. He was devoutly religious, and to a clergyman in New Jersey he wrote: "Were it not for my firm reliance upon and trust in Our Heavenly Father, I could not but be disheartened, but I feel that I am here in the performance of a solemn duty, and am assured that He, who has shielded me when Death claimed his victims all around me, will not desert me now. Pray for me and my little band—I feel assured that the prayer will be heard."

He traced the difficulties of his position: Fort Moultrie was surrounded by houses, which helped make it indefensible;

he could not remove the houses until an attack on him had actually begun; and, anyway, he did not have enough ammunition to waste any that way. But he and his command would do their best, and he was proud of the men under him. "Were you to see this little band, to note how zealously they attend to any duty I require of them, frequently voluntarily engaging in some work which, they know, I wish executed, how entirely they refrain from drinking, you would see that they were men who in the hour of trial would do their duty —For myself I can say frankly truthfully that I have not had a moment of despondency—I feel that He who made me will guide me through any trials there may be in store for me."[18]

To an acquaintance in Washington, Anderson wrote frankly that he despaired of the safety of the Union. If South Carolina could go out alone, he said, he would not mind seeing her "make the trial of exercising her sovereignty out of it," but he felt that this was a vain hope. "Other states will, however, follow her example and our glorious Confederacy will disappear from the galaxy of Nations, and be replaced by the uncertain lights of a milky way—Were it not for my trust in God, I would despair of extricating myself from my present critical position but I have no misgivings. He will teach me the way."[14]

The trials would be heavy, and matters by now had reached a point at which almost any accident could start a war. There was a sudden, ominous flurry on December 17, when Captain J. G. Foster, of the Corps of Engineers, present in Charleston to supervise the work that was being done on the forts, went to the Charleston arsenal to get some machinery that was needed at Fort Sumter. While there it occurred to him that forty muskets that were to have been transferred early in November had not actually been sent because of the uproar made at the time, and Foster had them shipped to Fort Moultrie. Since nothing that anyone did remained a secret in Charleston in these days, news of this immediately got around, and (as Foster might have foreseen) it raised much trouble. In Washington, Trescot got a frantic telegram announcing that if the arms were not immediately returned "a collision may occur at any moment," and Trescot went to Floyd's house, roused the Secretary from a sickbed, and had him send a telegram ordering the forty muskets sent back to the arsenal. The next day Trescot got a telegram from J.

Johnson Pettigrew, aide-de-camp to Governor Pickens. The governor was glad the arms were being returned, as otherwise there would have been great danger—and now it was imperative that there be no movement of troops from Fort Moultrie to Fort Sumter: "Inform the Secretary of War."[15]

Governor Pickens, as a matter of fact, had had his eye on Fort Sumter from the very first. He was inaugurated on December 16, and on the next day he sent a confidential agent—Major D. H. Hamilton, of the First Regiment South Carolina Volunteers—off to Washington to demand that Fort Sumter be given up. To spare the effusion of blood (said a letter which Pickens gave Major Hamilton for President Buchanan), it would be wise of the President to give the fort up and to let the South Carolina authorities take immediate possession, "in order to give a feeling of safety to the community." As a parting shot, Pickens added: "If something of the kind be not done, I cannot answer for the consequences."

Major Hamilton got to Washington, and Trescot took him to the White House, but his meeting with the President was not happy. James Buchanan felt that he had done about all he could properly be asked to do to keep the peace with South Carolina. He had been bitterly attacked in the Northern press in consequence, there was even talk of a Congressional investigation into his conduct . . . and, as Trescot hastily wrote to Governor Pickens, to press the Sumter matter now might drive him all the way over into the opposition camp. Pressured by Trescot, the governor withdrew the letter.[16]

Trescot had judged matters accurately. When the news that Pickens had withdrawn his request reached the White House, Buchanan was in the act of composing a letter that, for him, was blistering. In it he informed Governor Pickens: "As an executive officer of this Government, I have no power to surrender to any human authority Fort Sumter or any of the other forts or public property in South Carolina. To do this would on my part as I have already said be a naked act of usurpation. . . . If South Carolina should attack any of these Forts she will then become the assailant in a war against the United States. . . . I have, therefore, never been more astonished in my life, than to learn from you that unless Fort Sumter be delivered into your hands, you cannot be an-

swerable for the consequences." The letter was never finished
and was never sent. Dated December 20, it presumably was
drafted before Buchanan knew South Carolina had voted to
secede. It remained in the presidential files, silent evidence
that even with a Buchanan in the White House it was possible for South Carolina to press her luck too far.[17]

Governor Pickens, meanwhile, was on the alert. Reaching
Charleston while the secession convention was in session preparing for its momentous vote, he sent an engineer officer
to examine Fort Sumter in detail, conferred with a delegation
from the state legislature regarding the necessity for keeping
Federal troops out of the fort, and then, late at night, sent
for Captain Charles H. Simonton, of the Washington Light
Infantry, to give certain instructions.

The Washington Light Infantry was on duty patrolling the
area around the Federal arsenal, to keep munitions from being removed. Now its duties were to be broadened. Governor
Pickens told Captain Simonton that Major Anderson was believed to be thinking about moving his command to Fort
Sumter. This, he said, must be prevented at all hazards, although an actual conflict should be avoided if possible. Captain Simonton was to take a picked group from his command,
embark on a steamer that would be provided, and cruise back
and forth between Sumter and Moultrie. He was to hail every
boat that passed from one fort to the other, and if he found
United States troops on board he was to recite his orders—
namely, that a troop transfer was to be prevented no matter
what the cost. If the Federal officer in charge of any floating
detachment, having heard these orders, persisted in trying to
go to Fort Sumter, Captain Simonton was to resist by force,
sink the boat, and immediately occupy Fort Sumter himself.
He was to use his own discretion in accomplishing the end in
view.[18]

Captain Simonton embarked his command and got down to
it—and the narrowing-down process had reached its limit at
last. The power to make the decision which everyone else
had evaded lay now in the hands of two obscure subordinates, a major of United States artillery and a captain of
South Carolina infantry. Each man had been given discretionary orders. Between them, they could say whether there
would be a war.

3. An Action and a Decision

CHRISTMAS DAY in Charleston was rainy and disagreeable, but the rain stopped during the night and December 26 came in clear and sunny, with a pleasant warmth in the air. Having considered his situation in detail, Major Robert Anderson concluded that the "tangible evidence of a design to proceed to a hostile act" mentioned in his orders was as clear as need be, and he made up his mind: he would move the garrison over to Fort Sumter.

In his appraisal of the situation, Major Anderson had a number of points to consider. The work of repairing Fort Moultrie had gone well. A large force of civilian workers had been employed, the troublesome sand had been shoveled away from the parapets, the guns were properly mounted, and if the fort had a proper garrison it could probably be held against any assault. But that, of course, was the trouble: a proper garrison Fort Moultrie did not have and could not get, and under the circumstances the place could not be defended. It was hard enough just to keep out the idlers and the sight-seers. There was a crowd around all day long, from dawn until dusk—newspaper correspondents, militiamen, unending numbers of ordinary citizens, making sketches, taking notes, asking questions, prying into everything, being so busy and so numerous that the major had felt obliged to post guards and close his gates: a step that caused angry mutterings and led people to talk resentfully about hirelings and mercenaries. Members of the garrison were under constant strain; at one stage two of the officers, worn out by the need for everlasting watchfulness, had put their wives on duty on the parapet while they themselves tried to catch up on lost sleep. Worried, Captain Foster notified the War Department that two guard steamers were patrolling the waters around Fort Sumter, and Captain Doubleday believed that South Carolina refrained from seizing Fort Sumter at once only because the authorities felt that the construction job there might as well be completed with Federal money: why take over an unfinished fort when a finished one could be had for a little waiting?[1]

Since it was impossible to keep any secrets with a crowd

of inquisitive strangers watching everything and questioning everybody, Anderson kept his intentions to himself. December 26 began like any other day, except that the post quartermaster was ordered to charter some barges and schooners and have them drawn up by the sea wall as near the fort as might be. If the garrison left Fort Moultrie, the wives and children of the enlisted men would lose their quarters, so the quartermaster was to take them across the harbor to old Fort Johnson, on the south side, a fort which was no longer operational but which did contain some dilapidated living quarters. Meanwhile, rowboats such as were used to transport workmen to and from Fort Sumter were to be beached on another part of the water front; and, for the rest, the ordinary routine prevailed in Fort Moultrie that day, and at dusk Captain Doubleday walked up from his quarters to invite Major Anderson to come down and have a cup of tea.

It was no day for afternoon tea. Doubleday noticed that the other officers were standing about the major, acting as if they had just learned something big, and he understood what was on their minds when the major, ignoring the invitation to tea, told him: "Captain, in twenty minutes you will leave with your company for Fort Sumter."

Doubleday hurried off to muster his command, and while the men were collecting muskets and knapsacks, he stepped into his own quarters to tell Mrs. Doubleday to pack her belongings as fast as she could and slip out into the sand hills somewhere; he was convinced that the move to Fort Sumter would start a big fight, and he wanted her out of the line of fire. Mrs. Doubleday got her things together, went out the sally port, and took refuge in the house of the post sutler, moving from there to the home of the post chaplain; she would go next day to a hotel in Charleston, and would leave for the North as quickly as possible. Meanwhile, the families of the enlisted men went to the boats that were to take them to Fort Johnson, and as the twilight deepened, the officers and men of the Fort Moultrie garrison set off for their own boats.

On this evening the soldiers' luck was in, and the procession to the beach went unnoticed. The sun had gone down and the winter twilight was thick, the regular crowd of sightseers had dispersed, and the militiamen who ordinarily kept watching the fort seemed to have gone home to supper; the streets of the little town of Moultrieville were deserted, and the parade of two diminutive companies of men went unnoticed. The whole garrison was on hand, except for a rear guard left in Fort Moultrie—seven privates, four non-coms, and the post's doctor, a Pennsylvanian named Samuel W. Crawford. Crawford had been on the army roster for nine years with the rank of assistant surgeon, but tonight he was acting as a line officer and the role seems to have pleased him; once he got north he would transfer from the medical corps to the infantry, and he would end with a major general's commission. With him, to take more immediate charge of the rear guard's activities, was Captain Foster, who as an officer of the Corps of Engineers was not properly a member of the garrison.

At the water front, officers and men got into the boats as speedily as they could, and after arranging their baggage they shoved off. Back in Moultrie, Foster and Crawford had a couple of the fort's biggest guns loaded and trained out over the bay, ready to sink any secessionist guard boat that might try to interfere; and with this support the little flotilla steered for Fort Sumter.

It had not gone far before Doubleday saw one of the guard boats heading for his own craft. He had his men remove their coats and lay them over their muskets, which were on the thwarts beside them, and he himself took off his military cap and threw open his coat so that his brass buttons would not be seen; with luck, the people on the guard boat might fail to recognize these men as soldiers, would perhaps assume that this rowboat simply carried workers over to Fort Sumter.

The guard boat came closer, and at a distance of perhaps 100 yards it drifted to a stop, motionless paddle wheels dripping, officers on the upper deck peering through the dusk at the open boat. Farther away, apparently not seen from the guard boat, the rest of Anderson's boats kept on their way; Doubleday's men continued to row with the clumsy care of landsmen; and on the parapet of Fort Moultrie, back in the shore-line dark, Foster and Crawford and the enlisted men swung two ponderous Columbiads around and tried to get the South Carolina guard boat in their sights. At last the people on the guard boat concluded that nothing out of the ordinary was going on, the paddle wheels began to dip and splash again, and the steamer chuffed off. In fifteen min-

utes the small boats touched the esplanade in front of Fort
Sumter. The soldiers put on their coats and picked up their
muskets, formed rank on the open wharf before the main
gate, swung into column, and went tramping into Fort Sumter.[2]

Inside the fort were more than 100 carpenters, bricklayers,
stonecutters, and other construction workers, lounging about
with the day's chores at an end. These, without ceremony,
were herded out to the esplanade and tumbled into the boats
to return to Charleston before they were entirely clear as to
whether the fort was being occupied by soldiers of the United
States or soldiers of South Carolina. Anderson saw to it that
proper guards were posted, set details to work blocking some
of the open embrasures on the ground level, perfected his
defenses as well as he could with the means at hand. Then he
had two guns fired, to notify the remnant at Fort Moultrie
that the transfer had been completed. By the oddest chance,
old Mr. Ruffin was near when these guns were fired. He had
embarked on a steamer that afternoon to go down to Fernan-
dina, and he was a few miles from Fort Moultrie, standing
on the upper deck, when the sound of the guns went echoing
across the darkened harbor. It puzzled him, and in his diary
he wrote that "it was an unusual occurrence . . . I supposed
this firing at so unusual an hour must have been a signal for
something."[3]

A signal it was, to reverberate far beyond Charleston; bearing news, first of all, to the state authorities that they had
been tricked. The guard ships set their sirens wailing and
burned blue lights, and from lookout stations along the water
front, rockets soared into the night. At daybreak the South
Carolina troops moved into Fort Moultrie—which Foster,
Crawford, and their squad had of course evacuated—and a
little later in the morning Castle Pinckney also was seized.
The Federal arsenal in Charleston was taken over on December 30. Major Anderson, meanwhile, having satisfied himself
that everything that ought to be done tonight had been done,
hurried to write a note to his wife.

"Thanks be to God," he wrote. "I give them with my
whole heart for His having given me the will and shewn the
way to bring my command to this Fort. I can now breathe
freely. The whole force of S. Carolina would not venture to
attack us. . . . I have not time to write more—as I must make

my report to the Ad Gen. . . . Praise be to God for His merciful kindness to us. I think that the whole country north and South should thank Him for this step."[4]

In more formal vein he then wrote to Adjutant General Samuel Cooper, informing him that "I have just completed, by the blessing of God, the removal to this fort of all my garrison, except the surgeon, four non-commissioned officers and seven men." He had left orders, he said, to have the guns at Fort Moultrie spiked and the gun carriages destroyed, and he had told Captain Foster to destroy all of the ammunition which could not be moved to Fort Sumter. He added that "the step which I have taken was, in my opinion, necessary to prevent the effusion of blood."[5]

In his belief that both North and South would offer thanks for the move to Fort Sumter, Major Anderson had been overoptimistic. The news hit official Washington like an earthquake, the force of it great enough finally to compel President Buchanan to face up to unpleasant reality.

South Carolina's commissioners, chosen to negotiate for the cession of Federal property, had just reached the capital. They were men of high standing—Robert W. Barnwell, J. H. Adams, and James L. Orr—and Buchanan, who could find nothing in the book telling what a President should do when a state has declared itself independent, had consented to receive them on December 27. On the morning of that day, in preparation for this meeting, the commissioners were in deep conference with Trescot, who had at last resigned as Assistant Secretary of State and who was remaining in Washington as South Carolina's agent. The conference had hardly begun when the news from Charleston arrived, brought by the indignant Senator Louis Trezevant Wigfall, of Texas, burly duelist, master of Senate debate, a forceful battler for states' rights. The men expressed shocked disbelief. Trescot, who had seen much of Secretary Floyd of late, was sure that if Anderson had done this thing, he had done it without authority. At this moment Floyd himself entered, and when Trescot turned to him and remarked, "I will pledge my life, if it has been done, it has been done without orders," Floyd smiled confidently.

"You can do more," he told Trescot. "You can pledge your life, Mr. Trescot, that it is not so. It is impossible. It would be not only without orders, but in the face of orders."

Despite Floyd's assurances, the conference broke up and Trescot hurried to the Capitol building, where he broke the news to Jefferson Davis and Senator R. M. T. Hunter, of Virginia—two of the most respected of Southern leaders, men who stood firmly for Southern rights but who had never been numbered with the fire-eaters. The three men went to the White House, and presently were in conference with Buchanan himself.

As Trescot remembered it, Davis opened the conversation by asking Buchanan bluntly: "Have you received any intelligence from Charleston in the last few hours?" When Buchanan said that he had not, Davis said: "Then I have a great calamity to announce to you." He told the President what had happened—how Anderson and his garrison had moved to Fort Sumter, spiking guns and burning gun carriages behind them, even chopping down the Fort Moultrie flag staff as a departing gesture—and he added: "And now, Mr. President, you are surrounded with blood and dishonor on all sides."

Buchanan stood by the mantelpiece, crushing a cigar in one hand; then he sank into a chair, bursting out at last: "My God, are calamities never to come singly? I call God to witness, you gentlemen better than anybody know that this is not only without but against my orders. It is against my policy." This was all very well, but it was not enough. The visitors told Buchanan that he must do something, and do it quickly; South Carolina would unquestionably seize Fort Moultrie and Castle Pinckney, and would probably attack Fort Sumter as well, and only a prompt statement from the President that the status quo would be restored at once would insure peace. Buchanan, as Trescot saw it, seemed inclined to agree; then he demurred, said that he must consult with his cabinet, insisted that he could not condemn Major Anderson unheard. The visitors argued, but without avail, and at last they went out, Buchanan saying that his meeting with the South Carolina commissioners must be postponed. Then Buchanan went to talk with the cabinet.[6]

The cabinet had changed since the argument about the Charleston forts began. It was no longer split down the middle, unable to give solid advice to a President who relied more than most executives on the advice of his cabinet; it was taking a new form, moving rapidly toward a strong Unionist position. Howell Cobb, of Georgia, stout and shaggy and rumpled, one of the ablest and most forceful of all the Southern leaders, had resigned as Secretary of the Treasury on December 8, writing Buchanan manfully that "a sense of duty to the state of Georgia"—which was well on the road toward an act of secession—made it improper for him to remain any longer. "The evil," Cobb wrote sadly, "has now passed beyond control." He believed that Buchanan's administration would certainly be the last one under the old Union, and he added gracefully that history would unquestionably rank it "with the purest and ablest of those that preceded it." Cobb's resignation had been followed, within a week, by that of Lewis Cass, of Michigan, who quit as Secretary of State because he felt the administration ought to have sent reinforcements to Charleston. Cass was aging and querulous and he had been rather ineffective, but with the departure of Cobb the cabinet had lost one of its ruling spirits.[7]

In the general reshuffle that followed, Jeremiah Sullivan Black had become Secretary of State, and Philip F. Thomas, a former governor of Maryland, had been made Secretary of the Treasury. Black was Unionist and Thomas was pro-Southern, but Black had more drive, and Thomas would linger, powerless, for no more than a month before offering his own resignation. Floyd himself was on very shaky ground, for reasons not connected with the Charleston crisis; he had been asked to resign and would do so before the month ended. To replace Black as Attorney General, Buchanan had appointed a fierce little man with bristling whiskers, Edwin M. Stanton, a Washington lawyer, Ohio-born, who had lived for years in Pittsburgh—"the little black terrier," as Montgomery Blair dubbed him, a man with enough original force for two or three cabinets. Stanton, as it happened, was to attend his first cabinet meeting today.

So the cabinet which President Buchanan was about to consult regarding his latest of calamities was not at all the same cabinet which had been giving him divided counsel during recent weeks. It had not yet had its shakedown cruise, however, and although it would presently speak with a new voice, that voice had not been found. There would be several meetings before the administration's policy would at last be adjusted to the new situation which Major Anderson had created.

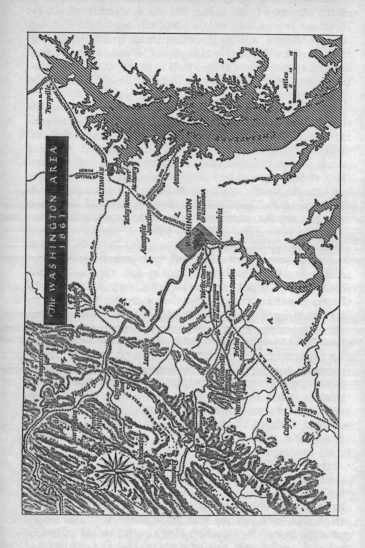

The Washington Area
1861

The cabinet, when President Buchanan sat down with it on the afternoon of December 27, was in a dither. Secretary Floyd was outspoken; Major Anderson had disobeyed his orders, a definite agreement had been fractured without good reason, and the Sumter garrison should be withdrawn at once, not merely from the disputed fort, but from Charleston harbor itself; such a move was the only way to prevent bloodshed and civil war.

Stanton believed that Buchanan at first was inclined to go along. Floyd and Jacob Thompson pressed him hard, asserting that the President had given a pledge which now was dishonored. There was "angry debate," lasting through several sessions, in the course of which Stanton (as Postmaster General Holt remembered it) announced that any President who would issue the kind of order Floyd was talking about would be guilty of treason. Buchanan raised his hands at this and said: "Oh no! Not so bad as that, my friend—not so bad as that." Buchanan himself wrote that he had received the news of Anderson's move "with astonishment and regret," fearing that it would drive the rest of the cotton states into secession and blight the tentative moves for conciliation which were afoot in Congress. He did not believe that South Carolina could have been ready to commit "the base perfidy" of attacking the forts, and he wanted to hear from Anderson before he did anything. At the same time, he felt that he could hardly restore the status quo "in consequence of the violent conduct of South Carolina in seizing all the other forts and public property in the harbor and city of Charleston."[8]

On December 28, Buchanan talked with the commissioners from South Carolina. He had made, they said, that agreement, early in December, with the South Carolina Congressional delegation, and Major Anderson had violated the faith of the President and of the United States government. Mr. Barnwell, a zealot whose intensity was as strong as Yancey's own, told him "at least three times" during the two-hour interview: "But, Mr. President, your personal honor is involved in this matter; the faith you pledged has been violated; and your personal honor requires you to issue the order"—the order, that is, pulling Anderson and the soldiers out of Fort Sumter. Buchanan, as Orr recalled it, fidgeted and wavered, crying out finally: "Mr. Barnwell, you are pressing me too importunately; you don't give me time to consider; you don't give me time to say my prayers. I always say my prayers when required to act upon any State affair."[9]

The real trouble was that the President and the South Carolina commissioners had different understandings of the agreement Buchanan had made earlier. To Barnwell and the others, the case was as clear as crystal; the President had made a promise which had been broken, and as a man of honor he could do nothing less than give in. To Buchanan, any pledge that had been made was ended when South Carolina seceded, and whether Anderson had done wisely or stupidly made no difference—no promise had been violated. And however the rights and wrongs may have been, the stormy meeting ended with nothing done. Buchanan did not order Major Anderson to get out of Fort Sumter.

Jeremiah Black had a little something to do with it. When the cabinet met to consider the calamity at Charleston, it was Black who remembered that Major Buell had taken certain instructions to Anderson two weeks earlier, and the memorandum which Buell had put on file in the War Department was brought up and examined. It was clear from this that whatever Anderson had done he had not violated his orders. He had been given discretionary powers and he had acted under them; he might have acted foolishly, but he had done nothing which his instructions from Floyd, as transmitted by Buell, did not permit him to do. If the government now meant to back down, it could not allege that the soldier in Charleston harbor had disobeyed his orders.[10]

Winfield Scott, old and infirm, but possessed still of a mind all his own, was beginning to make his voice heard. In all of the dealings between Washington and Fort Moultrie the general-in-chief of the army had been bypassed, and he complained bitterly that none of the orders and reports had come across his desk. His trouble, probably, came because he was aged and in bad health, and until December 12 he had his office in New York instead of in Washington; it had been easy to go around him, and during a crucial five weeks he had been more or less out of the picture. He would stay out of it no longer, however, and on December 28, the day when the South Carolina commissioners were accusing President Buchanan on a point of honor, Scott got off a stilted but perceptive memorandum to the Secretary of War:

"Lieutenant General Scott, who had had a bad night, and can scarcely hold up his head this morning, begs to express the hope to the Secretary of War— 1. That orders may not be given for the evacuation of Fort Sumter. 2. That one hundred and fifty recruits may instantly be sent from Governor's Island to re-enforce that garrison, with ample supplies of ammunition, subsistence, including fresh vegetables, as potatoes, onions, turnips; and 3. That one or two armed vessels be sent to support the said fort."[11]

A copy of this memorandum went to Buchanan. At just about the same time, Buchanan also received an extremely stiff letter from the South Carolina commissioners, who sent him a copy of the ordinance of secession and pointed out that they had been empowered to treat with the government of the United States for the transfer of forts, lighthouses, and other bits of property and to make any other arrangements necessary "for the continuance of peace and amity between this Commonwealth and the Government at Washington." The commissioners were not able to avoid a touch of arrogance. They remarked that they had been prepared to negotiate in a friendly spirit, in the assurance that all parties wanted "mutual respect, general advantage and a future of good will and harmony," which was just another way of expressing the bland assumption that the state's act of secession would of course be accepted at face value by all men of good will. This assurance, to be sure, had vanished in the face of recent developments in Charleston harbor. Therefore: "Until those circumstances are explained in a manner which relieves us of all doubt as to the spirit in which these negotiations shall be conducted, we are forced to suspend all discussions as to any arrangements by which our mutual interests might be amicably adjusted. And, in conclusion, we would urge upon you the immediate withdrawal of the troops from the harbor of Charleston. Under present circumstances they are a standing menace which renders negotiation impossible, and, as our recent experience shows, threatens speedily to bring to a bloody issue questions which ought to be settled with temperance and judgment."[12]

Buchanan was beginning to stiffen. Once again, he had been pushed a little too far—he *could* be pushed too far, and now he had a different cabinet, which was in almost continuous session during the days immediately following the news of Major Anderson's move. Buchanan remarked that the letter was "of the most extravagant character," and declared that the whole request "was not to be thought of for a moment."[13] The President had learned, too, that on December 27 the South Carolina authorities had already taken possession of nearly everything in sight except Fort Sumter —Fort Moultrie, Castle Pinckney, the customs house and post office—and soon would seize the Federal arsenal. The palmetto flag had been hoisted over all of these, and every Federal officer in the state, from collector of the port to postmaster, had resigned. The Federal government, in short, now had not one shred of sovereignty in all of South Carolina except for the place Major Anderson and his men were occupying, and beyond these precincts it did not have one civil or military officer in the state. There was perilously little for President and commissioners to negotiate about any longer. Things had begun to happen, and the area in which men might talk their way out of a problem had become very small indeed.

Under these circumstances, what reply could a harassed President make to the letter from the South Carolina commissioners? To compose one was difficult; to get the composition approved by a cabinet that was beginning to be as touchy and as stiff-backed as the secessionists themselves would be even harder. Buchanan tried, and on Saturday, December 29, his cabinet came together to consider what he had written. Apparently Buchanan tried desperately to find some middle course. He would not remove the troops from Charleston, but he seems to have felt that it might still be possible to get Anderson back to Fort Moultrie if the South Carolina people would make a few concessions, and he tried to make it clear that Congress, rather than the President, had final control over title to Federal property in a seceded state. All in all, nobody in the cabinet approved of what he had put on paper except for the Secretary of the Navy, Mr. Toucey, who liked the middle of the road even better than President Buchanan liked it. The Southerners thought it too harsh and the Unionists thought it too weak, and the cabinet meeting was filled with discord.[14]

Attorney General Stanton, abundantly equipped to cut his own trail through a meeting of this kind, presently took the floor and spoke bluntly and with much heat. (Everybody was talking heatedly to Buchanan these days; rarely has a President of the United States been addressed as sharply as Buchanan was being addressed just now.) Stanton poured out scorn on the commissioners from South Carolina.

"These gentlemen claim to be ambassadors," he said. "It is preposterous! They cannot be ambassadors; they are lawbreakers, traitors. They should be arrested. You cannot negotiate with them; and yet it seems by this paper that you have been led into doing that very thing. With all respect to you, Mr. President, I must say that the Attorney General, under his oath of office, dares not to be cognizant of the pending proceedings. Your reply to these so-called ambassadors must not be transmitted as the reply of the President. It is wholly unlawful, and improper; its language is unguarded and to send it as an official document will bring the President to the verge of usurpation."[15] Some years after this, Stanton said that Buchanan was pale as a ghost, tremulously wagging his head and waving his arms like a weak old man, and he added contemptuously: "It was a fight over a corpse." But although Stanton grew abusive—at one stage he told the President that if he gave up Fort Sumter he would be a greater traitor than Benedict Arnold and would deserve hanging—it apparently was Jeremiah Black who carried the day. That night, after the long argument had ended, Black made up his mind to resign from the cabinet unless Major Anderson were given proper support, and his threat (supported, it is said, by Stanton and Postmaster General Holt) seems to have been decisive. The President finally made up his mind. He would deal no more with the South Carolina commissioners and he would not order the soldiers to leave Fort Sumter. Whatever might come of it, the administration henceforward would resist secession.[16]

On Sunday, December 30, while Buchanan was at last reaching this conclusion, General Scott sent another of his dignified and melancholy notes:

"Lieutenant-General Scott begs the President of the United States to pardon the irregularity of this communication. It is Sunday; the weather is bad, and General Scott is not well enough to go to church. But matters of the highest national importance seem to forbid a moment's delay, and if misled by zeal he hopes for the President's forgiveness. Will the President permit General Scott, without reference to the War

Department and otherwise, as secretly as possible, to send two hundred and fifty recruits from New York Harbor to reenforce Fort Sumter, together with some extra muskets or rifles, ammunition and subsistence stores?"[17]

Winfield Scott was pathetically decrepit, but he still had an eye, and he could see that if the government was not going to give up Fort Sumter it had better get ready for a fight.

4. Footsteps in a Dark Corridor

THE AREA in which there would be room for quiet second thoughts was getting narrower and narrower; many small decisions were beginning to add up to one great decision. If the Mississippi commissioner had put things correctly when he told a Baltimore audience that secession was really a political maneuver designed to force concessions, the game was getting seriously out of control. Outright war could be averted now only if somebody backed down. As the tragic, confused, and dynamic year 1860 came to a close, there was not the slightest indication that anything of the kind was likely to happen.

Viewing the situation with an alert intelligence and from the vantage point of a family closely identified with the South Carolina secession movement, Mrs. Chesnut reflected that Major Anderson had provided a useful if dangerous stimulus. "The row is fast and furious now," she wrote in her diary. "They say if we had been left out in the cold alone, we might have sulked a while, but back we would have had to go, and would merely have fretted and fumed and quarreled among ourselves. We needed a little wholesome neglect. Anderson had blocked that game, but now our sister States have joined us and we are strong. I give the condensed essence of the table talk: 'Anderson has united the Cotton States. Now for Virginia!' Those who want a row are in high glee. Those who dread it are glum and thoughtful enough."[1]

No one in America dreaded a row more than President Buchanan, and he was as glum and thoughtful as anyone could have asked. He knew that the row could be much more easily started than stopped, and in his own way he had tried to apply the wholesome neglect Mrs. Chesnut was talking about. Now there could be no more neglect. What to do about secession would be the number-one order of business from now on, and as this became clear, it might also have been discerned that the cotton-state leaders, pressing just a little too hard, were about to lose the initiative. Until Major Anderson made his move, they had been in control, carrying less ardent Southerners along with them, forcing Northern leaders to keep step. Now the response to secession would be decisive. The challenge having been issued, everything would depend on what the challenged party was going to do about it.

Eventually this would put it up to Abraham Lincoln, if he had the capacity to act. He had been extremely busy ever since the election, negotiating about cabinet appointments, talking to a stream of callers at Springfield, carefully guarding a little list of possible cabinet appointees. (Much later he remarked that the list he drew up the day after election was essentially the list that was finally submitted to the Senate for confirmation, but at this time no one knew what names this list contained.) Beyond the matter of cabinet appointments, he was considering two pressing matters of high policy—what to do about a projected compromise in regard to slavery, and what to do about the seizure of government forts and arsenals.

Lincoln was willing to give the slave states as much consolation as they could get out of a stiffening of the fugitive slave law, but he would listen to no talk about any possible extension of slavery in the territories. On December 10 he wrote firmly to Lyman Trumbull: "Let there be no compromise on the question of *extending* slavery. If there is, all our labor is lost, and, ere long, must be done again. The dangerous ground—that into which some of our friends have a hankering to run—is Pop. Sov. Have none of it. Stand firm. The tug has to come, & better now, than at any time hereafter." In the same vein he expressed himself to William Kellogg a day later: "Entertain no proposition for a compromise in regard to the extension of slavery. The instant you do, they have us under again; all our labor is lost, and sooner or later must be done over." Congressman Elihu B. Washburne, of Illinois, had written to Lincoln from Washington, warning him that "the secession feeling has approached proportions of which I had but a faint conception when I saw you at Springfield" and asserting that few Westerners realized "the imminent peril which now environs us." To Washburne, in reply, Lincoln repeated the advice he had given Trumbull and Kellogg: "Prevent, as far as possible, any of our friends from demoralizing themselves and our cause by entertaining propositions for compromise of any sort upon 'slavery extension.' There is no possible compromise upon it . . . On that point hold firm, as with a chain of steel."[2]

He wrote in much more detail to Congressman John A. Gilmer, of North Carolina. Gilmer was known as a Southern moderate; so much so that Lincoln later tried to put him in his cabinet, both as a gesture of good will toward the South and as a means of enlisting at least a little Southern support for his new administration. Ten days before the South Carolina convention voted to secede, Gilmer wrote Lincoln with studied courtesy, asking if the President-elect could in advance of his installation "give the people of the United States the views and opinions you now entertain on certain political questions which now so seriously distract the country." Gilmer went on:

"For one politically opposed to you, and representing a Southern constituency, who, together with myself, did all we could (I trust honorably) to defeat your election, I feel that I presume a great deal . . . but the danger of the crisis, and my desire to have allayed, if possible, the apprehensions of real danger and harm to them and their peculiar institution which have seized the people of my section, I respectfully ask whether as President you will favor the abolition of slavery in the District of Columbia"—and, in fine, what position Lincoln would take on other aspects of the slavery controversy.

Lincoln was suspicious, not so much of Gilmer as of the use that might be made of any statement he might make. The same suspicion had kept him quiet during the campaign; in his anxiety to stand on his record he was refusing to utter any words of clarification or amity which might be misinterpreted. It was the caution perhaps of a lawyer rather than of a statesman. He marked his letter to Gilmer "strictly confidential," and he asked:

"Is it desired that I shall shift the ground upon which I have been elected? I cannot do it. You need only to acquaint yourself with that ground, and press it on the attention of the South. It is all in print and easy of access. May I be pardoned if I ask whether even you have ever attempted to procure the reading of the Republican platform, or my speeches, by the Southern people? If not, what reason have I to expect that any additional production of mine would meet a better fate? It would make me appear as if I repented for the crime of having been elected, and was anxious to apologize and beg forgiveness. To so represent me, would be the principal use made of any letter I might now thrust upon the public. My old record cannot be so used; and that is precisely the reason that some new declaration is so much sought."

Then to the specifics: on such matters as slavery in the District of Columbia, "I never have been, am not now, and probably never shall be, in a mood of harassing the people, either North or South." He would be flexible, in other words, on everything except "the territorial question," and on that he would not yield. It seemed to him that that was "the only substantial difference" between himself and such men as Gilmer, and he repeated the brooding sentence he had used in his letter to Alexander Stephens: "You think slavery is right and ought to be extended; we think it is wrong and ought to be restricted." To this he added: "For this, neither has any just occasion to be angry with the other."[3]

Wearily and without much hope, Congress was trying to work out some compromise, and committees from each house were considering the matter. No compromise plan offered any hope unless the Republican members would accept it, and Lincoln continued to advise Republican leaders that there could be no recession on the territorial issue. On all other points he was willing to be conciliatory. From Henry J. Raymond, of the New York *Times,* he was given a letter written by one William C. Smedes, of the Mississippi legislature. Mr. Smedes, reciting all of the abolitionist views which he believed the Republican nominee to represent, closed by remarking that if Lincoln were struck dead by lightning it could only be considered "a just punishment from an offended deity," and Lincoln wrote to Raymond: "What a very madman your correspondent Smedes is. Mr. Lincoln is not pledged to the ultimate extinction of slavery; does not hold the black man to be the equal of the white . . . and never did stigmatize their (i.e., the Southern states) white people as immoral and unchristian." To the New York Republican manipulator Thurlow Weed, he wrote that he did not believe any state could lawfully get out of the Union without the consent of the other states; and he resorted to a favorite phrase when he added that it would be the duty of the President and other members of his administration "to run the machine as it is."[4]

Secession, brought on by the great quarrel over slavery, was taking on more importance than its parent. In the face of what had been happening in Charleston, in the triangle neatly bounded in time and space by Secession Hall, the drifted sand dunes at Moultrieville, and Fort Sumter, it was perceptibly growing less and less important whether Northern states might yet agree to arrest and transport fugitive slaves, or whether the old Missouri Compromise line could be restored to life and driven west to the Pacific. Of greater immediate consequence was the question that was beginning to hammer insistently on the man in Springfield: What are you going to do about those forts? Governor Pickens and Major Anderson, between them, had immeasurably oversimplified the complicated issue that was dividing the nation. It was ceasing to be a far-ranging social and economic problem involving nations and races; now it could all be comprehended in a pentagonal enclosure of masonry containing fewer than fourscore professional soldiers, and in this perilous simplification it had become something so easy to see and so quickly identified with primitive emotions that it could pull men into war.

Lieutenant General Scott wanted very much to know what policy the next President was going to follow. Even before the South Carolina convention formally announced South Carolina's secession, the old general had suspected that the surrender of the Charleston forts would be demanded, and he suspected also that what South Carolina demanded, Buchanan would give; so Scott talked to Francis P. Blair, Sr., and, a day or so later, to Congressman Washburne, to learn if he could what Lincoln was apt to do about all of this.

Lincoln heard from both Blair and Washburne and wrote his replies before Major Anderson got out of Fort Moultrie, so that what he put in his letters to these men must be read in the light of the fact that he was expressing an opinion formed before any overt act had been taken. To Blair, Lincoln was quietly blunt:

"Yours giving an account of an interview with Gen. Scott, is received, and for which I thank you. According to my present view, if the forts shall be given up before the inaugeration, the General must retake them afterwards." To Washburne he wrote in similar words: "Last night I received your letter giving an account of your interview with Gen. Scott, and for which I thank you. Please present my respects to the General, and tell him, confidentially, I shall be obliged to him to be as well prepared as he can to either *hold,* or *retake,* the forts, as the case may require, at and after the inaugeration."[5]

These letters were dated December 21. Three days later Lincoln amplified his views slightly, in a letter to Lyman Trumbull, indicating that a surrender of the forts might make him do what the entreaties of friend and foe had not yet made him do—issue a public statement explaining what action he would take when he became President. His letter to Trumbull, dated December 24, said in part:

"Despatches have come here two days in succession, that the Forts in South Carolina, will be surrendered by the order, or consent at least, of the President. I can scarcely believe this; but if it prove true I will, if our friends at Washington concur, announce publicly at once that they are to be retaken after the inauguration. This will give the Union men a rallying cry, and preparation will proceed somewhat on their side as well as on the other."[6]

An interesting field for speculation opens briefly just here. What would have happened—how would the ever-changing situation in respect to slavery, secession, and the preservation of the Union have been affected—if in December the South Carolina commissioners had won everything they had asked for? Suppose that Buchanan had given them the forts, on their demand, and that Lincoln thereupon had announced publicly that as soon as he took office, the government would fight to regain what had been given away: what then? Everything since would have been very different—perhaps better, perhaps worse, certainly different.

No matter. Buchanan stood his ground, and the business did not at that moment come to a clash of arms. Lincoln continued to reflect on the course the Federal government ought to follow, and on December 29 he gave a glimpse of the way his mind was working in a letter to James W. Webb: "Yours kindly seeking my view as to the proper mode of dealing with secession was received several days ago, but, for want of time, I could not answer it till now. I think we should hold the forts, or retake them, as the case may be, and collect the revenue. *We* shall have to forego the use of the Federal courts, and *they* that of the mails, for a while. We cannot fight them into holding courts, or receiving the mails. This is an outline of my view; and perhaps suggests sufficiently, the whole of it."[7]

The letter revealed the danger point. The North could not make war over an abstraction, but it could easily make war to possess a fort or to hoist a flag on some disputed staff, and this actionable issue was coming nearer, like eerie footsteps coming down the empty corridor of a haunted house. The thing could really happen, now, and it could happen quickly.

Obviously neither Lincoln nor any other man at that hour could say with assurance just what this course would be three months later. The situation was not merely plastic; it had the smoky fluidity of molten ore, and good men were behaving like conspirators, plotting darkly just so that they could do their duty as they saw it. Until recently, an Assistant Secretary of State had been exerting himself in the interests of what he conceived to be a foreign power; an Attorney General on his first day in office had declared in cabinet meeting that the President was following a policy that looked like treason and might deserve hanging; the General of the Armies, bypassing both White House and War Department, was asking the President-elect whether there was likely to be a war after the present administration left office . . . and the President-elect was saying, clearly although not for publication, that there very probably would be one.

Or—was he, really? The words he was sending to Scott and to others would mean a fight, provided the people of South Carolina really meant the spirited things they were saying; provided, as well, that Lincoln himself did not between now and March come to some other point of view. For many months many men had been saying just a little more than they meant, doing so because overstatement is the universal language of politics, of salesmanship, of hard bargaining. The fact remains that it seemed to Lincoln at the end of December 1860 that the United States government must hold the forts it still had and regain the ones it had lost. In other words, he was saying that there was a point at which he, as President, would make war rather than consent to continuing dissolution of the Union; as he then felt and as the situation then looked, he would make war over the question of the forts. He might modify his position later, or the situation itself might change, but that was the way he was thinking ten weeks ahead of his inauguration. Whatever else it might do, the government at Washington was going to take a stand.

It was already taking it, as a matter of fact. Buchanan had come all the way around; Stanton and Black would not leave his cabinet, but would dominate it instead, and although the President would regard himself as little more than a caretaker, holding on in the White House until the new man came in, he would very definitely be a pro-Unionist caretaker.

Howell Cobb had left the cabinet, and now John B. Floyd was following him; and the South, which until recently had dominated both Buchanan and his cabinet, now had lost all but a trace of its old influence. Floyd left under the oddest circumstances, for reasons that had nothing to do with slavery, states' rights, or embattled forts, but his departure helped to tighten the lines.

Floyd, by clumsiness, had got himself into a rousing mess. The War Department had had extensive dealings with a western transportation firm, Russell, Majors, and Waddell, which had furnished supplies and transportation for which it had not been paid. Badly overextended, and left shaky by the panic of 1857, this firm had faced bankruptcy; to stave off disaster it had persuaded Floyd to issue, in advance, signed acceptances, indicating sums that were now or soon would be due from the government. Since appropriations had been delayed, these actually were worth nothing much, but for a time Russell, Majors, and Waddell were able to discount them with the banks. In the summer of 1860 this would work no longer, and resort was had then to a complaisant clerk in the Interior Department, who gave the firm $870,000 worth of bonds belonging to an Indian Trust Fund, taking Floyd's signed acceptances in return. The whole deal was of course grossly illegal, although Floyd personally profited not a penny out of it, and it had come to light just about the time when the crisis over Charleston's forts was developing. Buchanan had asked Floyd to resign. He had not asked him directly, because the President simply was not up to forthright action, but he had passed the word through the friendly offices of Vice-President Breckinridge. Stanton referred to the matter bitterly, in a heated cabinet meeting on December 28, when the question of ordering Anderson out of Fort Sumter was up for discussion; to Buchanan, he said that "no administration, much less this one, can afford to lose a million of money and a fort in the same week."[8]

Floyd at last sent in his resignation, going to elaborate lengths to show that he was quitting because he disagreed with top policy in regard to the forts. His departure was no great loss to anyone, but it did have the indirect result of giving Anderson solid backing in the War Department. To replace him, Buchanan appointed Postmaster General Joseph Holt Secretary of War, and Holt, a sour-visaged man of considerable force, was an all-out Unionist who stood unswervingly with Black and Stanton. Trescot realized at once what the shift meant, and on the last day of the year he sent a telegram to William Porcher Miles: "Holt is Sec War. That means civil War I do not know what reinforcements are sent but I believe the orders have been or will be sent immediately I have heard that the *Harriet Lane* light draught is under orders make every preparation for preventing entrance into the Harbor."[9]

As usual, Trescot was well informed. The *Harriet Lane,* a revenue cutter, would not be used, but action definitely was coming. Governor Pickens passed the warning along to Lieutenant Colonel Wilmot Gibbs De Saussure, commanding now at Fort Moultrie. To Colonel de Saussure, the governor sent a grim message:

"The authentic news from Washington not very favorable. Reinforcements *may be on their way.* I have ordered Capt. Cosle with his cutter to report to you, and to guard the outer entrance, to give you the earliest notice. All vessels to be stopped by him, if suspicious, or if supposed to have supplies or reinforcements for Fort Sumter— See him and give your orders. Be careful—and intercept all reinforcements if possible at all *hazards.*"[10]

On the same day, Major Anderson wrote a report to Adjutant General Samuel Cooper. South Carolina troops, he wrote, were erecting batteries on Morris Island, a sandy expanse of land on the south side of the entrance to the harbor, within easy cannon shot of Sumter itself: "I am at a loss what this means, unless it be that some armed vessel is expected here." He added that he was more than ever convinced that he had done the right thing when he moved to Fort Sumter: "Thank God, we are now where the Government may send us additional troops at its leisure." He was a little pinched for supplies. On moving to Fort Sumter, the troops somehow had failed to take along enough fuel, soap, or candles, "but we can cheerfully put up with the inconvenience of doing without them for the satisfaction we feel in the knowledge that we can command the harbor as long as our Government wishes to keep it."[11]

The government did, at last, definitely wish to keep it. President Buchanan had finally notified the South Carolina commissioners that he could have no further dealings with them—except, of course, in their private capacities as gentlemen of high character—and orders were out to send the sloop-of-war *Brooklyn* down with men and munitions as soon as she could be loaded. Suspecting what was coming, the commissioners notified Buchanan that they were going back to Charleston, and they added coldly: "If you choose to force this issue upon us, the State of South Carolina will accept it, and relying upon Him who is the God of Justice as well as the God of Hosts, will endeavor to perform the great duty which lies before her, hopefully, bravely and thoroughly." This letter went into the White House files with the notation: "This paper, just presented to the President, is of such a character that he declines to receive it."[12]

Up to this time, most of the displays of public anger and determination had come in the South, and there had been little to show that the average Northerner either knew or cared very much what was up. Now there were certain indications. Major Anderson began to hear from people in the North, old friends and total strangers together, and he was getting letters of sympathy, stray bits of well-meant advice, offers of support. A bricklayer in Baltimore wrote that he had read of a shortage of workmen; if the major wished, he would raise a corps of workers "who would not hesitate to lay aside the trowel if it became necessary and help to defend their country's flag." A New Yorker suggested that "citizen volunteers" charter a steamer and go South to "rescue the garrison & save the Fort," and Edward Hinks, of the Massachusetts militia, posed a blunt question: "In case of an attack

upon your command by the State (or would-be nation) of
South Carolina, will you be at liberty to accept volunteers?"[13]

Equally significant was a small ripple that briefly preceded
Secretary Floyd's departure from the cabinet.

Besides permitting the growth of a scandal over the dealings with Russell, Majors, and Waddell, Floyd had indulged
in some rather free and easy actions in connection with the
sale or transfer to the states of surplus Federal ordnance
supplies. In substance, it was alleged that as Secretary of
War he went to great lengths to put weapons in the hands
of states that were about to secede. Later investigation would
indicate that the amount of help thus given Southern states
was greatly exaggerated, and apparently an important factor
all along was simply Floyd's old habit of slipshod administration. But there were a few cases that did have a rather sinis-
ter cast, and one of these involved the transfer of heavy
ordnance from Pittsburgh to the Gulf Coast.

Under the prewar program, the government was building
forts at Galveston, Texas, and on Ship Island, Mississippi. It
would be many months before the Ship Island emplacements
would be ready for guns, and the fort at Galveston was years
away from completion, but late in October, Floyd directed
an ordnance captain to send guns to both places as quickly
as the Pittsburgh arsenal could deliver them. The shipments
would be substantial—110 Columbiads and eleven 32-pound-
ers—and when the shipments were about to be made, late in
December, the people of Pittsburgh learned about the deal
and protested. The steamboat *Silver Wave* was docked, ready
to take the weapons down the river; then the protest was
raised. A group of citizens telegraphed Buchanan that "great
excitement has been created in the public mind by this order," and begged that the order be countermanded at once:
"If not done we cannot be answerable for the consequences."
A delegation hurried to Washington to make protest in person, and Secretary Holt, who had at last replaced Floyd in
the War Department, canceled the shipment.[14]

This meant little enough, except as a straw floating down
the wind, in which capacity it meant a great deal. The people
of Charleston had shown anger and bitterness earlier in the
fall, when an attempt was made to move arms from the
Charleston arsenal to Fort Moultrie, and they had blocked
the move. There had been nothing especially surprising about

this: the people of Charleston had been passionately stirred for a long time and everybody knew it, and their reaction might have been anticipated. But now the people of Pittsburgh were beginning to behave in the same way, blocking the shipment of guns from government arsenal to government fort. The proud and vigilant anger that was on display in South Carolina was perhaps infectious, beginning to touch the hearts of men, not only in the cotton states, but far to the north as well.

5. The Strategy of Delay

THE NEW YEAR's reception at the White House looked very much the way New Year's receptions always looked. There were flowers and gay music, with well-dressed people moving up to give President Buchanan a smile and a hand-shake, each one repeating the formal "I wish you a happy New Year, Mister President"; and although the weather was bad, things seemed to be bright enough inside the mansion. But neither the President nor his guests had any illusions about the happiness that 1861 was likely to bring to the people who occupied this building, and Mr. Buchanan looked tired and unhappy, as if he had had about all the strain he could take. Mrs. Roger Pryor, wife of the fire-eating Congressman from Virginia, felt that "a gloomy foreboding of impending disaster" oppressed everyone, and she reflected unhappily that the familiar social world of the capital was having the last of its old get-togethers. So many people had already left for the far South, so many more would be leaving very soon: no matter what happened, the group that met here on January 1, 1861, would never come together again.[1]

As a harbinger of coming change, there was the improved morale of Lieutenant General Scott. Scott was in Washington now, and on New Year's Eve he confessed that he felt more cheerful than he had been able to feel for a long time. A mixed policy of force and conciliation, he believed, was what the country needed, and this policy was going to be applied. A soldier could at last understand what was expected of him, and what was expected of General Scott—as President Buchanan had told him the day before—was that he would immediately move to put reinforcements into Fort Sumter.[2]

The steam sloop *Brooklyn*—up to date, as wooden warships were rated at that time, less than three years old, a 2000-ton, propeller-driven, ship-rigged craft mounting twenty-two 9-inch Dahlgren smoothbores and two rifled pivot guns— lay in Hampton Roads; and on December 31 Secretary of the Navy Toucey, after a conference with the President, wired the commandant at the Gosport Navy Yard near Norfolk to fill the *Brooklyn* with provisions, water, and coal and hold the vessel ready for immediate service. At the same time General Scott, also at the President's direction, drafted orders for the commanding officer at Fort Monroe: 200 regulars, fully armed and equipped, and taking with them subsistence for at least ninety days, were to be prepared to embark on the *Brooklyn* as soon as the ship was ready for them. The move was not to be made just yet; the President had notified the South Carolina commissioners that he would treat with them no more, but he felt that the expedition should not sail until they had had time to digest this news and to make reply if they chose; but by January 3 the *Brooklyn* had stocked up at the navy yard and was anchored off Fort Monroe, ready for the soldiers.

Before the *Brooklyn* could sail, however, plans were changed. Buchanan felt that any officer who tried to take troops to Fort Sumter would need plenty of muscle, and the *Brooklyn* was a powerful warship; but Scott—reflecting, perhaps, on the impossibility of keeping the move a secret —concluded that it might be better to use a fast merchant steamer, which could possibly slip into Charleston harbor before anyone knew what was up, and so the *Brooklyn*'s orders were canceled. Instead, the side-wheel merchant steamer *Star of the West* was chartered in New York, 250 recruits from Governor's Island were sent aboard, plus food stuffs and ammunition, and on January 5 this vessel headed out past Sandy Hook, turned south, and made for Charleston.[3]

But nothing that was ever done in respect to Fort Sumter went quite as had been planned. Shortly after the *Star of the West* sailed, the War Department got a message from Anderson, who reported that he was in pretty good shape; he believed that he could hold the fort against any force likely to be brought against him, and "I shall not ask for any increase in my command, because I do not know what the ulterior views of the Government are." Anderson added that the South Carolina authorities were busily putting heavy guns in battery to sweep the entrance to Charleston harbor, and he remarked that "we are now, or soon will be, cut off from all communication, unless by means of a powerful fleet which shall have the ability to carry the batteries at the mouth of this harbor." This crossed a message which the War Department had just sent to Anderson, telling him that reinforcements were on the way and broadening his charter of authority: "Should a fire, likely to prove injurious, be opened upon any vessel bringing up re-enforcements or supplies, or upon tow-boats within the reach of your guns, they" [that is, Anderson's guns] "may be employed to silence such fire; and you may act in like manner in case a fire is opened upon Fort Sumter itself."[4]

This message did not reach Anderson, and he knew nothing about the relief expedition. His own message, however, gave the administration second thoughts. Scott telegraphed to New York to hold the *Star of the West* in port, but he was too late; the steamer was hull down beyond the Jersey highlands when his message arrived. Then the Navy Department sent new orders to Captain W. S. Walker, commander of the *Brooklyn*, telling him to put to sea and meet the *Star of the West* off the entrance to Charleston harbor. If he arrived in time, he was to have the merchant vessel return to New York; if there was any trouble, he was to give such assistance as he could; and if, on arrival, he found that the reinforcements had already been landed, he was to come back to Hampton Roads.[5]

Anderson was the only person who did not know what was being tried. The administration had done its best to keep the expedition a secret. The *Star of the West* was a vessel ordinarily on the New York-to-New Orleans run. She had been quietly chartered (for $1250 a day), and the soldiers and supplies had been put on board as unobtrusively as possible, and when the ship cleared there was nothing to show that she was not leaving on her regular run. But the news leaked out, as it was bound to do. On January 8 Governor Pickens, at Charleston, got a telegram from Senator Wigfall saying that troops were on the way, and on the same day a shore boat brought to Fort Sumter a newspaper giving the same information. Major Anderson and his officers read this with much interest, but were inclined to doubt the truth of it, the War Department's message not having reached them. They noticed that there seemed to be a flurry of signals between Charleston and the outlying batteries and sensed that something was up, but they had no solid information.[6]

Meanwhile the *Star of the West* moved on toward Charleston, with nobody on board knowing anything about the interchange of messages, leakage of information, order to the *Brooklyn,* or anything else that had happened since the ship left New York. Late on the afternoon of January 8 Lieutenant Charles R. Woods, of the 9th U. S. Infantry, commanding the troops on the steamer, mustered his men, issued arms and ammunition, and had everybody stand by. Around midnight the ship drew near the harbor entrance. All the harbor lights had been put out, except for one beacon on Fort Sumter itself, and the steamer drifted on the tide, "groping in the dark," as Lieutenant Woods wrote, her own running lights extinguished, until daybreak. Then, as soon as there was light enough to see, the *Star of the West* crossed the outer bar and steamed up the main-ship channel.

Ahead there was a guard steamer, which hoisted red and blue lights, sent up rockets, and started back into the harbor. The *Star of the West* kept on, keeping as close as possible to Morris Island in order to stay out of range of the guns on Fort Moultrie. On Morris Island the ship's lookouts could see a palmetto flag, but they saw no batteries there. The troops were sent below, an American flag was hoisted, and the steamer began to enter the harbor.[7]

On the parapet of Fort Sumter, Captain Abner Doubleday was on watch. Looking seaward in the half-light of a clear dawn he saw the steamer, studied it with his spy glass, identified it as an unarmed merchant vessel, and concluded that the newspaper story about the *Star of the West* must be true. And on Morris Island the South Carolina gunners —cadets from the Citadel, the state's military college— saw what he saw, reached the same conclusion, and went into action. South Carolina had not been bluffing: if the discharge of one gun might start a war, here was the gun, shotted and trained toward the target. An officer gave an order, a gunner jerked a lanyard, and there was a stabbing spurt of flame and a sudden burst of smoke, with a dull report echoing out to sea across the empty mud flats. A solid shot went across the bows of the *Star of the West,* which

hoisted a second, larger flag and kept on coming . . . and
Captain Doubleday dashed down the stairway to arouse
Major Anderson. The fort's drummers came tumbling out
to beat the long roll—that throbbing, stirring call to general
quarters, which would be heard all across America during
the next four years.[8]

Anderson came to the parapet and his gunners ran to their
stations. On Morris Island more guns were firing. Their first
shots were high. Then some gun crew corrected its elevation,
and a shot came ricocheting across the smooth water, low
and deadly, coming on business. It smashed into the side of
the steamer just below the fore chains, narrowly missing a
seaman who was taking soundings with a lead line. For
whatever it might mean to the country, a steamer flying
the United States flag and carrying United States troops
had been hit by hostile fire.

Anderson's men were at their guns, excited, jubilant with
the release from tension, waiting for the word. The *Star of
the West* came closer, nearing a narrow part of the channel
where she would have to make a left turn and expose her
unprotected side to the guns on Fort Moultrie, which could
break her to bits. Major Anderson stood on the rampart,
glass at his eye, studying—and thinking hard.

He had been told to defend himself if attacked, but he
had no instructions governing a case like this. (They had
been sent but they had never reached him, and the *Brooklyn*,
delayed in her own sailing, had not been able to join the
Star of the West: the major would have to make up his
own mind.) If he opened fire, the United States and South
Carolina would be at war. . . . An officer nudged him and
pointed across the harbor: Fort Moultrie now was opening
fire on the *Star of the West*, taking a few ranging shots, and
the officer urged that the fire be returned. Major Anderson
hesitated, plainly uncertain, an immense weight of responsibility resting on him.

Meanwhile, the skipper of the *Star of the West* had had
enough. Fort Sumter was not opening fire, and the cross-
fire from Morris Island and Fort Moultrie would unquestionably send the *Star of the West* to the bottom in short
order. The steamer reduced speed, swung about in a tight
circle, headed back for the open sea, and put on speed. Soldiers in Fort Sumter swore; at an eight-inch seacoast

howitzer, trained on the Morris Island battery, a gunnery sergeant stood with the lanyard in his hand, waiting for orders. And then, at last, Major Anderson made up his mind.

"Hold on—do not fire," he said. "I will wait. Let the men go to their quarters, leaving two at each gun. I wish to see the officers in their quarters."

Members of the garrison were disappointed and indignant. Captain Foster, of the engineers, ran down the stairs in open fury, throwing his hat on the ground and muttering something about "trample on the flag." Among the civilians who were still in Fort Sumter was the wife of one of the soldiers, and she ran to a loaded gun and reached for the lanyard, crying that she would fire the gun herself. Captain Doubleday gently drew her away, remarking that she had a good deal of courage. "Courage!" she snapped. "I should think, sir, a soldier's wife *ought* to have courage!"

The *Star of the West* went on out to sea, got past the bar, turned north, and started back for New York. The Southern guns ceased firing, and Major Anderson's officers, stirred and resentful, gathered in the major's room for a conference. Major Anderson asked for their advice.[9]

The moment of crisis had passed—and yet this crisis was permanent. Major Anderson had refused to blast a clear path for the *Star of the West,* but he still had his guns, he was the representative of a government whose flag had been fired on, and it seemed to him now that he should close the port, refusing to permit any steamer to enter or leave or even move about from the city to the South Carolina batteries. He raised the point. This, some of his officers argued, would most certainly be taken as an act of war, as fateful as if he had opened fire during the past hour; on the other hand, it appeared that an act of war had already been committed, every day counted—for the South Carolina authorities would assuredly build more batteries and put more guns in position —and perhaps the challenge should be accepted at once. As a matter of fact, Major Anderson by now had just about ceased to hope that war could be averted. To a friend in Washington he wrote, two days after this, that although his own sympathies were all with the South: "I have lost all sympathy with the people who govern this state. They are resolved to cement their secession with blood."[10]

In the end, it was agreed that Major Anderson should write to Governor Pickens and ask him if he had authorized his troops to fire on the *Star of the West*. If he replied that the action was official, then Fort Sumter could close the harbor. The officers went about their business and Major Anderson sat down to write.

Dating his note January 9, 1861, he addressed Governor Pickens with stiff formality: "Two of your batteries fired this morning upon an unarmed vessel bearing the flag of my government. As I have not been notified that war has been declared by South Carolina against the government of the United States, I cannot but think that this hostile act was committed without your sanction or authority. Under that hope, and that alone, did I refrain from opening fire upon your batteries." Accordingly: would the governor disavow the things his troops had done? If not, Major Anderson would regard it as an act of war, and "I shall not . . . permit any vessels to pass within range of the guns of my fort."

The governor's reply came back within hours, and it was equally stiff and formal. South Carolina was an independent nation; the action of the United States in putting troops in Fort Sumter, and then in sending reinforcements, was clearly an act of aggression; and the firing from Morris Island and Fort Moultrie was abundantly justified. If Major Anderson felt that he must use his own guns now, the responsibility was his own: "Your position in this harbor has been tolerated by the authorities of the State, and . . . it is not perceived how far the conduct which you propose to adopt can find a parallel in the history of any country, or be reconciled with any other purpose of your Government than that of imposing upon this State the condition of a conquered province."[11]

Governor Pickens had touched the point precisely. There was no parallel in the history of any country for the things that were being done these days, and neither governor, major, nor anyone else had any clear rules for guidance. Young Lieutenant J. Norman Hall, of the Sumter garrison, had taken Major Anderson's letter ashore under a flag of truce, and he reported that the city of Charleston was in an uproar—the word had gone about that Fort Sumter was about to bombard the town and that the lieutenant had

come ashore to give due warning, and an excited crowd
was on the streets. When he returned to his boat with
Governor Pickens's letter of reply, Lieutenant Hall was accompanied to the dock by one of the governor's aides and
an armed escort. On the dock he found anxious citizens
questioning his boat's crew and learning nothing.[12]

The citizens learned nothing because no final decision had
been made; there was nothing anyone could tell them. Both
Major Anderson and Governor Pickens were holding firm,
each man bound on a collision course, but there was still
time for second thoughts. On January 11 a steamer came out
to the fort bearing representatives from the governor—D. F.
Jamison, president of the secession convention, and Judge
A. G. McGrath, South Carolina's Secretary of State. The
representatives landed with some difficulty—their steamer
ran aground near the fort, and a small boat was sent out
to get them—and they went to Major Anderson's room,
giving him a letter in which Governor Pickens, moved by
"considerations of the gravest public character," urged the
surrender of Fort Sumter to the South Carolina authorities.

This was not quite the ultimatum it appeared to be. There
was discussion, in which Judge McGrath assured the Major
that "it is not an alternative that is offered to you by the
Governor, it is not peace or war that he offers in making
this communication to you; it is done more to give you an
opportunity, after understanding all of the circumstances,
to prevent bloodshed." Major Anderson replied that he was
glad to know this. He would not surrender the fort unless
his government told him to do so, but he wanted to prevent
bloodshed as much as any man could—and, in the end, he
would do this: he would send an officer to Washington to
report and to ask further instructions, and if the governor
wanted to send his own man to Washington, to demand the
fort's surrender at the top, the two men might go together.
He embodied these thoughts in a letter to Governor Pickens,
closing with an expression of his regret that "you have
made a demand with which I cannot comply."

It was so arranged, at last. Once more, the center of
gravity shifted from the fort to the White House. Something
faintly resembling a truce ensued. Arrangements were devised to send the women and children of the garrison to

New York, it was made possible for Major Anderson to get day-to-day supplies of fresh meat and vegetables from the Charleston markets, and both the demand for surrender and the threat to close the port were held in abeyance. Meanwhile, Governor Pickens's troops continued to build more batteries to bear on the fort and the entrance to the harbor, and the Fort Sumter garrison worked unceasingly to get more guns mounted, to block up embrasures that would not be used, and to get ready for a fight or a siege.[13]

A breathing spell, in short: brought on, perhaps, by a sudden realization in Charleston that an armed clash right now might be fatal to Southern hopes.

Once again, the secessionists had overplayed their hand. The South Carolina gunners who fired on the *Star of the West* had, in effect, invited the Federal government to start the war then and there if it wanted a war; but in plain fact a war begun just then could have been very one-sided. South Carolina was the only state that had actually seceded. (Mississippi was to vote for secession that very day, and Florida would follow the day after, but at the moment South Carolina stood alone.) There was no Southern Confederacy —no government, no chain of organization, no army except for the South Carolina militia: there was, in short, nothing to fight a war with, and this fact was beginning to dawn on the Southern leaders. Early in the month, Governor Pickens's chief military adviser had written earnestly "to express my conviction of the inexpediency of commencing actual hostilities, on our side, in our present wholly unprepared state," and he had said that "nothing but bloody discomfiture must attend the opening campaign."[14] After the meeting between Major Anderson and the governor's people, Jefferson Davis, in Washington, sent similar words of caution. Senator Davis had led troops in combat and he had been Secretary of War, and he understood that a shooting war was not to be begun lightly. To Governor Pickens he wrote soberly:

"The opinion of your friends . . . is adverse to the presentation of a demand for the evacuation of Fort Sumter. The little garrison in its present position presses on nothing but a point of pride & to you I need not say that war is made up of real elements. It is a physical problem from the solution of which we must need exclude all sentiment. I hope we shall soon have a Southern Confederacy, shall soon be ready to do all which interest or even pride demands, & in the fullness of a redemption of every obligation the more impatient will find indemnity for any chafing in the meantime they would have to endure. We have much of preparation to make both in military and civil organization and the time which serves for our preparation, by its moral effect, tends also towards a peaceful solution. . . . The occurrence of the *Star of the West* seems to me to put you in the best condition for delay so long as the government permits the matter to rest where it is—your friends here think you can well afford to stand still so far as the presence of a garrison is concerned, and if things should continue as they are for a month we shall then be in a condition to speak with a voice which all must hear & heed."[15]

Governor Pickens agreed, writing in reply that "the truth is I have not been prepared to take Sumter." The fort was strong, the state was weak, its military supplies were deficient, and everything was "on a small militia scale." He needed time. Let the Southern states form a government of their own, pooling their resources under a commander-in-chief— who, said the governor, should be Mr. Davis himself—and then something might be done; then it was to be hoped that "the slave holding race will present such a union as will secure the protection & development of our civilization in any emergency that may arise."[16]

The demand for the surrender of the fort, accordingly, would not be pressed. The situation would remain explosive, and if either side wanted a final decision, the gun was loaded and cocked, ready to hand; but Charleston would be uncharacteristically static, with the important developments taking place elsewhere.

There was, to be sure, a certain amount of continued sputtering. The man Governor Pickens sent to Washington was his Attorney General, J. W. Hayne, who was accompanied by Lieutenant Hall, from Fort Sumter. Hall made his report to the War Department, and Hayne delivered a letter to the White House. Buchanan, who refused to talk with Hayne in person, appears to have felt that a binding truce had been agreed to in Charleston, and that nothing could be done by either side until a formal reply to Governor Pickens's demand had been delivered to the governor. He let Secretary of War Holt write the reply, and Holt acted as if South Carolina had simply offered to buy Fort Sumter from the United States; he pointed out (to the intense irritation of Mr. Hayne) that the Federal government's title to the fort was "complete and incontestible" and remarked that the President had no Constitutional power to cede or surrender the place. For the rest, Sumter would not now be reinforced because Major Anderson did not think reinforcements were needed, but if the situation changed, reinforcements would be sent.[17]

Mr. Hayne was indignant. He sent an angry letter, not to Holt, but to President Buchanan himself, and he indicated that Southern pride was outraged by the notion that South Carolina was merely trying to buy a fort; it was difficult, he said, for him to see in this anything other than "an intentional misconstruction." South Carolina, he insisted, (growing somewhat shrill) was a separate and independent government: "and how, with this patent fact before you, you can consider the continued occupation of a fort in her harbor a pacific measure and parcel of a peaceful policy, passes certainly my comprehension."[18] The letter delivered, Mr. Hayne took himself off to Charleston. The interchange meant little, except that President Buchanan had made his administration's policy firm and official: there was no such thing as peaceful secession, and South Carolina (in the eyes of the government at Washington) was still legally a part of the Union. This President was not, after all, quite as weak as he looked; he had committed himself to a policy which Abraham Lincoln would continue when he reached the White House.

Meanwhile, the situation grew ever so much more complicated. Secession was spreading, and the creation of that Southern Confederacy which Senator Davis and Governor Pickens had been talking about drew steadily nearer. Mississippi left the Union on January 9, Florida went out on January 10, and Alabama followed on January 11. Eight days later Georgia seceded, to be followed a week later by Louisiana. Forts and arsenals were seized—without any armed clash, largely because most of the places taken over were held by nothing but caretaker detachments. Arsenals at Baton Rouge and Augusta and at Mount Vernon, Alabama, passed under state control, along with a string of forts—Pulaski, Ship Island, Morgan and Gaines, Jackson and St. Philip, Barrancas, Marion; all along the Southern coast the United States flag was coming down and state flags were going up, with enthusiastic militiamen moving in to take the place of Federal regulars.

It was a little confusing. A revolution was in progress, yet it was adhering to protocol as far as it could—clumsily, because protocol for such a situation had never been devised, but with the best of intentions. Just before Alabama seceded, a Congressman from that state wrote to Secretary Holt asking for the plan of the magazines in the Mount Vernon arsenal, and Holt replied, straight-faced, that he would cheerfully comply with this request "did not the interests of the service in the present condition of affairs forbid the publication of information of that description." Militia officers who seized the Federal installations solemnly gave receipts to the dispossessed, and Ordnance Captain Jesse L. Reno sent Holt a report explaining that he had not been able to hold the Mount Vernon arsenal because four companies of militia had clambered over the walls at daybreak and were upon him before he knew anything was up: "I trust the Department will not hold me responsible for this unexpected catastrophe."[19] His standing would remain good; he would become a major general and he would die in battle at South Mountain, in Maryland, a year and a half later.

There was an occasional mix-up. Moved by a false report that Federal troops were coming down on them, citizens of Wilmington, North Carolina, swarmed out on January 9 and seized Forts Johnston and Caswell, over the loud protests of the two caretakers—Ordnance Sergeant James Reilly, at Fort Johnston, and Ordnance Sergeant Frederick Dardingkiller, at Fort Caswell. A few days later Governor John W. Ellis sternly ordered the forts returned—North Carolina had not seceded, and there was considerable doubt whether it ever would—and the two ordnance sergeants, who had demanded receipts for the sequestered property, told the insurgents they would take the public property back "if there was none of it broken, or none of the ammunition expended." Sergeant Reilly notified the War Department that the men who had seized the forts "were not sustained by the people which brought them into it," and concluded his report with the remark: "I hope that the conduct of me and Sergeant Dardingkiller will be approved by the Department, as we took the responsibility of taking the stores back for the best interest of the public service." Governor Ellis notified Secretary Holt that his people were apt to make real trouble if any troops were sent to the two forts, and Holt gravely assured him that the government considered the forts entirely safe, "under the shelter of that law-abiding sentiment for which the people of North Carolina have ever been distinguished."[20]

As the cotton states, one after another, formally passed ordinances of secession, it became clear that not everyone in the deep South wanted to leave the Union. Even in Mississippi and Alabama there were men who argued boldly and with some public support against secession, and in the North men like Lincoln felt that there was a strong vein of loyalty to the Union all across the South if it could only be tapped. But this hope was largely a delusion. Loyalty to the Union did indeed exist, but the feeling that the states' claims ran deeper could sweep it away, and men who fought to keep secession from happening would support secession once it became a fact. In Alabama, Delegate Jeremiah Clemens told the state convention that secession was nothing more or less than treason, a great wrong which he would defeat if he could; but if secession was finally voted, "I am a son of Alabama: her destiny is mine . . . calmly and deliberately, I walk into revolution." In the same way the Mississippi anti-secessionist James L. Alcorn, having lost his fight, solemnly announced his decision in classical terms: "The die is cast—the Rubicon is crossed—and I enlist myself in the army that marches on Rome."[21]

The sheer sweep of dramatic events carried many men along. As had been the case with the marching Wide-Awakes in the North during the summer campaign, there was a rising sense of identification with a powerful movement; no one knew quite where the Southern states were going, but at least they were on the march and it was exciting to be a part of it. When the people of Mobile, for instance, celebrated the passing of the ordinance of secession by firing a 100-gun salute, setting off rockets and parading all across the downtown area to the sound of a brass band, they displayed an enthusiasm that was bound to be highly contagious. In Jackson, Mississippi, secession was celebrated by a parade led by a man swinging a large blue silken banner with one white star on its field; music-hall comedian Harry Macarthy saw it, was stirred, and quickly dashed off a song that was to be one of the great swinging battle songs of the Confederacy— "The Bonnie Blue Flag." All of Jackson sang it next day, and most of the South was singing it within weeks. The convention that voted Mississippi out of the Union voted also that the state's most distinguished son, Jefferson Davis, should be major general commanding the independent state's armed forces.

It was not entirely clear, even yet, just where all of the marching and singing and voting would take people. Secession was real, voted by men deeply in earnest—and yet there might still be room for an arrangement; the people of the North might yet give way when they understood that the people of the South really meant what they said. Congressmen J. L. Pugh and J. L. M. Curry, of Alabama, writing the day before their state's delegates voted for secession, said that their friends in the Northern and border states believed that "the secession of the cotton states is an indispensable basis for a reconstruction of the Union": it would put an end to coercion, and if the idea of coercion could be abandoned, perhaps all of the nation's troubles could somehow be solved.[22]

Yet the chance for harmony was growing very dim, one reason being that each faction expected someone else to make the compromises, another being that the drift of events carried its own hard logic. Buchanan's cabinet had now lost the last trace of pro-Southern feeling.[23] Jacob Thompson had resigned, his place as Secretary of the Interior being filled by Chief Clerk Moses Kelly, who was serving as acting secretary; and Philip Thomas, after one month's service as Secretary of the Treasury, had likewise quit, to be replaced by an energetic and uncompromising Unionist, former Senator John A. Dix, of New York. Dix lost very little time letting people know where he stood. Immediately after the secession of Louisiana, a Treasury agent went to New Orleans to see if anything could be saved from the wreckage. He found that the mint and the customs house had already been seized by state authorities, but he hoped that he could save the two revenue cutters that were berthed there, and he ordered them moved to New York. Captain J. G. Breshwood, of the cutter

McClelland, flatly refused, and when the agent reported this fact, Dix wired that he was to put the captain under arrest as a mutineer, following with the uncompromising order: "If anyone attempts to haul down the American flag, shoot him on the spot." The order made a stir in the North, where more and more people were in a mood to welcome a note of firmness, but it had no effect in New Orleans because it was never delivered. Captain Breshwood was not arrested, no one was shot, the cutter stayed where it was, and the flag did come down; the rising tide, having flooded forts and arsenals, had gone high enough to swamp a revenue cutter as well, and the Secretary's firm words had no effect.[24]

6. *"Everything, Even Life Itself"*

THE SENATE chamber was crowded on the morning of January 21. People had started moving toward the Capitol at daybreak, and by nine o'clock there was hardly standing room in the galleries or in the cloakrooms; there were foreign ministers in the diplomatic gallery, and when the doors to the outer halls swung open, the expectant faces of women, "like a mosaic of flowers," could be seen. As the routine business of the morning hour was disposed of, the chamber grew hushed, simple human curiosity blending with a tragic feeling that a long era in the nation's life was today being brought to a close. The Senators from the seceding cotton states were to speak their good-bys this morning; most notably, Senator Jefferson Davis, of Mississippi, gaunt and haggard, coming for the last time to this room where he had helped to make so much history.

Davis had been ill. He was tortured by agonizing migraine headaches that had kept him in bed for a week, and this morning his doctor had not thought him able to go to the Senate at all. Yet there was a fire in this man, a thin flame burning on the edge of darkness, and by its light he would follow the path of duty despite any imaginable physical weakness. He came in now, erect and deliberate, taking his final look at the Senate of a dissolving nation. His wife, Varina Howell Davis, watching from the gallery, felt that he gazed about him "with the reluctant look the dying cast on those upon whom they gaze for the last time." When he began to speak, his voice was low and he seemed to falter, but he gained strength as he went on and presently his words rang out firmly.

He had received satisfactory evidence, he told the Senators, that his state had formally declared its separation from the United States. His functions here, accordingly, were terminated; he concurred in the action of his people, but he would feel bound by that action even if he did not concur. He was offering no argument today. He had argued for his people's cause before now, had said all that he could say, and nothing had come of it. A conservative who loved the Union, he had cast his lot with his state, and he still hoped that there might be in the North enough tolerance and good will to permit a peaceful separation; but if there was not, "then Mississippi's gallant sons will stand like a wall of fire around their State; and I go hence, not in hostility to you, but in love and allegiance to her, to take my place among her sons, be it for good or for evil."

So it was time for good-bys, and the hush deepened as Davis spoke his valedictory:

"I am sure I feel no hostility to you, Senators from the North. I am sure there is not one of you, whatever sharp discussion there may have been between us, to whom I cannot now say, in the presence of my God, I wish you well. . . . Mr. President and Senators, having made the announcement which the occasion seemed to me to require, it only remains for me to bid you a final farewell."[1]

That night Davis prayed earnestly: "May God have us in His holy keeping, and grant that before it is too late peaceful councils may prevail." To a friend he wrote that his farewell had been wrung from him "by the stern conviction of necessity, the demands of honor"; his words "were not my utterances but rather leaves torn from the book of fate." To another friend he wrote, in more bitterness: "We have piped but they would not dance, and now the Devil may care." And to former President Franklin Pierce, in whose cabinet he had served, Davis confessed a deep pessimism and said bluntly that the Buchanan administration had mishandled the situation so badly that war was likely to be the result: "When Lincoln comes in he will have but to continue in the path of his predecessor to inaugurate a civil war, and leave a *soi disant* democratic administration responsible for the fact." He himself would go at once to Mississippi, and he did not know what the future might hold: "Civil war has only horror for me, but whatever circumstances demand shall be met as a duty and I trust be so discharged that you will not be ashamed of our former connection or cease to be my friend."[2]

It was over. With Davis, the other cotton-state Senators took their departure, and a few more of the frail threads that bound the Union together were snapped. The immediate effect was surprising, although quite logical. The deep South no longer had a voice in the national legislature, and as a result the long-impending measure to admit Kansas to the Union as a free state was promptly brought forward and passed. The Kansas issue had been at the very heart of the whole controversy; it had contributed much to the fury and suspicion that were now tearing the country apart; and here, on the heels of the first acts of that secession which it had done so much to bring about, it was at last settled, leaving its own bitter legacy. Old states were leaving, the first of the new states was coming in, and the country hereafter would look very different.

There was no way to undo what was being done; and yet the steady drift toward separation and war was subject to curious eddies and counter-currents, and the pattern refused to become clear. By February, six states had left the Union and one more, Texas, was about to follow; yet the slave states were far from united, and only the cotton states of the deep South—the Gulf Squadron, as men called them, with some bitterness—had taken the decisive step. It was beginning to be clear that the border and middle-South states were not ready to secede. Some of them would not go at all; others would go only if they were pushed. The slave empire was not monolithic, and it was beginning to crumble around the edges.

Early in January a roving commissioner from Mississippi addressed both houses of the legislature of slave-state Delaware, urging immediate secession and adherence to a Southern confederacy. The legislators heard him out, then unanimously adopted a resolution: ". . . we deem it proper and due to ourselves and the people of Delaware to express our unqualified disapproval of the remedy for the existing difficulties suggested by the resolutions of the legislature of Mississippi." In Maryland things were no better. Pro-slavery Democratic leaders urged Governor Hicks to call a special session of the legislature to consider an ordinance of secession, and Hicks flatly refused. Both Northern and Southern extremists, he remarked, had said that secession would lead to war, "and no man of sense, in my opinion, can question it." The governor had been ill, and he believed that he might not have long to live; "but should I be compelled to witness the downfall of that Government inherited from our fathers, established, as it were, by the special favor of God, I will at least have the consolation, in my dying hour, that I neither by word nor deed assisted in hastening its disruption."[3]

North Carolina, whose citizens had seized two forts in an excess of zeal and whose governor had promptly returned the forts to Federal control, held a plebiscite at the end of January. The legislature had presented a two-pronged bill for a state convention on secession; the voters could elect delegates to the convention, and at the same time they could say whether or not the convention ought to be held. In the end, they chose a substantial majority of Unionist delegates and also, by a narrow margin, voted against having a convention at all. The vote was not quite as solid a Unionist victory as it looked, because a great deal of the pro-Union sentiment would obviously evaporate if the Federal government made any move toward "coercion" of any Southern state. Still, for the moment, North Carolina was definitely refusing to join the procession.

In Tennessee the situation was somewhat the same. The legislature listened to much oratory, considered the problem at length, and at last resolved that delegates from all slave states ought to meet as soon as might be to work out some program by which Southern rights could be protected through amendments to the Federal Constitution. It resolved that if such a program could not be obtained, the formation of a new Southern confederacy ought to be undertaken, and it summoned a state convention to meet late in February to consider the matter of secession; but it provided also that if the convention should adopt an ordinance of secession, the action would not be valid unless the people of the state ratified it at a special election. Tennessee, in short, would wait a while. It was a slave state and its sympathies ran strongly with the men from the deep South, but it was not yet ready to go out of the Union.

Kentucky likewise would wait. Governor Beriah Magoffin told a commissioner from Mississippi that Kentuckians were strongly Southern in sympathy, and he predicted that if the Union broke apart, Kentucky would enter the Southern confederacy, but he believed that the prevailing sentiment "was unquestionably in favor of exhausting every honorable means of securing their rights within the Union." The legislature, considering the matter in the final week in January, recommended a national convention to work out a solution for the problem and suggested that Senator Crittenden's amendments might be a basis for a permanent settlement. In the direction of outright secession it moved not an inch.[4]

In Missouri, also, people wanted the situation clarified before they took any action. When the legislature convened in mid-January, the retiring governor, R. M. Stewart, remarked that the state "cannot be frightened by the past unfriendly legislation of the North, or dragooned into secession by the restrictive legislation of the extreme South," and the new governor, Claiborne Jackson, said that Missouri ought to stand with the other slave states but should remain in the Union as long as there was any hope of maintaining Constitutional guarantees regarding slavery. The legislature voted to summon a state convention for February 18, "to ascertain the will of the people," with a proviso that any secession ordinances would have to be ratified by a state-wide vote.

Sentiment in Arkansas seemed to be divided, with Unionists strong in the northwestern part of the state and secessionists from the cotton counties displaying eagerness for action. (One reason the people of the northwest hesitated about secession was the presence along the border of powerful Indian tribes, which were held under control only by the long arm of the Federal government.) Late in December the legislature called for an election on February 18, to determine whether there should be a convention to consider secession and to elect delegates if such a convention should be approved; meanwhile, secessionist leaders began to take things into their own hands. Early in February, disturbed by reports that the Federal government was going to reinforce the garrison at the Little Rock arsenal, several hundred armed citizens moved in to take possession of the place. Governor Henry M. Rector had had nothing to do with all of this, but to prevent an open fight he took control of this impromptu army and made formal demand, in the name of the state, for surrender of the arsenal. Captain James Totten, of the 2nd U. S. Artillery, a Pennsylvania-born regular, reflected on the matter for twenty-four hours and then agreed to turn the arsenal over to state authorities and to march his little detachment out of Arkansas—an action for which the grateful ladies of Little Rock presented him with a sword, along with a fancy scroll that told Totten: "You feared the danger of a civil war and the consequence to your country." Totten took the sword and, to the chagrin of the Little Rock ladies, wore it later as a Union brigadier general leading troops against the South.[5]

Only Texas was ready to act. Governor Sam Houston argued against secession, but late in January he yielded to pressure and called the legislature in special session. He was gloomy about what might happen, and to the secessionist leaders he had dark words of warning: "You may, after the sacrifice of countless thousands of treasure and hundreds of thousands of precious lives, as a bare possibility, win Southern independence, if God be not against you; but I doubt it." Texas, however, refused to listen to him, and on February 1 a state convention passed an ordinance of secession by the lopsided vote of 166 to 8.[6] Now there were seven states that considered that they had left the Union, and the formation of a new confederacy would proceed apace.

A great deal would depend on Virginia, traditionally a leader, a state with powerful Southern sympathies but also with a strong attachment to the Union. The new Southern nation that was struggling to be born needed Virginia as a man needs the breath of life. With Virginia it might in fact become a nation; without Virginia it could hardly, in the long run, hope to be more than a splinter; and Virginia was by no means ready to act.

Governor John Letcher addressed his state legislature on January 7, and he spoke broodingly, like a man who looks into a dark future but refuses to give up all hope. He had about abandoned the notion that the Union could be preserved; still, it was not too late to make the attempt, and at the very least Virginia might be able to get Federal guarantees that would justify her in rejecting secession. With somber insight, he put his finger on the fantastic central point: "It is monstrous to see a Government like ours destroyed merely because men cannot agree about a domestic institution." He felt that there should be a national convention of all the states, and he urged that a commission be sent to each of the Northern states (except those in New England, which he considered beyond the reach of reasonable appeal) to see whether they would agree to a program acceptable to Virginia. Such a program would include, roughly, guarantees of non-interference with the interstate slave trade, tightening of the fugitive slave laws, non-interference with slavery in the District of Columbia, Federal laws providing punishment for anyone who tried to get slaves to rise in rebellion, and a promise that the new administration would not, in the slave states, give Federal offices to anti-slavery characters.

For the rest, Governor Letcher made it clear that Virginia would resist coercion to the utmost. He would regard any attempt by Federal troops to pass through Virginia for the purpose of coercing any Southern state as an act of invasion, which Virginia would repel; a warning that contained teeth, since Washington could not easily send troops South without somewhere crossing Virginia's borders. Governor Letcher did not think there should be a state convention just yet, but the legislature disagreed. It adopted his plea for a national convention, and it invited all the states to send delegates to a meeting in Washington on February 4 "to unite with Virginia in an earnest effort to adjust the present unhappy controversies in the spirit in which the Constitution was originally formed and consistently with its principles," and it resolved that Virginia would resist any Federal step toward coercion; it also voted to call a state convention for February 13 to consider the matter of secession. At the same time it voted that if the attempt to bring about an adjustment of "the unhappy differences existing between the two sections of the country shall prove to be abortive," then Virginia ought to cast her lot with the slave states of the South.[7]

Virginia, in short, like the other border states, would wait and see, but while waiting it would make an honest effort to get the whole quarrel settled. The state was balanced on a knife edge. Of unconditional unionism it betrayed not a trace, except for the western counties beyond the mountains—

which, before long, would definitely be heard from—and it
had given fair warning that it would leave the Union unless
the present impasse got a strictly Southern solution; but it
had not yet acted, and in effect it had provided the country
with a little breathing spell, a brief extension of the time in
which the drift toward war might be halted.

But more than time was needed. Among the leaders on
both sides some evidence of an honest desire to make a compromise would have to appear unless the time gained should
be wasted, and this evidence was lacking.

Shortly after South Carolina seceded, Stephen Douglas had
written that "many of the Republican hordes are for disunion while professing intense devotion to the Union." And
he amplified this in another letter by remarking that many
Republican leaders "wish to get rid of the Southern Senators
in order to have a majority in the Senate to confirm Lincoln's
appointments." He himself had not quite given up hope for
a peaceful settlement, but he could never agree "that any
State can secede and separate from us without our consent,"
and he felt that no adjustment would work if it failed to
banish the slavery question from Congress forever."[8]

In the House of Representatives a committee of thirty-
three had been wrestling with the problem, and in January
this committee found itself unable to agree on anything.
Charles Francis Adams, of Massachusetts, dryly remarked
that no adjustment would satisfy the deep South unless it put
into the Federal Constitution "a recognition of this obligation
to protect and extend slavery"; and in the end the helpless
committee simply directed its chairman, stout Tom Corwin,
of Ohio, to present to the House, with such comments as he
cared to make, the principal resolutions the committee had
had under consideration. Corwin eventually managed to win
House approval of a resolution asking for repeal of the free
state "personal liberty laws" and faithful execution of the
fugitive slave laws, and late in February both Houses approved a constitutional amendment providing that the Constitution could never be amended in such a manner as to give
Congress the power to interfere with slavery in any slave
state. Yet this meant little, the projected amendment died of
simple inanition, and Corwin wrote to Lincoln that "Southern men are theoretically crazy . . . Extreme Northern men
are practical fools." If the several states, he said, were no

more ready to seek harmony than the members of the committee of thirty-three, "we must dissolve & a long & bloody civil war must follow." For whatever consolation there might be, he added: "I think, if you live, you may take the oath."[9]

In the Senate the aging Senator John J. Crittenden, of Kentucky, fought valiantly and without success for a plan by which the old Missouri compromise line would be restored and written into the Constitution for all time—no slave states to be formed in territory north of the parallel of thirty-six thirty, slavery to be permitted (at the option of the citizens) in any states to be formed from territory south of that line. But Crittenden could not even bring his proposition to a vote. He at last demanded that his compromise be submitted to the people of the entire nation in a solemn referendum, and as good an abolitionist as Horace Greeley wrote later that if this could have been done, the plan would almost certainly have carried with a large majority. But the Senate refused to vote on this suggestion, either, and any possibilities it might have offered were never put to the test. Crittenden argued for it with moving eloquence: "It will be an open shame to the Senate of the United States, an open shame to the Government of the United States, if, under such circumstances as now exist, this great Government is allowed to fall in ruins. . . . Peace and harmony and union in a great nation were never purchased at so cheap a rate as we now have it in our power to do. . . . The people will give good advice as to how this matter ought to be settled. . . . Balance the consequences of a civil war and the consequences of your now agreeing to the stipulated terms of peace here, and see how they compare with one another."[10]

This won no votes. In twelve months the country had heard much talk—too much, perhaps; it had lived too long in a cave of the winds, and now it seemed to be reaching a point where things done were more persuasive than things said. In the North, men could see that there was great danger, but they continued to hope that things might yet be settled peaceably; Major Anderson was a popular hero, partly because he had stood firm, but even more, apparently, because he had refrained from shooting when he had his loaded guns trained on a hostile target. There were odd cross-currents. Mayor Fernando Wood, of New York, was openly proposing that New York declare itself a free city, dealing with both North and South on a friendly basis and so offering "the only light and hope for a future reconstruction of our once blessed confederacy." Senator Seward was telling the Senate that the notion that a settlement could be worked out after peaceful separation looked like an admission that destruction must go before reconstruction, and he doubted that the Union could be saved "by some cunning and insincere compact of pacification." Abolitionist orators were openly welcoming secession, as if this convulsive step would at last take the great evil of slavery off forever beyond the horizon; but audiences were cool to this sort of talk, as if they were beginning to consider Union more important than slavery. The famous agitator Wendell Phillips told a Boston meeting that he was a disunion man, and that he hoped the slave states would leave the Union as quickly as possible; he was hissed and jostled, and police had to escort him out of the hall, and in Rochester a crowd broke up an abolitionist meeting, gave three cheers for the Union, and passed informal resolutions commending Major Anderson and General Scott.[11]

Meanwhile, one fact was becoming obvious. The Republicans had won the last election and were in the driver's seat. They had campaigned on the notion that there should be no extension of slavery in the territories and on that point they would not yield an inch. Their leaders were as unwilling to compromise as any cotton-state fire-eaters—with whom, indeed, they shared an extremely accurate understanding of what the election had really meant. A step had been taken which must ultimately mean the containment of slavery; unless this step were canceled, slavery could not be permanent but must eventually die. The Republican leaders would no more give up this point than men like Toombs and Davis would accept it. To win peace and a continued harmonious Union, Crittenden was in fact asking the people of the North to reconsider the verdict they had rendered at the polls. What the people themselves might have said if the proposition had finally come to them is beyond determination, but as a political proposition it was something the party leadership would not dream of embracing.

To outward appearances Lincoln, the President-elect, was doing nothing much more lofty than work on the selection of his cabinet, which was partly a matter of choosing his own administrative advisers and assistants and partly a matter of putting the new party together on an enduring basis. Privately, however, he was working against compromise. On January 28 the New York *Herald* reported him as saying that he would "suffer death" before accepting any compromise "which looks like buying the privilege of taking possession of this government to which we have a constitutional right." Correspondent Henry Villard wrote from Springfield that Lincoln was "firmly, squarely and immovably set against any compromise position that will involve a sacrifice of Republican principles," and Senator Charles Sumner exultantly wrote to Governor John A. Andrew, of Massachusetts, that Lincoln "is firm as a rock" against the Crittenden proposal. Sumner wrote out the words Lincoln had given him:

"Give them personal liberty bills & they will pull in the slack, hold on, & insist on the border state compromise—give them that, they'll again pull in the slack & demand Crit's comp.—that pulled in, they will want all that So. Carolina asks." To one pleader for compromise, Sumner wrote, Lincoln had said that "he would sooner go out into his back yard & hang himself"; and according to Sumner's letter, Lincoln had ended his interview with the flat statement: "By no act or complicity of mine shall the Republican party become a 'mere sucked egg—all shell—no principle in it.'" In a postscript, Sumner labeled this letter "private—except for the faithful."[12]

This did not mean that there could never be a compromise. Villard believed that Lincoln's firmness rested in large part on the belief that his election must be accepted first. Chosen by a minority of all the voters, he had nevertheless been chosen in the Constitutional manner, and the reporter wrote that "he desires to see the somewhat uncertain disposition of the border slave states yield to the rights of the majority, and obedience to the Federal Constitution and laws fully decided by his inauguration, before his friends shall make any move for reconciliation upon the basis of congressional enactments or Constitutional amendments." In informal conversations at this time, Villard said Lincoln expressed doubts about the possibility of retaining in the Union, by force, states that were determined to leave; he refused to encourage anti-slavery leaders who hoped that the whole secession crisis would somehow bring about the end of slavery, and he firmly believed that property in slaves was protected by the Constitution. Lincoln was under pressure, and he was showing it. On January 11, the Illinois politician W. H. L. Wallace wrote that "he is continually surrounded by a crowd of people," and said that "he looks care worn & more haggard & stooped than I ever saw him." Editor C. H. Ray, of the Chicago *Tribune,* a dedicated enemy of slavery, wrote that Lincoln was honest and patriotic enough for anybody, but that "more *iron* would do him no harm."[13]

It may be that by insisting on immediate secession the leaders of the Gulf Squadron had played their high trump too soon. The threat to secede had been a powerful weapon, but when secession became a visible fact rather than a threat, the argument was moved to a level where it was very hard to carry on negotiations. On most points affecting slavery, moderate Republican leaders like Lincoln were prepared to make some adjustments, but they would make no adjustments whatever on the question of union. Slowly but steadily the men of the North were beginning to realize that they were facing a new issue. Once they fully understood this point they would show a firmness that had not been anticipated.

Signs of this new firmness were appearing. On January 11 the New York legislature passed resolutions pledging full support to the President, in men and in money, in any action he might take to enforce the laws and uphold the authority of the Federal government. The resolutions also thanked the Union-loving citizens of those slave states that had not seceded; and, with a blithe incapacity to understand how these resolves might be regarded in the South, the New York authorities sent copies to the various Southern governors. Virginia's governor indignantly returned his copy with the curt request that no more communications of this kind be forwarded, and the Tennessee legislature asked Governor Harris to tell New York that if that state ever sent armed forces into the South, the people of Tennessee would resist "at all hazards and to the last extremity." But if the action of the New York legislature was tactless, it was indicative of a changing attitude, as was the fact that similar resolutions were presently adopted in Massachusetts, Wisconsin, and Ohio. The Pennsylvania legislature chimed in with the considered opinion that "the right of the people of a single state to absolve themselves at will, and without the consent of other states, from their most solemn obligations, and hazard the liberties and happiness of the millions composing this union, cannot be acknowledged."[14]

On the surface the Southern position looked weak. Of the fifteen slave states, only seven had voted to secede. The border states' reluctance to move hinted strongly that outside of the cotton belt the institution was in fact beginning to die, and that "containment" was actually beginning to take place. Yet this very weakness served to stiffen the spines of the secessionists. Time was running out, and the whole way of life that was based on slavery and symbolized by slavery's existence was threatened not so much by a recent Republican victory as by the inexorable passage of the years. To remain in the Union was to consent to the eventual transformation of Southern society. It was now or never, and this was the imperative that drove moderates like Davis down the trail blazed by extremists like Yancey.

Even though most of them owned no slaves and never would own any, the great mass of Southern people would follow when the final testing came. They identified themselves completely with a life and a land that seemed good to them; even more, they identified themselves with a dominant race which drew status and happiness from a rigid caste system whose dissolution, as far as they could see, would reduce their ordered existence to chaos. It was the massed presence of the mute and luckless Negro that exerted the real pressure. The average Southerner might not fight for slavery, but he would fight to the death to avert race equality. The average Northerner, in turn, even though he might share in this prejudice, would not understand the force it exerted—not until he tripped over it.

Nearly two years later, when the war that was now approaching was in full swing, a North Carolina mountaineer wrote to Governor Zebulon Vance a letter that expressed the non-slaveholder's point of view perfectly. Believing that some able-bodied men ought to stay at home to preserve order, this man set forth his feelings: "We have but little interest in the value of slaves, but there is one matter in this connection about which we feel a very deep interest. We are opposed to Negro equality. To prevent this we are willing to spare the last man, down to the point where women and children begin to suffer for food and clothing; when these begin to suffer and die, rather than see them equalized with an inferior race we will die with them. Everything, even life itself, stands pledged to the cause; but that our greatest strength may be employed to the best advantage and the struggle prolonged let us not sacrifice at once the object for which we are fighting."[15]

Real compromise was all but impossible. The most profound emotional force in the South was leading men to revolt against the whole trend of the times, and a tragically isolated society was preparing to risk everything in the attempt to preserve a past that was dissolving. Even if the Republican leaders had had the will to give the South the "guarantees" which it demanded, they actually lacked the power to do it, because those guarantees were out of any man's reach. War might come and great victories might be won, but the South was struggling for an unattainable.

Robert E. Lee was in Texas this winter, and late in January he wrote to his wife in gloomy foreboding:

"As far as I can judge from the papers we are between a state of anarchy & civil war. May God avert from us both. It has been evident for years that the country was doomed to run the full length of democracy. To what a fearful pass it has brought us. I fear mankind for years will not be sufficiently Christianized to bear the absence of restraint & force." To his daughter, a few days later, he added the words: "If the bond of the Union can only be maintained by the sword & bayonet, instead of brotherly love & friendship, & if strife & Civil War are to take the place of mutual aid & commerce, its existence will lose all interest with me. . . . I can however do nothing but trust to the wisdom & patriotism of the nation & to the overruling providence of a merciful God."[16]

CHAPTER FOUR

Two Presidents

1. The Man and the Hour

MONTGOMERY seemed an unlikely place for great events. It was a pleasant, unassuming country town, built on rolling hills at the head of navigation on the Alabama River, sheer bluffs rising from the water front, open marsh and meadowland stretching away on the far side of the stream. From the top of the bluffs Main Street, wide and sandy, went inland half a mile to the highest of the modest hills, where the white columns of a Greek revival capitol building rose as a landmark; a correspondent wrote that although the building was not particularly impressive, it nevertheless dominated the city, and he felt that it "stared down the street with quite a Roman rigor." There were shaded streets with fine residences, and a reporter for the New Orleans *Delta* enthusiastically reported that these showed "much architectural skill and beauty," with lawns and gardens and shrubbery "arranged in such order as to impress the beholder that these are the abodes of wealth, taste and refinement."[1] Montgomery, in short, was eminently suited to the part it had been playing—capital of a prosperous rural state, trading and commercial center for a thriving agricultural area. Now it had a new part to play. It was to become a world capital, in which men would say and do things that would affect American history for generations to come. On February 4, delegates from six of the states that had left the Union met in Montgomery to create and staff a government for the new Confederate States of America.

Montgomery was not old. It had existed for forty years, and so it was younger than many of the statesmen who assembled in it. Its central location commended it as a site for the South's great constitutional convention, and perhaps it was fitting that the new nation come to birth in a new country town (the cotton belt itself was new, only recently drawn from primeval wilderness, and of the seven states that would form the new Confederacy, only two had been in existence at the time of the American Revolution). But the city's facilities were plainly inadequate. There were two principal hotels, the Montgomery and the Exchange House, both of them overcrowded and expensive, and one (by the testimony of survivors) decidedly uncomfortable, not to say dirty. The capitol building itself, although handsome, was not nearly large enough, and it would soon be necessary to take space in a commercial building, letting the President of the Confederacy hold office in a hotel parlor. (A little later this month the new Secretary of State, beset by an applicant for office, angrily took off his top hat, held it out, and demanded: "Can you get in here, sir? That's the Department of State, sir!") The intense eagerness to shift the capital to Richmond, a few months later, probably came at least partly from the general realization that Montgomery just was not big enough to be the capital city of a great nation.[2]

Its inadequacy was not, however, immediately visible, for the great convention was not actually composed of a large number of delegates. Six states were represented at the start —Texas, the process of secession still incomplete, would be along a bit later—and these six sent but thirty-eight delegates, one of whom was delayed in his arrival. The other thirty-seven chose Howell Cobb, of Georgia, as their president and got down to work with a minimum of speech-making.

There was plenty for these men to do. They had to create a new nation, provide it with a constitution, name its chief executive, and then run the machinery which they had created; by turns they must be revolutionary committee, constitutional convention, electoral college, and national congress, all of these functions overlapping slightly, the specific legal authority for some of them being vague. This work had to be done under powerful pressures. There was first of all the pressure of time; it seemed essential to have the new government in operation, as a visibly going concern, by March 4, when the old government at Washington would install a new and presumably hostile President. It seemed advisable, also, to move fast in order to check the South Carolina hotheads, who were quite likely to provoke a fight with Major Anderson at Fort Sumter and thus bring on a war while the Confederacy was still in the act of getting born. There was pressure, too, from public opinion in the outer world. It must be shown that what was done at Montgomery was done by sober and conservative men who would make no disturbance unless malevolent outsiders thrust a cause of action upon them. The border states must not be frightened off. It must be proved, both to the satisfaction of the delegates themselves and to the skeptical eyes of the strangers up North, that secession was wholly legal, that this new nation was of entire and unstained legitimacy, and in short that this revolution was really no revolution but was simply the quiet assertion of undeniable rights by men who had suffered much with great forbearance.

All in all, it was a very large assignment, and it was discharged with speed and competence. The delegates met on February 4, got down to serious work on the following day, adopted a provisional constitution on February 8, named a provisional President on February 9, and had a government on the job and functioning within a week thereafter. Few American deliberative bodies have done so much so fast and so smoothly, with less time out for oratory.

Exactly how it was all done is not yet wholly clear, for this convention-congress voted at the start to conduct its more important deliberations in secret. When the convention became the Congress the habit was continued, and throughout the life of the Southern Confederacy the legislative branch did much of its work in executive session. In the long run this was undoubtedly a handicap; the open debate, the constant public examination of governmental policies and actions, out of which comes an informed public opinion, was very largely lacking, and the new government deprived itself of full grass-roots intimacy and understanding with the people back home—a deprivation that would finally be extremely costly. For the moment, however, there was no one to complain, except the reporters who were locked out, and also certain indignant ladies who had accompanied their husbands to Montgomery and now found that they could not sit in the galleries to watch, to listen, to applaud prettily, and to be admired. Alexander Stephens wrote long afterward that this was the ablest group of its kind he had ever seen, and he felt that the delegates "were not such men as revolutions or

civil commotions usually bring to the surface. They were
men of substance as well as of solid character—men of education, of reading, of refinement, and well versed in the
principles of government. . . . Their object was not to tear
down so much as it was to build up with the greater security
and permanency. The debates were usually characterized by
brevity, point, clearness and force."[3]

Whatever was said in debate, the fire-eaters said very little
of it. Never was a revolution made by men less revolutionary
in manner; the new nation was presented as if its birth had
been the mildest and most natural of events, and there was a
good deal of sentiment to name it The Republic of Washington—opposed, indeed, by some who argued that the name
should simply be the United States of America, as proof
that it was the Northern states that had really fractured the
old Constitution and destroyed the old Union. One member,
recalling that the convention was at all times "quiet, orderly,
dignified, with a deep sense of responsibility," wrote that
"there was a marked and purposed agreement with the Constitution of the United States." This, he said, was an attempt
to vindicate "the oft-repeated declaration that the States withdrew, not from the Constitution, but from the wicked and
injurious perversions of the compact."[4]

The provisional constitution (which differed only very
slightly from the permanent constitution of the Confederate
States, adopted a month later) was indeed the old familiar
United States Constitution with small but significant changes.

The famous "We, the people" opening sentence was modified so as to suppress the faint, haunting echo of Democracy's
trumpets; it was made clear that the people were acting
through sovereign and independent states rather than just as
people. Negro slavery was specifically mentioned, and was
given permanence; there never could be a law "denying or
impairing the right of property in Negro slaves," and slavery
was fully protected in territories then or later acquired. The
old fugitive slave law was retained, and its mealy-mouthed
locution about persons "held to service or labor" was straight-
ened out to read "slaves." The absence of true fire-eater influence, however, was visible in a constitutional prohibition
of the old African slave trade, which the more dreamy-eyed
visionaries of slave-state empire had talked of reviving, and

Congress was given power to prohibit the importation of slaves from non-seceding slave states.

But the delegates thought about much more than the simple protection of slavery. They tried, obviously, to build a government that would be better than the old one, and some of the reforms they brought forward had nothing at all to do with Southern rights. It was, to be sure, specified that there never could be a protective tariff, and Congress was barred from appropriating money for internal improvements, but most of the changes came from men who had been doing a good deal of abstract thinking on the way governments work. In some ways the President was given more power than in the United States; he could veto individual items in an appropriation bill without vetoing the entire bill, and Congress could appropriate money only by a two-thirds majority unless the appropriation had been specifically requested by the President. At the same time, however, the President was limited to a single six-year term, and Congress, if it chose, could give cabinet members seats on the floor of either house so that they could be questioned about departmental matters —a clear step in the direction of parliamentary authority after the British manner.[5]

To a certain extent, at least, this concern over improving the machinery of government reflected a feeling that an aristocratic society must, in the very nature of things, be able to govern itself better than a democracy. Undiluted democracy, indeed, was one of the things from which the cotton belt was seceding, as an editorial in the February issue of the *Southern Literary Messenger* made clear. The creation of the new Southern republic, said this magazine, would leave the states that remained in the old Union "absolutely at the mercy of an unprincipled, cold-blooded, tyrannical, remorseless horde of Abolitionists, whose anti-slavery creed but thinly disguises mob-law and agrarianism which surely overtakes all free society and which is the root of all Republican offending." Enlarging on this point, the editorial writer continued: "It is not a question of slavery alone that we are called upon to decide. It is the far greater question of civil liberty, of government of any sort. It is *free society* which we must shun or embrace."[6]

The new constitution was slightly odd in just one respect:

it said nothing whatever about the right of secession. The
states were recognized as sovereign powers, but whether any
one of them could leave the Confederacy as simply as it had
entered was left unmentioned; the right to secede may have
been an article of Southern faith from the cradle upward, but
it was not provided for in the Confederacy's basic charter.

In any case, the provisional constitution was adopted on
the night of February 8. (It would be submitted to the states
for ratification, and there would be a purely provisional government until February 22, 1862, but in effect the Confederacy would be a going concern as soon as it got its executive officers.) Things had gone with uncommon smoothness,
so far. If the same smooth unanimity could govern the choice
of a President, the world would be given a striking demonstration of the harmony and singleness of purpose which had
created the new nation.

The excesses of the old nominating conventions would be
avoided—which, considering the displays that had taken
place at nominating conventions during the preceding year, is
hardly surprising—and if men caucused earnestly in smoke-
filled rooms, they would at least do so out of the public gaze.
Their task would not be too difficult. This convention was of
manageable proportions. It now contained thirty-eight members, from six states, and all of its votes were to be cast by
states, with each delegation possessing one vote. Instead of
oratory from the floor, in the regular sessions, there would
be simple private discussions within the separate delegations.
It was generally agreed that the choice of a President ought
to be unanimous; if there should be a contest among two or
more candidates, it would be resolved before the business
came to a formal vote. Whenever four of the six delegations
had settled on a man, it would be time to vote.

There was a great deal of discussion, but no real campaigning, and apparently by unspoken agreement the delegates
shied away from the fire-eaters. Yancey was in town, and if
any man could claim to be the father of the new nation, he
was the man; but he was too much the extremist, the people
in Virginia and the other border states felt that he was dangerous, and he was not seriously considered for the presidency. The same was true of the elder Rhett, who was leader
of South Carolina's delegation. Rhett believed that he was

abundantly qualified for the post, but there was never much chance that he would be chosen, and he made no serious effort to get the place. It appeared that much would depend on how the Georgia delegation felt, and it was generally assumed that Georgia would offer the name of Howell Cobb; an assumption which led to a slight mix-up, which had far-reaching consequences. Cobb was a man of much stature, perhaps the ablest leader in the South—Stephens said afterward that if it had not been for Cobb, Georgia might not have seceded—but there was opposition to him in the other delegations. Many good secessionists felt that in the past he had shown altogether too much love for the Union, and in addition there were tag ends of old party animosities clinging to him, and when the state delegations began to talk candidacies on the night of February 8 (the President was to be chosen the next morning), members of at least three delegations, believing that Cobb would be named by Georgia, cast about for some other candidate. More or less inevitably, they gravitated toward Jefferson Davis.[7]

Davis was not present. Men on the Mississippi delegation knew that he did not want to be President. He presently held a major general's commission from Mississippi, he believed that his talents lay in the military field, and if the new Confederacy was to give him anything, he wanted command of the Confederacy's army—for which, indeed, everyone felt that he was highly qualified. At the same time, it was logical to consider him for the presidency. Like Cobb, he had national stature, and although he too had shown a deep attachment to the Union, he enjoyed the active support of one of the most active of the South Carolina fire-eaters, Robert Barnwell. In the belief that the business would come down to a choice between Cobb and Davis, at least three of the delegations that night agreed to vote for Davis.

The Georgia delegation, meanwhile, was not doing what people had expected it to do. Cobb had never been an active candidate. He had written to his wife when the convention opened that "the presidency of the Confederacy is an office I cannot seek and shall feel no disappointment in not getting," and on this night of February 8 he was repeating that "far from making an effort to obtain that position I have frankly said to my friends that I would greatly prefer not to be put

there." Learning that strong sentiment for Davis was developing, Cobb told other Georgians that he hoped Davis would
be chosen unanimously.[8]

The Georgia delegation was not quite ready to agree to
this. If they could not put Cobb over, they had another candidate in Robert Toombs, whom Stephens considered by far
the ablest man the convention could select. There were
those who said afterward that Stephens would have been
happy to be selected himself, but as a man who had supported
Douglas (who had talked of a high gallows for traitors),
Stephens was not quite the ideal candidate. Not realizing
that some of the state delegations were by now committed
to Davis, the Georgians at length agreed to vote for Toombs.

If they had come to this conclusion earlier, Toombs might
have become President of the Confederacy; the groups that
had swung to Davis had done so largely to head off Cobb,
and it is quite possible that they would have followed Georgia's lead if they had known Georgia was going to name
Toombs. Toombs was popular, and he was an attention-getter
in any company; an outspoken, hard-driving, tough-fibered
man, untidy, often breezily profane, his candidacy perhaps
weakened slightly by a rumor that he was drinking more
than he should. He was needling Cobb mercilessly these days,
and Stephens (with a slight trace of glee) wrote to a friend
that Toombs "never lets Cobb pass without giving him a
lick." One evening, at a gathering that included Cobb and
other delegates, Toombs announced that as Buchanan's Secretary of the Treasury, Cobb had done more for the Confederacy than any other man alive—he had left the Northern government without any money in the till, "he did not even
leave old 'Buck' two quarters to put on his eyes when he
died."[9] It was a characteristic Toombs outburst. Intensely
ambitious, Toombs wanted the presidency very much, and
one of the South's tragedies was the fact that it never quite
found how to put his undeniable talents to work.

When the convention assembled on the morning of February 9 and prepared to elect a President, the Toombs balloon
collapsed as soon as it became known that at least three of
the state delegations were going to vote for Davis. The
Georgians had committed themselves to Toombs in the belief that the field was open, and Toombs himself insisted that
there must be no contest on the floor; unless all the other

delegations were prepared to vote for him, he would not let his name be presented. There were last-minute scurryings-about; the desire for harmony won out, Toombs's name was withdrawn, and all six delegations voted for Jefferson Davis. Then, in a move that was more than a little surprising, but that apparently involved an attempt to give Georgia proper recognition, the convention unanimously elected Stephens Vice-President.

By afternoon the business was settled. The Confederacy had a constitution, it had a President (who would be sworn in as soon as he could get to Montgomery), and it had a Vice-President, and until the permanent constitution went into effect a year later, the convention would act as a unicameral legislature. The new nation was in being.

Under the surface the harmony was not perfect. The Rhetts grumbled that Jefferson Davis had never been an all-out secessionist, and in the Georgia delegation there were raised eyebrows about Stephens's election. Howell Cobb's younger brother, Thomas R. R. Cobb, himself a Georgia delegate, wrote that Stephens's victory was "a bitter pill to some of us but we have swallowed it with as good grace as we could." It seemed to the younger Cobb outrageous that "the man who has fought against our rights and liberty is selected to wear the laurels of our victory," and he concluded that it all stemmed from "a maudlin disposition to conciliate the Union men." Darkly, he went on to say that many secessionists were troubled by rumors that Davis himself was "a reconstructionist," and he believed that unless Davis thoroughly scotched such fears in his inaugural address, "we shall have an explosion here."[10]

Cobb need not have worried, for few men in the South now were less inclined toward reconstruction than Davis. The delegates at Montgomery were in a hopeful mood, feeling that the North might soon consent to a peaceful separation, but Davis was not deluded; he believed that there was going to be war and that it would be long and costly, and his reluctance to accept the presidency came in large part from his conviction that there would be work for the armies. When a Mississippi friend protested that war ought not to follow the peaceable withdrawal of a sovereign state, Davis replied that "it was not my opinion that war *should* be oc-

casioned by the exercise of that right, but that it *would* be."
(Even Stephens, as a matter of fact, saw things the same
way. Not long after his election as Vice-President he wrote
that he considered war certain. Every effort should be made
to avoid it, he said, but "we are told by high authority that
'offences must come' and I think this is one of the occasions
on which we may expect such a result.") There would be
times when Davis could fix his gaze so firmly on what he
hoped for that he would blind himself to what was actually
going on around him, but in the winter of 1861 he was a
most clear-sighted realist.[11]

His dismay at being made President was genuine. Varina
Davis told how she and her husband were in the garden of
Brierfield, their plantation home in Mississippi, making rose
cuttings, when a messenger brought Davis the telegram announcing that he was to be President of the Confederacy. He
read it with an expression that made her feel that some dreadful personal calamity had taken place, and when he told her
what the message said, he spoke "as a man might speak of
a sentence of death." The news in truth came to Davis as
no surprise, letters from the Mississippi delegates at Montgomery having kept him posted about the drift of things,
and he felt that he had no option but to accept: "The trial
was too great and the result too doubtful to justify one in
declining any post to which he was assigned, and therefore I
accepted." It took one day to set his affairs in order, to say
farewell to his slaves, and to take a last look at the plantation home which meant so much to him. Then Jefferson Davis
left for Montgomery.[12]

The trip was all enthusiasm and cheers and music, with
rear-platform speeches before jubilant crowds at way stations
and more formal talks here and there in larger cities. When
he talked, Davis did his best to warn his fellow citizens that
a time of trial lay ahead. At Vicksburg he remarked that he
had always been "attached to the Union of our fathers by
every sentiment and feeling of my heart," but that the separation had finally become inevitable; and although he hoped
that the separation might be peaceable, "I am ready, as I
always have been to redeem my pledges to you and the
South by shedding every drop of my blood in your cause."
A correspondent for the New York *Herald* was deeply impressed by events of the journey, and wrote a warning dis-

patch for his Northern readers: "There are two things notice-able in connection with the president's passage through the country—the unstudied, spontaneous, hearty enthusiasm with which he has been everywhere greeted, and the unanimous determination to stand by the new government. For whatever division there may have been before secession, there is now but one mind."[13]

Davis reached Montgomery on February 16, to be met at the train by an official delegation to whose greeting Davis responded with words of grim determination, which must have removed Thomas Cobb's last doubts.

"The time for compromise has now passed," said Davis, "and the South is determined to maintain her position and make all who oppose her smell Southern powder and feel Southern steel if coercion is persisted in." That evening, at the Exchange Hotel, Davis appeared on a balcony with Yancey to respond to the cheers of an expectant crowd with words of hope and flame.

"It may be," cried the new President, "that our career will be ushered in in the midst of a storm; it may be that as this morning opened with clouds, rain and mist, we shall have to encounter inconveniences at the beginning; but as the sun rose and lifted the mist it dispersed the clouds and left us the pure sunshine of heaven. So will progress the Southern Confederacy, and carry us safe into the harbor of constitu-tional liberty and political equality. We fear nothing . . . be-cause, if war should come, if we must again baptize in blood the principles for which our fathers bled in the Revolution, we shall show that we are not degenerate sons, but will re-deem the pledges they gave, preserve the rights they trans-mitted to us, and prove that Southern valor still shines as bright as in 1776. . . . I will devote to the duties of the high office to which I have been called all that I have of heart, of head, of hand."

Then, thinking of the armies that would march, and re-sponding to his own inner longing, Davis added: "If, in the progress of events, it shall become necessary that my services be needed in another position—if, to be plain, necessity re-quire that I shall again enter the ranks of soldiers—I hope you will welcome me there."

The crowd cheered mightily; then Yancey stepped forward,

to pay his own tribute to "the distinguished gentleman who has just addressed you." In Davis, said Yancey, the South had found "the statesman, the soldier and the patriot," and the South was thrice fortunate: "The man and the hour have met."[14]

It was Yancey's odd fate that he would be remembered by remote generations chiefly for that one remark: "The man and the hour have met." He was a passionate, intense person who had labored for years to create this new nation, one of the principal authors of a great drama which other men would enact; and he would go on into the shadows leaving little enduring trace of his own taut humanity except that on the balcony of a hotel in a little Southern city he had found the words to sum up, perfectly, the nobility and the tragedy of the Southern Confederacy and Jefferson Davis.

The man and the hour had been approaching each other by unlikely channels. The hour grew out of everything that a proud, self-centered, insecure society had been striving for in its attempt to ward off unwelcome change. The long argument over slavery in the territories, the resentment aroused by abolitionist taunts and by Northern aid for fugitive slaves, the fear and fury stirred by John Brown's raid and by the realization that many folk in the free states looked on Brown as a saintly martyr, the desperate attempt to preserve a pastoral society intact in a land being transformed by the Industrial Revolution—all of these had led to this hour in Montgomery, with banners waving and words of brave defiance shouted into the winter air. And the man who was meeting the hour, tense and erect, lonely and dedicated, looking without fear into a clouded future, was perhaps greater than the cause he embraced. He came from the Ohio Valley, cradle of a leveling democracy, born within a few months and a few miles of another Kentuckian, Abraham Lincoln, coming to manhood by a different course. He was a Mississippi planter at a time when the Mississippi planter was a hard man on the make rather than the exemplar of a cultivated pillared aristocracy, and yet somehow he transcended the limitations of his background and represented, once and for all, the nobility of the dream that his fellows believed themselves to be living by. Of all the men the Confederacy might have summoned, he was the man for this hour and for the hours that would follow.

2. The Long Road to Washington

JEFFERSON DAVIS was leaving Brierfield, saying good-by to his rose garden, his slaves, and his dream of military glory, traveling to Montgomery to begin a great hour on a hotel balcony amid cheers and torchlight. Similarly touched by destiny, Abraham Lincoln was beginning the same sort of journey at just about the same time, going from Springfield to whatever might await him in Washington. Like Davis, Lincoln had to say farewell to much; he was moving away from his own personal existence, he would belong from now on in every word and thought and deed to something larger than himself, and everything that had happened to him until now was no more than preparation for the years that lay ahead. He would meet, as he traveled eastward, flags and music and crowds of people eager to look and to cheer, just as Davis had met them; and although he and Davis would never come face to face, they would confront one another now through tumult and wind-driven smoke, the rival leaders of two nations in a land that could hold only one.

Early in February Lincoln closed his home, selling or storing his household furnishings, moving to Springfield's Chenery House for his last days in Illinois. Shortly after daybreak on February 11 he drove to the Great Western railroad station through a cold drizzle, and in the waiting room there he spent half an hour bidding farewell to friends. There was a crush of people all about, and Lincoln was pale, apparently gripped by deep emotion. He said little as men and women pumped his hand, and when he spoke, his voice seemed almost ready to break. After half an hour of it the train was ready, and the President-elect and his party went out to go aboard.

There were three cars—baggage car, smoker, and coach, with "a powerful Rogers locomotive" in front; the railroad time card warned that "it is very important that this train should pass over the road in safety." With Lincoln there was his son Robert, already dubbed "the Prince of Rails" by newspaper correspondents; his youthful secretaries, John G. Nicolay and John Hay; and Elmer Ellsworth, the slightly unreal amateur soldier who had drilled gaily dressed militia units and who had somehow won a place in the older man's heart; he would be killed in three months, and his body would lie in state in the White House. Also present were four professional soldiers, detailed by the War Department to be an escort and to look out for the safety of the President-elect. One of these was Colonel Edwin Vose Sumner, gruff and white-haired, who became an army officer before Lincoln entered his teens, an old-timer who would not survive the war. Others were Major David Hunter, Captain George Hazard, and energetic Captain John Pope, who would live to meet responsibilities too heavy for him. There were reporters, and political characters, and the New York *Herald* man noted that the cars were well stocked with "refreshments for the thirsty." Mrs. Lincoln, with the younger sons, Willie and Tad, would board the train at Indianapolis.

The crowd surged out of the waiting room as the party got on the train. Lincoln went to the rear platform, his tall hat in his fingers, and his fellow townsmen fell silent. He faced them, a somber, brooding figure, seemingly as reluctant as Davis had been to meet the incomprehensible burdens of the presidency. He spoke, finally, the last words he would ever speak in Springfield, not so much making a speech as thinking out loud.

"No one, not in my situation, can appreciate my feeling of sadness at this parting," he said. "To this place, and the kindness of these people, I owe everything. Here I have lived a quarter of a century, and have passed from a young to an old man. Here my children have been born, and one is buried. I now leave, not knowing when, or whether ever, I may return, with a task before me greater than that which rested upon Washington. Without the assistance of that Divine Being, who ever attended him, I cannot succeed. With that assistance I cannot fail. Trusting in Him, Who can go with me and remain with you and be everywhere for good, let us confidently hope that all yet will be well. To His care commending you, as I hope in your prayers you will commend me, I bid you an affectionate farewell."[1]

In this simple impromptu speech Lincoln was at his best. He would be at his worst in the speeches he would give between Springfield and Washington, and a thoughtful American who troubled to listen could have been excused for believing that a woefully unfit man was about to become President. As the special train moved eastward, it began to seem that all of the North was watching it, and whenever the train stopped, Lincoln had to show himself—precisely as Davis had to show himself on another train, far to the southward. Showing himself, he had to say something, and the art of saying nothing in an impressive way was one that he had not yet learned. Not having learned it, he fumbled badly, giving the impression at times of a man who simply did not understand the crisis or know what his own part in it ought to be. Few chapters in Lincoln's whole career are as melancholy to read about as the one that tells how he went from Illinois to Washington.

There were trackside crowds all along the route, but most of these expected little more than a bow and a waved hand from the train's rear platform. The first real test came at Indianapolis, where Lincoln had to leave the train and attend a reception at the Bates House. There was a dense, uncontrolled crowd here, and the New York *Herald* reporter noted disapprovingly that Lincoln had to force his way through the crush unaided: "no precautions had been taken to protect him from insolent and rough curiosity," and when he reached the supper room he had to wait half an hour for a sketchy meal. Having eaten, at last, Lincoln had to make a speech. For the first time since the election, he was addressing his fellow countrymen, and a carefully considered policy pronouncement might have been expected. What actually came out was nothing much better than the rambling spur-of-the-moment remarks of a politician who, finding himself in the presence of an enthusiastic crowd, feels obliged to "say a few words" without much regard to what the words mean or the echoes they may strike—one trouble, perhaps, being that he simply did not yet realize how far his lightest words now must echo.

The people of the South, Lincoln now said, seemed to be worried about coercion. But what was coercion? "Would the marching of an army into South Carolina, for instance, without the consent of her people, and in hostility against them, be coercion or invasion? I very frankly say, I think it would be invasion, and it would be coercion too, if the people of that country were forced to submit. But if the Government, for instance, simply insists on holding its own forts, or retaking those forts which belong to it"—just here he was interrupted by cheers—"or the enforcement of the laws of the

United States in the collection of duties upon foreign importations, or even the withdrawal of the mails from those
portions of the country where the mails themselves are
habitually violated; would any or all of these things be coercion? Do the lovers of the Union contend that they will resist
coercion or invasion of any state, understanding that any
or all of these would be coercing or invading a state? If they
do, then it occurs to me that the means for the preservation
of the Union they so greatly love, in their own estimation, is
of a very thin and airy character."

Interrupted again by applause, Lincoln went on to develop
this offhand study of the value of a secessionist's love for the
Union; a study that would have benefited greatly by deeper
thought and more careful phrasing. ". . . In their view, the
Union, as a family relation, would not be anything like a
regular marriage at all, but only a sort of free-love arrangement to be maintained on what that sect calls passionate attraction." This was greeted by laughter, and Lincoln presently continued: "Can a change of name change the right?
By what principle of original right is it that one-fiftieth or
one-ninetieth of a great nation, by calling themselves a
State, have the right to break up and ruin that nation as a
matter of original principle? . . . Where is the mysterious,
original right, from principle, for a certain district of the
country, with inhabitants, by merely being called a State, to
play tyrant over all its own citizens and deny the authority
of everything greater than itself?"[2]

The best that can be said for the Indianapolis interlude is
that at last it ended and the journey was resumed. That Lincoln or any other man should be asking himself questions
of that sort, in the baffling February of 1861, is not surprising, but that these questions, unedited and unanswered, should
find their way into a serious speech is staggering. (It was on
this day that the Southern Confederacy served formal notice
of its existence by inaugurating its Vice-President.) On succeeding days there were other crowds to be addressed, and
the result was not always more fortunate.

At Lawrenceburg, Indiana, on February 12, Lincoln was
on a different tack: "I have been selected to fill an important
office for a brief period, and am now, in your eyes, invested
with an influence which will soon pass away; but should my
administration prove to be a very wicked one, or what is

more probable, a very foolish one, if you, the PEOPLE, are but true to yourselves and to the Constitution, there is little harm I can do, *thank God!*" The next day he had more cheerful words for the Ohio legislature, at Columbus: "I have not maintained silence from any want of real anxiety. It is a good thing that there is no more than anxiety, for there is nothing going wrong. It is a consoling circumstance that when we look out there is nothing that really hurts anybody. We entertain different views upon political questions, but nobody is suffering anything."

He developed this notion further, as his train continued in its oddly zigzag course across the Middle West. At Rochester, Pennsylvania, someone called out to ask what he would do about the secessionists when he reached Washington and became President, and he replied: "My friend, that is a matter which I have under very great consideration." But the next day, at Pittsburgh, he told an audience: "Notwithstanding the troubles across the river, there is really no crisis springing from anything in the government itself. In plain words, there is really no crisis except an *artificial* one. . . . If the great American people will only keep their temper, on both sides of the line, the troubles will come to an end." His itinerary doubled back to Cleveland, where there was a long parade through slush and snow, leading to a speech in which this Pittsburgh theme was carried further:

"I think that there is no occasion for any excitement. The crisis, as it is called, is altogether an artificial crisis. . . . It has no foundation in facts. It was not argued up, as the saying is, and cannot, therefore, be argued down. Let it alone and it will go down of itself."[3]

. . . It was not going down very fast. On February 18 Jefferson Davis took the oath of office as President of the Southern Confederacy, and Lincoln told the New York State legislature: "It is true that while I hold myself without mock modesty the humblest of all individuals that have ever been elected to the Presidency, I have a more difficult task to perform than any one of them." In New York City on February 20 he paid his respects, obliquely, to Mayor Fernando Wood's suggestion that the metropolis set itself up as a free ctiy, declaring that "there is nothing that can ever bring me willingly to consent to the destruction of this Union, under which not only the commercial city of New York but the whole country has acquired its greatness"; and a day later, in Philadelphia, he returned to the notion that there was something artificial about the national crisis. He qualified this, however, by adding: "I do not mean to say that this artificial panic has not done harm. That it has done much harm I do not deny."

At least partial redemption from all of this came on Washington's Birthday when Lincoln spoke at Independence Hall, and reached above the say-a-few-words routine to touch the edges of genuine eloquence.

"I have never had a feeling politically that did not spring from the sentiments embodied in the Declaration of Independence," he said. "I have often inquired of myself, what great principle or idea it was that kept this Confederacy so long together. It was not the mere matter of the separation of the colonies from the motherland; but something in the Declaration giving liberty, not alone to the people of this country, but hope to the world for all future time. It was that which gave promise that in due time the weights should be lifted from the shoulders of all men, and that *all* men should have an equal chance. This is the sentiment embodied in the Declaration of Independence. Now, my friends, can this country be saved upon that basis? If it can, I would consider myself one of the happiest men in the world if I can help to save it. . . . If this country cannot be saved without giving up that principle—I was about to say I would rather be assassinated on this spot than to surrender it."[4]

Lincoln was eleven days away from Springfield, and he had not yet got to Washington. If the purpose of this excessively roundabout trip had been to let the people of the North look at him, something of value had perhaps been accomplished; otherwise it would have been a good deal better if the trip had been made as short as possible, adorned by no speeches or rear-platform appearances. The physical strain had been immense; Newspaperman Henry Villard estimated that Lincoln had spoken at least fifty times during one week, and said that the man was almost exhausted by the time he got to Buffalo. The New York *Herald*'s man said that Lincoln seemed too "unwell and fatigued" to take part in conversation when his train left Albany, and he paid him a condescending tribute: Lincoln seemed "so sincere, so conscientious, so earnest, so simple hearted, that one cannot help liking him," but the only answer to the unending speculation about what he was going to do, as President, had to be the simple statement: "Lincoln does not know himself yet." In the capital of the Southern Confederacy the Montgomery *Post* made propaganda out of its summing-up of Lincoln's trip:

"The more we see and hear of his outgivings on his way to Washington, the more we are forced to the conclusion that he is not even a man of ordinary capacity. He assumes to be insensible of the difficulties before him—treats the most startling political questions with childish simplicity, and manifests much of the disposition of the mad fanatic who meets his fate—not in the spirit of respectful Christian resignation, but with the insane smile of derision upon his lips, as if unconscious of the destiny that awaits him. We may readily anticipate that such a man will be the pliant tool of ambitious demagogues, and that his administration will be used to subserve their wicked purposes."[5]

Yet there had been something extremely impressive about the journey, not because of anything that was said, but because of the intense, almost desperate press of the people who came to listen. David Davis, who traveled with Lincoln, wrote that the whole trip across Indiana and Ohio had been "an ovation such as has never before been witnessed in this country." Wherever the train stopped there was a crowd, tense with excitement, and Davis believed that this was because of the times rather than the man. "I don't think that it is Lincoln's person or character that calls out the enthusiasm," he wrote. "It must be, that the present state of the country calls forth such an enthusiasm as has never been witnessed."[6]

The unhappiest part of the whole trip came at the end. Here Lincoln found himself in an episode that wobbled uncertainly between low comedy and outright tragedy, a singular affair which is not entirely clear even now and which proves nothing except that the public mind was in an excessively disturbed condition.

At Philadelphia, just before the Independence Hall appearance, Lincoln and his closest advisers were warned—solemnly, and apparently on excellent authority—that he would be murdered if he passed through Baltimore as scheduled on the afternoon of Saturday, February 23.

The first warning was received by Norman B. Judd, the Chicagoan who had been one of the Lincoln headquarters men at the Wigwam convention and who was now a member of the party traveling to Washington. To Judd, in his Philadelphia hotel room, at night, came two men with a tale to tell. One of the two was S. M. Felton, president of the Philadelphia, Wilmington, and Baltimore Railway, a sober man of business; and the other was the rising private detective Allan Pinkerton, who had a peculiar combination of energy and imagination—a combination that was taking him to the top of his chosen profession, but that would prove a decided handicap to the nation's principal army before a year was out. Felton had hired Pinkerton to investigate rumors that secessionist sympathizers in Baltimore planned to break railroad communications with the capital; a matter of concern to Felton, since his own railroad was likely to be involved. Investigating, Pinkerton had unearthed an elaborate assassination plot, which hinged on the related facts that railway interchange facilities in Baltimore were imperfect and that the city was full of turbulent characters whose sympathies were notoriously Southern. A through car from the North bound for Washington must be switched in Baltimore from Felton's railroad to the Baltimore & Ohio, and the transfer usually involved hauling the cars down a city street with horses. As Lincoln's schedule stood, this would take place on a Saturday afternoon: Baltimore authorities had neither gone through the routine of inviting him to visit their city nor had they made any arrangements for police protection, and according to Pinkerton, Lincoln would be mobbed and killed while he was moving from one railroad station to another.

Judd, Felton, and Pinkerton therefore urged him to cut his trip short, cancel further appearances in Pennsylvania, and go to Washington secretly that very night.

This Lincoln refused to do. He had commitments to speak in Philadelphia and in Harrisburg the next day, February 22, and he would not try to get out of them. (Apparently he could not quite make himself believe in the reality of this assassination story anyway.) He did agree that after he had spoken in Harrisburg he would give the business further thought.

Further thought was thrust upon him. At Harrisburg he was visited by young Frederick Seward, son of the Senator from New York from whom Lincoln had taken the Republican nomination and whom he had privately selected to be Secretary of State in his new cabinet. Frederick Seward brought impressive warnings from his father and from General Winfield Scott, both of whom had come upon the conspiracy story from sources independent of Pinkerton and both of whom believed that there definitely was substance to it. Like Judd and Felton, they were urging Lincoln to come down to Washington secretly so as to avoid the Saturday-afternoon transfer in Baltimore.[7]

A serious plot to kill Abraham Lincoln may or may not have existed. (Four years later an equally frothy situation did in fact produce a John Wilkes Booth, complete with loaded derringer; it would develop eventually that in a time of civil war the most grotesque improbabilities can be built on ugly facts.) Washington had been full of ominous rumors all winter. The War Department had gone to great lengths to build up a thoroughly loyal home guard in the District of Columbia to prevent a seizure of power by secessionist sympathizers, and Winfield Scott had remarked that the general tension was such that "a dog-fight might cause the gutters of the capital to run with blood." Just before Lincoln left Springfield, a citizen visited the old general to ask whether precautions had been taken to make sure that Congress could formally count the electoral vote; it was being rumored that a mob would rise and prevent it, thus (presumably) making it impossible for Lincoln to take office.

"I supposed I had suppressed that infamy," said General Scott. "Has it been resuscitated? I have said that any man who attempted by force or unparliamentary disorder to obstruct or interfere with the lawful count of the electoral vote for President and Vice-President of the United States should be lashed to the muzzle of a twelve-pounder and fired out of a window of the Capitol. I would manure the hills of Arlington with the fragments of his body, were he a Senator or chief magistrate of my native state!" Subsiding a little, the general added: "While I command the army there will be no revolution in the city of Washington."[8]

Both Scott and Seward, in any case, believed in the reality of the assassination plot, and Lincoln was persuaded that he ought to be cautious. Elaborate arrangements were made, and on the night of February 22 Lincoln and his close friend

Ward Lamon—a muscular fighting-man type from the prai-
ries, heavily armed with pistols and knives—quietly slipped
away from the Harrisburg hotel, took a train to Philadelphia, changed there to a Washington sleeper, and got through
Baltimore in the dead of night without incident. Lincoln
wore a soft felt hat in place of his usual stiff topper, and
Pinkerton accompanied the travelers and made certain security arrangements en route; and when the party reached
Washington and Lincoln went to Willard's Hotel, Pinkerton
hurried to a telegraph office to send a wire in clumsy code
to the people in Harrisburg: "Plums delivered nuts safely."
Whatever danger may have existed, it had been evaded. The
long trip was over, and Lincoln had arrived at the capital
city where he would spend the rest of his life.

This evasive action may have been necessary—may at
least have *seemed* necessary, the state of the public mind being what it was—but it brought Lincoln much derision.
There was something extremely undignified about a President-elect sneaking into Washington in the dead of night, and
the uneasy drama of the trip from Illinois, bad enough at
best, came to its end on this note of outlandish melodrama.
(Why Pinkerton thought it necessary to send his plums-nuts
wire is beyond explanation except that the man was an overgrown Tom Sawyer; once Lincoln had reached Washington,
there was no earthly reason for mystery.) Lincoln's act in
wearing a soft hat was promptly magnified into the story that
he had come into town disguised, garbed in a plaid Scotch
cap and cloak, and the fact that this story could be printed
and believed is simply another evidence that people were
ready to believe anything at all: if Lincoln had encased his
lanky six feet four in Scotch plaids, he would have been
about as inconspicuous as the Washington Monument, an
eye-catching target for the dullest of assassins. The whole
trip had been mishandled, and the ending was the worst of
all. The man on whom the nation's fate was to depend had
seemed to come to the capital like a clown.[9]

But it was what he had been saying that disturbed thoughtful men. Charles Francis Adams, of Massachusetts, wrote of
his misgivings in a letter to Richard Henry Dana, just before
Lincoln arrived:

"As yet," he said, "I can form no opinion of the character

of the Chief. His speeches have fallen like a wet blanket here. They put to flight all notions of greatness. But he may yet prove true and honest and energetic, which will cover a multitude of minor deficiencies."[10]

3. Colonel Lee Leaves Texas

THIS WAS a winter when Americans began long journeys, moving from the West toward the East, from the known to the unknown, going separately and independently but somehow making part of one great, universal journey. Jefferson Davis had set off on his travels, and Abraham Lincoln had started his; and before either man reached his goal, Robert E. Lee also began to move, pulled east by the same force that was pulling the other two. For a brief time all three men were on the road at once, each of them deeply troubled in spirit, knowing that duty might require him to do hard and painful things which he would prefer not to do.

In a singular way, Lee began his journey more in the mood of Lincoln than in the mood of Davis. Davis had fewer doubts than either of the others. He knew, broadly, what he was supposed to do, and he knew how to set about it, and he neither knew nor cared what it might cost him. Lincoln and Lee took more doubts with them—doubts not only about the future but about the precise parts they themselves might have to play. Each man would say things, in the early stages of this journey, that he would not have said later. Each man would find the dimensions of the crisis enlarging as he came closer to it, his own probable role growing as the crisis grew; and each man would grow with the crisis itself, shaped by it but at the same time giving shape to it, becoming finally larger than life-size, a different man altogether than the one who began the journey.

As lieutenant colonel of the 2nd regular cavalry, Lee was stationed at Fort Mason, Texas. The commander of the Department of Texas, Brigadier General David Emanuel Twiggs, had passed along orders just received from the War Department: Lieutenant Colonel Lee was detached from his command and was to report to the general-in-chief, in Washington, for orders. On February 13 Lee put himself and his worldly goods in an army ambulance and set out on the first leg of the trip, heading for San Antonio, site of department headquarters.

Lee's orders were slightly out of the ordinary. A regular reassignment to routine duty would call on him to simply report to the War Department and would not involve a personal call on Winfield Scott. It seemed probable that the general-in-chief had a special assignment for Lee, and this would almost certainly have something to do with the government's military plans regarding the Southern Confederacy. Lee frankly told a brother officer that if this were the case he would resign. Under no circumstances could he draw his sword against Virginia and her sons. (He was assuming, obviously, that Virginia would eventually find herself in the Confederacy.) To another officer who asked bluntly what Lee proposed to do, he replied: "I shall never bear arms against the Union, but it may be necessary for me to carry a musket in defense of my native state, Virginia, in which case I shall not prove recreant to my duty." How he could bear arms in Virginia's defense without bearing arms against the Union was not clear, but the situation itself was not clear either. Earlier, Lee had coldly written that "secession is nothing but revolution," but he had felt obliged to add that he saw no charms in "a Union that can only be maintained by swords and bayonets"; he apparently clung to a dim hope that he and his state could in some way manage to be neutral in the approaching conflict, and to an even dimmer hope that in the end there would be no war at all.[1]

This latter hope grew noticeably weaker before he even got out of Texas. If Virginia had not yet seceded, Texas had, and when Lee entered San Antonio, the revolution that he disliked so much was visible all over town in the form of marching men, excited crowds, and an unmistakable air of general hostility to the government of the United States. Lee discovered, in fact, that he might be a prisoner of war before he left San Antonio, even though no war existed. General Twiggs had surrendered his entire department to the recently seceded state of Texas.

Twiggs was seventy, Georgia-born, a veteran of the War of 1812 and the Mexican War; tall, red-faced, with heavy white hair and an ear-to-ear beard, possessor of a sword with jeweled hilt and golden scabbard voted him by Congress for gallantry in action. Twiggs was on the side of the South and he made no bones about it, and he had been trying for many weeks to get a clear set of policy instructions from the War Department. In this effort he had had no more luck than Major Anderson had had, in faraway Fort Sumter, but he lacked Anderson's uncompromising sense of duty, and when armed Southerners invited him to give up, he obeyed without demur. In Twiggs's behalf it must be said that he had done his best to give Washington fair warning.

Early in December he had told the War Department that Texas would unquestionably secede before the winter ended, and he asked: "What is to be done with the public property in charge of the Army?" He got no reply, except for a vague statement that the administration had confidence that his "discretion, firmness and patriotism" would stand the test. He twice repeated his request for instructions, remarking early in January that "the crisis is fast approaching and ought to be looked in the face," and on January 15 he wrote to Winfield Scott formally asking to be relieved from duty. On January 28 this request was granted, and orders were issued removing Twiggs from command of the Department of Texas and instructing him to turn the command over to Colonel Carlos A. Waite, of the 1st U. S. Infantry. The War Department, however, was in no mood to be precipitate, and instead of telegraphing these orders, it simply mailed them. Neither Twiggs nor anyone else in Texas knew that he had been relieved, and late in January, Twiggs bluntly told Washington that since he did not think that anyone wanted him to "carry on a civil war against Texas" he would, once the state seceded, surrender government property to the state authorities if the state authorities asked him to do so. He pointed out that he had asked four times for instructions without getting any answer.[2]

The orders relieving Twiggs and appointing Waite finally reached San Antonio on February 15. Waite unfortunately was sixty miles away, at Camp Verde, and Twiggs was conferring with certain commissioners from the state of Texas about the Federal government's arms and military installations under his control. The situation was fluid, not to say confusing. A state convention on February 1 had voted Texas out of the Union, but the action was subject to ratification by a vote of the people in a referendum to be held on February 23. Technically, if anyone wanted to make a point

of it, Texas was still in the Union, and there was at least
a chance that the electorate would not ratify the act of
secession. (It was not a very bright chance, and it would
turn extremely dull if, by election day, the Federal government's top military man in Texas had surrendered.) On the
night of February 15—on muleback and on horseback and
on foot, devoid of uniforms but armed and waving the
Lone Star flag—Texas state troops began marching into
San Antonio, converging on the plaza, orderly but determined; their commander was Colonel Ben McCulloch, a
redoubtable frontiersman who had been friend and neighbor
to Davy Crockett and who had fought brilliantly in the
Mexican War. By morning of February 16 a thousand of
these troops were in town, ready to underline the state
commissioners' demands on Twiggs. The meeting with the
commissioners was abruptly broken off. Twiggs surveyed the
situation, found armed Texans surrounding government installations, then with his staff went back into conference with
the commissioners, who demanded that he give up all military
posts and public property forthwith.

Twiggs made only a token resistance. He had been given
no instructions, he was heart and soul with the South, to
reject the demand would have meant bloody fighting in the
streets of San Antonio, and in any case he was seventy and
in poor health, not ideally fitted to become a martyr for a
cause in which he did not believe. By the middle of the day
he gave up, signing an agreement under which his troops
would collect their weapons, clothing, and camp equipment
and march out of Texas unharmed. Orders were prepared
and sent out along the 1200-mile line where the army's
frontier posts and forts were scattered—there were more
than 2600 Federal soldiers in Texas, dispersed in small detachments all along the frontier—and the troops in San
Antonio got under way at once, moving out of their quarters
with flag flying and band playing, to make their first camp
that evening on the edge of town. San Antonio contained a
number of Unionists, who watched the little procession in
impotent indignation, but most of the people were enthusiastic secessionists.[3]

In the midst of all of this excitement the ambulance containing Colonel Lee came into town and pulled up in front
of the Read House, where Lee was to stop. As Lee got out

of the wagon he noticed that the street was full of armed men, some of them wearing strips of red flannel on their shoulders to show that they were officers. A friend met him, the Unionist-minded Mrs. Caroline Darrow, whose husband was a clerk in army department headquarters. Lee asked her who these men might be.

"They are McCulloch's," she said. "General Twiggs surrendered everything to the state this morning and we are all prisoners of war." Lee stared at her, and she wrote afterwards that his lips trembled and his eyes filled with tears as he exclaimed: "Has it come so soon as this?"

Lee's position was embarrassing. If Mrs. Darrow's story was right, he himself might at this moment be some sort of prisoner, although technically, since he had been detached from his command and ordered to Washington, he was no longer on duty in Texas, and hence should not be included in any list of officers who had been surrendered. He entered the hotel, changed his uniform for unobtrusive civilian clothing, and went to department headquarters. There he found that the story was all too true. The state of Texas was in control, and its representatives intimated that Lee might not be given transportation to get out of Texas unless he immediately resigned his commission and joined the Confederacy. This proposal he instantly rejected. He was an officer in the army, his orders were to report in Washington, and those orders he would obey—and, on consideration, the Texans decided not to try to stop him.

. . . A fascinating "if" develops at this point. A few months earlier, in Twiggs's absence, Lee had been acting commander of the Department of Texas. If the secession crisis had come to a head then, or if Twiggs's return had been delayed past mid-winter, it would have been Lee and not Twiggs on whom the Texas commissioners would have made their demand for the surrender of government property. Without any question, Lee would have given them a flat refusal—in which case it might easily have been Lee, and not Major Robert Anderson, who first received and returned the fire of the secessionists, with San Antonio, rather than Fort Sumter, as the scene of the fight that began a great war. Subsequent history could have been substantially different.

However, it did not happen that way. Lee made his arrangements for transportation to the coast, where he could

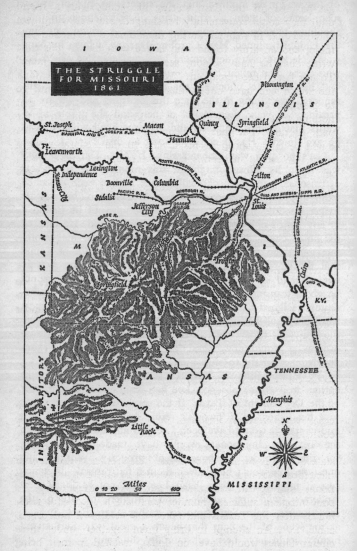

THE STRUGGLE
FOR MISSOURI
1861

get passage for the East, storing his goods with a friend until they could conveniently be shipped. He was withdrawn and reserved in manner during these final days in San Antonio, and an army friend who talked with him at this time wrote that he had "seldom seen a more distressed man." To this friend Lee remarked: "When I get to Virginia I think the world will have one soldier less. I shall resign and go to planting corn." To another friend, he said frankly that nothing that happened in Texas could swerve him from the path of duty, but that he believed his loyalty to Virginia ought to come ahead of his loyalty to the Federal government. He would make this clear, he said, to General Scott, and in the end he would do what Virginia did. If Virginia stayed in the Union, so would he; if Virginia went out, he would follow her, "with my sword, and if need be, with my life."[4]

He got to the coast, at last, on February 22, took a steamer to New Orleans, and reached his home at Arlington on March 1.

In Texas, meanwhile, secession became complete and final, Colonel Waite reached San Antonio on February 19, to take over the command of a department that no longer existed. The city was full of armed men, not all of them under complete control; there was a good deal of excited firing at nothing in the streets, and Northern men were making hasty arrangements to get their families and themselves out of the state. Everything the government owned in San Antonio was in the hands of the Texas authorities, and some of the army's outlying posts appeared to be in danger of attack by enthusiastic levies of citizen-soldiers. Colonel Waite, a Northerner with Northern instincts, found there was nothing he could do but accept the accomplished fact.

"No one at a distance can form a correct idea of the state of public feeling," he wrote. "The troops in this department are stationed at different camps or posts in small garrisons, and spread over a very large extent of country. To concentrate a sufficient number to make a successful resistance, after the Texans had taken the field, was not practicable. . . . An attempt to bring them together, under these circumstances would have, no doubt, resulted in their being cut up in detail before they could get out of the country. Under these circumstances I felt it my duty to comply with

the agreement entered into by General Twiggs and remove
the troops from the country as early as possible."[5]

At some of the remote camps there was infinite confusion.
The situation at Camp Cooper was typical. The probability
that Twiggs would do whatever Texas asked him to do was
recognized, even in advance of the surrender, and Captain
S. D. Carpenter, of the 1st U. S. Infantry, commanding at
Camp Cooper, warned his men on February 16 that the
place would very likely be attacked "by the identical persons
whose lives and property the Government have sent us here
to defend." In such case, he said, the garrison must defend
itself to the death: "In a strife like this we have but one
course to pursue, for each would rather lay his corpse to
molder upon the plain he defends than to drag it hence
to be the laugh and scorn of every honest lover of his country's glory." Three days later, however, Captain Carpenter
found himself obliged to eat his brave words, and to the
officer in command of the surrounding Texas troops he sent
a message of submission. Guided by "a spirit of patriotism
and loyalty to the Union, and by what I conceive to be the
counsels of the most enlightened of statesmen of the nation,
and also by what I understand to be the policy of the general commanding the department, after due consultation with
the officers of my command, I have determined to surrender
this camp to the State of Texas."[6]

In a sense all of this turmoil was unnecessary, because the
War Department was not looking for a fight in Texas any
more than General Twiggs was looking for one, and nothing
but the bureaucratic habit of trusting to the mails and letting time take care of itself kept this from being known to
everybody involved. On February 15, before McCulloch's
warriors had come trooping into San Antonio, the War
Department drafted instructions for Colonel Waite, who
would become Twiggs's successor as soon as he could reach
San Antonio. If Texas should secede (said these instructions), Waite must as quickly as possible "put in march for
Fort Leavenworth, the entire military force of your department." He was to use all army means of transportation, including camels—among the items of government property in
Texas were several dozens of these beasts, imported by Jefferson Davis when he was Secretary of War as likely burden-
bearers on the arid plains of the West—and any property

that had to be left behind was to be turned over to selected quartermasters, who would have the stuff sent on to New York by steamer at the earliest opportunity. The only trouble was that it seems to have occurred to nobody in Washington to send these orders by wire. If Twiggs had received them by February 16, as he might have done, he would have had at last the clear guidance that had been denied him, and everybody concerned would have been spared a good deal of mental anguish. But the orders were sent along by mail, and they did not reach San Antonio until March 1, when they meant nothing to anyone.

The scattered army detachments were on their way by this time. The state of Texas turned over twenty-six teams and wagons (transportation it probably had acquired by means of the Twiggs agreement) to help the movement along, and by the end of the month most of the men were on their way to the coast. Not all of Texas thought that the troops should be allowed to leave. The Federal commander at Camp Mason, which Colonel Lee had left just in time, got a curt note from the commander of a contingent of Texas Rangers, who told him bluntly: "I think the commissioners on the part of the State Of Texas are a set of jackasses in allowing the regular troops in leaving Texas with their arms; and, to be plain with you, if I had a sufficient force I would make all of you lay down your arms in short order, and if I can get men I will yet do it." Most of the troops finally made their way outside of the state, but more than 800 of them, including Colonel Waite, were captured and held as prisoners, to be released on parole a bit later. A San Antonio newspaper estimated that the army property seized was worth $1,209,500, not counting public buildings.[7]

The authorities in Washington from first to last lagged behind the movement of events in Texas. Long after he was completely unable to do anything about it, Colonel Waite received orders from General Scott to establish an entrenched camp at Indianola, on the Gulf Coast, with from 500 to 1200 men and supplies; the purpose of which, he was told, was "to keep a foothold in the State until the question of secession on her part be definitely settled among her own people, and, second, in case of conflict between them to give such aid and support to General Houston or other head of authority in the defense of the Federal government as

may be within your power."8 This came much too late. The
orders were signed on March 19, by which time Texas was
gone beyond recall. There was not the faintest chance that
Sam Houston would lead a counter-uprising, and even if he
had done so, there was not by this time anything Colonel
Waite could have done to help him.

Texas formally ratified the ordinance of secession on February 23, at a referendum election. The result surprised no
one. Secession carried by 46,129 votes to 14,697—figures
roughly the same as those by which Breckinridge had carried
the state over Constitution-and-Union Bell in the presidential
election. There may well have been more Unionist sentiment
in the state than these figures showed, but it had been
boxed in from the start. The secessionist leaders had acted
with drive and determination, the state convention by early
February had taken effective control of the state away from
Governor Houston, and the movement had acquired an irresistible momentum. General Twiggs's capitulation had
been the final touch; in plain fact Texas was out of the
Union before the election was held, and the voters did no
more than ratify something that had already happened.
Shortly after the election, the convention passed a resolution
thanking Twiggs "for his patriotism, moral courage and
loyalty to the Constitution of the United States, embracing
the rights and liberty of his native South." On March 2
Texas delegates reached Montgomery and the state was
formally admitted to the Confederacy. Georgia's Tom Cobb
wrote to his wife that "the Texas members are a very con-
ceited crowd and very little of enlarged statesmanship about
them."9

Now there were seven states in the Southern Confederacy,
and the secessionist tide had reached its crest; as a matter
of fact, it had for the moment expended all of its force.
There would be no more departures based simply on the belief that the election of a Republican President embodied
an unendurable menace to Southern institutions. Eight of
the fifteen slave states remained in the Union, and none of
them would go out unless and until the Federal government,
or the Confederate government, or the two of them together,
brought some new element into the equation. The South had
not acted as a unit. Only the cotton states had broken

away. The new "Southern nation" included only about half of the South.

Not even in the cotton states was the impulse to leave the Union as sweeping and unanimous as it came to seem. South Carolina had indeed been wholly united, but in the six states that followed her, there were fairly substantial numbers of people who, if they were not thick-or-thin Unionists, at least were not ready for immediate secession. Only Texas had submitted its ordinance of secession to a popular vote; in all the others the only thing resembling a referendum had been the election of delegates to state conventions, and here the figures make curious reading. A recent student of these elections has estimated that in Mississippi, Alabama, Georgia, and Louisiana at least 42 per cent of those who voted must be listed as opponents of immediate secession. Significantly, secession took place on a state-by-state basis, and the various efforts to have the matter considered by a general convention of Southern states all failed. Throughout, the leaders of the secession campaign had worked for speedy action, in order that the new government might be set up and in operation by the time the new administration took office in Washington.[10]

The Confederate government that was thus brought into being did not when it was established speak for the old South, and it was not in fact defending an old established culture. It represented rather the raw, bustling, new South which was making immense profits out of slave-produced cotton—basically a frontier society in which the acquisition of land and slaves stood as the visible symbols of prosperity and the ability to better one's position in the world. This society saw in the growth of abolitionism not merely a stirring-up of profound racial antagonisms but also a direct threat to the boom times that enabled an energetic go-getter to make his stake. The new government might come to represent much more than this later on, but this was its original basis. It would take actual violence—the firing of great guns, with battle smoke drifting out to sea—to broaden the base.

Handicapped as it was by imperfect communications and an inability to make any move quickly, Washington may have had some dim awareness of this fact. It is mildly interesting to note that the Federal government actually had much more at stake in Texas than it had at Fort Sumter; 2600 soldiers and a whole chain of army installations, as opposed to seventy soldiers and one unfinished fort. Logically, it would seem that if a stand were to be made, San Antonio rather than Charleston would be the place to make it. But Washington was marking time. It consented to the loss of Texas, and the Federal government did no more than issue, on March 1, a formal order stating that by direction of the President, General Twiggs was dismissed from the army "for his treachery to the flag of his country."

This infuriated Twiggs, who felt that he had properly followed a higher loyalty, and some weeks after Buchanan left office, the old general sent him a bitter letter: "Your usurped right to dismiss me from the army might be acquiesced in, but you had no right to brand me as a traitor. This was personal, and I shall treat it as such, not through the papers but in person. I shall more assuredly pay a visit to Lancaster" [in Pennsylvania, where Buchanan made his home] "for the sole purpose of a personal interview with you. So sir prepare yourself. I am well assured that public opinion will sanction *any course* I may take with you."[11]

In the language of Twiggs's time and place that meant a duel and nothing less. But Twiggs did not, in the end, go to Pennsylvania, and the country was spared the grotesque spectacle of a personal encounter between two seventy-year-olds. On the day Twiggs was dismissed from the army, Robert E. Lee reached his home in Arlington.

4. Talking Across a Gulf

WHEN LINCOLN reached Washington on February 23, with derisive newspaper articles repeating untruths about a Scotchplaid disguise, he had just nine days to prepare himself for the presidency. He needed more time. He had said, too easily, that nobody was being hurt, and although this was no more than a natural attempt to relieve public tension, it reflected a misconception of the situation. Lincoln overestimated the extent and power of Union sentiment in the South. He apparently failed to realize that the border states had by no means shelved the idea of secession for good and that what they did might in the end depend largely on what

he himself did. He could see clearly that the Southern Confederacy had been created by a comparatively small group
of expert operators, but he did not yet see that the Confederacy was much more than just the result of a smart
conspiracy. It was a new nation which, even though it stood
on very shaky legs, could not be talked out of existence.

His immediate problems were almost overwhelming. He
had to finish making his cabinet, he had to talk endlessly with
many important people, and he was under tremendous pressure from needy Republicans who wanted jobs under the new
government and who believed in going to the man at the top
to demand them. His rooms at Willard's Hotel were no
refuge. Everybody in Washington, seemingly, wanted to get
into them. He would have very little time to think.

Congress was in session, grappling with such Republican
platform planks as a new tariff bill, a Pacific railroad, and
internal improvements, doing nothing whatever either to
conciliate the offended Southern states or to enable the Federal government to deal forcefully with them. In Virginia a
secession convention was meeting under circumstances that
may have added to Lincoln's confusion. The outright secessionists had been able to elect only about thirty of the 152
delegates, but at least seventy of the rest of the delegates
were secessionists at heart—men who would vote the state
out of the Union the moment the trend of events in Washington displeased them. The convention now was marking
time, waiting to see what was going to happen farther north.[1]
And in Washington there was a peace convention, watched
anxiously both by Congress and by the Virginians, meeting
behind closed doors at Willard's and showing few indications
that it was going to accomplish anything.

Virginia was responsible for this convention's existence.
On January 19 the Virginia General Assembly had adopted
a joint resolution calling for a conference of all the states
in Washington, and the business had got under way on February 4. It was off to an unencouraging start, sharply criti-
cized by the press for meeting in secrecy, and its 131 members—distinguished Americans, but elderly, a little tired and
shopworn—spoke for only twenty-one of the states. None
of the seven states that had seceded was represented. Neither
were the West Coast states of California and Oregon, the
Southern state of Arkansas, nor the Middle Western states

of Wisconsin, Michigan, and Minnesota. It was no better than a pale copy of the true national convention which had been proposed in Congress immediately after the election, and the chance that it would devise a program that could pull the sections together and harmonize their bitter differences was very slight. The New York *Herald* had remarked, perhaps with some injustice, that the delegates "are for the most part the emanations of the grog-shop and other low influences which direct the politics of their respective states. They are, moreover, many of them political fossils, who would not have been disinterred but for the shock given to the Union by the secession movement." The *Herald* added that it was both "stupid and ungrateful" of the delegates to exclude the press from their sittings. Horace Greeley's New York *Tribune* was equally pessimistic although less brutal, predicting that "the Border State compromise convention" could do nothing useful: "The seceding states have taken no part in it, and their most influential statesmen and journals have already expressed their contempt for any such attempt to patch up a truce between them and the United States." Off stage, Michigan's tough Senator Zachariah Chandler was muttering that some of the Northern manufacturing states were altogether too nervous about the prospect of a fight, and was saying that "without a little bloodletting this Union will not, in my estimation, be worth a rush."[2]

From the start the delegates had trouble. Former President John Tyler presided, calling upon the convention to achieve "a triumph over party"—which, he believed, would cause "a long, loud shout of joy and gladness" to resound across the country—but when the resolutions committee got down to work, it was clear that a triumph over party would be hard to attain. Republican delegates from the North were consistently obstructionist, some of Virginia's representatives showed a substantial lack of enthusiasm, and it was three weeks before the resolutions committee could agree on a program—which, when it was unveiled, proved to be nothing more than a watered-down version of the compromise that Senator Crittenden had fought for so unsuccessfully in Congress. The old Missouri Compromise line would be extended to the West Coast, with slavery prohibited in territories north of the line and protected in territories south of it; Congress would be forbidden to interfere with slavery in states or territories, the fugitive slave law was to be stiffened (in a way no one quite understood), intricate restrictions were laid on the acquisition of additional territory by the United States—and, all in all, the program satisfied hardly anyone and was visibly inadequate to bear the load it would have to carry.[3]

Yet this conference was about all the hope that remained. The most anyone could say regarding the last four months was that war had not yet actually begun. No one had backed down or had a change of heart; it was just that the final shock that would produce explosion had not yet been delivered. As long as this peace conference remained in session, there might still be a chance to settle things. Men of good will were at least bound to make the effort.

Actually, the delegates were men calling across a wide gulf through an unquiet dusk. Misunderstanding was communicating with misunderstanding, and inadequate answers were being returned to meaningless questions. Lincoln met one evening, late in February, with a number of the delegates, but the conversations were not fruitful. When William C. Rives, of Virginia, told him soberly "Everything now depends on you," Lincoln replied that he could not agree. "My course," he said, "is as plain as a turnpike road. It is marked out by the Constitution. I am in no doubt which way to go. Suppose now we all stop discussing and try the experiment of obedience to the Constitution and laws. Don't you think that would work?" Lincoln's path might indeed be clear—to him, at least, if not to all of his fellow countrymen—but a general appeal for obedience to the Constitution meant nothing at all, because the Constitution meant such different things to different men.

From the sepulchral James A. Seddon, of Virginia, who would become Secretary of War in the Confederate government before two years were out, Lincoln in his turn got nothing to indicate that sectional understanding could yet be found if good men looked for it. Seddon, lean and pallid and intense, could do no better than lodge a broad bill of complaint against Yankeedom in general, as if Illinois and Massachusetts shared in one unshaded response to the intricacies of the slavery problem. The North (said Mr. Seddon) failed to suppress its John Browns and its William Lloyd Garrisons; it refused to execute the fugitive slave laws, and it nourished an incendiary press that advocated servile insurrection "and advises our slaves to cut their masters' throats." To this Lincoln replied that "a gentleman of your intelligence should not make such assertions," adding that the North did indeed maintain a free press, considering it necessary in a free society; and the whole exchange proved nothing, except perhaps that tidewater aristocracy and northwest democracy had very little to say to one another.

When William D. Dodge, of New York, inspired by some conciliatory remark, asked hopefully if Lincoln would "yield to the just demands of the South" and would refuse to go to war over slavery, Lincoln replied soberly that it would be his solemn duty to execute the office of President and defend the Constitution, continuing: "The Constitution will not be preserved and defended until it is enforced and obeyed in every part of every one of the United States. It must be so respected, obeyed, enforced and defended, let the grass grow where it may."

In deeply somber mood he told a New Jersey delegate that "in a choice of evils, war may not always be the worst" —a fairly grim sort of warning, considering the decisions Lincoln would have to make in the near future—and he went on (as one listener recalled it) to speak his mind on the underlying issue:

"As to slavery, it must be content with what it has. The voice of the civilized world is against it; it is opposed to its growth or extension. Freedom is the natural condition of the human race, in which the Almighty intended men to live. Those who fight the purposes of the Almighty will not succeed. They always have been, and they always will be, beaten."[4]

In all of this there was very little oil for the troubled waters. At about this time Senator Charles Sumner was writing to Governor John A. Andrew, of Massachusetts, that he believed Virginia would certainly leave the Union. The peace conference, Sumner felt, could do nothing to restore harmony, and everybody very soon would have to face "the question of enforcing the laws or retaking the forts—in other words of our existence as a Govt." If Lincoln stood firm, said Sumner, the Union cause could be saved; and, so far, "all that we see testifies to his character." As if he realized the powerful influences that would push the new President this way and that, Sumner added darkly: "But *he is a man!*" Two days later Charles Francis Adams, Jr., wrote to Governor Andrew that Sumner was far too excitable, and that the important question just now was not so much what Lincoln would do as what Seward would do. Everyone in Washington, said Adams, was waiting for a lead, and if Lincoln would support the conciliatory efforts that Seward was making, it might yet be possible to "save us the country without the loss of anything save many fair words."[5]

Seward was doing his best. He had spoken in the old days about a higher law and an irrepressible conflict, so that Southerners considered him an extremist who meant nothing but evil for the South. But the Seward who was about to become Secretary of State (and, as he then believed, the real leader and shaper of policy for an untried administration) was talking much more gently than the Seward who had been out to win a militant party's nomination for the presidency. Whether he was busy on the Senate floor and in its cloakrooms or was talking confidentially in the drawing rooms of the homes of friends, he seemed leisurely and unworried, sure that the country could be led out of its dire predicament. He said openly, early in February, that he thought the danger was over, and the elder Charles Francis Adams wrote that Seward semed to be the only Republican in the capital "who comprehends the nature and treatment of the present malady." As Adams saw it, the important victory had already been won, "the slave question is substantially settled by the last election," and the Republican leadership would commit an immense blunder if it let this be followed by an actual dissolution of the Union. The leadership must be moderate; instead of meeting the threat of secession by angry talk and threats, it must be ready to make the concessions that would encourage pro-Union men in the South and hold the loyalty of the border states, and if this involved giving the South a constitutional amendment with "safeguards" for slavery, what of it? Slavery itself was on the downhill road, and the important thing now was to deprive the secessionist movement of the support which it had to have in such states as Virginia. If this could be done, the movement would fail, "and we shall never again hear of secession as a *legal* remedy."[6]

To this, or something like it, Seward was addressing himself. One night Senator Douglas gave a dinner for the French Minister, Mercier. When the table was cleared and it was time for toasts, Seward called on the guests to fill their glasses to the brim and to be prepared to drain them to the bottom; and then, raising his own glass, he offered his toast— "Away with all parties, all platforms, all previous committals and whatever else will stand in the way of the restoration of the American Union." A little later, Senator Crittenden brought Seward into intimate conversation with Justice John A. Campbell, of the Supreme Court. Justice Campbell was a good Alabaman, born in Georgia, who would finally go with his state, once the sections came to a showdown; but he was a moderate on the slavery question, a man who still hoped to see the Union preserved, and now, in Senator Crittenden's presence, he explained his position to Seward.

Slavery, said Campbell, ought not to form a cause for a break-up of the Union. Slavery was a transitory institution. It would inevitably be greatly modified or abolished altogether in the course of time. Modification, in fact, was already taking place; for many years slavery had been steadily receding from the upper south to the rich plantation belt around the mouth of the Mississippi. That was where slavery was really thriving, and it would probably be a quarter of a century before that area's expanding needs for slave labor were fully met. Seward quietly interrupted: "Say fifty years." Campbell accepted the correction: fifty years, then, not twenty-five—fifty years, in all, before the institution would have reached the final limit of its development. Meanwhile, the most the slavery group could hope for was the continued protection of slavery in the states. In the territories the battle was lost—New Mexico, well south of the Missouri Compromise line, had been open to slave immigration for a full decade, and only twenty-nine slaves had been carried there. (Again Seward broke in: "Only twenty-four, sir.") Twenty-four: in ten years, under full protection of the laws. Was there any sense, asked the Justice, in letting the Union be destroyed over the question of slavery in the territories when slavery obviously was not going to establish itself in the territories in any case? Seward agreed that there was not.

The talk ended in nothing better than the glow of agreement between the Northerner and the Southerner. Seward walked over to a table and dealt himself a hooker of brandy, and Justice Campbell heard him tell Senator Douglas and Senator Crittenden that his latest information was that Governor Chase, of Ohio, would surely be in Lincoln's cabinet, but that Seward had no real assurance he himself would be in it. The point of this was that Chase was an anti-slavery stalwart as unyielding as Senator Sumner; if his place was sure and Seward's was not, the chance that the new administration would take a conciliatory position toward the South was slim indeed. Seward shrugged: What can I do? The Senators shook their heads and said they could see his situation.[7]

So the talk never led to anything: Seward and Campbell went their separate ways and the sections of the country did the same; yet there is a haunting, tantalizing quality to the report of this conversation, for it is one of the few lights of hope that comes down to us from the fated months that led up to the war. What Seward and Campbell were agreeing was that the slavery issue, considered rationally, had already gone past the flash point. Only in the Gulf states did slavery retain its old dynamic power, and even there it was beginning to live on borrowed time. It would inevitably come down to manageable proportions if men would only let it do so; Justice Campbell was saying that the anti-slavery men of the North had already gained what Lincoln said they wanted most of all—the assurance that slavery was inevitably on the road to extinction. It remained for reasonable men (in the quiet drawing room, between the intoned toasts and the final sip of brandy) to stop haggling over non-essentials and to agree on some way to make the institution's demise as seemly and as inexpensive as might be.

But it was being said too late and too privately. Here is what many leaders of the North and South should have been saying publicly, in political conventions and on campaign platforms, for a year and more. No one had done it. The climate in which a politician might find the courage to talk sober sense about the most emotion-ridden of all issues had not existed, possibly because no one had seemed to want it to exist. Instead of the great debate which might truly have shown people that the cause of their dreadful quarrel was slowly but surely evaporating, unseen, there had been desperate appeals to pride, to principle, to all of the moral imperatives that have a way of riding down the wind just ahead of the fatal bugle calls. Now a Southern Confederacy existed, a beleaguered fort was surrounded by dozens and scores of shotted guns in the Carolina swamps, a hopeless peace convention was consuming the last of its time with bumbling futilities . . . and off stage, unseen, not yet even in existence but surely fated to exist very soon, waited the terrible armies of unknowing boys who would presently be tramping their way across the bewildered country.

Seward and Campbell got nowhere. They were neither heard nor followed; and perhaps, when all is said and done, they could not have got anywhere no matter who might have heard or followed them. Perhaps it was not really possible for slavery to die peacefully and quietly, while everyone waited hat in hand for the mills of God to finish their grinding. Perhaps the essential fact about slavery was that it could neither be kept alive nor done to death *rationally*. Its foundations went far down into the pit, down to blackest wrong and violence, and when the foundations were torn out, wrong and violence would surely be loosed for a season. The institution's defenders had both overplayed their hands and overstayed their time.

One of Lincoln's troubles was the weight of the mechanical details which had to be borne by the first President elected by a new party. The Republican party on the eve of Lincoln's inauguration was less a political organization than an assemblage of separate factions each with its own leadership and its own shibboleths, loosely united by the requirements of a victorious campaign but enjoying only the vaguest basis for real unity. A great many of these men were much more concerned with party power than with the national crisis. They would cheerfully tear one another to shreds in the scramble for control, and to some of them, at least, secession was welcome because it got so many Democrats out of Washington. Altogether, with their intense rivalries, their hot ambitions, their driving attempts to win place and preferment, these men constituted the instrument through which Lincoln would have to try to govern a dissolving nation. If Lincoln felt that his first task was to get this instrument into some sort of order, so that when he took office he would at least have something to govern with, it is hard to criticize him. He may have failed to appraise the real temper of the South, but he at least knew the temper of his own party. He was undertaking now to bind the separate party factions together, and in this effort—for the first time since he left Springfield—he was beginning to show real statesmanship.

The first step of course was the selection of a cabinet, and here Lincoln was creating a coalition of antagonistic Republicans, trusting to his own powers of leadership and of decision to master the separate elements and to impose on the coalition his own policies. It was a daring step; he was going to surround himself with the very men who had fought against him at Chicago, and at least a few of these considered themselves stronger and wiser than he was and believed that they had more prestige and power in the party and with the voters. He would, for instance, have Seward for his Secretary of State, and his Secretary of the Treasury would be Salmon P. Chase: and these two men, so different in personality and outlook, were so bitterly opposed about the proper policy regarding slavery and secession that Seward a few days before the inauguration was doubtful whether he could serve at all and was considering a flat rejection of the cabinet post. (If Seward stayed out, the party would be split wide open, and the younger Adams was gloomily predicting that the party's cause and principles would be set back by a full ten years.) Seward was working hard for conciliation; Chase—devoted, self-righteous, ambitious, spokesman for the unyielding anti-slavery faction—was arguing that the South must first of all accept the fact of the Republican victory. Once the new party was in office with the controls in its hands, there would be time enough (as Chase saw it) to see about a reconstruction of the divided Union.

For Attorney General, Lincoln would have Edward Bates, of Missouri, a stolid border-state Unionist, Missouri's favorite son at the Wigwam. Also from the border-state tier came Montgomery Blair, of Maryland, son of the contentious old-line Jacksonian Francis P. Blair, a political feudist known irreverently in some quarters as "Death on a Pale Horse." Montgomery Blair would be Postmaster General; his selection meant that "the Blair family" would have influence with the new administration—altogether too much influence, its numerous rivals would complain. New England would be represented by Gideon Welles, of Connecticut, an observant, petulant, but fair-minded former Democrat, who would be Secretary of the Navy. Welles knew little more about the navy than the average politician who finds himself called upon to run the Navy Department, but he would prove a capable executive once he found his way around the department; he would also show rather more of an instinct for loyalty toward the man who appointed him than some of his colleagues would ever display.

The remaining two places represented political bargains allegedly made by Lincoln's managers at Chicago. Secretary of the Interior would be Caleb Smith, of Indiana, a party hack who represented a handful of votes at the Wigwam and nothing more; and the Secretary of War would be Pennsylvania's Simon Cameron, whom Lincoln appointed with deepest misgivings simply because the political heat which Cameron had been able to bring to bear seemed irresistible. Before the year was out, it would be clear that all of Lincoln's misgivings had been justified.

This, then, was the group that would serve as the new President's confidential advisers. It was a unique assortment. Five of the seven had been rivals of Lincoln for the party nomination; four of the seven had at one time or another been Democrats; not one of the lot came from Illinois or had enjoyed any intimacy with Lincoln before the campaign. Whatever else might be said of them all, it was at least true that they did represent the separate elements in the chaotic new party. If Lincoln could control them, he might have a strong government. Choosing these men, he had shown that he was either a complete political innocent or a man of such strength and subtlety that he felt no fear in surrounding himself with men as strong as himself.[8]

It would take time to see this. As February came to an end, men were trying to determine who was going to be the power behind the throne, taking it for granted that the new President was so weak that there would be such a power somewhere. Young Adams continued to hope that this power would be Seward, who was working constantly to keep Lincoln from falling under the control of the "iron-back Republican" combination symbolized by Chase. It was Adams's belief that his own father was at one time slated to go into the cabinet, and that Seward had felt obliged to sacrifice him in favor of Cameron in order to build a proper fence around Chase. Congressman Sherrard Clemens, of Virginia, concluded that the Republican party was already demoralized and disrupted; its factions could never work together, and Lincoln himself—"a cross between a sandhill crane and an Andalusian jackass"—was by all odds the weakest man who had ever been sent to the White House. Virginia, said Clemens, must presently secede because this President-elect was simply impossible: "He is vain, weak, puerile, hypocritical, without manners, without moral grace, and as he talks to you he *punches* you under your ribs. . . . He is surrounded by a set of toad eaters and bottle holders."[9]

Everyone wanted to know what the new government was going to do, but first it was necessary to know what the new government was going to be. No one knew. The true center of power was not yet visible.

5. Pressure at Fort Sumter

THE SOLDIERS had not yet been called into action but they were busy, and the materials to force a decision were piling up—in Fort Sumter, and on the mud flats that surrounded it in Charleston harbor. Major Anderson was doing what he could to perfect his defenses, mounting additional guns on the barbette, making his walls more solid by bricking up embrasures that could not be manned, removing stone flagging from the parade ground so that shells that might be thrown into the fort would bury themselves in the sand before exploding. He was also running short of fuel, and his men were dismantling temporary wooden barracks to get firewood. He believed that he might yet avoid a fight, and to a friend he wrote expressing the belief that "the separation which has been inevitable for months will be consummated without the shedding of one drop of blood." But the local papers kept printing reports that Federal reinforcements were on the way, and he feared this might lead hotheads to open an attack on him. Certainly the batteries that surrounded him were being strengthened day after day; under the circumstances he could do no more than hold on and, hoping for the best, prepare for the worst.[1]

The worst was taking shape before his eyes. South Carolina had put powerful weapons in position, its guard boats kept a night-and-day watch on the harbor, and it was becoming increasingly obvious that if Washington tried to reinforce him, it would have to mount a full-dress war expedition. Furthermore, the South Carolina authorities were becoming exceedingly impatient, and their impatience was almost as much a problem in Montgomery as in Washington. They wanted this fort captured, and they wanted it done before Abraham Lincoln should become President. South Carolina had forced the pace ever since the secession convention of December 20, and Governor Pickens could see no reason for a change in tactics.

Everybody but Pickens wanted to mark time. Washington could do nothing until the new administration came in, and whether it could do anything effective thereafter seemed an open question. Montgomery was in no better shape; it had to create a new government, and it did not want the first uncertain steps to be taken in the midst of a shooting war. But Governor Pickens wanted action, and he began demanding it before the Southern Confederacy even had a chief executive. On February 7 he sent a breathless telegram to Porcher Miles, at Montgomery: "There is danger ahead unless you give us immediately a strong organized government & take jurisdiction of all military defence we will soon be forced into a war of sections unless you act quickly it will be too late & reaction will commence which will inaugurate confusion & with it the most fatal consequences." A day later he sent a "did you get my telegram?" follow-up, asking whether the new government was sending commissioners to Washington to demand surrender of the forts and repeating "Every hour is now deeply important."[2]

Miles tried to restrain him, pointing out that South Carolina could no longer go it alone and offering both a sop and a warning for state pride.

"It seems to me," wrote Miles, "we ought not to attack Ft. Sumter without authority from the Confederate government. I cannot see that the short delay compromises the honor of the State in the least—if—when the attack is ordered—South Carolina troops alone engage in it. We do not ask our Confederate States to help us take it. But our attack necessarily plunges the new government into war with the United States and that before they (our Confederates) are prepared. This would be the inevitable consequence for surely the United States government as soon as we open with our batteries upon Sumter will be bound by every consideration to send relief and assistance to Major Anderson and his handful of men, who is holding his post by the express orders of his Government. Might not our attack be considered as 'making war' which the Provisional Constitution restrains a State from doing except in case of invasion?"

Miles went on: would not South Carolina's dignity suffer if she immediately began imploring the Confederacy to come to her aid? The delegates at Montgomery knew all about the situation at Charleston, and it was up to them to suggest what ought to happen next. Furthermore, Governor Pickens ought to realize that the President of the Confederacy would appoint his own general to take charge of the operation, because "a general of our appointment might not be acceptable to the President-elect and thus jealousy and distraction and inefficiency would result."[3]

The new government actually was losing very little time. On February 12 it resolved to take charge of "the questions and difficulties now existing between the several States of this Confederacy and the Government of the United States relating to the occupation of the forts, arsenals, navy yards and other public establishments," and three days later the Confederate Congress unanimously agreed to take possession of the disputed properties "either by negotiations or force, as early as practicable." President Davis, who had not yet formally been installed in office, was authorized to "make all necessary military preparations" for such a step. In return, Pickens sent the Confederate Congress a letter, reciting South Carolina's grievances in connection with the continued occupation of Fort Sumter and pointing out that Washington's denial of the state's right to take over the fort was in fact a denial of the state's independence. Arrangements to reduce the fort, he said, were just about complete, and he assumed that when they were completed, everyone would agree that the blow should be struck. He summed up his argument bluntly:

"Fort Sumter should be reduced before the close of the present administration at Washington. If an attack is delayed until after the inauguration of the incoming President of the United States, the troops now gathered in the capital

may then be employed in attempting that which, previous to
that time, they could not be spared to do. . . . If war can
be averted, it will be by making the capture of Fort Sumter
a fact accomplished during the continuance of the present
Administration, and leaving to the incoming Administration
the question of an open declaration of war. . . . Mr. Buchanan cannot resist because he has not the power. Mr. Lincoln
may not attack, because the cause of quarrel will have been,
or may be considered by him, as past." The governor
went on to say that if war did at last come he would of
course regret it, but it would simply show that "under the
evil passions which blind and mislead those who govern the
United States, no human power could have arrested the
attempted overthrow of these States."[4]

Jefferson Davis moved quickly to get the power of decision out of Governor Pickens's hands and into his own—
a feat that took a little doing. On February 23 Davis sent
Major W. H. C. Whiting, a West Point graduate and a
capable engineer officer, off to Charleston harbor to survey
the situation. After Whiting got there, Pickens sent Davis
another impatient dispatch: "We would desire to be informed
if when thoroughly prepared to take the fort shall we
do so, or shall we await your order; and shall we demand
surrender, or will that demand be made by you?" Back
promptly came a message from the new Confederate War
Department: "This Government assumes the control of military operations at Charleston, and will make demand of the
fort when fully advised. An officer goes tonight to take
charge." In more soothing vein, the message confessed that
South Carolina's perhaps excessive ardor, "natural and just
as it is admitted to be," would have to yield to "the necessity of the case." When the blow was struck it would have
to be successful, since the price of a failure would be disastrous; meanwhile, the officer who was being sent to Charleston to take charge would, on his arrival, muster into the
provisional service of the Confederacy the South Carolina
troops that were on duty at Charleston.[5]

In plain English, Davis was not going to have this job
ruined by a set of impatient politicians. He would take over
the negotiations regarding the possible surrender of Fort
Sumter—official representatives of his government were
already on their way to Washington to press the case with

Lincoln, or with Seward, or with anyone they could talk to—and he would get a competent soldier into Charleston to handle the military end of things. If a war was to begin at Fort Sumter, it at least would not begin just because some local bigwig gave way to blind enthusiasm. South Carolina would lead the parade no longer.

The implications of all this were clear enough, and bad enough. One way or another, Fort Sumter was going to be taken—if not today, then a little bit later. Washington could give up the fort or fight; the choice that was going to be presented to the new administration would be, simply, to back down or make war. And the choice would be offered, not by a lone state that was going its own way with blind arrogance, but by the South itself. The time for temporizing was just about over.

Meanwhile, efforts to assuage Governor Pickens continued. Porcher Miles wrote him a long letter, insisting that everyone in Montgomery agreed that the fort ought to be taken at the earliest possible moment and that it was necessary to "restrain the ardor of our troops for *a few days only*." The sole point that was bothering President Davis, said Miles, was the question: "Are we able with present preparations to take the fort?" On this point, he confessed, "we are all in the dark," but better light would be available very soon, and whenever it could be said that "our batteries can with reasonable certainty reduce Fort Sumter, we will do everything to hasten the attack."

Other words of caution came from, of all people, William L. Yancey, who found himself for the first time counseling moderation and delay. Yancey confessed that he had hoped South Carolina could take the fort before the Confederate government was organized, but that time had passed. "I can but give you the settled assurance of my mind," Yancey wrote to Pickens, "that if the Fort shall be assaulted without the orders of the Executive of the Confederate States, it will produce a confusion, an excitement, an indignation and astonishment here in the Confed. Congress that will tend to break up the new government."[6]

With Yancey himself talking so gently, even Governor Pickens might feel a little restraint. A more important factor, however, undoubtedly lay in the choice Davis made when

he sent a military commander to Charleston to take charge
of the operations in the name of the Confederate government. He selected a man whose personality and talents would
play a large part in the history of the Confederacy—the
dapper, self-confident, and gifted Creole, Pierre Gustave
Toutant Beauregard, recently a captain in the United States
Army, now a brigadier general in the provisional army of
the Confederate states. Beauregard was just the man to help
the Charlestonians digest the idea that a higher authority
was taking over.

Beauregard was in his early forties; small, vigorous, graceful, his graying hair maintained in glossy blackness by
judicious application of hair dye, a man who wore ex-
quisitely tailored uniforms with an air, pleasant but unsmil-
ing, with faultless manners. He bore a good professional
reputation; had been an engineer officer on Scott's staff in the
Mexican War, where he had been twice wounded and had
twice won brevets for gallantry, had served for one brief
week, in January of 1861, as superintendent of the Military
Academy at West Point, resigning that position to follow
his state, Louisiana, out of the Union. He had enough social
position to impress even the Charlestonians, and he immediately captivated not only Governor Pickens but everyone
else in South Carolina. Shortly after his arrival he wrote that
he was greatly pleased with the people of Charleston, "who
are so much like ours in La. that I see but little difference
in them."

Beauregard reached Charleston on March 3, met with
Governor Pickens and a concourse of leading citizens at the
governor's headquarters in the Charleston Hotel, and immediately got down to work. He was taken on long tours of
the military installations, during which he learned that all
of the "high-spirited gentlemen" who accompanied him had
made elaborate plans for the reduction of the fort; he listened
attentively, and was able to shelve these plans without giving
offense to the planners. It did not take him long to discover
that there was a great deal to be done.

Fort Sumter itself, he realized, would be "a perfect Gibral-
tar" if it were properly garrisoned and armed. The weakness of its garrison was his greatest advantage, and the obvious strategy was to make certain that the garrison remain

weak—in other words, to mount guns so that the Federal government would find it impossible to reinforce the place. Tactfully but firmly, he began to rearrange the batteries, concentrating on sealing off the harbor rather than on simply piling up the armaments that would fire on Fort Sumter itself. Along the sandy shores of Morris and Sullivan's islands he built new detached batteries, devised to control the seaward approaches. The defenses at Fort Moultrie were rebuilt, mortar batteries were put where the guns of Fort Sumter could not reach them, and Major Anderson's lookouts could see signs of new activity all around the harbor. Anderson and Beauregard, incidentally, were no strangers. Years ago, when Anderson was an instructor in artillery at West Point, Cadet Beauregard had been one of his students, and had shown such talent that Anderson had had him retained as an assistant instructor.[7]

Beauregard was sensitive to points of pride and honor. In effect he was making a complete change in the military installations around the harbor, but he was fully aware that the South Carolina troops he was commanding were not at all like the regular soldiers of the old army. They were, as he saw them, "gallant and sensitive gentlemen" who had left comfortable homes "to endure the privations and exposures of a solider's life" on bleak and comfortless islands where harsh winds from the sea kicked up annoying sand storms. Among the private soldiers were planters and the sons of planters, some of them the wealthiest men in South Carolina, proud as Lucifer, doing pick-and-shovel work in many cases alongside of their own slaves; and they had to be handled with some delicacy. This delicacy Beauregard had, and although he was undoing much that they had worked hard to do, they made no complaints. Instead they quickly made Beauregard their idol.[8]

Control of things at Charleston, accordingly, passed into the hands of the Confederate government with a minimum of difficulty, and Jefferson Davis had passed his first acid test. He had at least made it certain that the war would not be begun through sheer irresponsibility. The harebrained plan to start the shooting before Lincoln could take office, on the theory that this would somehow put the Federal government at a crippling disadvantage, had been quietly laid to rest. Thrust so suddenly into a position where he must create a new government against the most profound handicaps, Davis had won at least a little of the time he needed so desperately. He had had, too, his first encounter with a problem that was finally to prove insoluble, even though this first encounter had been successful—the necessity for adjusting the eternal clamor of states' rights to the overriding requirements of the central government.

Davis was formally inaugurated President on February 18, in an impressive ceremony on a platform built in front of the portico of the state capitol at Montgomery. There was a parade, with a six-horse team of matched grays pulling the presidential carriage, with brightly uniformed militia companies marching, with cannon firing salutes, and with 10,000 people crowding around to see and hear. When the party reached the platform, and Howell Cobb, as President of the Confederate Congress, presented a Bible and administered the oath of office, there was a breathless silence, in which Davis's "So help me God" rang out clearly. An impressionable correspondent for the New York *Herald,* deeply moved, wrote that "God does not permit evil to be done with such earnest solemnity, such all-pervading trust in His Providence, as was exhibited by the whole people on that day," and an Alabama lady wrote that the slim, erect figure of the new President made her think of General Andrew Jackson, "though he is much more a gentleman in his manners than the old General ever *wished* to be." The editor of the Montgomery *Weekly Advertiser* concluded that "if, after this, our enemies at the North shall persist in representing that the seceded states are not in earnest, they will fully entitle themselves to be recorded among those who having ears hear not and having eyes see not."[9]

In his inaugural address, Davis struck the note that he was to sound to the end of his days: secession was right, reasonable, legal, a peaceful exercise by the sovereign people of an unassailable liberty, a step taken from necessity rather than by choice. There was no real reason for any conflict between this new nation and the old one from which it had separated, and "if a just perception of mutual interest shall permit us peaceably to pursue our separate political career, my most earnest desire will have been fulfilled." Still, it was necessary for the Confederacy to be ready for anything: "If this be denied to us, and the integrity of our territory and jurisdiction be assailed, it will but remain to us with firm resolve to appeal to arms and invoke the blessing of Providence on a just cause." It was quite possible, he believed, that some states still in the Union would presently want to join the Confederacy, and the Constitution made full provision for this; but this new nation was permanent, and "a re-union with the States from which we have separated is neither practicable nor desirable."

For the rest: "It is joyous in the midst of perilous times to look around upon a people united in heart, where one purpose of high resolve animates and actuates the whole; where the sacrifices to be made are not weighed in the balance against honor and right and liberty and equality. Obstacles may retard, but they cannot long prevent, the progress of a movement sanctified by its justice and sustained by a virtuous people. Reverently let us invoke the God of our Fathers to guide and protect us in our efforts to perpetuate the principles which by His blessing they are able to vindicate, establish and transmit to their posterity. With the continuance of His favor ever gratefully acknowledged, we may hopefully look forward to success, to peace and to prosperity."

There was in all of this no trace of the fire-eater's bugle call, and no faintest hint of any call to the revolutionary barricades. Davis was appealing to the intellect rather than to the emotions. To Mrs. Davis he wrote that beyond the cheers and the smiles displayed by his audience he saw "troubles and thorns innumerable," and he outlined them briefly: "We are without machinery, without means, and threatened by a powerful opposition; but I do not despond, and will not shrink from the task imposed upon me."[10] He had made his inaugural address almost plaintive in its repeated assumption that no one who examined the facts could fail to see the complete reasonableness and justice of the Southern position. If the independence of the Confederacy could be talked into reality, these were the words that might do it. Under the circumstances as they were on February 18, 1861, they were probably the only words the new President could have used. There was nothing in them to touch the heart and quicken the pulse. Nothing of that kind was needed, because the Southern pulse was already beating about as fast as it well could.

Davis's insistence that the new government was permanent and that there would be no reconstruction of the Union was not put in his speech by accident. Amid all of the rejoicings that attended the construction of this new government, there was one haunting fear to disturb the slumbers of devout patriots—the prospect that the whole business might in the end turn out to be what optimists in the North had supposed it was, a political maneuver pure and simple that would end in a reconstruction of the old Union. The Charleston *Mercury* had been grumbling all winter, complaining that a reconstruction plan lay somewhere underneath everything the Montgomery convention had tried to do. Darkly it mused that in such case the South would have "the same battle to fight all over again," that "we will have run a round circle and end where we started." It was known that some of the slave-state leaders who were still in Washington had reconstruction in mind, and Stephen A. Douglas was actively working for such a development. Privately, he had drafted tentative terms: the independence of the Confederacy would be recognized, but the two governments would be bound together tightly in a commercial union, with common laws governing trade, commerce, navigation, tariffs, patents, and the like, with a president and a council to handle all economic matters and with each nation guaranteeing the defense of the other—a strange, probably impractical, but nevertheless interesting scheme for a dual republic which would tie two separate unions into one greater union. People who were close to Douglas were lobbying in Montgomery; among them the forceful and erratic George Sanders, the Kentucky-born political and financial fixer from New York, who had headed the lusty, expansive "Young America" movement during the 1850s and had had a good deal to do with the famous Ostend Manifesto. Big-bodied, powerful, with blue eyes and an air of disheveled energy, Sanders now seemed to be agitating for a rebuilding of the old Union.[11]

The cabinet that President Davis selected did not, in its composition, seem to offer the thick-and-thin secessionists a great deal of encouragement. By and large, it represented the conservative element. Carefully selected to give representation to each of the seceding states, it brought together a group of Southerners who were eminently respectable but not in the least revolutionary-minded. It included only one man who could be listed with the original fire-eaters—Robert Toombs, of Georgia, Secretary of State. Christopher Memminger, of South Carolina, was named Secretary of the Treasury after Robert Barnwell had declined a cabinet post— a thrifty, small-scale lawyer and politician, of whom the Rhetts complained that he had opposed secession up to the last moment. Leroy Pope Walker, of Alabama, was Secretary of War, and Stephen Russell Mallory, of Florida, was Secretary of the Navy. Postmaster General was John H. Reagan, of Texas, and former Senator Judah P. Benjamin, of Louisiana, was Attorney General. Davis remarked afterward that none of these appointees was on close personal terms with him at the time the cabinet was organized; two, indeed, were utter strangers to him, chosen on the recommendation of local political leaders.

One thing was clear: the cabinet did not represent the famous planter aristocracy. Three of its members—Memminger, Mallory, and Benjamin—had been born abroad. All of the cabinet appointees, at one time or another, had been Unionists, and two had opposed secession until their own states seceded. For better or for worse, Davis had not tried the experiment Lincoln was trying, of bringing in the most forceful leaders the nation's politics had to offer; none of these men had either the stature or the desire to take the reins away from the President and direct the government. The executive would be Jefferson Davis and no one else.[12]

Excluded from the top posts in the government, and living amid rumors that sooner or later the old Union might be put back together, the fire-eaters felt that they had ground for worry. The frantic effort to set off the guns in Charleston harbor may have represented a desire to put pressure on the Confederate government as well as on the government in Washington. Yet this worry was largely without solid foundation. The fire-eaters' biggest maneuver had been successful: the new government was established and operating before Lincoln took office, and from the moment he took the oath, the Republican President would have to face the hard fact that the Union had actually been broken. Furthermore, although Davis was talking about peace, he was ready to fight and knew that he almost certainly would have to fight, and there was a great deal of iron in him. He had handled his first big problem, that of getting South Carolina under control, with deft speed; he immediately addressed himself to the second, which had to do with the Federal government at Washington.

On February 25 Davis named three commissioners to go to Washington and negotiate for the surrender of Federal forts and other installations in secession territory. He chose his men carefully: A. B. Roman, of Louisiana, an old-line Whig who had supported Bell in the presidential election, Martin J. Crawford, of Georgia, who had been a Breckinridge supporter, and John Forsyth, of Alabama, a Douglas man. Representing the three principal wings of Southern politics, these men, Davis felt, ought to be able to win "the sympathy and cooperation of every element of conservatism with which they might have occasion to deal." The spirit of his inaugural address ran through his instructions to these commissioners: they were to go to Washington in the most friendly spirit and were to ask for the things to which the Confederacy obviously was entitled—recognition, surrender of forts, arsenals, and other public property, and a general settlement of debts and other disputed matters. Davis was assuming that the separation was permanent, and from this assumption he would not depart as long as there was the remotest chance that it could be made good.

His private opinion was that there would be a war, and his Congress swung around to this view somewhat reluctantly but fairly quickly. It empowered the Confederate President to summon and use the militia of the several states, and shortly afterward expanded this by providing for a Confederate army "to repel invasion" which would be composed of the militia and of at least 100,000 volunteers. It directed the Committee on Naval Affairs to consider the propriety of building ironclad frigates and gunboats, it provided for the establishment of a general staff for the army, it passed elaborate regulations to govern the rank that might be given to former officers in the United States Army, and it devised a national flag. On March 4, 1861, this flag was formally hoisted to the staff over the capitol building in Montgomery.[13]

6. First Inaugural

THERE WAS a gale during the night, but it blew itself out before dawn and March 4 came in cloudy, raw, and gusty, with streaks of moderate warmth. The correspondent for *Harper's Weekly* believed that there were 25,000 visitors in Washington and said that many of them had been unable to find sleeping quarters. Newspaperman Henry Villard remarked that although the city did not contain one good restaurant, it had "no end of bar rooms," most of which were doing a fine business, and he felt that the city looked like an untidy overgrown village, indolent and unfinished but crowded and somehow vibrant with life. Most of the streets were unpaved and muddy, and the open plaza east of the Capitol was cluttered with castings and building blocks for the still incomplete dome. Beyond this litter, as day came in, a battery of regular artillery casually unlimbered and took position in full view of the temporary platform where Abraham Lincoln would presently take the oath as sixteenth President of the United States.

In this expression there was a trace of mockery, because the states obviously were no longer united. The man from Illinois was about to become President of something, but a precise definition was lacking. What drew so many people to Washington today, what kept the country's attention centered on the place, was the hope that the impending ceremony, the man himself, and the words that he would speak might bring clarification. For good or for ill, today was likely to be a turning point.

By nine in the morning most of the visitors seemed to be crowding Pennsylvania Avenue near Willard's Hotel, where the President-elect was staying, and within an hour the street was practically blocked. The procession would be elaborate, with decorated floats, including a huge wagon draped in bunting and labeled "Constitution," bearing thirty-four pretty girls representing the several states that, it was hoped, would soon reassemble in sisterly affection. There would be marching delegations from this place and that, along with parade marshals, members of the Committee on Arrangements, and carriages for judges, diplomats, and other dignitaries who would presently be riding up to the Capitol. It was noticed that a good many soldiers were in evidence.[1]

Many of these were District of Columbia militiamen, called to duty because Washington had heard so many rumors of possible violence. It was whispered that someone would try to shoot the President, or that an armed mob would swarm out to break up the parade and prevent the inauguration, and the harassed government was doing its weary best to be on the alert. There were groups of riflemen on the roofs of buildings overlooking the line of march, and in the wings of the Capitol itself there were riflemen in every window that overlooked the platform where the oath would be taken; what might happen if these considered that they saw something subversive and opened fire on the dense crowd was something that, happily, was never put to the test. There were also regular troops—600 or more of them, all that the government could conveniently assemble—and squads of cavalry patrolled street intersections, with more cavalry ready to ride beside the presidential carriage and a detachment of engineer troops ready to march just ahead. Two days earlier James Buchanan had explained all of this to Congress. These troops, he said, had been called to Washington "to act as a *posse comitatus* in strict subordination to the city authority for the purpose of preserving peace and order in the city of Washington, should this be necessary before or at the period of the inauguration." There was also a carriage to bear Lieutenant General Scott up to a command post by the artillery east of the Capitol.[2]

General Scott was disturbed and slightly confused—as, indeed, were most of his fellow countrymen. He had said, firmly enough, that he would manure the Virginia hills with fragments of the body of any person who tried to keep the ceremony from taking place, and this much he could infallibly do; beyond it, however, he was at a loss, and he had just made this fact clear in a letter to William H. Seward—who for his own part was at a loss also; he was not, as this day began, at all certain whether he would or would not take a place in Lincoln's cabinet. Scott told Seward that it seemed to him the new government could do one of four things. It could adopt the Crittenden peace plan and wait for the dissident states to return to the Union; it could blockade the ports of the Southern states, collecting import duties outside the harbors and in general waiting for a break; it could raise huge armies and beat the Confederacy into submission, winning at last "15 devastated provinces" that would have to be garrisoned for generations at immense cost . . . or it could simply give up and say to the seceded states "Wayward Sisters, depart in peace!"[3]

This from the general of the armies. From the Congress there could come no immediate help, for after a winter in which it had done little more than orate passionately, Congress had adjourned. It had refused to pass certain "force bills," which would have authorized the President to call out the militia to recover or defend Federal property and which would also have empowered him to follow Scott's second suggestion and close the ports in the Confederate states; in a final spasm of activity it had approved an amendment to the Constitution which would have outlawed any future Constitutional amendment empowering Congress to interfere with slavery—an amendment that would go forever unratified and would, in the crush of events, be quietly forgotten. The Senate had been summoned into special temporary session, so that the new President's appointments could be confirmed, and it was busy this morning with some last-minute business; and President Buchanan, two hours away from his return to private life, had gone to the Capitol with his cabinet to attend to any final bills that might be offered for his signature.

Secretary of War Holt reached this meeting late. He had with him a new and highly disturbing dispatch from Major Anderson, in Fort Sumter, which he thought Buchanan and the cabinet ought to know about. Major Anderson was saying that he could not remain at Fort Sumter very much longer unless the government sent him more supplies; much worse, he was also saying that Beauregard had mounted so many guns around the harbor and had his defensive preparations so well in hand that the Federal government would need a force of 20,000 men if it tried to come in and reinforce its lost garrison.[4] Obviously the status quo, which had wobbled so uneasily for months, was on the point of total collapse; equally obviously there was nothing the out-going administration could do with this unwelcome news but pass it along to Abraham Lincoln and let him make of it what he could. Buchanan returned to the White House to prepare for the inauguration parade.

He would be relieved to depart from Washington; before the day ended he remarked that if Lincoln was as glad to get into the White House as he himself was to get out of it, Lincoln must be the happiest man alive. Yet Buchanan was not oppressed by any great feeling that he had failed in a time of high crisis. He felt that he had done his best and he believed that his best had been fairly good, and he summed up what he had done with the statement: "I acted for some time as a breakwater between the North and the South, both surging with all their force against me." He was turning over the government to Lincoln without having made a single admission of the right of secession and without having committed Lincoln to hold even an informal conversation with the commissioners from Montgomery. The border slave states were still in the Union. Anderson was still in Fort Sumter (even though his dispatch, read this morning, indicated he could not possibly stay there much longer), and Buchanan had firmly asserted the Federal government's right to keep him there. All in all, the departing President felt he had not done too badly. One week after his term ended he wrote to a friend that his administration had been successful in its foreign and domestic policy—to which, incredibly, he calmly added, apparently as an afterthought, "unless we may except the sad events which recently occurred." No human wisdom, he added, could have prevented these sad events; he had done his best, and he believed that posterity would do him justice.[5]

In any case, he would not slink out of Washington as a broken and defeated weakling. When he returned to his home in Pennsylvania, the citizens of Lancaster would greet him with cheers and a brass band, with militia to escort an open barouche in a parade through the downtown streets, and he would respond with a graceful speech climaxed by the devout cry: "May God preserve the Constitution and the Union." Many people in Washington would remember him with fondness. Mrs. Roger Pryor, wife of the erratic fire-eater from Virginia, would recall him as a regular visitor at Dr. Gurley's Presbyterian church on Sundays: greeting him at the doorway, after services, she would always tell him: "A good sermon, Mr. President," to which his invariable reply was: "Too long, madam, too long." He was tall, with a pink complexion and silky white hair, and some defect in vision caused him to stand with his head cocked on one side, like

an inquisitive bird. Like all presidents, he had found political
job seekers a trial, and he had protested once that "they give
me no time to say my prayers," but he had kept a certain
amount of serenity through all the pulling and hauling of the
secession winter. In December, at the time South Carolina
was cutting the silver cord, he had written to Publisher
James Gordon Bennett: "I have never enjoyed better health
or a more tranquil spirit than during the past year. All our
troubles have not cost me an hour's sleep or a meal's vict-
uals." Now it was about over. Leaving the White House, he
would pick up Lincoln at Willard's, take him to the Capitol,
see and hear the inauguration ceremonies, escort the new
President back to the White House, and then start for home,
hoping only "to perform the duties of a good citizen and a
kind friend and neighbor."[6]

Buchanan's open carriage drew up in front of Willard's
some time after twelve o'clock. Lincoln came out, in top hat
and frock coat, escorted by Senators Edward D. Baker, of
Oregon, and James A. Pearce, of Maryland, and with cavalrymen for outriders and a company of regulars tramping just
ahead, the party left for the Capitol. Lincoln had had a hard
morning, with deserving Republicans desiring office clinging
to him like leeches. Meeting correspondent Villard sometime
that day, Lincoln confessed: "It was bad enough in Springfield, but it was child's play compared with this tussle here.
I hardly have a chance to eat or sleep. I am fair game for
everybody of that hungry lot." But his chief problem this
morning was with a man who apparently did not want a job,
rather than with the multitude who did want jobs. Seward
had notified him, a day earlier, that on full reflection he
found that he could not accept the post of Secretary of State
which Lincoln had offered him—the real trouble being that
Seward did not want to sit in the same cabinet with his rival,
Chase. While the procession was forming, Lincoln dealt with
this. He said: "I can't afford to let Seward take the first
trick," and he scribbled a note for his secretary to copy and
deliver. In this note he asked Seward to reconsider his withdrawal: "The public interest, I think, demands that you
should; my personal feelings are deeply enlisted in the same
direction." The note was delivered, and that afternoon Seward had another change of heart and agreed to serve.[7]

None of the anticipated acts of violence took place. The

presidential carriage got to the Capitol without trouble, and
the preliminary ceremonies went off smoothly. Buchanan and
Lincoln entered the Senate chamber arm in arm to see Hannibal Hamlin, of Maine, sworn in as Vice-President; an observer said that Buchanan was pale and nervous, and that
Lincoln, tight-lipped, was "grave and impassive as an Indian
martyr." Mr. Hamlin became Vice-President, and presently
the party walked out to the platform that had been built over
the east portico to the Capitol. Ancient Chief Justice Roger
Taney, frail as a withered leaf, was waiting with a Bible to
administer the oath. Stephen A. Douglas was in the group
on the platform; by happy chance, when Lincoln took his
seat and found that he had no handy place to lay his stovepipe hat, Senator Douglas stepped forward, said "Permit me,
sir," and took the hat from him, holding it throughout the
rest of the ceremony. This gesture from the leader of the
Northern Democracy, cherished by later historians, was observed by Murat Halstead, here to cover the inaugural for
his Cincinnati *Commercial* just as he had covered the conventions, and in his story Halstead mused aloud: "Doug must
have reflected pretty seriously during that half hour, that instead of delivering an inaugural addres from the portico he
was holding the hat of the man who was doing it."[8]

A good omen, possibly—like the sunlight that came out
brightly as Lincoln stepped up to deliver his inaugural address? Most welcome, if so, for other good omens were lacking. Lincoln was addressing a nation that had broken into
two pieces, with additional fractures visibly indicated for the
near future. No matter what he said, men would read their
own hopes and fears into his speech. Hoping for peace, he
was face to face with a crisis that could hardly be settled
peaceably unless one side or the other went off in full retreat
—a thing that was in the highest degree unlikely. The deep
shadow that hung over this first inaugural of America's most
eloquent President was the simple fact that Lincoln was trying, this morning, to do with words that which words could
not possibly do.

The speech would be studied, analyzed, and taken apart
sentence by sentence wtih devout care—by nervous Americans in that first week of March 1861 and by historians in
every decade since then—and nobody ever found in it anything particularly surprising. There was not in it, either

(there could not have been, by any possibility under heaven), the magical phrase that would quell the rising hurricane and, by the power of its logic, the beauty of its structure, or the nobility of its thought, bring a divided nation back to amity, understanding, and peaceful intent.

Lincoln's first inaugural, in short, did not achieve the impossible. As a state paper, it was excellent; it contained moving passages, soft words of conciliation, closely reasoned appeals for forbearance and brotherhood—and these would have no effect whatever. Lincoln argued that secession was illegal, ruinous, and in the long run physically impossible; the argument meant no more than Jefferson Davis's argument, in his own inaugural a few weeks earlier, that secession was legal, right, and completely inevitable. The gist of the speech, the part that set the pattern for the time that was to follow, was in a few sentences that constituted the new President's statement of intent. He considered the Union unbroken, no matter what had been said and done at Charleston, at Montgomery, or elsewhere, and he would act on the assumption that the states that said they were out of the Union were eternally in it.

Consequently: "The power confided to me, will be used to hold, occupy, and possess the property, and places belonging to the government, and to collect the duties and imposts."[9] He hoped to do all that he proposed to do without having any trouble, and if there was going to be fighting, the people who considered themselves out of the Union would have to start it, but he would stand on this position. Between Canada and the Rio Grande there was just one nation; he was its chief executive, and he would behave accordingly.

This was the heart and center of the trouble. The crisis was not the fact that Major Anderson and eighty hungry soldiers occupied Fort Sumter, with black cannon staring at them and the pulse of coming violence beating steadily. That was no more than the symptom. The crisis came because seven states (for the most complex of reasons) had declared themselves out of the Union and had made it clear that they would willingly fight in order to stay out. Lincoln was saying now that they were not out and that everything he did would rest on the assumption that they could not possibly go out. All of the rest of his speech—his Constitutional argument, his offer of a flexible attitude in respect to the slavery problems, his plea for harmony, his soft-spoken appeal to "the mystic chords of memory" stretching from half-forgotten battlefields to the hearts of living men—might as well have gone unspoken. He could have peace by consenting to a division of the Union and he flatly refused to get it on that basis. The rest was in the hands of the unrelenting gods. Thirteen years earlier he had told the Congress, of which he was then a member, that "it is a quality of revolutions not to go by *old* lines, or *old* laws; but to break up both and make new ones." Old lines and old laws had at last been broken, and presently everyone would see what came of it.

Lincoln was not in any sense occupying new ground. It had been clear enough for a long time, to anyone who cared to ponder on the man and his record, that he did not believe in and would never recognize the right of secession, and the men in the cotton states had never deceived themselves about the matter; in a queer way, it appears that the people of the Confederacy that winter had interpreted Lincoln better than many Northerners had been able to do. What this speech did was pin a general principle down to an exceedingly specific case: when Lincoln said that he would "hold, occupy and possess" the government's property, he meant Fort Sumter, and everybody knew it.[10]

He did not necessarily mean that he was going to do anything in particular about it. The government already held, occupied, and possessed Fort Sumter. It would simply go on doing so, accepting the symbolism that made this one fort represent all of the material and spiritual values that were at stake between the two governments. Major Anderson would be completely passive. If he stayed where he was and kept his flag flying, that would be enough. When Lincoln told the secessionists: "You can have no conflict without being yourselves the aggressors," he was simply reminding them about Major Anderson. If there was going to be a war, the Confederacy would have to start it.

The new President had chosen his ground with strategic intelligence. Unfortunately, he had also chosen it with incomplete knowledge. He was staking his whole policy on the belief that Fort Sumter could be held as long as need be; and two hours before he got up to make his speech, the War Department had received the major's announcement that this was no longer true. Anderson could stay in Fort Sumter only a short time unless all the power of the government were actively used in his behalf. The key point in Lincoln's plan had been knocked loose before he even took the oath of office.

The oath was taken, after the speech. Ancient Taney, black-robed and stooped, came forward with the open Book, administering the oath to a new President for the eighth time in his career; knowing, as he did it, that his Dred Scott decision and most of the policies he had stood for were fading out as this tall man from Illinois took the new office. Lincoln took the oath, bent and kissed the Book, and the Marine Corps band began to play, the crowd cheered, and the battery of regular artillerymen began to fire a salute. Haughty Senator Sumner remarked to the younger Charles Francis Adams: "Hand of iron: velvet glove," the carriage and the cavalcade moved back down town, and Abraham Lincoln was President of the United States.[11]

Men construed the speech, as Senator Sumner had done, according to their own ideas. Bennett's New York *Herald* remarked that it meant everything to everybody; "the most extreme Southern men regard it as meaning war . . . while the more conservative men of the border states view it as conciliatory." The *Herald*'s man in Richmond reported that secessionists there "regard it as equivalent to a declaration of War" and said that Virginia's Unionists, saying little, were disappointed. Northern Republicans, according to the *Herald*, were delighted, and Northern Democrats were worried. George Templeton Strong, the New York diarist, correctly noted that the speech had "a clang of metal in it," and Henry Adams took a lofty look at the new President, pitied him because he did not know how to wear white kid gloves, and permitted himself to conclude that "no man living needed so much education as the new President but that all the education he could get would not be enough." Martin J. Crawford, one of the Confederate commissioners in Washington, wrote to Robert Toombs that everything would depend on what Lincoln thought the border states would swallow; "whatsoever the Republican party can do without driving out Virginia it will do, and such coercive measures as the new Administration may *with safety* adopt it will most certainly."[12]

Southern newspapers and public men had many things to say about the inaugural, but T. R. R. Cobb, in Montgomery, expressed the inner fact of the matter when he wrote, on this same March 4: "We are receiving Lincoln's inaugural by telegraph, it will not affect one man here, it matters not what it contains." From the grim duelist Louis T. Wigfall, of Texas, who had stayed in Washington to hear what the new President had to say, came a wire: "Inaugural means war . . . Be vigilant." The Montgomery *Weekly Advertiser* agreed that Lincoln's speech meant that "war, war, and nothing less than war, will satisfy the Abolition chief," and the Charleston *Mercury* was even more outspoken: "If ignorance could add anything to folly, or insolence to brutality, the President of the Northern States of America has, in this address, achieved it. A more lamentable display of feeble inability to grasp the circumstances of this momentous emergency could scarcely have been exhibited. . . . The United States has become a mobocratic empire and the Union of the States is now dissolved."[13]

The speech undoubtedly disappointed men of the border states, who devoutly longed for peace and who had innocently supposed that Lincoln would insure it by basing his policy on a deliberate acceptance of the "sad events" to which Buchanan was referring. Thinking so, they had been hoping for an impossibility, failing to realize that the North as well as the South contained determined men who would fight rather than knuckle under—men who had already made up their minds, and who stood at the very center of the force that had made Lincoln President. Facing the mere threat of secession, these men might have been conciliatory enough; facing the actual fact of secession, they were not conciliatory at all, and they were men whose outspoken feelings Lincoln could by no means ignore.

As early as February 2 the legislators of the state of Michigan, refusing to send delegates to the unhappy peace conference, had resolved that the secessionist states were "in open rebellion against the government" and had pledged all of the state's men and money to the government's support, with a rider saying that "concession and compromise are not to be entertained or offered to traitors." In Minnesota, a week earlier, the legislature had passed a similar resolution, asserting that secession amounted to revolution and would precipitate civil war and declaring that Minnesota would support "with men and money" the most vigorous effort Washington could make to assert its supremacy. In Wisconsin, Governor Alexander Randall had warned the legislature on January 10 that it might presently be necessary to vote men and means "to sustain the integrity of the Union and thwart the designs of men engaged in organized treason," and even in Ohio, where there were many Democrats deeply sympathetic to the South, the legislature that winter had voted that "the power and resources" of the state would be used "for the maintenance of the civil authority, Constitution and laws of the general government."[14]

These were fighting words as grim as anything that had been said at Charleston or Montgomery. They came from men without whose support Lincoln could not have become President. These men expected him to do whatever he had to do to maintain the Union, and his pledge to "hold, occupy and possess" Fort Sumter and any other forts that had not already fallen was the absolute minimum he could have offered them. The pressure that was on him was as strong as the pressure that rested on Jefferson Davis, and it ran in precisely the opposite direction; and, like Davis, he shared in the inner convictions of the men from whom the pressure came. To suppose that he could admit the legality and the reality of secession and put the desire for peace above the desire for Union was, quite simply, to imagine a vain thing.

At any rate, the speech and the oath-taking and the rest of the ceremony finally ended. The crowd that gathered in front of the Capitol had been orderly enough, although one reporter felt that it had shown very little enthusiasm; but at least the vigilant riflemen had not been needed, and there had been no disorder. When Lincoln began to speak, and fitted steel-rimmed spectacles on his nose so that he could read his manuscript, some leather-lunged citizen had shouted: "Take off them spectacles—we want to see your eyes." A little later there was a brief disturbance when some other witness fell out of a tree, with a loud cracking of branches.[15] Otherwise all had gone smoothly, and by mid-afternoon Lincoln was in the White House, the duly qualified President of whatever might remain of the United States. He had stated his position flatly; he would make no overt acts but he would hold Fort Sumter, and the Confederacy would have to make the next move.

Waiting for him was the one bit of news he had not had

when he took this position—Major Anderson's message. Fort Sumter could not be held without an overt act. Presidential policy would have to be revised before it could be put into effect; the all-important next move would be made in Washington rather than in Montgomery. What Lincoln had just said might make interesting reading in the history books of some later day; what he would do in the immediate future would determine what sort of history was going to be written.

CHAPTER FIVE

Into the Unknown

1. Two Forts and Three Agents

GUSTAVUS VASA FOX was tall and stout, an energetic bearded man who presented a blend of the breezy sea dog of legend and the canny businessman of shore-side reality. He was just forty, an Annapolis graduate who had spent fifteen years in the navy; he had swallowed the anchor while in his mid-thirties to go into the textile business in Massachusetts, and as March began he was a behind-the-scenes figure of considerable importance in Washington. This was partly because of his political connections—his wife was sister to the wife of Montgomery Blair, the only man in the cabinet just now who believed that Fort Sumter ought to be reinforced no matter whose toes were stepped on—and partly because Fox himself had studied the matter and believed that he knew how to get supplies and men into Fort Sumter in spite of General Beauregard.

Men who believed that they knew exactly what to do and how to do it were rare. President Lincoln, who was still digesting the fact that the foundation stone for his whole policy had been removed overnight, was assuredly not one of them. His confidential advisers had had time for nothing more than a hurried glance around, and such a glance was not likely to show anything beyond the disordered concourse of office seekers. The President and his cabinet met, very briefly, on the evening of March 6, the day after the Senate had confirmed cabinet appointments, but the affair had been less a cabinet meeting than a simple get-together at which men shook hands and exchanged stereotyped cordialities. The fact that the perennial crisis at Charleston had at last entered the final stage—that the question of Fort Sumter had abruptly, by a monstrous twist of fate, become the only question that really mattered—was still a secret. The secret would be presented to the cabinet in due course. Meanwhile, Lincoln had to wrestle with two questions: Could Major Anderson be reinforced? If so, should he be reinforced? On the first question, at least, Fox could perhaps shed light.

Early in February, while the unpleasant taste of the *Star of the West* fiasco was still fresh, Fox had been called to Washington by Winfield Scott, at Montgomery Blair's suggestion, to devise some means for getting reinforcements to Major Anderson. As an old navy man, Fox distrusted the idea that the warships could simply hammer their way into the harbor whenever the administration nerved itself to make the attempt, and he had worked out a scheme which he believed would make a stand-up fight unnecessary. Send down your men and supplies (he said) by transports, with men of war for escort. In the thickness of a dark night, put men and goods into whale boats, landing craft, small barges, or whatnot, have shallow-draft tugboats to take them in tow, and get them up to the Fort Sumter wharf before South Carolina knows what is going on. If guard boats or soldiers in rowboats try to interfere, the warships can drive them off. By daylight the fort will have everything it needs, and the secessionist gunners can do as they please: Fort Sumter will be secure.[1]

In its essentials this plan had been accepted, and at Buchanan's direction the War and Navy departments had set aside men and ships for a Fort Sumter relief expedition. But the expedition had never been sent, because—as Lincoln was learning on his first full day in office—Major Anderson himself had concluded that it was not needed.

The major had been most explicit. After the *Star of the West* had been driven away, he told the War Department that he hoped it would make no effort to put supplies into the fort, because it "would do more harm than good." Early in February he wrote that although it was always possible for a small party to slip in by stealth—precisely the point around which Fox was building his own plan—the harbor defenses had been improved so that an entrance could be forced only by a substantial fleet.[2] The War Department, in turn, instructed the major to send word if he needed anything, and in the absence of any further word assumed that everything was all right. Anderson had sent many reports since then, but none of them had indicated any special change in his situation (except that a steady, ominous tightening of pressure was perceptible, as Beauregard gave South Carolina's effort professional direction), and as far as Washington knew, Fort Sumter contained all the soldiers and rations it would need for a long time to come. Now, out of a clear sky, had come this startling report, which in effect said, or at least appeared to say, that it was impossible for Major Anderson to stay at Sumter and equally impossible for the government to help him.

Any ideas Gustavus Fox had, accordingly, would be considered. Yet before he could pass on these, Lincoln had to reflect that Sumter was not the only fort to be held, occupied, and possessed. Most Federal installations along the coast, from Charleston to the Rio Grande, had passed into Confederate hands, but Lincoln's government still held four. There was Sumter, to begin with. There were also Fort Taylor, at Key West, Florida, and Fort Jefferson, a gloomy rock of a place far offshore in the Dry Tortugas—places which it was important for the government to keep, but so remote that the Confederacy was not likely to raise a fuss about them. And there was, finally, Fort Pickens, at the entrance to Pensacola harbor in Florida.

Potentially, Fort Pickens offered a case that was fully as explosive as that of Fort Sumter. It also offered the Federal government one advantage that was absent at Fort Sumter; it was permanently reinforceable. A United States warship, as a matter of fact, with a company of regulars aboard, was even now anchored within musket shot of Fort Pickens, and the regulars could be sent ashore in a matter of minutes. Furthermore, whereas Fort Sumter lay well inside of Charleston harbor, and so could be isolated as soon as enough Confederate batteries were in place—a matter to which General Beauregard had been systematically attending for weeks— Fort Pickens lay on the seacoast, out at the harbor's entrance. Confederate guns might conceivably pound it into submission, or it might be stormed if enough assault troops were put on Santa Rosa Island, the forty-mile expanse of sand and underbrush on which the fort had been sited; but the place could never be isolated as long as the United States had a navy.

Fort Pickens's history during the last three months had been a good deal like Fort Sumter's, the difference lying chiefly in the fact that the people of Florida were milder than the people of South Carolina, and that Fort Pickens was more remote than Fort Sumter. When 1861 began, Pickens, like Sumter, was empty. United States troops present in the vicinity included no more than forty-odd artillerists, commanded by middle-aged Lieutenant Adam J. Slemmer, quartered on the mainland in barracks that were clustered about ancient Fort Barrancas, part of which had been built by the Spaniards in the long ago. When Florida seceded and prepared to seize all available government property, Slemmer took a leaf from Major Anderson's book and got his men over to Fort Pickens—just in time, too, for the state troops seized Fort Barrancas, occupied the United States Navy Yard near by, moved into Fort McRee at the harbor mouth facing Fort Pickens, and began to build new batteries. Slemmer knew his case was hopeless if the Southerners made an all-out attack. His little company had been reinforced, after a fashion, by thirty sailors who got away when the navy yard was taken, bringing his total manpower to eighty-one, and he had plenty of supplies; but in its present condition Fort Pickens was vulnerable to an infantry assault and its tiny garrison would be overwhelmed if the Southerners used their available manpower in an all-out attack.

On January 12 the Florida authorities first demanded the surrender of the fort. Slemmer had rejected this demand, but it was common knowledge that an attack was being planned, and in consequence it was much to Slemmer's advantage when Florida's Stephen R. Mallory—a United States Senator, in January: in March, Jefferson Davis's Secretary of the Navy—worked out a deal with President Buchanan. Under this deal the North would not reinforce Pickens and the South would not attack it. Both sides were fortifying, but neither side did any shooting. In many ways the case of Pickens and Pensacola was like the case of Sumter and Charleston, except that nobody worked up a great head of steam about it. Potentially, the cases were exactly parallel, with the Federal government occupying a fort in a seaport that (as secessionists saw it, at any rate) belonged to a foreign power. One fort would make just as good a test case as the other. So far Fort Sumter had drawn all of the emotion, but there was plenty to spare for Fort Pickens if any-one made an issue of it.

At the end of the first week in March the Fort Pickens situation was endurable but complicated, the chief complication being that no one in Washington was entirely clear about the deal Buchanan had made back in January. The Navy Department of course knew that U.S.S. *Brooklyn,* swinging to her anchor chain half a mile from the Fort Pickens sally port, still contained a company of soldiers who belonged in the fort but had not been put there because the administration, two months earlier, had felt that it was advisable to keep them afloat for a while yet. In an absent-minded sort of way the department probably realized that the commanding officer of the U.S.S. *Sabine,* Captain H. A. Adams, who also commanded the squadron, had been instructed on January 30 not to put the soldiers ashore "unless said fort shall be attacked or preparations shall be made for its attack." But nobody in Washington quite realized (and this was typical of the confusion and general fogginess which lay upon the capital as the new administration took over) that as far as Captain Adams knew, these orders of January 30 were still binding unless the Navy Department specifically canceled them.[3]

Since January the situation at Pensacola had changed. The Confederacy had taken over. The thousands of Southern troops at Pensacola were now under the command of Brigadier General Braxton Bragg, a dour martinet who was an exceedingly capable trainer and organizer of troops but who, in action, was to show a bewildering knack for following moments of genuine achievement with moments of inexplicable incompetence; a baffling character, who would retain Davis's confidence long after he had lost that of practically everyone else in the South. Like Beauregard, Bragg had been busy, and he had many guns in position along the water front. He was darkly pessimistic, writing to his wife that "our troops are raw volunteers, without officers, and without discipline, each man with an idea that he can whip the world," and he did not see how the fort could be taken without a regular siege. But he was whipping his men into shape, and by mid-March the only thing around Pensacola that had not changed was the January 30 order in Captain Adams's desk.[4]

However that might be, Fort Pickens had a powerful claim

on the new President's attention. Lincoln apparently was about to lose so much more than he could afford to lose at Fort Sumter; at Fort Pickens, quite possibly, he could get all of it back.

The Fort Sumter problem had always been loaded. If the Lincoln administration gave up the fort without a fight, the Confederacy was virtually independent; no one thereafter— in the North, in the South, or anywhere else—would see much reason to think that this government would or could maintain the Union. On the other hand, if the administration mobilized army and navy and fought its way into Charleston harbor, it immediately became the aggressor, validating all of the anguished complaints about coercion of the South; and it would certainly lose the border states en bloc. Its only possible course was the one that had been set forth in the inaugural—to stay in Fort Sumter peaceably, leaving only after the other side had brought on a fight. And this only possible course was, according to Major Anderson's dispatch, about to be lost.

But Fort Pickens was different. This fort could be reinforced to the limit of capacity, without the need for firing a shot. Furthermore, the reinforcements—or enough of them, at any rate, to show what the policy was going to be—were immediately available and could be put into the fort in short order. The test of the administration's determination to "hold, occupy and possess" its remaining forts could be made at Fort Pickens just about as well as at Fort Sumter. If the place were immediately reinforced, the government's will would be unmistakable. The Fort Sumter problem could be disposed of at leisure. If Captain Fox's plans looked good, Major Anderson could be reinforced and supplied; if not, Major Anderson could be withdrawn and no great harm would have been done.

Accordingly, on March 12, U.S.S. *Mohawk* was sent off to make a quick run to Pensacola. It bore a dispatch from General Scott, signed by E. D. Townsend, assistant adjutant general of the army, addressed to Captain Israel Vogdes, captain of the company of regulars which had been resting aboard U.S.S. *Brooklyn* for so many weeks, and the dispatch read as follows:

"At the first favorable moment you will land with your company, re-enforce Fort Pickens, and hold the same till fur-

ther orders. Report frequently, if opportunities present themselves, on the condition of the fort and the circumstances
around you."

On the same day, General Scott wrote that "as a practical
military question the time for succoring Fort Sumter with
any means at hand had passed away nearly a month ago." In
the general's opinion it would take four months to collect
the needed warships, and from six to eight months to raise
and discipline the troops—5000 regulars and 20,000 volunteers. The fort's surrender, from starvation or under assault,
was, he felt, merely a question of time. On this day, too,
Fox's detailed plan was brought before the President, who
liked it and found that most of the cabinet also liked it; and
on March 15 Lincoln sent to each cabinet member a note:

"Assuming it to be possible to now provision Fort Sumter,
under all the circumstances is it wise to attempt it? Please
give me your opinion in writing on this subject."[5]

The assumption that it was possible to put provisions into
the fort doubtless owed much to Fox, who seemed to be the
only optimist in town. With the new administration less than
a fortnight old, most of Washington was already taking it
for granted that Fort Sumter would be given up. For two
days, newspaper correspondents had been telling their papers that the cabinet had agreed to evacuate the fort. The
Baltimore *American*'s story was explicit: "The battle of the
cabinet has been fought and Mr. Seward has triumphed. The
cabinet has ordered the withdrawal of Major Anderson from
Fort Sumter." Edwin M. Stanton, who had lent so much vigor
to the closing weeks of Buchanan's administration, wrote to
Buchanan that Lincoln had not yet come to any decision on
the matter—Seward, Bates, and Cameron, he said, were pulling him one way, and Chase, Welles, and Blair were pulling
in the opposite direction—but he felt that what was coming
was clear enough: "It is certain that Anderson will be withdrawn." Rumors of surrender were printed in Charleston,
and were believed inside Fort Sumter; hospital supplies and
other movables were packed, by way of preparation for the
move. Some of Anderson's people thought that they could
see the besieging Confederates beginning to relax—obviously
because they expected to get Fort Sumter without further effort. (The relaxation was only temporary, if indeed it existed

at all. Beauregard was profoundly skeptical about Yankee intentions.)[6]

The Washington correspondent who spoke of the anticipated withdrawal as a victory for Seward had put his finger on one of the real oddities of the situation. Seward, who had tried at the last minute to avoid entering the cabinet at all, was doing his best to run things now that he was in it. The papers had a way of referring to him as "Lincoln's Premier," and it was widely believed—by Seward himself, most of all— that Seward would be the real boss of the administration. And Seward, who had won Southern hatred years earlier by talking glibly of an irrepressible conflict, believed now that everything could be settled if the government let go of Fort Sumter in the right way. The stories that Anderson would be withdrawn were almost certainly being planted by Seward. At the very time when Lincoln was asking the ministers to say whether or not Fort Sumter should be provisioned, Seward was quietly passing the word to the Confederate commissioners that the fort was going to be surrendered. Captain Fox was not going to get any support from the Secretary of State; neither, for that matter, was Major Anderson . . . nor the dedicated Union men of the North, who had put this administration in office in the first place, who in the Northwest had seen secession as no better than rebellion and treason, and who if a fight at last came would be the men on whom the government would have to rely the most. Ben Wade, the ruthless anti-slavery extremist from Ohio, was furiously declaring that withdrawal would wreck the Republican party and the administration throughout the Northwest, and he was said to have told Lincoln bluntly: "Give up fortress after fortress and Jeff Davis will have you a prisoner of war in less than thirty days." In New England many Republicans felt the way prominent editor Joseph Hawley, of Connecticut, felt. Hawley had just written to Gideon Welles that he could see why Fort Sumter must be given up, but that the idea brought tears to his eyes, and he had then burst out: "I will gladly be one of the volunteers to sail into that harbor past all the guns of hell rather than see the flag dishonored and the government demoralized."[7] A tension was rising in the North, and the longer the business of the forts hung in the balance, the higher it would be, matching the merciless tension that already was tormenting the South.

Lincoln's cabinet did not think Sumter ought to be relieved. Of all the members, only Montgomery Blair was flatly and without qualifications in favor of sending provisions down to Major Anderson. Secretary Chase, to be sure, was for it, with encircling ifs and buts; he admitted later that just now he favored letting the seven seceded states "try the experiment of a separate existence rather than incur the evils of a bloody war," and his endorsement of the relief plan was trimmed down until it was actually no endorsement at all. Even Gideon Welles believed that the administration had best let well enough alone. "An impression has gone abroad," he wrote, "that Sumter is to be evacuated and the shock caused by that announcement has done its work. The public mind is becoming tranquillized under it, and will become fully reconciled to it when the causes which have led to that necessity shall have been made public and are rightly understood." Secretary of War Simon Cameron recited the heavy weight of professional opinion which held that the only thing to do with Major Anderson was to call him home, and wrote that since "the abandonment of the fort in a few weeks, sooner or later, appears to be an inevitable necessity, it seems to me that the sooner it be done the better." He went on to say that he liked Captain Fox's plan and would support it except that he believed it would bring on a war.[8]

In effect, all of the cabinet except Blair opposed the plan to send relief to Major Anderson, and Lincoln—still painfully new in the office, and surrounded by advisers most of whom believed that they on the whole were wiser and more experienced than himself—did not feel that he could go ahead in face of all that opposition. He was not, however, ready to give up. If his election and his own convictions meant anything at all, he had to make a stand somewhere. For the moment he would postpone a final decision. Meanwhile, he needed to know everything he could know about the exact situation, both in Fort Sumter and in Charleston itself.

As a first step, the President seems to have called on Mrs. Abner Doubleday, who was then living in Washington, to see what light the letters she was getting from her husband might shed. Of all of Major Anderson's officers, Doubleday was probably the most wholehearted in his belief that the fort ought to be held in spite of everything, but his letters could tell the President little except the condition of the garrison and the state of its preparations for defense.[9] Lincoln needed something broader than this, and he sent down three men to get the information he needed.

The first of these was Captain Fox himself. Lincoln talked to him on March 19, and two days later Fox reached Charleston. He went to see Governor Pickens, explained his mission, and said that he would like to talk to Major Anderson—not to give him any orders, but simply to find out what his situation really was. Governor Pickens agreed, and shortly after dusk a Confederate guard steamer dropped Fox on the wharf at Fort Sumter.

Anderson was pessimistic. He thought it was too late for the government to relieve him except by landing troops on Morris Island and storming the batteries there—an operation which, as General Scott had pointed out, would take a large army and a powerful fleet—and he made it clear that his supplies were getting very low. He and Fox agreed that Fox must tell the President that the troops could not stay in the fort after April 15 unless more supplies were received. While the men talked, the splashing of a rowboat's oars could be heard somewhere off in the darkness, although no boat could be seen. Fox drew the major's attention to this, indicating that small boats might reach the fort at night without damage, but Anderson felt that this was not good enough—Fort Moultrie had at least thirteen guns bearing on the wharf where the boats would have to unload, and he did not think the chances were very bright. Fox insisted that he did not actually tell Anderson about his plan, although Anderson apparently got a fairly clear idea of what was in the wind. (A little later the Confederates accused Fox of acting in bad faith, since he had assured Governor Pickens he was not bringing Anderson any orders. Fox insisted that he had lived up to the agreement, but said that it did not matter: he considered that a state of war already existed, and felt that it was entirely legitimate for him to deceive "the enemy" in any way he could.) In any case, Fox presently returned to Washington and prepared to tell Lincoln what he had learned.[10]

A second emissary was Stephen A. Hurlbut, an Illinois

lawyer and Republican leader whom Lincoln had known for years. Hurlbut reached Charleston March 24, shortly after Fox started back to Washington, concerned less with finding out about Major Anderson's position than with ascertaining just how the people of Charleston felt about everything. He talked to old James L. Petigru, who by now was recognized as the only Union man in the state, talked also with businessmen and politicians whom he knew, and returned full of unrelieved gloom. He found in Charleston no vestige of attachment to the Union, and told Lincoln bluntly that "there is positively nothing to appeal to—the sentiment of national patriotism, always feeble in Carolina, has been extinguished and over-ridden." Nothing the government could do short of unqualified recognition of South Carolina's independence and complete surrender of Federal jurisdiction, he felt, would satisfy Charleston, and Beauregard would unquestionably stop even a boat containing nothing but bacon and hardtack. As far as Hurlbut could see, the case of Fort Sumter was hopeless; the only thing Lincoln could do was hold on to Fort Pickens—and "if war comes, let it come."[11]

The third man Lincoln sent to Charleston was Ward Lamon, a close personal friend, newly appointed Federal marshal for the District of Columbia. Lamon and Hurlbut went south together, but parted once they reached Charleston. Lamon learned nothing Lincoln did not already know, but he did manage to muddy the waters slightly. He talked to Governor Pickens and to Major Anderson, and gave both men the definite feeling that troops at Fort Sumter were going to be withdrawn. Sympathetic to the South, Lamon almost certainly exceeded his authority; writing about it long afterward, he was notably reserved regarding the messages he had been supposed to give the governor and the major—if indeed he had been supposed to do anything more than take soundings—but he was looked upon in Charleston as the President's authorized agent, and Anderson reported to the War Department that what Lamon told him led him to believe "that orders would soon be issued for my abandoning this work." Whatever Lamon may have said, he at least brought back to Washington Governor Pickens's flat warning that "nothing can prevent war except the acquiescence of the President of the United States in secession and his unalterable resolve not to attempt any reinforcement of the

Southern forts." In substance, his report to the President was about like Hurlbut's: even the arrival of a boatload of provisions would touch off a fight.[12]

The three men returned to Washington separately, and Lincoln called a new cabinet meeting to consider the situation. Meanwhile, there were two additional complications. General Scott submitted a memorandum advising against the plan to reinforce and hold Fort Pickens; and Captain H. A. Adams, the senior naval officer at Pensacola, saw the orders the U.S.S. *Mohawk* had brought down and refused to honor them. Captain Adams pointed out that he was still bound by the January 30 orders from the Secretary of the Navy, which said he was not to put troops ashore unless the fort was under attack or clearly about to be attacked. What the War Department might write to Captain Vogdes was interesting, but it did not affect him. He would stand by the old orders, and he and the soldiers would remain aboard ship. In some anxiety, Captain Adams wrote to the Navy Department: "I beg you will please send me instructions as soon as possible, that I may be relieved from a painful embarrassment."

For the moment, nobody in Washington knew about this. When the news did come, Secretary Welles wrote bitterly that Adams was technically justified, although Welles felt that "a faithful and patriotic officer would have been justified in taking a reasonable responsibility." Meanwhile, President and cabinet would reconsider the Fort Sumter problem.[13]

2. *Memorandum from Mr. Seward*

WILLIAM HOWARD RUSSELL, correspondent for the London *Times*, found Abraham Lincoln a more impressive figure than he had anticipated. He was long, craggy, strong, and awkward, as everyone said he was, but to study his "strange, quaint face and head, covered with its thatch of wild republican hair" was to get an impression of kindness and good sense, and although "the mouth was made to enjoy a joke," there was plenty of firmness in it. Russell liked it when Lincoln told him that the *Times* was one of the greatest powers in the world, and he also liked the President's whimsical addition—"in fact, I don't know anything which has much more power, except perhaps the Mississippi River." Greeting a convocation of diplomats at the White House, Lincoln apparently had to restrain an impulse to shake hands with everybody; smiling good-naturedly, he bowed instead, and his bow was ungainly, jerky, "a prodigiously violent demonstration," as Russell felt, which "had almost the effect of a smack in its rapidity and abruptness." All in all, Russell felt that by the standards of European society, Lincoln was hardly a gentleman, but no one who saw him could fail to take a second look at him.

After paying a more or less formal call at the White House, Russell was invited to a state dinner, held on the evening of March 28—the first affair of the kind for the new administration. The Englishman scanned the cabinet members with frank curiosity. Secretary Chase, clearly, was distinguished and intelligent, a man of power and energy; Cameron seemed able and adroit, with deep-set eyes over a thin mouth; Welles did not look like much, although Russell was assured that he was a man of ability even though he hardly knew one end of a ship from the other; and Blair was a hard, lean Scotchman, with a head that might be "an anvil for ideas to be hammered on." Russell admitted he was agreeably disappointed in Mrs. Lincoln. She was pleasant, nicely gowned, and carried herself with dignity, and altogether seemed to be much more of a person than unkind secessionist ladies in Washington were saying she was. Russell noted that General Scott had come to the dinner but did not stay, having been compelled by some indisposition to retire.[1]

Scott's retirement was perhaps advisable. He had just given Lincoln a memorandum that was about to raise a storm; it was so disturbing that when the party at last ended, Lincoln asked the cabinet members to remain and listen to it. As he read it, Lincoln seemed agitated, as well he might. Having previously urged that Fort Sumter be abandoned, Scott now was advising the same thing in respect to Fort Pickens, and was basing his advice, not on military considerations, but on straight political grounds.

It seemed doubtful, the general had written, "whether the voluntary evacuation of Fort Sumter alone would have a decisive effect upon the States now wavering between adherence to the Union and secession. It is known, indeed, that it would be charged to *necessity*, and the holding of Fort Pickens would be adduced in support of that view. Our Southern friends, however, are clear that the evacuation of both the forts would instantly soothe and give confidence to the eight remaining slaveholding states, and render their cordial adherence to the Union perpetual. The holding of Forts Jefferson and Taylor, on the ocean keys, depends on entirely different principles, and should never be abandoned; and, indeed, the giving up of Forts Sumter and Pickens may be best justified by the hope that we should thereby recover the State to which they geographically belong by the liberality of the act, besides retaining the eight doubtful states."

Seward had assured Russell a few days earlier that "we will give up nothing we have" and had insisted that the line laid down in the inaugural (to hold, occupy, and possess) clearly expressed administration policy. Now the general of the armies was saying that this policy must be abandoned, and when the President finished reading the memorandum, there was a brief, stunned silence. Less than a fortnight earlier the cabinet had agreed, almost to a man, that Fort Sumter ought to be abandoned, but in the days since then the urge to "soothe and give confidence" to the slave states that remained in the Union had grown perceptibly weaker. Blair spoke up angrily to say that General Scott was far out of line; he was "playing the part of a politician, not a general," and as far as Blair could see, there was no military reason to give up Fort Pickens. The meeting ended at last, with the understanding that the cabinet would reassemble the next day and that each member once more would submit in writing his ideas concerning what ought to be done.[2]

By noon of March 29, when the cabinet came together, it was evident that there had been a change of heart. General Scott's surprising pronunciamento about Fort Pickens seemed to have thrown the whole business into sharper relief. Secretary Chase, who had wavered uncertainly at the first meeting, had been purged of his doubts. If war would come from an attempt to provision Fort Sumter, he wrote, it would come just as certainly from an attempt to keep Fort Pickens. He himself was definitely in favor of retaining Fort Pickens; by now he was "just as clearly in favor of provisioning Fort Sumter." If the attempt to send rations to Major Anderson should be resisted by military force, Anderson should be reinforced: "If war is to be the result I perceive no reason why it may not be best begun in consequence of military resistance to the efforts of the administration to sustain troops of the Union stationed under the authority of the government in a fort of the Union in the ordinary course of service."

Chase spoke for most of his colleagues. Attorney General Bates hedged slightly; he would reinforce Fort Pickens, but as to Sumter, his best judgment was that "the time is come either to evacuate or relieve it." Caleb Smith still remained where he had been at the first cabinet meeting—he wanted the government to pull out of Fort Sumter—and in this he did no more than reflect the attitude of his politician guardian, Secretary Seward. For Seward, despite the firm words he had uttered to correspondent Russell, wanted Major Anderson withdrawn.

Seward was fully prepared to have the Federal government take a stand that would mean war, but he believed that Fort Pickens rather than Fort Sumter was the place where the stand ought to be taken. He felt (as he wrote the President) that the notion of coming to Major Anderson's relief by force of arms was simply impractical and hence ought not to be tried. "The dispatch of an expedition to supply or re-enforce Sumter," he asserted, "would provoke an attack and so involve a war at that point. The fact of preparation for such an expedition would inevitably transpire, and would therefore precipitate the war—and probably defeat the object. I do not think it wise to provoke a civil war beginning at Charleston and in rescue of an untenable position." Fort Pickens, however, was a different case: "I would at once and at every cost prepare for a war at Pensacola . . . to be taken however only as a consequence of maintaining the possession and authority of the United States."[3]

The ordinary human eye could not quite follow all that Secretary Seward was doing in the weeks immediately following Lincoln's inauguration, and his course in connection with the Sumter-Pickens business was downright subterranean. During the winter Seward had become, in the Senate, the Republican party's semi-official voice of moderation, the conciliator who thought a peace by compromise and adjustment possible to attain. More recently he had been playing the same part with a more official touch, playing it as if he could make as well as enunciate administration policy. If he was now drawing a sharp distinction between a war begun at Charleston and a war begun at Pensacola, he was speaking

partly from principle, partly in support of promises already
made (by grapevine) to Jefferson Davis's representatives,
and partly as a bid to lodge the effective final authority of
the new administration in the hands of the Secretary of
State—Seward's hands.

Two days before this momentous cabinet meeting, Seward
had talked in confidence with the sympathetic Charles Francis Adams, whom he was naming (with the President's approval) United States Minister to Great Britain. Adams noted
in his diary that Seward "spoke of the President kindly and
as gradually coming right," but this qualified approval was
followed by words of sharp criticism. The President, said
Seward, had "no system, no relative ideas, no conception of
his situation," and showed "little application to great ideas"—
all of which made things most difficult for his Secretary of
State. Not long after this meeting, Adams wrote gloomily
that the country seemed to be drifting into war, and he certainly reflected Seward's feeling if he did not actually echo
it when he added: "I see nothing but incompetency in the
head. The man is not equal to the hour."[4]

Observing the inauguration of Jefferson Davis, Mr. Yancey, of Alabama, had discerned a happy meeting of the man
and the hour. Observing the first three weeks of Lincoln's
administration, Mr. Adams, of Massachusetts, had been able
to see nothing of the kind. The incompetency that he did
see might perhaps be remedied if Secretary Seward acted
fast and with firmness, and this much Seward was quite eager
to do. Seward used two instruments: a memorandum for the
President, written out in his own hand and saying astounding
things with an air of superior detachment; and a competent,
hard-working captain in the army's Corps of Engineers,
Montgomery Meigs, who had ideas about Fort Pickens along
with a refreshing readiness to behave irregularly in irregular
times like the present.

Seward got to work with Meigs first. He began on March
29, not long after the new orientation of the cabinet had
been manifest, taking him to the White House and introducing
him to President Lincoln; the purpose of the meeting apparently being little more than to register Captain Meigs on
the mind of the President as a loyal soldier who knew what
to do about this Florida fort. (Meigs told the President that
Fort Pickens most certainly could be held, provided the navy

had not already given it away.) After the brief meeting at the White House Seward explained the situation to Meigs.

All men of sense, the Secretary said, knew that a war must come. He wanted to see "the burden of it"—by which, apparently, he meant the onus of starting it—fall upon those who by rebellion had provoked it. He had always wanted the troops withdrawn from Fort Sumter, which he considered too close to Washington. He wanted to have the real showdown at Fort Pickens, and possibly along the Texas coast as well, where Sam Houston might conceivably restore Texas to her duty if properly supported by United States troops. (On the latter point, Seward was indulging in one of the vainest of all the vain hopes of the 1860s.) But whatever happened elsewhere, Fort Pickens was to be held, and Captain Meigs was to develop his plans in that connection.[5]

March 31 was a Sunday, and Captain Meigs was getting ready to go to church when Colonel Erasmus Keyes, military secretary to General Scott, interrupted him and took him off to see Secretary Seward, who had precise orders: Col. Keyes and Captain Meigs were to commit to paper a suitable plan for relieving and holding Fort Pickens and were to take it to the White House and submit it to the President by four o'clock that afternoon. Keyes and Meigs went over to the War Department, compared notes, found that their views on Fort Pickens were in harmony, and by half-past two had their plan drafted. It did not seem likely that they could get the paper to General Scott, win his approval, and then get to the White House by four o'clock, so they left Scott out of it and went directly to see the President. Lincoln listened to their plan, approved it, and told them to take it to General Scott and tell him this was something the President wanted imperatively: "I depend on you gentlemen," said Lincoln, "to push this thing through." Off to see Scott went the two officers. Scott made no objection to anything; Secretary Seward came in, and as Meigs remembered it, "the matter was talked over and resolved upon."[6]

Resolved upon, be it noted, by the Secretary of State. Simon Cameron, the Secretary of War, who held actual authority over Scott, Keyes, Meigs, and the troops that were to be dispatched, had been bypassed. It was Seward who was selecting officers, taking them to the White House, visiting the general-in-chief and expediting matters generally. Presi-

dent Lincoln had made up his mind to reinforce Fort Pickens, but it was Seward who was translating the decision into
action. The plan itself was simple enough. A transport would
land soldiers and stores at Fort Pickens, on the seaward
side; at the same time a warship, cleared for action, would
steam in through the harbor entrance and keep the Confederates from interfering. Nothing was being done through
channels. (Seward had even picked the naval officer to command the warship, bustling Lieutenant David Dixon Porter,
without saying anything to Secretary Welles about it, and
was drafting orders for the President to sign in that connection.) The incompetency in administration which had so
grieved Mr. Adams would at least be given a different guise
by the intense dynamism of the Secretary of State.

There was always a chance, of course, that Lincoln himself would fail to realize where the authority was being exercised, and Seward had written a memorandum to give the
President guidance. This document, headed "Some Thoughts
for the President's Consideration," landed on Lincoln's desk
on April 1. The President had, on that day, other matters
demanding his consideration; years later the editor of his
papers found twenty-four documents for April 1, referring
to appointments or to the planned expeditions. Now there
was this one: as completely fantastic a note as any American
President ever received from his Secretary of State.

Seward began by baldly remarking: "We are at the end
of a month's administration, and yet without a policy, either
domestic or foreign." This, to be sure, he conceded, was un-
avoidable, but now was the time for action; "further delay
to adopt and prosecute our policies for both domestic and
foreign affairs would not only bring scandal on the Administration but danger upon the country."

For domestic policy, Seward went on, the big thing was
to "change the question before the public from one upon
slavery, or about slavery, for a question upon union or disunion. In other words, from what would be regarded as a
party question to one of Patriotism or Union." Fort Sumter
had somehow got itself identified with the slavery issue as a
matter of party politics; forget about it, therefore, concentrate heavily on retention of the Gulf Coast forts, recall all
warships from foreign stations to be prepared for a blockade,
and thus "raise distinctly the question of *Union* or *Disunion*."

Foreign policy should be vigorous. France and England had been pressing Mexico for payment of certain debts, and Spain had been meddling with affairs in Santo Domingo; explanations should be demanded at once, agents should be sent through Canada, Mexico, and Central America to arouse a "continental spirit of independence against European intervention," and if the governments from which explanations were demanded returned unsatisfactory answers, war should be declared. Then, clipping his argument off into terse paragraphs, Secretary Seward got down to bed rock:

"But whatever policy we adopt, there must be energetic prosecution of it.

"For this purpose it must be somebody's business to pursue and direct it incessantly.

"Either the President must do it himself, and be all the while active in it, or

"Devolve it on some member of his Cabinet. Once adopted, debates on it must end and all agree and abide.

"It is not in my especial province.

"But I neither seek to evade nor assume responsibility."[7]

As President of the United States, Abraham Lincoln received his full share of odd letters, all of them demanding something and demanding it with especial fervor because the times were so perilous. Until this first day of April, the oddest of his letters was possibly one that came to him from a certain Amalia Majocchi Valtellina, an opera singer who found herself at a dead end in Rahway, New Jersey, and who demanded that the President assume the mortgage on her villa there so that she could go back to Italy and resume her career. "The orrible future of our situation, fright me," she had written. "I have tryd to find some persons in Rahway, to hold the mortgag; but hunapply, in the hard time, is impracticable. The thought com to me, to lay our circumstances, to your Excellency . . . I confess my temerity, but our situation is orrible and frightful, that make me daring, hoping in your Noble heart a favorable answer."[8]

Thus Signora Valtellina, whose plea went unanswered. Now there was Secretary Seward, who felt, as did the singer, that the situation was "orrible and frightful" and who knew just what the President ought to do about it—and who offered a suggestion that was quite as fantastic on its own level as the one she had offered. Secretary Seward had to be answered.

It was a busy day at the White House, but Lincoln lost no time in writing a reply.

As far as he could see, he wrote, the administration had a perfectly clear and definite policy—the one set forth in the inaugural about the determination to hold, occupy, and possess government property in areas where people believed they had seceded: the determination, in other words, to maintain an unbroken Union. At the time this policy was enunciated, it had had Seward's express approval, and it had governed the administration's actions ever since. Furthermore, it was hard for the President to understand how the reinforcement of Fort Sumter "would be done on a slavery, or party issue, while that of Fort Pickens would be on a more national and patriotic one." As to foreign policy, the demanding of explanations, the making of war, and so on: "I remark that if this is to be done, *I* must do it." Then Lincoln summed it all up in words that even an infatuated power seeker was bound to understand:

"When a general line of policy is adopted, I apprehend there is no danger of its being changed without good reason, or continuing to be the subject of unnecessary debate; still, upon points arising in its progress, I wish, and I suppose I am entitled to have the advice of all the cabinet."[9]

It is not entirely clear whether Lincoln gave Seward the letter to read or simply let him have the gist of it verbally, but in either case he made his point: Lincoln would run the administration and he would also run the cabinet; policy was what he said it was, and the execution of it lay in his own hands. It would take the Secretary a few days to assimilate this, but he would do it eventually and no soreness would remain; in the end there would be more of human warmth and liking between Lincoln and Seward than between Lincoln and any other members of the cabinet. Once put firmly in his place, Seward would fill that place loyally and with much of the competency that Mr. Adams prized so highly.

It would not appear just yet, however. First Seward would have to extricate himself and his government from the tangle that he had been so industriously creating, and before this could be done, there would be a windy mess, which, if it did not actually help to start the war, at least had a good deal to do with the way in which the war was started. Seward was badly overextended. He had made unequivocal promises, at a time when he and others supposed that their fulfillment would rest entirely with him, and he was abruptly learning that he could not deliver what he had said he would deliver. Greatly deceiving himself, he had deceived others, and the memory of the deception would linger for many years, adding to a bitterness and misunderstanding that would have been almost too strong even without this final addition.

Meanwhile the whole business meant delay and a general slowing-down, and the administration was at last aware that it was in a desperate race with time. Major Anderson could keep his flag flying for two more weeks, which meant that Lincoln had precisely a fortnight to show that his inaugural address, his adminstration policy, and he himself had to be taken seriously. When Major Anderson hauled down his flag, everything would be over—unless, before the flag was struck, some imposing and unmistakable act made clear to everyone the government's fixed determination to do what it had said it was going to do. This act might have taken place at Fort Pickens; could not now, because the new expedition could not possibly reach the place before Major Anderson's time expired. Whatever would be done must be done at Fort Sumter, and unless it were done more deftly than there was any reason to think possible, the mere doing of it would cause a war.

3. *"If You Have No Doubt . . ."*

SECRETARY SEWARD grossly deceived Jefferson Davis's representatives, but they at least met him halfway. They were men prepared to be deceived. Believing firmly that any reasonable man must eventually concede the justice of the Southern cause and the independence of the Confederate states, they would find plausible any words that hinted they were right. Reaching Washington shortly after Lincoln's inauguration, they took it for granted that both Seward and Cameron meant to follow a peace policy and they assumed that these men would carry Lincoln with them. As early as March 6 Commissioner M. J. Crawford informed Secretary Toombs that "the President himself is really not aware of the condition of the country and his Secretaries of State and War are to open the difficulties and dangers to him in cabinet today."[1]

On March 11 the commissioners—Mr. Crawford, Mr. Roman, and Mr. Forsyth—made formal application for a meeting with Secretary Seward, at which they hoped to arrange for the surrender of Fort Sumter and the recognition of Confederate independence. Seward of course could not see them without tacitly admitting that they somehow represented something which was entitled to deal with the Secretary of State. He talked instead with their emissary, Senator R. M. T. Hunter, of Virginia, and he wrote a memorandum, addressed to no one, which seems to have reached the commissioners' hands. In it Seward was quite starchy. The Secretary of State, he wrote, saw in the events that had recently taken place in the South, "not a rightful and accomplished revolution and an independent nation, with an established government, but rather a perversion of a temporary and partisan excitement to the inconsiderate purposes of an unjustifiable and unconstitutional aggression upon the rights and authority vested in the Federal government."[2]

Having delivered this message, Senator Hunter retired from the scene. His place as go-between was taken by the eminent Justice Campbell, who had talked so earnestly (and so sensibly) with Seward a few weeks earlier about the absurdity of letting the slavery quarrel develop into war. Campbell quickly found that despite those stiff words about unjustifiable and unconstitutional aggression, Seward was extremely reasonable. The commissioners had been in town no more than a week before they were convinced that Fort Sumter was going to be surrendered. They were convinced because Seward had flatly and without qualification told Campbell that this was going to happen.

Campbell talked with Seward on March 15—the day on which Lincoln had asked the members of his cabinet to give him their written opinions regarding the advisability of provisioning Fort Sumter. Speaking as one old friend to another, Campbell remarked that he was about to write to Jefferson Davis. What should he tell him?

"You may say to him," said Seward, "that before that letter reaches him"—here Seward broke off to ask him how long it took to get a letter from Washington to Montgomery. Three days, he was told. Seward then went on, his promise made all the more convincing because he had interrupted himself to ask that little question—"you may say to him that before that letter reaches him, the telegraph will have informed him that Sumter will have been evacuated."[3]

This was as explicit as anything could be, and the word was passed along. When the telegraph failed to convey the information Seward had said it would convey, the aggressive Robert Toombs grew impatient, and the commissioners soothed him with a confident message: "If there is faith in man we may rely on the assurances we have here as to the status. Time is essential to a peaceful issue of this mission. In the present position of affairs precipitation is war." They also telegraphed innocently to Beauregard, asking if Fort Sumter had been surrendered yet.[4]

Beauregard, who never appears to have taken a great deal of stock in the stories that were coming out of Washington, of course replied that there had been no surrender. Back to Seward went Justice Campbell. Seward assured him that the resolution to abandon the place had passed the cabinet, and that its execution was up to the President; he himself did not know just what had caused the delay. The next day Seward told Campbell that the policy was a hard one, opposed by many influential Republicans, but that the decision stood. The fort would be given up; also, there would be no change in the status of things at Fort Pickens.

Monday, April 1, at last. The cabinet has reversed itself, the plan for the relief of Fort Pickens has been drawn up and approved, and Seward has given the President that memorandum concerning what ought to be done and who ought to be doing it; and Justice Campbell comes once more to talk with Seward. Campbell has had an inquiry from Governor Pickens, brought on by the governor's recent chat with Ward Lamon; Pickens wants to know what the latest word about Fort Sumter may be.

. . . There is perceptible here a faint change in the wind, which Justice Campbell hardly noticed at the time but thought about later. Seward was as smooth and jaunty as ever, but his promises were just a little narrower. There was no design to reinforce Fort Sumter, he insisted; Campbell could tell Governor Pickens that although the President might indeed desire to send reinforcements, he would not do so. Campbell replied that the people of South Carolina, the gov-

ernor no less than everybody else, were notoriously touchy.
If they learned that Lincoln even wanted to send help to
Major Anderson, they might start shooting. Seward at once
said that he would run right over and see the President. Justice
Campbell was to wait for him.

After "some minutes," as Campbell remembered it, Seward
came back and wrote out a message which, he said, Campbell could properly send off to the governor of South Carolina. The message read: "I am satisfied the Government will
not undertake to supply Fort Sumter without giving notice to
Governor Pickens." Either because he was satisfied with this
or because he believed that it was the best he could get,
the Justice departed. He still had no notion that anyone was
being deceitful. Years later, however, he wrote that he finally
came to believe that Seward in all of their talks "was deliberately and intentionally false."[5]

It was a curious business, that April 1 conversation.
Whether Seward, in his brief absence from his office, actually
saw the President; whether, if he did see him, he then learned
that his bid to take over control of the government had been
rejected; whether, seeing Lincoln or not seeing him, he had
begun to realize that the policy in regard to Fort Sumter
was about to take a right-angle turn—to these questions there
is no certain answer. But the promise he finally gave Campbell
that day was not at all the promise he had been reciting
so convincingly all through the preceding fortnight. Until
now, Seward had been saying that Fort Sumter would be
given up: now he was merely saying that if the government
decided not to give it up, it would promptly tell the governor
of South Carolina. If the Confederate authorities had studied
the contrast, they might have seen in it something profoundly ominous. Whatever Seward may have intended, he
had given what amounted to a clear warning that something
drastic was about to happen.

The final decision had not yet been made: or, if made,
had not been committed to paper; but rumors were beginning to circulate. After all, the army and navy people in
New York were preparing two expeditions, one to be sent
to Fort Pickens, the other to stand by for possible use at
Fort Sumter, and the news was getting around. The Confederate commissioners passed the rumors on to Toombs,
saying that "the war wing presses on the President"; then,

having possibly received some echo of Seward's amazing proposal for a foreign war to take off the heat at home, they reported that "high circles" in the capital believed that the preparations were aimed at Spain, "on account of the Dominican affair." Not being completely daft, they added that of course the expedition which was fitting out might be ordered to the Confederate coast: "Hence we would say strengthen the defenses at the mouths of the Mississippi."[6]

Somewhere between April 1 and April 4, Abraham Lincoln made up his mind. He would fulfill the pledge in his inaugural, and he would fulfill it actively, not passively; that is, he would take his stand at Fort Sumter. He had won a majority of the cabinet over to his way of thinking, he had shown his Secretary of State who was boss, and the time for drift and reflection was over. On April 4 Lincoln called Gustavus Fox to the White House and gave him the news.

Fox had been in New York, making preliminary arrangements for the Fort Sumter expedition but getting no orders about it, and he had returned to Washington to see what was going to happen. When he reached the White House he was taken to President Lincoln, who told him that the government would definitely send supplies to Major Anderson and that Fox was the man to take them there. A special messenger, said Lincoln, was going down to give Governor Pickens due notice, and to tell him that no troops would be landed if the delivery of the provisions was not opposed; the messenger, said the President, would reach Charleston long before Fox could get there. Lincoln also gave Fox formal orders from Secretary of War Cameron: Fox was to put supplies and soldiers aboard ship at New York and go to the entrance of Charleston harbor, where he was to try to put rations into Fort Sumter. If armed forces opposed him, he was to report to the senior United States naval officer present, and this officer would have orders from Secretary Welles to use his entire force to batter his way into the harbor. When this had been done, Fox was to land both troops and supplies. A message was going to Major Anderson over Cameron's signature telling him what was being attempted and ordering him to hold out, if he could, until the relief expedition arrived. There was a qualifying sentence saying that a complete, last-ditch-last-man resistance was not expected of him; the major was authorized to surrender if necessary to save the lives of his command and himself.

Action was what Fox had been wanting and now it was going to start, but he felt obliged to point out to the President that they were cutting things rather fine. Anderson had said he could not possibly hold out beyond April 15. Fox had to go to New York, charter at least one steamer, get it properly fueled and supplied, load it with soldiers and army freight, and then steam 632 miles from Sandy Hook to Charleston. He was not sure there would be time enough. Lincoln told him to do the best he could, and explained about the naval arrangements. Secretary Welles was sending down the warships *Powhatan, Pocahontas,* and *Pawnee,* along with the revenue cutter *Harriet Lane,* which the Treasury Department was making available; these vessels would be cruising off the bar at the entrance to Charleston harbor when Fox got there and would (it was hoped) be powerful enough to force their way into the harbor if force had to be used.[7]

Fox hurried back to New York, where he chartered the crack liner *Baltic* and (after losing half a day persuading a resident army colonel that this Fort Sumter business was real) got troops and supplies aboard. He also engaged the tugs *Uncle Ben* and *Yankee,* and he would be ready to sail on April 9.

The expedition he was leading had been substantially augmented since he first suggested it. Originally the big idea had been to slip a boatload of provisions into the harbor by a stealthy dash at night, relying on speed and deception to get the supplies to Fort Sumter before the Confederates knew what was up; now all question of surprise was given up, Governor Pickens was being officially notified in advance that the thing was going to be tried, and four warships were going along with orders to open fire if there was any trouble. Clearly enough the entire concept of the operation had changed. A month earlier the underlying idea had been to uphold Major Anderson and his garrison; now it was nothing less than to uphold the breadth and depth of Federal authority over an unbroken Union. The first might have been done by a quick dash with nobody looking; the second would mean nothing unless seen by all the world, and if General Beauregard's cannon might help call the world's attention to it, that would be up to General Beauregard. The first had been nothing more than a play for time. This was a frank avowal that time had run out.

Table stakes, in other words. Sending the outrider down to Governor Pickens, Lincoln was shooting the works. He was not forcing a war, but he was serving notice that he would fight rather than back down; more, he was setting the stage in such a way that Jefferson Davis, if he in his turn preferred to fight rather than to back down, would have to shoot first. Lincoln had been plainly warned by Lamon and by Hurlbut that a ship taking provisions to Fort Sumter would be fired on. Now he was sending the ship, with advance notice to the men who had the guns. He was sending warships and soldiers as well, but they would remain in the background; if there was going to be a war it would begin over a boatload of salt pork and crackers—over that, and the infinite overtones which by now were involved. Not for nothing did Captain Fox remark afterward that it seemed very important to Lincoln that South Carolina "should stand before the civilized world as having fired upon bread."[8]

By contrast there was the case of Fort Pickens. The program in respect to that fort had not gone smoothly, because Captain Adams insisted that he was still bound by orders which everyone in Washington had overlooked, but the hitch caused by all of this made little difference in the end; a special messenger, Lieutenant John L. Worden, of the navy, was sent down overland with revised orders, Captain Vogdes's company was landed, more troops and abundant supplies came down from New York just as Captain Meigs had proposed, and by the end of the month the government had 1100 men in Fort Pickens and the danger that Braxton Bragg would sweep the place into the sea was gone forever.[9] Fort Pickens got the muscle and the direct action, and Fort Sumter got the careful handling, the worrying, the intricate maneuvering—and, exposed to the first flash of fire, the fuse that led straight to the main magazine.

The Fort Sumter expedition would sail just as soon as Captain Fox had everything in order, and yet somewhere in his mind Lincoln seems to have held a faint hope that some peaceful arrangement might yet be made. The Virginia convention, which might or might not vote the Old Dominion out of the Union, was still in session, and even before Lincoln became President, he had explored the possibility of a deal. To William C. Rives, one of the Virginia delegates, Lincoln had in February offered to abandon Fort Sumter if the convention would adjourn *sine die* without passing an ordinance of secession. Now, even as he was concluding that the Sumter expedition must go forward, it appears that Lincoln, in one form or another, renewed this offer.

There is a certain mystery that still hangs over most of the things that happened during the first week in April 1861, but it seems reasonably clear that Lincoln got word to Richmond that he would like to talk with some Unionist-minded delegate to the secession convention, and on April 4 John B. Baldwin came to see him. To him, Lincoln apparently repeated what he had said to Rives six weeks earlier —he would swap a fort for a state and consider it a good bargain. The deal could not be made: Baldwin was in no condition to bind the secession convention, adjournment could easily be followed by the calling of a new convention, and in studying what passes for a record of the conversation, one gets the feeling that neither man could quite understand the pressures that bore upon the other. About all that can be said with real assurance is that the negotiation, whatever might conceivably have come of it, got nowhere. One is left with a haunting feeling that everyone might have been much better off if this particular avenue had been explored earlier and much more vigorously.[10]

Meanwhile there was a final, comic-opera mix-up which had no especial effect on the course of history but which does stand as a striking illustration of the strange way in which the administration conducted its business during the first half-dozen weeks of its tenure.

In selecting naval vessels to meet Captain Fox off the entrance to Charleston harbor, Secretary Welles had specified that the steamer *Powhatan* be flagship of the force, and *Powhatan*'s skipper, Captain Samuel Mercer, received orders to that effect. Secretary Seward, however, was backing the Fort Pickens expedition, and he wanted *Powhatan* for this service. Furthermore, he wanted *Powhatan* commanded by Lieutenant Porter, who was working closely with Captain Meigs in the project. Orders were accordingly prepared relieving Mercer and putting Porter in his place, and Seward took these orders to the White House and got Lincoln's signature on them. It appears that the President signed without quite realizing what he was signing, and it is wholly certain that Secretary Welles, who supposed that he had full authority to assign warships and officers, knew nothing at all about the business.

Powhatan was due to sail from New York on April 6. Just before sailing time, Porter appeared, flourished Lincoln's order, dispossessed Mercer (over the latter's strong objection), and assumed command of the warship. Mercer got on the wire to the Navy Department, and Welles indignantly hurried to the White House, collecting Seward en route. There were explanations, complaints, and at last an abashed admission by the President that the order to Porter should never have been issued. Welles was told to wire New York, restoring Mercer to *Powhatan*'s command, and he immediately did so. Porter, however, refused to pay any attention to this order, on the ground that he had been put in command of the warship by the President of the United States and could be relieved by no lesser authority. In the end he sailed *Powhatan* off for Pensacola in spite of everybody, depriving the Fort Sumter expedition of better than 25 per cent of its naval strength. In the long run this made little difference; what mattered at Charleston was that the shooting began there, and the result would have been the same even if *Powhatan* had been present.[11]

Secretary Seward was coming to the end of his period of assumption of authority; the end was not graceful and the aftermath was not good. John A. Campbell and the Confederate commissioners were beginning to suspect that the Secretary had been playing games with them, and on April 7 Campbell sent to Seward a melancholy letter of inquiry. There were increasing rumors, he said, that the government was mounting some sort of expedition for the Confederate seacoast, and although the Justice continued to believe that this could not be aimed at Fort Sumter, he did feel that something ought to be said or done to quiet the rising excitement. He included in his letter a quotation that was more apt than he perhaps realized: "Such government by blind-man's buff, stumbling along too far, will end by the general over-turn." Seward immediately sent a reply: "Faith as to Sumter fully kept—wait and see."

It is hard to be sure just what faith Seward believed that

he was talking about. An official messenger had already left for Charleston with a word from the President to Governor Pickens, and Seward knew it; he knew, as well, that Fox would be sailing in forty-eight hours, and that his convoying warships had already left. Deceiving Campbell, he was still deceiving himself, for he appears to have been convinced, even at this late hour, that everything would at last wind up in peace, harmony, and joyful reunion. On the night after he wrote that message for Justice Campbell, Seward chatted with Russell, of the London *Times,* over the whist table in Seward's house and assured the correspondent that even the secessionists would presently understand that the administration had no aggressive intent. "When the Southern states see that we mean them no wrong—that we intend no violence to persons, rights, or things," he told Russell, "they will see their mistake and one after another they will come back into the Union." This happy turn of events, he said, would take place within three months. A Secretary of State is of course entitled to plant untruths in a great newspaper if that will advance his country's interests, but in this case it may be that Seward really meant what he was saying. The belief that a huge, untapped reservoir of Unionist sentiment in the South would yet wash away all traces of secession was a long time dying.[12]

There had been too much loose talk, and the whole administration had been weakened by it. Mr. Stanton wrote to his good friend Buchanan at this time that hardly anyone in the capital had any confidence in the new regime. "A strong feeling of distrust in the candor and sincerity of Lincoln personally, and of his Cabinet has sprung up," he declared. "If they had been merely silent and secret, there might have been no ground of complaint. But assurances are said to have been given, and declarations made, in conflict with the facts now transpiring in respect to the South, so that no one speaks of Lincoln or any member of his cabinet with respect or regard."[13]

It was on April 7 that Justice Campbell was assured that the faith had been fully kept in connection with Fort Sumter. Technically, this was perhaps correct, in a limited sort of way. Campbell's last promise from the Secretary had been the pledge that the government would not try to provision the fort without first telling the governor of South Carolina;

and on April 8 a War Department clerk named Robert S. Chew showed up in Charleston bearing instructions written by President Lincoln which read thus:

"You will proceed directly to Charleston, South Carolina; and if, on your arrival there, the flag of the United States shall be flying over Fort Sumpter, and the Fort shall not have been attacked, you will procure an interview with Gov. Pickens, and read to him as follows: 'I am directed by the President of the United States to notify you to expect an attempt will be made to supply Fort Sumpter with provisions only; and that, if such attempt be not resisted, no effort to throw in men, arms or ammunition will be made without further notice, or in case of an attack upon the Fort.' "[14]

Chew delivered his message that evening. It probably surprised no one except the unhappy commissioners in Washington; the Confederate authorities both in Montgomery and at Charleston had taken very little stock in the fine reports that had been coming down from the North. As early as April 2, Beauregard had been warned by Secretary of War Walker that "the Government has not at any time placed any reliance on assurances by the Government in Washington in respect to the evacuation of Fort Sumter, or entertained any confidence in the disposition of the latter to make any concession or yield any point to which it is not driven by absolute necessity." Beauregard was instructed that he should be as active and alert "as if you were in the presence of an enemy contemplating to surprise you."[15]

Charleston immediately passed Chew's message along to Montgomery, where President Davis and his cabinet considered it. It was clear that there could be but one answer; possession of Fort Sumter was as much a cardinal point of Davis's policy as of Lincoln's. Strangely enough, it was the impetuous, hard-driving Robert Toombs who was reluctant to act. When the telegram was first shown to him he remarked: "The firing upon that fort will inaugurate a civil war greater than any the world has yet seen; and I do not feel competent to advise you." The discussion went on for a long time—this was not a matter to be settled on the spur of the moment—and Toombs paced the floor, hands clasped behind him, staring off at nothing. Finally he stopped, faced President Davis, and urged against opening fire.

"Mr. President," he said, "at this time it is suicide, murder, and will lose us every friend at the North. You will wantonly strike a hornet's nest which extends from mountains to ocean, and legions now quiet will swarm out and sting us to death. It is unnecessary; it puts us in the wrong; it is fatal."[16]

It would be hard to put, in one paragraph, a better explanation of the tactical insight behind Lincoln's decision to send Captain Fox down to Charleston harbor.

On April 10 the discussion had been concluded, and if Davis had ever had any serious doubts about what his course should be, he had resolved them. On this morning Secretary Walker sent Beauregard his instructions:

"If you have no doubt of the authorized character of the agent who communicated to you the intention of the Washington Government to supply Fort Sumter by force you will at once demand its evacuation, and if this is refused proceed, in such manner as you may determine, to reduce it."[17]

4. The Circle of Fire

THE SIEGE had been carried on in earnest, but it had been like a formalized ritual carried on between friends. The Federal soldiers in the fort and the South Carolina soldiers who encircled it maintained polite relations while they got ready to kill each other, and when the big guns they were lining up went off by accident, or were fired in the wrong direction, letters of apology were quickly sent and gracefully acknowledged.

The guns had been doing a good deal of firing all winter long. Fort Sumter and South Carolina were still at peace, but their gun crews had to be exercised and there was need for target practice. Delegates to the South Carolina convention cruised about in the harbor by steamboat at the end of March, watching the discharge of guns in the different batteries, noting the way heavy shell could be exploded squarely over the deep-water channel—and, after the firing had ended, enjoying "a very handsome collation" of chicken salad, sandwiches, and cake and wine. Passing Fort Sumter on the way home, the delegates could see Federal officers on the parapet, and believed Anderson himself was surveying them with a telescope.[1]

Now and then there were accidents. Anderson's men mounted a ten-inch Columbiad as a mortar in the parade ground, pointing it at Charleston's fabled park, The Battery; to see if the alignment was correct, they got Major Anderson's permission to fire one shot with a greatly reduced charge. The reduction in the charge was insufficient; the gun threw its projectile in a soaring parabola that almost landed it in downtown Charleston, and there was a flurry of intense excitement, with officers coming out under flag of truce to ask the major if he was really starting the war. Explanations and an apology followed, and the excitement died down. Similarly, a few days later, some inexpert gun layer in Beauregard's gun crews fired a shot that actually nicked a corner of Fort Sumter itself. Again there were flags of truce, inquiries, and apologies. On April 3, when the tension had appreciably risen, the little schooner *Rhoda B. Shannon,* carrying ice down from Boston to Savannah, came blundering up the channel toward Charleston harbor and was promptly fired on, one ball splitting her mainsail. Anderson's drums beat his men to quarters, and at least five of his officers demanded that he open fire on the nearest Confederate battery; Anderson temporized, sent an inquiry ashore under a flag, learned that the schooner's captain had simply lost his way and that he carried nothing the Sumter garrison wanted in any case, and the incident was closed.[2]

Once, early in the spring, Mrs. Anderson came down from New York for a visit, bringing with her Peter Hart, who had been a sergeant in Anderson's company in the Mexican War. Mrs. Anderson felt that with so much disaffection everywhere her husband ought to have one man on whom he could rely implicitly, so she was bringing him this former sergeant. Reaching Charleston, she went to Governor Pickens, who immediately gave her a pass to go to the fort; he did not think he could issue a pass for Sergeant Hart—after all, the man constituted reinforcements, of a sort—but Mrs. Anderson talked him into it, and a Confederate guard boat took her and the former sergeant out to the fort. A Federal sentry cried a challenge as the boat neared the fort, and a

Confederate officer took up his speaking trumpet and called: "Mrs. Major Anderson!" Back came the summons: "Mrs. Anderson, advance"—and the major's wife and the ex-soldier whom he could trust came on to the wharf, and Major Anderson ran out crying "My glorious wife!"

The visit was very brief. There was no talk about home, children, or any other personal matters; Mrs. Anderson simply explained about Sergeant Hart, the sergeant was folded into the Sumter garrison, and Mrs. Anderson got into the guard boat, returned to Charleston, and went back to New York. With the help of the governor of South Carolina and a former sergeant of United States artillery, her mind had been made easier.[3]

Late in March, Anderson and Beauregard had an odd exchange. It had been printed that the Yankees were going to withdraw the Sumter garrison and that Beauregard had said that he would not permit this unless Anderson first surrendered, and Anderson's feelings were hurt. He wrote to Beauregard about it in protest, and both Beauregard and Governor Pickens replied politely that nothing of the sort had been said or contemplated. Anderson wrote back that he knew Beauregard could not have said such a thing, and the amenities were properly preserved.[4]

A Northerner who visited Charleston that winter found that he was greeted without any particular hostility: the people he talked with all asked if the North really intended coercion and closed by saying that everyone in South Carolina hoped for a peaceful separation—peaceful, but of course a separation. He looked on with interest at the drill of the home guard, a modestly uniformed assortment of elderly men, some of them with white hair, and was told that this was a volunteer police force, raised to overawe the Negroes during the absence on military service of most of the city's young men. One Charlestonian explained that the illiterate Negro slaves, knowing nothing of anything that happened ten miles away from them, had somehow caught on to the fact that big things were stirring in the land. . . . "Our slaves have heard of Lincoln—that he is a black man, or black Republican, or black something—that he is to become ruler of this country on the fourth of March—that he is a friend of theirs and will help them." Hence it was essential for the state to establish its independence, so that the black folk would know that this legendary Lincoln could do nothing for them; essential, as well, for the home guard to come out and drill, while the younger men manhandled the big guns out in the marshes.[5]

So the winter wore away: guns firing harmlessly, officers exchanging dignified notes, elderly guards drilling under the Carolina sun, Negroes mysteriously hearing something, amateur soldiers toiling to learn the cruel skills of a new profession—and nothing irrevocable was actually happening. But now the pace was quickening, and it would never go any more slowly. Lincoln had made up his mind and sent his message, Secretary Toombs had voiced his grim doubts, Davis had come to his own conclusion and sent a message of his own—and on the night of April 8 the steamer *Baltic* left her New York wharf, dropped down the bay, and anchored until dawn just inside of Sandy Hook. The warships and tugs had gone on ahead, separately. *Baltic* would sail in the morning, there would be a rendezvous off the Charleston bar, and it was conceivable that the Sumter garrison would get fresh provisions.

Gustavus Fox, aboard *Baltic*, had few doubts about his mission, several doubts about Major Anderson. When he visited Fort Sumter, he had supposed that he would find a straightforward soldier, thinking only of his soldierly duty and hoping his government would send him help in time. To such a man Fox would have told everything he knew— about the projected relief expedition, about the eddying cross-currents in Washington, about Lincoln himself. But he felt that he had found a man who was "on the other side, politically as well as in a military point of view"; as a Massachusetts-born Unionist, Fox could neither understand nor sympathize with the American of conflicting loyalties.[6]

Anderson, whose loyalty to the Federal government never wavered for a moment, had doubts of his own. He doubted that the relief expedition would work, and he wrote to the War Department: "I fear that its result cannot fail to be disastrous to all concerned." He felt that Washington should have told him about it earlier; Fox had done no more than hint at it, and Lamon had convinced him that the thing would not be tried. "We shall strive to do our duty," said the major, "though I frankly say that my heart is not in the war which I see is thus to be commenced."[7]

One man who had no doubts was Beauregard. He was a soldier whose loyalty lay with his duty. He had come to Charleston to form what he called "a circle of fire" around Fort Sumter; the circle was formed, and he would set it aflame whenever he was told to do so, content to follow the destiny of his state. To a Northern friend he wrote that his state had called on him for his services; he had given them, "not through a false ambition or a desire to see my name (badly spelt) in print, but because I consider it my solemn duty." He hoped sooner or later to be able to retire to a farm near New Orleans, with his family, his books and a few friends around him. Meanwhile, "whether this *revolution* results in peace or war—I will take as my only guide a clear conscience and a fearless heart."[8] Now he had his orders from Secretary Walker, and he would carry them out.

Another man untroubled by doubts was Roger Pryor, the Virginia Congressman, who came down to Charleston, was serenaded on the evening of April 10, and spoke with unrestrained passion to the serenaders who stood in the street in the spring dusk under his hotel balcony.

"Gentlemen, I thank you, especially that you have at last annihilated this cursed Union, reeking with corruption and insolent with excess of tyranny," cried Pryor. "Thank God, it is at last blasted and riven by the lightning wrath of an outraged and indignant people. Not only is it gone, but gone forever." South Carolina had taken the lead, but Virginia would surely follow. A great storm of cheers arose when Pryor shouted his words of advice: "I will tell you, gentlemen, what will put her in the Southern Confederation in less than an hour by Shrewsbury clock—strike a blow! The very moment that blood is shed, old Virginia will make common cause with her sisters of the South."

The news that Sumter was to be reinforced was out, and words like Pryor's were what Charleston wanted to hear. At midnight alarm guns were fired from Citadel Square, signal for the reserves to assemble, and all night long there were the beating of drums and the tramping of feet as company after company formed up—in the open streets, armories being lacking—and moved off to their posts. It was reported that a United States fleet lay off the bar, in the

windy dark, and signal lights were seen, or were believed
to have been seen, atop Fort Sumter.[9]

On the morning of April 11—cloudy, with a mild breeze,
although a heavy swell out at sea kept Captain Fox's
steamer tossing most uncomfortably on its way down from
New York—Beauregard set about the composition of the
formal demand for Fort Sumter's surrender. He had it finished by noon, and soon after that a boat with a white flag
shoved off from a Charleston wharf and headed for the fort.
It carried two of Beauregard's aides—Colonel James Chesnut, until December a United States Senator from South
Carolina, an aristocrat of aristocrats, whose wife was keeping
a diary that would be famous; and Captain Stephen D. Lee,
a West Point graduate recently resigned from the United
States Army, a man who would win fame and high position
as a Confederate officer. With them was Lieutenant Colonel
James A. Chisholm, aide-de-camp to Governor Pickens. In
due course the boat reached the fort. The officers came on
the wharf and were taken inside, and to Major Anderson
they gave General Beauregard's message.

During the war that was about to begin, various generals
would write demands for surrender. This document, however, had a tone all of its own. It had the dignity and the
odd, formal politeness of an age that was ending; it was,
furthermore, pure Beauregard from start to finish, as if it
had been written partly to make a demand on Major Anderson, partly to satisfy Beauregard's own sense of what was
correct, and partly for the appraisal of history. It might
have been a restrained argument addressed to a wayward
friend rather than a trumpet blast announcing violence. It
read:

"Sir: the Government of the Confederate States has hitherto foreborne from any hostile demonstration against Fort
Sumter, in the hope that the Government of the United
States, with a view to the amicable adjustment of all questions between the two Governments, and to avert the calamities of war, would voluntarily evacuate it.

"There was reason at one time to believe that such would
be the course pursued by the Government of the United
States, and under that impression my Government has refrained from making any demand for the surrender of the
fort. But the Confederate States can no longer delay assum-

ing actual possession of a fortification commanding the entrance of one of their harbors, and necessary to its defense and security.

"I am ordered by the Government of the Confederate States to demand the evacuation of Fort Sumter. My aides, Colonel Chesnut and Captain Lee, are authorized to make such demand of you. All proper facilities will be afforded for the removal of yourself and command, together with company arms and property, and all private property, to any post in the United States which you may select. The flag which you have upheld so long and with so much fortitude, under the most trying circumstances, may be saluted by you on taking it down."[10]

The three Southern officers waited alone for perhaps an hour, while Anderson called his officers together, read the message to them, and asked for their comments. The officers said about what they could have been expected to say, and no one bothered to make a record; they were professional soldiers in a fort which they had been ordered to keep, and to surrender on demand would have been unthinkable. Major Anderson composed a reply to General Beauregard. Like the letter he had just received, what the major wrote had dignity, courtesy, and firmness, and yet there was in his note a flavor faintly odd—as if his voice, had he been saying this instead of writing it, would have quavered just a little.

"General," wrote Major Anderson, "I have the honor to acknowledge the receipt of your communication demanding the evacuation of this fort, and to say, in reply thereto, that it is a demand with which I regret that my sense of honor, and of my obligations to my Government, prevent my compliance. Thanking you for the fair, manly and courteous terms proposed, and for the high compliment paid me, I am, general, very respectfully, your obedient servant, Robert Anderson, Major, First Artillery, Commanding."

This letter was given to the Confederate officers, and they started back to their boat, Major Anderson walking with them. At the edge of the wharf he asked whether Beauregard would open fire at once, without giving further notice. Colonel Chesnut hesitated, then replied: "No, I can say to you that he will not, without giving you further notice." Anderson said he would take no action until he was fired upon; then, moved by the thought that had been preying on his mind for many days—the almost complete exhaustion of the fort's supply of food—he burst out: "If you do not batter us to pieces we will be starved out in a few days."

The remark seems not to have registered, right at first, and the Southern officers got into their boat. Then Colonel Chesnut did a double-take: if the major had said what the colonel thought he had said, there might be no need to open a bombardment. Quickly Colonel Chesnut asked Major Anderson to repeat his last remark. Major Anderson did so, and Colonel Chesnut asked if he might include this in his report to General Beauregard. The major was not enthusiastic about having that casual remark put in a formal report, but he said that he had stated a fact and the colonel could do as he liked.[11]

Like a good subordinate, Beauregard passed the whole business on to the Confederate Secretary of War, telegraphing the text of Anderson's written response and adding the remark to Colonel Chesnut. To show that he wanted Montgomery to say whether the bombardment should be called off, Beauregard ended his telegram with the single word: "Answer."

Jefferson Davis was perfectly willing to call off the shooting, but he wanted something better than Major Anderson's offhand remark on the wharf. Beauregard was informed, in a telegram signed by Secretary Walker but undoubtedly composed by President Davis, that he had better get it in writing.

"Do not desire needlessly to bombard Fort Sumter," said the telegram. "If Anderson will state the time at which, as indicated by him, he will evacuate, and agree that in the mean time he will not use his guns against us, unless ours should be employed against Fort Sumter, you are authorized thus to avoid the effusion of blood. If this or its equivalent be refused, reduce the fort as your judgment decides to be most practicable."

Neither Davis nor Beauregard could overlook the chance that somebody might be trying to pull a fast one. Major Anderson was saying that he would be starved out very soon, but while the major seemed to be a truthful man, Washington of late had been a hotbed of deceit and falsehood. It was known that food was on its way to Fort Sumter. Some sort of Yankee ships—warships, transports, or whatnot—were known to be cruising to and fro off the Charleston bar, and

Captain H. J. Hartstene, of the Confederate navy, had just said that in his opinion it was quite possible for these ships to send supplies to Major Anderson at night in small boats. All in all, this was no time for Southerners to be too confiding. To cancel the attack because Major Anderson was about to starve, and then to find that his larder had just been filled and that he could hold out indefinitely, would be a very poor way to begin the Confederacy's struggle for independence.[12]

Beauregard undertook to nail it down. He wrote another letter to Major Anderson, and at eleven o'clock on the night of April 11 the three aides got into their boat once more and started for Fort Sumter, reaching the wharf a little after midnight. Major Anderson took the letter they gave him and once more called his officers into council.

The only real question was the length of time the garrison could hold out, on the food that was available. One week earlier, Lieutenant Hall had made a tabulation. The fort then contained ⅔ of a barrel of flour, 5 barrels of hard bread, just under a barrel of rice, 100 pounds of sugar, 25 pounds of coffee, ¹⁄₆ of a barrel of salt, 24 barrels of salt pork, 2 barrels of vinegar, 40 pounds of hominy grits, and ½ a barrel of corn meal. To eat this there were in the fort 15 commissioned officers (including 3 from the Corps of Engineers), 74 enlisted men, and 1 functionary listed as a mail carrier. There were also 43 civilian employees whom Major Anderson had been trying to send ashore but whom he was compelled to keep because the South Carolina authorities would not let him get rid of them—figuring, no doubt, that these men would serve the South by helping to consume the major's food. Most of the stuff Lieutenant Hall had listed was gone by now, and the best judgment Major Anderson could get was that the garrison might possibly hold out for five more days. On the last three of those days there would be no food whatever.

One more letter to General Beauregard, then: Major Anderson would evacuate the fort on April 15, if General Beauregard would furnish him with transportation, and Major Anderson would not before that date open fire—*provided* that the Confederates did not commit, or seem obviously about to commit, some hostile act against Fort Sumter or against the United States flag, and provided also that Major Anderson did not in the meantime receive new instructions or provisions from his government. This was reduced to writing, and the message was given to the Southern officers, who were waiting in one of the casemates of the fort.

Major Anderson's answer was of course no answer at all, as far as the Confederacy was concerned, since it really committed him to nothing, and Beauregard's aides did not even feel that they needed to make the long trip back to Charleston to get Beauregard's verdict. (Consistently with the pattern that had been followed all along, the final activating decisions would be made by remote subordinates, exercising authority that had been delegated down the long chain of command.) With Colonel Chesnut dictating, Captain Lee writing it down, and Lieutenant-Colonel Chisholm copying the reply as fast as Captain Lee got it down—they were a busy trio, as Chisholm admitted afterward, for a few candle-lit minutes there in the casemate—Major Anderson got his reply in five minutes: "By authority of Brigadier General Beauregard, commanding the Provisional Forces of the Confederate States, we have the honor to notify you that he will open the fire of his batteries on Fort Sumter in one hour from this time." As the note carefully stated, it was then 3:20 on the morning of April 12.[13]

Since Major Anderson and several of his officers were present when Colonel Chesnut dictated all of this, the written reply was no surprise. Major Anderson studied it, and Captain Lee thought he was profoundly moved: "He seemed to realize the import of the consequences, and the great responsibility of his position." Major Anderson walked out on the wharf with the three Southerners and saw them into their boat. Shaking hands with them, he murmured: "If we never meet in this world again, God grant that we may meet in the next." The boat moved off in the darkness, and Major Anderson and his officers went through the fort, arousing the sleeping soldiers, telling them that the battle was about to start, and warning everybody to stay under cover until further notice; Anderson would not try to return the fire until daylight. Most of the officers went to the barbette to take a last look around.[14]

There were bonfires and torches going in all of the Confederate camps and batteries. Sumter was ringed by an almost complete circle of flickering lights, with darkness off to seaward; clouds hid the stars, and there was a hint of rain in the air. From batteries and camps came a jumble of far-off sounds, as soldiers fell in line for roll call, trundled guns into position, made all of the other last-minute preparations. In a Charleston bedroom Colonel Chesnut's wife waited in an agony of suspense. Her husband had told her what was going to happen; she looked out over the dark harbor with the twinkling lights on its rim, listening. . . .

The three aides went ashore at old Fort Johnson, where Major Anderson had once thought he could quarter the families of the married members of his garrison. A Confederate battery was there now, and the officers gave their orders to its commander, Captain George S. James, who had a seacoast mortar tilted at the proper angle; it was to be the signal gun which would tell the encircling troops, the city of Charleston, and the world at large that the most momentous bombardment in American history had begun.

Roger Pryor had gone out to the fort with the military aides, although he had remained in the boat while the others went inside. Now he came in to Captain James's battery, and the captain bowed to him and asked him if he would like to have the honor of firing the first gun. (The blow Pryor had been asking for was about to be struck. It would have the exact result he had predicted, pulling Virginia into the conflict and into the Confederacy, and into a long, tragic bloodletting. It would also make a true prophet out of Robert Toombs.)

Pryor seemed as emotionally disturbed as Major Anderson. His voice shook as he told Captain James: "I could not fire the first gun of the war," and Captain James passed the order on to Lieutenant Henry S. Farley. Then Pryor and the three aides got back into the boat and set off for Charleston, to make report to General Beauregard. Before the boat had gone very far, they told the oarsmen to stop rowing, and the boat drifted in utter silence for ten minutes while the men looked toward Fort Johnson. Lieutenant Farley was a little late, but it made no difference. At 4:30 there was a flash of light and a dull explosion as he fired the mortar. Arching high in the night, the shell could be traced by its glowing red fuse. A gunner on Morris Island thought it looked "like the wings of a firefly." It hung in the air, started down, and exploded squarely over Fort Sumter. The boat resumed its journey. In her bedroom, Mary Chesnut went to her knees and prayed as she had never prayed before.[15]

5. White Flag on a Sword

IN THE moment of its beginning the Civil War was an improbable spectacle to make the pulse beat faster. The guns flashed on the rim of the night like holiday fireworks, the fuses of the soaring shells drew red lines across the dark sky, and there was a romantic unreality to the hour of long-awaited action. The young men who fired the cannon, like the people in Charleston who stood on the water front, leaned out of windows, or climbed to the house tops to watch, felt that something great was beginning and they were glad to be part of it. Hard knowledge of war's reality would come later; at the hour of its dawn, with a new day's light coming in from the open sea, and a thin haze rising to soften the hard outlines of fort and city and mounded batteries, the war had an incredible and long-remembered beauty.

Beauregard's men had been on the alert since midnight. By the guns little pyramids of shells had been built. In the hot-shot furnaces fires had been lit, so that solid shot could be heated and driven like glowing coals into the woodwork of Major Anderson's stronghold. Officers who had been told what the schedule was kept looking at their watches while they waited for the signal gun. Along the sand dunes on Morris Island sentries peered out to sea, expecting to discover at any moment boatloads of armed Yankees; logically, a relief expedition would land troops on this island to storm the batteries so that ships might reach the fort undamaged, and the infantry was waiting. Beauregard had obtained and mounted searchlights of a sort, but these lit up nothing except the tumbling surf close inshore, and they were not being used. Somewhere out in the darkness there were Confederate picket boats, which would set off blue rockets if any hostile craft approached.[1]

The flash and the report of the first shell sent a flutter of nervous movement through all of the batteries, as gun crews hurried to open fire, and there was much postwar argument about who fired next. (The veterans argued that Captain

James's opening gun was not really the first gun of the war;
it was merely a signal gun, and the next gun was the first
one fired with intent to do harm. Captain James took no part
in these arguments, because he was killed in action in the
fall of 1862 at South Mountain, in Maryland.)

The next gun to be fired may have been one in Fort Moultrie, or it may have been another of Captain James's pieces,
or it may conceivably have been one of the guns on Cummings Point, the northern tip of Morris Island, a scant three
quarters of a mile away from Fort Sumter. Sentimentalists
always insisted that it was a gun in the iron battery—a set of
heavy-duty Columbiads protected by an armored shield, at
Cummings Point—and said that it was fired by that legendary hero of the secessionist movement, Edmund Ruffin; and
inasmuch as the war began in a stir of sentiment and returned
its memories to a sentimental mist afterward, that story was
very widely accepted, both then and later.

Ruffin was certainly present as a soldier that night, and he
did fire one of the first guns. The old gentleman had presented
himself to Captain George Cuthbert, of the Palmetto Guards,
two days earlier, asking permission to volunteer—with certain conditions. He would be a gunner, but if the Yankees
made a landing, he claimed the right to serve in the infantry
that was to drive them back into the sea; and his term of
service would expire once the Confederate flag floated over
Fort Sumter. He was accepted, the oldest and surely the
most appealing of all of Beauregard's soldiers on opening
day.

A youthful volunteer who saw him could never forget the
looks of him—an old man, his gray hair worn long and done
up in a queue in the style of the eighteenth century; six feet
tall, or close to it, slender and straight as an Indian brave,
his uniform coat buttoned to his throat, joining his company
with a musket in one hand and a carpet bag in the other, accepted by his comrades in arms as an ornament but taking his
duties most seriously. The night before the action began, the
rest of the company got together and agreed that Ruffin ought
to fire the first gun, and when Captain Cuthbert told him
about it, Ruffin was greatly pleased. He slept that night without removing his uniform, and when the drums called the
men to action stations just before four in the morning, the
old patriot hurried to his post. After the signal gun was fired,

Ruffin pulled the lanyard of his piece, firing the first shot from this particular battery; and if several guns in other emplacements fired before this battery did, the flavor of the legend was not harmed. Someone took a photograph of the old man in full uniform a day or so later, and it was circulated all over the South, a propaganda piece of immense power. They do not make old men much more fiery than Edmund Ruffin.[2]

He had no monopoly on patriotic ardor, and if there is a wild and unreal beauty to the first hours of the war, much of it comes from the spirit with which the intense Southerners went into action. Quite typical of the lot was boyish D. Augustus Dickert, who was a member of "Captain Walker's company, from Newberry, South Carolina," and who stood at the opposite end of the scale of ages; he was just fifteen, and he had been on his way to school one morning when Captain Walker's company marched past, all brass buttons, palmetto cockades, bright uniforms, and music, and he forgot about school and hurried off to enlist. When he first applied, he was rejected because he was too young—inside of three years the Confederacy would be reaching out for boys of fifteen, whether or no, but in the hour of its beginning there was youth to spare—but he went on to Charleston anyway, slipped past the guards to Morris Island, and made connections. He was put to work, along with all the others, building fortifications, used wheelbarrow and shovel for the first time in his life, and found that his excitement, his sense of being a part of something glorious and uplifting, survived even this drudgery. Now he was a unit in Beauregard's little army, helping to tighten the vise on the hated fort as the stars grew dim and the morning light slowly became stronger.[3]

The Confederate bombardment was heavy—by the innocent standards of April 12, 1861, anyway—and it was fairly effective, considering the fact that every shot was being fired by amateur gun crews. Some of the gunners tried to sweep the open parapet of the fort, firing too high at first but improving their aim as the daylight grew. Others tried to explode shells on or just over the open parade ground inside the fort, and still others attacked the solid masonry walls. Beauregard had laid out a routine in advance, and his men followed it. In Captain James's command, the opening mortar had hardly been fired when his engineers exploded a mine to destroy a house that blocked the field of fire of a battery the captain had posted on a little hill. The smoke and debris from this explosion had no sooner settled than this battery was in action. (Long afterward, men from this battery insisted that neither Fort Moultrie, Edmund Ruffin, nor anyone else fired before they did.) Beauregard's aides reached Beauregard with their formal report of Major Anderson's refusal to accept terms long after the firing had started, but it made no difference.

Fort Sumter itself, meanwhile, was strangely silent, firing not a gun in reply, and some of the Confederate gunners were disturbed—the Yankees ought to be firing back. The only sign of life from the fort as the full light of day came was the fact that the flag was flying. (It had been hoisted during the night, immediately after Colonel Chesnut had served notice that the shooting was about to start.) Anderson kept his men under cover throughout the early hours of the bombardment. Around seven o'clock they were given breakfast—salt pork and coffee. Then, at 7:30, the drums beat the assembly, and the men were paraded in spite of the intermittent explosions of Confederate shell. Anderson divided the garrison into three reliefs, or shifts, ordered specified batteries to be manned, and opened fire.[4]

In laying out his battle plan, Anderson was under difficulties. He had more guns than he could use; short of supplies, he was also woefully short of men, and he could neither maintain a proper volume of fire nor use his most powerful weapons. His only chance, actually, was to lie low as much as possible and try to hold out until Captain Fox's relief expedition reached him. (Its arrival, if indeed it showed up at all, would present a new set of problems, but they could be met when the time came.)

Fort Sumter itself was solid enough—brick walls five feet thick, rising forty feet above the water, designed to carry three tiers of guns. The two lower tiers were in casemates: that is, each gun was fully protected, in a roomy compartment of heavy masonry, firing through a comparatively small embrasure or gunport. The third tier was on top, on what military jargon of that day called the terreplein, or barbette, the guns completely in the open, firing over a parapet that was their only protection. Anderson had forty-eight guns in position, half of them in casemates on the lower tier, the rest mounted on the barbette; none had been put in the second tier, and the casemates there were bricked up. The casemate guns, unfortunately, were the weakest of the lot—32-pounders and 42-pounders, firing nothing but solid shot. The heavy Columbiads and eight-inch howitzers, which could fire shell and had much greater range and smashing power, were all on the barbette. Not all of the guns would bear on any proper target, and Anderson did not have nearly enough men to fire all of his guns in any event, even though most of the civilian workers who had had to stay in the fort agreed to carry powder and shot or to serve in the gun crews.

The major's biggest handicap was that he could not afford to have very many casualties. He had 128 men, forty-three of whom were civilians, and he had to figure that after a day or so of bombardment Beauregard might send out infantry in boats, after dark, to take the place by storm. For that kind of fighting the Confederates had a huge advantage in numbers; Beauregard commanded probably 7000 men, and with the war actually begun he could get reinforcements without difficulty. The Federals had done their best to get ready for him. The wharf was mined and could be blown to bits at a moment's notice, heavy shells converted to hand grenades were distributed behind the parapet, and various infernal machines—each of which had a keg of gun powder as its operating mechanism—were ready to be dropped on any intruders; all in all, the little garrison could give an assaulting party a very warm welcome. But it would be touch and go, at best, and if any appreciable number of Anderson's men became casualties the case would be utterly hopeless. No matter what happened the major had to keep his men protected.[5]

Now the only guns with which he could make any effective reply to Beauregard's fire were the Columbiads and howitzers on the open barbette. The Confederates were already showing a dismaying ability to explode shell just above the fort and they had at least seventeen mortars firing; it was as certain as anything could be that Yankee gun crews on the barbette would take a very hard beating. Anderson would lose men much more rapidly than he could afford to lose them if he tried to keep the barbette guns in action.

As a result, Anderson ordered all hands under cover; he would use only the casemate guns in the lower tier, and although this meant that he could fire nothing but solid shot and could hardly hope to silence any of the guns that were firing at him, it could not be helped. His gun crews would be pretty well protected; if Fox should try to bring in reinforcements—the topmasts of the Federal warships could be seen on the horizon, and Sumter's flag had been dipped to show that they had been recognized—then the heavy guns could be manned to beat down Confederate fire and make it possible for the reinforcements to get to the fort. Until then the barbette guns would be left all alone, loaded but unmanned.

(One minor nightmare that plagued the Federal officers was the thought that if armed men in boats approached the fort in pitch darkness, there would be no sure way to tell whether they were reinforcing Federals or attacking Confederates. It would be terrible to obliterate a party of friends; it would be fatal to let enemies get to close quarters unharmed. The war was not half a day old before men began to see that fighting a foe who speaks the same language as one's friends can present special problems.)

With Captain Doubleday in general charge, Anderson's first shift went on duty, and six of the lower-tier guns opened fire. The fire was almost completely ineffective. Shooting at the iron-clad battery on Morris Island, the Federals quickly discovered that their solid shot hit the shield and bounded off harmlessly, and after a time they left that target altogether and began shooting at Fort Moultrie. Here their luck was no better. Beauregard's engineers had given the old fort a protective coating of cotton bales and sand bags many feet thick, with more cotton bales used as shutters to close the embrasures between shots; nothing that Sumter's guns could do seemed to have the slightest effect. Doubleday's gun crews were hot and irritable, and the sight of a crowd of civilian spectators on the beach of Sullivan's Island, well out of the line of fire and enthusiastically pro-Confederate to the last man and woman, was more than two of the old regular army sergeants could bear. When no officer was around they swung two of their 42-pounders about and fired at this crowd. Luckily, their shots were high—they smashed into the Moultrie House, which was flying a hospital flag but which contained no wounded, no Confederate having yet been hit—and the crowd scattered in vast haste. Naturally enough, the

Charleston papers next day discoursed on the barbarity of Yankees who shot at civilians and hospitals.[6]

There were other incidents. Once a veteran sergeant stole up to the barbette and, all by himself, fired every gun that bore on Fort Moultrie. He hit nothing, and he had to scamper back downstairs in a hurry before he could be detected, but the Confederates thought Anderson was beginning to use his heavy guns and shot at the parapet with everything they had. Another time two sergeants crept to the barbette and fired a ten-inch Columbiad at the iron battery on Cummings Point. It was a near miss; encouraged, they reloaded, and although it was impossible for the two of them to run the huge gun back into proper firing position, they tried one more shot. The recoil made the huge gun turn a backward somersault, and all seven and a half tons of it left its carriage and crashed halfway downstairs, almost mashing one of the sergeants. The two managed to creep away safely, and once more the Confederates swept the barbette with shell and solid shot. . . . Sergeants in the Sumter garrison, apparently, averaged fairly tough.[7]

Meanwhile, the fort was taking a bad pounding. On Morris Island the Confederates had an English Whitworth gun, a breech-loader of immense power, sent over as a gift by a South Carolinian who lived in London. This gun began to gouge big chunks out of the fort's southeast corner, showing an amazing capacity for destroying first-class masonry; luckily for the Federals it soon ran out of ammunition, or the wall would have been breached then and there. Shell and red-hot shot set the wooden barracks on the parade ground on fire, and the fire-fighting details were whistled into action. Seeing the rising smoke, the Confederates increased their rate of fire, and the men fought the flames while ten-inch shell burst overhead. The blaze was put out, rekindled, put out again, started again, put out once more; shell fragments wrecked water tanks that had been installed under the barracks roof, and the deluge helped quench the flames—and sent choking clouds of steamy smoke all through the casemates as an added trial for the men at the guns. Major Anderson noticed that leading the fire fighters in their dangerous work was Sergeant Peter Hart, doing his best to live up to the role Mrs. Anderson had chosen for him.[8]

The day wore away, Beauregard's guns chipping steadily at the fort, Anderson's guns replying ineffectively; and out at sea Gustavus Fox came steaming up in the liner *Baltic* and discovered that for all the good he could do he might as well have stayed in New York.

Fox had come down from Sandy Hook in a twisting gale, and early on the morning of April 12 he met the warship *Pawnee* and the revenue cutter *Harriet Lane* cruising on station a dozen miles east of Charleston harbor. When Fox said that he was going to reprovision Fort Sumter and asked for an escort, Commander Stephen C. Rowan, of *Pawnee,* refused to go along; his orders were to stand by and await the arrival of the more powerful warship *Powhatan* (long gone by now on her way to Pensacola, with impish David Porter on the quarter deck), and if he went blundering in on his own he might start a civil war. Neither Rowan nor Fox nor anyone else on the open sea knew that the shooting had already started.

Fox stood in toward the bar with *Harriet Lane* plugging along cheerfully in his wake, and he presently learned that Commander Rowan's scruples were out of date. The brisk wind brought him tag ends of ragged powder smoke, and the bumping echoes of the firing of great guns, and it was all too evident that the war had begun. The same thing dawned on Rowan before long, and he brought *Pawnee* in at full speed, calling out to Fox as his ship came abreast that he wanted a pilot—he was going to go into the harbor and share in the fate of his brethren of the army. Fox went aboard *Pawnee* and managed to persuade Rowan that the government expected no such sacrifice; he explained the orders that governed his own conduct, and the three ships hove to and waited for *Powhatan*. With that ship, Fox believed, he could do something about forcing an entrance, or sending in a small-boat expedition; without it, he could do nothing. The weather continued bad, with a high wind and a heavy sea. A number of merchant ships came up and anchored, awaiting the result of the bombardment; from Morris Island the cluster of masts made the Confederates think that a large Federal fleet lay just offshore, and Beauregard alerted the island command to be prepared to resist a storming party on the beaches that night.[9]

There would be no storming party, and Fox's sense of frustration kept rising. *Baltic* tossed restlessly on the swell all night, waiting for *Powhatan;* the soldiers aboard the liner were seasick, but they were made to practice getting in and out of small boats just the same, and Fox wrote admiringly of the behavior of the army's Lieutenant Robert O. Tyler, who helped organize the detail although he himself was as seasick as anyone. The morning of April 13 came in foggy, with the sea as ugly as ever; trying to get close in shore, *Baltic* ran aground briefly on Rattlesnake Shoal, but got off undamaged. From *Pawnee*'s deck a huge column of black smoke could be seen rising from Fort Sumter, its base lit now and again by the flash of Anderson's guns. Fox concluded that there was no use waiting for *Powhatan* any longer, but he found that he could not go through with his small-boat program either; none of the tugs had arrived, and the naval officers all insisted that no open boats carrying any load at all could reach Fort Sumter in the prevailing seas.

U.S.S. *Pocahontas* came along shortly after noon, and Fox learned at last what had happened to *Powhatan*. Refusing to give up, he commandeered a schooner from among the flotilla of sea-going idlers that had collected, planning to build a night expedition around her; but his preparations had not advanced very far before the lookouts reported that Major Anderson's flag was no longer flying, and before dusk Fox learned that it was all over.[10]

In the fort, things had been going from bad to worse. The night had been uneasy, with sentries looking anxiously for approaching boats, hoping they could tell the difference between a relief expedition and a landing party; every ten minutes all night long a Confederate mortar would toss a shell into the fort, just to keep everybody on the alert. With daylight on April 13 the bombardment was resumed, and it seemed to the Federals that the Confederate fire was heavier than ever. Flames broke out again, the officers' quarters were destroyed, all of the casemates were full of blinding smoke, and the men at the guns wore wet rags over their faces, and staggered to the embrasures between shots for a breath of air. It seemed likely that the blaze would reach the magazine before long, and powder barrels were moved into the casemates; in the heavier bombardment this was no safe place, and some of the barrels were thrown into the harbor. At noon the flagstaff was shot down. A new one was improvised, and Lieutenant G. W. Snyder and Sergeant Peter Hart went topside and managed to fasten it to a gun carriage on the shell-swept barbette.[11]

The Confederates saw the flag come down, and saw the heavy smoke clouds going up, and correctly deduced that Major Anderson was in trouble. Beauregard ordered up a small boat with a flag of truce, and sent his aide, Captain Lee (with Porcher Miles and Roger Pryor for company), out to the fort to ask the major if he needed assistance: a courtly offer of help to an enemy, and also a tactful way of inquiring whether the Federal should not now surrender. Captain Lee set out on his mission, saw the flag hoisted again, turned to go back to the shore, then noticed that the United States flag had been lowered and that a white flag had been hoisted. Once more he turned about and made for the fort, where he found himself taking part in an amusing, unimportant, and wholly characteristic little farce.[12]

During the height of the contest, while Lieutenant Snyder and Sergeant Hart struggled to get the flag flying, and the gun crews stumbled through the smoke to maintain some sort of fire, a cannoneer in a lower-tier casemate, going to the muzzle of his piece to reload, saw a strange fellow looking in the embrasure—a burly civilian with a swarthy, piratical face, red sash and sword belt incongruously belted about his middle, a naked sword with a white flag knotted about the blade gripped in one hand—altogether a wholly improbable-looking figure. This man announced that he was Colonel Wigfall, recently United States Senator from Texas, now an aide to General Beauregard; he wanted to see Major Anderson, and he wanted even more to get safely inside the fort because he was at the moment squarely in the line of Confederate fire—"Damn it, they are firing at me from Fort Moultrie." After a certain amount of discussion he was led to Major Anderson; the rowboat that had brought him out, manned by a white man and a colored boy, remained tied up at the wharf. Colonel Wigfall addressed the Federal commander with bluff heartiness:

"Major Anderson, I come from General Beauregard. It is time to put a stop to this, sir. The flames are raging all around you and you have defended your flag gallantly. Will you evacuate, sir?"

The major was ready to call it quits. Washington had specifically told him that a last-ditch sacrifice was not expected of him. He had defended his flag long enough to meet all requirements; his magazine might explode before long, his cartridges were nearly all gone, and with flames and glowing embers all over the place, it was impossible to make new ones, and, besides, the main gate had been blown in and a storming party could overrun the fort any time it cared to make the effort. Anderson said he would surrender on the terms originally proposed—that he be allowed to salute his flag and then, with all the honors of war, take his men and their personal property back to New York. Wigfall said that this was a deal: "Lower your flag, and the firing will cease. I will see General Beauregard and you military men will arrange all the terms." Anderson reflected that his men were at the point of exhaustion, and it seemed to him that Wigfall's coming was providential. Down came the United States flag, and up went the white flag of surrender.

At this point Captain Lee and his two civilian companions got to the fort. Presented to Major Anderson, Lee said that Beauregard had sent them to offer assistance, if assistance happened to be needed, and to find out what all of this raising and lowering of flags meant. Anderson, puzzled, explained that he had just surrendered to Colonel Wigfall, whereupon his three visitors exchanged baffled looks; then they explained that although Wigfall did belong to Beauregard's staff, he had not seen the general for two days and had come out to the fort strictly on his own hook. Anderson muttered: "Gentlemen, this is a very awkward business," which stated the case accurately; he had just surrendered to a man who had no authority either to demand or to receive a surrender. Anderson ordered the white flag hauled down and the national flag raised; the fighting would be resumed.[13]

In the end, though, things were arranged. Captain Lee suggested that everything be left as it was while they got in touch with Beauregard; Anderson wrote out his understanding of the terms on which he and Wigfall had agreed; the Confederates took this letter to the general and made explanation, and in two or three hours—white flag still flying, and all the guns silent—they came back and it was settled. The surrender was official, as of that moment, but on the next day Anderson could hoist his flag, salute it, haul it down again, and march forth to board one of Captain Fox's steamers. The fighting was over . . . there had been too much of it for this one seaport town to contain, and it had brimmed over the rim; it would run all across the South, and into the North as well, going on and on until nobody could see any end to it.

The liner *Baltic* drew too much water to come in over the bar, and so the steamer *Ysabel* was sent in to take off the garrison. Shortly after the noon hour on Sunday, April 14, the final ceremony was held, the men of the garrison looking glum, Major Anderson near to tears with emotion, Charleston harbor all crammed with boats full of people, local wherrymen doing a land-office business rowing sight-seers past the fort at fifty cents a head. There would be this final salute . . . but things that were planned in connection with Fort Sumter always went awry.

The salute was being fired by one of the big guns on the barbette. Some burning fragment of a powder bag was caught by the wind and dropped on a pile of ready cartridges behind the piece, and there was a sudden explosion—and the only loss of life caused by the great battle of Fort Sumter took place here and now, twenty-four hours after the fighting had stopped. (One of the fantastic things about Fort Sumter was that about 4000 shells were fired altogether, without killing anyone on either side.) Private Daniel Hough, a regular artillerist, was instantly killed, and five other soldiers were wounded, one so gravely that he died a few days later in a Charleston hospital. Private Hough was buried in the fort, with a company of South Carolina volunteers presenting arms and a Confederate naval chaplain conducting services. Then the band struck up "Yankee Doodle," the United States troops marched out to the waiting transport, the Confederate and Palmetto flags soared to the top of the flag pole, and guns all around the harbor fired a jubilant salute. Beauregard came out to make formal inspection of the fort, along with Governor Pickens and other notables. Captain Lee, examining the place with the professional eye of a military engineer, found it badly damaged and estimated that it would cost at least $350,000 to make suitable repairs.[14]

Out at sea, the transports and the warships steamed north for Sandy Hook.

6. The Coming of the Fury

DINING WITH three cabinet members not long after the fall of Fort Sumter, Winfield Scott expressed complete confidence in Northern victory, but doubted that there would be an early end to the nation's troubles. For a long time to come, he said, it would require the exercise of all of the powers of government "to restrain the fury of the noncombatants."[1]

This fury was an elemental force that swept through North and South in precisely the same way, and it was going across the land like a flame. It did not look like fury at first; it was wild, laughing, extravagant, armed with flags and music and the power of speech, groping insistently for heavier weapons. The coming of war had released it. Something unendurable had ended; the uncertainty and the doubt were gone, along with the need to examine mind and heart for unattainable answers, and a Boston merchant looked about him at the crowds, the waving banners, and the general jubilation and wrote: "The heather is on fire. I never before knew what a popular excitement can be." The London *Times*'s Mr. Russell, stopping in North Carolina on his way to Charleston, saw the same thing—"flushed faces, wild eyes, screaming mouths," with men shouting so stridently for Jefferson Davis and the Southern Confederacy (to which North Carolina had not yet attached itself) that the bands playing "Dixie" could not be heard. Men slapped strangers on the backs, women tossed bunches of flowers from windows, and in Richmond a crowd paraded to the Tredegar Iron Works under a Confederate flag, dragged a cannon to the steps of the state Capitol, and fired a salute. Some fundamental emotion had slipped the leash; it would control both President Lincoln and President Davis, and yet at the same time it was a force which the two men themselves would have to control in order to make war.[2]

Dazzled by the overwhelming public response to the news that one flag had gone down and another had gone up, ordinarily sensible men gave way to uncritical vaporing. Youthful John Hay, the somewhat condescending ornament of the White House secretariat, looked at a company of untried Northern militia and wrote: "When men like these leave their horses, their women and their wine, harden their hands, eat crackers for dinner, wear a shirt for a week and never black their shoes—all for a principle—it is hard to set any bounds to the possibilities of such an army." Hard indeed; particularly so since exactly the same sort of men were doing exactly the same things in the South for a diametrically opposed principle, creating boundless possibilities of their own. Leroy Pope Walker, the Confederate Secretary of War, told a serenading crowd in Montgomery that the Confederate flag "will, before the first of May, float over the dome of the old capitol in Washington," and he went on to say that if Southern chivalry were pushed too far, the flag might eventually rise over Faneuil Hall in Boston. The eminent German-American Carl Schurz wrote admiringly that "millionaires' sons rushed to the colors by the side of laborers," and correspondent Russell noted that barefooted poor whites in the deepest South were whooping it up for Confederate independence as loyally as the wealthiest planters.[3]

Through the fall and winter, events had seemed to move slowly, as if fate wanted to give men a chance to have second thoughts about what was being done. Now everything began to go with a rush, and what was done would be done for keeps. White House routine had gone about as usual on April 13, when Anderson was driven to surrender. Lincoln received visitors, signed papers, worried about patronage. The cabinet met briefly, but in the absence of conclusive news it could do very little. During the morning Lincoln met with a delegation from the Virginia secession convention. What this convention would inevitably do was strongly indicated by the news in the morning papers; Roger Pryor had cried "Strike a blow!" and the blow had been struck, once and for all. Still, there was time for a word from the President, and Lincoln had written out a brief statement: a cautious indication of future policy, saying much less than was on the President's mind.

If it proved true, he said, that Fort Sumter had actually been attacked, he would perhaps suspend the delivery of United States mails in the states that claimed to have seceded, for he believed that the commencement of actual war against the government justified and perhaps required such a step. He still considered all military posts and property in the seces-

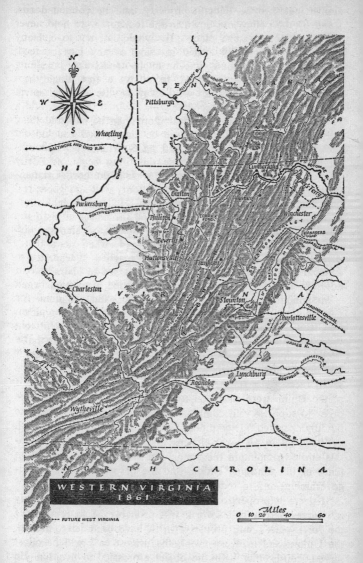

WESTERN VIRGINIA
1861

- - - FUTURE WEST VIRGINIA

Miles
0 10 20   40   60

sionist states to be Federal property, and he continued to stand by the policy laid down in the inaugural—to hold, occupy and possess such places. He would not try to collect duties and imposts by armed invasion of any part of the country, but at the same time he might conceivably land an armed force, in case of need, to relieve a fort along the borders. . . . The delegates went away as wise as when they came but probably no wiser.[4]

Lincoln would do a great deal more than he had told the Virginians that Saturday, because he clearly had concluded that the time for temporizing had gone. Whatever might or might not have been done, once the firing began at Fort Sumter, Lincoln was ready to make war. If the border states could stand the shock and would go along, well and good; if not, they could go where they chose. He would fight the theory and the fact of secession with all the power at his disposal, letting what had happened at Charleston stand as a declaration of war. On Sunday, April 14, when news that Anderson had hauled down his flag reached Washington, Lincoln met with his cabinet again, and talked to his military advisers, and on Monday morning he issued a proclamation —an announcement that the war was on, and a statement (as far as one could be made at this moment) of the policy that would guide him in the conduct of that war. It went to the country on April 15. After reciting the obvious fact that "combinations too powerful to be suppressed" by ordinary law courts and marshals had taken charge of affairs in the seven secessionist states, it announced that the several states of the Union were called on to contribute 75,000 militia "in order to suppress said combinations and to cause the laws to be duly executed." It continued:

"I appeal to all loyal citizens to favor, facilitate and aid this effort to maintain the honor, the integrity, and the existence of our National Union, and the perpetuity of popular government; and to redress wrongs already long endured.

"I deem it proper to say that the first service assigned to the forces hereby called forth will probably be to repossess the forts, places, and property which have been seized from the Union; and in every event, the utmost care will be observed, consistently with the object aforesaid, to avoid any devastation, any destruction of, or interference with, property, or any disturbance of peaceful citizens in any part of the country.

"And I hereby command the persons composing the combinations aforesaid to disperse and retire peaceably to their respective abodes within twenty days from this date.

"Deeming that the present condition of public affairs presents an extraordinary occasion, I do hereby, in virtue of the power in me vested by the Constitution, convene both Houses of Congress. Senators and Representatives are therefore summoned to assemble at their respective chambers, at 12 o'clock noon, on Thursday, the fourth day of July, next, then and there to consider and determine such measures, as, in their wisdom, the public safety, and interest may seem to demand."5

This was clear enough, and it went substantially beyond the threat to suspend the mail service and reinforce beleaguered garrisons which he had mentioned to the Virginia delegation two days earlier. It was a flat announcement that the unbroken Union would be fought for, a promise that slavery would not be disturbed—the word "property" had a very specific meaning in those days—and a clear indication that this President would aggressively use all of his powers right up to the hilt. It was mid-April now, and Congress would not meet until early in July. Until then, Abraham Lincoln would be the government, free to act as he chose with no restraint except the knowledge that he would have to give Congress an accounting ten or eleven weeks later—by which time everything Congress did would be done under the incalculable pressure of wartime emergency.

As an experienced politician, Lincoln had looked to his fences before he acted. The Republicans were bound to support him; he was also assured that his decision to go to war would be publicly endorsed by Stephen A. Douglas, which meant that the Democratic party in the Northern states would support the war.

On Sunday evening Congressman George Ashmun, a Massachusetts Republican, called on Douglas at the Senator's home in Washington and urged him to go at once to the White House and tell the President he would do all he could to help him "put down the rebellion which had thus fiercely flamed out in Charleston harbor." Douglas demurred; Lincoln had been firing good Democratic office-holders, many of them friends of Douglas, in order to make jobs for Republicans, and, anyway, Douglas was not sure that Lincoln wanted any advice from him. Ashmun insisted and at last won Douglas over, with the help of Mrs. Douglas, and the two men went to the White House. Lincoln received them cordially, and read to Douglas the proclamation he would issue in the morning. Douglas endorsed it wholeheartedly, but told Lincoln to call out 200,000 men instead of 75,000. Reflecting on the bruises he had received in the Charleston convention at the hands of the cotton-state leaders, Douglas warned: "You do not know the dishonest purposes of those men as well as I do." The President and the man who had opposed him then went to a map, and Douglas pointed to strategic spots that ought to be strengthened—Washington, Harper's Ferry, Fort Monroe, and the muddy Illinois town of Cairo, at the junction of the Ohio and Mississippi rivers. They parted at last, and Douglas wrote out and gave to the Associated Press a brief statement, telling the country that although he remained a political opponent of the President, "he was prepared to sustain the President in the exercise of all his Constitutional functions to preserve the Union and maintain the Government and defend the Federal capital."[6]

For a few months, at least, the Democratic party in the North would support the war, and in this third week of April it seemed that all of the North was an enthusiastic and patriotic unit. The heather was truly on fire. There were "war meetings" everywhere, mayors made speeches, citizens paraded, and military recruiting stations were swamped. State governors who had worried for fear they could not meet the enlistment quotas set by the War Department found they had many times as many applicants as the quotas would accommodate, and began to wonder how they could pacify all of the indignant voters who wanted to go to war and could not be accepted. City after city named committees of public safety, the committee members usually having the loftiest of motives and the haziest of ideas as to their duties. A Southern woman temporarily resident in New England wrote to friends that the intense fervor that was sweeping Massachusetts was not patriotism but simple hatred for the South, but she felt that these Yankees were in earnest whatever their motive, and she voiced a warning: "I would not advise you of the South to trust too much in the idea that the North-

erners will not fight, for I believe they will, and their numbers are overwhelming."⁷ Sober businessmen of Cincinnati
met and agreed that they would ship no more goods south—
an agreement that languished and died in due course, for
Cincinnati was to be an active supply depot for Confederate
smugglers of contraband throughout the war.

But if the proclamation moved the North to a wild, almost
discordant harmony, it knocked Virginia straight out of the
Union and turned the war into a life-or-death affair for the
whole nation.

Lincoln had said that to trade a fort for a state, Sumter
for Virginia, might be an excellent bargain, although his
efforts to drive such a bargain had been tardy and ineffective. Now both fort and state were gone, and their joint departure meant that the war would be long and desperate.
Without Virginia the Southern Confederacy could not have
hoped to win its war for independence; with Virginia the
Confederacy's hopes were not half bad, and they would get
even better when people realized that Virginia would come
equipped with Robert E. Lee. American history has known
few events more momentous than the secession of Virginia,
which turned what set out to be the simple suppression of a
rebellion into a four-year cataclysm that shook America to
the profoundest depths of its being. Once the proclamation
was out, Virginia's departure was almost automatic.

People in Richmond were celebrating the fall of Fort
Sumter before they saw Lincoln's proclamation, and a mass
meeting on April 15 resolved "that we rejoice with high,
exultant, heartfelt joy at the triumph of the Southern Confederacy over the accursed government at Washington."⁸ In
the midst of this jubilation came the news that the accursed
government expected Virginia to provide three regiments of
infantry for the purpose of destroying the joyously congratulated Confederacy. To a proud tidewater people who
had seen Yankee coercion in the mere fact that the United
States flag had been flying over a fort in South Carolina, this
call for troops—this obvious, bluntly stated determination to
make war—looked like coercion triply distilled and outra-
geously unbearable. Virginia's refusal to join the Confederacy
during the winter had never meant anything more than a
desire to wait and see, a thin hope that the deep South might
yet get all it wanted without having to establish a brand-

new nation. Having waited, Virginia now had seen; the thin little hope was dead; and Virginia would be out of the Union just as soon as the most meager formalities could be attended to.

Virginia's Governor Letcher gave abundant warning of what was to come when, on April 16, he sent Lincoln a reply to the request for militia.

"In reply to this communication," said the governor, "I have only to say that the militia of Virginia will not be furnished to the powers at Washington for any such use or purpose as they have in view. Your object is to subjugate the Southern States, and a requisition made upon me for such an object—an object, in my judgment, not within the purview of the Constitution or the act of 1795—will not be complied with. You have chosen to inaugurate civil war, and having done so, we will meet it in a spirit as determined as the Administration has exhibited toward the South."

As Governor Letcher felt, so felt most of the other border-state governors, and messages of angry defiance poured in on Lincoln as soon as his call for troops was received. From Kentucky, Governor Beriah Magoffin telegraphed: "Kentucky will furnish no troops for the wicked purpose of subduing her sister Southern states." Governor John W. Ellis, of North Carolina, wired that the request for troops was so shocking that he could hardly believe it to be genuine: it was both a violation of the Constitution and a "gross usurpation of power," he would have no part of it, and "you can get no troops from North Carolina." From Governor Isham G. Harris, of Tennessee, came the statement: "Tennessee will not furnish a single man for purpose of coercion, but 50,000 if necessary, for the defense of our rights and those of our Southern brethren." Governor H. M. Rector, of Arkansas, said that his state would send no troops; the people of Arkansas would "defend to the last extremity their honor, lives and property against Northern mendacity and usurpation." And Governor Claiborne F. Jackson, of Missouri, refusing to join in "the unholy crusade," telegraphed to Lincoln that his call for troops was "illegal, unconstitutional, and revolutionary in its object, inhuman and diabolical, and cannot be complied with."[9] It had seemed of the first importance to hold the border states in the Union, but within the week following Major Anderson's surrender it looked as if the border might go over to the Confederacy en bloc. The nation that was going to war to preserve its unity might well find the war lost before it had fairly begun.

Most important of all was Virginia; and in Virginia, it quickly developed, the overwhelming majority of the people (east of the Blue Ridge, at any rate) felt precisely as Governor Letcher felt. Virginia's secession convention had never adjourned, and the call for troops galvanized it into quick action. On April 17 the convention passed an ordinance of secession. Technically, this would become effective only if a majority of the voters of the state ratified it at a special election called for May 23, but by now there was not the slightest chance that the voters would reject it and everyone took it for granted that Virginia had made an irrevocable decision. Until the action at Fort Sumter, there had been a good Unionist majority in the convention, but Delegate W. C. Rives wrote to a friend in Boston that "Lincoln's unlucky and ill-conceived proclamation" had caused an immediate reversal. The ordinance passed by a vote of 88 to 55, most of the pro-Union votes being cast by delegates from the western part of the state, beyond the mountains. Governor Letcher promptly issued a proclamation pointing out that seven states had already "solemnly resumed the power granted by them to the United States," asserting that Lincoln's call for troops was unconstitutional and a grave threat to Virginia, and summoning all of the state's volunteer regiments or companies in the state to stand by for an immediate call to active duty.[10]

The governor was moving fast, but the people of Virginia were moving even faster. Some of the military units Governor Letcher was talking about had not only assembled ahead of time but were on the move to smite the Yankees by the time he got out his proclamation. Henry A. Wise had been governor of Virginia at the time of the John Brown affair—had questioned the old man after the collapse of the uprising, and had in effect caused Brown to be convicted of treason and hanged—and the Fort Sumter crisis and what followed it turned his mind immediately to Harper's Ferry. On the evening of April 15, before Governor Letcher had even had time to make his defiant reply to Lincoln's demand for troops, Wise arranged a conference, in Richmond, of as many militia officers as he could find, and worked out a plan to get an armed force into Harper's Ferry to seize the government arsenal there. With this advance planning, a force of perhaps 1000 armed men was put in motion the moment the convention passed the ordinance of secession, and by the evening of April 18 this force was drawn up within four miles of the historic little town.

United States authority at the arsenal was represented by First Lieutenant Roger Jones and forty-two regular infantrymen. (By one of the remarkable coincidences common to this war, Lieutenant Jones was a cousin of Robert E. Lee.) It was utterly impossible for this company to stay there; not only were the Federals badly outnumbered, but Harper's Ferry (as other officers were to discover, later in the war) was practically indefensible anyway. The town lay at the bottom of a cup, with high mountain ridges on every side, and unless its garrison could hold all of these ridges, which would take a very large force, an assailant could shell the place into submission without much trouble. Jones set fire to the arsenal and armory that night and put his command on the road for Pennsylvania, and the next morning the Virginia troops marched in. The government buildings had been destroyed, but the machinery with which military rifles were made was not badly damaged, and it was promptly moved farther south to make arms for the Confederacy. Several thousand rifle barrels and gun locks were salvaged, and the Virginians settled down to hold Harper's Ferry and the country roundabout. In a short time they got a new commander—an ungainly professor from the Virginia Military Institute, a cold-eyed West Pointer who had fought in the Mexican War and who turned out to be a secretive and hard-boiled stickler for discipline; a colonel in Virginia's service by the name of Thomas Jonathan Jackson.[11]

It had been just one week since Beauregard's guns opened on Fort Sumter, and already Virginia was in the war. Either Lincoln had discounted Virginia's action in advance, or (which seems much more probable) he had grossly overestimated the amount of Unionist sentiment in this and other border states. Neither Lincoln nor Seward had been able to see that this Union sentiment was purely conditional; it existed as long as no strain was put upon it, but when a real test came it fell apart. The emotional drive was all-important, and in this part of the country the Government

of the United States, the very concept of the United States
as a nation, could look like an interfering third party standing between a man and the object of his deepest loyalty. . . .
The fury was on the land, and men all over America were
responding to impulses that came up from the greatest
depths.

Among them, Robert E. Lee.

Reaching his home, Arlington, at the beginning of March,
Lee had reported to the War Department on March 5, immediately after the inauguration ceremonies were out of the
way. He had been placed on waiting orders, which seems
to have been General Scott's way of keeping him where he
would be available for immediate use in case of emergency.
(Of all the officers in the army, Lee was the one Scott regarded most highly.) On March 16 Lee was made colonel
of the 1st U. S. Cavalry, an appointment which he promptly
accepted. Since then nothing had happened. Lee had had
a waiting period of approximately seven weeks—as odd a
period, one would suppose, as his entire life contained. He
had been educated for service in the United States Army and
he had spent all of his life in that service; now the sections
of the nation had drifted into war, and as a recently promoted officer in the army, Lee might expect to be called
on to lead troops against the South. His own state, Virginia,
had not seceded, and in Texas Lee had said that he would
do what Virginia did. He had also said that he thought perhaps he would resign and "go to planting corn." Lee had
waited at Arlington, hoping for the best.

When he first saw Scott—sometime between March 5 and
the day he was given his promotion, apparently—he asked
the old general what was going to happen; for his part, he
said, he could not go into action against the South, and if
that kind of action was coming, he wanted to know so that
he could resign at once. Scott reassured him. This was at
the time when Seward was talking conciliation, Lincoln's
cabinet was almost a unit in opposing reinforcements for
Fort Sumter, Lincoln seemed to be in no mood to force
the issue, and Scott told Lee he believed there would be a
peaceful solution. Lee clung to this assurance. Even on
April 15, the day Lincoln issued his call for troops, Lee retained some shred of optimism. An Alexandria clergyman
whom Lee visited that evening said that Lee "was not en-

tirely in despair." Lee that night apparently voiced some belief that things would come out all right, for the minister wrote: "I hope his view may prove correct. But it seems to be against probabilities."[12]

The probabilities caught up with Lee almost immediately. On April 18, the day Virginia's troops were moving on Harper's Ferry, the day after the convention had voted for secession, Lee was called into conference in Washington by Francis P. Blair, Sr., who asked him point-blank if he would take command of the United States Army. Blair made it clear that he was asking this question with the full approval of President Lincoln. Afterward, Blair wrote that Lee expressed a certain devotion to the Union and said that he could not make up his mind without first consulting General Scott; Lee himself, after the war, said that he told Blair he could take no part in any invasion of the South, and he added that he went to see Scott simply to tell him what his decision had been. In any case, he called on Scott as soon as he left Blair and told him what had happened.

The meeting with Scott was brief. Lee told Scott that he was going to resign and admitted that the struggle was hard. He did not believe in secession, he said, and if he owned every slave in the South he would free them all if that would bring peace; but to fight against Virginia was not in him. Lee went back to Arlington. Two days later he wrote a formal letter of resignation and sent it to the War Department, asking that it be made effective at once.

Those two intervening days appear to have been days of emotional upheaval rather than of intellectual analysis. To his sister, Mrs. Anne Marshall, of Baltimore, Lee wrote that the whole South "is in a state of revolution" and that Virginia had been drawn into it. He himself could see no necessity for this state of things, but his course seemed clear: "I have not been able to make up my mind to raise my hand against my relatives, my children, my home. I have therefore resigned my commission in the Army, and save in defense of my native State, with the sincere hope that my poor services may never be needed, I hope I may never be called on to draw my sword." To his brother, Captain Sydney Smith Lee, of the Navy, he wrote in much the same vein; he had thought to wait until Virginia's voters had passed on the ordinance of secession, but the war had actually begun and he might at any moment be ordered to do things which he could not conscientiously do. Accordingly, "save in defense of my native State I have no desire ever again to draw my sword." The same phrase about drawing his sword only in defense of his native state had appeared in his letter of resignation addressed to Simon Cameron. In a letter which she wrote to friends at about this time, Mrs. Lee said: "You can scarcely conceive the struggle it has cost Robert to resign to contend against the flag he has so long honored disapproving, as we both do, the course of the North & South, yet our fate is now linked with the latter & may the prayers of the faithful for the restoration of peace be heard. . . . We shall remain quietly at home as long as possible."[13]

This would not be very long. Two days later a delegation sent by the Virginia authorities invited Lee to go to Richmond. He went at once, and on April 23 he was made commander of Virginia's armed forces. The time of waiting was over; Lee had not so much made up his mind as followed his heart. In this he was doing what most of his fellow Americans were doing.

In Boston, George Ticknor wrote to a friend in England: "We have been slow to kindle; but we have made a Nebuchadnezzar's furnace of it at last, and the heat will remain, and the embers will smoulder, long after the flames that now light up everything shall cease to be seen or felt."[14]

CHAPTER SIX

The Way of Revolution

1. Homemade War

THE SOUTHERN Confederacy had been in existence a little more than two months, and in that time it had made much progress. By the middle of April it had acquired both a fort and a state which it had not had before. Its credit was good, subscriptions of $8,000,000 having been received on a national loan that asked for $5,000,000; a new and much larger issue would be launched very shortly. The Post Office Department was about ready to go into business despite a lamentable lack of proper stamps; courts had been set up in most of the states, and there would soon be a patent office, it being evident that the Yankees had no monopoly on the inventive genius. The Confederate State Department was already in action, and long before Sumter was fired on it had sent commissioners abroad to explain secession to the powers of Europe and (it was devoutly hoped) to win recognition and treaties of friendship, commerce, and navigation.

Significantly, the principal commissioner was William L. Yancey. The prince of fire-eaters was being sent far away from the nation he had done so much to create; he was entrusted with the most delicate of diplomatic missions, not so much because anyone supposed that he had a talent for diplomacy—his enormous skill lay in the rough-and-tumble of American politics—as because he might be an embarrassment if he stayed at home. Leaders who could eat fire had served their turn. The destiny of the Confederacy now was in the hands of more moderate men who were prepared to emphasize the eternal logic and justice of Southern secession, ready to meet force with unmeasured force if need be but still abiding in the faith that reasonable men must eventually accept the Confederacy at its own valuation.

Yancey and his fellow commissioners, Pierre A. Rost, of Louisiana, and A. Dudley Mann, of Georgia, were to work especially on Great Britain. Secretary of State Toombs, himself a man of action who would soon find the dignity of his office too confining, had given detailed instructions. They were to reveal to the British statesmen the complete and undeniable legitimacy of the new Confederate nation; they were also to remind them that this nation was where most of Britain's cotton came from, and were to hint delicately that the supply would probably be cut off in case of a long war. It was hoped, in Montgomery, that this reasonable presentation would be enough. Editor Rhett, of Charleston, was complaining that Yancey ought to have authority to bait the net properly, offering to the British nation of shop-keepers irresistible trade concessions in return for a binding offensive and defensive alliance, but the government was playing a more sober game.[1]

Davis's attitude was revealed in his address to a special session of the Provisional Congress of the Confederate states, called together after the long dispute at Fort Sumter finally exploded into actual war. "All we ask is to be let alone," he cried. The moment Lincoln showed himself ready to adopt a let-alone policy, "the sword will drop from our grasp and we shall be ready to enter into treaties of amity and commerce that can but be mutually beneficial." For the time being, however, the sword must be held. The Confederacy had 19,000 men in the field—at Charleston and at Pensacola, in Fort Pulaski below Savannah, in Fort Morgan at Mobile, and in Forts Jackson and St. Philip at the mouth of the Mississippi—and it was sending 16,000 more to Virginia. It was preparing to organize and equip an army of 100,000 men, and as long as the United States showed a desire to subjugate the South, "we will continue to struggle for our inherent right to freedom, independence and self govern-ment." But there could be no reasonable doubt of final success of the cause.[2]

Davis would have no fire-eaters setting the pace. A man of profound self-control, he would avoid the unpredictable violence of revolution; he would play this by the book. Both Presidents would, as a matter of fact, until it became impossible to play it that way any longer. One of the saddest facts about the nation's final plunge over the brink is that even after the fighting had actually started, both Davis and Lincoln responded to some dim, deeply held feeling that perhaps the point of no return had not really been passed, that there might yet by some miracle be a bloodless solution and a healing. Long afterward the Confederate President's wife, Varina Howell Davis, remembered how her husband took the news that Major Anderson had surrendered Fort Sumter. His first remark was that he was glad so little blood had been shed. Then, most strangely, he remarked: "Separation is not yet, of necessity, final. There has been no blood spilled more precious than that of a mule." And Lincoln, in this same month of April, talking to a group of "frontier guards" at the White House, said an equally unexpected thing: "I have desired as sincerely as any man—I sometimes think more than any other man— that our present difficulties might be settled without the shedding of blood. I will not say that all hope is yet gone."[3]

Separation not yet final, hope not yet gone . . . but each man had set himself a task which he would not give up, had taken a position to which he would cling with the most uncompromising tenacity. More than that: the immense emotion that was welling up from bottomless deeps in the hearts of people all over the country was stronger now than any President and would carry America beyond all formalities and restraints. The country had entered upon a revolution, even though it was not quite clear just who was making the revolution or whom the revolution was directed against, and it would at last wring from Lincoln the bitter cry (in which austere Davis might well have joined) that he could not claim to have controlled events but must admit rather that events had controlled him.

Revolution sets soldiers fighting civilians, and it can pick a city street for a battlefield. So it was now. This was civil war, a time of overthrow and destruction and rising savagery, and the first real fight came when a senseless riot went rolling across Baltimore, with men in uniform and men not in uniform stretched dead on the pavement after it had passed . . . and with a new forced draft applied to Nebuchadnezzar's furnace.

The border states had been considered the key pieces in

the secession crisis, and in some ways Maryland was the most important of the lot. If Maryland went out of the Union (Virginia having gone already), the national capital would be wholly cut off and the government could be imprisoned by its foes, in which case the government would probably lose the war for sheer inability to function. At any cost whatever, the Lincoln administration had to keep Maryland in the Union—with a gun at the nape of the neck, if in no other way.

Cotton-state agents who came proselytizing for additions to the Confederacy in the weeks just after South Carolina seceded had a thin time of it in Maryland; the state listened politely but refused to respond. Although the Mason and Dixon line formed its northern boundary, Maryland was only half southern; it was Dixieland along the eastern shore, but it was straight Pennsylvania west of Baltimore, and Baltimore itself was partly a southern city and partly a trading center of the northern type, prospering because it was both a gateway to the Middle West and an outpost of eastern finance. In a time of civil war a state thus divided was certain to have trouble, and Maryland got its full share at a very early stage.

When Lincoln called for troops, Maryland's Governor Thomas H. Hicks, Unionist-minded but fully aware that very careful handling was called for, hurried to Washington and got from Secretary Cameron and General Scott a promise that Maryland's militia would be used only inside the state and in the District of Columbia. He passed this assurance on to the people of Maryland, and in a sober proclamation he warned that "the consequences of a rash step will be fearful" and urged everyone to refrain from words or deeds that might "precipitate us into the gulf of discord and ruin gaping to receive us." Maryland would furnish her quota of troops, giving the government a conditional but invaluable loyalty which might or might not last for the duration of the war.[4]

The trouble that Governor Hicks foresaw came almost at once. Washington needed troops, being almost totally undefended, and because Washington's only railroad connection with the North was the railroad line that came down from Baltimore, the troops Washington got had to cross Maryland. The first contingent reached the capital on April 18, the day the Harper's Ferry arsenal was lost; a detachment of 460 Pennsylvania volunteers, whose seeming unreadiness led John Hay to comment acidly on the "unlicked patriotism" that came in "ragged and unarmed," and a company of regulars brought from Indian-country posts in Minnesota. These came down from Harrisburg, were alternately hooted and cheered as they went through Baltimore, and reached Washington without incident, but their passing stung the sensitivities of the numerous Southern sympathizers in and around Baltimore. This transit of troops bent on coercion of the South was an outrage, and if there was any more of it, Baltimore's Southerners would take steps. Rumors of coming violence reached Washington, and Secretary Cameron warned Governor Hicks by telegraph that "unlawful combinations of misguided citizens" proposed to use force to keep troops from coming to Washington. This warning might have done some good, except that no one in the War Department told either Governor Hicks or Mayor George William Brown, of Baltimore, when the next contingent of troops was due to pass through Baltimore. The local authorities, who knew without being told by Cameron that something was likely to pop, thus lacked the one bit of knowledge that would enable them to take effective precautions.[5]

The next troops reached Baltimore on April 19; the 6th Massachusetts, a full-strength militia regiment which arrived on a special train, reaching the President Street station of the Philadelphia, Wilmington, and Baltimore railroad a little before noon. There was, to repeat, no through rail connection with the Baltimore & Ohio line to Washington; as a makeshift, cars were hauled cross-town, one at a time, by teams of horses, along a street railway line that led to the Baltimore & Ohio's Camden Street station, and as these cars went trundling along the streets, the unlawful combinations of the misguided swung into action.

Moving as rapidly as possible—which was not, after all, much faster than a brisk walk—nine cars made the trip without serious trouble. The way was lined with hostile crowds, which quickly got larger and more unruly; there were jeers and hisses, stones were thrown, and emotional temperatures grew hotter and hotter, and at last people dumped sand on the track, piled anchors on top of the sand, and effectively blocked the right of way. Stranded at the President Street station were four companies of the regiment and the regimental band, perhaps 220 men in all. With them was an extremely unhappy body of embryonic soldiers from Pennsylvania; 800 men belonging to various military companies in Philadelphia, unarmed and lacking uniforms, not belonging to the state's organized militia, led by officers who had never been formally commissioned—a patriotic but utterly ineffective outfit, of no conceivable use in this crisis, hoping to get to Washington and to be of some service there. The band and the Philadelphians stayed at the railroad station, awaiting developments; the four companies of the 6th Massachusetts shouldered muskets and set out for the Camden Street station on foot.

The march began badly and ended in catastrophe. There were hostile crowds all along President Street, throwing stones, cheering for Jefferson Davis, uttering throaty groans for Abraham Lincoln, and denouncing uniformed Yankees. Someone in the crowd unfurled a Confederate flag, and the shower of stones increased. Mayor Brown got to the scene, placed himself at the head of the column, and appealed to the crowd to keep the peace.

He was heeded only briefly. Then the stone-throwing was resumed, citizens jostled the soldiers and tried to wrest their muskets away from them, and some officers shouted an order to double-quick in the hope that the soldiers could get out of there before the busines grew serious. This seemed to make matters worse instead of better, for the running Yankees looked like chicken-hearted fugitives who dared not fight, and in no time at all there was a full-scale riot and men who had merely been trying to hurt began to try to kill each other. Shots were fired, from the ranks and from the sidewalks—in all of the tumult no one was ever certain just who fired first—and Mayor Brown, sensibly concluding that his presence protected neither the soldiers nor the citizens, stepped out of the column.

A detachment of police arrived at last. (It would have been there from the beginning if Secretary Cameron's people had bothered to tell the governor or the mayor when the 6th Massachusetts was going to arrive.) Enough order was restored to enable the battered companies to reach the Camden Street station and board the cars for Washington. As the troop train at last steamed out, there was one final incident, which the people of Baltimore would remember for a long time. A group of men near the track voiced a cheer for Jefferson Davis, and some soldier or soldiers fired through the car windows in reply, killing an eminently respectable merchant named Robert W. Davis, who had had no part whatever in the rioting. Back at the President Street station the unlucky companies from Pennsylvania were badly beaten before the police could take charge; not knowing what else to do, the police at last sent the men back to Philadelphia—profoundly unhappy men, who had shed blood but had acquired no glory, suffering the final ignominy of being sent home by the police.

The Massachusetts regiment had had casualties: 4 men killed and 36 wounded, not to mention about 130 who had disappeared in all the excitement but who, presumably, would eventually reappear. (This of course would include the members of the band, which had received contusions at the railroad station along with the Pennsylvanians.) The citizens of Baltimore had an even worse casualty list—12 men dead and an undetermined number injured. The first fatalities of the war had been recorded.[6]

Some time that evening the 6th Massachusetts got to Washington. It left behind it a Baltimore that was all but on fire with indignation, and many of those who were angry were not secessionists at all. There were men who argued that the troops were as much to blame for the fighting as the sidewalk crowds, the War Department's handling of the business had been inexcusably inept, and Mayor Brown believed that the killing of Davis, the cheering but non-violent merchant, kept many citizens from feeling "a keener sense of blame attaching to themselves as the aggressors." The Baltimore Police Board met that evening and agreed that there would be an even worse riot if any more troops came through the city; to prevent it, the bridges connecting Baltimore by rail with the East must be burned, and Governor Hicks reluctantly concurred. A special committee was sent off to Washington to tell Lincoln about it.

Lincoln would accept what had to be accepted, and he would go out of his way to support men like Governor Hicks and Mayor Brown, who were doing their best in an extraordinarily difficult situation; he wrote to them, thanking them for their efforts to keep the peace and promising that to the extent possible, troops coming to Washington would be ordered to bypass Baltimore. Thus the immediate effect of all of this was that the Baltimore secessionists had won; they had isolated the capital of the United States, and the Federal government had lost the first battle of the war. Acutely conscious of this fact, Lincoln insisted that his underlying policy must be understood. The Federal government would do what it had to do to insure its survival, and if need be it would be very tough about it. When a committee of leading citizens came to the White House to protest that it was an insult and a provocation to bring Federal troops across Maryland, Lincoln returned a blunt answer. Washington had to have soldiers, he said, and the soldiers were neither moles that could tunnel under the ground nor birds that could fly through the air; they had to go on foot, and to reach Washington they had to march across Maryland, which they would do no matter who did not like it. "Keep your rowdies in Baltimore," said the President, "and there will be no bloodshed. Go home and tell your people that if they will not attack us we will not attack them; but if they do attack us we will return it, and that severely."[7]

Over the long pull this policy would be made effective, but for the immediate present the administration was almost completely helpless. It was cut off, receiving no troops and suddenly discovering that it could send out no orders—secessionists in Baltimore, encouraged by the destruction of the railroad bridges, had seized the telegraph offices. Below the Potomac, Virginia seemed bent on making war with energy and dash, and it was perfectly possible that Virginia troops might at any moment march into Washington, capturing President and cabinet and paralyzing the central nervous system of the whole Federal government. Lincoln had at his immediate command very little to prevent a stroke of this kind —a bare handful of regulars, a few District of Columbia home-guard regiments that might or might not prove to be Unionist at heart, the battered 6th Massachusetts, and the incomplete Pennsylvania regiment that had preceded it. Until reinforcements arrived, the capital was all but defenseless. With telegraphic communication broken, the administration could not know what the rest of the country was doing. It could only trust that help was on the way. Journalist Bayard Taylor, casting about in Washington at this time, found that every conversation ended with the anxious question: "Why don't the troops come on?"

Taylor talked with Lincoln, and was encouraged to see in him "that solemn, earnest composure which is the sign of a soul not easily perturbed"; but Lincoln in fact was profoundly perturbed, as genuinely worried perhaps as at any time in all the war. His presidency seemed to exist in a vacuum. Troops from New York and Rhode Island were supposed to be on their way, but they had vanished into a silent mist that enfolded all of the North. Reviewing the 6th Massachusetts, he put his aching bewilderment into words: "I begin to believe there is no North. The 7th New York regiment is a myth. The Rhode Island troops are another. You are the only real thing."[8]

Winfield Scott had told a War Department functionary, just before the Baltimore riot, that if Washington's railroad connections with the North were broken for as much as ten days, the capital would be brought to the edge of starvation and would probably fall into the hands of the secessionists. The city seemed to be entering a state of siege; hundreds of barrels of flour, pork, beans, and sugar were stacked up in the General Post Office and in the basement of the Treasury Building, and strange bands of volunteer rangers stumped about Capitol and White House to protect government from treason. Some of these were residents of Kansas, brought together by the lanky frontier orator James H. Lane, given the collective title of "Frontier Guards" and quartered for a time in the White House itself. Even more improbable was the "Strangers' Guard," transients from the principal hotels, rounded up, armed, and put to work by the redoubtable Cassius M. Clay, of Kentucky, the stalwart duelist who by sheer toughness had managed to survive an extended career as active abolitionist in a slave state. Clay showed up at the White House wearing three revolvers and a bowie knife. He had his men stalking the downtown streets after dark; Washington was at bottom a southern city, containing many citizens who would gladly co-operate with an invading force from Virginia, and there was quite literally no telling what might happen. John Hay reported that the President spent much time staring from the White House windows at the Potomac. It was supposed that some of the northern regiments that could not reach Washington by rail might come in, roundabout, by water.[9]

Lincoln saw steamers at last on April 23, when the U.S.S. *Pawnee* and a transport came up the river and docked at the Washington Navy Yard, but instead of bringing help they brought tidings of a new disaster. The Gosport Navy Yard, near Norfolk, then as now the country's most important naval base, and usually referred to simply as the Norfolk Navy Yard, had been seized by armed Virginians, along with several warships, a first-rate dry dock, and much useful machinery, and an immense quantity of guns and ammunition. The loss was not only expensive but humiliating. The yard had simply been fumbled away.

Commandant at Norfolk was Commodore Charles S. Mc-Cauley, a brittle shell-back of sixty-eight—he had been born during the presidency of George Washington, and had gone to sea before either Lincoln or Davis was born—and although he was brave and loyal, the outbreak of civil war was just too much for him. He wanted to do the right thing, but nothing in naval tradition told him what the right thing was in a time like this. In substance, the old commodore never knew what hit him.

He had at his command 800 sailors and marines, along with a collection of warships that were mostly either museum pieces or cripples. There were the huge line-of-battle ship *Pennsylvania*, once mounting 120 guns, unarmed now, serving as a receiving ship, and three smaller ships of the line—*Columbus* and *Delaware*, three-deckers built to the standards of Trafalgar, and *New York*, which was still on the stocks. (The navy had been leisurely dawdling away at her construction for twenty years and more.) These ships were completely useless. There were also two sailing frigates, *Columbia* and *Raritan*, out of order but fairly serviceable if repaired, and there were the 22-gun sloops *Plymouth* and *Germantown*, and the little dispatch boat *Dolphin*. Most important of all, there was the big steam frigate *Merrimack*, one of the most powerful warships afloat, laid up waiting for extensive engine-room repairs.

Early in April, Secretary Welles had begun to worry about all of this property, and he sent the navy's chief engineer, Benjamin F. Isherwood, down to make temporary repairs on *Merrimack*'s engines; and on April 11 he ordered Commander

James Alden to take command of *Merrimack* and bring her up to Philadelphia. Isherwood got the engines fixed, Alden went aboard and raised steam, and then Commodore Mc-Cauley—under the influence, said Isherwood, of "liquor and bad men"—gave way to nervous doubts. He had been told, over and over, that aggressive action by the Federal power might drive Virginia into secession (a condition that Virginia was just about to enter anyway), and he countermanded Welles's orders and refused to let *Merrimack* sail. Alden and Isherwood came back to Washington to report.[10]

Then things began to get complicated. Virginia's convention passed the ordinance of secession, and the people of Norfolk sank old hulks in the Elizabeth River to keep the Yankee warships from getting out; they did it inexpertly and the channel remained open, but it showed what was in the wind. Governor Letcher sent state troops to Norfolk under Major General William B. Taliaferro, and Washington dispatched U.S.S. *Pawnee*, a regiment of Massachusetts infantry from Fort Monroe, Captain Horatio G. Wright, of the Corps of Engineers, and two commodores, Hiram Paulding and G. J. Pendergast, with somewhat vague orders to get the ships out, see to the security of the yard, and in general present a solid front to the menace of secession.

All of this was too much for Commodore McCauley. A number of his officers had resigned to go off and join the Confederacy; the watchmen at the navy-yard gates, similarly motivated, had also quit; the whole city was bristling with aggressive hostility; and Taliaferro's men were putting up batteries in preparation for a bombardment. The old man believed that the navy yard could not be defended, and on the evening of April 19 he ordered every warship in the place scuttled. (The smoke from the burning arsenal at Harper's Ferry was still in the air, wounded men still lay on the streets in Baltimore, and now this: the revolution was moving fast this week.) Just as the ships settled toward the bottom, the relief expedition arrived, *Pawnee* towing the sailing frigate *Cumberland*, which carried the troops. The officers in charge could do nothing now but acquiesce in McCauley's decision; it was agreed that the job of destruction should be completed on the evening of April 20, and the navy yard should then be evacuated.

The moon came out to give light for the work. Captain

Wright laid a mine to destroy the dry dock. The scuttled ships, which had touched bottom with their upper works still above water, were set on fire. Detachments were put to work throwing shell and solid shot into the water—a completely fruitless task, since the Confederates fished them all out as soon as the Federals went away—and all of the shops and other buildings in the place were set on fire. Smoke went up to hide the moonlight, the black clouds streaked with red from the mounting fires; a correspondent for the New York *Times* remarked that the burning of the *Pennsylvania* made a spectacular sight, with flames twining masts and rigging and issuing from 120 gun ports. Poor old McCauley, moved by heaven knows what remnant of the tradition that a captain ought to go down with his ship, wanted to destroy himself, perishing in the conflagration that was destroying his command, but was talked out of it. Naval officer in charge of setting fire to things was a Captain Charles Wilkes—a lanky, thwarted genius, brilliant, opinionated, erratic and unlucky: a man who would in due time make his own strange contribution to this war. To Wilkes, as he moved through the smoky night, came a group of Marines asking him to refrain from burning the Marine barracks; the sergeant of the guard had a hen setting on twelve eggs in the guardroom and he hoped that the brooding fowl might not be disturbed. This was a homemade war, and all ranks of the professionals tended to be a bit confused.[11]

The Federals got away at last, leaving fire and embers behind them, and *Pawnee* and *Cumberland* moved down to Hampton Roads and anchored under the guns of Fort Monroe. As the Confederates moved into the smoldering navy yard, General Taliaferro complained bitterly that the burning of the buildings and the warships was "one of the most cowardly and disgraceful acts which ever disgraced the Government of a civilized people." (One of the characteristic aspects of this utterly confusing war was the general feeling, among active secessionists, that it was somehow perfidious and unnaturally evil for the Federal government to resist when warlike measures were taken against it.) He grew less wrathful, presumably, when he learned that the act of destruction, although base, was incomplete. The mine that Captain Wright had planted had failed to explode, and the dry dock was intact. So was most of the important machinery and equipment elsewhere about the premises, and nothing that was really needed seemed to be hurt beyond repair. Nearly 1200 heavy-duty cannon had been captured; the Federals had tried to spike them but had worked in too much haste, and the weapons could easily be restored to usefulness; they would arm Confederate forts all over the South, from Roanoke Island to Vicksburg. And *Merrimack* could be refloated and rebuilt; a matter that would presently be attended to.[12]

2. Arrests and Arrests Alone

DURING FOUR years of war, Washington came to know many hours of despondency, but it never again seemed quite as lost and as helpless as it felt between April 19 and April 25. In retrospect it is clear that the situation was not really as bad as it looked, but at the time the Federal government appeared to be face to face with final disaster. Edwin M. Stanton, temperamentally fitted to see things at their worst, assured his good friend James Buchanan that he simply could not give him an adequate description of the panic—which, he added, "was increased by reports of the trepidation of Lincoln that were circulated through the streets." Families were packing their goods and preparing to leave, women and children were being sent away, and the price of food stuffs (said Stanton, who liked to pick up his basket and do the family marketing) had risen to famine levels. Willard's Hotel looked deserted, and the desolate calm of an out-of-season holiday descended on the capital. If this time of trial brought Lincoln little help, it at least gave him temporary relief from the swarm of hungry Republicans looking for government jobs.[1]

There were plenty of problems to occupy Lincoln's mind even without the job hunters. The soldiers who were so desperately needed were on the way, but getting them would compel the government to take steps regarding the situation in Maryland. Many of these steps would be extra-legal, and before all of them were taken Lincoln would stretch the Constitution to the limit—beyond the limit, in the opinion of Chief Justice Taney—but there was no help for it. There were no rules now except the ancient law of survival. What had to be done would be done, and now and then some odd-looking instruments would be used.

Among these was the eminent Massachusetts politician Benjamin F. Butler. Gross, shifty, and calculating, Butler had been a prominent Democrat, and at the Charleston convention (so long ago, now, so irrevocably lost in the past) he had worked long, hard, and fruitlessly to win the Democratic Presidential nomination for Jefferson Davis. Now he was a brigadier general, leading troops south to fight against that same Davis; and on April 20 a steamer carrying Butler and the 8th Massachusetts Infantry dropped anchor at Annapolis, forty miles by rail from Washington.

Annapolis was the capital of Maryland and it contained Governor Hicks, who was thoroughly loyal to the Union but was almost distracted by the thought of what the dedicated pro-Confederates in his state might do if they saw any more Federal troops moving south on coercive missions. It seemed at the moment as if all of Maryland might go aflame, just as Baltimore had, and Hicks begged Butler to keep his men on their boat. He also sent an impassioned telegram to Lincoln, describing it in a companion message to Secretary Seward: "I have felt it to be my duty to advise the President of the United States to order elsewhere the troops now off Annapolis and also that no more may be sent through Maryland. I have also suggested that Lord Lyons [the British minister in Washington; a functionary whom Robert Toombs would have loved to see enmeshed in this war] be requested to act as mediator between the contending parties of our country to prevent the effusion of blood."[2]

This day was Saturday. Over the weekend, Hicks conferred extensively with Butler, while the Massachusetts soldiers lounged about in crowded idleness aboard their steamer. Governor Hicks discovered something that other men would discover later—that Ben Butler, however grave his deficiencies as a military man, was highly skilled in argument and negotiation; was also a man who never hesitated to use all of the authority that he believed himself to possess. By Monday morning, April 22, Butler had things settled his way, and he brought the 8th Massachusetts ashore. As the men were landing, another steamer came in with the 7th New York, and this regiment also came ashore. As a brigadier, Butler as-

sumed command of everybody, after certain spirited protests
from the officers of the New York regiment.

From Annapolis a branch line of the Baltimore & Ohio ran
twenty miles westward to intersect the Baltimore–Washington line at a point called Annapolis Junction. Track and
bridges on the Annapolis branch had been sabotaged, and the
only rolling stock at Annapolis consisted of one damaged
locomotive; but the Massachusetts regiment was full of mechanics—one soldier discovered that he had actually helped
to make the engine that needed repairs—and Butler put track
and engine gangs to work, with two companies of infantry
thrown out to guard against secessionist interference. Orders
came in from the War Department by special messenger;
Butler was to remain in Annapolis, assuming responsibility
for keeping this route to the capital open, and troops were
to come on to Washington. The 7th New York plodded along
the track to the junction, got aboard a waiting train there,
and went steaming on to Washington. There it detrained,
formed ranks, and went tramping along Pennsylvania Avenue toward the White House. The date was April 25, just ten
days after Lincoln had issued his call for troops.

The 7th New York was a crack militia regiment, neatly
uniformed, priding itself on the precision of its drill, the ex-
cellence of its brass band, the high social standing of its officers and enlisted men, and the general snap and sparkle of
its military behavior. It had left New York after a two-mile
parade down Broadway, and because of the emergency it
moved in light marching order, leaving behind much camp
equipment, including 1000 velvet-covered camp stools. One
of its members wrote of the "terrible enthusiasm" with which
New York sent its first regiment off to war—cheers so loud
the regiment could hardly hear its own band, citizens pressing close to pound soldiers on the back, ladies tossing handkerchiefs from windows or, more bold, stepping out from
the curb to tap a soldier's wrist with a pair of gloves . . . "it
was worth a life, that march." (The soldier who wrote thus
was a young man named Theodore Winthrop: he would die
in battle before this spring was over, paying his own price
for the march that stirred him so much.) Now the regiment
was in Washington, knowing its supreme moment. It came
down the great avenue under its flags, stepping along as if it

were the finest regiment in the world, the advance guard of many more to come. Washington's week of panic was over.[3]

This was all very well, but the fundamental insecurity remained. The border states appeared to be exploding like a string of firecrackers, and if Maryland exploded with them—which, considering what had happened in Baltimore, seemed quite likely—the administration and the capital city and the war itself could be lost all in one lump. Ben Butler and the militia had merely opened a temporary road. That road now must be made permanent, broad enough to give every Northern state free access to the capital. The administration had to make certain of Maryland's loyalty to the Union, or, if the loyalty proved inadequate, at least of Maryland's subservience. President Lincoln and Governor Hicks would see about it.

Against them was the power of a blazing sentiment, built on an old fondness and raised now by violence to story-book intensity. The bond that pulled American states into the Confederacy was always more a matter of emotion than of cold logic, and from Baltimore to the Gulf the emotional response to the nineteenth of April was unrestrained. What the North saw as a mob scene looked in the South like a legendary uprising, with gallant heroes brutally done to death by the ignorant soldiers of a cruel despotism. All of the sense of romance that attached itself to the Southern cause was centered now on Maryland, and the state was pictured as a tragically beset heroine whose ultimate rescue must come if the world made any sense at all. James Ryder Randall, a Marylander-in-exile, wrote a passionate apostrophe—"The despot's heel is on thy shore, Maryland!"—and the song was sung all across the South as an inspiring battle hymn. The Confederate Congress would, in time, vote that no treaty of peace would ever be signed that did not permit Maryland to enter the Confederate nation. To this welling forth of sentiment, there was a responsive reaction among all Marylanders who felt kinship with the South.

Maryland's legislature was in adjournment at this time, and Governor Hicks was undoubtedly willing to have it stay that way, but now his hand was forced. Ardent and influential friends of the South were demanding that the legislature assemble at once in Baltimore, and a proclamation calling such a meeting had been issued over the name of State Senator Coleman Gellott. The proclamation had no legal standing

whatever, but this was a spring in which legalities meant very
little; a rump session meeting in Baltimore, which in the days
immediately following the riot seemed to be as pro-Confederate as Richmond itself, might do incalculable things and
make them stick. Weighing all of the possibilities, Governor
Hicks concluded that the best way to head off an uncontrol-
lable, self-summoned and self-instructed rump session was
to have a regular session called in the regular way, so he
ordered the legislature to convene on April 26. Inasmuch as
Annapolis, the capital, was occupied by Federal troops, he
specified that the meeting take place in the city of Frederick,
forty miles west of Baltimore. Frederick had been selected
after careful thought; it was well over in western Maryland,
where most people were Unionists and the legislators would
not be meeting under pressure of a secessionist gallery.

When the legislature assembled, the governor assured it
that "the only safety of Maryland lies in preserving a neutral
position between our brethren of the North and of the
South." Maryland, he pointed out, had violated the rights
of neither section, wished everybody well but still prized the
Union, had done nothing to start the war, and hoped that
the war would end as quickly as possible. In consequence:
neutrality.[4]

After some debate the legislature agreed with the governor.
It passed a resolution asserting that it lacked the constitutional
power to adopt an ordinance of secession, and it pointedly refrained from calling a state convention, which could adopt
such an ordinance; in effect, it refused to go for secession,
and the chance that Maryland would formally leave the
Union was dead. The legislature named commissioners to
discuss with the Federal authorities arrangements "for the
maintenance of the peace and honor of the State and the security of its inhabitants," and it named committees to visit
both Lincoln and Davis. There were certain rumblings while
this went on. The lower house urged Lincoln to make peace,
and at length resolved that "the state of Maryland desired
the peaceful and immediate recognition of the independence
of the Confederate States." Mere resolutions, however, the
Federal government could take in its stride. The important
thing was that Governor Hicks had kept Maryland in the
Union.[5]

In all of this, Governor Hicks had help from Washington,

and the kind of help he got was clear indication that Lincoln was prepared to be ruthless. It had taken the President a long time to make up his mind, after a winter in which he had seemed to sway uncertainly with varying breezes, but at last he had hardened, and now he had come to one of the fateful decisions of the Civil War. He would fight secession with any weapon he could lay his hands on, no matter what the weapon might be; facing what he looked upon as a revolutionary situation, he would use revolutionary means to cope with it. He had said, so recently, that all hope was not yet gone, but the hope that remained now (as a loyalist Northerner might see it) was nothing better than the hope that those who had risen against this administration might yet confess their error and submit. His answer to those who denied the power of the Federal government was simply to assert (backing the assertion by force) that that power could, in time of crisis, be wholly unlimited.

When he first learned that Governor Hicks was convening the legislature, Lincoln seriously considered arresting the entire membership in order to prevent the meeting. The matter was discussed with the cabinet, and Lincoln at length rejected it. On April 25 he made this rejection official in a letter to General Scott: the dispersion of the legislature, he wrote, "would *not* be justifiable, nor efficient for the desired object." He set forth the reasons briefly: "First, they have a clearly legal right to assemble; and we cannot know in advance that their action will not be lawful and peaceful. And if we wait until they shall *have* acted, their arrest or dispersion will not lessen the effect of their action. Secondly, we *can* not permanently prevent their action."

Two days later he followed this with another note to the old general: "You are engaged in repressing an insurrection against the laws of the United States. If at any point on or in the vicinity of the military line, which is now (or which will be) used between the city of Philadelphia and the city of Washington, via Perryville, Annapolis City and Annapolis Junction, you find resistance which renders it necessary to suspend the writ of habeas corpus for the public safety, you, personally or through the officer in command at the point where the resistance occurs, are authorized to suspend that writ."[6]

This was not just talk. Military rule descended on the Baltimore area. People could be arrested (and a good many were) simply because an army officer believed that they were up to something hostile, and the courts could not help them. Mayor Brown, who was bitterly opposed to all of this, wrote afterward that the mere display of Confederate colors—in shop windows, on children's garments, or wherever—was prohibited, and he specified other items of harshness: "If a newspaper promulgated disloyal sentiments, the paper was suppressed and the editor imprisoned. If a clergyman was disloyal in prayer or sermon, or if he failed to utter a prescribed prayer, he was liable to be treated in the same manner, and was sometimes so treated. . . . Very soon no one was allowed to vote unless he was a loyal man, and soldiers at the polls assisted in settling the question of loyalty." The mayor went on to say that Unionists generally approved of these steps but that many people were greatly worried by this loss of constitutional liberties; in the arguments, friendships were resolved, close relatives became estranged, "and an invisible but well-understood line divided the people."

To this situation General Butler made massive contributions. (In point of fact, Butler was exactly the sort of man the founding fathers had in mind when they stiffened the Constitution to prevent an abuse of military authority.) Early in May, Butler took troops over to occupy Relay House, just southwest of Baltimore, the vitally important junction point where the railroad line to Washington joined the Baltimore & Ohio Railroad's main line to the West. At Relay House, Butler heard that treason was rife in Baltimore, and that Federal and State laws were being flouted by, as he put it, "some malignant and traitorous men." He promptly marched troops into Baltimore, seizing and fortifying the commanding height of Federal Hill overlooking the harbor and the business district, and he issued a proclamation whose general effect was that the Federal power was now in charge. He found and confiscated quantities of arms, arrested (among other people) the well-known inventor and builder of railway locomotives, Ross Winans, and took possession of a contraption Winans had built which the daily press described as a "steam gun."[7]

Butler was enjoying himself. Carl Schurz saw him at this time and reported that the man was little less than fantastic; he wore the gaudiest of militia uniforms, set off with much gold braid, and adopted an overdone air of high authority, a curt and peremptory manner of speech and action, which struck Schurz as exactly the sort of thing a certain type of actor would indulge in on the stage. After every passage-at-arms with his subordinates, Butler would glance around to make sure that his visitor was duly impressed. Still, Schurz confessed, Butler was quite an operator, and with all of his foibles he kept things moving.[8]

General Scott had not authorized the occupation of Baltimore, and as a stiff old regular he found Butler hard to take, anyway; he sent the man an angry rebuke, telling him to issue no more proclamations and remarking that it was a Godsend that the move had not touched off a wholesale fight, and on May 15 Butler was relieved of his command and sent down to take charge of the quieter post at Fort Monroe. He took with him an admonitory note from the general-in-chief: "Boldness in execution is nearly always necessary, but in planning and fitting out expeditions or detachments, great circumspection is a virtue." Butler's place at Baltimore was taken by Major General George Cadwalader, who was a much milder man than Butler but who nevertheless quickly got himself involved in a case that the lawyers would study and talk about for many generations to come.[9]

For although the government had removed Butler, it had not disavowed the things he had done. What was afflicting Maryland just now was not really Ben Butler at all; it was the growing weight of Federal authority, directed by an administration that would assert and use any power necessary to ensure the government's survival. Federal troops remained in control, and military law continued to be applied; and in this month of May a man named John Merryman was in Baltimore getting recruits for a military company that was going to go south and fight for the Confederacy. Cadwalader heard about him, or at least his subordinates heard about him, and Merryman was arrested and locked up in Fort McHenry—that historic fort where Francis Scott Key had seen a starry flag by the dawn's early light and had made a song about it—and Merryman's lawyers went to Chief Justice Taney, who was then in Baltimore, to get him out.

The arrest of Merryman was precisely the kind of act which the government could not, in any ordinary circumstances, perform, and there were laws to govern such cases.

Justice Taney promptly issued a writ of habeas corpus, and a United States marshal ventured off to serve it; could not, because the way was blocked by soldiers; returned to the Chief Justice with a report from General Cadwalader stating that Merryman appeared to be guilty of treason and that he, General Cadwalader, was authorized by the President to suspend the writ in such cases. Taney cited the general for contempt, and the marshal went to serve an attachment on him, only to find once again that armed soldiers made his job impossible. Taney could do nothing further, except to announce that Merryman ought to be discharged immediately and that "the President, under the Constitution of the United States, cannot suspend the privilege of the writ of habeas corpus, nor authorize a military officer to do it."

But Lincoln controlled the soldiers and Taney did not, and the arrest stuck. Explaining his position in a message to Congress a few weeks after this happened, Lincoln discussed the legal points briefly. The Constitution, he said, provided that the privilege of the writ might be suspended in cases of rebellion or invasion if the public safety required it; the government (that is, the President) had "decided that we have a case of rebellion, and that the public safety does require the qualified suspension of the privilege of the writ" and that was that. Furthermore: "Are all the laws, *but one,* to go unexecuted, and the government itself go to pieces, lest that one be violated?" Merryman would remain under arrest (for a time, at least), as would many others, and the state of Maryland would remain in the Union.[10]

Some time later Governor Hicks reviewed the whole business in a speech before the United States Senate, to which he was elected in the middle of the war. The act of suspension, he said, was necessary. "I believe that arrests and arrests alone saved the State of Maryland not only from greater degradation than she suffered, but from everlasting destruction," he said. "I approved them then, and I approve them now; and the only thing for which I condemn the Administration in regard to that matter is that they let some of these men out."[11]

The drastic quality of Lincoln's policy needed to be realized. Democratic governments, both before and since, have died of less. Lincoln had been ready to disband a popular legislature by force of arms, refraining not so much because it was wrong as because it did not seem to be expedient. He had suspended, in one troubled area, all of the hard-won protections which law erects between the helpless citizen and the government—courts, trial by jury, the intricate due-process safeguards against arbitrary arrest and imprisonment. He had flatly defied the Supreme Court, using the army to nullify the court's pronouncements. Years earlier he had written that it is the quality of revolutions to break up the old lines and the old laws and to make new ones. Now he was showing how this worked.

Some of his enemies could see the necessity for this sort of action and wanted his principal rival to copy it. The editor of the Richmond *Examiner*, reflecting on the tasks that lay ahead of the Confederate government, wrote a paragraph that Lincoln might have adopted as an argument in his own justification.

"No power in executive hands can be too great, no discretion too absolute, at such moments as these," said an editorial in the *Examiner* on May 8. *"We need a dictator.* Let lawyers talk when the world has time to hear them. Now let the sword do its work. Usurpations of power by the chief, for the preservation of the people from robbers and murderers, will be reckoned as genius and patriotism by all sensible men in the world now and by every historian that will judge the deed hereafter."[12]

Whatever might be said, either by sensible contemporaries or by latter-day historians, the thing worked in Maryland, and the chief reason why it worked may have been that Maryland did after all contain a pro-Union majority. What was done—by President Lincoln, by Governor Hicks, even by the ineffable General Butler—was effective because in the long run it somehow corresponded with what most of the people dimly wanted. Ruthlessness, then, is acceptable as long as it is ultimately acceptable to the majority . . . the shakiest of moral principles, but the one on which a great war began.

3. Diplomacy Along the Border

VISITING THE capital of the Confederacy a little more than a fortnight after the fall of Fort Sumter, Mr. Russell, of the London *Times*, sensed that he was looking at a people who might make a fabulous war. He disliked much that he saw, to be sure. He found Montgomery sultry and primitive, as dull and lifeless as a town in the middle of Russia, and the universal chewing of tobacco appalled him almost as much as the slave pens and the callous crowds at the slave auctions; yet the men who lived amid all of this were prodigious. They were tall, lean, and uncouth, but "they are not peasants," and indeed Russell believed that a real peasant or even an authentic dull-eyed rustic, in the European understanding of the word, was nowhere to be found. The poorest men dressed and acted like the wealthiest, even though dress and manner might be a poor imitation, and both rich and poor expressed anger at the insulting tyranny that was being attempted by the government at Washington.

Significantly, everyone seemed to feel that this government represented a malignant faction rather than the Northern people as a whole. (The South had its delusions as well as the North this spring.) Men spoke of the Federal authorities as "Lincolnites," "Black Republicans," "Abolitionists," and so on, as if usurpers held power in Washington, destroying national unity even before secession took place. The Confederate Congress Russell found as impressive as the people themselves. Its capitol was "one of the true Athenian Yankee-ized structures of this novo-classic land," and its members somehow looked like old-time Covenanters, massive, earnest men inspired by a strong faith; altogether, "they were like the men who first conceived the great rebellion which led to the independence of this wonderful country—so earnest, so grave, so sober and so vindictive." In this, Russell agreed with Varina Davis, who was writing to a friend that the men in this Congress "are the finest looking set of men I have ever seen collected together—grave, quiet and thoughtful looking men with an air of refinement." Mrs. Davis felt that they offered a refreshing contrast to the Northerners who sat in Congress at Washington.

Congress impressed Russell more than the President did. He found Mr. Davis slight, erect, clearly a gentleman, wearing "a rustic suit of slate-colored stuff" with a black silk handkerchief at his neck; a man with a reserved, rather severe manner, with a square jaw, high cheekbones, and thin, flexible lips, one of the deep-set eyes nearly covered with a film—the man suffered from excruciating attacks of neuralgia, and had lost the sight of this eye. Davis seemed confident and he spoke with decision, but Russell thought he looked haggard and worn. Here again he agreed with Mrs. Davis, who felt that the President was working altogether too hard and said that he protested against the time he lost at meals; "he overworks himself and all the rest of mankind."[1]

There was reason for overwork, for much had to be done. The great surge of Southern enthusiasm for the war was unchecked by any realization of what actual war was going to mean, and although Davis and the professional soldiers knew very well that the new troops needed much more training and equipment than it was yet possible to give them, the public at large was impatient for action. In Richmond, Lee was trying desperately to get such fundamental necessities as gun carriages, ammunition, and the machinery to make cartridges and percussion caps. People were urging him to invade the North, although he knew this to be impossible in view of "the want of instruction of the men and the inexperience of officers," and one patriot complained to Secretary of War Walker that Lee "wishes to repress the enthusiasm of our people," and asked: "Is our cause not in danger of demoralization?"[2]

It seemed to the authorities that the cause might be in danger of worse than that. When Lincoln issued his call for troops, he gave the Southern "combinations" twenty days to lay down their arms and go home. The twenty days expired on May 5; would not the Federals immediately invade Virginia, once that date was passed? Technically, to be sure, Virginia was not quite out of the Union. Her ordinance of secession would not be effective until the voters ratified it at a special election called for May 23. But Virginia and the Confederacy had already signed "a convention of alliance," under which Confederate troops were sent to Virginia and put under Lee's command, Lee in turn getting his orders from Montgomery, and there was not the slightest doubt that the act of secession would be upheld by a sweeping majority. There were many Confederate soldiers in the state, but they were not ready for a real fight.

Alexandria, the historic town which lay almost across the river from Washington—the obvious target for the first Federal thrust—offered a case in point. The Confederate commander there was Lieutenant Colonel A. S. Taylor, of the

Virginia Volunteers, and his orders were to hold Alexandria "unless pressed by overwhelming and irresistible numbers"; but on May 5 Colonel Taylor got his men out of there without waiting to be pressed. He explained that his command consisted of 481 untrained men, many of them unarmed, none of them possessing more than a few rounds of ammunition. Living in Alexandria, they "were becoming almost useless from home influences"; they were scattered all over town, and to assemble them in any one place with any speed at all was entirely out of the question. So Colonel Taylor ordered a retreat, and it was mortally hard to blame him very much—except for the fact that the Federals were no more ready to invade than he was to defend. Alexandria went unoccupied for some days, and then the Confederates got some better-prepared troops back into the place.[3]

Meanwhile, the Congress at Montgomery could at least make the war official. On May 6 Davis announced that he had approved and signed "an act recognizing the existence of war between the United States and the Confederate States," this act having been adopted by Congress three days earlier. It merited examination. Neither in tone nor in content was it a declaration of independence. Independence was taken for granted; this was a declaration of war, pure and simple, the kind of document one full-fledged nation might issue against another, and its "whereas" clauses were devised to justify war and not revolution. It recited the acts that amounted to war: all of the Confederate government's attempts to establish friendly relations with the United States, and to settle points at issue "upon principles of right, justice, equity and good faith" had been rebuffed; the government at Washington refused to talk about these things, refused even to listen, and was now mustering troops "to overawe, oppress and finally subjugate" the Southern people. The government at Montgomery was telling the world that it was engaging in war with a foreign power, not in insurrection.[4]

In Washington the line was drawn with equal sharpness: the United States was fighting to suppress a rebellion, and the only issue was this challenge to its national unity. On the same day Davis made his announcement, Secretary Seward released for publication the text of instructions which he had given to William L. Dayton, the United States Minister to

France, and what he had to say collided head-on with what had been said at Montgomery.

"You cannot be too decided or too explicit," Seward had written, "in making known to the French government that there is not now, nor has there been, nor will there be any— the least—idea existing in this Government of suffering a dissolution of this Union to take place in any way whatever. There will be here only one nation and one government, and there will be the same republic and the same Constitutional Union that have already survived a dozen national changes and changes of government in almost every other country. These will stand hereafter, as they are now, objects of human wonder and human affection."[5]

The quality of human wonder and affection was, in the North, a reality that Lincoln could feel and rely on, but along the tormented border it had worn very thin and now it was shredding away entirely. Whatever of wisdom or of folly there had been in Lincoln's call for troops, the call had driven the process of political fission to a conclusion. It had abruptly ended the time in which men of divided sympathies could wait and hope for the best; it had brought about a second secession, far more significant than the first, giving the Confederacy a strength and a broad emotional base which the cotton states alone could never have had.

For the thesis of the government at Montgomery now had as much deadly vitality as the thesis of the government at Washington. This struggle would be two things at once, in desperate earnest—insurrection and foreign war. The aims of the opposing governments could never be harmonized. If men held to the opinions they were adopting now, the thing would have to be fought to a finish. The lean and tenacious muscularity that had so impressed Mr. Russell on his travels meant that the finish was very far away.

Virginia had gone out of the Union with considered speed, a gun in each hand. Maryland had been kept in place only by careful handling and the use of force. Kentucky and Missouri were lurching unsteadily, might do anything, stood at the moment in perilous equilibrium, unpredictably explosive. North Carolina, Tennessee, and Arkansas peeled off without delay and went with the Confederacy, giving it eleven states in place of its original seven; giving it, also, a very substantial portion of the continental mass of the original nation.

These three states that seceded so defiantly once the shooting started had refused to secede earlier in the year, and men like Lincoln and Seward had misinterpreted the refusal, believing that it reflected a firm and enduring loyalty to the Union. Actually, this loyalty had been all festooned with qualifying clauses. If the Federal government showed endless patience in negotiation, if it gave ground on every major point at issue, if in short it accepted the essential rightness of the secessionist position and behaved accordingly, then this Unionist sentiment would hold firm, and on this highly conditional loyalty a highly conditional Union might be reconstructed. The call for troops left the ordinary Southern Unionist high and dry.

In North Carolina a pro-Union majority which had existed during the winter evaporated overnight. One of the Unionist leaders in the state complained bitterly: "Lincoln prostrated us. He could have devised no scheme more effectual than the one he has pursued to overthrow the friends of the Union here. . . . Lincoln has made us a unit to resist until we repel our invaders or die." On April 15 state troops seized Fort Macon, on the outer banks, and the next day the Wilmington Light Infantry occupied Fort Caswell and Fort Johnston at the entrance to the Cape Fear River—the same two forts that had been seized by an inspired citizenry, and returned to the Federal government with stiff apologies, early in the year. Governor Ellis called the legislature into special session, and the legislature immediately authorized him to give military help to Virginia. Then it summoned a secession convention to meet on May 20. If technicalities mattered, North Carolina would not join the Confederacy until May 21, but technicalities did not matter. To all intents and purposes the state was out of the Union as soon as the call for troops was issued. As a practical matter, once Virginia left the Union, North Carolina was bound to go.[6]

The story was very much the same in Tennessee. Two months earlier the state had shown a strong majority against secession, and even Governor Harris, as dedicated to Southern rights as Governor Letcher himself, had thought that the cause was lost. The events of April 15, however, gave the cause a vigorous rebirth. Governor Harris defied Lincoln and convened the legislature, and the legislature authorized him to make an alliance with the Confederacy, declared Tennessee's independence, and then voted to submit the question of entering the Confederacy to a popular vote. This election would occur on June 8, but by the end of the first week in May it was obvious that Tennessee had left the Union.

Tennessee's case, as a matter of fact, was rather special. Slavery here was not quite like slavery in the deep South. In the mountainous eastern section it hardly existed at all, and even in the more populous west it had been subtly modified. Completely and unmistakably Southern, Tennessee nevertheless looked in some ways like a Northern state that had unaccountably acquired the habit of slavery; or, just conceivably, it represented an evolutionary stage in the development of slave society which no other Southern state had yet reached. Western Tennessee had big plantations in the traditional style, and it had poor whites and shiftless tenant farmers, also after the old tradition, yet its population was not really divided into two sharply contrasting classes, the rich planters and the poor whites; its distinguishing characteristic was the presence of a strong, growing middle class, which owned few slaves, operated family-sized farms with success, developed small but healthy industrial plants in towns and cities, and all in all prospered happily despite the presence of slavery.

This was the state that had contributed John Bell, the Constitutional Union candidate, to the last presidential campaign. Like Bell, its majority wanted the Union to live but identified itself with the South when the final pinch came. Bell and others had signed an appeal in mid-April pleading for peace and a reunited country, but events were too much for them. Before the month was out, Bell was making a speech at Nashville declaring that he would stand by the South and would defend it against "the unnecessary, aggressive, cruel, unjust and wanton war" which Washington was preparing. He had spoken for compromise, and there had been no compromise; now he was accepting war because there did not seem to be anything else that he could do, but he was doing it sadly, and the war cruelly broke him. In the deep depression of spirit with which he met the onset of hostilities, Bell differed from the Tennessee majority.[7] Like Virginia, this state, which had refused to secede in the absence of an overt act at Washington, went out with enthusiasm when the time to go out at last came, responding to an emotional tie that was far more compelling than a mere abstract reverence for the Union. There was a strange significance in the fact that these two states, Virginia and Tennessee, which had tried to avert war, gave the Confederacy more soldiers and the war more battlefields than any other states.

They were alike, also, in that they suffered their own sectional divisions. Western Virginia refused to respond to the secessionist impulse, showed a Unionist sentiment that was robust enough to stand the shock, and would presently—in a wholly extra-legal way, abetted by Washington—perform its own act of secession, breaking away from Virginia and clinging to the Union as a bob-tailed but finally acceptable new state. Eastern Tennessee would not go so far, but it was strong for the Union; it held a convention, denounced governor and legislature for making the alliance with the Confederacy, and sent in a memorial asking that the eastern counties be allowed to form a new state. Eastern Tennessee would be a problem to both Presidents—to Davis because it represented a disloyal area giving aid and comfort to the enemy; to Lincoln because it kept asking for armed help which he was not able to provide.

Arkansas slipped out of the Union almost without argument. In March a state convention had rejected secession by the close vote of 39 to 35, and had called a special election for August to enable the electorate to choose between secession and "co-operation"; the whole action meaning nothing more than the fact that before Fort Sumter was bombarded a majority in Arkansas favored compromise rather than secession. The call for troops put the game in the hands of the pro-Confederates, who acted without delay. The state convention reassembled on May 6, condemned the "inhuman design" of the Lincoln administration, canceled the August election, and voted for secession by a lop-sided 69 to 1. The sole dissenter was an Ozark mountaineer named Isaac Murphy; here, as elsewhere in the South, loyalty to the Union seemed to have its only solid roots in the mountain country, where few people owned slaves and where the independent mountain men tended to be somewhat suspicious of the doings of political leaders from the lowlands. The all but unanimous vote in the convention probably overstated the extent of pro-Confederate sentiment, but this was only a matter of degree. By May 18 delegates from Arkansas were seated in the Confederate Congress; technically, Arkansas was the ninth state to join the Confederacy.[8]

Where the business really became complicated was in Kentucky, which was emotionally a part of the South and geographically a part of the Middle West; a tragically divided commonwealth, whose distraction was symbolized by the fact that it was the native state of Jefferson Davis, who was creating a new nation; of Abraham Lincoln, who was calling the country to arms to destroy that nation; and of Senator Crittenden, who had worn himself out all through the winter and spring trying to find a formula that would make both the new nation and its destruction by force unnecessary. Each of these men spoke for something fundamental in the state's character, something that had become essential to the state's personality. There was the devotion to the old South, the South of the half-unreal but magically compelling tradition, and there was also the devotion to the Federal Union and to the Northern and Western states that had drawn so many settlers from Kentucky's soil; and there was, finally, the deep attachment to the great Henry Clay tradition of compromise and peaceful adjustment. With this last there existed, strangely, a conflicting tradition, as strong as any—the tradition of violent action, dating back perhaps to the Indian fighting that had run up and down the dark frontier like a flame, coming down through the feudists and the knife fighters and the wild young men who went armed to political caucuses and polling places. Kentucky wanted conflicting things, and what it wanted it was apt to reach out for with a muscular hand.

At the start Kentucky reached out for nothing. The firing at Fort Sumter and the summoning of troops left the state momentarily paralyzed, unable to adjust itself to the collapse of peace. Senator John C. Breckinridge, who had been the fire-eaters' candidate for President in the last election, and whose sympathies were clearly with the Confederacy, remained in the United States Senate and hoped that outright war might yet be avoided. Senator Crittenden continued to talk of compromise and hoped that Kentucky might be the medium through which North and South could at last negotiate terms. Governor Magoffin, who had used strong words to reject Lincoln's call, summoned the legislature in special session, saw that only a minority of the legislators shared his secessionist views, and came out at last with a proclamation of neutrality. (The United States Constitution provided for a state's neutrality no more than it provided for a state's secession, or for the coercion of one state by another, but the Constitution this spring was subject to all manner of extemporized interpretations. This was Governor Magoffin's.)

"I hereby notify and warn all other states, separated or united, especially the United and Confederate States," said the governor, addressing the legislature on May 20, "that I solemnly forbid any movement upon Kentucky soil, or occupation of any post or place therein for any purpose whatever, until authorized by invitation or permission of the legislative and executive authorities. I especially forbid all citizens of Kentucky, whether incorporated in the State Guard or otherwise, making any hostile demonstrations against any of the aforesaid sovereignties, to be obedient to the orders of lawful authorities, to remain quietly and peaceably at home, when off military duty, and refrain from all words and acts likely to provoke a collision, and so otherwise conduct that the deplorable calamity of invasion may be averted; but meantime to make prompt and efficient preparation to assume the paramount and supreme law of self-defense, and strictly of self-defense alone."[9]

These were fine words if Governor Magoffin could make them stick, but the odds were against him. From the Alleghenies all the way to the Mississippi River, Federal and Confederate armies could get at each other only by crossing Kentucky, and the state's neutrality was bound to have a short life—all the more so since this neutrality came from an even balance between opposing forces within the state rather than from a settled belief in neutrality for its own sake. At the same time, it was up to Lincoln and Davis to move with extreme care, for one false move could easily turn Kentucky from a neutral into an outright enemy, and this could be fatal. The danger was greater for the Federals. If the Ohio River should be the northern boundary of the Confederacy, Confederate independence was all but assured. Lincoln was said to have remarked that while he hoped to have God on his side, he had to have Kentucky; a little later he wrote that to lose Kentucky was about the same as to lose the whole game. Davis said, long afterward, that Kentucky might have been able to remain neutral if she had been physically stronger than either of the contestants, or if she had had a moral influence which all men would be obliged to respect. As things were—the Civil War being real, and not just a war of words—the hope to remain neutral struck Davis as "utterly impracticable."[10]

The tactics by which Lincoln had compelled Maryland to remain in the Union would be ruinous in Kentucky; the state was different, the situation was different, and the administration's program had better be different, too, as Lincoln was the first to realize. In Maryland there had been no time for delicacy or finesse. The Baltimore secessionists had put their hands on the government's windpipe, the grip had been broken by the unabashed use of sheer power, and the administration would go to any imaginable lengths to keep that particular hand-hold from being regained. Nobody was gripping anything, in Kentucky. Direct action would spoil everything. This state had to be wooed.

The wooing would be largely negative. Officially, Lincoln would leave Kentucky strictly alone, as far as he could and as long as he could, and he saw to it that this was clearly understood. Before April ended, some of Kentucky's leading Unionists, worried lest the policy applied in Maryland might also be used in Kentucky, sent Lincoln's old-time friend Garrett Davis to Washington to sound the President out, and to Garrett Davis, Lincoln talked freely. He did not intend (he said) to send military or naval forces into any state unless the people of that state were in open resistance to the laws and authority of the United States. More specifically, he had in mind no military operations that would make it necessary to send troops across Kentucky. "If Kentucky," Davis wrote to a friend in Louisville, "made no demonstration of force against the United States, he would not molest her."[11]

Yet although he would abstain from molestation, Lincoln could not be inert. Jefferson Davis could take a passive attitude toward Kentucky; as long as the state remained neutral, it was a great shield for the deep South, protecting the Confederacy better than a whole cordon of forts would do. The Federal approach had to be more positive. Kentucky not only must be prevented from going over to the Confederate side; somehow, a majority of her citizens must be led to give active approval to the war for the Union.

There would be a propaganda drive, with speeches, news-

paper articles, and the organization of Unionist clubs and
societies. Here Lincoln could get help from one of Louisville's influential citizens, Joshua Speed, who was his own
intimate friend; also from another Louisville resident, Joseph Holt, who as Secretary of War during the final months
of Buchanan's regime had given Unionist stiffening to that
unhappy man's cabinet. And Major Robert Anderson, the
hero of Fort Sumter, the regular-army officer with Southern
sympathies and Unionist convictions, was by great good fortune a Kentuckian: he would be sent west, promoted, given
authority to raise troops of Kentucky volunteers, but instructed to remain for the present north of the Ohio River.
For the time being, at least, the state's neutrality would be
technically respected.

Respected, at any rate, on the surface. Both sides were
surreptitiously, but without much genuine secrecy, trying to
arm their adherents in Kentucky. Before May was over, Anderson wrote to Lincoln that he had talked to Joshua Speed,
who bore a letter of introduction from the President men-
tioning the matter of providing arms for the faithful; "I will
carefully attend to the performance of that duty," Anderson
promised. One Kentuckian who was most active in this connection was a burly, arrogant giant of a man named William
Nelson, who had been a lieutenant in the navy but who believed he could better serve the Union by returning to his
native state and getting Unionists there in shape to fight. Nelson took leave of absence from the navy and went to Louisville without definite instructions, with the understanding that
he would do whatever seemed most likely to be helpful. He
got 5000 stand of arms into Kentucky, working with a committee of local Unionists. When the time came to use those
weapons, Nelson would resign from the navy and become a
general in the army. Governor Magoffin was organizing and
equipping the state militia; thousands of secessionists were
enrolling, and although the militia was ostensibly preparing
to defend neutrality, few people doubted that the governor
wanted it to go in eventually on the Confederate side. To
balance this force, home-guard units of pro-Union sentiments
were being set up in towns all across central and northern
Kentucky, and "Lincoln rifles" were given these levies, quietly, by night. The state was developing two sets of troops,
which might or might not some day come to blows.[12]

. . . To the President of the United States, Kentucky represented a chance to atone for an earlier miscalculation. Lincoln had moved too fast in connection with the other border states; his call for troops—embodying, as it did, the conclusion that secession must be destroyed by force of arms—had cost him four states, might yet cost still more. Kentucky could perhaps be saved. Much would depend on the kind of handling it was given. Much would depend also on what happened in Missouri, the uncertain anchor of the whole border tier, its vast land mass banked up west of Kentucky and Illinois, lit now by uncertain lightning flashes of violence. Kentucky would get diplomacy and soft words, but Missouri would get the hard hand that had beaten down secession in Maryland.

4. Collapse of Legalities

MISSOURI MIGHT go anywhere at all. The only safe prediction was that it would produce a great deal of trouble for somebody, perhaps for both North and South together, certainly for its own people. A slave state jutting north of the old Missouri compromise line, it was a blend of the South and the Middle West, admiration for the Confederacy existing side by side with devotion to the Union. In the West there were the spirited "border ruffians" who had made life so interesting for free-state settlers during the days when Bleeding Kansas was a national problem; in St. Louis there were many thousands of unassimilated German immigrants who cared nothing for the Southern tradition and were the dedicated foes of chattel slavery. (One of the baffling factors in the Missouri situation was the fact that its Unionists included both conservative pro-slavery men and zealous abolitionists, who distrusted one another about as much as they distrusted the secessionists.) The state was so far from Washington and Montgomery that both Federal and Confederate governments had to rely on the judgment and decisions of men on the spot; and, in the luck of the draw, these included certain very forceful characters who believed in direct action.

Among them was Claiborne Jackson, the governor; tall, angular, determined, an ardent Southern-rights man in his middle fifties, with a firm, straight mouth framed by a clean-shaven upper lip and a square lower jaw fringed with whiskers that ran from ear to ear in a sweeping crescent. Jackson had been elected in the fall of 1860. A Democrat, he had supported Douglas because the Missouri Democracy was solidly in the Douglas camp, but he really belonged in the secessionist wing of the party. He tried to take Missouri out of the Union early in 1861, at the time the cotton states went out, but lost the fight when the voters, electing delegates to a state convention, chose a Unionist majority. Jackson waited, returning to the fray when Lincoln called for troops. On April 17 Jackson sent his bristling refusal to Washington; and on the same day he wrote a letter to Jefferson Davis, entrusting it to two captains in the state militia, Colton Greene and Basil W. Duke, and proposing a plan of action which might put Missouri in the Confederacy despite the unfortunate result of the recent election. (American political leaders always respect the will of the majority, but in time of crisis they sometimes have even greater respect for the way an accomplished fact can force a majority to change its mind.)

Jackson's plan had to do with the United States arsenal in St. Louis. This institution contained a good store of weapons —probably 30,000 infantry muskets, by the best estimate, together with ammunition and other items of equipment— and if state troops controlled by a secessionist governor could get those arms, the Federal power in Missouri would be overthrown. Jackson was asking Davis for the loan of some field artillery, along with a few mortars if possible.

"Missouri," he wrote, "has been exceedingly slow and tardy in her movements hitherto, but I am now not without hope that she will promptly take her stand with her Southern sister states. The Arsenal at St. Louis, now under the command of an abolition officer, it is feared will be greatly in our way—in the event of active hostilities being commenced against the Confederate States. To remove this obstacle it will probably become necessary to have a few large guns to batter down its walls and drive out our enemies."[1]

Governor Jackson anticipated, correctly, that President Davis would be helpful, and he set about plans to use the guns the Confederacy was sending to him. A state law authorized him to call the militia into camp for drill and instruction; accordingly, the governor ordered a militia general named D. M. Frost (a good man, but a shade mild in his manner for a time like this) to get his brigade together and put it in camp on the hills overlooking the arsenal. When the guns arrived, Frost could take the arsenal and its priceless military stores.

The guns would be forthcoming. Davis wrote to Jackson admitting that "a generous but misplaced confidence has, for years past, prevented the Southern States from making the preparation required by the present emergency," which meant that the Confederate government was short on ordnance supplies. However, two 12-pounder howitzers and two 32-pounder guns, with ammunition, were available and were being sent, and as an old soldier Davis felt they should be sufficient. "These, from the commanding hills, will be effective, both against the garrison and to breach the inclosing walls of the place," he wrote. "I concur with you as to the great importance of capturing the arsenal and securing its supplies. . . . We look anxiously and hopefully for the day when the star of Missouri shall be added to the constellation of the Confederate States of America."[2]

So far, so good; until the ordnance reached him, Governor Jackson was going to be most circumspect. He had called a special session of the legislature, to meet on May 3, and he would tell the legislature that although Missouri's interest and sympathies were identical with those of the other slave states, Missouri "at this time has no war to prosecute." It was merely necessary for the state to spend money arming for its own defense. Before the legislature met, he wrote frankly to a friend: "I do not think Missouri should secede today or tomorrow, but I do not think it good policy that I should publicly so declare. I want a little time to arm the state, and I am assuming every responsibility to do it with all possible dispatch. Missouri should act in concert with Tennessee and Kentucky. They are all bound to go out, and should go together if possible. . . . Nothing should be said about the time or the manner in which Missouri should go out. That she ought to go and will go at the proper time I have no doubt."[3]

Thus ran the plan of Governor Jackson; perfectly feasible, carried on below the surface, with as much secrecy as was possible in a time and place where complete secrecy was all but impossible; a plan that might wreck the old Federal Union beyond repair. Working against the governor, like military engineers counter-mining far underground, were men fully as ruthless and determined, with a plan of their own.

One of these was the hard-drinking, hard-fighting Frank Blair—Francis P. Blair, Jr., son of redoubtable Old Man Blair, of Washington, brother to Postmaster General Montgomery Blair, and himself a Republican Congressman from Missouri; a man who was considered a moderate on the slavery question but who was rarely moderate on anything else. Another was the soldier whom Jackson had mentioned in his letter to President Davis as the abolitionist officer who controlled the arsenal—Captain Nathaniel Lyon, fiery, with bushy red hair and whiskers, remembered by an old army acquaintance as "wild and irregular . . . a man of vehement purpose and of determined action";[4] precisely the man to work under the direction of Frank Blair in a situation in which all the rules were off and no holds were barred. These two had a pretty clear idea of what Governor Jackson was up to, and to his conspiracy they erected a counter-conspiracy of their own. That neither the governor's plan of action nor their own had any basis in ordinary legality was wholly characteristic of the atmosphere of the spring of 1861.

Blair had thought about the arsenal as promptly as Governor Jackson had, and he went into action just as soon as the Republican administration came into office—as soon, that is, as his own copper-riveted political connections with the White House would be of service. Lyon was then in command at Fort Riley, Kansas; a harsh disciplinarian, disliked by his soldiers because of the ferocious punishments he inflicted, known as a man of almost fanatical devotion to the Union.[5] Blair pulled strings, and Lyon was transferred to St. Louis and made commandant of the arsenal. Blair then bethought himself of the Wide-Awakes, the Republican marching clubs that had tramped the streets, singing and chanting and carrying banners, during the presidential campaign. He had organized a number of these in St. Louis, enrolling chiefly the Germans; these he now turned into an irregular sort of home guard, and Lyon helped to give them military drill—some of the units, it was reported, put in eight hours a day at it. Since they were wholly outside the

tables of State or Federal military organization, it was impossible to equip them at public expense, but uniforms and
other items of the soldiers' outfit were bought with money
raised from anti-Confederates in the East. For arms, Blair
kept his eye on the stacks in Captain Lyon's arsenal.

His resources were not yet exhausted. The top army commander in the St. Louis area was Brigadier General William
S. Harney, an old Indian-fighting type with a good military
record, but not quite the man (as Frank Blair saw it) to
defend the government's interests in Missouri at a time like
this. Harney was as loyal to the Union as any regular officer
need be, but he would always abide by army regulations,
and the regulations made no provision for the sort of thing
Blair and Lyon were considering. Blair tugged at his strings
once more, and Harney was temporarily relieved from his
command and ordered to Washington: whereupon Lyon
got orders from the War Department instructing him to
arm loyal citizens, protect the public property, and muster
into service four regiments of Missourians. The loyal citizens
and the four regiments would of course be Frank Blair's
Germans, and the public property would be chiefly the
weapons in the arsenal.[6] (In Baton Rouge, Louisiana, a
steamboat was taking aboard bulky boxes labeled "marble,"
and consigned to a St. Louis address. In the boxes were the
siege guns and howitzers that Davis was sending to Governor
Jackson to enable Jackson to take possession of this same
public property. This artillery, as it happened, came originally
from a Federal arsenal in Baton Rouge, seized by Louisiana
troops earlier in the winter.)

Governor of Illinois at this time was Richard S. Yates, a
stout Republican who was deeply disturbed by the thought
of a Confederate state along his own state's western border,
and who was even more disturbed by the fact that the Mississippi River, the corn belt's traditional traffic artery to the
outside world, now flowed through militantly foreign territory. He would do anything he could to help Unionists
gain the upper hand in St. Louis, and now—by prearrange-
ment with the Blair-Lyon team—he sent Captain James H.
Stokes, of the Illinois militia, down to St. Louis on a steamer
to help get those muskets out before Governor Jackson
could seize them. Captain Stokes took his steamer to the
wharf on the night of April 25, and before daylight more

than 20,000 muskets and 110,000 cartridges had been put aboard. The steamer then went upstream, got to a railhead at Alton, on the Illinois side, and trans-shipped the arms to Springfield. (There was a great to-do about this in the Northern press, with colorful accounts of how an elaborate ruse was employed to foil a secessionist mob which wanted to prevent the transfer. It made a good story, full of melo-drama, doubtless welcomed by a Northern public that was beginning to understand that there was a war on and ex-pected a little excitement in the public prints; but it was pooh-poohed by the editor of the Missouri *Republican,* a loyalist paper in St. Louis, who wrote that no secessionist mob had even tried to keep the weapons from being shipped, and said the midnight transfer "could just as well have been done in the daylight.")[7]

By the end of April the muskets were gone, except for those that had been retained to arm Blair's German regi-ments and other "loyal citizens," and General Frost's state troops had not yet made their camp on the site commanding the arsenal. Lyon accordingly put his own new troops on the chosen site, and when Frost's men were assembled, on May 6, Frost put them in camp in a grove on the western edge of St. Louis. In honor of the governor this place was known as Camp Jackson: it was a pleasant clearing with a good board fence around it, its principal roadways were named for Jefferson Davis, General Beauregard and Fort Sumter, and on spring evenings the camp was thronged by "the fairest of Missouri's daughters" who strolled about "in company with their sons, brothers and lovers." A big United States flag floated above General Frost's tent, and altogether the camp looked like the scene of any peacetime militia muster, except that the militiamen and their visitors all did seem to have strong secessionist leanings. Also, on the night of May 8, the load of munitions from Baton Rouge reached St. Louis, and guns and ammunition were quietly hustled out to camp.

Governor Jackson unfortunately was a little late. The Federal arsenal now was guarded by several regiments of troops, and although these soldiers were complete amateurs, the same was true of the militiamen who had been called together to oppose them. Even though the Confederate ar-tillery had been received, there was no very good place to put it. General Frost's little brigade was actually at a loose end. It went on with its drill, while the governor and the general waited to see what would happen next.[8]

Now the business took on a farce-comedy coloration. Captain Lyon wanted to see for himself what the state troops were up to. (Legally, these troops had every right to be where they were, but Lyon angrily referred to them as "a body of rabid and violent opposers of the general government" and said that they were "a terror to all loyal and peaceful citizens.") Accordingly, Lyon rigged himself up in the most improbable of disguises—black bombazine dress, veil, market basket, and whatnot—got into a buggy with a Negro coachman, and had himself driven all through the camp, ostensibly Frank Blair's mother-in-law out to see the sights, peering darkly through the veil for signs of subversion and rebellion, reinforcing his conviction that Camp Jackson menaced the integrity of the Union and must be dealt with immediately.

William Tecumseh Sherman was living in St. Louis at this time, a retired army officer working as superintendent of a street railway company. He knew Lyon from old army days, and when he heard about this flamboyant act of espionage he refused to believe that it had really happened. Lyon, he pointed out, had "a full rough beard and a shocking head of hair" and was just about the last man in North America to play the part of female impersonator. Also, said Sherman, Camp Jackson was pretty much open to all visitors, and anyone could have strolled through the place at any time without trouble. Apparently, however, Lyon really made the visit, complete with gown, veil, and gloomy suspicion, and immediately afterward he and Blair concluded that the time for action had come.[9]

On May 9 four of Blair's home-guard regiments were drawn up at the arsenal to receive ammunition. Sherman saw them there, saw Lyon running about (in proper regimentals once more, fortunately) with his hair in the wind and his pockets full of papers, and Sherman assumed that things were about to happen. General Frost, who had been hearing things, made the same assumption, and on May 10 he wrote to Lyon saying he understood that Lyon planned to attack Camp Jackson. General Frost said, with dignity, that this was hard to believe. Surely no United States officer would attack law-abiding citizens who were carrying out their Constitutional function of organizing and instructing a body of state militia? The message reached Lyon by messenger just as he was preparing to march; he contemptuously refused to receive it and started for Camp Jackson, with two companies of regulars and several thousand of the German guards. Southerners who watched the detachment start out eyed the Germans with contemptuous disdain. One man wrote that these recently enrolled soldiers "did not march so much as shuffle along" and felt that they looked apathetic and uncomprehending; felt, too, an eerie sense "of something silently fatal, bewildering, crushed, ghastly." Lyon got his men out to the camp early in the afternoon, and sent in a peremptory demand for surrender. Frost surrendered, under protest, there being by this time nothing else that he could do.[10]

Frost might have done several things if he had acted earlier. He might have attacked the arsenal in spite of the odds against him as soon as the ordnance from Baton Rouge reached him. He might have fortified Camp Jackson and made ready to fight it out there. He might have retreated, to gain time and strength for a showdown later on. But by the afternoon of May 10 it was too late for him to do any of these things, and the real trouble seems to have been that he simply did not understand the kind of game that was being played. He had been preparing to do an extra-legal thing—seize a United States arsenal by force of arms —and he had relied, for protection, on the very legalities that were being disregarded. He had never quite managed to get down to business; his camp had been informal, easy-going, romantic, a "fashionable rendezvous," as one sympathizer called it, where "all was forgotten save youthful vanity, impossible ambitions, flirtations."[11] Frost's note to Captain Lyon had the muted ring of General Taliaferro's complaint, at Norfolk, where the burning of abandoned warships and machine shops seemed cowardly and disgraceful; it was not *legal* for the United States Army to attack state militia; men ought to go by the rules. But the rules were collapsing all over the land, and General Frost was helpless, and so Captain Lyon's men went through Camp Jackson, lining up prisoners and assembling the captured war material.

Lyon hastily checked on what he had captured; 50 officers and 639 enlisted men, 3 siege guns, 1 mortar, 6 brass field pieces, 1200 rifled muskets, and an assortment of ammunition, equipment, and whatnot, along with 30 or 40 horses. Nothing would do now but to march the prisoners down to the arsenal so that they could be properly paroled. The procession was formed, regular troops leading the way, followed by German home guards, the prisoners surrounded by armed men; late in the afternoon the military band sounded off and the troops began to move.[12]

A great many people had come out to watch, and the troops moved through an increasing throng. Sherman believed that the bulk of the spectators were simply curious folk who wanted to see what was going on, but there were many loyal Southerners on the scene, and as the files of unhappy prisoners came tramping along, the crowd became more and more hostile. People surged off the sidewalks, jostled the moving troops, cheered for Jefferson Davis, and called down curses on all Dutch soldiers. (Good Southerners in St. Louis never referred to these Unionist Germans as Germans; they always called them Dutchmen, or Hessians, usually with a select string of qualifying adjectives.) One thing that gave Southern-minded folk in St. Louis a particular sense of outrage was the feeling that General Frost's youthful soldiers represented chivalry, breeding, an aristocracy of birth and manners, and that it somehow was deeply wrong—almost unthinkable—for regular-army scum and clumping foreigners to presume to dictate to them. When news of the march to Camp Jackson circulated through the town, a woman told Sherman there would be bloodshed, because Frost's men came from the best families in St. Louis, had much pride, and would fight to the death rather than surrender. Sherman remarked that "young men from the best families did not like to be killed better than ordinary people," but this did not console her very much. The regular soldiers who led the procession presently leveled their bayonets to force a passage. They opened a path without serious trouble, but the German regiments behind them lacked the regulars' tough discipline, and when the crowd menaced them with revolvers, they reflected that they carried loaded weapons themselves and got ready to use them.[13]

They boiled over into outright violence before long, just

as a similar situation had brought violence in Baltimore. When the crowd saw the files of prisoners, flanked by armed men, what little restraint there was vanished entirely. A woman screamed "They've got my lover!" and ran close to spit on one of the guards; the guard turned on her with his bayonet and chased her down the street, wholly ignoring the storied sanctity of Southern womanhood. A drunken man with a revolver tried to break through the cordon, was pushed violently away, and began to fire, wounding an officer. Some of the Germans fired in reply; then the column wavered to a halt and suddenly the firing was general. In the beginning, it was said that most of the soldiers fired in the air, hoping to frighten the crowd into retreat, but this did not last long, and many of the bullets found human targets. In a little open square Sherman stood watching, with his small son at his side. When the firing began, he pulled the boy to the ground and lay over him to protect him; he estimated that at least 100 bullets passed over them before the firing died down. Smoke clouds drifting across the pavement veiled the movement of running men and women, and there was a wild uproar of musket fire, shouts, screams, hoarse cries of command, and the clatter of hurrying feet.[14]

It came to an end after a while, and the soldiers were able to finish their trip to the arsenal. No one ever made a really accurate count of the casualties, but it appeared that at least twenty-eight people had been killed or mortally wounded, with many more receiving lesser hurts. Most of those shot were civilians, some of whom had come out to do nothing more than see what was going on; a child had been killed in its mother's arms, a woman was dead, at least three of the prisoners had been shot—by whom, nobody ever quite knew. The soldiers had had losses, too. Captain Constantine Blandovski, of the Third Volunteer regiment, had been mortally wounded while his company was standing at rest, a man from Poland dying in a haphazard battle no one had planned, others from Europe dying with him. Death had struck at haphazard and from a clear sky, and the terror was remembered. One citizen said that up to the moment of actual violence the soldiers had passed silently, except for the unending shuffle of heavy feet, their presence all the more frightening because they looked so awkward. Emerging from his cellar after the riot ended, this man found a dead "Hessian" sitting on the sidewalk, his back against the house, a bullet hole in his head; near-by a servant with mop and bucket was scrubbing bloodstains from the sidewalk. Farther down the street there was a little fruit stand, run by an Italian who probably knew and cared as little about secession and unionism as any man in America. A stray bullet had killed him, and the cries of his widow and children hung in the empty street.[15]

St. Louis was a wild town that night. Thousands of people were on the streets, asking for news, prepared to make news on their own account. Groups paraded back and forth, shouting, brandishing weapons, now and then firing in the darkness, some carrying the United States flag, others bearing the flag of the Confederacy. Proprietors of saloons, restaurants, and theaters prudently shut up shop, fearing a general riot. A store selling firearms was raided, and fifteen or twenty rifles were carried off before the police could disperse the mob. Somehow, general rioting was averted, but trouble broke out afresh the next day when one of the German regiments, marching from the arsenal to its mustering place, fell afoul of an angry crowd at Fifth and Walnut streets. In the senseless firing that resulted, from six to twelve persons were killed—some of them, it was believed, soldiers hit by wild shots fired by their own comrades.[16]

The militiamen captured at Camp Jackson were duly released, paroled prisoners of war. Nobody quite understood what kind of war this was, but a war of some sort unquestionably had begun—it had taken lives, it had its formal roster of men taken prisoners, and the kind of neutrality Kentucky had been enjoying was going to be forever impossible for Missouri.

5. Symbolism of Death

THE MONTH that followed the bombardment of Fort Sumter settled it. Resorting to violence, the country now had to abide by the results of violence; the fury that had been invoked would grow great, with gunfire in the streets, armed riders on the country roads, undisciplined militia driven on toward the great test of battle. The secession of the cotton states might, just possibly, have ended simply as a political-pressure play. But the second secession changed all of that. States like Virginia and Tennessee were taking part in no pressure play. They went out to stay out, a terrible finality implicit in their action. The confused and brutal struggle for the border states was a logical consequence—logical, because the only logic that prevailed now was the rough logic of chaos itself.

This logic can lead to unexpected conclusions. Blair and Lyon had won the civil war in St. Louis before it really got started, which was just what they set out to do, but as far as the rest of the state was concerned, they had won nothing; they had simply made more civil war inevitable. The fighting in St. Louis was clear warning that the middle of the road was no path for Missourians. No longer would carefree militiamen lounge picturesquely in a picnic-ground camp, serenading the girls while they waited for glory and an easy triumph. Now they would fight, and other men would fight against them, and no part of the United States would know greater bitterness or misery. Here was a state still close to the frontier, where men were predisposed to violence and where half a decade of dispute over the slavery issue had created many enmities, the lines of hatred running from farm to farm and from neighbor to neighbor. Altogether, it was a bad state in which to ignite a civil war.

The seismic shock of what happened in St. Louis on May 10 struck the state legislature first. That body was in session at Jefferson City, the state capital, and until about six o'clock on the evening of May 10 it had seemed to be safely Unionist. It had long since refused to vote for secession, providing instead for a state convention which had solidly beaten an ordinance of secession and had voted for a benevolent neutrality more or less on the Kentucky model; but when the first dispatch from St. Louis arrived, the legislature was galvanized into swift, pro-Confederate action. It might even have voted to take the state out of the Union, if it had not previously delegated authority in that respect to the state convention; as it was, it gave the Union cause a sharp defeat, passing a military appropriation bill which the Unionists had bitterly opposed. This bill authorized the governor—Claiborne Jackson, against whose secessionist ambitions the whole Blair-Lyon blow had been aimed in the first place—to spend $2,000,000 to repel invasion; it also put every able-bodied man in the state in the militia, made the militia strictly subject to officers appointed by the governor, and made criticism of the governor an offense that could be punished by court-martial. Having done this, the legislature adjourned for the evening, only to be called back into session by messengers at midnight, a violent thunderstorm raging, church bells ringing, anxious citizens braving the storm to see what new crisis had developed. Word had just come in that 2000 troops were leaving St. Louis to march on the state capital, and the governor had called the legislators into secret session.

That midnight session was eerie; tense, shadowed, poised halfway between the desperate and the ludicrous. Almost everybody came to the meeting armed, some men excessively so. Rifles were stacked in the aisles, or leaned against the desks; some members sat in their places with guns between their knees, and some wore heavy belts to which were fastened revolvers and bowie knives; and there were armed guards at the doors. The tension was allayed when it became known that the Osage bridge, which must be crossed by any despotic Dutch levies that intended to enter Jefferson City, had been burned. There would be a breathing spell, then. The solons voted to send the state treasure to some safe place out of town, voted to do the same with the state's supply of powder, and then adjourned for the night, their weapons unused. In the morning it was learned that the march on the capital was not taking place after all.[1]

All across the state men were choosing their sides, and many who had been tacitly supporting the Union went over to the Confederacy; among them, most importantly, Sterling Price, the state's leading citizen, former Congressman, former governor, soldier in the Mexican War, a high-minded man of lofty ambitions—one of the "conditional Unionists" who found the conditions imposed by Frank Blair too much to stomach. He called the St. Louis affair "an unparalleled insult and wrong to the state" and pronounced for the Confederacy, and Governor Jackson promptly commissioned him a brigadier general and put him in charge of the state militia. Price took charge of the state troops that were being called up, spurred Confederate recruitment, ordered guns mounted to control navigation on the Missouri

River, and sparred for time to get substantial forces organized. In southwest Missouri other secessionist levies were
raised; and in the southeast corner of the state, near the
great river, an energetic eccentric named M. Jeff Thompson
collected several thousand informally organized guerrillas
and got ready to harass the Yankees, issuing proclamations
the while. (Thompson rode about his camps on a spotted
stallion called Sardanapalus, attended by a huge Indian orderly named Ajax; he cruised the river periodically in a
tugboat which he denominated his flagship, and wrote that
the Confederate authorities could crush the St. Louis
Unionists without trouble if they would just burn all the
breweries and declare lager beer contraband of war; "by
this means the Dutch will all die in a week and the Yankees
will then run from this State.")[2]

For an uneasy fortnight the Federal authorities seemed to
be in a conciliatory mood. General Harney, who had been
temporarily removed from his command so that Lyon could
work with Blair, was returned to St. Louis, and he did his
sober-minded best to restore order. He refused to disavow
the capture of state troops at Camp Jackson, but he announced that he did not want to interfere in any way with
the governor or other state authorities and warned that
he would "suppress all unlawful combinations of men,
whether formed under pretext of military organizations or
otherwise." He wanted to dissolve the German home guards,
but was persuaded (by Frank Blair) that he lacked authority
to do this. Then he entered into a formal truce with General Price and Governor Jackson—an odd sort of nonaggression pact, under which Federal troops would stay
out of territory held by state troops, and both sides would
work to preserve the peace; an excellent idea if preservation of the peace was the principal end in view, but by this
time both sides had other goals. Two delegations of St.
Louis Unionists hurried off to Washington to see Lincoln,
one delegation urging that General Harney be sustained, the
other demanding that he be thrown out.

Harney deserves a little more sympathy than he usually
gets. He was an old-school army officer, completely loyal
and deeply conscientious, operating now in a situation which
no man of his background and training could easily understand. Rather clumsily, the War Department tried to coach

him. In a letter that may have been drafted by Lincoln, the adjutant general notified Harney that despite the truce a good many Unionist citizens in Missouri were being driven from their homes by effervescent secessionists. "It is immaterial," said the letter, "whether these outrages continue from inability or indisposition on the part of the State authorities to prevent them. It is enough that they devolve on you the duty of putting a stop to them summarily by the force under your command." Harney was warned to take no stock in the peaceful professions of the state authorities; these men, he was told, were really disloyal and would maintain the peace only when they lacked the power to disturb it. Whatever happened, he must suppress any movement that seemed to be hostile to the Federal government. Meanwhile, unknown to Harney, Lincoln sent to Frank Blair a curious and irregular document—a paper giving to Blair full authority to remove Harney from his command whenever Blair considered it necessary. Lincoln confessed that he was not entirely satisfied with this document, doubted its propriety, and hoped that Blair would not have to use it; Harney had already been removed and then reinstated, and if he were removed once more, people would think the administration did not know its own mind. "Still," the President concluded, "if, in your judgment, it is *indispensable*, let it be so."[3]

Before very much time passed, Blair did consider it indispensable. He was informed that Governor Jackson had invited the governor of Arkansas to send troops into Missouri, he noticed that Confederate levies were being organized all over the state—and on May 30, "feeling that the progress of events and the condition of affairs in this State make it incumbent upon me to assume the grave responsibility of this act," he called on Harney, presented the letter, and told the old general that he was out, with Nathaniel Lyon, now a brigadier general, taking his place. Harney went into hurt retirement; he wrote to the adjutant general that his confidence "in the honor and integrity of General Price, in the purity of his motives and in his loyalty to the Government, remains unimpaired." It seemed to Harney that the manner of his removal had "inflicted unmerited disgrace upon a true and loyal soldier," and he felt that his motives had been impugned by "those who clamored for blood." A stout Southerner living in St. Louis wrote angrily that "Frank Blair is dictator" and felt that the whole affair was simply the violent extension of a political quarrel: "The Republicans are as grandiose & sneering as if they had won a great victory. It is only a political one—they are below par socially." From Washington, Postmaster General Montgomery Blair wrote to Frank Blair that it was "not so much disunion as hostility to the Republicans" which gave Governor Jackson most of his support, and he warned his brother "not to arrest the Union feeling by making it too visibly your property."[4]

Lyon assumed his new duties on May 31, and Jackson and Price got ready for trouble. They held the machinery of state government, and they needed time to finish their preparations; and time was the one thing Lyon did not propose to let them have. The Unionists held St. Louis, with perhaps 10,000 troops at their disposal, and despite the shock caused by the Camp Jackson affair, a majority of Missourians leaned toward the Union. The Unionists had the initiative, and Lyon proposed to use it.

There were people in the state who still hoped that neutrality could be maintained, and they arranged for a meeting between Governor Jackson and General Price and General Lyon. Lyon issued a formal safe-conduct, and on June 11 Jackson and Price came to St. Louis to see him. The meeting lasted several hours and was stormy; it could hardly have been anything else, since the conferees wanted incompatible things and were men of deep conviction and strong passion. Governor Jackson offered to disband the state troops and remain neutral if the Federals would disband the St. Louis home guards and promise to move no troops into any part of the state not already occupied by Federal soldiers. Lyon hotly refused, demanding that the militia be sent home but refusing to disband the home guards, and finally saying flatly that he would see every last Missourian dead and buried before he would agree that the state government could impose any restriction whatever on the Federal authority within the state. "This means war," he told the governor and the militia general. "One of my officers will conduct you out of my lines in an hour."

Returning to Jefferson City, Governor Jackson tried to pick up the pieces. He began by issuing a proclamation tell-

ing the people of Missouri that the Blair-Lyon team proposed
to reduce the state "to the exact condition of Maryland."
He called out 50,000 militia, and although he asserted that
Missouri was still a member of the Federal Union, he insisted that its citizens were "under no obligations whatever
to obey the unconstitutional edicts of the military despotism
which has introduced itself at Washington, nor submit to
the infamous and degrading sway of its wicked minions in
this State." He concluded: "Arise, then, and drive out
ignominiously the invaders who have dared to desecrate the
soil which your labors have made fruitful and which is
consecrated by your homes."[5]

The war was taking a fantastic shape. Missouri was still
in the Union, lying outside of the direct line of fire between
the two sections, a majority of its people (as far as anyone
could tell, in this state of profoundly mixed sentiments) still
loyal to the Union; yet its government and the national
government were fighting one another. Governor Jackson's
appraisal was accurate enough. Things were indeed following
the pattern that had been set in Maryland, and there was no
Constitutional precedent for anything that was happening.
State governors do not ordinarily negotiate with foreign nations for arms with which to seize Federal arsenals, nor
do regular-army officers commonly set out to destroy a
legally constituted state militia. Now these things had happened, and because they had happened they would make
other things happen, equally extraordinary.

Lyon lost no time. He was impetuous and intolerant, driving on to enforce his own will, the will of Frank Blair, and
ultimately the will of the determined President in Washington, of whom skeptical patriots had said, only a short time
before, that they feared he lacked iron. Lyon put his troops
on the march while Governor Jackson was still drafting his
proclamation, and on June 14 he moved into Jefferson City,
seizing the machinery of state government and sending Jackson and Price off in hasty retreat. With hardly a pause,
Lyon pushed on fifty miles to Boonville, which was the
concentration point for the state militia—the militia that, if
given time to assemble, organize, and equip itself, would be
a powerful force for the Southern Confederacy. On June
16 there was a brief fight at Boonville, in which some 1700
men led by Lyon met a smaller contingent of state troops;

a hard little fight between untrained forces, with a good deal of shooting but very few casualties, which ended in the complete rout of the militia. Lyon's little army occupied Boonville, while Jackson and Price headed for the extreme southwestern corner of the state to make an effort to rally new forces. Lyon halted to organize and outfit his troops for further adventures; he notified Washington that he would hold Boonville, Jefferson City, and the line of the Missouri River, and that he himself would presently move on to Springfield, far to the south.

This fight at Boonville, the slightest of skirmishes by later standards, was in fact a very consequential victory for the Federal government. Governor Jackson had been knocked loose from the control of his state, and the chance that Missouri could be carried bodily into the Southern Confederacy had gone glimmering. Jackson's administration was now, in effect, a government-in-exile, fleeing down the roads toward the Arkansas border, a disorganized body that would need a great deal of help from Jefferson Davis's government before it could give any substantial help in return. In Missouri as in Maryland, the Lincoln administration had taken the important first trick; had taken it by displaying an uncomplicated readiness to disregard all of the ancient rules of the game. Ardent Southerners might still believe that the Yankees would not really fight, but they were at least beginning to see that the Yankees had a government that knew exactly what it wanted and would stop at nothing to get it.[6]

The Confederate government also knew exactly what it wanted, as far as that was concerned, and it would pay the ultimate price to get it, if necessary, but it was playing a very different sort of game. It was fighting to conserve, not to destroy; far from engaging in revolution, it was taking the most ancient rules and giving them a literal interpretation, and everything that it did would be done in the strictest observance of those rules. Its very existence was justified by the belief that the states which composed it had a legal and moral right to do what they had done. It was this government's first article of faith that it was completely and eternally Constitutional—Constitutional, not by the writ devised at Montgomery, but by the older Constitution which Lincoln said that he was making war to preserve. The very essence of secession was the desire to maintain unaltered a society, an order of things, which the world was threatening to change, and no government on earth had a more sincere and dedicated desire to uphold the established formulas. Strict constructionists had made secession in the first place; having made it, they could not be other than what they had always been.

In the early stages—in the canvassing and negotiating which led up to secession, and in the time when the existence of the new nation was being proclaimed—this had been an immense advantage. Men who persuasively say and obviously believe that they are religiously following the most hallowed laws do not look dangerous, and even men who disagree with them will not quickly prepare to fight against them. But now, with war on the land, this scrupulous insistence on Constitutionality was a handicap. It ruled out flexibility of action. The ruthlessness which would strike quickly, cunningly, beyond the law, was not possible, because the new government was legalistic, and in a situation where irregular action was imperative, it had to follow the forms. Furthermore, it was naturally bound to assume that the rival goverment, the one at Washington, would also follow the forms: to believe otherwise would be to admit a revolutionary situation existed, in which case the argument that the Confederacy was Constitutional rather than revolutionary would fall to the ground. One result of all this was that the Confederacy had lost Missouri.

Missouri, in any case, was very far from the center of Jefferson Davis's interest just now. The fatality which beset both governments so much of the time was keeping his attention centered principally on the East; on Virginia, the most powerful and welcome of new states to join the Confederacy, and on Richmond, Virginia's capital and now, by vote of the Confederate Congress and seemingly by the common consent of all Southerners, the capital of the Confederacy as well.

The Confederate Congress adjourned on May 21, after voting to make Richmond the new capital: a move which was both a gesture of defiance and a sign of confidence. To put the center of the new government a scant hundred miles from the center of the old government was to invite invasion. The Confederacy would function on its most exposed frontier; at the time the move was made, there was very little to keep Federal warships from steaming up the James River and bombarding the capital, and invading Yankees would find Richmond ever so much nearer than Montgomery—or, for that matter, Atlanta, which had hoped it might be chosen. But in a way the move was forced. Howell Cobb explained it, in a speech at Atlanta, saying that Confederate troops had already gone to Virginia and that the government wanted to follow them: "In the progress of the war further legislation may be necessary, and we will be there, that when the hour of danger comes we may lay aside the robes of legislation, buckle on the armor of the soldier, and do battle beside the brave ones who have volunteered for the defence of our beloved South." The Montgomery *Weekly Advertiser* had protested that the move was preposterous, "utterly at variance with the dictates of prudence and sound policy," but it confessed that it was probably necessary for President Davis to be near the front, so that he might take command of the armies in person if need be; and, anyway, Virginia was the state above all others whose secession had given the Confederacy an appearance of breadth and permanence, and to go to Richmond was to indicate full reliance on Virginia's solidity.[7]

The real trouble with the move was not so much that it put the Confederate capital on the firing line as that it compelled the Confederate government, over the long pull, to see the whole war in terms of military action in tidewater Virginia. The enormous importance of the West, of the Mississippi Valley, of Missouri and Kentucky and Tennessee, would be inevitably diminished, in the government's eyes, by the tremendous battles that would be fought within a day's ride of the capital. The focus of vision would be narrowed, and a price would be paid for it.

Meanwhile, on May 23, Virginia formally voted to secede. Inasmuch as the state had actually gone to war as soon as its convention passed the ordinance of secession, the verdict finally registered at the polls (overwhelmingly for secession, throughout most of the state; strongly against it, in the thirty-nine counties west of the Alleghenies) made little practical difference, except that it at last pushed the Federal government into direct action. Willing to cut across restraints elsewhere, Lincoln had abided by all of the rules in respect to Virginia. Not until the voters themselves had ratified secession would he move. Once ratification came, however, he moved quickly. Long before dawn on the morning of May 24 he sent eight regiments across the Potomac to seize Alexandria and Arlington Heights and to establish a firm bridgehead on secession soil. The first invasion of the South was under way. It was not much of an invasion and it did not occupy much of the South, but it was a symbol. A great many young men must die before it was finished.

Much would die with them; including a way of looking at life and seeing nothing but its freshness and the fact that it was made to be spent, a special notion of how things might be with the spirit when the ultimate challenge is faced, a feeling for the overtones that can haunt a man's hearing as he goes down the long pathway into the dusk. This also was symbolized, as Federal troops first put their feet on Virginia soil. Among the eight regiments that went across the river (it was two o'clock in the morning and there was a big moon to shimmer on the water and to put mysterious shadows under the dark trees) there was a rowdy, untamed, and not too noteworthy outfit known as the New York Fire Zouaves: a regiment of amateurs led by an amateur, going down to the Alexandria wharves by boat in search of a war that would be all youth and flags and easy valor and rewarding cheers; not destined to be hardened by fire into the company of the elect. The colonel was luckier than the rest. He was named Elmer Ellsworth, and he would die before the illusion had a chance to fade, leaving a name that would live longer than the cold facts required.

Ellsworth was twenty-four; an odd young man, by profession a Chicago patent attorney (it seems the last job on earth for this particular man) and by chosen avocation a drill-master of irregular troops, a wearer of bright uniforms, a dedicated play actor; remembered now because death met him very early, and because there was something in him that had won the affection of Abraham Lincoln. He had trained a patent-leather militia company before the war, winning plaudits, and he had come east on the same train with Lincoln, half bodyguard and half pampered nephew-by-election; when war came, he had helped to recruit a new regiment from among the New York volunteer firemen, had seen it clothed in the brilliant uniforms copied from the French Zouaves—baggy red knickers, russet leather gaiters,

short blue jacket over a big sash, a red fez for the head, and
a go-to-hell grin for the face—and now he was leading
the first invasion of the South, taking his men in to occupy
Alexandria.

Before the regiment started out, Ellsworth had written a
final letter to his parents. (A romantic, off for the wars,
would write a "final letter" before any move whatever,
casting an innocently calculated shadow for posterity and
for himself.) He felt, he said, that "our entrance to the city
of Alexandria will be hotly contested," but he was unworried:
"thinking over the probabilities of the morrow and the
occurrences of the past, I am perfectly content to accept
whatever my fortune may be." The entrance, as it turned out,
was not contested at all. Such Confederate troops as had been
in and around Alexandria had decamped, and the invading
host got in unopposed; but Ellsworth's own fortune was not
diminished thereby. Leading his men down the empty streets,
Ellsworth came to a hotel, the Marshall House, and on
top of this there was a flagpole flying the Confederate flag.
A challenge, obviously; and Ellsworth, followed by soldiers,
went inside, hurried to the roof, and with a knife borrowed
from a private soldier cut down this emblem of rebellion
and started back for the street with the flag tucked under his
arm.

In a shadowy hallway he met the proprietor of the inn,
a solid Virginian named James T. Jackson, who perhaps
had not the clearest conception of what war might mean
but who knew that he was not going to be pushed around
by any bright young man in red pants; and Jackson produced a shotgun and killed Ellsworth by sending a charge
of buckshot through his body, being himself killed a few
seconds later by one of Ellsworth's Zouaves, who first shot
the man and then, for good measure, ran his bayonet through
him. All of these deeds were final; that is, Ellsworth and
Jackson stayed dead, and the flag stayed down from the
flagpole; and the North suddenly found itself with its first
war hero. Ellsworth's body lay in state in the White House,
mourned by President Lincoln, and a rash of editorials,
poems, sermons, speeches, and quick-steps enshrined him
as well as might be.[8]

The war was new. The two deaths were utterly meaningless, although Ellsworth had precisely the end he would

have chosen for himself. He died while the day was still bright, a flag under his arm, his name and his uniform still bright. It was a springtime of symbols. Ellsworth meant little alive, much in his coffin, symbolizing a national state of mind, a certain attitude toward the war that would quickly pass and would never return. And so, for that matter, did the innkeeper, Mr. Jackson.[9]

6. Before the Night Came

LONG SHADOWS stole across the land as spring turned into summer. A darkness that would last four years was beginning. The untaught armies were gathering, small fights were erupting on the fringes like ominous flashes of lightning, and here and there people died. The deaths were isolated, almost meaningless, so far. They came in bewildering encounters where men hardly knew why they killed. A child and a fruit peddler were slain in St. Louis, a man of business in Baltimore, a hotel keeper and a stage-struck officer of Zouaves in Alexandria; victims, these folk and others, of stray picket-line firing far out on the edge of things, their deaths the first sullen drops of rain striking heavily just ahead of an unimaginable storm. Among those who died now was Stephen A. Douglas, who had tried to keep the war from coming but who, when it came, found himself rallying men to fight in it, and who died on the eve of the great battles.

Douglas died in Chicago on June 3. He was forty-eight, a man who could have been useful to the nation in the time just ahead; he was the one leader of them all who might, just possibly, have come to serve as a bridge between the two nations—might have done so, except that the chasm now was too wide for bridging—and when the end came, he was broken financially, physically, and emotionally. Ever since Fort Sumter he had been speaking for the Union cause, rallying to its service thousands of Westerners who might not have rallied without him. Now he was down, stricken with rheumatism, stricken too with typhoid fever, and it was clear that death was near. He received the last rites of the Catholic Church. Once he rallied long enough to dictate a final letter—a letter addressed to Virgil Hicox, chairman of the Democratic state committee in Illinois, meant for all the men who had believed in Douglas so deeply. In this letter he stoutly urged these men to stand firmly for the Union in this strange war which "is being waged against the United States for the avowed purpose of producing a permanent disruption of the Union and a total destruction of its government." He had hoped for peace, he said, had hoped that there still remained in the South a body of men who loved the Union and would make their voices heard, but he had come to believe that the secessionists were determined "to obliterate the United States from the map of the world." No man, said Douglas, could be a true Democrat now unless "he is a loyal patriot."[1]

This was about the last of him. Just after daylight on the morning of June 3 he sank back on his pillow. With long pauses between each word—words wrenched from him by who knows what final moment of despair?—he murmured "Death . . . death . . . death." He roused briefly, when someone asked him if he had any final message for his two sons. "Tell them," he said, with a flash of his old spirit, "to obey the laws and support the Constitution of the United States." His lovely wife, Adele Douglas, sat by the bedside holding his hand, sobbing convulsively. Through the shutting mist Douglas seems to have heard someone in the room whisper a fear that the dying man was suffering greatly. He whispered: "He . . . is . . . very . . . comfortable." Then, in a few moments, he was gone.[2]

He was going to be missed, and tributes were paid to his memory. The War Department, seeing "a national calamity" in his death, ordered regimental colors draped in black crepe. In the Senate, Orville Hickman Browning, of Illinois, saw "something almost sublime" in the way Douglas had spoken for the Union cause, and felt that Douglas had achieved "a conspicuous niche in the temple of fame." And far to the south little Alec Stephens, Vice-President of the Confederacy, wrote to his brother that he almost wished Douglas "had lived longer or died sooner." If there had been no Douglas, said Stephens, the Charleston convention in the spring of 1860 would not have divided and there would have been no disunion; but now—"Had he lived he might have exerted great power in staying the North from aggressive war. I can but think this would have been his position. He would have been against attempted subjugation. He would have been for a treaty of recognition & for peace."[3]

Alec Stephens may have been right, but it was too late. He himself knew pessimism. Speaking at Augusta, Georgia, he confessed that the war was bound up with deep consequences, "not unto us but to the people of the North." The end, as far as he could see, was clouded in darkness, but he believed that to those who had begun the war the worst consequences would come. Looking north, now that Douglas was gone, he saw only anarchy. "How long will they be able to war against us? I tell you it will be until we drive them back. There is no hope for us, there is no prospect for an early and speedy termination of the war until we drive them back."[4]

Alec Stephens spoke out of the growing shadows. The little pale star had a fragile strength, but no hands to smite; he could see disaster on its way, but he could neither lead his people out from under it nor help them move straight on into it with the hard purpose to salvage what might be saved from disaster's wreckage; he could see too much and dare too little, and the iron was not in him. Of all the leaders, two men had the terrible capacity to make men love them and to strike with unrestrained fury—Robert E. Lee and Abraham Lincoln. These two would be followed to the bitterest end, to the sorrow, the glory, and finally the salvation of their common country. The others would do what was in them to do and pass on. Eventually the two great antagonists would dominate the stage.

Meanwhile, other men would have their say. One of them was Ben Butler, of Massachusetts, a man seemingly appointed now, in the infinite Providence of God, to cast his own strange ray of revealing light on the way the war must go. To the relief of everyone, Butler had been lifted out of Maryland and had been set down, by the Federal War Department, at Fort Monroe, at the tip of the Virginia peninsula. Here, trying to be an administrator and a warrior, succeeding imperfectly in each, he would bring up for definition the one thing both sides did not want mentioned just now—the deep underlying wrong of human slavery. Meaning nothing more than a good lawyer's shrewdness, he helped to define the war.

Into Butler's lines, late in May, came three fugitive Negro slaves, men whose master had had them using pick and shovel to erect a battery for Confederate guns. Their arrival was unwelcome. The fugitive slave law remained on the books; legally, General Butler was required to deliver these chattels up to their lawful owner, and nobody in Washington had so much as hinted that he might do something different. The lawful owner turned out to be a Colonel Charles Mallory, in the Confederate service, and Colonel Mallory wanted his possessions returned to him. Butler, wholly devoid of feeling, had a lawyer's cunning; had also, apparently, an instinct for the inner meaning of things. Property of men in rebellion against the United States, he held—spades, wagons, farms, whatnot—could be taken over by the national authority as contraband of war; these three colored men were indisputably property, owned by a man in a condition of unrelieved rebellion, and they were, accordingly, *contrabands*. General Butler would hold them and use them. He had given a word to the national language and an idea to the national administration, and the word and the idea would go on working.[5]

Other Negroes came, in the days that followed, and Butler presently told the War Department that he would keep these people and use them, letting the strong men build wharves, dig trenches, build roads, and do similar things, having the women cook meals and launder clothes, suffering the children to exist: "As a matter of property to the insurgents it will be of very great moment, the number I now have amounting, as I am informed, to what in good times would be of the value of $60,000." At least a dozen of the fugitives, he learned, had been building batteries on Sewell's Point, commanding the approaches to Norfolk; and so Butler argued that "as a military question it would seem to be a measure of necessity to deprive their masters of their services."

Unquestionably; and when Major J. B. Cary, of the Confederate army, came to see General Butler, and suggested that the Constitution required the general to deliver up errant slaves under the fugitive slave act, Butler had a ready answer. "I replied that the fugitive slave act did not affect a foreign country, which Virginia claimed to be, and that she must reckon it as one of the infelicities of her position that in so far at least she was taken at her word." Secretary of War Cameron, another man who knew his way in and out of the entanglements of legal verbiage, promptly wrote: "Your position in respect to the Negroes who came within your lines from the service of the rebels is approved. The Department is sensible of the embarrassments which must surround officers conducting military operations in a State by the laws of which slavery is sanctioned."[6]

The matter was not really simple. Legally, the United States government did not recognize secession; legally, therefore, the laws of the United States still applied, including the one which said that runaway slaves must be returned to the people who owned them. At the same time, Butler had agreed that slaves were property, and he was permitted to make use of the property of Rebels. Nobody was going to touch the institution of slavery. It was official policy, signed and sealed by Abraham Lincoln and the Congress, that the object of the war was not to end slavery but simply to restore the Union. But the people who were property under the laws of states which had declared themselves out of the Union could be held and used . . . and, all in all, General Butler was right and he would be supported.

The news got about the plantation grapevine, and before long the general found himself harboring dozens, scores, and hundreds of fugitive slaves. He put all who were able-bodied to work, and in spite of himself he found himself, within weeks, controlling a "contraband camp" with 900 inhabitants. He advanced, at one time this spring, into the Virginia village of Hampton, from which point, before long, he was obliged to withdraw; when he withdrew, huge numbers of Negroes (who had been working for him, in Hampton) followed him, pursued, as Butler believed, by gray-clad soldiers who threatened to shoot the men "and to carry off the women who had served us to a worse than Egyptian bondage."

Butler wrote to the War Department for guidance. (His tongue may have been in his cheek at the time, but nevertheless he wrote.) He had, he said, treated able-bodied Negroes "as property liable to be used in aid of rebellion" and so as contraband of war. Now he had many of these people on his hands. Were they in fact property? If so, whose property were they? Their owners had abandoned them, or had been legally bereft of them. He, who now possessed them, did not own them and did not want to own them; were they now, therefore, property at all? "Have they not become, thereupon," he asked, as plaintively as if he had deep convictions on the mat-

ter, "men, women and children? . . . I confess that my own
mind is compelled by this reason to look upon them as men
and women. If not free born, yet free, manumitted, sent forth
from the hand that held them never to be reclaimed."

Secretary Cameron agreed. He wrote a reply which went
all the way around Robin Hood's barn to insist that the war
was being fought to preserve the Union and protect the Constitutional rights of all citizens, one of these rights being the
right to repossess slaves who had fled from servitude; but at
the same time, "in states wholly or partly under insurection-
ary control," things were a bit different. Congress, very significantly, had recently held that slaves employed in hostility
to the United States were no longer slaves. To be sure, in a
state like Virginia (where there were slave owners who still
professed loyalty to the Union) the case might be difficult.
Still, the War Department felt that "the substantial rights of
loyal masters are still best protected by receiving such fugitives, as well as fugitives from disloyal masters, into the Service of the United States, and employing them under such
organizations and in such occupations as circumstances may
suggest or require." At the same time, the General must be
careful to do no proselytizing. His troops must not encourage
"the servants of peaceable citizens in a house or field" to run
away and join up with Uncle Sam. He must be passive; and,
in his passivity, he must be firm.[7]

That settled that; which is to say that it affirmed Butler's
right to receive fugitives, to put them to work, and to turn
an unreceptive ear to all complaints. For the rest, however,
instead of settling anything at all, it started much which
would demand a deeper settlement later. This early in the
war—before a single fight of any consequence had taken
place between organized troops, before either side had got
much beyond stating the eternal justice and rightness of its
chosen position—slaves were being recognized as men, wom-
en, and children, and in that notion slavery had a loophole
wide enough to march all of Egypt's fugitives, on their way
through whatever Red Sea might await them. A new road
was being traveled, and it would be impossible to go down it
very far without confronting, finally, the question of emancipation.

Down this road Lincoln would go one cautious step at a
time. Supporting Butler's theory about contrabands, he would

apply it where he had to, but he would make no general rule for all army officers. He was caught now, by his own doubts, and by the demands of the border states, where there were men who held slaves but who were standing firmly for the Union. In his inaugural address he had said that he would execute all of the laws, including the one relating to fugitives from servitude. In Washington, slavery existed under his very eyes; slavery, the attempt to escape from it, and the stern repression of such attempts. The same War Department which had upheld Butler's ingenious theory would pass on to the Federal commander in northern Virginia a note in which the President had given thought to the cases of slaves who ran away from masters in the District of Columbia and, guided by an obscure but sound instinct, had tried to find refuge in the military camps. "Would it not be well," the President had asked, "to allow owners to bring back those which have crossed the Potomac with our troops?" General Scott felt certain that the district commander shared with him the wish that the President might carry out all of his Constitutional functions; at the same time, he warned that "the name of the President should not at this time be brought before the public in connection with this delicate subject."[8]

The district commander was discreet. He was Irvin McDowell, serious, well-intentioned, hard-working, deeply unlucky; a husky, squarely built professional, who had served with credit in the Mexican War and in peacetime assignments thereafter, a man who neither sought nor gained popularity, something of a protégé of Secretary Chase, well liked by General Scott. A major since 1856, he had been made brigadier general in the middle of May, and now he commanded what was about to become an army of invasion. The odds were against him. He had had staff assignments throughout his army career and had never commanded troops in the field; now he had a badly mixed collection of militia regiments which he must somehow turn into an army, and because no one quite understood the problems he was facing he was as a man doomed to make bricks without straw. Through no particular fault of his own he would be remembered as architect of one of the most ignominious defeats in American military history. A total abstainer, he would be accused of drunkenness; a soldier who ignored all political considerations, he would be accused of heretical softness toward the South;

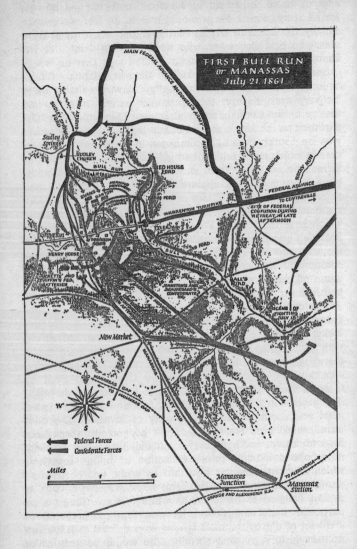

FIRST BULL RUN
or MANASSAS
July 21, 1861

and, all in all, he would have reason to regret that he ever heard of this war. Now he would hew to the line scrupulously, and if the War Department told him to bring fugitive slaves back to their owners, he would do it without a second thought.[9]

He did not have a great deal of time to get ready for his military operations, for his objective was visibly taking shape before everyone's eyes this June. This objective, of course, was to be the Confederate capital, whose capture, as hopeful Northerners believed, secession and the Confederacy could not long survive; and the Confederate capital now was the city of Richmond, not more than 100 miles away and apparently ripe to be taken. A New York *Tribune* correspondent, near the end of May, found Richmond "in the most fearful state of agitation." Troops from the South were arriving at the rate of 500 or 600 a day, but most of them were very young, "entirely inexperienced, ill-clad and ill-armed," and they would need a great deal of drill "before they will be able even to present a respectable front in a pitched battle." Venturing into an expression of personal opinion which gives him rank as one of the very worst prophets of the entire war, the *Tribune* man wrote that General Lee, who commanded at Richmond, was "an inferior officer in vigor of mind and energy of character" and he predicted that "the mildness of his disposition will lead him to prefer negotiations to battles." He added that recruits with and without uniform were parading the streets at all hours, and that nearly all of the soldiers chewed tobacco.[10]

McDowell's troops could have been described in practically the same terms; which is to say that they were very young, totally without experience, untrained, poorly equipped, and in all conceivable respects quite unready for campaigning; a fact which, at the beginning of June, seemed to be apparent to no one in the high command except to McDowell himself. Adam Gurowski, the caustic and intransigent *émigré* who held down a small job in the State Department and wrote copiously in a diary meant for early publication, was writing now in lofty disparagement about Northern military preparations. "Weeks run, troops increase," he wrote, "and not the first step made to organize them into an army, to form brigades, not to say divisions; not yet two regiments maneuvering together. What a strange idea the military chief or chiefs, or department, or somebody, must have of what it is to organize an army." As a result of this, he believed, "the loss in men and material will be very considerable before the administration will get on the right track."[11]

He was not the only pessimist. Secretary Seward himself, taking stock in the middle of May, felt a certain gloom, partly because he was not allowed to control things. To his wife Seward wrote sadly that he was "a chief reduced to a subordinate position" and that he was under attack because he had been working for the organization of a powerful army, although "it is only from an army so strong as to dishearten the traitors that we can hope for peace or union." The military secretary to the governor of Ohio, noting that excellent men of business were eager to make money out of the war, wrote in disgust that "scoundrels get contracts because they have money; have money because they are scoundrels." The word was out that Pennsylvanians with good connections were getting a good deal from Secretary Cameron; it was said that already "there is evidently much feeling between Lincoln and Cameron" and that Lincoln had received so many complaints about Pennsylvania contracts that he "intended to have the matter examined." William T. Sherman, brought east and given a colonel's commission, meditated gloomily about the likelihood of "absolute national ruin and anarchy," and wrote that Americans might "degenerate into a new brand of men, struggling for power and plunder." Mr. Stanton told former President Buchanan that "the peculation and fraud" so visible in Washington "have created a strong feeling of loathing and disgust"; Stanton felt the country early in June was in greater danger than ever before.[12]

Jefferson Davis, meanwhile, had arrived in Richmond. He was unwell, and the long trip up from Montgomery had been an ordeal; he tried to keep to his bed while the slow train clanked along, but had to rouse himself at each whistle stop and show himself, responding to cheers and serenades and the salutes of military companies. Physically very trying, the trip at least showed the President that his country was enthusiastic for the war. The wife of Senator Wigfall recorded that the whole country looked like a military camp, "all as jubilant as if they were going to a frolic instead of a fight," and the Richmond *Enquirer* believed that the trip "has in-

fused a martial feeling in our people that knows no bounds."
At Richmond there was a parade, with much handshaking,
and the weary President had to go to a hotel balcony and address an enthusiastic crowd. He said what was expected of
him, said it gracefully and with spirit: "I look upon you as
the last best hope of liberty. . . . Upon your strong right
arm depends the success of your country . . . remember
that life and blood are nothing as compared with the immense interests you have at stake. . . . To the last breath of
my life, I am wholly your own." He was at last permitted to
retire and get a little rest.[18]

He was on the frontier, and although serious fighting had
not yet begun, it would obviously come in the near future;
it would come in Virginia first of all, and Virginia was full
of vulnerable points. The state formally turned its armed
forces over to the Confederate government—which, for the
moment, left General Lee with an empty title and nothing
much to do—and the President must begin by taking stock.
He found that he had between 35,000 and 40,000 troops immediately available. There were 7000 in and around Norfolk,
where the great naval base must be made secure, and where
engineers were already raising and preparing to refit the sunken
steam frigate *Merrimack*. Five thousand or more were on
the lower peninsula, guarding the approach to Richmond between the James and York rivers, there were perhaps 2700
in the vicinity of Fredericksburg, and between 7000 and
8000 were at Manassas, a day's march from Washington;
Beauregard had come up from Charleston, his arrival in
Richmond the occasion for a great ovation, and he was in
command at Manassas, where much was expected of him.
Harper's Ferry and the lower Shenandoah Valley were held
by nearly 8000 men, and there were between 5000 and 6000
in Richmond itself, the number rapidly increasing as new
levies arrived for organization and training.[14]

All of these points needed immediate attention. In Richmond a captain of engineers named E. Porter Alexander,
who would become a notable artillerist in the years just ahead,
wrote that Governor Letcher had done little to prepare the
state for proper defense and said that "Davis was greatly deceived before his arrival here about the state of affairs." The
President, Alexander believed, was moving fast, making many

improvements; Richmond was "so full of men & uniforms you could hardly walk the streets," and if the Yankees would hold off just a little longer, things would work out all right— "I don't think the Yanks can ever get to Richmond now. Should they try it they would be 'feted.'" Lee himself, his occupation for the moment gone, wrote to his wife that he did not know what his own position would be: "I should like to retire to private life, if I could be with you and the children, but if I can be of any service to the State or her cause I must continue." At Manassas, Beauregard was calling Virginians to arms, announcing that Lincoln, "a reckless and unprincipled tyrant," was invading Virginia's soil with irresponsible "abolition hosts" which had abandoned all rules of civilized warfare; "they proclaim by their acts, if not on their banners, that their war-cry is 'beauty and booty.'" One of his staff officers believed that Davis's appearance at Richmond had put fresh energy into war preparations, said that reinforcements were coming, and wrote: "Our regiments here are superbly drilled & equipped."[15]

. . . There still was daylight, but it would not last much longer. There was abroad, in the North and in the South, an odd expectancy, a feeling almost of exaltation. From a Confederate troop camp at Lynchburg, Virginia, Lieutenant Colonel Edmund Kirby Smith sensed it and was moved and disturbed by it. Writing to his mother, he spoke of what he felt: "Surrounded by military preparations, with troops arriving and departing daily, with the tramp of armed men and the rapid roll of the drum ringing hourly in my ear, I feel as if the realities of war were fast closing upon us—and when I see the best blood of our country enrolled, the youth of sixteen and the aged side by side, the statesman, planter and minister of the gospel in the ranks, my heart throbs with anxiety. I deprecate a contest which must be baptised in the blood of all we hold dear and good in the land." Out on the Illinois prairie, a young man preparing to enlist wrote that "it is worth everything to live in this time," and stated his reliance on a faith he could not define: "It seems to me almost like a disgrace not to be in the ranks when there is so much at stake." From the Shenandoah Valley, a very youthful Virginia recruit wrote to his mother that he too saw great things in the balance: "If the North subjugates the South I never want to live to be 21 years old; when I am at that age, to be regarded as an effective citizen of my state, I want to breathe the breath of a freeman or not breathe at all." The historical society which preserves this letter records that its writer, presumably before reaching his majority, was killed in action.[16]

CHAPTER SEVEN

To the Fiery Altar

1. War in the Mountains

GEORGE BRINTON MCCLELLAN had almost all of the gifts. He was young, sturdy, intelligent, and up to a certain point he was very lucky. A short man with a barrel chest, a handsome face, and the air of one who knew what all of the trumpets meant, he won (without trying much more than was necessary) the adoration and the lasting affection of some very tough fighting men who tended to be most cynical about their generals. He had too much, perhaps, and he had it too soon and too easily; life did not hammer toughness into him until it was too late, and although many men died for him, he never quite understood what their deaths meant or what he could do with their devotion. For a time he served his country most ably.

Born in Pennsylvania, McClellan was thirty-five when the war began. He had been graduated from West Point in 1846, number two in his class, a magnetic and brilliant young man; he won three brevets for gallant and meritorious conduct in the Mexican War, served as War Department observer in the Crimea in the middle fifties, and then resigned from the army, as a captain, to go into business. In business he did well, had been successful as vice-president of the growing Illinois Central Railroad, and in the spring of 1861 was president of the Eastern Division of the Ohio & Mississippi. He found himself, in the middle of May, major general of volunteers (and, a short time afterward, major general of regulars as well) commanding the Department of the Ohio—the states of Ohio, Indiana, and Illinois, along with a part of western Pennsylvania and the dissident section of western Virginia. It was up to him to organize and then to use the troops raised in this area, and he did these things with smooth competence.[1]

McClellan had an observant gaze, and at the end of May there was much for him to look at. Across the Ohio River, going eastward from Kentucky, was Virginia. Virginia was basically a tradition and a state of mind, but it was also a vast geographical expanse, running from the Atlantic beaches and the Chesapeake capes west beyond the Blue Ridge and along the Ohio River; a huge territory of immense strategic importance, offering to the young general and to the national authority both a threat and an opportuniy.

The threat was self-evident. To get west from Washington it was necessary to use the Baltimore & Ohio Railroad, and this road lay almost completely at Virginia's mercy. It entered Virginia at Harper's Ferry, followed the Potomac past Cumberland, Maryland, and at last plunged into Virginia's western mountains on its way to the Ohio Valley. At the town of Grafton, Virginia, the railroad forked, sending one branch northwest to the Ohio at Wheeling and the other, almost due west, to the same river at Parkersburg. Thus it ran through secession territory, and was subject to interruption; was totally interrupted, in fact, at the end of May, with armed Confederates holding the line from Harper's Ferry to Cumberland, and with the prospect that everything west of Cumberland would also be lost just as soon as the Richmond government could get a substantial force over into the Alleghenies. The section east of Cumberland would of course be regained by the Union forces, sooner or later, in the natural course of things; it was close to the capital, and if the Federal armies could do anything at all, they could eventually make this part of the line tolerably secure. But this would do the Union cause no good if the Confederates continued to hold western Virginia, and to the people of Ohio this was a matter of great importance. They not only wanted direct communication with the national capital; even more they wanted to be able to send their produce to the eastern market at Baltimore. Since Ohio was the most populous state in the West, and had furnished most of McClellan's troops, Ohio could make its wishes felt.

But although western Virginia menaced the Federal cause, it also promised it substantial gains. Its people were largely Unionist. For years they had felt like Virginia's stepchildren,

believing that the state was run by tidewater folk for tidewater's benefit; a great many of them had ceased to identify
themselves strongly with Virginia, precisely as Virginia itself
had lost its feeling of identity with the Federal Union, and
they had voted against secession. Now they were planning a
secession of their own; they would break away from Virginia
and become either a brand-new state or, if the war lasted,
the legally dominant section of the old one. Either way they
meant trouble for Jefferson Davis, and the Lincoln administration would help them if it could.

All of this was as clear to McClellan as anything needed
to be. He got, in addition, a slight nudge from General Scott.
Late in May a detachment of Confederate infantry moved
into the railroad junction town of Grafton, and Scott telegraphed McClellan to do something about this, if he could—
to protect the railroad and also to "support the Union sentiment in western Virginia." McClellan got under way without lost motion. From his headquarters in Cincinnati on
May 26 he issued a proclamation, inviting mountaineer Virginians to "sever the connection that binds you to traitors"
and to show the world that "the faith and loyalty so long
boasted by the Old Dominion are still preserved in western
Virginia."[2]

He got a good response. The Wheeling *Intelligencer*, strong
for the Union, reported that the arrival of the first Federal
troops "has been one continued ovation" and said that people in every house greeted the soldiers by cheering and by
waving hats and handkerchiefs, women who could do nothing better waving sunbonnets and aprons. The Federal soldiers who made up the advance responded with cheers and
hat-wavings of their own, and concluded that this was going
to be a fine war—an innocent conclusion which they modified
later. By May 30 they had occupied Grafton, and four days
later, led by an Indiana volunteer, Brigadier General T. A.
Morris, they attacked and routed a small Confederate force
at Philippi, fifteen miles south.

The fight at Philippi was a very small thing, as battles went
—no Unionists were killed, and hardly any Confederates—
but it was a propaganda victory of some magnitude. The
western Virginia Unionists were so encouraged that they held
a convention at Wheeling on June 11, voted to nullify the
ordinance of secession, declared that the offices of the state

government at Richmond were vacated, and named Francis H. Pierpont governor of the "restored" government of Virginia. To the Confederates the fight was a combination of tragedy and abysmal farce. Their untrained troops at Philippi had been caught entirely by surprise and fled in utter disorder, leaving behind almost all of their equipment and, in some cases, their very pants, and a cold rain came down to complete the dampening of their spirits. The Federals referred exultantly to the affair as "the Philippi races"; the Confederate government sent in a new commander, Brigadier General Robert S. Garnett, and ordered a court of inquiry, which found that the surprise that had been suffered was inexcusable. General Lee wrote that he hoped the thing "will be a lesson to be remembered by the army through the war."[3]

McClellan wanted to keep moving. In a broad way he had two objectives—to protect the Unionists and the railroad in western Virginia, and to drive a column across the Alleghenies and into tidewater Virginia by the back door—and he would use two principal columns of attack. One would go on from Philippi, and this column he himself would accompany. The other would leave the Ohio River farther south, moving up the valley of the Great Kanawha River and aiming, ultimately, at the town of Staunton, at the upper end of the Shenandoah Valley. On the map, this latter route looked like a promising avenue of invasion; actually the difficulties of moving across a thinly settled mountainous country were so great that to the end of the war the Federals were not able to make effective use of it. This column he entrusted to a new brigadier, an Ohio-born politician who would display some talent for military affairs, Jacob D. Cox.

McClellan himself joined the northern column late in June. He had a knack, common among generals on both sides in the early days of the war, for issuing inspiring proclamations, and he unloaded one now: "Soldiers! I have heard that there was danger here. I have come to place myself at your head and to share it with you. I fear now but one thing—that you will not find foemen worthy of your steel. I know that I can rely upon you." He went on, more soberly, to warn his men that they were not to make war on civilians, announcing that looters and marauders "will be dealt with in their persons and property according to the severest rules of military law."[4]

Foemen worthy of their steel the Union troops would even-

tually find—no Federal army invading Virginia was ever disappointed in that respect—but the Confederates were under
profound handicaps. General Garnett, taking over his command at Huttonsville, forty miles south of Philippi, found
that he had twenty-three companies of infantry, "in a miser-
able condition as to arms, clothing, equipments, instruction
and discipline." He considered this command "wholly in-
capable, in my judgment, of rendering anything like efficient
service," but he would do his best. Two turnpikes came down
from Federal territory, crossing through passes in Rich and
Laurel mountains, a few miles north and west of his camp.
If the Federals occupied these, Garnett would be locked out
of the action completely; wondering why the invader had
overlooked these points, he moved up to hold the places
himself, and did his best to get reinforcements and supplies
and to give his men the rudiments of military training and
discipline. He was inclined to believe that he would not be
attacked, simply because the enemy "has as much of the
northwestern country as he probably wants," but Lee warned
him not to take too much for granted, suspecting that Mc-
Clellan planned a major invasion. Garnett would continue
to be outnumbered, but Lee hoped that he could hold the invaders in check "by skill and boldness."[5]

By the beginning of July, McClellan commanded an imposing force. All in all, he had perhaps 20,000 men—new troops,
all of them, but further along in their training and infinitely
better equipped than the men who would oppose them. About
5000 of his men McClellan had strung out over a 200-mile
stretch of back country, guarding roads and bridges and supply dumps. General Morris, moving down from Philippi, had
between 4000 and 5000; he thought he ought to have more,
but McClellan rebuked him sternly: "Do not ask for further
reinforcements. If you do I shall take it as a request to be
relieved from your command and return to Indiana. I speak
officially. The crisis is a grave one, and I must have generals
under me who are willing to risk as much as I am, and to be
content to risk their lives and reputations with such means
as I can give them. Let this be the last of it." McClellan and
his principal lieutenant, a tough ex-regular, Brigadier General
William S. Rosecrans, moving in separate but co-ordinated
columns, had about 10,000 men. To oppose these numbers,

Garnett had been able to assemble no more than 5000 men, posted at the passes in Rich and Laurel mountains.[6]

It took McClellan longer to get this host moving than he had anticipated, and on July 5 he wrote the War Department that "the delays that I have met with have been irksome to me in the extreme, but I feel that it would be exceedingly foolish to give way to impatience and advance before everything was prepared." Everything considered—the newness of his troops, the difficulty of the country, the inexperience of everybody who had anything to do with supply and transportation—McClellan actually got ready fast. His machine began to roll twenty-four hours after he sent this dispatch, and by July 10 his men were in contact with the Confederate outposts. The next day, after conferring with McClellan, Rosecrans led his column off to a bold flanking move up the difficult slopes of Rich Mountain; got to the top after hard climbing but no fighting, struck the Confederate rear, and drove the defenders off helter-skelter, taking prisoners, seizing guns and camp supplies, and effectively cracking General Garnett's defensive line. Garnett pulled his right wing back from Laurel Mountain; McClellan's troops followed, overtook Garnett's rear guard July 13 at Corrick's ford, on a branch of the Cheat River, smashed the rear guard, and killed Garnett himself. The Federals moved on and occupied the town of Beverly, and McClellan reflected that with a little help he might go slicing all the way down to the Virginia-Tennessee border, seizing the Confederacy's vital lead mines at Wytheville, Virginia, breaking the railroad that ran from Richmond all the way through Tennessee, and in general inflicting a grievous wound on the Confederacy. He reflected also that eastern Tennessee, like western Virginia, contained a great many good Unionists, and he wrote enthusiastically to the War Department: "With the means at my disposal, and such resources as I command in Virginia, if the Government will give me ten thousand arms for distribution in Eastern Tennessee I think I can break the backbone of secession. Please instruct whether to move on to Staunton or on to Wytheville."[7]

Washington did not want him to be too hasty, but it was most happy with what he had done. General Scott sent hearty congratulations: "The general-in-chief, and what is more, the Cabinet, including the President, are charmed with your ac-

tivity, valor and consequent successes. . . . We do not doubt
that you will in due time sweep the rebels from Western Virginia, but we do not mean to precipitate you, as you are fast
enough." (If McClellan had had the gift of second sight he
would have taken the last twelve words of that dispatch, had
them engraved in bronze, and hung them in his tent; never
again would the War Department talk to him that way.)
While he waited to see what would be wanted of him next,
McClellan congratulated his soldiers on what they had done.
On July 16, in orders sent to all his regiments, he let them
have it: "Soldiers of the Army of the West! I am more than
satisfied with you. You have annihilated two armies, commanded by educated and experienced soldiers, intrenched in
mountain fastnesses fortified at their leisure. . . . You have
proved that Union men, fighting for the preservation of our
Government, are more than a match for our misguided and
erring brethren. . . . In the future I may still have greater
demands to make upon you, and still greater sacrifices for
you to offer. It shall be my care to provide for you to the
extent of my ability; but I know now that by your valor and
endurance you will accomplish all that is asked."[8]

The soldiers took this at face value. Most of them had not
actually fought at all, and the ones who did fight had everything their own way, and a young Ohio officer wrote that
"our boys look forward . . . to a day of battle as one of
rare sport." The local secessionists, he said, had taken to the
hills, the Union troops looked and felt like conquerors, and
the retreating Confederates scared the mountain people by
assuring them that the Federals shot civilians, ravished wom-
en, and burned barns. To boys from the flat Ohio and Indiana country, the mountain scenery was magnificent; there
were "ravines so dark that one could not guess their depth;
openings, the ends of which seemed lost in a blue mist; others
so steep a squirrel could hardly climb them . . . mountain
streams, sparkling now in the sunlight, then dashing down into apparently fathomless abysses." Shortly before the affair at
Rich Mountain, McClellan had written to his wife that his
successes would probably be due to maneuvers, and that "I
shall have no brilliant victories to record." He added that he
would be glad "to clear them out of West Virginia and liber-
ate the country without bloodshed, if possible." A body calling itself the Virginia legislature, composed of representatives

from the western Unionist counties, met in Wheeling, voted funds to carry on the war for the Union, and named two men as United States Senators—apparently on the theory that the only part of Virginia which now had legal existence was the part west of the mountains, the part which had been wrested away from the Confederacy. Washington would approve of this action, recognizing Governor Pierpont, seating the new Senators; later on, when western Virginia declared itself a separate state and sought admission to the Union, that action would be recognized. Virginia's loss would be made permanent.[9]

In this, the Federal government's insistence that states' rights meant nothing whatever when opposed to the rights of the nation was carried a long step further. In Maryland the government had choked off secession by sending in troops, by suspending civil rights, and by standing ready to imprison the state legislature if necessary. In Missouri it had made war on the troops of a state which had not seceded and had driven the legal governor off in desperate flight. Now it would calmly break a state in half, turning to its own advantage a hump-backed act of secession which was even more irregular than the original act of secession which Washington was fighting to suppress. It was giving the war a shape—this early, with serious fighting not yet begun—which would make a compromise peace, a settlement by negotiation, all but impossible.

That the Confederate cause had had a serious set-back was quickly recognized in Richmond. Hurried efforts were made to get more troops over into the Kanawha Valley, where the city of Charleston was occupied by the Federals on July 25; if the invaders could not be driven out, they must at least be kept from coming any further. (Before long, Lee himself would be sent over the mountains to take charge of things.) Jedediah Hotchkiss, a talented Confederate engineer who would become one of Stonewall Jackson's most trusted aides, wrote after the war that this West Virginia campaign gave the Federals lasting advantages. Washington now controlled navigation in all the headwaters of the Ohio, had control of valuable coal and salt mines, and could establish advance military posts which would be a problem to the Confederacy throughout the war. From these posts, said Hotchkiss, the Federals were constantly threatening "Virginia's interior lines of communication through the Great Valley and the lead mines, salt works, coal mines, blast furnaces, foundries and other important industrial establishments in and near the grand source of military supplies, thus requiring the detaching of large numbers of troops to watch these Federal movements." In addition, Virginia had lost much territory, important revenues, and a good recruiting ground for troops; and, finally, the "bogus government" at Wheeling was strengthened and made permanent.[10]

A collateral gain was that the North now had an authentic military hero in General McClellan. Good stay-at-home patriots who had been uneasy because the war seemed to be going so slowly had something to cheer about, and they dazzled themselves by the tributes they paid. The Louisville *Journal* probably spoke for most Unionists when it published a breathless, starry-eyed tribute, saying that McClellan's victory was like a perfect work of art that left nothing to be desired in conception or in execution. "McClellan set out to accomplish a certain definite object," said the *Journal*. "With that precise object in view he gathers his forces and plans his campaign. Onward he moves, and neither wood, mountain nor stream checks his march. He presses forward from skirmish to skirmish, but nothing decoys or diverts or forces him from the trail of the enemy. . . . There is something extremely satisfactory in contemplating what might be called a piece of finished military workmanship by a master hand."[11] Many others were singing the same song. Whatever else might happen, General McClellan was obviously destined for a higher command.

Federal officers began to understand that being part of an army of occupation brings subsidiary problems. During their stay in the mountain valleys the Confederate troops had impressed supplies with a free hand, doing it all the more roughly because the farmers they were despoiling were arrant Unionists. Now those who had been despoiled were coming to the Federal authorities demanding justice and compensation; they came, as one quartermaster officer wrote, "like so many hungry wolves, with a pertinacity that knew no bounds." As a sample, this officer mentioned a claim for $625.15 presented by one Lewis Stoops, from the town of Jackson. Stoops claimed damages for the loss of his house, five apple trees, two plum trees, and two peach trees, along with "bedsteds, chears & table, and other Furniture," various tools, a clock, a brass kettle, a set of harness, and the loss of his crop, and he set forth his grievance breathlessly: "Sir, the within account is the amt of Damages I sustained by the infernal secession outbrake at Jackson, and would be glad if you can intersead in refunding back my losses, the Rebles called on me to fight for the South, as I was a Southern man, I told them Nay, they made me leave my home, then I enlisted. They then burnt my House and I am now in the service of the United States service."[12]

The Federals also began to learn about bushwhackers— Southern-minded residents who took to the woods with rifle and ammunition, sometimes organizing into bands that broke telegraph lines, tore up railway tracks, burned bridges, and ambushed supply wagons, sometimes operating alone, shooting straggling soldiers or Unionist civilians impartially and in general making life a burden for everyone. An indignant Federal officer, somewhat biased, wrote that the average bushwhacker "kills for the sake of killing and plunders for the love of gain," and said that "parties of these ferocious beasts, under cover of darkness, frequently steal into a neighborhood, burn the residences of loyal citizens, rob stores, tan yards, and farmhouses of everything they can put to use, especially arms, ammunition, leather, clothing, bedding and salt."[13] West Virginia was in fact learning what Missouri was learning, what Kentucky and Tennessee would learn a bit later—that the fabled war between brothers could take a very ugly turn when it was brought down to isolated neighborhoods where people had divided minds and quick tempers.

Among the officers to whom the Confederate government gave the task of repairing the damage west of the mountains was the former governor of Virginia, Henry A. Wise. Wise was a brigadier general now, he was popular in the western part of the state, he had been raising a body of troops known as Wise's Legion, and he was sent west to make war. He would find himself, before long, in bitter rivalry with John B. Floyd, the former Secretary of War, who was also a brigadier general, who was also raising troops and making war west of the mountains, and who out-ranked General Wise; and the sharp antagonism between these two ardent patriots would create a problem that would add gray hairs to the head of General Lee, who presently was given the almost impossible task of trying to get the two men to work in double harness.

General Wise was all for the war, but he could see that terrible times lay just ahead. Shortly before he went west he addressed an audience in Richmond in strange, impassioned words touched with a grim prophetic fury. He rejoiced that the war had come, he said, because it would be a war of purification.

"You want war, fire, blood to purify you," he cried, "and the Lord of Hosts has demanded that you should walk through fire and blood. You are called to the fiery baptism, and I call upon you to come up to the altar."[14]

Wise had been governor of Virginia when old John Brown made his terrifying descent on Harper's Ferry. Wise had gone to the scene, had talked to the wolf-like prisoner, had seen to it that he was tried, convicted and hanged; and in what he said now there was the strongest echo of John Brown's last words. Facing the scaffold, Brown wrote a hard warning: "I, John Brown, am now quite *certain* that the crimes of this *guilty* land will never be purged *away* but with blood." John Brown had seen it; now Henry Wise was seeing the same thing. All men would see it, as they took the road toward the fiery altar.

2. The Laws of War

THE FIRST session of the thirty-seventh Congress of the United States met in Washington on July 4. This Congress had been called in haste to convene at leisure. President Lincoln had ordered a special session immediately after the surrender of Fort Sumter, but he had given it eighty days to assemble. These days having passed, the Congress finally was meeting, and Cincinnati Editor Murat Halstead wrote moodily that neither Congress nor the capital city looked quite as it had when the last session ended.

Washington itself was so full of soldiers that the uniformed crowds, the dusty lines of military wagons, the hurrying officious colonels and couriers, had ceased to be a novelty. The bright new uniforms were beginning to be stained with sweat and dirt, gilt shoulder straps were becoming tarnished, the baggy red pants of the Zouaves "look as if they had been used to swab the guns at the Navy yard"; there had been no military action here, no advance, nothing to stir the blood and create excitement, and Washington had concluded that "masses of soldiers, in a state of stagnation, are not especially interesting."

Congress had lost something, too, legislators in the mass being, basically, no more interesting than soldiers. Specifically, Congress had lost its fire-eaters: the cotton-belt statesmen, the picturesque and aggressive Southerners who had dominated the scene for so long. Even their opponents would miss these men. "What," asked Halstead, "will our New England brethren do without an opportunity of denouncing the peculiar institution in the presence of its devotees?"[1] As it happened, the brethren would make out fairly well, for slavery still had defenders here; among them John C. Breckinridge, still a Senator from Kentucky, which was as much a part of the Union as Ohio or Massachusetts. Yet something had come to an end. This Congress was new, and different, and what was said in it about slavery would be said in a different way, with different results.

The attack on slavery was no longer a mere exercise in forensics. Men who had recently been colleagues, joining in that exercise, giving and taking blows in hot debate without arousing deep personal antagonisms, had at last become avowed enemies. It was beginning to be hard for Unionists who distrusted slavery all along to escape the feeling that the argument over slavery touched something so fundamental and dangerous that it must eventually create a deadly and permanent hostility. A debate on slavery now must, inevitably, be in one way or another a debate on the way in which the Union itself could be saved. The old days were gone forever. Never again could the fight about slavery be carried on as it had been carried on in the days before slavery's principal spokesmen had abandoned the arena.

There still were optimists; men who had hopes, not merely for the Congress of the United States, but for the national peace itself, for the restoration of good feeling and the dissolution of destructive angers. Among these was the chaplain of the House of Representatives, the Reverend Mr. T. H. Stockton, who offered prayer as the new session opened.

"Oh Lord our God," he intoned, "if there must be war—oh, that there might be peace!—but if there must be war, if

Thou dost indeed ordain and sanction war, may it not be a bloody and ruinous war. May it rather be an armed, mighty, irresistible migration—a migration of true love . . ."[2]

It was a vain hope. The immense enthusiasm that had swept across both North and South after the Fort Sumter bombardment was at bottom a demand for action. The armies must meet, head-on, to fight it out. A Washington reporter who was passing advice along to Samuel L. M. Barlow, the New York Democratic leader and man of affairs, was writing this spring that the Lincoln administration could not conceivably resist the public pressure for a vast military campaign; if it tried to resist, he believed, there would be a military dictatorship. The people of the North, in short, wanted a fight; the *National Intelligencer,* a pro-Union paper, long established, was losing so many subscribers because of its moderate position that its proprietor felt he must change his editorial policy or go out of business. "They who labor for a peaceful adjustment," warned Barlow's correspondent, "must calmly await the ebb of the Deluge. . . . Reason & moral courage must remain as yet in abeyance if they would render politic & efficient service."[3]

Saturnine Count Gurowski, that frequently self-deceived observer, asserted that Seward himself still hoped for compromise. Seward, said Gurowski, "disbelieved in the terrible earnestness of the struggle," and continued to hope that "he shall be able to patch up the quarrel." Seward was a moral dictator, who led Lincoln by the hand and, "having complete hold of the President, weakens Lincoln's mind by using it in hunting after comparatively paltry expedients."[4] Gurowski did not quite know what was going on. Lincoln was out of his leading strings; he would address Congress now, and from his address and what it evoked in Congress would emerge the shape of the war itself. It would slowly become evident that when they committed themselves at last to secession, not as a threat but as an accomplished fact armed for violence, the devoted men who wanted to preserve the Southern way of life had made a tactical error. The ultimate fate of their cause would be largely determined by what was done in Washington. Leaving Washington forever, they had fatally surrendered the initiative. Now their enemies would seize it.

The Republicans had firm control over both houses of

Congress. Of forty-eight Senators, they now had thirty-two;
of 176 in the House, they had 106. The House began by
electing Galusha Grow, of Pennsylvania, speaker. (His chief
opponent was the same Frank Blair who had labored so
powerfully, and so irregularly, for the Federal cause in Missouri.) Grow made his own warlike position clear in a brief
address in which he declared that "if the republic is to be dis-
membered and the sun of its liberty must go out in endless
night, let it set amid the roar of cannon and the din of battle,
when there is no longer an arm to strike or a heart to bleed
in its cause."[5] Then, on July 5, the two houses met in joint
session to hear a message from the President of the United
States.

In the message which he sent up to the Capitol, Mr. Lincoln had a good deal to say. He had done a great many extraordinary things since Congress last met, and now he must
give an accounting. Specifically, he had called out the militia; he had blockaded the ports of the seceded states; he had
called for 42,000 volunteers for three-year terms; he had
authorized an increase of 22,000 in the regular army and of
18,000 men in the navy; he had authorized suspension of the
writ of habeas corpus; and he had committed the government
to the expenditure of large sums. It might not be necessary
for Congress to give formal approval to all of these steps;
men like Senator Breckinridge argued that it could not and
there were Unionists who argued that it should not, since doing it might imply that the actions had originally been illegal.
But at least a tacit approval was needed. The President had
to be sure Congress would go along.

For his justification he relied largely on the history of recent events, which he recited: secession, seizure of forts,
bombardment of Fort Sumter, attack on Harper's Ferry and
the Gosport Navy Yard, the creation of an "insurrectionary
government." These things, he felt, had no possible motive
except a desire to destroy the authority of the Federal Union,
and they compelled Americans to ponder on haunting questions. Could "a government of the people by the same people" maintain itself against domestic foes? Or, put more
sharply: "Must a government, of necessity, be too strong for
the liberties of its own people, or too weak to maintain its
own existence?"

All of this, he went on, had led him to exert the war power

of the government, and he left no room for doubt about
where he would strike the first blow. The rival government
had established its capital in Richmond. "The people of Virginia have thus allowed the giant insurrection to make its
nest within her borders; and this government has no choice
left but to deal with it, *where* it finds it." Just as clearly, he
indicated what he would do about the strange new government which was proclaiming itself in western Virginia, saying that "these loyal citizens" must be recognized and protected "as being Virginia." He denied that there was such a
thing as a right of secession, and denied as well that any of
the border states could be neutral; their neutrality, he said,
could help no one but disunionists and was "treason in effect."
(This last shaft, clearly, was aimed at Kentucky, where Lincoln did not need to tread quite as delicately as he had earlier.
In a Congressional election on June 30 Kentucky had elected
nine Unionists and only one States' Rights candidate, and the
Union cause had gained a big majority in the popular vote,
92,000 against 37,000.)

The recital of causes went on, and the involved justification of things done, followed by the blunt assertion "this is
essentially a people's contest" and the pledge that it would be
fought until the visible authority of the people's government
had been fully restored. Then, at last, came the pointed request—not for a blank check covering war measures taken
in haste, but for a grant of $400,000,000 in money and
400,000 soldiers in uniform.[6]

Here was a new estimate of the war's dimensions, out on
the table for all men to see. The struggle in which the nation
was involved had begun without a plan; it had been a formless war, so far a very small one, almost inactive, its ultimate
potentialities unexplored. Lincoln was giving it a form and
a plan; he would develop its full potential and make it great
—partly because the pressure was on him, and partly because
the war, of itself, had reached its moment of transition. So
far it had been a muddle touched with violence. Now it was
something that must either be abandoned or transformed. If
secession was not to be accepted, it must be recognized as
something infinitely greater than a mere local disorder created
by "combinations too powerful to resist," which a few ninety-
day militia regiments could handle.

Lincoln still had things to learn. He restated his old belief that the Confederacy somehow spoke for a minority: "It may well be questioned whether there is, today, a majority of the legally qualified voters of any State, except perhaps South Carolina, in favor of disunion. There is much reason to believe that the Union men are the majority in many, if not in every other one, of the so-called seceded states." Actually there was no real reason to believe anything of the kind; yet this unfounded faith was undoubtedly one of the things that led Lincoln, in this same speech, to speak of the terms on which the old Union could be reconstructed after secession had been destroyed: "The executive deems it proper to say, it will be his purpose, then as ever, to be guided by the Constitution and the laws; and that he probably will have no different understanding of the powers and duties of the Federal government, relatively to the rights of the States, and the people, under the Constitution, than that expressed in the inaugural address." Here, if anyone had seen it, was a promise of an easy peace, with continued life for slavery. Apparently no one saw it. The lights were fading; it was beginning to be hard to see things clearly unless they had bulk and a sharp outline.

Sharp outlines were very evident in Congress, where once conservative men used harsh words and spoke with a heat which, in the old days, only the abolitionists had used. Congress would obviously vote the men and the money Lincoln had asked, and when border-state men protested that this huge war program seemed to be aimed at outright subjugation of the South, Senator Jacob Collamer, of Vermont, had an answer for them. The classic meaning of the verb "to subjugate," he pointed out, meant to compel beaten enemies to pass under a yoke—*sub juga*. He himself did not want to make anyone pass under a literal yoke, but subjugation in the modern sense, he said, was exactly what he was looking for. When Senator Lazarus Powell, of Kentucky, tried to amend an army-supply bill with a rider stipulating that troops could not be used to interfere in any way with African slavery, he was promptly voted down. James Dixon, of Connecticut, warned him that if it came to a pinch, "and it should turn out that either this government or slavery must be destroyed," the conservative people of the North would unhesitatingly destroy slavery. Senator Henry S. Lane, of Indiana, made it even more pointed: ". . . let me tell gentle-

men that although the abolition of slavery is not an object
of the war, they may, in their madness and folly and treason,
make the abolition of slavery one of the results of this war."

That word "treason" was used often. One day the Senate
found itself considering a measure to expel eight Southern
Senators who had left the chamber months earlier to go with
the Confederacy. Since the seats of these eight men had already been declared vacant, and since their former occupants
had not the faintest desire to return, the resolution would have
no practical effect, and one Senator objected to it: he knew
the men in question and they were honorable men, while the
act of expulsion implied moral turpitude. Senator Joseph A.
McDougall, of California, replied that the resolution ought
to pass. There was no question of turpitude; the absentees
had simply committed treason, and "treason was always a
gentlemanly crime, and in ancient times a man who committed it was entitled to the axe instead of the halter." For
whatever it might be worth, the resolution was adopted.

There were still men who shared Lincoln's belief that most
Southerners were Unionists at heart. Congressman John A.
McClernand, of Illinois, a Douglas Democrat once known as
a good friend of the South, declared that this was really a
war of liberation rather than of conquest—"as the Federal
flag advances toward the heart of this rebellion, thousands
and tens of thousands of loyal men in the seceded States will
be found rallying around it ready to uphold it." However,
Mr. McClernand would leave nothing to chance, and he
brought in a resolution which was quickly passed that "this
House hereby pledges itself to vote for any amount of money
and any number of men which may be necessary" to win the
war. Congressman John Hickman, of Pennsylvania, was grimmer; if half a million men could not destroy the Confederacy,
he would vote for a million, and in the end "this government will be preserved and the gallows will eventually perform its office." Even grimmer was Owen Lovejoy, of Illinois,
an old-time abolitionist who would stop at nothing. He was
willing to wipe out the Southern nation, he said, just as Rome
had wiped out Carthage: "If there is no other way to quell
this rebellion, we will make a solitude and call it peace."

A great deal of this, to be sure, was just talk without much
solidity behind it. Tough Andrew Johnson—an East Tennes-
sean who remained in the Senate even though his state had

formally left the Union—offered a resolution stating that the war had been forced upon the country by Southern disunionists and that the Federal government was fighting neither to subjugate Southern states nor to interfere with slavery but simply to maintain the Constitution and uphold the Union. Senator Breckinridge objected that the South had forced no war on anybody, and remarked that after listening to what his colleagues had been saying, he believed this really *was* a war for subjugation; but in the end the Senate adopted Johnson's resolution with only five dissenting votes, and shortly afterward the House passed it by a thumping 121 to 2.[7]

The lines were not yet firmly drawn. Most good Unionists were disturbed by the talk of conquest and subjugation, and although the Congress was overwhelmingly in favor of going on with the war, it was willing, within limits, to be moderate. But Northern men of good will, friendly to the South, had no firm ground to stand on. Their problem was defined by Samuel F. B. Morse, the distinguished inventor of the telegraph, who despised abolitionists, believed that the South had suffered genuine wrongs, and said that he would do nothing to support the war beyond paying his taxes. By its "inappeasable, implacable, stubborn resolve of *permanent* disunion," he wrote to a friend, the Confederacy had hamstrung Northerners who felt as he felt. The Southern leaders "have struck at friends and foes alike, and left their friends without their support to battle it with fanaticism alone"; they had thus given to their worst enemies "the prestige of the flag of the Union, the war cry of liberty, the enthusiasm of Revolutionary recollections, the plausibility of defence of government and the semblance of justice to the outcry of treason." This, it seemed to him, was "an unwise, a most disastrous step."[8]

Not quite all of the friends of the South in this Congress felt hamstrung. One who insisted on being heard was a handsome, gifted Democrat from Ohio, a good lawyer and an orator of repute—Clement Laird Vallandigham, of Dayton, known as a supporter of Southern rights ever since the war with Mexico and still firm in the faith. On July 12 Vallandigham offered a resolution in the House: ". . . before the President shall have the right to call out any more volunteers than are already in the service, he shall appoint seven commissioners, whose mission it shall be to accompany the Army

on its march, to receive and consider such propositions, if
any, as may at any time be submitted from the executive of
the so-called Confederate States, or of any one of them, looking to a suspension of hostilities, and the return of said
States, or any one of them, to the Union and to obedience to
the Federal Constitution and authority." He was voted down
—his resolution gained twenty-one votes—and when, a few
days later, he offered further motions to censure the President for acts performed before Congress met, his resolutions
were quietly tabled. The war machine had rolled over him,
but it left him undaunted. In a New York speech in the fall
of 1860 he had promised that he would never vote "one dol-
lar of money whereby one drop of American blood should be
shed in a civil war," and to this stand he would cling. If war
weariness ever seized the North, Vallandigham would give it
a rallying point and a means of expression.[9]

In plain fact the Congress did not yet quite know its own
mind. It had accepted Andrew Johnson's motion, disavowing
any intent to subjugate the South, and insisting that it had
no desire to interfere with slavery; it had also supported the
drastic steps Lincoln had taken, it had voted the men and
the money for an all-out war, and it had made it clear that
it expected men and money to be used vigorously. Then, before the session ended, it got entangled with the same problem that had confronted General Butler—the fact that slavery
was a central factor in the Southern war effort, impossible to
ignore even though top policy said that it must be ignored. It
found itself considering a bill "to confiscate property used
for insurrectionary purposes," and one section of this bill
said that slaves used in the Confederate war program should
be declared free.

This touched the untouchable, and it led to much oratory.
Even Republicans agreed that the Federal government lacked
power to interfere with slavery in the states. They had voted,
all but unanimously, that they did not propose to try to interfere with it. Now they were about to provide that in certain cases they would interfere, that some slaves could and
would be given their freedom by direct intervention of the
Federal authority. Apparently the thing was unconstitutional
all around; apparently, also, it was necessary.

Border-state men protested bitterly, arguing that the section "amounts to a wholesale emancipation of the slaves in

the seceding or rebellious states." Not so, replied Congressman John Bingham, of Ohio; it applied only in cases where owners were directly using their slaves, or letting others use them, to overthrow the government. Such men were traitors, and "I aver that a traitor should not only forfeit his slave but he should forfeit his life as well." Yet the Constitution was explicit in its definition of treason, and it said that there could be no forfeiture of a traitor's goods "except during the lifetime of the offender." This forfeiture would apply forever. How now? Would this not "furnish those in arms against the Government a pretext for misrepresenting the purposes and objects of this war," which the Congress had just defined as being something very different?

The answer came, at last, from the Republican leader of the House, Thaddeus Stevens, who in the years ahead would raise his voice again and again to call down woe upon the South; crippled Thad Stevens with his ill-fitting wig and his burning eyes, a bitter, implacable man, a mixture of idealism and hatred, sometimes a radical for human rights and sometimes a straight Pennsylvania Republican in the most traditional meaning of the words. Stevens now evoked the policy on which, in the end, the question of slavery would be handled.

"I thought the time had come," he said, "when the laws of war were to govern our action; when constitutions, if they stood in the way of the laws of war in dealing with the enemy, had no right to intervene. Who pleads the Constitution against our proposed action? Who says the Constitution must come in, in bar of our action? It is the advocates of rebels, of rebels who have sought to overthrow the Constitution and trample it in the dust—who repudiate the Constitution. . . . I deny that they have any right to invoke this Constitution, which they deny has any authority over them, which they set at defiance and trample under foot. I deny that they can be permitted to come here and tell us we must be loyal to the Constitution."[10]

Considering the fact that the war was hardly three months old, and that the time of desperate expedients was still far ahead, these were very powerful words. If this kind of guidance were to be followed, almost anything could happen. The laws of war run all the way to the farthest horizon; in the last analysis they say, simply: "Do what you think needs to be done to win." Unless General McDowell, who, oppressed by many doubts, was about to take his army down toward Richmond, could quickly win a decisive and final victory, the war might lead in a direction not contemplated by any of the people who had started it.

The section in regard to slavery was at last adopted. Considered by itself, it was narrow enough; it said no more than that any master who let his slave be used by the Confederacy on direct military work—building forts, digging trenches, restoring warships or navy yards, and so on—would lose his title to that slave once and for all. In a way, and with careful restrictions, it simply endorsed the essence of Ben Butler's curbstone opinion about contrabands. But it might be a precedent.

Two things this Congress had done that would set a pattern for the struggle; things which could mean that it would be a shattering upheaval rather than just a war. It had in effect voted to put all of the resources of the North into the contest. These resources were immense, or would be when they were finally marshaled, and the Confederacy could not begin to match them; in a long war they would be decisive, provided that the will to use them continued. In addition, Congress had taken a confused but revolutionary step toward making this a war that would swallow up slavery as well as secession; it had at least hinted that when it dealt with slavery it would be guided by the harsh necessities of the case rather than by the Constitution. In the months ahead these necessities would become exceedingly demanding.

3. A Head Full of Fire

PERHAPS THE great comet meant something. It swung into view early in July, it was believed to be the most brilliant in half a century, and an awed observer in Connecticut said that "both head and tail were seen simultaneously." The tail, he said, was "in the form of a bright streamer, with sides nearly straight and parallel." The New York *Herald*, irreverently ready to see an omen in almost anything, wrote solemnly about the "celestial visitor that has sprung upon us with such unexampled brilliancy and magnitude," and said the thing was a burden for the timid, "who regard it with fear, looking upon it as something terrible, bringing in its train wars and desolation."[1]

This was as it might be, the time of war and desolation having arrived. To a crippled scientist who was trying just then to blow up two Yankee warships (he was a trained observer well qualified to judge such matters), the comet was at least useful. It was a bright beacon which men in rowboats, afloat on a perilous tide at midnight, could use as a guide while they tried to place infernal machines where they would do the most harm. The observer was Matthew Fontaine Maury, a commander in the Confederate States Navy, and in a way his presence on this expedition of derring-do was a portent more meaningful than Thatcher's comet itself.

Maury was one of the few Americans of that day with a true international reputation. He perhaps had done even more than the clipper-ship designers themselves to speed the progress of wind-driven ships across the world's oceans. A studious, thoughtful man, he had worked at his desk in Washington so effectively that every ship captain in the western world was deeply in his debt; he was, in fact, one of those quiet world-shrinkers who make the planet smaller and, simply by taking effective thought, bring the distant races and nations of man closer together. Virginia-born, he had become a midshipman in the United States Navy in 1825, had served at sea for fourteen years, and then, while on leave, had been in a stagecoach accident which left one leg permanently lame. Supposedly unfit for duty afloat, he had been appointed, in 1842, superintendent of the navy's Depot of Charts and Instruments, with responsibility as well for direction of the Naval Observatory and Hydrographical Office, and in this post he became one of the navy's most useful officers. He studied not only the stars but winds, ocean currents, and the logs of thousands of mariners; and presently, year after year, he was publishing wind and current charts, sailing directions, studies in oceanography, and the like, whose net effect was to show ship masters what courses would enable them to make the fastest passages. (It was said that his work knocked forty-five days from the average sailing time between New York and San Francisco.) He was honored at home and abroad, and although in the 1850s some petty rivalry among the brass-bound old salts in the Navy Department put him on the shelf, he was quickly restored to duty and promoted to commander.

When secession came, he was in his middle fifties, a staunch Southerner but no extremist; on Lincoln's inauguration he wrote that it was each man's duty to follow his state, if his state should go to war—"if not, he may remain to help on the work of reunion." Virginia went to war and Maury followed Virginia, and shortly thereafter Secretary Mallory gave him a Confederate commander's commission and put him in charge of harbor defenses. Maury began experimenting with electric mines, and early in July he set out on an attempt to put some of those mines to use. He was a pleasant-spoken man, short, stout, and ruddy, still afflicted with that game leg, going out after years at a desk to try his hand at a sea-going exploit in the John Paul Jones style.[2]

This happened down off Sewell's Point, Virginia, where the James River flows out into the broad reach known as Hampton Roads. Anchored in the stream, along with other men-of-war, were the Federal warships U.S.S. *Minnesota* and *Roanoke*. Maury wanted to sink them, and he had been studying them through a spy glass. A guard boat, puffing steam, circled about them night after night, and the chances looked bad; and on a Sunday he saw the church flag floating above the national emblem, and it bothered him. His daughter, Betty, to whom he told the story a few days later, said that "when he thought that those men were worshiping God in sincerity and truth, and no doubt think their cause as righteous as we feel ours to be, his heart softened toward them for he remembered how soon he would be the means of sending many of them to eternity." But Sunday night came, and the guard boat apparently was off duty, so Maury went out in a skiff, four other skiffs following him, an officer and four oarsmen in each boat. They had an arrangement of kegs full of powder, connected by long lines, and the idea was to get up-tide from the warships and set these powder kegs adrift; they would float down, the long lines would be caught by the warships' anchor chains, the kegs would drift on and touch the vessels' sides—and then, by some intricate trigger mechanism, the powder would explode and the ships would go to glory.

When he got back, Maury told his daughter about it and

she put his words down in her diary: "The night was still, clear, calm and lovely. Thatcher's comet was flaming in the sky. We steered by it, pulling along in the plane of its splendid train. All the noise and turmoil of the enemy's camp and fleet were hushed. They had no guard boats of any sort out, and as with muffled oars we began to near them we heard seven bells strike." Then came anti-climax. The mines were set adrift, the anchor chains caught the lines on schedule, the powder kegs went in against the black wooden hulls—and the triggers failed to work. Maury and his men rowed away and waited for an explosion that never came, and Betty Maury wrote: "Thank God, for if it had Pa would have been hung before now. At the first explosion the calcium light at Fortress Monroe would have been lit, and the little steamer—whose steam was up, they could hear her—would have caught them in a few minutes."

Nothing happened. Maury escaped, as did U.S.S. *Minnesota* and *Roanoke*, and apparently the United States Navy never knew what it had missed. Maury believed that on a second try he could make the mines work, but there was no second try. The Confederate government had a genius on its hands and did not quite know what to do with him, and Betty Maury considered it an outrage "that they allowed so celebrated, valuable and clever a man as my father to risk his life in such an expedition." She noted, also, that "Papa looks preoccupied and low-spirited. Says it is more and more palpable that the men at the head of this Government are not the men for the times."[3]

The men at the head of the government were doing their best, under extreme difficulties, but the mere fact that they had a man like Maury in their service meant something. They had other men, too, who had broken off promising careers to stake all they had on the success of the new nation. Among them was a handsome six-footer named Albert Sidney Johnston, Kentucky-born, a graduate of West Point, veteran of the Mexican War, former colonel of the 2nd U. S. Cavalry, a man esteemed so highly in Washington that when Lee decided he could not take the job of second-in-command to Winfield Scott, the place was offered to Johnston. Johnston, by now commanding the Department of the Pacific with headquarters at San Francisco, an old soldier getting on for sixty, turned the offer down and resigned his commission. He stayed on for two weeks, so that his successor could take his place, and he was horrified to learn that the War Department (remembering what Twiggs had done in Texas) suspected that he would turn California over to the Rebels unless he was closely watched; and now he was coming east to Richmond, cross-country, hoping that Jefferson Davis somehow would be able to make use of him in the Confederate army. Nothing had been promised to him; just thought he could be of some service.

There was another Johnston—Joseph Eggleston Johnston, a sprightly and courtly little Virginian in his fifties who, when war came, was quartermaster-general of the United States Army, with the rank of brigadier. He had a trim gray goatee, a knack for winning the adoration of men who worked for him, and an indefinable quality that led soldiers to refer to him as "the gamecock"; he was both kindly and touchy, and although his superiors sometimes found him hard to get along with, his inferiors never did. He would pace his office in the War Department, thinking hard, and when an aide came in to remind him of some unfinished business, he would bite the aide's head off—and then, before the man had left the room, would apologize so pleasantly that the aide would feel no hurt. One morning, a few days after Fort Sumter, he went in to see Secretary Cameron; came out a bit later, head bowed, tears in his eyes, to collect his belongings and go away. Cameron recalled that Johnston had told him he must resign and go south; he owed everything to the United States government, it had educated him and honored him, but he must go with his state. "It was ruin, in every sense of the word," said Cameron, remembering what the gamecock had told him, "but he must go." Johnston went—to Richmond, where Mr. Davis made him a Confederate brigadier and sent him off to command troops in the Shenandoah. An admiring soldier, looking on when Johnston took command, considered him both an intellectual and a fine horseman, and wrote: "He sat his steed like a part of the animal, and there was that about him which impressed us all with the idea that he was at home in the management of an army as well as of a horse."[4]

. . . The historian Francis Parkman, considering the state of the war two years later, marveled that an adversary "with means scarcely the tithe of ours" could not only hold the Northern invader at bay but could twice show the ability to take the war into the Northland itself. The reason, he believed, was that the Confederacy—"ill-jointed, starved, attenuated"—had, nevertheless, "a head full of fire." It had claimed the allegiance of some great men, men who had much to lose and much to offer, and the fight between Confederacy and Union came down to "strong head and weak body against strong body and weak head."[5] Parkman named no names, and he did not need to. The Confederacy had Lee, and the Johnstons, and Maury, and others like them, and they had not turned their lives upside-down lightly: they would stick to the finish, they would carry lesser men with them, and a new nation whose cause these men had chosen had some important assets. . . .

And this was the counter-weight which the South was putting into the scales against the massive force which the Northern President and Congress were evoking, in the month of July 1861. The South did not have the strength in mine, factory, counting house, or field which the Northern states had, nor did it own, far down in reserve, waiting to be accepted and used, the overriding moral force of the anti-slavery cause. Yet it did have, somewhere, in an area beyond easy definition, the power to draw the loyalty of some very remarkable men—who, before they got through, might do great things with the lean, restless countrymen whose muscularity had so impressed Mr. William Russell. It could summon a man like Maury to steer a rowboat across a dark tide by the light of a comet, on a mission which ought to have been given to some twenty-five-year-old lieutenant; it could bring an Albert Sidney Johnston across the continent, riding toward destiny and a fated bullet on the off chance that he might be of some service; and its ability to command such men was a factor as significant, in the national response to the laws of war, as anything Thaddeus Stevens might call on the Federal Congress to do. Alec Stephens had looked without regret on the broken Union and had boasted "We are the salt of the concern."[6] Men like those would make his boast look as if it contained some substance.

Mr. Davis seemed unworried, although there was much

that might have worried him. He went before the third session of the provisional Congress in Richmond on July 20 to welcome the states of Virginia, North Carolina, Tennessee, and Arkansas to the Confederacy and to pay his respects to the talk and the legislation that had been coming out of the Federal Capitol. These, he said, "strip the veil behind which the true policy and purposes of the Government of the United States had been previously concealed; their odious features now stand fully revealed; the message of their President and the action of their Congress during the present month confess the intention of subjugating these States by a war whose folly is equalled by its wickedness." The Confederacy was getting ready for them. Crops were good: the yield of grain in the recent harvest was the largest in Southern history, such export staples as cotton, sugar, and tobacco were coming along well, and "a kind Providence had smiled on the labor which extracts the teeming wealth of our soil." Army recruiting was flourishing, and "the noble race of freemen who inhabit these states" was volunteering "in numbers far exceeding those authorized by your laws." The people of the South, in short, were thoroughly aroused, and Northern talk of subjugation was utter folly. The President stated both the faith and the determination of the Southern people with the defiant assertion: "Whether this war shall last one, or three, or five years is a problem they leave to be solved by the enemy alone; it will last till the enemy shall have withdrawn from their borders—till their political rights, their altars and their homes are freed from invasion. Then, and only then, will they rest from this struggle, to enjoy in peace the blessings which with the favor of Providence they have secured by the aid of their own strong hearts and sturdy arms."[7]

Mr. Davis's confidence seemed justified; his new government, with everything to do and little to do it with, had accomplished a good deal, and when he spoke, it had upward of 110,000 men under arms, not counting home guards and militia. But although volunteers were coming forward in an enthusiastic flood tide, there were not nearly enough weapons for them, and there was no possibility that the shortage could be overcome in the immediate future. Joe Johnston, up in the Valley, was calling for reinforcements, and a week before he addressed Congress, Davis had felt compelled to explain to the general that there were no reinforcements because men could not be armed. "From Missi. I could get 20,000 men who impatiently wait for notice that they can be armed," he wrote. "In Georgia numerous tenders are made to serve for any time, any place, and to these and other offers I am still constrained to answer I have not arms to supply you."[8]

This was a hard message to send to a soldier whose army was in contact with the enemy, but there was no help for it. At Manassas, Beauregard was calling for troops even more insistently than Johnston was, and although he was getting a few, he was not getting nearly as many as he believed he needed, and one of his staff officers was angrily complaining that the President and the War Department would send no help "unless it is *dug out of them.*" With bitter cynicism, he wrote: "I hear that the Prest. will send re-enforcements here. Perhaps tomorrow 4000 will arrive. We want 15,000."[9]

This explosion was natural enough, in view of the fact that the Federals were obviously about to start an offensive campaign, but it was unjust because there was nothing whatever that Davis could immediately do as far as equipment was concerned. The North also had a shortage of arms just now, but it would be overcome as soon as the country got itself organized for war; the case in the Confederacy was different because the South had so little to organize. The very machinery of government had been improvised—improvised in a land whose fundamental faith was that the government which governs least is best—and this machinery was attempting to operate in a land where the financial and industrial base for a large-scale war simply did not exist. The lack of guns was the first symptom of a deficiency which could never really be overcome and which, if the war went on long enough, would be fatal.

The South, to be blunt, had a grave shortage of capital and of manufacturing capacity. Its wealth consisted largely of land and slaves. In 1860 it had produced a little less than 10 per cent of the total of American manufactured articles. The shortage of hard money was already being felt; the different state governments, overextended by money spent in the early days of secession, were being obliged to borrow in a very bad money market. Specie payments to individuals were being suspended, treasury notes based on state credit were being issued, and the Congress at Richmond within a month would be authorizing the issuance of $100,000,000 in Confederate treasury notes so that it could reimburse the states for what they were spending on war preparations. The touch of inflation was beginning to be felt before the war was well begun.

Mr. Davis had spoken with pride of the promising production of export staples. To possess a large surplus of cotton, tobacco, and sugar was good, provided that the export markets could in fact be reached, but there were difficulties. The Southern carrying trade had been conducted largely in Northern vessels, which were no longer at hand. The Northern market itself was of course gone: two months ago Davis had signed a law prohibiting the export of cotton except through the seaports, which Northern ships could not enter. Europe remained, and Commissioners Yancey, Mann, and Rost were overseas reminding the British and the French about all of that cotton. They were getting no hint that actual recognition would be extended, and they probably did not expect to, but the cotton business looked more promising. In Paris the Count de Morny, believed to be in the confidence of the Emperor Napoleon, had assured them (as they recently reported to Richmond) that "as long as we produced cotton for sale, France and England would see that their vessels reached the ports where it was to be had." In London the British Foreign Minister, Lord John Russell, had indicated that his government would go no farther than its declaration extending the rights of belligerents to the Confederate states, but the commissioners felt that this attitude might change if "the necessity for having cotton becomes pressing."[10] The necessity was not yet pressing. There had been a big carryover of cotton stocks overseas—so heavy that New England textile mills would actually be able to import some from Europe during the year ahead—but time might tell a different story. The great supply of export staples was unquestionably a long-term asset, but right now it did nothing to relieve the shortage of war goods.

There were Southerners, then and later, who argued that President Davis should have had his government buy all of the cotton in the South, rush it to Europe, and use the proceeds to buy munitions, warships, and industrial equipment. Theoretically the idea was sound enough, but as a practical matter it was all but out of the question. A far-reaching action of that kind was almost unthinkable in a new nation which owed its existence, primarily, to the belief that the central government ought to have and to use as few powers as possible. So immense a purchase would have given the inflationary wave much impetus. The ships to carry the cotton did not exist. For the moment it seemed best to leave the cotton where it was. Let Europe get hungry for it.

In addition there was the Yankee blockade. Although this now was not much more than a nuisance, it was imperceptibly but inexorably tightening, week by week. Secretary Welles had. told the Federal Congress that the navy had twenty-two blockaders in service along the Atlantic Coast and twenty-one more on duty in the Gulf. It had already bought twelve steamers and chartered nine more, and was giving them guns; as combat ships they would be of no account, but as blockaders they would be quite serviceable. Contracts had been let for the building of twenty-one gunboats, to be delivered in ninety days, and a number of larger warships were under construction. Since anything that would float and carry a gun could halt an unarmed merchantman, even sailing ships were being chartered, armed, and put into service, and most of the warships in the overseas squadrons were being recalled.[11] The blockade was extremely loose right now and it never would become airtight, but in the long run it would produce strangulation.

Business in the South presented contrasts this summer. Some lines were almost in collapse. In Mississippi, a Vicksburg businessman was complaining that "there is no business doing. The shelves are bare—the merchants lolling on the counters. There is no money, no credit, and provisions scarce and dear."[12] But other lines were booming. The trade in arms, shoes, clothing, and anything else the army might use was going at a great rate. Along the Kentucky border, business was exceptionally lively. As a neutral state, Kentucky offered a notable field for trade with the Yankees, and the opportunity was not being missed. (As Lincoln had perceived, neutrality here was a positive asset to the South.) Confederate agents were in Europe, or on their way there, to buy arms—finding themselves, more often than not, in direct competition with Federal agents who had gone abroad to do the same thing.

To buy at home or abroad the goods the army needed was one thing; to move them to the places where the army wanted them was quite another. Lacking a financial and industrial system equal to the demands of a large war, the South lacked also a proper transportation system. It had many railroads but no real railroad network, because hardly any of its railroads had been built with through traffic in mind. Most of them had been conceived as feeder lines, to move cotton to the wharves at river towns or at seaports, and they had been built in many different gauges so that no interchange of cars was possible. On the map Richmond had good rail connections with the rest of the Confederacy, but it was not possible to send a loaded freight car from the deep South to Richmond. At numerous junction points each car had to be unloaded, the freight moved cross-town by dray and then reloaded on different cars, and if there was any sort of delay (which was usually the case), the freight had to be stored in a warehouse until the delay was over. There could be no smooth flow of freight traffic; it was bound to move slowly and jerkily, with more or less spoilage and wastage along the way.

This handicap, to be sure, existed also in the North. But there it was not so serious. It had been recognized earlier, and it was being removed; and the significant point was that in the North it *could* be removed, but that in the South it could not. The South was almost helpless in this respect. Nearly all of its locomotives, rails, spikes, car wheels, car bodies, and other items of equipment had come from the North. The famous Tredegar Iron Works at Richmond could make some of these things, but it could not make nearly enough, and, besides, it was swamped now with war orders. The South would have to get through the war on the railroad layout it had when the war began: a layout which was inadequate even at the start and which could never be properly repaired or maintained. As the nation's need for an adequate transportation system increased, the system would grow weaker and weaker and there was no earthly help for it. Much freight would of course move in wagons along country roads, in the age-old way, but the same pinch would apply here; the wagons came from Yankee shops, and replacements would have to be improvised out of inadequate means. The Confederacy's transportation problem, like its problem of finance and production, was fundamentally insoluble unless the war could be kept short.[13]

These problems, indeed, were so grave and pointed so surely toward final defeat that one is forced to wonder how the founding fathers of the Confederacy could possibly have overlooked them. The answer perhaps is that the problems were not so much unseen as uncomprehended. At bottom, these were *Yankee* problems; concerns of the broker, the money changer, the trader, the mechanic, the grasping man of business; they were matters that such people would think of, not matters that would command the attention of aristocrats who were familiar with valor, the classics, and heroic attitudes.[14] Secession itself had involved a flight from reality rather than an approach to it. Howell Cobb had spoken for his class when, in February, he declared that the South's near-monopoly on cotton production was an asset stronger than armies or navies. "We know," he said, "that by an embargo we could soon place not only the United States but many of the European powers under the necessity of electing between such a recognition of our independence as we require or domestic convulsions at home."[15] Essentially, this was the reliance of a group which knew a little about the modern world but which did not know nearly enough and could never understand that it did not know enough. It ran precisely parallel to Mr. Davis's magnificent statement that the duration of the war could be left up to the enemy—the war would go on until the enemy gave up, and it did not matter how far off that day might be.

The trouble was that it did matter. It mattered enormously. Mr. Davis was assuming that courage and dedication, because they burned so brightly, would make up for all other deficiencies. This they might very well do for a time, but their magic would grow a little bit less compelling, week by week and month after month, and if the war went on indefinitely, the day would certainly come when other matters would become dominant. The head so full of fire could make an inadequate body surpass its limitations only for a time.

4. The Road to Bull Run

PERHAPS A SULLEN desire to avenge the beating at Big Bethel
had something to do with it. So did General McClellan's glittering triumph in the western Virginia mountains, the entice-
ment of victory being added to the sting of defeat. Running
just beneath these was the impatient anger of the non-com-
batants, sensed by General Scott from the beginning, taking
fire now that the war was actually under way; the whole creating an atmosphere in which an unready army was driven into battle by an impulse which nobody knew how to resist. Bull
Run was the consequence.

Big Bethel came first. This was an unremarkable little fight
which took place a few miles below Yorktown, Virginia, on
June 10, brought on because the Federal power was clumsily
flexing its muscles. It would hardly be remembered even as a
skirmish except that it was the first real trial by combat.
Militarily, it affected the course of the war not at all, and
yet because it brought a feeling of humiliation to people who
had supposed the war would be won easily, it helped to create a certain state of mind.

Ben Butler commanded Federal troops in and around Fort
Monroe, at the tip of the Virginia peninsula, and early in
June he learned that the Confederates had built a battery at
a river crossing, near a church known as Big Bethel, eight
miles from Butler's own outposts, thirteen miles from the
historic village of Yorktown. He was by no means ready to
begin a real campaign, but it seemed to him that these Rebels
ought to be driven away, and he mounted an expedition to
do this; a complicated affair which involved a night march
and the convergence of four separate regiments on the point
to be attacked. He considered that proper precautions had
been taken; the troops were to shout the watchword "Boston," and one group would wear white badges on its sleeves
so that the others would recognize it. These devices failed; the
advancing soldiers could not even recognize the roads they
were supposed to take and they went straggling up to the
scene of action after a premature encounter in which two
Federal regiments had fired briskly into each other. An officer who reached the place at dawn reported that disorganized

men were wandering all about, "looking more like men enjoying a huge picnic than soldiers awaiting battle."

When the attack at last was made it failed miserably. Young Theodore Winthrop, the ardent New Englander who had thought that the joy of marching down Broadway under the flags was worth life itself, tried to lead an assault through a swamp; waved his sword, shouted "Come on, boys—one more charge and the day is ours!" and was immediately shot to death. Lieutenant J. T. Greble, of the regular artillery, was killed, the first regular-army officer to die in this war, working his guns while the Confederates squatted in the underbrush and maintained a relentless fire; their commander wrote that they "seemed to enjoy it as much as boys do rabbit shooting." In the end the Federals fled back to their base, utterly routed, leaving seventy-six dead and wounded men behind them. The Confederates had lost but eight, and trophies from the battlefield were displayed in Richmond shop windows to delight the patriotic.[1]

The situation on the Virginia peninsula remained precisely as it had been before, but the situation in Washington began to change. Was the war not being bungled? There had been riots in Baltimore; now there was humiliating defeat on the battlefield; a fortnight earlier there was the death of Elmer Ellsworth, arousing powerful emotions; and on the heels of all of this there came McClellan's advance in the west, a demonstration, apparently, that when things were handled with energy, the war news could be good. Lincoln's secretaries wrote afterward that "overstrained enthusiasm was slowly changing into morbid sensitiveness and a bitterness of impatience which seemed almost beyond endurance." Before long, Horace Greeley's New York *Tribune* was repeating "Forward to Richmond! Forward to Richmond!" demanding that the Confederate capital be taken before the Confederate Congress could assemble on July 20. Opinionated Count Gurowski spoke for many when he wrote, with all the certainty of the doctrinaire: "The people's strategy is best; to rush in masses on Richmond; to take it now, when the enemy is there in comparatively small numbers. . . . So speaks the people, and they are right; here among the wiseacres not one understands the superiority of the people over his little brain."[2]

To rush in masses upon Richmond might be well, provided the masses were in shape to make the rush, although the ghost of Theodore Winthrop could have testified that something more than enthusiasm was needed. General Scott had a better grasp of the matter. Understanding something of the way in which wars are won, he had worked out a plan to win this one—a plan whose essentials, finally applied, would at last actually win it—but the rising tension all around him would compel him to resort to expedients. Doubting that the thing could be done all in a rush, he began to seem unduly cautious and slow; a failing made even worse by his belief that Richmond was not really the best place to rush upon anyway.

Scott put his plan together early in the spring, the genesis of it, apparently, being a letter from General McClellan. McClellan wrote to him on April 27, suggesting that the nation's major offensive effort be made from the Middle West. Hold the line of the Ohio and the upper Mississippi firmly (said McClellan) and then, with an army of at least 80,000 men, strike eastward by way of the Great Kanawha Valley to Virginia and Richmond, or possibly drive down across Tennessee toward Montgomery. This, he said, could be combined with a thrust by an eastern army through Charleston and on into Georgia, the ultimate goal of everybody being the Gulf Coast and the cities of Pensacola, Mobile, and New Orleans. McClellan thought all of this should be done quickly. ("The movement on Richmond," he wrote, in words that may have returned to haunt him a year later, "should be conducted with utmost promptness.")

Scott replied on May 3. His chief objection to this plan, he said, was that it proposed to subdue the seceded states by piece-meal, instead of overwhelming them in one broad, co-ordinated campaign. He pointed out, also, that the government was going to rely on three-year volunteers instead of on the ninety-day militia regiments; there would be time, therefore, to organize properly for the long pull. Then he set forth his own scheme: blockade the Confederate coast rigorously, send a powerful army (accompanied by gunboats) down the Mississippi, seize New Orleans with an amphibious expedition coming up from below, and establish a firm grip on the Mississippi all the way to the Gulf. The object of this, he wrote, was "to clear out and keep open this great line of communication . . . so as to envelop the insurgent states and bring them to terms with less bloodshed than by any other plan." It would be necessary to give the volunteers at least four and one-half months of training, river gunboats must be built, and much equipment would have to be assembled; Scott believed that the big drive down the river could not begin before the middle of November. Then he added a note of warning:

"A word now as to the greatest obstacle in the way of this plan—the great danger now pressing upon us—the impatience of our patriotic and loyal Union friends. They will urge instant and vigorous action, regardless, I fear, of consequences."[3]

They were already doing it, although the pressure for instant and vigorous action, strong enough even then to worry General Scott, was nothing compared with what it would be by July. It would become something Federal officers would feel all through the war; McClellan himself would be under its cruelest compulsion before the year was out, and any general who at any time seemed reluctant to rush in masses, pell-mell, upon the enemy would risk intense criticism and the loss of his job. Even now Scott could feel it, and could see that it was going to increase—one indication being the reception his plan got. President Lincoln liked it, to be sure; the more so, perhaps, because he was a Westerner who knew the profound importance of the Mississippi Valley. Other people, however, did not. The proposal leaked out, military secrets at that time being less than sacred, and it brought Scott a good deal of derision. Newspapers called it "the Anaconda plan," and something about the picture of heavy serpentine coils slowly constricting the life out of the enemy struck many patriots as ridiculous. There was no dash to it, nothing to stir the pulses; it had no room for "Forward to Richmond" or for the decisive rush of inspired masses, and the last thing anyone wanted to think about was the prospect of a long war.

The business began to come to a head late in June, when General McDowell submitted a plan of operations to the War Department.

McDowell was not concerned with broad strategy. He commanded what was called the Department of Northeastern Virginia, with headquarters at Arlington, in the pillared house occupied until recently by Robert E. Lee, and he knew that he was expected to take action against the enemy in his immediate front. This enemy was General Beauregard, who had an army drawn up in front of Manassas Junction, thirty-odd miles from Washington, behind a sluggish stream known as Bull Run. McDowell had nothing resembling an adequate staff, but his intelligence service was good, and he had an only mildly exaggerated count of Beauregard's numbers: about 25,000 of all arms, he believed, with perhaps 10,000 more up in the Shenandoah Valley led by Joe Johnston. Since there was a railroad line from Manassas to the Valley, Johnston could quickly come to Beauregard's aid when the Yankees moved. Let the Federals along the upper Potomac, then, keep Johnston so busy that he could send no help; McDowell himself, with 30,000 men in column and another 10,000 in reserve, could march down to give Beauregard a battle.

McDowell's plan was a workmanlike job. He knew that his militia regiments were poorly trained and, in almost all cases, were commanded by men totally without experience in war. He would organize them, therefore, into small brigades (which later would be grouped into divisions), each brigade to be led by a regular-army colonel, each colonel to be assisted by as many junior regulars as might be available, "so that the men may have as fair a chance as the nature of things and the comparative inexperience of most will allow." He had no grandiose ideas about taking Richmond; he said flatly that "the objective point in our plan is Manassas Junction," and because he felt that his raw troops would be more likely to stick together in advance than in retreat, he specified that once the move began, there should be no backward step. On June 29 Lincoln called his cabinet and his military advisers to the White House to consider this plan.

General Scott did not like it. Repeating what he had told McClellan, he told Lincoln that he "did not believe in a little war by piece-meal"; he wanted the Anaconda scheme, with the decisive campaign going down the Mississippi in the autumn—"fight all the battles that were necessary, take all the positions we could find and garrison them, fight a battle at New Orleans and win it, and thus end the war." He leaned, it must be confessed, on the old delusion: the South contained many Union men, and these would come forward once the Mississippi was opened and the blockade was made tight, and "I will guarantee that in one year from this time all difficulties will be settled." In any case, Scott's program looked too remote. President and cabinet clearly wanted action now, in Virginia, and Scott withdrew his opposition and listened while McDowell laid a map on the table and explained just what he proposed to do. McDowell's exposition was soldierly and lucid, and his plan was approved. He was told to start his forward movement on July 9.[4]

This would crowd things, July 9 being only ten days away. Haste seemed necessary, however, because in about a fortnight the ninety-day terms of many of the militia regiments would begin to expire; better use the men while they were still available. In the end the target date proved unattainable. New regiments were still coming in, including some of the three-year volunteers, and it took time to fit them into the new army's organization. It took even more time to find all of the wagons, horses, and harness for the supply trains. McDowell had only eight companies of cavalry and practically no engineer troops; and, all in all, there was a good deal of point in Scott's notion that the summer ought to be spent in the slow task of getting ready. It would be several days after July 9 before McDowell could get his unwieldy force on the road.

If this force were to do its job, the Confederate army in the Shenandoah had to be kept out of action, and this was up to Major General Robert Patterson, who had some 14,000 troops in Maryland along the upper Potomac in the general vicinity of Hagerstown. Patterson was sixty-nine, a veteran of the War of 1812 and of the Mexican War. He came from the militia rather than from the regulars, and he had spent most of his life as a businessman, successful and prosperous; he owned sugar and cotton plantations in the South and textile mills in the North, he had helped to promote the Pennsylvania Railroad, and he had interests in Philadelphia steamship lines, and he was on duty now as a major general of volunteers, serving a three-month term like the rest of the militia. Handicapped though he was by age, he was a stout old smooth-bore, and in the middle of June he had wanted to cross the Potomac and clear the lower Shenandoah Valley of Rebels at least as far as Winchester. Scott turned down his plan rather brusquely, took the few regulars Patterson had away from him, and sent a series of rather confused orders which left the old general somewhat muddled.

In the end Patterson got the picture: McDowell was going to advance, and Patterson was to keep Johnston occupied. The picture was still fuzzy, however. Scott seemed to be saying that Patterson must fight Johnston but that he must be very careful, and if it was too risky to pursue the enemy, he ought to think about coming down the Potomac Valley toward McDowell instead; the sum of it seemed to be (as far as Patterson could see) that he was to make warlike demonstrations and delay the enemy, but that he was not to take undue chances. A reverse or even a drawn battle would encourage the enemy, "filling his heart with joy, his ranks with men and his magazines with voluntary contributions." The two old generals, conferring along the length of the telegraph wire, just were not getting through to one another.[5]

The Confederates were suffering from a little confusion of their own, although in the end this was not so expensive. Early in June, Beauregard had written to President Davis urging that they work out a detailed strategic plan, but Davis warned him that because they were so outnumbered they must first see what the Yankees were up to; "the present position and unknown purpose of the enemy require that our plan should have many alterations." The unknown purpose became clear enough before long. Beauregard had plenty of spies in Washington and they kept him posted, and anyway the Northern newspapers were printing detailed stories telling what McDowell was going to do, and Beauregard soon was very well aware that he was about to be attacked. Full of expedients, he laid plans for his battle—Napoleonic plans, based, as he said, on what Napoleon did at Austerlitz. They were excellent, although as things worked out no single part of them could ever be put into operation. Beauregard's role was simply to hold on and stand the hammering until Johnston could join him.[6]

Johnston, on his part, was suffering from some unease. McClellan seemed about to break through the mountains from the west, and Patterson might cross the Potomac in force at any minute; and although Lee warned him that to give up Harper's Ferry "would be depressing to the cause of the South," Johnston considered the place indefensible—and on June 15 he evacuated the historic little town and retreated to Winchester. (Patterson considered this a ruse. An outpost commander warned him that "there may be a deep-laid plot to deceive us," and Patterson wired Scott: "Design no pursuit; cannot make it.") Johnston reconsidered a little, after his retreat, and moved twelve miles forward to Bunker Hill, where he took position and regained a measure of confidence. The threat from McClellan evaporated, and Johnston watched to see what the Federals might do next.[7]

He was well served by his lieutenants. One of them was that singular genius, Brigadier General Thomas J. Jackson, a shy man full of ferocious Presbyterianism, born to fight; and Jackson put over a sly trick on the Baltimore & Ohio Railroad people, confiscating trains that ran through Harper's Ferry and depriving the road at last of forty-two locomotives and 386 freight cars. Most of these were wrecked and thrown into the river, but Jackson was able to haul fourteen locomotives and a few boxcars overland, by road, with horses for motive power, all the way to the town of Strasburg, where they could be put on the Manassas Gap Railroad and added to the Confederacy's stock of railroad equipment.[8] Johnston also had some cavalry, commanded by a bearded young West Pointer named James Ewell Brown Stuart—Jeb Stuart, who would be known to fame a little later, a man who was both an unconscionable show-off and a solid, hard-working, and wholly brilliant commander of light horse. He wore an ostrich plume in his hat, he had a gray cloak lined with scarlet, and he kept a personal banjo player on his staff, riding off to war all jingling with strum-strum music going on ahead, and before he got killed (which came in the final twilight several years later) he gave the Yankees a very bad time of it. Johnston used Stuart these days to befuddle the already confused General Patterson, and no one could have done it better.

Patterson had good ground for complaint, considering everything. He never knew exactly what Washington wanted him to do. He had been told to make warlike movements and he had been told to be very careful lest evil befall him, and no one ever quite said, in so many words: Fight Joe Johnston, and even if you get licked we will win down on the Manassas plain. Patterson tried to get into action, and he got his army down to the Potomac and took it across. It made a bright picture—a six-hour parade of men tramping down to the river, bands playing, splashing through the bright water and moving off into the wooded valleys on the Virginia side—and presently the army was confronting armed Confederates at Bunker Hill. Johnston had been warned that the big push was on in front of Beauregard, and he must go down and help; and to do this he must first either beat Patterson or deceive him grossly. The latter part looked simpler. Johnston sent Stuart forward to take care of it. On July 16, Patterson's advance fought a little skirmish with Stuart's people, and then Patterson sidled over to Charlestown, where John Brown had been tried and hanged two years earlier. Patterson's army was composed mostly of three-months men, and the time of many of these men was expiring, and when he thought everything over, he reported that "it would be ruinous to advance, or even to stay here, without immediate increase of force." He was now twenty miles away from the Confederates, who were about to leave for Manassas Junction, and he would stay where he was, meaning everything for the best but accomplishing nothing whatever, confronting absolute vacancy with an army that could have been of much service elsewhere; a deserving man who might have done fairly well if he had ever understood just what was expected of him.[9]

So Joe Johnston started down to join Beauregard, and Beauregard talked to his spies and read the daily papers and evolved a Napoleonic plan, and Jeb Stuart shuttled cavalrymen back and forth and caused a good Federal army to remain inactive in the Shenandoah Valley, while McDowell's army pulled itself together and went tramping across the Potomac bridges in front of Washington. General Scott, unable to fight the kind of war which he dimly saw was needed, did what he could to give strength to McDowell's elbow; and everybody on each side was more or less helpless, caught up by the fact that the armies at last were in motion. In Richmond, President Davis hurried through his dealings with Congress because he felt that he ought to get where there was going to be fighting, and in Washington, President Lincoln watched the troops moving south and mulled over whatever thoughts may have come to him; and fifty or sixty thousand young men in assorted uniforms, knowing nothing whatever about war, got ready for the first big test which lay just ahead of them. And although it was not possible to see this at the time, the hard fact was that nobody really had control of anything. The armies had begun to move. Events were moving with them. The war itself had begun to move. The great political conventions, the campaigns, the meetings and oratory and half-hearted negotiations, had all come down at last to this. Men were going to fight.

In spite of Patterson's failure, McDowell still had plenty of time if he had been able to use it. He got his army of 34,000 men in motion on July 16, a week after the target date, and Beauregard was less than thirty miles away. Johnston's advance, as things developed, would not reach Beauregard until July 20, and most of his troops would not come in until July 21; at a minimum, McDowell had four days to get to the scene and fight his battle. Later in the war, when the troops knew how to march, and generals and their staffs knew how to handle them, this would have been more than time enough, but at this time no one knew anything; from general down to ninety-day private, everybody was green. McDowell's troops had come in slowly, and when the march began McDowell had never set eyes on a great many of his regiments, which in turn had never in their existence moved in brigade formation. Supply arrangements had been badly fouled up, and when the column started out, the wagon trains that had to carry all of its supplies were still in process of organization; when the head of the army began to move, the tail of it was still being put together. A worse beginning could hardly have been made.

Knowing that raw troops could not stand surprise, McDowell warned his subordinates that to stumble on an enemy battery or entrenchment unexpectedly "will not be pardonable in any commander." This was sound enough, but combing the woods and fields with advance patrols to prevent surprise caused still more delay, and although each part of the column tended to move a little faster than the part just behind it, even the men out in front went very slowly. By the first evening the advance reached Fairfax Court House, drove out some Confederate pickets, and made camp. McDowell ordered the army to pursue vigorously on the following day, only to discover that the soldiers "were too much exhausted to do so."[10] With all of its other troubles, this army simply was not physically fit. Such training as the men had been given had not hardened them. They had never had to make a driving cross-country march, carrying full equipment, in July heat, and it was a very different thing than tramping back and forth for an hour or so on the parade ground. Their officers did not know how to make things easier for them. There were long halts when the regiments stood, sweating mightily, in the dust—halts that were as tiring as marching, because nobody told the men to break ranks, stretch out, and catch forty winks. On the second day a six-mile march was the best the army could do.

Of discipline most regiments really had none at all, as various Virginia civilians began to learn. Fairfax Court House was cruelly ransacked. Vacant houses were plundered, some were burned, and guffawing militiamen went spraddling up and down the streets with crinoline underskirts and ruffled drawers pulled on over their uniforms. With bland understatement, one of these lads wrote that this town, when the army camped there, "wore the softened aspect of a carnival." There was more looting at Germantown, where men shot pigs and snatched up chickens, and went through houses to steal things for which they had no use. One soldier ambled off after his regiment carrying a feather bed in all the July heat; another, for some unimaginable reason, bore a sledge hammer; a third carried a huge looking-glass. Part of the army's weariness came out of senseless romping.[11]

With all of its difficulties the army did keep moving. Despite the billowing dust, and the disorderly swarms of thirty men who broke ranks whenever a regiment passed a brook or a pool, it made an impressive martial picture, especially to the men who, moving as a part of all of this, had never before seen thousands of soldiers on the march. Mile after mile, the swaying column kept going, dust overhead, sunlight flashing from musket barrels, officers and couriers impressive on horseback, every man feeling that he was moving toward something unknown and tremendous . . . it had a touching quality, this blind and ill-managed advance.

By July 18 the advance guard, led by Brigadier General Daniel Tyler, of the Connecticut militia, got to the hamlet of Centreville, where the Confederates until recently had had a strong point. The town itself was nothing much. An officer in the 69th New York held that it was "the coldest picture conceivable of municipal smallness and decrepitude," and wrote scornfully: "It looks for all the world as though it had done its business, whatever it was, if it ever had any, full eighty years ago, and since then had bolted its doors, put out its fires and gone to sleep."[12] The soldiers found the Confederate trenches empty, scouted around for wells and cisterns, and then were called back into ranks again; General Tyler wanted to know whether Bull Run, which lay just a few miles ahead, was held by the Confederates in force.

He sent a brigade forward to find out—to make a reconnaissance in force, as the military jargon had it—and the brigade got down to the stream at Blackburn's Ford, blundered into a sharp fire by artillery and by infantry, lost eighty men, and saw one of its militia regiments go running back to Centreville in panic. The Rebels were there, all right, and word went back to the high command. During the next two days McDowell hauled up the rest of his army, and he concluded that his best move was to circle off to the northwest and get around the Confederates' left flank.

The Confederate army that was waiting for him was in no better shape than his own as far as training and discipline went, except that it did not contain any ninety-day regiments whose time was about up. McDowell had many of these; a few, learning on the literal eve of battle that their ninety days had been spent, insisted on marching off to the rear despite McDowell's earnest entreaties. Beauregard had nearly 25,000 men, drawn up in a line eight miles long on the far side of Bull Run. He had most of his strength on his right, and he was planning to make a grand left wheel, hitting the invader in the flank; he reported that his men were "badly armed and suffering from the irregularity and inefficiency of the Quartermaster's and Commissary's Departments," but he believed they would do well enough. They did have one advantage: they had not had to tire themselves out and disrupt their organization with a long and wearing march. Like McDowell, Beauregard was worried for fear his men could not tell friend from foe once the fight began—in each army some men wore blue and others wore gray, there were all manner of fancy-dress uniforms in use, and some Confederates had no uniforms at all. McDowell had ordered that the United States flag be displayed constantly in all units, and Beauregard hoped that the ladies of Richmond might contribute colored scarves which his men could loop over their shoulders. The ladies did their best, but the supply was short, and what resulted was a sort of rosette which men were asked to pin to their coats. Beauregard noted that a good many of his regiments had no flags at all.

It was going to be, in short, a battle of amateurs, and both commanders knew it. Looking back long afterward, Beauregard believed that a special weight rested on both sides: "There was much in this decisive conflict about to open not involved in any after battle, which pervaded the two armies and the people behind them and colored the responsibility of the respective commanders. The political hostilities of a generation were now face to face with weapons instead of words."[13]

5. *Dust Clouds Against the Sky*

COMING DOWN from Washington, the Warrenton turnpike ran a little south of west; a dusty straight road that passed through looted Fairfax Court House, climbed the slopes around Centreville, and then dropped down to the valley of Bull Run, where a brown river moved southeast in slow loops with a fringe of marshy underbrush, briar patches, and spindly trees on each bank. The turnpike crossed Bull Run on an arched stone bridge, and although the stream was not wide, this little bridge was marvelously long just now; it connected two different time spans, running from the United States into a country which, for all anyone then knew, might not even exist; it spanned darkness and mystery, and in the Federals' camps it was widely believed that the bridge was heavily guarded and was mined for destruction.

At two o'clock on the morning of July 21 a bright moon shone down on the brown river, the white roadway, the green rolling countryside, and the unremarkable town of Centreville itself, and by its uncertain light there was a great stir and movement. The regiments of McDowell's army were forming up and moving down to the roadway, their polished muskets making a faint frosty glitter in the moonlight. They left small campfires burning, where they had cooked the earliest of breakfasts, and on every hillside these fires twinkled and blinked as men passed back and forth in front of them, harnessing six-horse teams for gun carriages and caissons, getting wagons and ambulances ready to move. An impressionable soldier who looked down on the scene said that the great column of soldiers seemed to fill the roadway without a break, flowing up, down, and along "like a bristling monster lifting himself by a slow, wavy motion." Troops which were to be held in reserve lined the roadside to watch, calling to the marching men to bring back souvenirs—a "traitor's scalp," for choice, or at the very least a palmetto button. The men who marched were full of state pride, and they bragged about the fine deeds which this day would be done by Massachusetts, or New York, or Ohio. Like the Southern boys whom they were about to meet, their feelings of loyalty and patriotism were translated ultimately in the homely terms of what a man could see from his own attic window. In each soldier's heart the nation was very small and intimate . . . big enough to be worth dying for, but familiar enough to be loved personally.[1]

The direct route from Centreville to Manassas ran off mainly south by west, crossing Bull Run by a number of fords —Mitchell's, Blackburn's, McLean's, Union Mills. Nearly all of Beauregard's army was waiting in this area, snugly posted behind the river in good defensive positions, and McDowell had no intention of making a head-on attack. He wanted to get beyond the Confederate left, which appeared to be anchored along the Warrenton Pike at the stone bridge, and so he had his men moving out at two in the morning in the flat white light of the moon, marching toward the positions from which they could take the Rebels by surprise. Some would be retained in the vicinity of Centreville, in reserve. A few would go down to the lower fords just to put in an appearance and make Beauregard think something was apt to happen there. A much larger contingent would move straight off for the stone bridge, under instructions to fire cannon and make other warlike noises, so that the Confederates on the left would look fixedly at the bridge and would pay no attention to anything that might be going on farther upstream.

Farther upstream was where things really would happen. McDowell would take 14,000 men off on a wide circle to the right, coming to Bull Run at a ford by a place known as Sudley Springs, several miles north and west of the stone bridge. Crossing here, this force could march south and come in well behind the Confederate flank, and if the job were done right, it ought to roll up the whole Confederate army like a rug. In addition, this flanking column could send parties over to break the railroad line that ran down from the Shenandoah Valley, thus keeping Johnston's men from coming to Beauregard's assistance.

It was a good plan, and it went into operation attended by equal parts of good luck and bad luck.

For good luck there was the fact that Beauregard so far had done just what McDowell would have wanted him to do. He had planned to use his own right to strike the Federal left flank, and although headquarters staff work right now was so hopelessly tangled that this movement would never get off the ground, the mere fact that it had been in contemplation meant that most of the Confederate army was massed on the right, where there was going to be no fighting at all. There were very few men up where the Yankee blow was about to land; hardly anyone, indeed, except for a rough-and-ready colonel from South Carolina named Nathan G. Evans, known to his old-army friends as Shanks, a West Point graduate and a former officer of dragoons. He was facing the stone bridge with two small regiments, a handful of cavalry, and a little artillery, possibly 1100 men in all, and unless he was both alert and tough there was nothing to keep McDowell's flank attack from doing just what McDowell wanted it to do.

For bad luck, there was the fact that Joe Johnston was already on hand. He out-ranked Beauregard and so he was in top command, although he had not been able to do much more than give a general approval to the dispositions that had already been made. He had brought some of his men with him, most notably a brigade of Virginia troops under Jackson. The rest of his men would come in during the day. (Poor old Patterson had been hopelessly fooled; he was up in the Harper's Ferry territory, no more than a corporal's guard of armed Confederates being within many miles of him.) As luck would have it, when Johnston's troops detrained, they would have good roads leading to the Confederate left, just where they could most effectively meet the Federal offensive.

So McDowell's army began to move, and its movement was as painful and as halting as all of the moves that had gone before. The flanking column came down from Centreville just behind the division of General Tyler, which was going

to make the big demonstration in front of the stone bridge,
and Tyler's men took a very long time getting past the cross-
roads where the route to Sudley Springs swung off to the right.
So the men in the divisions of S. P. Heintzelman and David
Hunter who were to be the main striking force, having been
pulled out of bed shortly after midnight, had to stand in the
road for hours before they had gone three miles from camp;
and after they got on the road that led upstream, things were
not a great deal better, and the hike was jerky, with spurts
of activity coming in between bewildering pauses. Daylight
came, and the soldiers saw that the meadows and bottom
lands were full of blackberry bushes, and they sauntered off
to pick the ripe berries on the sensible theory that they might
as well be doing this as standing around waiting. There was
supposed to be a place where the road forked, with the two
forks leading down to two separate fords, and the leading
division was supposed to go by the right-hand fork while the
second division took the one to the left; but the fork either
did not exist or it went completely unnoticed, and the whole
column went plowing on along one narrow road, and it was
eleven o'clock and after before the whole force was over Bull
Run.

Meanwhile, General Tyler moved up to the stream and early in the morning he opened fire—a slow, desultory cannon-
ade which did little more than announce that the Yankees had
got up early. Miles to the southeast, Johnston and Beauregard
waited at army headquarters, supposing that Beauregard's own
offensive would very soon be moving, recognizing in the firing
of Tyler's guns a demonstration and nothing more. But far off
to the left, Beauregard had a smart staff officer, Captain Edward Porter Alexander, of the Corps of Engineers, and
Alexander was prowling about full of curiosity and resentment, inspired by the fact that the second shell fired by Tyler's
gunners had ripped through the tent where Alexander was
sleeping. He saw the sunlight glittering from the muskets and
brass guns in the Federal columns and he wigwagged a message to warn Evans that the enemy was about to land on his
flank. Evans investigated, verified the report, and passed the
word on to headquarters, which was somewhat skeptical;
then, leaving four companies to watch the stone bridge—
where, he concluded, the Yankees were not trying to do anything in particular—Evans took the rest of his command and

two pieces of artillery over the fields to the north. By a little after nine o'clock he had his men drawn up on an open farm half a mile north of the turnpike, a regiment from South Carolina and another from Louisiana, and when the head of the Federal column appeared over the hills, these boys opened fire. After much jolting and creaking and many false starts, the war had at last begun.[2]

McDowell had made a good plan and except for delays here and there he was executing it tolerably well; but he was leading an army bigger than the one Winfield Scott had commanded in Mexico and neither he nor his subordinates knew quite how to go about it, and so the great attack came in by driblets, a series of well-intentioned taps rather than one heavy smash. The head of his column consisted of four regiments, one from New Hampshire, two from Rhode Island, and one from New York, the lot of them commanded by an imposing-looking colonel with magnificent sideburns, Ambrose E. Burnside, who was accompanied today by the wealthy young governor of Rhode Island, William Sprague. (In this innocent early morning of the war it seemed perfectly natural for a governor to accompany his state's troops, to encourage them, and perhaps to lend a hand with their leadership.) These soldiers had been on their feet for six hours and they were tired and hungry, and afterward they remembered the opening of the battle as slightly unreal. They had tramped past a cabin where an excited woman kept shouting that there were enough Confederates up ahead, including her own husband, to whip the lot of them, and when the firing began, the men were fascinated and a little appalled by the strange whirring noise the bullets were making just overhead. Getting from a long column of fours into a fighting line two ranks deep and four regiments wide was an intricate business, and Burnside's soldiers did it clumsily. One man fell off a rail fence and broke his bayonet, and others were showered with chaff and bits of dead grass when a shell blew up a haystack behind which they had been huddling; and when at last the men were deployed, they lay on their stomachs and began to return the Rebels' fire, shooting wildly but making an impressive racket.[3]

Shanks Evans's men were badly outnumbered and they were every bit as green as Burnside's, but they could hold their own against an attack no more resolute than this one.

Yet as the morning wore on, things got a good deal tougher. Two first-rate regular batteries reached the scene and began to hammer the Confederate line, and the sluggish Federal marching column was slowly but steadily pushing men up to the zone of action. (The colonel commanding one Federal division, a grumpy old regular named Samuel P. Heintzelman, noticed when he crossed at Sudley ford that there seemed to be no higher officers around to tell him what to do; he was even more disturbed to see, off to the west, immense clouds of smoke against the clear sky, and he believed that this meant that Johnston's army was coming in from the Shenandoah.)[4] Burnside's men managed to make two attacks and were knocked back, disorganized and through for the day, but other men were coming up to take their place, and Evans's men were badly cut up and out of order, too; and Evans, seeing at last that he could not stay where he was without help, sent back desperate appeals for reinforcements. Up to the rescue came a brigade from Johnston's army, men from Mississippi, Alabama, and North Carolina led by Brigadier General Barnard Bee, a first-rate soldier who had a certain gift for making a memorable phrase. Stiffened, the Southerners held, and from the rear, Confederate artillery began to pound the Federal advance.

Back by the ford McDowell was trying to add weight to his attack. He got Heintzelman's command forward, and he sent word downstream to Tyler to make more of a fight of it. The stone bridge itself struck Tyler as a bad place to cross, but half a mile above it he had a brigade led by cross-grained Sherman—the same who had been an unhappy bystander during the street fighting in St. Louis—and Sherman found a place where his men could wade across the river. He got them over, and brought them into the fight on the left of McDowell's line, other regiments from Tyler's command following him. The pressure grew heavier and heavier, and before noon the Confederates were overpowered. They ran back, going clear across the turnpike, splashing through a muddy creek known as Young's branch, and climbing the slope of an imposing hill to the south, a hill which took its name from a family named Henry, which had a farmhouse on the crest. Here they found help—South Carolina troops led by that legendary planter Wade Hampton, and a couple

of Georgia regiments under a Colonel Francis S. Bartow—
and on the level top of the hill they made a new line. Federal
skirmishers kept peppering them, and north of the turnpike
an overpowering mass of troops was obviously regrouping
for a new attack. If this Confederate line should break, the
whole Confederate flank would be gone and the Federals
would have won the battle.[5]

By this time the Confederate high command had caught on
to what was happening. Johnston had sent forward those
elements of his own army that were at hand; now he was seeing heavier and heavier dust clouds from the direction of
Sudley Springs, and he realized that the decisive action was
going to be fought near the turnpike, just west of the stone
bridge. He began to order troops from the right over to the
left, letting Beauregard's planned offensive collapse of its
own weight, and at last, growing more and more uneasy, he
gestured toward the north with a toss of his head and
snapped: "The battle is over there—I am going." He got on
his horse and went galloping toward the Henry house hill.
Beauregard (who had been having doubts of his own) delayed only long enough to order more of the men on the
right to go post-haste over to the left, and then mounted and
raced after him. Just before the two men got to the scene of
action, the five Virginia regiments led by Brigadier General
Jackson marched up and took position. Jackson carefully
posted them far enough away from the brow of the hill so
that the Federals would have to get all the way to the top
in order to shoot at them effectively.[6]

From the Confederate right to the left was a long way, the
roads were bad, and the day was very hot, and the raw Confederate regiments hurrying over to get into the fight were
no better at cross-country marching than the Yankees had
been. Men tramping forward with fixed bayonets broke ranks
to go out in the fields and eat blackberries. (No one ever tal-
lied the number of boys who died that day with blackberry
stains on their lips; it would make a good footnote to military history, if the proper figures could ever be gathered.)
The on-coming Confederates stopped to drink at little brooks,
they gaped at the wounded men who were drifting to the
rear, and they plodded on through dust so thick that no man
could see much more than the back of the man in front of

him. (One officer, seeing from a hill top a billowing dust cloud off to the northwest, where the road from the Shenandoah came in, believed that this meant that Patterson's Federals were coming in, and felt that the battle probably was lost.) In effect, Johnston and Beauregard were trying to realign their entire army in the middle of a battle and it was slow work. The whole fight had suddenly become a struggle for the Henry hill; it was being waged, on both sides, by boys who were tired, hot, and thirsty, who in all of the marching had lost all sense of direction.[7]

On the hill top the tempo was picking up after a brief lull. It was close to noon now, and the Federal line was very long; those two fine regular batteries were firing effectively, the Federal regiments were edging forward, and the Confederate line wavered. Evans's weary brigade was disorganized, and Bee's men were sagging toward the rear; they suffered, apparently, from the weakness common to all green troops—the tendency to fire and then to drop back a few feet before reloading for another volley—and Bartow was appealing to the pride of his two regiments. Flag in his hand, he cried out: "General Beauregard says you must hold this position —Georgians, I appeal to you to hold on!" Then a Yankee bullet found him and he fell dead. An increasing number of men from the firing line drifted back to a little ravine, and Beauregard was there, rallying them; a Federal shell exploded under his horse, killing the animal, leaving the general unhurt. Farther to the rear, Johnston was trying to get fresh troops up to the line; and the Henry house plateau was full of smoke and crashing noise and sudden death, with the Federals visibly gaining the upper hand. If Beauregard could stiffen his men enough to hold on until the men Johnston was calling showed up, well and good; if he could not, disaster was at hand.[8]

Then came a dramatic moment, to live in legend, giving the American story one of its unforgettable names. Of the 6000 Confederate soldiers on this broad hill top, at least half had lost their organization and were out of the fight; only Jackson's brigade and Wade Hampton's South Carolinians remained in line, waiting for the final onslaught. General Bee was trying desperately to reorganize his men; all of his field officers were down, and he seemed to command no more than a fragment, and he rode to Jackson and said, despairingly: "General, they are beating us back." Wholly unperturbed, Jackson replied: "Sir, we will give them the bayonet." Bee rode off through the smoke to an unwieldy tangle of stragglers, stood erect in his stirrups, and gestured with his sword to the solidity of Jackson's brigade. "Look!" he shouted. "There is Jackson standing like a stone wall! Rally behind the Virginians!"

It was Bee's final contribution. A bullet struck him in the abdomen, knocking him off his horse with a mortal wound; but at least some of his men responded and sorted themselves out into a fighting line, and the rallying cry was always remembered. Jackson would be Stonewall, thence forward and forever.[9]

Later in the war, after he had become very famous, Jackson insisted that the nickname really belonged to his brigade rather than to himself; it was the firmness of the men in the ranks, he said, that saved the day on the Henry house hill, and after Jackson's death the Confederate government officially designated this unit the Stonewall Brigade. Yet the instinct that led men to give the name to the general was sound, for this was a battle in which—more, perhaps, than in any other fight in the war—much depended on the brigade and division commanders. The soldiers themselves were first-rate men, but they were pitifully untrained, and they needed leadership far more than battle-tested veterans would ever need it. In most units, in both armies, the leadership which ordinarily comes from company and field officers was almost non-existent. In the blind turmoil of battle, companies and regiments were fragmented and lost; they had to have a man on horseback to pull them together and tell them what to do. Jackson's Virginians were not better men than the confused thousands all about them—except that they had Jackson. With him, they were a stone wall, immovable in a dissolving world.

. . . Wholly characteristic is the adventure that befell young Captain Delaware Kemper, who commanded a Virginia battery off on the Confederate left. Momentarily detached from his battery, Captain Kemper stumbled into the middle of a Yankee regiment in a smoke-filled thicket and he was ordered, with a dozen muskets leveled at him, to surrender. He replied that he would give up his sword to a qualified officer, but his captors explained that all of their officers had vanished and they did not know where to find any others. Stiffly, Captain Kemper insisted that he would surrender only to an officer; and so he and the Yankees set off through the woods to find one—blundering, at last, into a Confederate regiment, which released Captain Kemper and sent the unofficered Federals off in headlong flight.[10]

Mid-afternoon came, and of the 18,000 Federals who had crossed the river, McDowell was able to get perhaps 10,000 lined up for an assault on the Henry house hill. He was isolated from the rest of his army; Tyler never did manage to force his way across the stone bridge, although a good many of his men had gone across by Sherman's ford, and there was an open gap between the attacking column and the troops east of Bull Run. The gap could have been closed. Tyler's troops could have swept across the bridge without great trouble, and upstream Burnside's soldiers lay idle in a safe wooded hollow, resting from their morning's work; they could have marched downstream almost unopposed, uncovering the bridge and linking the two halves of the army. It seems to have occurred to no one that these things ought to be done.

At last McDowell's line moved forward. There were four brigades in line, and yet the assault was made by separate regiments, rather than by one solid mass; try as they would, McDowell's officers seemed unable to bring their brigades in as co-ordinated units. To stiffen the attack, McDowell sent those two regular batteries forward, instructing their commanders, Captains J. B. Ricketts and Charles Griffin, to get onto the high ground just south of the Henry house and pound the Confederate line at close range. Ricketts and Griffin did as they were told, but they got ahead of the line of infantry and were exposed to a deadly fire of musketry, some of which came from infantrymen who huddled behind the Henry house, which stood near the brow of the hill. The Federal gunners fired a few rounds at the house to dislodge them; in the process they killed eighty-four-year-old Mrs. Judith Henry, mistress of the house, who lay a helpless invalid in one of the bedrooms and who died when shells crashed through the walls and exploded in her bedroom.[11]

Federal infantry was sent forward to support the batteries,

Ellsworth's famous Fire Zouaves and a battalion of United States Marines, but Jeb Stuart had brought his Virginia cavalry regiment down from the valley and he led a hot charge along the turnpike, crashing straight through the Fire Zouaves and scattering them. The marine detachment was composed wholly of recruits who had been in service no more than three weeks, and when Confederate fire hit them, they broke and ran for the rear. Gruff Heintzelman tried to rally the fleeing Zouaves and marines but could not; he wrote afterward that the men would run a hundred yards, turn around and fire wildly toward the front, and then run some more, their discipline wholly gone. A Confederate regiment in blue uniforms came close to the Federal guns, which held their fire, thinking these men were Northerners; the Confederates fired a volley at close range, and a Union officer watching the business from afar through field glasses wrote that "it seemed as though every man and horse of that battery just laid right down and died right off."[12]

McDowell himself was on the hill top now, climbing to the upper floor of the Henry house for a better view. His men crossed the plateau, were driven back, reformed, tried it again. Off to the west new Union brigades crossed the turnpike and marched up the valley to outflank the Confederate line, and it seemed as if Union victory might be at hand. But the attack was much less solid than it looked. A Confederate officer coming to the front met a friend and asked how things were going, and was given the confident answer. "Them Yankees are just marchin' up and bein' shot to hell." A newspaper correspondent in the Confederate ranks scribbled that "for one long mile the whole valley is a boiling crater of dust and smoke," and in this murky fog the Union advance wholly lost its cohesion. Strong Confederate reinforcements came up on the left: Jubal Early's brigade, from Beauregard's right, and a brigade from Johnston's army led by Edmund Kirby Smith, just off the train. These got on the flank of the Federal advance and crumpled it. Beauregard led a counter-attack across the Henry house hill, the Federal batteries were overrun—and suddenly the whole Union army was in retreat, heading for the fords and safety.[13]

McDowell and his officers did their best to reorganize the men and make a stand, but the effort was hopeless. These untrained regiments had simply been used beyond their capacity and they had fallen apart. One officer estimated that by this time there were more than 12,000 Federals on the field who had entirely lost their regimental organization; they could no longer be handled as troops because men and officers were not together. Captain D. P. Woodbury, of the Corps of Engineers, noted the profound difference between veterans and raw recruits: "An old soldier feels safe in the ranks, unsafe out of the ranks, and the greater the danger the more pertinaciously he clings to his place. The volunteer of three months never attains this instinct of discipline. Under danger and even under mere excitement he flies away from his ranks and looks for safety in dispersion." The vast majority now was looking for safety, and there was nothing McDowell or anyone else could do but try to herd the disorganized crowd back out of range.[14]

As a matter of fact, much the same sort of thing had happened to a good part of the Confederate army. Porter Alexander, riding to the rear just after the moment of victory, wrote that he found so many panicky stragglers behind the lines that he would have believed the Confederates had been defeated if he had not already seen them winning. President Jefferson Davis came up from Richmond, reaching Manassas and leaving the cars just about the time when the tide was turning, and he got the same impression. To a mounted aide he remarked grimly that "fields are not won where men desert their colors as ours are doing," and as he rode through a dense throng of displaced soldiers near a field hospital, he undertook to rally the men, crying: "I am President Davis! Follow me back to the field!" Stonewall Jackson was near by, getting a wound in his hand dressed. His doctor told him what the President was saying, and Jackson shouted: "We have whipped them! They ran like sheep! Give me 5000 fresh men and I will be in Washington City tomorrow!"

A Confederate battery drew up on the turnpike to hammer the retreating Federals. Riding along on one of the gun carriages was indomitable old Edmund Ruffin, who had hiked by himself all the way over from his post on the Confederate right, carrying his musket. When the first gun was unlimbered, the gunners asked the old man to fire it. He jerked the lanyard, and planted a shell in the middle of a flying tangle of Federal soldiers who were running madly for the rear.[15]

6. Death of the Minute Man

PROBABLY IT would not have been quite so bad if the battle had not been fought on a Sunday. Because it was Sunday a great many people in Washington had nothing to do, and numbers of these precious folk had taken carriages, packed lunches, and ridden down through Centreville to make a picnic where they could have the pleasure of watching a battle. They had been coming down all morning and they had planted themselves on the easy slopes between Bull Run and the little brook known as Cub Run, a mile or so east of the battlefield, and there they stayed through the long afternoon, unable to see much except for the rising billows of gun smoke and the casual coming and going of military traffic along the highway, hearing the great crash of battle and entertaining themselves with the exchange of groundless rumors. Among them were Union officers who, having in one way or another got lost from their commands, elected to stay here among the holiday-makers, offering portentous explanations of the goings-on from which they had disengaged themselves. Many ladies were present, in their brightest summer frocks. Also present, by the best estimate one can make, were six United States Senators and at least ten Congressmen.

These holiday-makers were there, in substantial numbers, because it never occurred to the authorities to keep them from coming. They were there because curiosity and the strange notion that war was an exciting pageant had led them to suppose that it might be stimulating to watch (from a safe seat in the gallery) while young men killed one another. They were there, in short, because America did not yet know what it was all about; and because they were there they contributed mightily to the fact that an overstrained army driven from the field in defeat dissolved into a wild and disorderly rout which no man could stop.

At first it was just a retreat—broken, out of control, dismaying to the eye of a regular soldier, but a retreat rather than a screaming runaway. The men who had been driven from the Henry house hill and from the wooded country to the west were so confused and disorganized that it was impossible to get them to do any more fighting, but they had not fallen into self-accelerating panic. They had simply had all they were going to take, and they wanted to get back to some place where people would no longer be shooting at them, some place where they could sort themselves out, get something to eat and drink, and, above all things, lie down for a while. Some of them waded Bull Run where Sherman's brigade had crossed at noon, and the rest went up to the Sudley ford and came back roundabout, and they moved with an odd, beaten-up, almost casual briskness—not losing any time, but not exactly running, either. They had a rear guard—a regiment of regular infantry, a little cavalry, and a good battery—and the Confederates were not pressing them very hard. McDowell sent over to his far left, east of the little river, and brought up Louis Blenker's brigade and other troops to keep the Rebels from surging over the stone bridge, and he believed that at Centreville he could perhaps pull things together and make a stand.[1]

But although it was only three miles from the bridge to Centreville, they were very bad miles and bad things happened on them. The picnickers had been noticing that increasing numbers of stragglers were drifting back along the highway, and as late afternoon came, these clotted groups got bigger and thicker, grimy men slouching along with or without weapons, accompanied by lumbering caissons, battery wagons, guns, and drifting white-topped wagons, moving with a little more urgency, overflowing at times from the road into the fields. It began to occur to the spectators that it would be well to get home, and the holiday carriages came wheeling down from the hillsides to get into the road; and before long the highway was full and there was a fine traffic jam in the making. The jam came, at last, partly by enemy action and partly by spontaneous combustion. Exultant Confederates near the stone bridge were firing cannon now and then, and one shell—it may have been the one fired by old man Ruffin himself—came arching in over everything and wrecked a wagon in the middle of the little bridge by which the main highway crossed Cub Run.

The bridge was blocked. Drivers on the Centreville side of it whipped up their horses to get out of danger, and drivers on the Bull Run side incontinently did the same, getting guns and wagons and carriages into a complete tangle, with horses rearing and kicking, teamsters swearing, ladies from Wash-

ington beginning to scream, the press of civilian vehicles constantly feeding in new elements which killed any faint hope
that this traffic jam could be resolved. Some carriages trundled down to the little stream, lurched up on the far side,
and made off for Washington as fast as maddened horses
could take them. Here and there a mounted officer took fire
along with all the rest and tried to ride through everything
at a bucketing gallop. People who were moving on foot began to run, and off to the rear frightened men were yelling
that Confederate cavalry was coming up to kill and maim—
and, all at once, utter panic descended on everybody in
sight.

The great drifting mass of fugitive soldiers, already out
from under what little discipline they had ever known, moved
faster and faster and became a wild, frantic, scrambling mob
which generated its own unendurable pressure. Teamsters
cut their horses loose and scrambled on their backs to ride
to safety, leaving guns, caissons, and military supplies for
anyone who cared to pick them up. Ambulances carrying
wounded men to hospitals were left by the roadside. Soldiers
who had thought they were too exhausted to do more than
put one heavy foot in front of another found they could run
very nimbly, and they dropped whatever they were carrying
—muskets, haversacks, canteens, anything—so that they
could run even faster. It was gabbled up and down the wild
rout that armed Rebels were close behind; for some odd
reason, the pursuing Confederates, believed to be as ruthless
as Cossacks, were all thought to be riding black horses and
frightened men were forever shouting: "Black horse cavalry!
Black horse cavalry!"[2]

McDowell still had troops fit for service. Colonel Theodore
Runyon's division, 5000 men or more, had been held in reserve east of Centreville, and it was brought forward to this
little town and posted on the hill there, along with twenty
guns. Blenker's brigade, bringing up the rear, was in good
order, and there were other usable formations from what had
been the extreme left. Major George Sykes came in with his
battalion of regulars, men dead on their feet but still in good
order. A little before six in the evening McDowell sent a wire
to Washington, explaining that he had been driven from the
battlefield and adding that "we have now to hold Centreville
until our men can get behind it." But the men who got be-

hind Centreville refused to stop, and a little later McDowell was compelled to report: "The larger part of the men are a confused mob, entirely demoralized. It was the opinion of all the commanders that no stand could be made this side of the Potomac." Still later he had to admit that efforts to pull the army together at Fairfax Court House had failed; "many of the volunteers did not wait for authority to proceed to the Potomac but left on their own decision." There was nothing for it, he confessed, but to fall back all the way to Arlington and dig in to hold the Potomac River bridges.[3] By far the bigger part of his army had simply gone out of existence and it would be days before it could be reconstituted.

In Washington, General Scott sent word to McDowell that he was getting reinforcements and wrote stoutly: "We are not discouraged." But the dimensions of the disaster were visibly expanding, and the old general became genuinely alarmed. The navy was asked to send a warship over to Alexandria to command the Potomac with its guns. Authorities in New York and Pennsylvania were urged to send troops forward as quickly as possible. The commander of troops at Baltimore was alerted, lest that city rise in open revolt. To McClellan, far off in the Virginia mountains, went an order to move over into the Shenandoah Valley at once "and make head against the enemy in that quarter." This was countermanded, a few hours later, and McClellan was told to stay where he was until further notice; reinforcements would be sent to him from Ohio. Then, at two o'clock in the morning, a third wire went to McClellan: "Circumstances make your presence here necessary. Charge Rosecrans or some other general with your present department and come hither without delay." McDowell's defeat was beyond remedy. The government wanted a winner.[4]

Meanwhile the jubilant Confederates were taking stock of their victory and were trying to see whether it could not be made even bigger. The last of the beaten Federals were driven from the field of battle, cavalry was ordered forward to harass the retreat, and from the extreme right, troops were told to move up to Centreville with all speed. Yet there was a good deal of confusion, most of it arising from the fact that to an untrained army, overwhelming victory can be almost as great a shock as overwhelming defeat. False reports of a Union counter-stroke caused the troops on the right to do a good deal of useless maneuvering, and when the misunderstanding was cleared up it was too late and too dark to do anything. On the main highway the "black horse cavalry" which had caused so much panic was not actually strong enough to overpower McDowell's rear guard. The squadrons reached the site of the original traffic jam at Cub Run, seized the military booty which had been abandoned there, captured large numbers of stragglers (including one life-sized U. S. Congressman, who was sent off to Richmond), and in the end could do little more than speed the departing Federals on their way. At Johnston's headquarters President Davis met with Johnston and Beauregard and other officers to appraise what had been gained and to see whether anything more could be done.

The victory looked big enough, in all conscience. Mr. Davis wired the War Department that "our forces have won a glorious victory," saying without exaggeration that "the enemy was routed and fled precipitately" with heavy loss. Beauregard recorded the capture of twenty-eight guns, thirty-seven caissons, a huge quantity of ammunition, and seemingly endless amounts of small arms, accouterments, blankets, hospital stores, haversacks, wagons, ambulances, and other valuable items. Something like 1300 prisoners had been taken. There were a great many dead Yankees on the field—close to 500 of them, it would develop, when all the returns were in—and there was something about the way in which McDowell's offensive had collapsed which led the more hopeful to feel that Southern independence had been just about gained.[5]

The high command was not deceived. Both Beauregard and Johnston knew that their army had had a very rough time of it; to organize, within an hour or two, an effective force that could drive on through the night in real pursuit seemed to them out of the question. Still, if the President ordered it, they would try it.

Mr. Davis was disposed to order it. Around eleven o'clock a staff officer came in bearing a report from another officer who said that he had gone all the way to Centreville and who reported that the Yankees were rushing through that hamlet in a state of total panic; and Mr. Davis dictated an order for immediate pursuit. Then came second thoughts. Someone recalled that the officer who sent in this report was an old army man whose nickname had always been "Crazy"— an eccentric, given to wild excitement, not altogether to be trusted. The dictated order was not issued. It was agreed, finally, that at dawn infantry should be sent forward to make a reconnaissance in force, and the conference came to an end. The victorious army would rest. Later it could move on and occupy the territory which the Federals were so hastily abandoning.[6]

There was much argument about this, later on. In the light of fuller knowledge it came to seem that the war might really have been won then and there if the routed Federals had been pressed vigorously. Stonewall Jackson had said that with 5000 fresh troops he could be in Washington by the next day, and although he went unheard at the time— and even if he had been heard, he then lacked the stature to make his words listened to—many Confederates eventually came to believe that inaction on the night of July 21 had wasted a glorious victory. In the end it was even held that it was President Davis who was chiefly responsible.

The thing can be seen more clearly now, with much hindsight, than it could be seen then, and it appears that the Confederacy really lost very little. Washington was not actually open to a sudden easy capture by any force that could have been brought against it on July 22 or July 23. Most of McDowell's army had indeed been blown apart, but even on the night of the disastrous retreat he still had close to 10,000 men who had fought little or not at all, who were still responsive to as much discipline as any volunteer army then possessed, and who had not given way to panic. The Potomac at Washington is wide and deep, and if Johnston's army was to enter the capital, it would have to use the bridges. Enough troops were at hand to hold those bridges until reinforcements could come down from the North. Johnston could have had his army follow on McDowell's heels, but almost certainly he could have done little more than he finally did do—occupy the Centreville ridge in force, build fortifications there, hold the place throughout the winter, and keep his outposts close enough to the Potomac so that on clear days they could see the unfinished dome of the Capitol building. The notion that the Confederate army could have walked into Washington within twenty-four hours will hardly bear analysis.[7]

Yet it was the wild, unreasoning panic of the Union army that was remembered, and the memory of it became an important factor in the war which had at last begun. Because there had been this panic, publicly displayed for all to see, burning deep into the consciousness of an overconfident people, things hereafter would be done differently. Nothing less than this, probably, could have stirred the North so profoundly. When the helpless fighting lines sagged away from the murky slopes of the Henry house hill and streamed off to look for safety, the country at last began to wake up to reality.

Washington saw the worst of it. The sorry picnic crowd which came back all bedraggled and frightened had seen none of the valor and endurance which the soldiers had displayed on the field of battle. They had seen only the disgraceful runaway, to which by their own presence they had contributed so greatly, and their stories lost nothing in the telling. Most of the newspaper correspondents had been caught up in the rout—among them Mr. Russell, of the London *Times*, who wrote so graphically about what he had seen that Northerners denounced him as a defeatist and a pro-Confederate—and their accounts showed the beaten army at its worst. Furthermore, all of the broken troops hurried straight to Washington, where everyone could see them. They came shambling in all through July 22 while a sullen rain came down, each man a visible proof of disaster, sauntering in singly, in disordered squads, downcast, streaked with dirt, almost out of their heads with weariness, a huge audience watching each and all.

Walt Whitman wrote that the downtown streets were crowded with civilians, who stared in silence at this formless procession. At least half of the lookers-on, he said, were secessionists, grinning triumphantly. By noon Washington was "all over motley with these defeated soldiers—queer-looking objects, strange eyes and faces, drench'd (the steady rain drizzles on all day) and fearfully worn, hungry, haggard, blister'd in the feet." Some people set out food and drink, standing in the rain for hours to give hungry men refreshment; yet most of the soldiers seemed to want rest more than anything else. They flopped down on sidewalks, on the steps

of houses, on vacant lots, in the lee of fences and store buildings, and fell asleep in the rain. The barrooms meanwhile began to fill with officers, each one reciting his own story of
catastrophe, each one (since men are human) putting the
guilt off his own shoulders and blaming other people. The
crush at Willard's roused Whitman's special wrath. "There
you are, shoulder-straps!" he wrote. "But where are your
companies? Where are your men? Incompetents! never tell of
chances of battle, of getting stray'd, and the like. I think
this is your work, this retreat, after all. Sneak, blow, put on
airs, there in Willard's sumptuous parlors and barrooms, or
anywhere—no explanation shall save you. Bull Run is your
work; had you been half or one-tenth worth your men, this
would never have happened."[8]

There was some point to Whitman's remarks. The Union
army had actually done as well as anyone had any right to
expect, and if at last it had collapsed, the fault lay much
more with its company and regimental officers than with the
men in the ranks. More than a fourth of the army had never
been put into action at all. The ones who did fight lost between 450 and 500 in killed, more than 1100 men wounded,
and between 1500 and 1800 missing in action—captured,
most of these latter, many of them wounded, a few of them
killed. By the bloody standards of later battles these losses
were not excessive, but they were not light, either; for troops
that were almost totally unready for battle, they were extremely impressive. Confederate losses were smaller, but they
were equally impressive. Between one fourth and one third
of the Confederate army had not fought at all; the casualty
list ran to about 400 killed, more than 1500 wounded, and
thirteen missing. The battle had lasted for more than seven
hours. On both sides it had been fought by men so poorly
trained that it was almost impossible for them to maneuver
under fire. The wonder is, not that the affair broke up in a
rout, but that it lasted as long as it did and was fought with
so much courage and determination.[9]

What Washington saw the whole country saw. To timid
people, the defeat and the rout looked like the end of everything. Horace Greeley, who had shouted "Forward to Richmond!" so long and so hard that McDowell's advance had
come to seem a move undertaken to satisfy an editor, was
unhinged by the news. A week after the battle he wrote Lin-

coln a letter full of almost incoherent woe. He suspected that the cause was lost. "On every brow," he cried, "sits sullen, scorching, black despair. . . . If it is best for the country and for mankind that we make peace with the Rebels at once and on their own terms, do not shrink even from that." He confessed himself "hopelessly broken," and begged the President to tell him what he should do. His state of mind was all the worse, perhaps, because for two days his New York *Tribune* had been playing up the battle as a great Union victory. When he got around to editorializing on the subject, he wrote: "We have fought and been beaten. God forgive our rulers that this is so; but it is true, and cannot be disguised." He demanded that the cabinet be dismissed so that the President could have better advisers, and concluded with an optimism which he did not feel: "Our banner, now drooping, will soon float once more in triumph over the whole land. With the right men to lead, our people will show themselves unconquerable. Onward, then, to victory and glory."[10]

Fortunately for the Union cause, Greeley's reaction was not typical. A Connecticut clergyman, in a sermon delivered a week after Bull Run, preached from a text in Proverbs, asserting that "adversity kills only where there is a weakness to be killed," and paid his respects to the likes of Greeley in bitter words: "We want no newspaper government, and least of all a newspaper army. . . . Let the government govern, and the army fight, and let both have their own counsel, disturbed and thrown out of balance by no gusty conceit or irresponsible and fanatical clamor."[11]

The government would govern: its first task being to make certain that the panic which had broken up first the army and then Horace Greeley should not also infect the administration. This task it met quickly. On the night after the battle, when President and cabinet members sat down with General Scott to assess the news, somebody brought in a report that the victorious Rebels had occupied Arlington and would soon be in Washington itself, and old General Scott met this head-on. "It is impossible, sir!" he exploded. "We are now tasting the first fruits of a war and learning what a panic is. We must be prepared for all kinds of rumors. Why, sir, we shall soon hear that Jefferson Davis has crossed the Long Bridge at the head of a brigade of elephants and is trampling our citizens under foot! He has no brigade of elephants: he cannot by any possibility get a brigade of elephants!" Lincoln himself spent a sleepless night, but his first-hand knowledge of disaster simply strengthened his determination to get on with the war. John Nicolay reflected the President's attitude when he wrote to his wife, two days after the defeat: "The fat is all in the fire now and we shall have to crow small until we can retrieve the disgrace somehow. The preparations for the war will be continued with increased vigor by the Government."[12]

The first task was to make Washington safe and to reassemble the army. The War Department established rallying points for the nucleus of each broken regiment and announced that rations would be issued at those points and nowhere else—on the sensible theory that the hungry men would at least go to the spots where they knew they would be fed. State governors sent forward new troops in response to urgent appeals, and within twenty-four hours Secretary Cameron was able to reassure a citizens' committee in New York: "The Department is making vigorous efforts to concentrate at this point an overwhelming force, and the response from all quarters had been truly patriotic. A number of regiments have arrived since last evening. There is no danger of the capital nor of the Republic." Lincoln and Seward crossed the river to inspect the troops that held the Arlington lines. When they returned to Washington, Lincoln got pencil and paper and wrote out his own program for the immediate future—the basis of it, apparently, a set of notes he had scribbled on the night the news of the defeat first reached him. He was an unmilitary man, called on now to solve an immense military problem, and his memorandum reflected his own inexperience and his insistence that the country get itself organized for a real war. It read:

"1. Let the plan for making the Blockade effective be pushed forward with all possible despatch.

"2. Let the volunteer forces at Fort Monroe & vicinity—under Genl. Butler—be constantly drilled, disciplined, and instructed without more for the present.

"3. Let Baltimore be held, as now, with a gentle, but firm, and certain hand.

"4. Let the force now under Patterson, or Banks, be strengthened, and made secure in its position.

"5. Let Gen. Frémont push forward his organization, and operations in the West as rapidly as possible, giving rather special attention to Missouri." [John Charles Frémont, the famous "Pathfinder" of the West and the Republican party's candidate for President in 1856, had been made major general and ordered to St. Louis to take charge of the western theater of operations.]

"6. Let the forces late before Manassas, except the three months men, be reorganized as rapidly as possible, in their camps here and about Arlington.

"7. Let the three months forces, who decline to enter the longer service, be discharged as rapidly as circumstances will permit.

"8. Let the new volunteer forces be brought forward as fast as possible, and especially into the camps on the two sides of the river here."

Four days later he wrote a postscript to this program:

"When the foregoing shall have been substantially attended to—

"1. Let Manassas Junction (or some point on one or the other of the railroads near it) and Strasburg, be seized, and permanently held, with an open line from Harper's Ferry to Strasburg—the military men to find the way of doing these.

"2. This done, a joint movement from Cairo on Memphis; and from Cincinnati on East Tennessee."[13]

Some of these things could be done at once, and some of them could not be done for a long time, but at least the President was blocking out a program for action. Stanton might indeed be writing, as he was, to ex-President Buchanan that "the imbecility of the Administration" had brought on misfortune and disgrace, and that the administration probably would not be reorganized properly "until Jefferson Davis turns out the whole concern,"[14] but things were beginning to move. Out of catastrophe the government, with the support of the people back home, was settling down to make real war.

It was the beginning of wisdom; wisdom paid for by tragedy and disillusion, with later increments to be bought in the same way. Scott had complained that the thrust at Manassas was an attempt to make war by piece-meal, but he had not been listened to; too many men had supposed that the war would be won by the ninety-day recruit, the fabulous

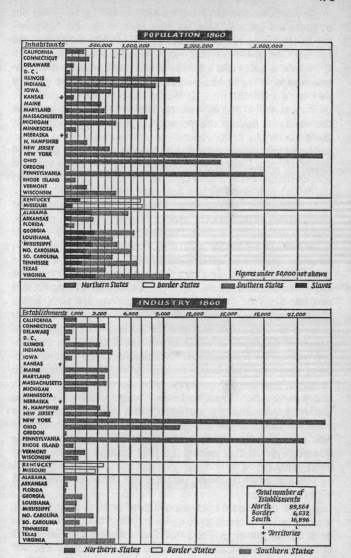

POPULATION 1860

Inhabitants 500,000 1,000,000 2,000,000 3,000,000

CALIFORNIA
CONNECTICUT
DELAWARE
D. C.
ILLINOIS
INDIANA
IOWA
KANSAS +
MAINE
MARYLAND
MASSACHUSETTS
MICHIGAN
MINNESOTA
NEBRASKA +
N. HAMPSHIRE
NEW JERSEY
NEW YORK
OHIO
OREGON
PENNSYLVANIA
RHODE ISLAND
VERMONT
WISCONSIN
KENTUCKY
MISSOURI
ALABAMA
ARKANSAS
FLORIDA
GEORGIA
LOUISIANA
MISSISSIPPI
NO. CAROLINA
SO. CAROLINA
TENNESSEE
TEXAS
VIRGINIA

Figures under 50,000 not shown

▨ Northern States   ▢ Border States   ▨ Southern States   ■ Slaves

INDUSTRY 1860

Establishments 1,000 3,000 6,000 9,000 12,000 15,000 18,000 21,000

CALIFORNIA
CONNECTICUT
DELAWARE
D. C.
ILLINOIS
INDIANA
IOWA
KANSAS +
MAINE
MARYLAND
MASSACHUSETTS
MICHIGAN
MINNESOTA
NEBRASKA +
N. HAMPSHIRE
NEW JERSEY
NEW YORK
OHIO
OREGON
PENNSYLVANIA
RHODE ISLAND
VERMONT
WISCONSIN
KENTUCKY
MISSOURI
ALABAMA
ARKANSAS
FLORIDA
GEORGIA
LOUISIANA
MISSISSIPPI
NO. CAROLINA
SO. CAROLINA
TENNESSEE
TEXAS
VIRGINIA

Total number of
Establishments
North   99,564
Border   6,532
South   16,896
+ Territories

▨ Northern States   ▢ Border States   ▨ Southern States

minute man who would leave his plow in the furrow, rush out
to smite the foe, and then go back and get on with his plowing as if nothing had happened. That hope had been trampled
to death by the mob that came streaming back from Cub
Run to the sidewalks of Washington, and it was dead beyond hope of resurrection. Never again would the country
rely on the minute man. It would have to rely hereafter on
its own strength and endurance, taking the time to organize
the strength, finding the patience to use it, summoning up
from the depths of its collective soul the dedication to go on
to the end no matter what the end might be. Out of Bull Run
would come an effort so prodigious that simply to make it
would change America forever. In the dust and smoke along
the Warrenton Road an era had come to an end.

In Richmond the victory was received with deep but quiet
thanksgiving. The cheering crowds, the clanging church bells,
and the thunderous salutes that had greeted the fall of Fort
Sumter and the act of secession were not in evidence; the
sense of relief and reborn confidence apparently went too
deep. The Confederate Congress solemnly resolved "that we
recognize the hand of the Most High God, the King of Kings
and the Lord of Lords, in the glorious victory with which
He hath crowned our arms," and Editor E. A. Pollard felt
that the look in men's eyes and the joy in men's hearts "composed an eloquence to which words would have been a mockery." Generals Johnston and Beauregard issued a joint statement thanking the people of the South "for that patriotic
courage, that heroic gallantry, that devoted daring" which
had won the day. The Charleston *Courier* admitted that "the
enemy fought bravely and well," but asserted that "their
valor could not resist the courage of men under the inspira-
tion of a grand and holy cause." Savoring the victory, many
Southerners felt that everything they wanted had practically
been gained.[15]

Too many felt that way, perhaps. Bull Run gave the North
a reawakening, but it gave the South overconfidence; the
legend of the minute man seemed here to have been verified,
and there was a good deal of feeling that he now might get
back to his plowing. President Davis wrote long afterward
that "members of Congress, and notably the Vice President"
(between whom and Mr. Davis there was at last little love
lost) "contended that the men should be allowed to go home

and attend to their private affairs while there were no active operations, and that there was no doubt but that they would return whenever there was to be a battle." General Johnston wrote confidentially to Davis that the victory had temporarily disorganized his army: "Everybody, officer & private, seemed to think that he had fulfilled all his obligations to country—& that before attending to any further call of duty, it was his privilege to look after his friends, procure trophies, or amuse himself. It was several days after you left us before the regiments who really fought could be reassembled." Mr. Trescot, who had held a watching brief for South Carolina in Washington early in the winter, said angrily that the victory would be the country's ruin.[16]

Yet there was, under this, a growing understanding of the terrible reality of war. Robert E. Lee wrote to a cousin that the South would continue the war "as long as there is one horse that can carry his rider & one arm to wield a sword." He added, grimly: "I prefer annihilation to submission. They may destroy but I trust will never conquer us."[17] Wounded men were brought back to Richmond: only a few, compared with the dreadful floods to come later in the war, but many more than the people of Richmond had ever expected to see. The first ambulance trains entered the city at twilight in a pelting rain, and men and women who knew only that there had been a glorious victory came out and saw for themselves what glory and victory could cost. The walking wounded were stumbling along beside the ambulances, heads bandaged or arms in slings, sometimes helped by a comrade. Then the men on stretchers were carried out, maimed and soiled, pallid, staring at nothing, gripping the side bars of their stretchers to keep from crying out; and the people stood and watched, while lanterns flickered in the wet dusk and there was little sound but the ambulance wheels on the stones, the unbroken drip of the rain, and here and there a quick exclamation from someone in the crowd who saw a friend.[18]

There were the dead to be brought back as well: the dead, and the news of their dying. Even while the city hummed with the talk of victory, Varina Davis had to go and tell Mrs. Bartow that Colonel Bartow had been killed. (It seems the man had had a premonition; before the battle he told Tom Cobb he knew that he would die.) Mrs. Bartow saw the truth in her caller's eyes and sank down on a chair, pulling a shawl over her face, asking quietly: "Is it bad news for me? . . . Is he dead?" A day or two later the colonel's body was carried through the streets to the cemetery, a military band playing a dirge, riderless horse with stirrups crossed in an empty saddle following the coffin, Mrs. Bartow fainting at the sight. There were many funerals; Mary Chesnut wrote that "it seems we are never out of the sound of the Dead March in Saul."[19]

On the Northern side, too, there had been men who had foreknowledge of their own death, and there were women to mourn. Major Sullivan Bullen, of Illinois, was killed in the battle, and just before it he had written to his wife, Sarah, to tell her that he believed he was going to be killed and to express a tremulous faith that could see a gleam of light in the dark: "But O Sarah! if the dead can come back to this earth and float unseen around those they loved, I shall always be near you in the gladdest days and in the gloomiest nights, advised to your happiest scenes and gloomiest nights, *always, always,* and if there be a soft breeze upon your chest it shall be my breath, as the cool air fans your throbbing temple it shall be my spirit passing by. Sarah do not mourn me dead; think I am gone and wait, for we shall meet again."[20]

Hundreds of thousands of women, before the war ended, would feel as Mrs. Bartow and Mrs. Bullen felt. Bull Run was an incident, a beginning, a warning that people all across the land must draw on their deepest reserves of strength. The South would in time rise above the victory just as the North would rise above the defeat; and rising thus, they without realizing it found a desolate but illimitable common ground. They had to learn the same lesson together, sharing, despite their angry separation, in the experience of a tragedy that knew no sectional limits. Denied all other unity, they would come at least to the desperate enforced unity of men and women caught up by suffering and hope, by courage and despair; this much would belong to everyone. The war had become national.

Notes

Chapter One: SPRINGTIME OF DECISION

1. The City by the Sea

1. The most detailed and graphic account of the Charleston convention which this writer has found is in Murat Halstead's engaging book, *Caucuses of 1860*, which has been drawn on liberally in the preparation of this and succeeding chapters. The description of Yancey at the Charleston Hotel is found on pp. 5-6; the book is cited hereafter as Halstead. Much reliance was placed also on material found in various manuscript collections which, even when not cited in corroboration of specific statements in the text, were invaluable in providing an understanding of the convention and the men who participated in it. Among the manuscript sources consulted in the preparation of this account were the S. L. M. Barlow Papers, at the Huntington Library; the James Buchanan Papers, at the Historical Society of Pennsylvania; the C. C. Clay Papers, at the Duke University Library; the Stephen Douglas Papers, at the Illinois State Historical Library; the John A. McClernand Papers, at the same depository, and the Joseph Gillespie Papers, at the Chicago Historical Society.

2. Dwight Dumond: "William Lowndes Yancey," in the Dictionary of American Biography" (cited hereafter as D.A.B.), Vol. XX, 592-95.

3. Dumond, op cit.

4. Halstead, 12-13.

5. D. E. Huger Smith, *A Charlestonian's Recollections,* 63; New York *Times,* issues dated April 27, April 28, and May 1, 1860; Avery Craven, *The Growth of Southern Nationalism,* 323-24; Allan Nevins, *The Emergence of Lincoln,* Vol. II, 203-4 (cited hereafter as Nevins); Roy Nichols, *The Disruption of American Democracy,* 288; Robert Molloy, *Charleston: a Gracious Heritage,* 1-2, 26-29.

6. Halstead, 4-5.

7. Cf Craven, op cit, 323: "A place worse than Charleston, South Carolina, in which to hold the convention could not have been selected." See also Dumond, *The Secession Movement, 1860-1861,* 4: "Not all of the men of the South were state-rights men, nor was the doctrine of state rights confined to that section of the country; but that doctrine was the constitutional refuge of the secessionists; and the fundamental cause of secession was the threatened extinction of slavery."

8. Halstead, 1-3.

9. Richmond *Dispatch,* issue dated April 24, 1860.

10. New York *Times,* April 27, 1860; Halstead, 5-7, 13.

11. Halstead, 3-4, 6.

2. *"The Impending Crisis"*

1. French Ensor Chadwick, *Causes of the Civil War, 1859-1861,* 90.

2. Congressional Globe, 36th Congress, First Session, Vol. I, 3; Chadwick, op cit, 91.

3. For a sketch of Helper's life, see D.A.B., Vol. VIII, 517-18; also Ulrich Bonnell Phillips, *The Course of the South to Secession,* 113-14, 154-55, and Craven, op cit, 250. Helper's *The Impending Crisis of the South; How to Meet It,* 155-56, urged Southerners to boycott all business and professional men who owned slaves, to hold "no fellowship with them in religion—no affiliation with them in society," and said that slaveholders should be given no recognition at all "except as ruffians, outlaws and criminals." In a later book, *Nojoque: Question for a Continent,* Helper voiced what must be the most bitter anti-Negro diatribe ever written in America. The passage quoted in the text (*Nojoque:* 105) concludes that Negroes "are not upon the earth to be loved and preserved, but, under the unobstructed and salutary operation of the laws of nature, to be permitted to decay and die, and then to disappear, at once and forever, down, down, deep down, in the vortex of oblivion!"

4. Helper, *The Impending Crisis of the South,* 21, 22, 25. For Blair's work on the *Compend,* see John Sherman, *Recollections of Forty Years in the House, Senate and Cabinet,* Vol. I, 169.

5. Sherman, op cit, 169-70.

6. Congressional Globe, 36th Congress, First Session, Vol. I, 17.

7. Ibid, 21, 44, 45, 82-83.

8. John B. McMaster, *A History of the People of the United States from the Revolution to the Civil War*, Vol. VIII, 434. (This work is cited hereafter as McMaster.)

9. Congressional Globe, 36th Congress, First Session, Vol. I, 658, 935.

10. Ibid, III, 2156. For an excellent summary of the situation as it developed in this session of Congress, see Craven, 313-16, 341.

11. Congressional Globe, 36th Congress, First Session, Vol. III, 2155-56.

12. Benjamin Thomas, *Abraham Lincoln*, 201-2; Roy Basler, *The Collected Works of Abraham Lincoln* (cited hereafter as Basler), Vol. III, 256, 534.

13. Halstead, 102; Congressional Globe, as above, Vol. I, 914.

14. Congressional Globe, Vol. I, appendix, 203-4; James Ford Rhodes, *History of the United States from the Compromise of 1850 to the Final Restoration of Home Rule in the South in 1877* (cited hereafter as Rhodes), Vol. II, 439. Reading the record of scenes like this, and the earlier row over the speakership, one sees so much passion and unrestrained invective that one is almost surprised the war did not come earlier than it did.

15. Nevins, Vol. II, 189-91.

16. Chadwick, *Causes of the Civil War*, 125; Congressional Globe, 36th Congress, First Session, Vol. IV, 2848-49.

3. Star after Star

1. Halstead, 5, 18-19.

2. Ibid, 10.

3. Ibid, 23-25.

4. Craven, 320-21, 327; Dumond, *The Secession Movement, 1860-1861*, 33; John Witherspoon DuBose, *The Life and Times of William Lowndes Yancey*, 362-63.

5. Laura W. White, *Robert Barnwell Rhett: Father of Secession*, 157.

6. Rhodes, Vol. II, 357.

7. Halstead, 25-28.

8. Nevins, Vol. II, 214-15; Halstead, 43-44; Edward Stanwood, *A History of the Presidency from 1788 to 1897*, Vol. I, 266-69.

9. Pamphlet in the Newberry Library, "Speech of the Hon. William L. Yancey of Alabama, Delivered in the National Democratic Convention"; Halstead, 47-48.

10. Halstead, 48-50.

11. Ibid, 52, 58-59, 61.

12. Richmond *Dispatch,* May 5, 1860; Montgomery *Weekly Advertiser,* May 16, 1860; Nichols, op cit, 303-4.

13. Halstead, 67-68, 71, 75.

4. *"The Party Is Split Forever"*

1. Emerson Davis Fite, *The Presidential Campaign of 1860,* 110-11; Halstead, 76; B. F. Perry, *Biographical Sketches of Eminent American Statesmen,* 148.

2. Official Proceedings of the Democratic National Convention, 74-75; Halstead, 85-87.

3. Halstead, 97-98.

4. Benjamin F. Butler, *Butler's Book,* 138-40; Halstead, 88, 92; Nichols, 308-9.

5. New York *Times,* May 2, 1860.

6. Richmond *Dispatch,* May 7, 1860.

7. Henry A. Wise to William Sergeant, May 28, 1858, in John G. Nicolay and John Hay, *Abraham Lincoln: A History,* Vol. II, 302. (Cited hereafter as Nicolay & Hay.)

8. Halstead, 101-3.

9. Jefferson Davis, *Relations of the States: Speech of May 7, 1860,* 13-14.

10. Congressional Globe, 35th Congress, First Session, Vol. I, 18.

11. Richard Malcolm Johnston and William Hand Browne, *Life of Alexander H. Stephens,* 365.

12. Ibid, 355-56.

5. *The Crowd at the Wigwam*

1. Halstead, 120.

2. Ibid, 208-12; Rhodes, Vol. II, 454. Note that Dumond (*The Secession Movement,* 94) insists that this group actually adopted "a distinctly Southern platform." He remarks: "It was not an endorsement of Federal supremacy, nor of majority rule, but rather of state rights and constitutional protection for the rights of minorities."

3. P. Orman Ray, *The Convention that Nominated Lincoln,* 5-8, 15.

4. Ibid, 11, 13-14.

5. Halstead, 122, 140.

6. Willard L. King, *Lincoln's Manager, David Davis,* 134-36. According to Don G. Fehrenbacher, in *Chicago Giant: A Biogra-*

phy of Long John Wentworth, 177, David Davis had previously written to Lincoln recommending Wentworth's talents as a political manager: "You ought to have got him long ago to 'run' you."

7. King, op cit, 134. For a succinct discussion of the different candidates and their prospects when the convention opened, see William E. Baringer, *Lincoln's Rise to Power,* 204-7.

8. King, 138; telegram, Davis and Dubois to Lincoln, May 15, 1860, photostat in the Lincoln Collection, Chicago Historical Society.

9. Francis Fisher Browne, *The Every-Day Life of Abraham Lincoln,* 232-33.

10. Halstead, 129.

11. Ray, op cit, 19, 21.

12. Ibid, 22-23; Halstead, 131, 138-39.

13. Ray, 25-26; Halstead, 140.

6. Railsplitter

1. King, 139.

2. For a careful weighing of the evidence on this point, see King, 137.

3. Halstead, 141.

4. Thomas Haines Dudley, a delegate from New Jersey, was one of the group meeting in Davis's headquarters suite, and he wrote a detailed account of the night's operations—"Report on Republican National Convention of 1860—Caucuses etc leading to nomination of Lincoln"—which has been followed in the preparation of this chapter. The manuscript is in the Thomas Haines Dudley Papers in the Henry E. Huntington Library, San Marino, Calif.

5. For the generally accepted version of the deal with the Cameron men, see Carl Sandburg, *Abraham Lincoln: The Prairie Years,* Vol. II, 341-42. Alexander K. McClure *Abraham Lincoln and Men of War Times,* 29-30 insists that the Pennsylvania delegation caucused and voted to swing to Lincoln because of the pressure exerted by Governor Curtin and the influence of the Indiana delegation's action; he asserts (139) that the Lincoln managers definitely made a deal with Cameron but that they simply bought something they were going to get anyway. King's version is in his *Lincoln's Manager,* 140-41, 162-64.

6. Halstead, 143-44.

7. Ibid, 144-45.

8. For all of the foregoing, the Halstead account (149-51) is a graphic and detailed bit of reporting.

9. Ray, op cit, 37.

10. Addison G. Procter, "Lincoln and the Convention of 1860: an Address Before the Chicago Historical Society," 10-12.

11. Halstead, 153.

Chapter Two: DOWN A STEEP PLACE

1. Division at Baltimore

1. Letter of Lee to Major Earl Van Dorn, July 3, 1860, in the R. E. Lee Papers, Library of Congress.

2. cf Nichols (320): "The great majority of Americans no longer wished to compromise."

3. Halstead, 160; Nichols, 314.

4. Halstead, 176, 185.

5. Ibid, 154-56.

6. Dumond, 81-82; Nichols, 316; Halstead, 185.

7. This account follows Halstead, who gives the text of Douglas's letter to Dean Richmond and quotes liberally from the debates. (Halstead, 187-99.)

8. Ibid, 205-6.

9. For a résumé of the voting statistics and an excellent analysis of their significance, see Nichols, 321. Douglas's letter to Richardson, and Richardson's remarks on it, are from Halstead, 207.

10. Halstead (citing a news story in the Baltimore *Sun*), 217-25.

11. Ibid, 227.

2. The Great Commitment

1. Since the Civil War ended, practically every conceivable interpretation of its causes and significance has been advanced. An almost indispensable survey and summary of these varying opinions can be found in Thomas J. Pressly's *Americans Interpret Their Civil War*. Highly recommended also is Howard K. Beale's *What Historians Have Said About the Causes of the Civil War* (Theory and Practice in Historical Study; a Report of the Committee on Historiography, Bulletin 54, 1946, Social Science Research Council.) Two sharply contrasting analyses which this

writer found stimulating and informative are Avery Craven, *The Coming of the Civil War* (second revised edition, 1957) and Nevins, Vol. II, 462 et seq.

2. "The general period in American history from 1825 to 1860 was one of vast material growth and expansion. But it was also one in which the wealth and power of the few grew disproportionately to that of the many. Democracy was not functioning properly. . . . Injustice, lack of material prosperity, loss of equality or failure to achieve American purposes—all became matters of moral significance and evidence of God's plan thwarted." (Craven, "The Coming of the War Between the States: an Interpretation," *Journal of Southern History*, Vol. II, No. 3, 305.)

3. "The localization of a great manufacture so distant from its sources of supply was as radical an innovation in industrial geography as was Arkwright machinery in industrial mechanics." (Victor S. Clark, *History of Manufactures in the United States*, Vol. II, 1.)

4. Clark, op cit, 2.

5. Ibid, 7.

6. cf Charles and Mary Beard (*The Rise of American Civilization*, Vol. II, 6-7): "The amazing growth of northern industries, the rapid extension of railways, the swift expansion of foreign trade to the ends of the earth, the attachment of the farming regions of the west to the centers of manufacture and finance through transportation and credit, the destruction of state consciousness by migration, the alien invasion, the erection of new commonwealths in the Valley of Democracy, the nationalistic drive of interstate commerce, the increase of population in the north, and the southward pressure of the capitalistic glacier, all conspired to assure the ultimate triumph of what the orators were fond of calling 'the free labor system.' This was a dynamic thrust far too powerful for planters operating in a limited territory with incompetent labor and soil of diminishing fertility."

7. Frederick Law Olmsted, *A Journey in the Seaboard Slave States in the Years 1853-1854, with Remarks on Their Economy*, Vol. I, 19-20. See also Ulrich B. Phillips, *The Course of the South to Secession*, 152-53.

8. Mary Boykin Chesnut, *A Diary from Dixie* (cited hereafter as Mrs. Chesnut), 10-11, 21-22, 142.

3. By Torchlight

1. Nicolay & Hay, Vol. II, 284-85.

2. William E. Baringer, *Campaign Technique in Illinois—1860;*

Illinois State Historical Society Transactions for the Year 1932, 249.

3. Ibid, 253-56.

4. *The Railsplitter* was published between Aug. 1 and Oct. 27, 1860. The quotations in the text are from a reprint by the Abraham Lincoln Bookshop, Chicago.

5. Baringer, op cit, 261.

6. Undated paper marked "Form of a reply prepared by Mr. Lincoln with which his private secretary was instructed to answer a numerous class of letters in the campaign of 1860," in the John G. Nicolay Papers, Library of Congres.

7. Memorandum dated Nov. 5, 1860, in the Nicolay Papers.

8. Craven, *The Growth of Southern Nationalism*, 346.

9. "Speech Delivered by William H. Seward at St. Paul, Sept. 18, 1860," a pamphlet printed by the Albany *Evening Journal*.

10. Chadwick, *Causes of the Civil War*, 127.

11. Ibid, 128, citing *The National Intelligencer* for Oct. 5, 1860.

12. Edmund Ruffin Diaries, Vol. IV, 677, 682; in the Library of Congress.

13. Emerson David Fite, *The Presidential Campaign of 1860*, 314, 317-18.

4. Little Giant

1. There is a brilliant analysis of this situation in Craven's *Growth of Southern Nationalism*. Pointing out that the Industrial Revolution had already pronounced the doom of slavery, Craven remarks (340): "Douglas had simply recognized inevitable trends and had adjusted his course to them. But because Southern men resented what 'progress' had done to them, they saw in Douglas the symbol of it all and hated him accordingly. By rejecting him they were attempting to repudiate the great forces of change that threatened their civilization."

2. George Fort Milton, *The Eve of Conflict*, 492; *The Campaign Plain Dealer and Popular Sovereignty Advocate*, Cleveland, issue of Sept. 1, 1860. (This is an interesting Douglas campaign paper, counterpart of the Republican Party's *Railsplitter* mentioned in the previous chapter. Facsimile reproductions are published by Lincoln College, Lincoln, Ill.)

3. Milton, op cit, 493; Fite, *The Presidential Campaign of 1860*, 282.

4. Howard Cecil Perkins, *Northern Editorials on Secession*, 38-39, 71.

5. Lucille Stillwell, *John Cabell Breckinridge*, 82-83.

6. King, *Lincoln's Manager*, 154-55, 158-59.

7. Diary of Edmund Ruffin, Vol. IV; Dwight L. Dumond, *Southern Editorials on Secession*, quoting the Charleston *Mercury* of Oct. 11, 1860.

8. Dumond, op cit, 185; Dunbar Rowland, *Jefferson Davis, Constitutionalist: His Letters, Papers and Speeches*, Vol. IV, 540.

9. Nicolay & Hay, Vol. II, 306-7.

10. Ibid, 307-14.

11. Milton, *The Eve of Conflict*, 500.

5. Verdict of the People

1. Paul Angle, *Here I Have Lived: a History of Lincoln's Springfield, 1821-1865*, 251-53; John G. Nicolay to his wife, Nov. 8, 1860, in the Nicolay Papers.

2. McMaster, Vol. VIII, 476, 478-79; Rhodes, Vol. III, 118.

3. Johnston and Browne, *Life of Alexander H. Stephens*, 564-65.

4. Ibid, 370-71; Basler, Vol. IV, 146, 160. In the former book, Lincoln is quoted as saying ". . . while we think it is wrong and ought to be abolished." The quotation in the text is from Basler.

5. Memorandum dated at Springfield, Nov. 15, 1860; from the Nicolay Papers.

6. New York *Tribune*, Nov. 9, 1860.

7. Dunbar Rowland, op cit, Vol. IV, 541.

8. Henry Villard, *Lincoln on the Eve of '61*, 17.

9. Donn Piatt, *Memories of Men Who Saved the Union*, 30, 33-34.

6. Despotism of the Sword

1. Winfield Scott, *Memoirs of Lieut. General Scott, LL.D., Written by Himself*, Vol. II, 609; James Buchanan, *The Administration on the Eve of the Rebellion*, 99, 287-88; Mss. copy of Scott's views, inscribed "To the Hon. E. Everett with the respects of his friend—W.S." in the Edward Everett Papers, Massachusetts Historical Society.

2. Buchanan, op cit, 104; Brevet Major General Emory Upton, *The Military Policy of the United States*, 224; A. Howard Meneely, *The War Department, 1861*, 21-22, 24-26.

3. Philip Gerald Auchampaugh, *James Buchanan and His Cabinet on the Eve of Secession*, 130; Nicolay & Hay, Vol. II, 36-63, quoting from the diary of John B. Floyd.

4. Auchampaugh, op cit, 132-34.

5. Attorney General Black's opinion is from George Ticknor Curtis, *Life of James Buchanan*, Vol. II, 319-24. (Cited hereafter as Curtis.)

6. Letters of Thomas L. Drayton, dated Nov. 10 and Nov. 23, 1860, and letter of R. L. Ripley, dated Nov. 7, 1860, all in the Edwin M. Stanton Papers, Library of Congress.

7. Letter of William Henry Trescot dated Nov. 17, 1860, in the Robert N. Gourdin Papers, Duke University Library; letter of Trescot dated Nov. 19, in the Edwin M. Stanton Papers; Mrs. Chesnut, 28.

8. James D. Richardson, *Messages and Papers of the Presidents*, Vol. VII, 3157-69.

Chapter Three: THE LONG FAREWELL

1. The Union Is Dissolved

1. *Journal of the Convention of the People of South Carolina, Held in 1860-61*, 3-5; John Amasa May and Joan Reynolds Faunt, *South Carolina Secedes*, 5-7.

2. Journal of the Convention, 18; Frank Moore, *The Rebellion Record: a Diary of American Events* (cited hereafter as Moore's *Rebellion Record*), Vol. I, 3; New York *Times*, Dec. 18, 1860.

3. New York *Times*, Dec. 19 and Dec. 20, 1860.

4. Journal of the Convention, 46-47, 53; Nicolay & Hay, Vol. III, 13.

5. James Petigru Carson, *Life, Letters and Speeches of James Louis Petigru, the Union Man of South Carolina*, 361, 364.

6. Diary of Edmund Ruffin, Vol. IV, 713 ff.

7. Nicolay & Hay, Vol. III, 11-12.

8. Samuel Wylie Crawford, *The Genesis of the Civil War; the Story of Sumter, 1860-61* (cited hereafter as Crawford), 54-55; New York *Times*, Dec. 20 and Dec. 22, 1860.

9. May and Faunt, *South Carolina Secedes*, 18-19.

10. Journal of the Convention, 325-31, 332-44.

11. Letter of William Porcher Miles dated Dec. 20, 1860, in the Robert N. Gourdin Papers.

12. New York *Times*, Dec. 22, Dec. 24, 1860.

13. Moore's *Rebellion Record*, Vol. I; Diary, 3; Documents, 1.

14. Mrs. Roger Pryor, *Reminiscences of Peace and War*, 110-

12; Buchanan's letter of Dec. 20 to James Gordon Bennett, in the James Buchanan Papers, Historical Society of Pennsylvania.

2. A Delegation of Authority

1. *The War of the Rebellion: a Compilation of the Official Records of the Union and Confederate Armies*, Vol. I, 68-69. (This invaluable compilation is hereafter cited as O.R. Unless otherwise noted in the citation, the volumes are from Series I.)

2. O.R., Vol. I, 70-72.

3. There is a good brief sketch of Anderson in D.A.B., Vol. I, 274-75. His orders are in O.R., Vol. I, 73.

4. Anderson's first report from Fort Moultrie, Nov. 23, 1860, O.R., Vol. I, 74; Crawford, 6-7; *Battles and Leaders of the Civil War* (hereafter cited as B & L.), Vol. I, 40.

5. O.R., Vol. I, 74-77

6. Ibid, 78-79.

7. Ibid, 81-82.

8. Crawford, 37-40. The letter from the South Carolina delegation to President Buchanan is in the William Porcher Miles Papers, Southern Historical Collection, University of North Carolina. On the back of this document is a note apparently in Buchanan's handwriting, containing the statement: "I objected to the word 'Provided' as this might be construed into an agreement on my part which I never would make. They said nothing was further from their intentions. They did not so understand & I should not so consider it."

9. O.R., Vol. I, 82-83.

10. Crawford, 71-74; O.R., Vol., I, 89-90.

11. Buchanan, 106; O.R., Vol. I, 103.

12. Letter of Major Anderson to Dr. G. T. Metcalfe, Dec. 15, 1860, in the A. Conger Goodyear Collection, Historical Manuscripts Division, Yale University Library.

13. Letter of Major Anderson to the Rev. Mr. R. B. Duane, Dec. 19, 1860, in the Goodyear Collection.

14. Letter of Major Anderson, Dec. 12, 1860, to a friend whose name is not decipherable, in the Robert Anderson Papers, Library of Congress.

15. Crawford, 77-78.

16. Ibid, 81-84.

17. Unfinished draft of letter dated Dec. 20, in the James Buchanan Papers, Historical Society of Pennsylvania.

18. Crawford, 88.

3. An Action and a Decision

1. Crawford, 95; O.R., Vol. I, 106-7; Abner Doubleday, *Reminiscences of Forts Sumter and Moultrie in 1860-61*, 49-50.

2. Doubleday, op cit, 60-64; also in B. & L., Vol. I, 44-45.

3. Captain James Chester, *Inside Sumter in '61*, in B. & L., Vol. I, 51-52; Diary of Edmund Ruffin, Vol. IV, 718.

4. Eba Anderson Lawton, *Major Robert Anderson and Fort Sumter 1861*, 8.

5. O.R., Vol. I, 2.

6. Crawford, 142-44; quoting liberally from Trescot's diary, to which Crawford apparently had access but which is no longer available. Buchanan's own account of his meeting with the South Carolina commissioners is in his book, *The Administration on the Eve of the Rebellion*, 181-82.

7. Auchampaugh, 66-67; Crawford, 37. A copy of Cass's letter of resignation, and a memorandum thereon by Buchanan, both in Buchanan's handwriting, are in the Buchanan Papers, Historical Society of Pennsylvania.

8. Crawford, 146; Chadwick, *Causes of the Civil War*, 213; George C. Gorham, *Life and Public Services of Edwin M. Stanton*, Vol. I, 158; Buchanan, 180-81.

9. Crawford, 148, giving the text of a letter he received in 1871 from James L. Orr with details of the meeting.

10. Crawford, 146.

11. Winfield Scott, *Memoirs*, Vol. II, 613; O.R., Vol. I, 112.

12. O.R., Vol. I, 109-10.

13. Buchanan, 182.

14. Nicolay & Hay, Vol. III, 74.

15. Frank A. Flower, *Edwin McMasters Stanton*, 88.

16. Document of John Codman Ropes dated 1870, setting forth an interview he had had with Stanton in 1869, in the Horatio Woodman Papers, Massachusetts Historical Society; Rhodes, Vol. III, 231; Crawford, 151.

17. O.R., Vol. I, 114.

4. Footsteps in a Dark Corridor

1. Mrs. Chesnut, 4-5.

2. Basler, Vol. IV, 149-51.

3. Letter of John A. Gilmer dated Dec. 10, 1860, in the Robert Todd Lincoln Papers; Basler, Vol. IV, 151-52.

4. Basler, Vol. IV, 154, 156.

5. Ibid, 157, 159.

6. Ibid, 162.

7. Ibid, 164-65.

8. For a brief discussion of Floyd's odd course, see D.A.B., Vol. VI, 482-83; also Nevins, Vol. II, 372.

9. Telegram, Trescot to Miles, marked showing receipt at Charleston Dec. 31, 1860, in the William Porcher Miles Papers.

10. Gov. Pickens to Lieut. Col. De Saussure, dated Dec. 31, 1860, in the Wilmot Gibbs De Saussure Order Book, Southern Historical Collection, University of North Carolina.

11. O.R., Vol. I, 120.

12. Ibid, 120-25; Curtis, 446.

13. Letters of H. Pollock dated Dec. 30; of Charles A. Hamilton, dated Dec. 28, and of Edward Hinks, dated Dec. 26, from the Robert Anderson Papers, Library of Congress.

14. Rhodes, Vol. III, 239-241; Meneely, *The War Department, 1861,* 43-45; note from Buchanan to Floyd dated "Christmas Evening," enclosing a telegram from citizens of Pittsburgh, in the James Buchanan Papers, Historical Society of Pennsylvania.

5. The Strategy of Delay

1. Mrs. Roger Pryor, *Reminiscences of Peace and War,* 115; Nichols, *Disruption of American Democracy,* 438, quoting a letter from the wife of Senator W. M. Gwin of California.

2. Brig. Gen. Charles P. Stone, describing a New Year's Eve conversation with Gen. Scott, in B. & L., Vol. I, 9; O.R., Vol. I, 119.

3. Buchanan's account of the sequence of orders relative to the dispatch of the *Brooklyn* is contained in his letter of Jan. 9, 1861, to Jacob Thompson, copy in the James Buchanan Papers, Historical Society of Pennsylvania. The change of plans which led to use of the *Star of the West* is set forth in Buchanan's *The Administration on the Eve of the Rebellion,* 189-91. A somewhat different version is in Winfield Scott's *Memoirs,* Vol. II, 620-21.

4. O.R., Vol. I, 132, 133.

5. Official Records of the Union and Confederate Navies in the War of the Rebellion (cited hereafter as N.O.R.) Vol. I, 220.

6. O.R., Vol. I, 130-31, 252; Crawford, 133, 139.

7. O.R., Vol. I, 9-10, containing the report of Lieut. Charles R. Wood, 9th U. S. Infantry.

8. Doubleday, *Reminiscences of Forts Sumter and Moultrie,* 102.

9. Crawford, 184-85; B. & L., Vol. I, 61; Miss A. Fletcher,

Within Fort Sumter, or, A View of Major Anderson's Garrison Family for One Hundred and Ten Days, 14.

10. Crawford, 187; copy of Major Anderson's letter to W. A. Gordon, dated January 11, 1861, in the James Buchanan Papers, Historical Society of Pennsylvania.

11. The letters exchanged by Major Anderson and Governor Pickens are in O.R., Vol. I, 134-36.

12. Crawford, 189.

13. O.R., Vol. I, 137-38, 143-44; Crawford, 191-94, 209; Doubleday, op cit, 117.

14. Nicolay & Hay, Vol. III, 118-21.

15. Letter of Jefferson Davis to Governor Pickens, dated Jan. 20, 1861, in the Miscellaneous Papers, Huntington Library.

16. Letter of Governor Pickens to Jefferson Davis, dated Jan. 23, 1861, in the Goodyear Collection.

17. Curtis, Vol. II, 451; Buchanan, 194-96; O.R., Vol. I, 166-68.

18. Crawford, 231-33.

19. O.R., Vol. I, 326-27.

20. Ibid, 474-76, 484-85.

21. Dumond, *The Secession Movement*, 204; Dunbar Rowland, *History of Mississippi, the Heart of the South*, Vol. I, 781.

22. Appleton's *American Annual Cyclopaedia, 1861*, 10-11; O. R., Series Four, Vol. I, 46-47; Rowland, *History of Mississippi*, Vol. I, 783-84, 790.

23. On Jan. 19, 1861, the Springfield (Mass.) *Republican* remarked that the Buchanan cabinet had become about as sectional as that of Abraham Lincoln could ever be, and predicted that "the policy of the outgoing administration by the 1st of March will have become precisely that of the incoming one"—a very fair appraisal. Two weeks earlier the politically observant Edward McPherson, clerk of the House of Representatives, wrote that "the Prest is under better influences . . . he more clearly sees his duty. The mutterings of the mighty North have reached him." (Letter of McPherson to Francis Lieber, dated Jan. 2 and 3, 1861, in the Francis Lieber Collection at the Huntington Library.)

24. Appleton's *Annual Cyclopaedia, 1861*, 428-29.

6. Everything, Even Life Itself

1. Varina Howell Davis, *Jefferson Davis: A Memoir, by His Wife*, Vol. I, 696-98; Congressional Globe, 36th Congress, Second Session, Part I, 487.

2. Varina Howell Davis, Vol. I, 699; copy of a letter from Jefferson Davis to Anna Ella Carroll, dated March 1, 1861, in the Anna Ella Carroll Papers, Maryland Historical Society; letter of Davis to Clement C. Clay, dated Jan. 19, 1861, in the Clement C. Clay Papers, Duke University Library; Dunbar Rowland, *Jefferson Davis, Constitutionalist*, Vol. V, 37-38.

3. Moore's *Rebellion Record*, Vol. I, Diary, 9, Documents, 17-18.

4. Appleton's *Annual Cyclopaedia, 1861*, 395, 538, 677; Dumond, *The Secession Movement*, 220-22, 223.

5. Appleton's *Annual Cyclopaedia, 1861*, 477; Pulaski County Historical Review, Vol. V, Number One; Arkansas *Gazette*, Feb. 16, 1861; the J. M. Keller Papers, in the files of the Arkansas History Commission; Jack B. Scroggs, "Arkansas in the Secession Crisis," in the Arkansas Historical Quarterly, Vol. XII, Number Three.

6. Nevins, Vol. II, 425-27. In a lengthy letter to J. M. Calhoun, Commissioner from Alabama, Houston acidly remarked that "we have to recollect that our conservative Northern friends cast over a quarter of a million more votes against the Black Republicans than we of the entire South." (O.R., Series Four, Vol. I, 77.)

7. Appleton's *Annual Cyclopaedia, 1861*, 728-29; O.R., Series Four, Vol. I, 77.

8. Letter of Douglas to A. Belmont, dated Dec. 25, 1860, in the Douglas Papers, Chicago Historical Society. See also a very similar letter of his in the Lanphier Papers, Illinois State Historical Library.

9. Gilbert G. Glover, *Immediate Pre-Civil War Compromise Efforts*, 112-13; Edward McPherson, *The Political History of the United States of America During the Great Rebellion*, 57; David C. Mearns, *The Lincoln Papers*, Vol. II, 406.

10. Congressional Globe, 36th Congress, Second Session, Part One, 237-38, 267.

11. Ibid, 341-44; New York *Herald*, Jan. 8 and Jan. 12, 1861; Moore's *Rebellion Record*, Vol. I, Diary, 15; Carlos Martyn, *Wendell Phillips: the Agitator*, 306.

12. New York *Herald*, Jan. 28, 1861; Henry Villard, *Lincoln on the Eve of 1861*, 58-59; letter of Charles Sumner, dated Jan. 21, 1861, from the Papers of John A. Andrew, Massachusetts Historical Society.

13. Villard, op cit; also *Memoirs of Henry Villard*, Vol. I, 145; W. H. L. Wallace, letter to "Dear Ann" dated Jan. 11, 1861, in

the Wallace-Dickey Papers, Illinois State Historical Library; letter of C. H. Ray, dated Jan. 17, 1861, in the John A. Andrew Papers.

14. McMaster, Vol. VIII, 510-11.

15. O.R., Vol. XVIII, 772-73.

16. Letter of Lee to Mrs. Lee, dated Jan. 23, 1861, and Lee's letter to "My Precious Agnes," dated Jan. 29, 1861, in the Robert E. Lee Papers, Library of Congress.

Chapter Four: TWO PRESIDENTS

1. The Man and the Hour

1. T. C. De Leon, *Four Years in the Rebel Capitals: an Inside View of Life in the Southern Confederacy, from Birth to Death,* 23-24; New Orleans *Delta,* Feb. 22, 1861.

2. De Leon, op cit, 24, 33; Burton J. Hendrick, *Statesmen of the Lost Cause,* 89-90.

3. "Correspondence of Thomas Reade Rootes Cobb, 1860-1862," in Publications of the Southern History Association, Vol. XI, 160-63; Alexander H. Stephens, *A Constitutional View of the Late War Between the States,* Vol. II, 325.

4. J. L. M. Curry, *Civil History of the Government of the Confederate States, with Some Personal Reminiscences,* 42-44, 50; E. Merton Coulter, *The Confederate States of America,* 20-21; Hendrick, op cit, 85.

5. For a detailed comparison of the United States and Confederate Constitutions, see Jefferson Davis, *Rise and Fall of the Confederate Government,* Vol. I, 648-73. Howell Cobb believed at the time that the Confederate Constitution was "the ablest instrument ever prepared for the government of a free people." Taking the United States Constitution as the basis for action, he said, "we have written down in the language of truth and simplicity the principles which an honest construction of that instrument has long pronounced its true meaning." (Journal of the Congress of the Confederate States of America, Vol. I, 153.)

6. *Southern Literary Messenger* for February 1861, 152.

7. R. Barnwell Rhett, *The Confederate Government at Montgomery,* in B. & L., Vol. I, 99 ff; Alexander Stephens, Vol. II, 328-333.

8. "Correspondence of Robert Toombs, Alexander H. Stephens and Howell Cobb": annual report of the American Historical Association for the Year 1911, Vol. II, 536-37.

9. Johnston and Browne, *Life of Alexander H. Stephens*, 385-86.

10. "Correspondence of Thomas Reade Rootes Cobb," 171-78.

11. Davis, *Rise and Fall*, Vol. I, 230, 236-37; Johnston and Browne, 387.

12. Varina Howell Davis, *Jefferson Davis*, Vol. II, 18; postwar letter of Jefferson Davis, dated June 4, 1878, in the Franklin Stringfellow Papers, Virginia State Historical Society.

13. Montgomery *Post*, Feb. 20, 1861; New York *Herald*, Feb. 23, 1861.

14. Appleton's *Annual Cyclopaedia, 1861*, 127; Montgomery *Weekly Advertiser*, Feb. 16, 1861; New York *Herald*, Feb. 23.

2. The Long Road to Washington

1. Paul Angle, *Here Have I Lived*, 260; Basler, Vol. IV, 190; New York *Herald*, Feb. 12, 1861; James G. Randall, *Lincoln the President*, Vol. I, 274-75.

2. New York *Herald*, Feb. 12, 1861; Basler, Vol. IV, 193-96.

3. Basler, Vol. IV, 197, 204, 208, 210-11. Southern newspapers made hay with some of these remarks. The Montgomery *Post* Feb. 20, 1861 asked sharply: "What means this civil commotion, these war-like preparations, this tearing down and building up of government? is it all imaginary—all a mere phantom fleeing before our distorted visions? The results of the future will develop how much of reality there is contained in this 'artificial crisis.'" The Natchez *Courier* Feb. 13, 1861, was moved to lament: "Alas! for our country's welfare! We have no Washington; no Clay; no Webster! The eagles have fled; the serpents crawl to eminence where eagles hardly dare to fly."

4. Basler, Vol. IV, 226, 230-33, 238, 240-41.

5. Villard, Memoirs, Vol. I, 151; New York *Herald*, Feb. 20, 1861; Montgomery *Post*, Feb. 22, 1861.

6. Letter of David Davis to Mrs. Davis, dated Feb. 17, 1861, from the David Davis Papers, Illinois State Historical Library.

7. The fantastic story of the assassination plot is excellently summarized in Randall, Vol. I, 286-89, and in Benjamin Thomas, 242-44.

8. L. E. Chittenden, *Recollections of President Lincoln and His Administration*, 37-39.

9. The furore raised by the soft hat and the cloak, transformed by rumor into plaid wrapper and tam o'shanter, could have been even worse if an idea which Secretary John G. Nicolay apparently toyed with had come to anything. In the Nicolay Papers at the Library of Congress there is a letter to Nicolay from one A. H. Flanders of New York, dated Jan. 27, 1861, reading as follows: "I wrote you a line yesterday from Philada. stating that I had ascertained that I could certainly get the coat of mail made in that city. . . . I shall be very happy to get this done for Mr. Lincoln if he will accept of it, and really hope he will not go to Washington without it. I am confident I can get it done without anyone knowing it is for him." A picture of Lincoln in a coat of mail would be worthy to stand beside the one which shows the mountain man, Jim Bridger, in a suit of armor.

10. Letter of C. F. Adams to R. H. Dana, dated Feb. 18, 1861, in the Dana Papers, Massachusetts Historical Society.

3. Colonel Lee Leaves Texas

1. B. & L., Vol. I, 36, n; Douglas Southall Freeman, *R. E. Lee*, Vol. I, 421.

2. O.R., Vol. I, 579-82, 584. There is a sketch of Twiggs in D.A.B., Vol. XIX, 83.

3. Twiggs's report, dated Feb. 19, 1861, is in O.R., Vol. I, 503-4. For the orders he issued, see the same volume, 515-16.

4. A very graphic if somewhat biased description of the doings at San Antonio and of Lee's arrival there is Mrs. Caroline Baldwin Darrow's *Recollections of the Twiggs Surrender*, B. & L., Vol. I, 33 ff.

5. Col. Waite's report, O.R., Vol. I, 521-22.

6. Report of Capt. S. D. Carpenter, O.R., Vol. I, 541-43.

7. O.R., Vol. I, 589, 595; B. & L., Vol. I, 39.

8. O.R., Vol. I, 598-99.

9. O. M. Roberts, *Texas* (Vol. XI of Clement A. Evans' *Confederate Military History*), 26; "Correspondence of Thomas Reade Rootes Cobb," 253; Dumond, *The Secession Movement*, 209.

10. A thoughtful analysis of the different votes on secession is in David M. Potter, *Lincoln and His Party in the Secession Crisis*, 208-15.

11. O.R., Vol. I, 597; Twiggs to Buchanan, dated March 30, 1861, in the Edwin M. Stanton Papers.

4. Talking Across a Gulf

1. Henry T. Shanks, *The Secession Movement in Virginia, 1847-1861,* 153-54.

2. New York *Herald,* Feb. 5, 1861; New York *Tribune,* Feb. 6; Congressional Globe, 36th Congress, Second Session, Part Two, 1247.

3. L. E. Chittenden, "A Report of the Debates and Proceedings in the Secret Sessions of the Conference Convention," 16; Nichols, *The Disruption of American Democracy,* 484; also Crafts J. Wright, "Official Journal of the Conference Convention Held at Washington City, February 1861."

4. Chittenden, *Recollections of President Lincoln and His Administration,* 72-76.

5. Letter of Charles Sumner to Governor Andrew, dated Feb. 20, 1861; letter of Charles Francis Adams, Jr., to Andrew, dated Feb. 22, 1861; both in the John A. Andrew Papers.

6. Letter of Charles Francis Adams to R. H. Dana, dated Feb. 9, 1861, in the Dana Papers.

7. Unsigned mss. paper of John A. Campbell, marked "memorandum relative to the Secession movement in 1860-61," in the Memorial Literary Society, Richmond.

8. The best concise summary of Lincoln's cabinet selections seems to this writer to be in Thomas' *Abraham Lincoln,* 232-35.

9. Letter of C. F. Adams, Jr., to R. H. Dana, dated Feb. 28, 1861, in the Dana Papers; letter of Sherrard Clemens to an unnamed recipient, dated March 1, 1861, in the William P. Palmer Civil War Collection, Western Reserve Historical Society.

5. Pressure at Fort Sumter

1. Crawford, 290; O.R., Vol. I, 183-84; B. & L., Vol. I, 53-54.

2. Telegrams from Governor Pickens dated Feb. 7 and Feb. 8, 1861; from the William Porcher Miles Papers, Southern Historical Collection, University of North Carolina.

3. Letter of Miles to Governor Pickens dated Feb. 9, 1861, American Art Association Catalog, Manuscript Room, New York Public Library.

4. Journal of the Congress of the Confederate States of America, Vol. I, 46-47, 55-58; printing the text of the resolutions and of Gov. Pickens' lengthy letter.

5. O.R., I., 258-59.

6. Letter of Miles to Governor Pickens dated Feb. 20, 1861,

in the Goodyear Collection; letter of Yancey to Governor Pickens dated Feb. 27, 1861, in the Yancey Papers, Library of Congress.

7. Alfred Roman, *The Military Operations of General Beauregard* (a book which is virtually Beauregard's autobiography), Vol. I, 25, 30; T. Harry Williams, *P. G. T. Beauregard, Napoleon in Gray*, 49, 54; Edward A. Pollard, *The First Year of the War*, 50; O.R., Vol. I, 25-27; John S. Tilley, *Lincoln Takes Command*, 161.

8. Roman, *Military Operations*, Vol. I, 29.

9. "Correspondence of Thomas Reade Rootes Cobb," 182; New York *Herald*, Feb. 23, 1861; *Harper's Weekly*, March 9, 1861; Montgomery *Weekly Advertiser*, Feb. 20, 1861.

10. Davis, *Rise and Fall*, Vol. I, 232-36, giving the text of his inaugural. His appealing note to his wife is from Varina Howell Davis, *Jefferson Davis, a Memoir*, Vol. II, 32-33.

11. The complaint of the *Mercury*—a journal singularly hard to please—is from Moore's *Rebellion Record*, Vol. I, Documents, 30. For the reference to Douglas, see Milton, *The Eve of Conflict*, 540-41.

12. Davis describes the making of his cabinet in his *Rise and Fall*, Vol. I, 241 et seq. Clifford Dowdey argues that Davis's cabinet choices were the sort an ordinary politician would make in time of peace but were not fitted for the stormy times that lay ahead: "However just they all considered their cause, it was revolution. Revolutions must succeed by force, or fail. They have no *status quo* in which to exist and not be won." (*Experiment in Rebellion*, 13.) It should be pointed out, of course, that Davis knew from the start that he was going to have to fight; it was just that he never saw himself as a revolutionist. As Roy Nichols remarks, the clubby Senatorial managers from the old government were comfortably in control. (*The Disruption of American Democracy*, 469-71.)

13. Davis, *Rise and Fall*, Vol. I, 246, 305-7; Journal of the Confederate Congress, Vol. I, 10 1-2; Pamphlet, "Confederate Flags," Confederate Museum, Richmond.

6. First Inaugural

1. *Harper's Weekly*, March 16, 1861, 165-66; Memoirs of Henry Villard, Vol. I, 154.

2. Charles P. Stone, *Washington on the Eve of the War*, in B. & L., Vol. I, 20, 24-25; Curtis, *Life of James Buchanan*, Vol. II, 494.

3. Winfield Scott, *Memoirs*, Vol. II, 625-27.

4. Buchanan, *The Administration on the Eve of the Rebellion,* 211; Curtis, Vol. II, 497.

5. Curtis, Vol. II, 509, 667; letter of Buchanan to James Gordon Bennett, dated March 11, 1861, copy in the James Buchanan Papers, Historical Society of Pennsylvania.

6. Curtis, Vol. II, 509; Mrs. Roger Pryor, *Reminiscences of Peace and War,* 47, 56; letter of Buchanan to Bennett, Dec. 20, 1860, in the James Buchanan Papers, Historical Society of Pennsylvania.

7. Memoirs of Henry Villard, Vol. I, 156: *Harper's Weekly,* March 16, 165; Nicolay & Hay, Vol. III, 371-72.

8. *Harper's Weekly,* p 166; Cincinnati *Commercial,* March 11, 1861. For a discussion of the credibility of this anecdote, see Allan Nevins, "He Did Hold Lincoln's Hat," in *American Heritage,* Vol. X, No. 2, 98-99.

9. It is interesting to note that in the first draft of this address, written during January 1861, Lincoln made the more aggressive statement: "All the power at my disposal will be used to reclaim the public property and places which have fallen; to hold, occupy and possess," etc, etc. (Basler, Vol. IV, 254.) In December he had written to Francis P. Blair, Sr., "According to my present view if the forts shall be given up before the inaugeration, the General must retake them afterward"; and to the former Whig Congressman Peter H. Silvester of Springfield he had written "If Mr. B. surrenders the forts, I think they must be retaken." (Basler, Vol. IV, 157, 160.) At least partly on Seward's urging he removed from the speech as finally delivered the pledge to "reclaim" what had already been lost. Shortly after the inauguration Charles Francis Adams, Jr., wrote that Seward had talked to him about the importance of his effort to get that one word taken out. (Diary of Charles Francis Adams, Jr., entry for March 11, 1861, in the Massachusetts Historical Society.)

10. Justice John A. Campbell wrote that Lincoln's address was "an incendiary message—one calculated to set the country in a blaze," but added that he believed its recommendations "will be allowed to slide." Campbell predicted that Major Anderson would soon be withdrawn from Fort Sumter and he hoped that in the end "a reunion may be affected or be permitted." (Letter of Justice Campbell to his mother, dated March 6, 1861, in the Alabama Department of Archives and History, at Montgomery.)

11. Isabel Wallace, *Life and Letters of General W. H. L. Wallace,* 100-1; Diary of Charles Francis Adams, Jr., entry for March 4.

12. New York *Herald,* March 5 and 6, 1861; Diary of George

Templeton Strong, Vol. III, 106; *The Education of Henry Adams,* 107; Martin J. Crawford to Robert Toombs, in the Robert Toombs Letterbook, South Caroliniana Library, from Allan Nevins' notes.

13. "Correspondence of Thomas Reade Rootes Cobb," 253; O.R., I, 261; Montgomery *Weekly Advertiser,* March 5, 1861; Charleston *Mercury,* March 5, 1861.

14. Appleton's *Annual Cyclopaedia, 1861,* 470, 472, 556, 757.

15. New York *Herald,* March 5, 1861.

Chapter Five: INTO THE UNKNOWN

1. Two Forts and Three Agents

1. O.R. Vol. I, 197, 198-205; memorandum dated March 4, 1861, in Buchanan's handwriting, in the James Buchanan Papers, Historical Society of Pennsylvania.

2. Jeremiah S. Black's report to Lincoln, March 5, 1861, in the J. S. Black Papers, Vol. 35, Library of Congress.

3. N.O.R., Vol. IV, 74. The situation at Fort Pickens during the winter and early spring is sketched by J. H. Gilman, "With Slemmer in Pensacola Harbor," B. & L., Vol. I, 26-32.

4. Braxton Bragg to Mrs. Bragg, letter dated March 11, 1861, in the Braxton Bragg Papers, Missouri Historical Society.

5. N.O.R., Vol. IV, 90; O.R., Vol. 1, 196-205.

6. Springfield *Republican,* March 14, 1861, quoting the Washington correspondent of the Boston *American;* letter of E. M. Stanton to Buchanan, March 16, 1861, in the Buchanan Papers, Historical Society of Pennsylvania; Crawford, 373; O.R., Vol. I, 196; Roman, *Military Operations,* Vol. I, 36.

7. Joseph Hawley to Gideon Welles, March 12, 1861, in the Goodyear Collection, Yale University Library.

8. O.R., Vol. I, 196-205; reports of Blair and Welles in the Goodyear Collection; letter of Chase to B. J. Lossing, dated Aug. 24, 1866, also in the Goodyear Collection.

9. Doubleday, *Reminiscences of Forts Sumter and Moultrie,* 130. At the end of March, Doubleday was writing to his wife: "If government delays many days longer it will be very difficult to relieve us in time, for the men's provisions are going fast." (Letter of March 29, 1861, in the Robert Todd Lincoln Papers.)

10. Crawford, 371; N.O.R., Vol. IV, 247, giving Fox's report; O.R., Vol. I, 211; letter of Gustavus Fox to General Crawford, dated May 10, 1882, in the Goodyear Collection.

11. Hurlbut's report to Lincoln, March 27, 1861, in the Robert Todd Lincoln Papers.

12. Ward Hill Lamon, *Recollections of Abraham Lincoln, 1847-1865*, 68-79; O.R., Vol. I, 237.

13. Nicolay & Hay, Vol. IV, 110; Gideon Welles, Diary, Vol. I, 29.

2. *Memorandum from Mr. Seward*

1. William Howard Russell, *My Diary North and South*, 20-27.

2. Nicolay & Hay, Vol. III, 394-5; O.R., Vol. I, 200-1; Crawford, 365.

3. Nicolay & Hay, Vol. III, 429-33. The cabinet members' replies are in the Robert Todd Lincoln Papers.

4. Diary of Charles Francis Adams, entries for March 28 and March 31, 1861, in the Massachusetts Historical Society.

5. Montgomery Meigs, "The Relations of President Lincoln and Secretary Stanton to the Military Commanders in the Civil War," *American Historical Review*, Vol. XXVI, No. 2, 299-300.

6. Ibid, 300.

7. Nicolay & Hay, Vol. III, 445-48; Basler, Vol. IV, 316.

8. David Mearns, *The Lincoln Papers*, Vol. I, 447-50.

9. Basler, Vol. IV, 316-17.

3. *"If You Have No Doubt . . ."*

1. Robert Toombs Letterbook, letter of Crawford dated March 6, 1861, in the Trescot Papers, South Caroliniana Library, Nevins' Notes.

2. Moore's *Rebellion Record*, Vol. I, Documents, 47.

3. Undated notes by John A. Campbell in the Southern Historical Society Papers, New Series, Vol. IV, 31-37.

4. O.R., Vol. I, 277.

5. Campbell's notes, as cited in Note Three, above; Edward Younger, ed., *Inside the Confederate Government: the Diary of Robert Garlick Hill Kean, Head of the Bureau of War*, 112-13; Dunbar Rowland, *Jefferson Davis, Constitutionalist*, Vol. V, 95-96. In the William H. Seward Collection of the Rush Rhees Library, University of Rochester, there is a long letter which Justice Campbell wrote to Seward on April 13, 1861, setting forth his version of the long negotiations.

6. O.R., Vol. I, 284; N.O.R., Vol. IV, 256-57.

7. N.O.R., Vol. IV, 248-49; O.R., Vol. I, 235.

8. *Confidential Correspondence of Gustavus Vasa Fox,* Vol. I, 34-35.

9. Rhodes, Vol. III, 345, 356; Nicolay & Hay, Vol. IV, 7, 11-13.

10. Anyone curious enough to trace the sequence of events in this situation can find a wealth of material. See Tyler Dennett, ed., *Lincoln and the Civil War in the Diaries and Letters of John Hay,* 30; Rev. R. L. Dabney, "Memoir of a Narrative Received of Col. John R. Baldwin, of Staunton, Touching the Origin of the War," in Southern Historical Society Papers, Vol. I, No. 6, 443-55; Report of the Joint Committee on Reconstruction at the First Session, 39th Congress, 102-5; New York *Tribune,* Nov. 6, 1862, quoting a speech by Charles S. Morehead, former governor of Kentucky, printed on Oct. 13 in the Liverpool *Mercury;* Allan B. Magruder, "A Piece of Secret History: President Lincoln and the Virginia Convention of 1861," *Atlantic Monthly,* Vol. XXXV, April, 1875.

11. Letter of Gideon Welles to I. N. Arnold, Nov. 27, 1872, photostat in the Lincoln Collection, Chicago Historical Society; letter of Capt. Samuel Mercer to Welles, April 8, 1861, in the Goodyear Collection, Yale; undated letter of Montgomery Blair to S. L. M. Barlow, in the Barlow Papers, Huntington Library; Gideon Welles, "Fort Sumter: Facts in Relation to the Expedition Ordered by the Administration of President Lincoln for the Relief of the Garrison in Fort Sumter," *The Galaxy,* Vol. X, No. 5, 620-21, 630-35.

12. Dunbar Rowland, *Jefferson Davis, Constitutionalist,* Vol. V, 95-96; letter of Campbell to Seward, April 7, 1861, in the William H. Seward Papers, Rush Rhees Library, University of Rochester; Russell, *My Diary North and South,* 34.

13. Letter of Stanton to Buchanan, April 11, 1861, in the Buchanan Papers, Historical Society of Pennsylvania.

14. Basler, Vol. IV, 323-24.

15. O.R., Vol. I, 285.

16. Crawford, 421, quoting a letter from L. P. Walker, Confederate Secretary of War; Pleasant A. Stovall, *Robert Toombs,* 226.

17. O.R., Vol. I, 297. One week before this, President Davis wrote a revealing letter to Braxton Bragg, commanding Confederate forces at Pensacola, giving his views on the matter of the forts: "It is scarcely to be doubted that for political reasons the U.S. govt. will avoid making an attack so long as the hope of

retaining the border states remains. There would be to us an advantage in so placing them that an attack by them would be a necessity, but when we are ready to relieve our territory and jurisdiction of the presence of a foreign garrison that advantage is overbalanced by other considerations. The case of Pensacola then is reduced to the more palpable elements of a military problem, and your measures may without disturbing views be directed to the capture of Fort Pickins and the defense of the harbor." (Letter of Davis to Bragg, April 3, 1861, marked "unofficial"; in the Palmer Collection of the Western Reserve Historical Society.) This letter is especially interesting in view of the charge that Lincoln plotted darkly to "provoke" the Confederacy into starting a war which it otherwise would not have fought.

4. The Circle of Fire

1. Letter of Chesley D. Evans to Mrs. Evans, March 31, 1861, in the Southern Historical Collection, University of North Carolina.

2. B. & L., Vol. I, 56; O.R., Vol. I, 237-38, 273.

3. Benson J. Lossing, "Mem. of Visit of Mrs. Anderson to Fort Sumter," in the Goodyear Collection at Yale.

4. Letter of Anderson to Beauregard, March 26, 1861, in the Goodyear Collection.

5. Unsigned article, "Charleston Under Arms," in the *Atlantic Monthly* for January 1861, 488-96.

6. Fox to Gen. Crawford, May 10, 1882, in the Goodyear Collection.

7. O.R., Vol. I, 294.

8. Letter of Beauregard to Maj. J. G. Barnard, March 18, 1861, in Letterbook No. 3, the Beauregard Papers, Library of Congress.

9. Edward McPherson, *The Political History of the United States of America During the Great Rebellion*, 112; Moore's *Rebellion Record*, Vol. I, Diary, 21-22.

10. O.R., Vol. I, 13; Crawford, 422.

11. O.R., loc cit; Crawford, 423-24. In the Houghton Library at Harvard University, in the papers of the Massachusetts Commandery, Military Order of the Loyal Legion of the United States, there are three notebooks bearing the penciled record of hearings held in the fall of 1865 on Major Anderson's illness and retirement. They contain Anderson's testimony on the bombardment of Fort Sumter, and have been consulted extensively in the

preparation of this chapter. Anderson testifies here that he made the remark about being starved out "jocosely."

12. O.R., Vol. I, 299, 301.

13. The text of Major Anderson's reply is in O.R., Vol. I, 14. There is a copy of the report of Col. A. R. Chisholm in the Palmer Collection of the Western Reserve Historical Society. In his testimony before the retirement board, Major Anderson said he suspected that Beauregard "wanted to tie my hands" by stipulating that the major should not open fire prior to the evacuation of the fort. It may be worth noting that Major Anderson's reply, and the decision to open fire, were not referred to the Confederate government. On April 12, after the bombardment had been going on for hours, Secretary of War Walker wired Beauregard: "What was Major Anderson's reply to the proposition in my dispatch of last night?" Beauregard wired back. "He would not consent. I write today." (O.R., Vol. I, 305.)

14. Stephen D. Lee, The First Step in the War, B. & L., Vol. I, 76. A typed booklet containing portions of his diary bearing on the events of this night is in the Stephen Dill Lee Papers, Southern Historical Collection. At the retirement hearing Major Anderson said he carefully checked his watch with the watches of the Confederates and told them: "Well, Gentlemen, at half past four you will open your fire upon me. Good morning."

15. B. & L., Vol. I, 76; Martin Abbott, The First Shot at Fort Sumter, Civil War History, Vol. III, No. I; Robert Lebby, The First Shot on Fort Sumter, The South Carolina Historical and Genealogical Review, Vol. XII, No. 3, 143-45; D. Augustus Dickert, History of Kershaw's Brigade, 24; Mrs. Chesnut's Diary, 35.

5. White Flag on a Sword

1. Wilmot Gibbes De Saussure, Order Book, in the Southern Historical Collection.

2. Diaries of Edmund Ruffin, Vol. IV, 797-98; Avery Craven, Edmund Ruffin, Southerner, 215-17, 219; Dickert, History of Kershaw's Brigade, 29.

3. Dickert, 17-21.

4. Major Anderson's testimony before the retirement board in the Massachusetts Commandery papers, Houghton Library.

5. The figures for the Fort Sumter garrison are Major Anderson's; a return dated April 4, 1861, in the Anderson Papers, Library of Congress. Accuracy in regard to the Confederate figures is impossible. The Charleston Mercury on May 14, 1861, used the figure of 7000; Gov. Pickens, shortly before the battle, esti-

mated Beauregard's strength at 6000 (O.R., Vol. I, 292); Rhodes, Vol. III, 355, quotes Russell of the London *Times* as putting the total at 7025. For a good description of Fort Sumter, see John Johnson. *The Defense of Charleston Harbor, Including Fort Sumter and the Adjacent Islands,* 17. The fort's guns are listed in the report of Capt. J. G. Foster, O.R., Vol. I, 18-19. See also B. & L., Vol. I, 58-60.

6. B. & L., Vol. I, 67-68.

7. Ibid, 69-70.

8. Major Anderson's testimony, Massachusetts Commandery papers, Houghton Library; B. & L., Vol. I, 71.

9. Fox's report, N.O.R., Vol. IV, 249.

10. Ibid, 249-50.

11. Major Anderson gives a graphic account of all of this—with due emphasis on the role of Sergeant Hart—in his testimony in the Massachusetts Commandery papers.

12. Diary in the Stephen Dill Lee Papers, Southern Historical Collection, University of North Carolina.

13. Report of Capt. J. G. Foster, O.R., Vol. I, 22-24; Crawford, 441-42; B. & L., Vol. I, 71-73. Russell gives a fine picture of the ineffable Wigfall in *My Diary North and South,* 46.

14. Crawford, 446-47; diary in the Stephen Dill Lee Papers; Charleston *Daily Courier,* April 15, 1861; Miss A. Fletcher, *Within Fort Sumter,* 64-66.

6. The Coming of the Fury

1. Letter of W. S. Rosecrans to Gen. Marcus J. Wright, March 1, 1892, in the Eldridge Collection, Huntington Library.

2. George Ticknor, *Life, Letters and Journals of George Ticknor,* Vol. II, 433; John B. McMaster, *A History of the People of the United States During Lincoln's Administration,* 35; Russell, *My Diary North and South,* 41-42.

3. John Hay, *Lincoln and the Civil War,* 14; McPherson, *Political History of the United States,* 114; Carl Schurz, *The Reminiscences of Carl Schurz,* Vol. II, 223; Russell, 42.

4. Nicolay & Hay, Vol. IV, 71; Basler, Vol. IV, 330.

5. Basler, Vol. IV, 331-32.

6. Nicolay & Hay, Vol. IV, 80-84; letter of Congressman George Ashmun to Isaac N. Arnold, printed in the Cincinnati *Daily Commercial,* Oct. 28, 1864. Ashmun was present when Lincoln and Douglas had their talk, and he wrote a clear and complete account of it.

7. Mrs. D. Geraud Wright, *A Southern Girl in '61*, 52-53. The author, a daughter of Senator Wigfall, quotes from a letter written by a friend in Providence, R.I.

8. McMaster, Lincoln, op cit, 35.

9. For the replies of the governors, see O.R., Series Three, Vol. I, 70-83.

10. Appleton's *Annual Cyclopaedia, 1861*, 735; Moore's *Rebellion Record*, Vol. I, Documents, 70; letter of W. C. Rives to Robert C. Winthrop, April 19, 1861, in the Robert C. Winthrop Papers, Massachusetts Historical Society.

11. O.R., Vol. II, 3-4; John D. Imboden, *Jackson at Harper's Ferry in 1861*, in B. & L., Vol. I, 111-18; Charlotte Judd Fairbarn, "Historic Harpers Ferry," pamphlet, 41-42.

12. Douglas Southall Freeman, *Robert E. Lee*, in D.A.B., Vol. XI, 122; diary of Cornelius Walker, D.D., entry for April 15, 1861, in the Confederate Memorial Literary Society, Richmond.

13. Capt. Robert E. Lee, *Recollections and Letters of General Robert E. Lee*, 24-28; letter of Mrs. Lee to Mrs. G. W. Peter, written apparently in April, 1861, on deposit in the Maryland Historical Society. Lee's account of his talks with Blair and Scott is set forth in memoranda by Col. William Allan, who discussed the matter with Lee in 1868 and 1870, in the Southern Historical Collection, University of North Carolina.

14. Ticknor, op cit, 434.

Chapter Six: THE WAY OF REVOLUTION

1. Homemade War

1. Journal of the Congress of the Confederate States of America, Vol. I, 89, 93, 114-15; N.O.R., Series Two, Vol. III, 191-95; R. Barnwell Rhett, *The Confederate Government at Montgomery*, B. & L., Vol. I, 109-10.

2. Journal of the Congress of the Confederate States of America, Vol. I, 160-69.

3. Varina Howell Davis, *Jefferson Davis: a Memoir*, Vol. II, 80; Basler, Vol. IV, 345.

4. O.R., Series Three, Vol. I, 79-80; Appleton's *Annual Cyclopaedia, 1861*, 444.

5. Nicolay & Hay, Vol. IV, 105; O.R., Vol. II, 577; George William Brown, *Baltimore and the Nineteenth of April, 1861*, 43. Brown was mayor of Baltimore at the time and he says that notice of the coming of the troops was "purposely withheld" from the city authorities. Two days before the Baltimore riot, General Scott and Secretary of War Cameron sent an unidentified agent north to speed the dispatch of troops and to take measures to safeguard Washington's railroad connections, which, the agent was told, were liable to be broken in Baltimore. Reaching Baltimore, the agent was told by loyalist citizens that the passage of state troops would almost certainly cause a riot but that regulars could go through Baltimore without difficulty; "They could not see or admit that, when sworn into the service of the United States, they were no longer State troops but U.S. troops—or militia in the service of the Government." This agent's report is in the Cameron Papers, Library of Congress.

Incidentally, John Hay seems to have done the Pennsylvania contingent an injustice in his remark about "unlicked patriotism." This contingent was composed of five militia companies—from Lewistown, Allentown, Pottsville, and Reading—which were well-trained and disciplined, by the standards of that day, and which on their arrival in Washington mounted guard around the Capitol after being greeted by President Lincoln. In its march across Baltimore this battalion was hooted and stoned by a mob; it is asserted that the first blood shed in the Civil War was shed by Nicholas Biddle, a former slave serving as an officer's orderly, who was hit in the head by a brick-bat. I am indebted to Dr. S. K. Stevens, executive director of the Pennsylvania Historical and Museum Commission, and to Mr. Charles McKnight of Fork, Maryland, for information about these troops.

6. George William Brown, op cit, 44-46, 49-53; Col. Edward F. Jones in O.R., Vol. II, 7-9.

7. Appleton's *Annual Cyclopaedia, 1861*, 56-57; O.R., Vol. II, 9-11; Basler, Vol. IV, 340-42.

8. Nicolay & Hay, Vol. IV, 107-8, quoting Taylor but giving no source; *Memoirs of Henry Villard*, Vol. I, 170.

9. Report of War Department agent in the Cameron Papers, as cited in Note Five, above; Appleton's *Annual Cyclopedia, 1861*, 752; Nicolay & Hay, Vol. IV, 106-7; John Hay, *Lincoln and the Civil War*, 6-11.

10. Nicolay & Hay, Vol. IV, 144-45; Appleton's *Annual Cyclopaedia, 1861*, 535; Diary of Gideon Welles, Vol. I, 43-44.

11. Nicolay & Hay, Vol. IV, 146-47; N.O.R., Vol. IV, 288-90;

New York *Times*, April 26, 1861; Welles, Vol. I, 45-47; John Sherman Long, "The Gosport Affair, 1861," *Journal of Southern History*, Vol. XXIII, No. 2, 169.

12. N.O.R., Vol. IV, 306-9; J. Thomas Scharf, *History of the Confederate States Navy from Its Organization to the Surrender of Its Last Vessel*, 132.

2. *Arrests and Arrests Alone*

1. "A Page of Political Correspondence: Unpublished Letters of Mr. Stanton to Mr. Buchanan," *North American Review*, November 1879. On April 26, 1861, just after the tension was relieved, John G. Nicolay wrote to his wife that for some days after the Baltimore riot "Our intercourse with the outside world was cut off. We heard frequently from Baltimore and different parts of Maryland, but the news had little of encouragement in it. Uniformly, the report was that all heretofore Union men had at once turned secessionists, and were armed and determined to the death to prevent a single additional northern officer crossing the soil of Maryland. . . . We were not only surrounded by the enemy but in the midst of traitors." (John G. Nicolay Papers, Library of Congress.)

2. Nicolay & Hay, Vol. IV, 135; Letter of Gov. Hicks to Secretary Seward, April 22, 1861, in the William H. Seward Collection, University of Rochester.

3. Nicolay & Hay, Vol. IV, 155-57; unsigned article apparently by Theodore Winthrop, "The New York Seventh Regiment: Our March to Washington," *Atlantic Monthly*, June 1861.

4. Appleton's *Annual Cyclopaedia, 1861*, 444-46; Journal of the Congress of the Confederate States, Vol. I, 189; New York *Times*, April 30, 1861; Rhodes, Vol. III, 388.

5. McPherson, *A Political History of the United States of America During the Great Rebellion*, 9.

6. Nicolay & Hay, Vol. IV, 166; Basler, Vol. IV, 344.

7. George William Brown, *Baltimore and the Nineteenth of April, 1861*, 94-95; O.R., Vol. II, 29-30.

8. Carl Schurz, *Reminiscences*, Vol. II, 223-25.

9. O.R., Vol. II, 28-30; Butler, *Ben Butler's Book*, 237, 240.

10. Nicolay & Hay, Vol. IV, 174; Basler, Vol. IV, 429-30. For an excellent discussion of this case, see James G. Randall, *Constitutional Problems Under Lincoln*, 84, 120-21, 161-62. The Merryman case was eventually transferred to civil authority and at last was dropped. (O.R., Series Two, Vol. II, 226.)

11. Congressional Globe, 37th Congress, Third Session, Part 2, 1372-73, 1376.

12. Cited in Moore's *Rebellion Record*, Vol. I, Diary, 61.

3. Diplomacy Along the Border

1. Russell, *My Diary*, 65-68; letter of Varina Howell Davis to Clement C. Clay, in the Clay Papers at the Duke University Library.

2. O.R., Vol. II, 39.

3. O.R., Vol. II, 23-27.

4. Journal of the Congress of the Confederate States, Vol. I, 180-81, 188.

5. Moore's *Rebellion Record*, Vol. I, Documents, 193.

6. J. G. de Roulhac Hamilton, ed., *The Correspondence of Jonathan Worth*, Vol. I, 143; Joseph Carlyle Sitterson, *The Secession Movement in North Carolina*, 239 ff.

7. Appleton's *Annual Cyclopaedia, 1861*, 676-77, 680; Chase C. Mooney, "Some Institutional and Statistical Aspects of Slavery in Tennessee," in the *Tennessee Historical Quarterly*, Vol. I, 228; Moore's *Rebellion Record*, Vol. I, Documents, 72, 137.

8. Appleton's *Annual Cyclopaedia, 1861*, 22-23; O.R., Series Four, Vol. I, 294; Series One, Vol. I, 687; Ted R. Worley, "The Arkansas Peace Society of 1861; a Study in Mountain Unionism," in the *Journal of Southern History*, Vol. XXIV, No. 4, 445.

9. Moore's *Rebellion Record*, Vol. I, Documents, 264-65. Gov. Magoffin's course in the spring and summer of 1861 was perhaps as unsatisfactory to the governor himself as it was to the partisans who tugged at him so violently. E. Merton Coulter (*The Confederate States of America*, 45) considers Magoffin "a thorough-going Secessionist" who did his level best to take Kentucky out of the Union; James G. Randall, on the other hand, felt that Magoffin "may be described as anti-Lincoln rather than fully pro-Confederate." (*Lincoln the President*, Vol. II, 4.)

10. Jefferson Davis, *The Rise and Fall of the Confederate Government*, Vol. I, 386.

11. Letter of Garrett Davis to George D. Prentice, in the Congressional Globe, 37th Congress, Second Session, Appendix, 82-83.

12. Nicolay & Hay, Vol. IV, 235-36; O.R., LII, Part One, 140-41. There is an illuminating examination of the confusing Kentucky situation in Edward Conrad Smith, *The Borderland in the Civil War*, 263 ff.

4. Collapse of Legalities

1. Letter of Gov. Jackson to Jefferson Davis, April 17, 1861, in the Jefferson Davis Papers, Duke University Library.

2. Thomas L. Snead, *The First Year of the War in Missouri,* B. & L., Vol. I, 264 ff; O.R., Vol. I, 688.

3. Letter of Gov. Jackson to J. W. Tucker, April 28, 1861, in the James O. Broadhead Papers, Missouri Historical Society. For the May 3 message to the legislature, see Moore's *Rebellion Record,* Vol. I, 55.

4. The characterization is William Tecumseh Sherman's, in his *Memoirs,* Vol. I, 172.

5. There is an engaging and sharply critical sketch of Lyon written by a former trooper in the 1st U. S. Cavalry, Robert Morris Peck, *Rough Riding on the Plains.* Trooper Peck remarks that when this regiment learned, late in the summer of 1861, that Lyon had been killed in action, "the almost invariable verdict was 'Well, the old son of a gun is "punished properly" at last.' " I am indebted to Mrs. Raymond Millbrook of Detroit for calling this little-known book to my attention.

6. Rhodes, Vol. III, 393-94; Nicolay & Hay, Vol. IV, 208-9; O.R., Vol. I, 669-70.

7. Chicago *Tribune,* April 29, 1861; letter of William Hyde of the St. Louis *Republican* to William McKendree Springer, in the Springer Papers, Chicago Historical Society.

8. Thomas L. Snead, op cit, 264-65; John Fiske, *The Mississippi Valley in the Civil War,* 13-15; O.R., Vol. III, 4.

9. The story is given in detail in Fiske, 16-17. After the war, Sherman wrote to John G. Nicolay expressing deep skepticism about the entire episode and remarking that although he himself had been in St. Louis at the time he had heard nothing about it. Nicolay's answer apparently satisfied him, however, for he wrote "Your proof is conclusive." (Letters of W. T. Sherman dated Feb. 4 and April 2, 1882; letter of Nicolay dated March 24, 1882; in the John G. Nicolay Papers.) The story obviously can be taken or left alone, at the reader's option.

10. O.R., Vol. III, 4-6; Sherman, *Memoirs,* Vol. I, 172; Snead, 265; Francis Grierson, *The Valley of Shadows,* 225-26. This seems as good a place as any to remark that the Grierson book is a little classic which deserves a wider reading than it has been getting.

11. Grierson, 228. For a discussion of Frost's course, see Col.

John C. Moore, "Missouri," in Vol. IX, *Confederate Military History*, 32-33.

12. O.R., Vol. III, 4-5.

13. Sherman, *Memoirs*, Vol. I, 173; Robert J. Rombauer, *The Union Cause in St. Louis*, 223. One of the German soldiers wrote: "When the hauty young Americans were taken into custody by the second regiment, composed of Germans, and as prisoners were marched to the arsenal, their rage knew no bounds. But to no avail. They simply were prisoners, and the Dutch, as we were generally called, were masters of the situation." (Diary of John T. Buegel, 3rd Missouri Volunteer Infantry, in the J. N. Heiskell Collection, Little Rock, Ark.) Shortly after Lyon's exploit an ardent St. Louis secessionist wrote: "My blood boils in my veins when I think of the position of Missouri—held in the Union at the point of Dutchmen's bayonets. I feel outraged —you may imagine how hard it is for men to endure it." (Letter signed A L to "Dear Sister," dated May 20, 1861, in the Civil War Papers of the Missouri Historical Society.)

14. Galusha Anderson, *A Border City During the Civil War*, 98-99; Rachel Sherman Thorndike, ed., *The Sherman Letters: Correspondence Between General and Senator Sherman from 1837 to 1891*, 119-20; Rombauer, *The Union Cause in St. Louis*, 233.

15. Rombauer, 234; Thomas L. Snead, *The Fight for Missouri*, 171; Grierson, 230-31.

16. Moore's *Rebellion Record*, Vol. I, Documents, 234-36; Rombauer, 239; James Peckham, *Gen. Nathaniel Lyon*, 162.

5. Symbolism of Death

1. William Ernest Smith, *The Francis Preston Blair Family in Politics*, Vol. II, 47-48; Rombauer, 243; Fiske, op cit, 21.

2. Snead, *The First Year of the War in Missouri*, B. & L., Vol. I, 266; D.A.B., Vol. XV, 216-17; Rombauer, 258; letter of Jeff Thompson to Charles M. Thompson, May 29, 1861, Civil War Papers Mo. Hist. Soc.

3. Nicolay & Hay, Vol. IV, 216; Basler, Vol. IV, 372-73, 387; O.R., Vol. III, 375.

4. Francis P. Blair, Jr., to Lincoln, May 30, 1861, in Nicolay & Hay, Vol. IV, 222; O.R., Vol. III, 383; Letter from A L to "Dear Sister," in the Civil War Papers of the Missouri Historical Society; James Peckham, *General Nathaniel Lyon*, 226. On May 17, Montgomery Blair wrote to his brother about the prospective removal of Harney and the promotion of Lyon: "I have had

great difficulty in accomplishing these matters. . . . The Secy of War was against both." (Francis P. Blair, Jr., Papers, Library of Congress.)

5. Snead, *The First Year of the War in Missouri*, B. & L., Vol. I, 267; Moore's *Rebellion Record*, Vol. I, 363-64.

6. There is a thoughtful discussion of the Missouri situation in Edward Conrad Smith, *The Borderland in the Civil War*, 221-240. Smith inclines to the view that it was Gen. Harney who blocked out the most practical policy for this troubled state, and he feels that Lyon's seizure of the militia camp in St. Louis was an expensive mistake: "No one can know what would have happened if the camp had been allowed to continue until the close of the day, or if the men had been allowed to go to their homes to spread secessionist propaganda and later to enlist with the armies of the South. But from the events which immediately followed the affair, one is forced to the conclusion that it was a political blunder of the first magnitude, which occasioned inestimably more damage to the cause of the Union than could have resulted from allowing it to continue." (*The Borderland*, 238.)

7. Appleton's *Annual Cyclopaedia, 1861*, 140; Montgomery *Weekly Advertiser*, May 11, 1861. For a discussion of the pros and cons of the move to Richmond, see E. Merton Coulter, *The Confederate States of America*, 100-2.

8. Nicolay & Hay, Vol. IV, 310-12; O.R., Vol. II, 40-42; B. & L., Vol. I, 179, editor's footnote on Ellsworth; New York *Tribune*, May 26, 1861; John Hay, "A Young Hero: Personal Reminiscences of Col. E. E. Ellsworth," in *McClure's Magazine*, March 1896; Ellsworth's letter to his parents, *Harper's Weekly*, June 8, 1861, 357; Basler, Vol. IV, 385-86. In the Ellsworth Papers at the Chicago Historical Society there is an account of Ellsworth's death written by George H. Fergus, who was a lieutenant in Company E of the Fire Zouaves. Fergus insists that Ellsworth did not enter the hotel to take down the flag; "He went in so that he could get a view of the situation from the cupola." According to Fergus, Ellsworth made his survey and then, almost as an afterthought, cut down the flag before he returned to the street.

9. In view of the innumerable eulogies that have been written on Ellsworth, it should be remembered that the whole affair looked very different in the South. Commenting on the occupation of Alexandria, the Richmond *Examiner* printed the following: "One trait of true heroism has signalized this unhappy affair. A citizen of Alexandria, named Jackson, lacked the prudence

to haul down the flag of his country, which streamed over his
dwelling. That band of execrable cut-throats and jailbirds, known
as the 'Zouaves of New York,' under the chief of all scoundrels,
called Col. Ellsworth, surrounded the house of this Virginian
and broke open the door to tear down the flag of the South.
The courageous owner of that house neither fled nor submitted.
He met the favorite hero of every Yankee there in the hall,
he alone, against thousands, and shot him through the heart! As
a matter of course, the magnanimous soldiery surrounded him
in his own violated home. But he died a death which Em-
perors might envy, and his memory will live in history, and
in the hearts of his countrymen, through endless generations."

6. Before the Night Came

1. Letter of Senator Douglas to Virgil Hicox; from the collection of Elsie O. and Philip D. Sang, River Forest, Ill.

2. Rhodes, Vol. II, 414; George Fort Milton, *The Eve of
Conflict*, 567-69.

3. Congressional Globe, 37th Congress, First Session, 30-31;
letter of Alexander Stephens to his brother Linton, June 7, 1861,
in the Stephens Papers, Brady Memorial Library, Manhattanville
College of the Sacred Heart, Purchase, N.Y.

4. Moore's *Rebellion Record*, Vol. II, Documents, 282-83.

5. Rhodes, Vol. III, 466; O.R., Vol. II, 648-51; James Parton,
With Butler in New Orleans, 127.

6. O.R., Vol. II, 649, 653; Series Three, Vol. I, 243.

7. Moore's *Rebellion Record*, Vol. II, Documents, 437-38,
493. Cf Bell Irvin Wiley, *Southern Negroes, 1861-1865*, 176.

8. Nicolay & Hay, Vol. IV, 390-91.

9. O.R., Vol. II, 653. McDowell's personality and pre-war
career are sketched in D.A.B., Vol. XII, 29-30.

10. New York *Tribune*, May 27, 1861.

11. Adam Gurowski, *Diary*, Vol. I, 41.

12. Frederick W. Seward, *Seward At Washington*, Vol. II,
575; Diary of William T. Coggeshall, military secretary to Gov-
ernor Dennison, entry for May 23, 1861, in the Illinois State
Historical Library, Springfield; letter of W. W. Orme to Leonard
Swett, May 14, 1861, in the David Davis Papers; W. T. Sherman
to Charles Ewing, June 22, 1861, in the Ewing Family Papers,
Library of Congress; Stanton to Buchanan, June 8, 1861, in the
North American Review for November, 1879.

13. Dunbar Rowland, *Jefferson Davis, Constitutionalist*, Vol. V,
102-4; Varina Howell Davis, *Jefferson Davis*, Vol. II, 74-75;

letter of Mrs. Wigfall to her daughter, May 30, 1861, in the Wigfall Family Papers, University of Texas.

14. Jefferson Davis, *Rise and Fall,* Vol. I, 340; O.R., Vol. II, 927-29, giving Lee's report on the situation at the time of the transfer. For a detailed appraisal, see Freeman's *R. E. Lee,* Vol. I, 521, 527.

15. Letters of E. Porter Alexander to his wife, dated June 4, 6 and 8, 1861, in the E. P. Alexander Papers, Southern Historical Collection; *Recollections and Letters of General Robert E. Lee,* 35; O.R., Vol. II, 907; letter of John S. Manning to Mrs. Manning, June 9, 1861, in the Williams-Chesnut-Manning Papers, Southern Historical Collection.

16. Letter of Edmund Kirby Smith to his mother, May 29, 1861, in the E. Kirby Smith Papers, Southern Historical Collection; letter of William Culbertson Robinson to Charles Abbot, May 29, 1861, in the William Culbertson Robinson Papers, Illinois State Historical Library; undated letter, written in May or June, 1861, from James H. Langhorne to his parents, in the Langhorne Family Papers, Virginia State Historical Society.

Chapter Seven: TO THE FIERY ALTAR

1. War In the Mountains

1. McClellan's autobiography, *McClellan's Own Story,* goes into detail on his activities during the first months of the war. In the Oberlin College Library there is a copy of this book once owned by Jacob D. Cox, the Ohio Republican politician who was closely associated with McClellan in the early days in Ohio, and who later in the war became a competent general in his own right; and Cox wrote a number of pungent marginal notes, commenting on McClellan's narrative, which are often worth examination. As a sample: on page 43 of his autobiography, McClellan remarks that Unionists in the west at the start of the war lacked organization, arms, supplies, money and officers, to say nothing of a general policy and a directing head, and adds: "It fell to me, perhaps more than to any one person, to supply those pressing wants, and at this distance I may say that the task was not unsatisfactorily performed." Cox questions this, marginally, writing: "Where was the governor?"

2. O.R., Vol. II, 49-50, 652. For a general account of the West Virginia situation, see Jacob D. Cox, *McClellan in West Virginia,* in B. & L., Vol. I, 126 ff.

3. Moore's *Rebellion Record,* Vol. I, Documents, 296-98; O.R., Vol. II, 66-67, 72-74; Charles Leib, *Nine Months in the Quartermaster's Department; or The Chances for Making a Million More,* 14-15; John C. Nicolay, *The Outbreak of the Rebellion,* 144; Appleton's *Annual Cyclopaedia, 1861,* 743-44.

4. O.R., Vol. II, 197-98.

5. Ibid, 236, 242.

6. Cox, *McClellan in West Virginia,* 130-31; O.R., Vol. II, 208-9.

7. O.R., Vol. II, 201, 206; Cox, op cit, 132.

8. Scott's message of congratulations is in O.R., Vol. II, 204. McClellan's message to his troops, 236.

9. John Beatty, *Memoirs of a Volunteer, 1861-1865,* 21, 23, 31; *McClellan's Own Story,* 59; Appleton's *Annual Cyclopaedia, 1861,* 743-44.

10. Jed. Hotchkiss, Virginia, Vol. III, *Confederate Military History,* 61-62.

11. Moore's *Rebellion Record,* Vol. II, Documents, 296.

12. Charles Leib, *Nine Months in the Quartermaster's Department,* 33-35.

13. Ibid, 126-27.

14. Jed. Hotchkiss, Virginia, Vol. III, *Confederate Military History,* 59-60; Moore's *Rebellion Record,* Vol. I, Documents, 323-24.

2. *The Laws of War*

1. Murat Halstead in the Cincinnati *Daily Commercial,* July 1, 1861.

2. Congressional Globe, 37th Congress, First Session, 2.

3. Letter from T. J. Barnett to S. L. M. Barlow, May 27, 1861, in the Barlow Papers, at the Huntington Library.

4. Adam Gurowski, *Diary,* Vol. I, 63-64, 66.

5. Congressional Globe, 37th Congress, First Session, 4-5; Rhodes, Vol. III, 441.

6. Basler, Vol. IV, 421-41.

7. For the speeches and general debate in both houses of Congress, the writer has relied on the extensive verbatim reports in the American *Annual Cyclopaedia, 1861,* 232, 234-36, 239-42, 244.

8. Morse to Dr. James Wynne, May 2, 1861: from the

Samuel F. B. Morse Papers, Library of Congress: notes from Allan Nevins.

9. Congressional Globe, 37th Congress, First Session, 54, 97, 130.

10. Appleton's *Annual Cyclopaedia, 1861*, 246-50.

3. A Head Full of Fire

1. Appleton's *Annual Cyclopaedia, 1861*, 43; New York *Herald*, July 4, 1861.

2. D.A.B., Vol. XII, 429-31.

3. Diary of Betty Herndon Maury, entry for July 10, 1861, in the Library of Congress; Moore's *Rebellion Record*, Vol. II, Diary, 21; N.O.R., Vol. IV, 566-67.

4. Notes by W. G. Cobb, in the Cameron Papers, Library of Congress; mss Recollections of C. D. Fishburne, in the Southern Historical Collection.

5. "Letters of Francis Parkman," edited by Wilbur R. Jacobs, Vol. I, 163.

6. Moore's *Rebellion Record*, Vol. II, Documents, 282-83.

7. Journal of the Congress of the Confederate States, Vol. I, 272-75.

8. Davis to Johnston, July 13, 1861, in the Joseph E. Johnston Papers at the Huntington Library.

9. Letter of John S. Manning to Mrs. Manning, July 7, 1861, in the Williams-Chesnut-Manning Papers, Southern Historical Collection.

10. James D. Richardson, *Messages and Papers of the Confederacy*, Vol. II, 34-38, 40.

11. Congressional Globe, 37th Congress, First Session, Appendix, with report of the Secretary of the Navy, 7-9.

12. *National Intelligencer*, July 9, 1861, quoting a letter from Vicksburg dated June 16, 1861.

13. For a thorough examination of the Confederacy's economic weakness, see Charles W. Ramsdell, *Behind the Lines in the Southern Confederacy*. He concludes (p 103) that the "industrial weakness of the South was one of the decisive factors in its defeat. . . . The colonial economy which had been so characteristic of Southern business before the war had left the country without sufficient fluid capital or coin to sustain the currency." Even more pointed is the verdict of John Christopher Schwab (*The Confederate States of America, 1861-1865: a Financial and Industrial History of the South During the Civil War*, 2-3): "The North was industrially much more advanced, its manufac-

tures were vastly more extensive, its urban population was more numerous, its trade more advanced, its transportation system more highly developed—in a word, its resources were far superior to those of the South, and were the cause of the final overthrow of the Confederate government." The editor of the *Cologne Gazette,* in Germany, wrote shortly after the outbreak of the war that "the poverty-stricken Don Quixotes of the Southern plantations gave battle to the roaring windmills and smoking chimneys of the wealthy North," and remarked that the Confederacy was "in arms against the spirit of the century." (Quoted in Moore's *Rebellion Record,* Vol. I, Documents, 265-66.)

14. Not long before the bombardment of Fort Sumter, the British correspondent William Howard Russell dined with the Confederate commissioners in Washington and wrote: "Mr. Lincoln they spoke of with contempt; Mr. Seward they evidently regarded as the ablest and most unscrupulous of their enemies; but the tone in which they alluded to the whole of the Northern people indicated their clear conviction that trade, commerce, the pursuit of gain, manufacture, and the base mechanical arts, had so degraded the whole race, they would never attempt to strike a blow in fair fight for what they prized so highly in theory and in words." (*My Diary,* 31)

15. American *Annual Cyclopaedia, 1861,* 157.

4. The Road to Bull Run

1. O.R., Vol. II, 77-82, 93-97; Joseph B. Carr, *Operations of 1861 about Fort Monroe,* B. & L., Vol. II, 150; Felix Gregory De Fontaine, "Shoulder to Shoulder," *Century Magazine,* No. VI, Vol. I, 443; Moore's *Rebellion Record,* Vol. I, Documents, 360-61.

2. Nicolay & Hay, Vol. IV, 319-20; New York *Tribune,* June 26, 1861; Adam Gurowski, *Diary,* Vol. I, 56.

3. O.R., Vol. LI, Part One, 338-39, 369-70, 387.

4. O.R., Vol. II, 718-21; Nicolay & Hay, Vol. IV, 322-24; E. D. Townsend, *Anecdotes of the Civil War in the United States,* 55-57.

5. O.R., Vol. II, 158-59, 163, 166-69, 187, 661, 691-96. This dreary exchange of messages is confusing enough to the modern student, and it is easy to see how it confused its authors. In his testimony before the Committee on the Conduct of the War, Patterson makes it clear that he precisely obeyed what he understood Scott's orders to be, and it is hard to feel that he alone was responsible for the fact that he never quite grasped

what Scott wanted him to do. (Report of the Joint Committee on the Conduct of the War, Part II, 1863, Bull Run, 5-7, 104). There is a sketch of Patterson's career in D.A.B., Vol. XIV, 306-7.

6. O.R., Vol. II, 485, 923; Vol. LI, Part Two, 688. For a sharp critique of Beauregard's plan, see T. Harry Williams, *Beauregard*, 75-80. The New York *Tribune*, particularly in its issues of July 17 and 18, 1861, appears to have given about all the information regarding McDowell's plans that Beauregard could have needed, and although the feminine spies in Washington are sometimes credited with having had a decisive influence on the battle of Bull Run it does not seem to this writer that their romantic activities really made very much difference. (It ought to be remembered, in this connection, that no part of the plans which Beauregard is said to have drawn up as a result of the information thus received was ever actually put into operation.) In his July 17 message to Davis announcing that a major engagement was imminent, Beauregard simply said, "The enemy has assailed my outposts in heavy force," making no mention of the supposedly all-important messages received 24 hours earlier from Washington. (Roman, *Military Operations*, Vol. I, 90). McDowell's advance was so heavily publicized all around that Beauregard would have had to be exceedingly stupid (which he decidedly was not) to have remained in ignorance of it.

7. O.R., Vol. II, 472, 686, 691, 901.

8. B. & L., Vol. I, 122-23.

9. Rev. A. M. Stewart, *Camp, March and Battlefield; or, Three Years and a Half with the Army of the Potomac*, 15; O.R., Vol. II, 168.

10. O.R., Vol. II, 303-5.

11. George Wilkes, *The Great Battle*, 6-7; Francis F. Meagher, *Last Days of the 69th in Virginia*, 6; D. G. Crotty, *Four Years Campaign in the Army of the Potomac*, 20. McDowell's report on the battle of Bull Run recites the difficulties of the march, and asserts that the men were more wearied by the obstacles in the road and the slow pace set than by the distance covered. McDowell adds that the men were "unaccustomed to marching, their bodies not in condition for that kind of work, and not used to carrying even the load of 'light marching order'." (O.R., Vol. II, 323-24.) Cf Colin R. Ballard, *The Military Genius of Abraham Lincoln*, 56: "The Federals were really defeated by their own exhaustion."

12. Meagher, op cit, 10.

13. Roman, *Military Operations*, Vol. I, 74-75; B. & L., Vol. I, 203.

5. Dust Clouds Against the Sky

1. George Wilkes, *The Great Battle*, 17-19; Edmund C. Stedman, *The Battle of Bull Run*, 15-17.

2. O.R., Vol. II, 318-19, 326, 559; E. Porter Alexander, *Military Memoirs of a Confederate*, 30-31; Joseph Mills Hanson, *Bull Run Remembers*, 4.

3. Elisha H. Rhodes, *The First Campaign of the Second Rhode Island Infantry*, 18-19; Martin A. Haynes, *A History of the Second Regiment, New Hampshire Volunteer Infantry*, 23-24.

4. Mss diary of Samuel Heintzelman, Library of Congress, 36-37.

5. O.R., Vol. II, 319, 349, 369, 559; Hanson, loc. cit.; Francis F. Wilshin, *Manassas*, 11-12.

6. Alexander, *Military Memoirs*, 33-35; Johnston's report, O.R., Vol. II, 474-75.

7. McHenry Howard, *Recollections of a Maryland Confederate Soldier and Staff Officer under Johnston, Jackson and Lee*, 34-38; W. W. Goldsborough, *The Maryland Line in the Confederate States Army*, 19-20; Alexander, 32-33.

8. Richmond *Enquirer*, Aug. 9, 1861; letter of Gen. Beauregard to the editors of the *Century Magazine*, Aug. 1, 1884, in the Palmer Collection, Western Reserve Historical Society. Porter Alexander, whose account of the fight on the Henry House plateau is especially vivid, remarks: "New troops going into action are very prone to 'fire and fall back'—to touch and let go —as one handles a piece of hot iron when uncertain how hot it may be." (*Military Memoirs*, 33.)

9. Alexander, 35; Richmond *Enquirer*, Aug. 9, 1861.

10. T. B. Warder and James W. Catlett, *Battle of Young's Branch, or Manassas Plain*, 74-76.

11. John W. Imboden, *Incidents of the First Bull Run*, in B. & L., Vol. I, 234-35; Hanson, 5.

12. Edwin S. Barrett, *What I Saw at Bull Run*, 20-21; Hanson, 6; O.R., Vol. II, 347-48, 391-92, 403; Alexander, 39; Col. William W. Averell in Report of the Joint Committee on the Conduct of the War, Part II, 1863, 216.

13. Hanson, 6-7; Wilshin, 14-15; Moore's *Rebellion Record*, Vol. II, Documents, 95; Charles Minor Blackford, in Susan Leigh Blackford's *Letters from Lee's Army*, 25.

14. McDowell's report, O.R., Vol. II, 319-20; Captain Wood-

bury, ibid, 334. After telling how the discipline of the Union troops collapsed during the retreat, Woodbury remarks: "We cannot suppose that the troops of the enemy had attained a higher degree of discipline than our own, but they acted on the defensive, and were not equally exposed to disorganization."

15. Alexander, 41-42; Davis, *Rise and Fall*, Vol. I, 349-50; Mss Diary of Edmund Ruffin, Library of Congress; Avery Craven, *Edmund Ruffin, Southerner*, 230. There are different versions of Jackson's remark about the need for a speedy pursuit. T. Harry Williams is inclined to skepticism, and Frank Vandiver (*Mighty Stonewall*) says that "caution must be used" regarding it. The remark does seem to be wholly in character with Jackson's aggressive attitude.

6. Death of the Minute Man

1. McDowell's report, O.R., Vol. II, 321. W. T. Sherman (ibid, 370-71) wrote that "there was no positive order to retreat, although for an hour it had been going on by the operation of the men themselves," and Brig Gen. Robert C. Schenck reported (360) that the retreat "seemed to me to be occasioned more by the fears of frightened teamsters, and of hurrying and excited civilians (who ought never to have been there) than even by the needless disorder and want of discipline of straggling soldiers." The classic account of the picnic and the rout is of course William Howard Russell's. His story of his own adventures at Bull Run begins on page 163 of *My Diary*.

2. Sarah Ellen Blackwell, *A Military Genius: Life of Anna Ella Carroll*, Vol. I, 77-79; Russell, 168-70; Albert Gallatin Riddle, *Recollections of War Times*, 48-51.

3. O.R., Vol. II, 316.

4. Ibid, 747-53.

5. Beauregard's report, ibid, 497; report of M. L. Bonham, 519; Davis to Adjutant General Cooper, 987; Roman, *Military Operations*, Vol. I, 111.

6. Roman, Vol. I, 114; Davis, *Rise and Fall*, Vol. I, 352-53; Alexander, 49. Alexander was present at the conference; he identifies the staff officer as Major R. C. Hill, adding: "Nothing that he had ever done had justified his nickname, but it arose from something peculiar in his eye, tones and manner, all suggestive of suppressed excitement."

7. This writer is strongly inclined to agree with Johnston's conclusion (*Narrative of Military Operations*, 60-61): "Considering the relative strength of the belligerents on the field,

the Southern people could not reasonably have expected greater results from their victory than those accomplished: the defeat of the invasion of Virginia, and the preservation of the capital of the Confederacy." In the autumn of 1861 Johnston wrote to Davis listing the reasons why his army did not advance on Washington: "The apparent firmness of the U.S. troops at Centreville, which checked our pursuit—The strong forces occupying the works near Georgetown, Arlington & Alexandria—The certainty, too, that General Patterson, if needed, would reach Washington with his army of more than 30,000 sooner than we could—& the condition & inadequate means of the army in ammunition, provision & transportation, prevented any serious thoughts of advancing against the capital." (Letter to President Davis, Nov. 10, 1861, in the Joseph E. Johnston Papers, Manuscript Department, Duke University Library.) In this explanation Johnston, to be sure, greatly overstates the "firmness" of the Federals at Centreville and the size of Patterson's army, but the other obstacles were very real. Jubal Early wrote after the war that "it was utterly impossible for any army to have captured Washington by immediate pursuit," pointing out that even if a pursuit had been made "it would have been very difficult to cross the Potomac at all." (*Autobiographical Sketch and Narrative of the War between the States*, 40.)

8. *The Complete Writings of Walt Whitman*, Vol. IV, 32-36. It should be borne in mind that although Whitman presented a graphic and apparently authentic account of the post-battle scene in Washington, he himself was not an eyewitness.

9. The figures are the best estimate this writer can make after examining the varying totals given in different sources. See *Battles & Leaders*, Vol. I, 194-195; O.R., Vol. II, 327, 570, and Vol. LI, 17-19; Thomas L. Livermore, *Numbers and Losses in the Civil War in America*, 77; Frederick Phisterer, *Statistical Record of the Armies of the United States*, 213.

10. Nicolay & Hay, Vol. IV, 365-66; New York *Tribune*, July 21 and 22, announcing a great Union victory, and July 23 with editorial lamentations.

11. Horace Bushnell, "Reverses Needed. A Discourse Delivered on the Sunday after the Disaster of Bull Run, in the North Church, Hartford," 8.

12. Nicolay & Hay, Vol. IV, 352-54; E. D. Townsend, *Anecdotes of the Civil War*, 58-59; John G. Nicolay, letters to Mrs. Nicolay dated July 21 and July 23, 1861, in the Nicolay Papers, Library of Congress.

13. O.R., Vol. II, 756; Nicolay & Hay, Vol. IV, 357, 368; Basler, Vol. IV, 457-58.

14. Stanton to Buchanan, July 26, 1861, in the Buchanan Papers, Historical Society of Pennsylvania.

15. *Richmond During the War; Four Years of Personal Observation,* by "a Richmond Lady" who seems to have been Mrs. Sallie A. Putnam, 63; Journal of the Congress of the Confederate States, Vol. I, 275-76; E. A. Pollard, *The First Year of the War,* 116; O.R., Vol. II, 574; Moore's *Rebellion Record,* Vol. II, Documents, III.

16. Davis, *Rise and Fall,* Vol. I, 443; letter of Johnston to Davis, Aug. 3, 1861, in the Joseph E. Johnston Papers, Duke University; Mrs. Chesnut's Diary, 92.

17. R. E. Lee, in a letter to a relative, July 27; mss. on deposit in the Maryland Historical Society.

18. De Leon, *Four Years in Rebel Capitals,* 123-24.

19. Mrs. Chesnut's Diary, 88; letter of T. R. R. Cobb, in Southern Historical Society Papers, Vol. XXVIII, 288.

20. Letter of Sullivan Bullen to Sarah Shumway Bullen, July 14, 1861, in the Chicago Historical Society.

Bibliography

THE BIBLIOGRAPHY for this volume, prepared by E. B. Long, consists of four parts. I. Resources. The libraries, historical societies, archives, colleges, universities, battlefields, forts, and other institutions that contributed to this volume. (Others will be named in later volumes.) Also this stands as grateful acknowledgment and recognition of the many persons who aided us in these places at the time of our visits. II. Primary manuscript collections made use of for this book. III. Newspapers. IV. Books, pamphlets, and periodicals.

SECTION I: *Resources*

The persons listed herein were those associated with these institutions at the time of our visit.

Abraham Lincoln Book Shop, Chicago, Ralph G. Newman, Margaret April, and Richard Clark.

Adjutant General's Office, State of Louisiana, Jackson Barracks, New Orleans, La., Thomas Harrison.

Alabama State Department of Archives and History, Montgomery, Ala., Peter Brannon.

Annan, David H., Chicago, Ill., private collection.

Arkansas History Commission, Little Rock, Ark., J. H. Atkinson, Orville W. Taylor, Francis I. Gwaltney.

Armstrong, Loring, Elmhurst, Ill., private collection.

Atlanta Historical Society, Atlanta, Ga., Allen P. Julian.

Bancroft Library, University of California, Berkeley, Calif., Mrs. Julia H. Macloed, Miss L. M. Ignacki.

Eugene C. Barker Texas History Center, University of Texas, Austin, Tex., Miss Winnie Allen.

Beauvoir, Biloxi, Miss., home of Jefferson Davis.

Boston Athenaeum, Boston, Mass., Miss Margaret Hackett.

Boston Public Library, Boston, Mass., Rare Book Dept., Zoltan N. Hardszti, John Alden, Louis Ugalde.

Brown University, John Hay Library, Providence, R.I., John R. T. Ettlinger, Mrs. Norma Kacen.

California Historical Society, San Francisco, Calif., James deT. Abajian.

California, University of, Berkeley, Calif., Library, Henry N. Smith, Frederick Anderson.

California, University of, at Los Angeles, Library, Dept. of Special Collections, Wilbur J. Smith, James Mink.

Charleston Library Society, Charleston, S.C., Miss Virginia Rugheimer.

Chicago Historical Society, Paul M. Angle, Miss Margaret Scriven.

Chicago Public Library, Gertrude Gscheidle, Herbert Hewitt, and others.

Chicago, University of, Harper Library, Robert Rosenthal.

Civil War Round Tables in numerous cities and their many, many members who always co-operate in every way possible.

Cockrell, Monroe F., Evanston, Ill., private collection.

Concordia Teachers College Library, River Forest, Ill., Albert Huegli, Cornell J. Kusmik.

Confederate Memorial Hall, New Orleans, La., Kenneth Urquhart.

Confederate Memorial Literary Society, Richmond, Va., also known as Confederate Museum or White House of the Confederacy, Miss India W. Thomas, Miss Eleanor Brockenbrough.

Dallas Historical Society, Dallas, Texas.

Duke University Library, Durham, N.C., Manuscript Department, Miss Mattie Russell, Mrs. Virginia R. Gray, Miss Sarah Gray.

Essex Institute, Salem, Mass., Mrs. Charles Potter, Mrs. Thomas Barrow.

Fort Pickens, Pensacola, Fla.

Fort Sumter National Monument, Charleston, S.C.

Georgia Historical Society, Savannah, Ga., Walter C. Hartridge, Mrs. Lilla M. Hawes.

Hanaford, G. E., Oak Park, Ill., private collection.

Harvard University, Houghton Library, Cambridge, Mass., W. H. Bond.

Harvard University, Widener Library, Cambridge, Mass.

Haverlin, Carl, New York, private collection.

Heiskell, J. N., Little Rock, Ark., private collection, Mrs. Margaret Ross.

Henry E. Huntington Library and Art Gallery, San Marino, Calif., John E. Pomfret, Allan Nevins, Norma B. Cuthbert, Mary Isabel Fry, Gertrude Ruhnka, Helen Mangold, and many others.

Illinois State Historical Library, Springfield, Ill., Clyde Walton, Margaret Flint, James Hickey, Howard Rissler, and others.

Johnston, J. Ambler, Richmond, Va., private collection.

Lebold, Mrs. Foreman M., Chicago, Ill., private collection.

Library of Congress, Washington, D.C., David C. Mearns, C. Percy Powell, Willard Webb, Roy Basler, John J. de Porry, and many others.

Lincoln Memorial University, Dept. of Lincolniana, Harrogate, Tenn., the late Robert Kincaid, William Taylor, Wayne C. Temple.

Lincoln National Life Foundation, Fort Wayne, Ind., R. Gerald McMurtry, Louis Warren.

Little Rock University, Little Rock, Ark.

Louisiana State Dept. of Archives, Louisiana State University, Baton Rouge, La., Virgil Bedsole.

Manassas National Battlefield Park, Manassas, Va., Francis Wilshin.

Manhattanville College of the Sacred Heart, Brady Memorial Library, Purchase, N.Y., Rev. Mother E. Mulqueen, Mother Eleanor O'Byrne, Mother Gertrude Buck.

Maryland Historical Society, Baltimore, Md., Francis C. Haber.

Massachusetts Historical Society, Boston, Mass., Stephen T. Riley, Miss Winifred Collins, Warren Wheeler, Malcom Freiberg.

Meine, Franklin J., Chicago, Ill., private collection.

Mercantile Library, St. Louis, Mo., Clarence E. Miller.

Military Historical Society of Massachusetts, Boston, Mass., Miss Agnes Scanlon.

Military Order of the Loyal Legion of the United States, Massachusetts Commandery, Boston, Mass., Preston Lincoln.

Military Order of the Loyal Legion of the United States, Philadelphia, Pa., Mrs. Stephanie Benko.

Mississippi Department of Archives and History, Jackson, Miss., Miss Charlotte Capers.

Missouri Historical Society, St. Louis, Mo., Charles van Ravenswaay, Mrs. Francis Stadler, Mrs. Ellen Harris, Mrs. Brenda R. Gieseker.

Museum of the City of New York, Philip Rees.

National Archives, Washington, D.C., Dallas Irvine, Victor Gondos and others.

Nevins, Allan, Huntington Library, San Marino, Calif., private collection.

Newberry Library, Chicago, Stanley Pargellis, Ben C. Bowman. In addition to their invaluable library, an office was graciously provided the Director of Research.

Newman, Ralph, Chicago, private collection.

New York Historical Society, New York.

New York Public Library, Manuscript Division.

Northwestern University Library, Evanston, Ill., Robert Harvey, Felix Pollak.

Oak Park Public Library, Oak Park, Ill., Lester Stoffel.

Oberlin College Library, Oberlin, Ohio.

Owen, Charles Norton, Chicago, Ill., private collection.

Peacock, John R., High Point, N.C., private collection.

Pennsylvania Historical and Museum Commission, Harrisburg, Pa., S. K. Stevens, Sanford W. Higginbotham, Henry Eddy, Miss Martha L. Simonetti, Frank Evans.

Pennsylvania, The Historical Society of, Philadelphia, Pa., R. N. Williams II.

Princeton University Library, Manuscript Division, Princeton, N.J., Alexander P. Clark.

Rochester, University of, Rush Rhees Library, Rochester, N.Y., Dept. of Special Collections, Miss Margaret E. Butterfield, Mrs. Evelyn Yost.

The Philip H. & A. S. W. Rosenbach Foundation, Philadelphia, Pa., William McCarthy.

Russell, Don, Elmhurst, Ill., private collection.

Sang, Philip D., and Elsie O., River Forest, Ill., private collection.

Seward, Wm. H., Home, The Foundation Historical Association, Inc., Auburn, N.Y.

Shedd, Charles, Pittsburg Landing, Tenn., private collection.

Sinnott, James Butterfield III, New Orleans, La., private collection.

Smith, Ray D., Chicago, private collection.

South Carolina Historical Society, Charleston, S.C., Samuel G. Stoney, Mrs. Gertrude T. Prior.

Southern California, University of, Los Angeles, Calif., Lloyd Arvidson, Helen Azhderian.

Southern Historical Collection, University of North Carolina Library, Chapel Hill, N.C., James Patton, Mrs. Carolyn Wallace.

Stanford University Library, Palo Alto, Calif., Julius Barclay.

Tennessee State Library and Archives, Nashville, Tenn., William

T. Alderson, Jr., Mrs. Isabelle Howell, Mrs. Frank Owsley, Mrs. Gertrude Parsley, Robert T. Quarles, Daniel M. Robison.

Texas State Archives, Austin, Tex., Dorman H. Winfrey, Mrs. Mary Osburn.

Tufts University, Eaton Library, Medford, Mass., Joseph S. Komidor, Miss Hilda F. Harris.

Tulane University, Dept. of Archives, New Orleans, La., Mrs. Connie Griffith.

Turner, Justin G., Los Angeles, Calif., private collection.

Valentine Museum, Richmond, Va., Edward Davis, Mrs. Ralph Caterall, Miss Elizabeth Dance.

Virginia State Historical Society, Richmond, Va., John M. Jennings, Howson W. Cole, James A. Fleming, Wm. M. E. Rachal.

Virginia State Library, Richmond, Va,, Randolph W. Church, William J. Van Schreeven, John W. Dudley, Marvin D. Evans.

Virginia, University of, Alderman Library, Manuscript Division, Charlottesville, Va., Robert Stocking.

Waitt, Robert J., Richmond, Va., private collection.

Western Reserve Historical Society, Cleveland, Ohio, William P. Palmer Collection and regular collection, Meredith B. Colket, Jr., Mrs. Alene Lowe White, Mrs. Mary Ruth Russell.

Wisconsin, State Historical Society of, Manuscript Division, Clifford Lord, Leslie Fischel, Mrs. Josephine Harper.

Yale University Library, Historical Manuscripts Division, New Haven, Conn., Howard Barnard Gottlieb, Miss Marjorie Gray Wynne.

SECTION II: *Manuscript Collections*

This lists the primary manuscript collections used as sources. It includes only the major collections which were consulted; individual documents which were referred to are cited separately in the footnotes.

Diary of Charles F. Adams, Jr., Massachusetts Historical Society.

Alcorn Papers, Southern Historical Collection, University of North Carolina.

E. P. Alexander Papers, Southern Historical Collection, University of North Carolina.

Col. William Allan Collection, Southern Historical Collection, University of North Carolina.

Robert Anderson Papers, Miscellaneous Letters, New York Public Library.

Robert Anderson Papers, Library of Congress.

Robert Anderson Retirement Hearing Notebooks, Massachusetts Commandery of the Military Order of the Loyal Legion, Houghton Library, Harvard University.

Robert Anderson Letters, the A. Conger Goodyear Collection, Yale University Library.

Mrs. Robert Anderson, Account of Visit to Fort Sumter, as recorded by Benson J. Lossing, the A. Conger Goodyear Collection, Yale University Library.

John A. Andrew Papers, Massachusetts Historical Society.

Isaac N. Arnold, The Life of Abraham Lincoln, extra illustrated, Huntington Library.

Nathaniel Banks Papers, Essex Institute Library, Salem, Mass.

Francis Channing Barlow Papers, Massachuetts Historical Society.

S. L. M. Barlow Papers, Huntington Library.

Battles and Leaders of the Civil War, extra illustrated, Huntington Library.

Beauregard Letters, Palmer Collection, Western Reserve Historical Society, Cleveland.

Beauregard Papers, Library of Congress.

P. G. T. Beauregard Papers, Duke University Library.

Letters of P. G. T. Beauregard, A. Conger Goodyear Collection, Yale University Library

Letters of Asa Beethan, Library of Congress.

Diary of Berry Greenwood Benson, Southern Historical Collection, University of North Carolina.

John Milton Binckley Papers, Library of Congress.

Jeremiah Sullivan Black Papers, Library of Congress.

Papers of Francis P. Blair, Jr., Library of Congress.

Letters of Montgomery Blair, A. Conger Goodyear Collection, Yale University Library.

Papers of the Blair Family, Library of Congress.

Blair-Lee Papers, Princeton University Library.

Letters of Mrs. John Boyle, Library of Congress.

Bradlee and Sears: Letters to and from the South; Palmer Collection, Western Reserve Historical Society.

Braxton Bragg Papers, Missouri Historical Society, St. Louis, Mo.

Braxton Bragg, letters to his wife, Library of Congress.

Mrs. Braxton Bragg, letters to her husband, Barker Texas History Center, University of Texas.

Thomas Bragg Diary, Southern Historical Collection, University of North Carolina.

Felix Brannigan Letters, Library of Congress.

Mason Brayman Collection, Chicago Historical Society.

John C. Breckinridge Papers, Chicago Historical Society.

James O. Broadhead Papers, Missouri Historical Society.

Campbell Brown, Notes, Tennessee State Library and Archives.

G. Campbell Brown, Papers, Huntington Library.

John Brown Diary, the J. N. Heiskell Collection, Little Rock, Ark.

John Brown Papers, Chicago Historical Society.

Joseph E. Brown Papers, Massachusetts Commandery of the Military Order of the Loyal Legion, Houghton Library, Harvard University.

James Buchanan, Miscellaneous President File, New York Public Library.

James Buchanan Papers, the Historical Society of Pennsylvania, Philadelphia, Pa.

James Buchanan Papers, Library of Congress.

James Buchanan Papers, Pennsylvania Historical and Museum Commission, Division of Public Records, Harrisburg, Pa.

James Buchanan Letter, Andre de Coppet Collection, Princeton University Library.

John T. Buegel Diary, the J. N. Heiskell Collection, Little Rock, Ark.

Sullivan Bullen Letters, Chicago Historical Society.

J. Howard Burnham Letters, the J. N. Heiskell Collection, Little Rock, Ark.

William Butler Papers, Chicago Historical Society.

R. K. Call Letters, Huntington Library.

Papers of Simon Cameron, Library of Congress.

George Washington Campbell Papers, Library of Congress.

John A. Campbell Letters, Alabama Department of Archives and History.

John A. Campbell Manuscript, Confederate Memorial Literary Society, Richmond, Va.

John A. Campbell Letters, the A. Conger Goodyear Collection, Yale University Library.

Campbell-Colston Papers, Southern Historical Collection, University of North Carolina.

Richard L. Campbell Letters, Mississippi State Department of Archives and History.

Anna Ella Carroll Papers, Maryland Historical Society.

Charleston, S.C., Board of Health, Daily Meteorological Observations, National Archives.

Chase Collections, the Historical Society of Pennsylvania.

Col. W. H. Chase Papers, Palmer Collection, Western Reserve Historical Society.

Col. A. R. Chisholm, Journal of Events before and during the bombardment of Fort Sumter, Palmer Collection, Western Reserve Historical Society.

Civil War Letters, Barker Texas History Center, University of Texas.

Civil War Papers, Missouri Historical Society, St. Louis, Mo.

C. C. Clay Papers, Duke University Library.

Sherrard Clemens Letters, Western Reserve Historical Society.

T. R. R. Cobb Letters, the Historical Society of Pennsylvania.

Diary kept by William T. Coggeshall as military secretary to Governor Dennison; Illinois State Historical Library, Springfield, Ill. Gift of Mrs. Foreman M. Lebold.

Comments of Gen. Jacob D. Cox on "McClellan's Own Story," from Cox's copy of the McClellan Book in the Oberlin College Library, Oberlin, Ohio.

Letterbook of the Commission Appointed for the Manufacture and Purchase of Arms and Munitions of War; for the Virginia State Legislature; Huntington Library.

Confederate Papers, Barker Texas History Center, University of Texas.

Jay Cooke Collection, The Historical Society of Pennsylvania.

Abel H. Crawford Letters, Tennessee State Library and Archives.

Samuel W. Crawford Papers, A. Conger Goodyear Collection, Yale University Library.

Letters of John Crittenden, Barker Texas History Center, University of Texas.

Caleb Cushing Correspondence, Nevins' Notes.

Charles A. Dana Papers, Duke University Library.

Richard Henry Dana and Family Papers, Massachusetts Historical Society.

C. C. Danley Letters, J. N. Heiskell Collection, Little Rock, Ark.

David Davis Papers, Illinois State Historical Library.

Jefferson Davis Papers, Duke University Library.

Jefferson Davis Papers, Palmer Collection, Western Reserve Historical Society.

Jefferson Davis Postwar Manuscripts, Confederate Memorial Hall, New Orleans, La.

Jefferson Davis Letter, Rosenbach Foundation, Philadelphia, Pa.

Jefferson Davis Letter, Nevins' Notes.

Jefferson Davis Letter, the Historical Society of Pennsylvania.

Davis and Beauregard; A. Conger Goodyear Collection, Yale University Library.

Eugene Delano Notes, Nevins' Notes.

Wilmot Gibbes DeSaussure, Order Book; Southern Historical Collection, University of North Carolina.

Stephen A. Douglas Papers, Chicago Historical Society.

Stephen A. Douglas Papers, Illinois State Historical Society.

Stephen A. Douglas Letter, Elsie O. and Philip D. Sang Collection.

Charles D. Drake mss. autobiography, Missouri Historical Society, St. Louis.

Paul Pecquet Du Bellet, typed mss., The Diplomacy of the Confederate Cabinet of Richmond and its Agents Abroad, being memorandum notes taken in Paris during the Rebellion of the Southern States from 1861 to 1865; Library of Congress.

Thomas Haines Dudley Papers, Huntington Library.

W. T. Duganne, mss. The Story of the Confederate Navy.

James B. Eads Papers, Missouri Historical Society.

Eldridge Collection, Huntington Library.

Ellsworth Papers, Chicago Historical Society.

Ralph Waldo Emerson mss. remarks, Sumner Autographs, Houghton Library, Harvard University.

David C. Williams Papers, the Clara Bertha Eno Collection, Arkansas History Commission, Little Rock, Ark.

Letters of Chesley D. Evans, 1860-1861, Southern Historical Collection, University of North Carolina.

Edward Everett Papers, Massachusetts Historical Society, Boston.

Ewing Family Papers, Library of Congress.

Letters of A. B. Fairfax, Barker Texas History Center, University of Texas.

James Fenton Recollections, Western Reserve Historical Society.

Recollections of C. D. Fishburne, Southern Historical Collection, University of North Carolina.

Letters of G. V. Fox, the A. Conger Goodyear Collection, Yale.

W. B. Franklin Papers, Library of Congress.

Joseph Gillespie Papers, Chicago Historical Society.

Gilpin Papers, Bancroft Library, University of California.

Political Associates of Abraham Lincoln, the A. Conger Goodyear Collection, Historical Manuscripts Division, Yale.

Thomas J. Goree Papers, Louisiana State University Department of Archives, Baton Rouge, La.

Robert N. Gourdin Papers, Duke University Library.

U. S. Grant Papers, Huntington Library.

U. S. Grant Letters, Rosenbach Foundation, Philadelphia.

Justice Horace Gray Papers, Library of Congress.

William Granville Gray Letters, Valentine Museum, Richmond.

Rose O'Neal Greenhow Papers, Manuscript Department, Duke University Library.

Diary of John Berkley Grimball, South Carolina Historical Society, Charleston, S.C.

Groner Collection, Southern Historical Collection, University of North Carolina.

George Harrington Papers, Missouri Historical Society.

A. C. Haskell Papers, Southern Historical Collection, University of North Carolina.

Frank A. Haskell Papers, State Historical Society of Wisconsin.

O. M. Hatch Papers, Illinois State Historical Library.

Gary W. Hazleton, mss. Abraham Lincoln, Edward S. Bragg Papers, Palmer Collection, Western Reserve Historical Society.

Samuel Heintzelman Diary, Library of Congress.

Anson G. Henry Papers, Illinois State Historical Library.

Governor Hicks Papers, Maryland Historical Society.

John Lyon Hill Diary, Virginia State Historical Society.

Joseph Holt Letter, A. Conger Goodyear Collection, Yale University Library.

Jed Hotchkiss Papers, Library of Congress.

R. M. T. Hunter Papers, Alderman Library, University of Virginia.

Irregular Books, 1861-1865; Registers of Letters Received, Record Group 107, Inventory 38; National Archives, War Records, Old Army.

Joseph E. Johnston Papers, Duke University Library.

Joseph E. Johnston Papers, Huntington Library.

Journal Magnolia Plantation, Southern Historical Collection, University of North Carolina.

Albert Kautz, mss., Bancroft Library.

J. M. Keller Papers, Arkansas History Commission.

Diary of Francis Milton Kennedy, Southern Historical Collection, University of North Carolina.

William Keyser Papers, Maryland Historical Society, Baltimore.

Horatio King Papers, Library of Congress.

Langhorne Family Papers, Virginia State Historical Society.

Lanphier Papers, Illinois State Historical Library.

Mary Custis Lee Letter, Rosebach Foundation.

Mary Custis Lee Letters, Virginia State Historical Society.

Lee Headquarters Papers, Virginia State Historical Society.

R. E. Lee Papers, Duke University Library.

R. E. Lee Letters, Huntington Library.

Lee Family Papers, Brock Collection, Huntington Library.

R. E. Lee Papers, Library of Congress.

R. E. Lee Letters, Maryland Historical Society, Baltimore.

R. E. Lee Letters, Palmer Collection, Western Reserve Historical Society.

Civil War Journal, the Stephen Dill Lee Papers, Southern Historical Collection, University of North Carolina.

Francis Lieber Collection, Huntington Library.

The Lincoln Collection, Chicago Historical Society.

Robert Todd Lincoln Papers, Library of Congress; microfilm at the Chicago Historical Society.

T. S. C. Lowe, Aeronautic Report, National Archives.

George B. McClellan Papers, Library of Congress.

John A. McClernand Papers, Illinois State Historical Library.

McCook Family Papers, Library of Congress.

Hugh MacRae Letters, Duke University Library.

John McRae Letterbooks, State Historical Library of Wisconsin.

Thomas F. Madigan Collection, Nevins' Notes.

S. R. Mallory Diary, Southern Historical Collection, University of North Carolina.

Betty Herndon Maury Diary, Library of Congress.

Matthew Fontaine Maury Papers, Library of Congress.

Christopher G. Memminger Letters, Rosenbach Foundation.

Christopher G. Memminger Papers, Southern Historical Collection, University of North Carolina.

Meteorological Registers, Naval Observatory, Washington; Weather Bureau Records, Agriculture and General Branch, National Resources Division, National Archives.

William Porcher Miles Letters, New York Public Library.

William Porcher Miles Papers, Southern Historical Collection, University of North Carolina.

William Porcher Miles Letter, A. Conger Goodyear Collection, Yale University Library.

Papers of the Massachusetts Commandery, Military Order of the Loyal Legion of the United States, Houghton Library, Harvard University.

Miscellaneous Papers, Huntington Library.

Miscellaneous Soldiers' Letters, C.S.A. Archives, Duke University Library.

Diary of James H. M. Montgomery, Library of Congress.

Orlando Hurley Moore Papers, Bancroft Library, University of California.

Samuel F. B. Morse Papers, Library of Congress.

Allan Nevins, research notes and manuscripts.

Newhall Family Letters, Boston Public Library.

Nicholson Collection, Huntington Library.

John G. Nicolay Papers, Library of Congress.

Kie Oldham Collection, Arkansas History Commission.

Williamson Simpson Oldham Memoirs, Barker Texas History Center, University of Texas.

Ord Papers, Bancroft Library, University of California.

Patrick Henry O'Rorke Papers, Manhattanville College of the Sacred Heart, Brady Memorial Library, Purchase, N.Y.

William P. Palmer Civil War Collection, Western Reserve Historical Society, Cleveland, Ohio.

Payroll of Slaves, Virginia State Library.

Edward Pendleton, mss., Library of Congress.

William Nelson Pendleton Papers, Southern Historical Collection, University of North Carolina.

Pickens-Bonham Papers, Library of Congress.

F. W. Pickens Letters, A. Conger Goodyear Collection, Yale University Library.

F. W. Pickens Papers, Chicago Historical Society.

F. W. Pickens Papers, Duke University Library.

Pickett Papers, Library of Congress.

Franklin Pierce Letter, the Massachusetts Commandery, Military Order of the Loyal Legion, Houghton Library, Harvard University.

L. M. Pipkin; Four Papers on the Civil War, transcribed by the Historian's Office, Military Department, State of Louisiana; originals held by Louisiana State Museum Library.

Leonidas Polk Letters, Palmer Collection, Western Reserve Historical Society.

David D. Porter Papers, Huntington Library.

John H. Reagan Papers, Texas State Library, Archives Division, Austin, Tex.

Register of Officers Arriving in Washington, 1861, National Archives.

William Culbertson Robinson Papers, Illinois State Historical Library; through courtesy of Ralph Newman.

W. S. Rosecrans Papers, UCLA Library.

Thomas L. Rosser Papers, Alderman Library, University of Virginia.

Diary of Edmund Ruffin, Library of Congress.

Letters of John F. Sale, Virginia State Library, Richmond, Va.

Frank A. Sanborn, mss., Chicago Historical Society.

Winfield Scott Letter, Greer Collection, the Historical Society of Pennsylvania.

William H. Seward Papers, the Rush Rhees Library, University of Rochester, Rochester, N.Y.

William H. Seward Papers, Chicago Historical Society.

William H. Seward Papers, Library of Congress.

William T. Sherman, Memoirs, personal copy with handwritten notes, Northwestern University Library.

Diary of Michael Shiner, Library of Congress.

William Dunlop Simpson Papers, Duke University Library.

Caleb B. Smith Papers, Huntington Library.

E. Kirby Smith Papers, Southern Historical Collection, University of North Carolina Library.

Letters of Augustine Smythe, South Carolina Historical Society, Charleston, S.C.

Homer B. Sprague Diary, Library of Congress.

William McKendree Springer Papers, Chicago Historical Society.

Edwin M. Stanton Letters, John Hay Library, Brown University.

Edwin M. Stanton Papers, Library of Congress.

Hannah C. Stearns Papers, Houghton Library, Harvard University.

Papers of Alexander Stephens, Manhattanville College of the Sacred Heart, Brady Memorial Library, Purchase, N.Y.

Diary of William H. Stewart, Southern Historical Collection, University of North Carolina.

Franklin Stringfellow Papers, Virginia State Historical Society, Richmond, Va.

J. E. B. Stuart Papers, Huntington Library.

Papers of Oscar J. E. Stuart and Family, Mississippi State Department of Archives and History, Jackson, Miss.

Papers of Charles Sumner, Houghton Library, Harvard University.

Papers of Charles Sumner, Huntington Library.

Papers of Gen. Thomas W. Sweeney, Huntington Library.

Telegram on opening of war from Charleston, Chicago Historical Society.

Papers of Eli Thayer, Widener Library, Harvard University.

Diary of Gilbert Thompson, Library of Congress.

Robert Toombs Letters,, Palmer Collection, Western Reserve Historical Society.

S. C. Turnbo, mss., History of the 27th Arkansas Confederate Regiment, the J. N. Heiskell Collection, Little Rock, Ark.

Robert H. Turner, "Recollections of the Virginia Convention of 1861," Virginia State Historical Society, Richmond, Va.

Mark Twain Papers, University of California Library.

E. A. Valentine Letters, Valentine Museum, Richmond, Va.

Papers of C. S. Venable, Barker Texas History Center, University of Texas.

Virginia in 1861, unsigned memorandum, Western Reserve Historical Society.

War letters of C. I. Walker, Barker Texas History Center, University of Texas.

Cornelius Walker Diary, Confederate Memorial Literary Society, Richmond, Va.

W. H. Walker, mss., Palmer Collection, Western Reserve Historical Society.

Wallace-Dickey Papers, Illinois State Historical Library.

Papers of Gideon Welles, Huntington Library.

Papers of Gideon Welles, Illinois State Historical Library.

Papers of Gideon Welles, Library of Congress.

Gideon Welles, draft of an article, The Collector, Nevins' Notes.

Horace White Papers, Illinois State Historical Library.

Wigfall Papers, University of Texas.

Charles Copland Wight Diary, Virginia State Historical Society.

Williams-Chesnut-Manning Papers, Southern Historical Collection, University of North Carolina.

William B. Wilson, mss., Lincoln File, Huntington Library.

Robert C. Winthrop Papers, Massachusetts Historical Society, Boston.

Henry A. Wise, Miscellaneous Papers, Massachusetts Historical Society.

Horatio Woodman Papers, Massachusetts Historical Society.

John L. Worden Statement, Palmer Collection, Western Reserve Historical Society.

William L. Yancey Papers, Library of Congress.

Papers of Richard Yates, Illinois State Historical Library.

SECTION III: *Newspapers*

Extensive use has been made of newspapers covering the period treated in this book. In many cases, quotations have been made from newspaper articles or editorials reprinted in such books as Moore's *Rebellion Record,* McMaster's *A History of the People of the United States,* Perkins' *Northern Editorials on Secession,* Fite's *Presidential Campaign of 1860,* Dumond's *Southern Editorials on Secession,* etc. In addition, individual copies or microfilms of the following journals were consulted:

The Arkansas Gazette, Little Rock, Ark.

Arkansas True Democrat, Little Rock, Ark.

Berryville (Va.) *Conservator*.

Campaign Plain Dealer and Popular Sovereignty Advocate.

Charleston Daily Courier.

Charleston Mercury.

Chicago Democrat.

Chicago Tribune.

Cincinnati Daily Commercial.

De Bow's Review.

Frankfort (Ky.) *Commonwealth*.

Harper's Weekly.

Lexington (Ky.) *Observer and Reporter*.

The Liberator.

Montgomery (Ala.) *Daily Mail*.

Montgomery Daily Post.

Montgomery Weekly Advertiser.

Montgomery Weekly Confederation.

Montgomery Weekly Mail.

Montgomery Weekly Post.

Natchez (Miss.) *Courier*.

National Intelligencer, Washington, D.C.

New York Daily Tribune.

New York Herald.

New York Leader.

New York Times.

New York Times Book Review.

New York Weekly Tribune.

The Railsplitter, Cincinnati, Ohio.

Richmond Dispatch.

Richmond Enquirer.

Richmond Examiner.

Richmond Whig.

Richmond Whig & Public Advertiser.

Sacramento Union.

Southern Literary Messenger.

Southern Watchman, Athens, Ga.

Springfield (Mass.) *Republican*.

Squatter Sovereign, Havana, Ill.

Terre Haute (Ind.) *Daily Express*.

Washington (Ark.) *Telegraph*.

West Virginia Hillbilly.

Winchester (Va.) *Times*.

SECTION IV: *Books, Pamphlets, and Periodicals*

Abbott, Martin, The First Shot at Fort Sumter, Civil War History, March 1957.

A Cycle of Adams Letters 1861-1865, edited by Worthington Chauncey Ford, two vols., Boston, 1920.

Adams, Charles Francis, Charles Francis Adams by His Son, Boston, 1900.

Adams, Charles Francis, The Memorial Address of Charles Francis Adams, of Massachusetts on the Life, Character, and Services of William H. Seward, New York, 1873.

Adams, Charles Francis, Richard Henry Dana, A Biography, Boston, 1890.

Adams, Charles Francis, Studies Military and Diplomatic 1775-1865, New York, 1911.

Adams, Charles Francis, Trans-Atlantic Historical Solidarity; Lectures Delivered Before the University of Oxford in Easter and Trinity Terms 1913, Oxford, 1913.

Adams, Henry, The Education of Henry Adams, Boston, 1918.

Adams, Henry, Great Secession Winter of 1860-61, Proceedings of the Massachusetts Historical Society, Vol. XLIII, Boston, 1910.

Adams, John and John Quincy, Selected Writings of John and John Quincy Adams, edited by Adrienne Koch and William Peden, New York, 1946.

Alleged Assault on Senator Sumner, Report No. 182, House of Representatives, 34th Congress 1st Session, Washington, 1856.

Alexander, Edward Porter, Military Memoirs of a Confederate, New York, 1907.

The American Annual Cyclopaedia and Register of Important Events of the Year 1861, New York, 1866 (known as Appleton's Cyclopaedia).

American Military History 1607-1953, Department of the Army ROTC Manual, July 1959.

Anderson, Galusha, A Border City During the Civil War, Boston, 1908.

Anderson, Osborne P., A Voice from Harper's Ferry, Boston, 1861.

Anderson, Robert, An Artillery Officer in the Mexican War 1846-47, Letters of Robert Anderson, New York, 1911.

Anderson, Robert, Fort Sumter Memorial, New York, 1915.

Anderson, Thomas McArthur, The Political Conspiracies Preceding the Rebellion or The True Stories of Sumter and Pickens, New York, 1882.

Angle, Paul, Here I Have Lived; A History of Lincoln's Springfield 1821-1865, New Brunswick, 1935.

Angle, Paul M., Lincoln in the Year 1858, Springfield, 1926.

Anspach, Frederick, The Sons of the Sires; A History of the Rise, Progress, and Destiny of the American Party, and Its Probable Influence on the Next Presidential Election, Philadelphia, 1855.

Auchampaugh, Philip Gerald, James Buchanan and His Cabinet on the Eve of Secession, Lancaster, Pa., 1926.

Ballard, Colin R., The Military Genius of Abraham Lincoln, New York, 1952.

Bancroft, Frederic, Calhoun and the South Carolina Nullification Movement, Baltimore, 1928.

Bancroft, Frederic, The Life of William H. Seward, New York, 1900.

Barbee, David R. and Bonham, Milledge L., Jr., Fort Sumter Again, Mississippi Valley Historical Review, XXVIII, 1941.

Baringer, William Eldon, Campaign Technique in Illinois—1860, Springfield, 1932.

Baringer, William E., A House Dividing; Lincoln as President Elect, Springfield, 1945.

Baringer, William, Lincoln, Lincoln's Rise to Power, Boston, 1937.

Barnard, J. G., The C.S.A., and the Battle of Bull Run, 1862.

Barnes, Thurlow Weed, Memoir of Thurlow Weed, two vols., Boston, 1884.

Barrett, Edwin S., What I Saw at Bull Run, Boston, 1886.

Basler, Roy, Abraham Lincoln; His Speeches and Writings, Cleveland, 1946.

Basler, Roy, Editor, The Collected Works of Abraham Lincoln, eight vols., New Brunswick, N.J., 1953.

Bassett, John Spencer, Anti-Slavery Leaders of North Carolina, Baltimore, 1898.

Bates, David Homer, Lincoln in the Telegraph Office, New York, 1907.

Bates, Edward, The Diary of Edward Bates, Washington, 1933.

Battles and Leaders of the Civil War, Johnson, Robert Underwood and Buel, Clarence Clough, editors, four vols., New York, 1887.

Beale, H. K., What Historians Have Said about the Causes of the Civil War, Theory and Practice in Historical Study, New York, 1946.

Beard, Charles A. and Beard, Mary R., The Rise of American Civilization, 2 vols., New York, 1947.

Beatty, John, Memoirs of a Volunteer 1861-1865, New York, 1946.

Beauregard, G. T., The Battle of Bull Run, Battles and Leaders of the Civil War.

Beauregard, Gen. P. G. T., A Commentary on the Campaign and Battle of Manassas of July, 1861, New York, 1891.

Beebe, Gilbert J., A Review and Refutation of Helper's "Impending Crisis," Middletown, N.Y., 1860.

Benton, Thomas Hart, Historical and Legal Examination of that part of the Decision of the Supreme Court of the United States in the Dred Scott Case, which declared the Unconstitutionality of the Missouri Compromise Act, and the Self-Extension of the Constitution to Territories, Carrying Slavery Along with it, New York, 1857.

Berger, John, The Private History of a Campaign That Failed, Civil War History, March, 1955.

Bernardo, C. Joseph and Bacon, Eugene H., American Military Policy, Its Development Since 1775, Harrisburg, 1955.

Betts, Samuel R., Opinion of Hon. Samuel R. Betts in the Cases of the Hiawatha and Other Vessels Captured as Prizes, New York, 1861.

Beveridge, Albert J., Abraham Lincoln 1809-1858, Boston, 1928.

Bevier, R. S., History of the First and Second Missouri Confederate Brigades, 1861-1865, St. Louis, 1879.

Bigelow, John, Retrospections of an Active Life, two vols., New York, 1909.

Blackford, Susan Leigh, Letters from Lee's Army, New York, 1947.

Blackwell, Sarah Ellen, A Military Genius; Life of Anna Ella Carroll of Maryland, Vol. I, Washington, 1891.

Blaine, James G., Twenty Years of Congress; From Lincoln to Garfield, two vols., Norwich, Conn., 1884.

Boston Slave Riot, and Trial of Anthony Burns, Boston, 1854.

Botts, John Minor, The Great Rebellion; Its Secret History, Rise, Progress, and Disastrous Failure, New York, 1886.

Boucher, C. S., The Nullification Controversy in South Carolina, Chicago, 1916.

Bowditch, William I., The Rendition of Anthony Burns, Boston, 1854.

Boynton, Charles B., The History of the Navy During the Rebellion, two vols., New York, 1867.

Britton, Wiley, Union and Confederate Indians in the Civil War, Battles and Leaders of the Civil War.

Brown, E. R., The Twenty-Seventh Indiana Volunteer Infantry in the War of the Rebellion 1861 to 1865; First Division 12th and 20th Corps., 1899.

Brown, George William, Baltimore and the Nineteenth of April, 1861, Baltimore, 1887.

Browne, Francis Fisher, The Every-Day Life of Abraham Lincoln, Chicago, 1913.

Browning, Orville H., The Diary of, edited by Theodore Calvin Pease and James G. Randall, Springfield, 1927.

Bruce, Robert V., Lincoln and the Tools of War, Indianapolis, 1956.

Buchanan, James, The Administration on the Eve of the Rebellion, London, 1865.

Buckingham, J. S., The Slave States of America, London, about 1842.

Buell, Augustus, The Cannoneer, Washington, 1890.

Buell, Don Carlos, Operations in North Alabama, Battles and Leaders of the Civil War.

Burgess, John W., The Middle Period, 1817-1858, New York, 1905.

Bushnell, Horace, Reverses Needed. A Discourse Delivered on the Sunday after the Disaster of Bull Run, in the North Church, Hartford, 1861.

Butler, Benjamin F., Butler's Book, Boston, 1892.

Calhoun, John C., Works of John C. Calhoun, six vols., edited by Richard K. Cralle, New York, 1883.

Campbell, James E., Sumner-Brooks-Burlingame-or-the Last of the Great Challenges, Ohio Archaeological and Historical Publications, Vol. XXXIV, Columbus, 1926.

Campbell, John Archibald, The Administration and The Confederate States—letters and correspondence between Hon. John A. Campbell and Hon. Wm. H. Seward, all of which was laid before the Provisional Congress on Saturday by President Davis, 1861.

Campbell, John A., Papers of Hon. John A. Campbell—1861-1865, Southern Historical Society Papers, October 1917.

Campbell, Mary R., Tennessee and The Union, 1847-1861, Reprinted from The East Tennessee Historical Society's Publication, No. 10, 1938.

Carnathan, W. J., The Proposal to Reopen the African Slave Trade in the South, 1854-1860, South Atlantic Quarterly, October 1926.

Carr, Joseph B., Operations of 1861 About Fort Monroe, Battles and Leaders of the Civil War.

Carroll, Anna Ella, The Star of the West; or, National Men and National Measures, James French and Company, Boston, 1857.

Carroll, Anna Ella, The Great American Battle; or, the Contest between Christianity and Political Romanism, New York, 1856.

Carroll, Joseph Cephas, Slave Insurrections in the United States, 1800-1865, Boston, 1938.

Carson, James Petigru, Life, Letters and Speeches of James Louis Petigru, The Union Man of South Carolina, Washington, 1920.

Caskey, Willie Malvin, Secession and Restoration of Louisiana, University, La., 1938.

Casler, John O., Four Years in the Stonewall Brigade, Guthrie, Oklahoma, 1893.

Catton, Bruce, Glory Road, Garden City, New York, 1952.

Catton, Bruce, Mr. Lincoln's Army, Garden City, New York, 1951.

Catton, Bruce, A Stillness at Appomattox, Garden City, New York, 1953.

Catton, Bruce, This Hallowed Ground, Garden City, New York, 1956.

Census Reports, U.S., various.

Chadwick, French Ensor, Causes of the Civil War, 1859-1861, New York, 1906.

Channing, Edward, The United States of America, New York, 1897.

Channing, Edward, A History of the United States, New York, 1925.

Charleston Under Arms, The Atlantic Monthly, April 1861.

Chase, Salmon P., Diary and Correspondence of, Washington, 1903.

Chase, Salmon P., Inside Lincoln's Cabinet; The Civil War Diaries of Salmon P. Chase, edited by David Donald, New York, 1954.

Chesnut, Mary Boykin, A Diary from Dixie, New York, 1929.

Chester, James, Inside Sumter in '61, Battles and Leaders of the Civil War.

Childs, Arney Robinson, The Private Journal of Henry William Ravenel, Columbia, S.C., 1947.

Chittenden, L. E., A Report of the Debates and Proceedings in the Secret Sessions of the Confederate Convention, for Proposing Amendments to the Constitution of the United States, held at Washington, D.C., in February, A.D., 1861, New York, 1864.

Chittenden, L. E., Recollections of President Lincoln and His Administration, New York, 1891.

Clark, Victor S., History of Manufactures in the United States, 2 vols. New York, 1929.

Clark, Walter, Histories of the Several Regiments and Battalions from North Carolina in the Great War 1861-'65, Raleigh, 1901.

Clarke, James Freeman, A Discourse on Christian Politics, Boston, 1854.

Clay, Henry Speech of the Hon. Henry Clay of Kentucky, On Taking Up His Compromise Resolutions on the Subject of Slavery, as reported by the *National Intelligencer,* New York, 1850.

Clemens, Will M., Mark Twain, Chicago, 1894.

Clement, Edward Henry, The Bull Run Rout, In Proceedings of the Massachusetts Historical Society for March 1909, Cambridge, 1909.

Cobb, Thomas R. R., Member of the Secession Convention of Georgia, of the Provisional Congress, and a Brigadier-General of the Confederate States Army. Extracts from Letters to his Wife, February 3, 1861-December 10, 1862, Southern Historical Society Papers, Vol. XXVIII, Richmond, 1900.

Cobb, Thomas Reade Rootes, The Correspondence of Thomas Reade Rootes Cobb, 1860-1862, Washington, 1907.

Cohn, Davis L., The Life and Times of King Cotton, New York, 1956.

Coit, Margaret L., John C. Calhoun, American Patriot, Boston, 1950.

Cole, Arthur Charles, The Irrepressible Conflict 1850-1865, New York, 1934.

Coleman, Mrs. A. M. B., The Life of John J. Crittenden, two vols., Philadelphia, 1871.

Colton, Calvin, The Life and Times of Henry Clay, two vols., New York, 1846.

Commager, Henry Steele, The Blue and the Gray, two vols., Indianapolis, 1950.

Commager, Henry Steele, Documents of American History, New York, 1949.

Confederate Flags, Richmond.

The Confederate States Almanac and Repository of Useful Knowledge for 1862, Vicksburg, Miss., 1861.

Congressional Globe, Washington, various volumes.

Connelley, William E., A Standard History of Kansas and Kansans, Chicago, 1918.

Connor, Henry G., John Archibald Campbell, Boston, 1920.

Conway, Moncure Daniel, Autobiography, Memories and Experiences, Boston and New York, 1904.

Coulter, E. Merton, The Confederate States of America, 1861-1865, Baton Rouge, 1950.

Cowley, Charles, Leaves from a Lawyer's Life Afloat and Ashore, Lowell, Mass., 1879.

Cox, Jacob D., McClellan in West Virginia, Battles and Leaders of the Civil War.

Cox, Jacob D., War Preparations in the North, Battles and Leaders of the Civil War.

Craven, Avery, The Coming of the Civil War, New York, 1942. Also second Revised Edition, New York, 1957.

Craven, Avery, Coming of the War between the States; An Interpretation, The Journal of Southern History, Aug., 1936.

Craven, Avery, Edmund Ruffin, Southerner, New York, 1932.

Craven, Avery, The Growth of Southern Nationalism 1848-1861, Baton Rouge, 1953.

Craven, Avery, The Repressible Conflict 1830-1861, University, Louisiana, 1939.

Craven, Avery, Slavery and the Civil War, The Southern Review, Vol. IV, 1938-39.

Crawford, Samuel Wylie, The Genesis of the Civil War; The Story of Sumter 1860-61, New York, 1887.

Crenshaw, Ollinger, The Slave States in the Presidential Election of 1860, Baltimore, 1945.

Criswell, Robert, Uncle Tom's Cabin Contrasted with Buckingham Hall, the Planter's Home, or A Fair View of Both Sides of the Slavery Question, New York, 1852.

Croly, Herbert, The Promise of American Life, New York, 1914.

Cross, Nelson, Life of General Grant: His Political Record, Etc., New York, 1872.

Crotty, D. G., Four Years Campaign in the Army of the Potomac, Grand Rapids, 1874.

Curry, J. L. M., Civil History of the Government of the Confederate States with some Personal Reminiscences, Richmond, 1901.

Curtis, Francis, The Republican Party, New York, 1904.

Curtis, George Ticknor, Life of James Buchanan, two vols., New York, 1883.

Curtis, Newton Martin, From Bull Run to Chancellorsville; the Story of the Sixteenth New York Infantry, New York, 1906.

Cutts, J. Madison, A Brief Treatise Upon Constitutional and Party Questions, The History of Political Parties, as I Received It Orally from the Late Senator Stephen A. Douglas, of Illinois, New York, 1866.

Dabney, Rev. R. L., D.D., Memoir of a Narrative Received of Colonel John R. Baldwin, of Staunton, Touching the Origin of the War, Southern Historical Society Papers, June 1876.

Dana, Charles A., Recollections of the Civil War, New York, 1898.

Darrow, Mrs. Caroline Baldwin, Recollections of the Twiggs Surrender, Battles and Leaders of the Civil War.

Davis, Jefferson, Calendar of the Jefferson Davis Postwar Manuscripts in the Louisiana Historical Association Collection, New Orleans, 1943.

Davis, Jefferson, Lord Wolseley's Mistakes, The North American Review, October 1889.

Davis, Jefferson, Relations of States, Speech of the Hon. Jefferson Davis of Mississippi, Speech of May 7th, 1860, Baltimore, 1860.

Davis, Jefferson, The Rise and Fall of the Confederate Government, two vols., New York, 1881.

Davis, Varina Howell, Jefferson Davis, A Memoir, by His Wife, two vols., New York, 1890.

De Fontaine, Felix Gregory, Shoulder to Shoulder, The XIX Century, Vol. First, Charleston, S.C., 1861.

De Leon, T. C., Four Years in Rebel Capitals; An Inside View of Life in the Southern Confederacy, from Birth to Death, Mobile, Ala., 1890.

Derry, Joseph T., Confederate Military History, Georgia, Vol. VI, Atlanta, Georgia, 1899.

Diary of a Public Man, And a Page of Political Correspondence Stanton to Buchanan, Rutgers University Press, 1946.

Dickens, Charles, American Notes, The Biographical Edition of the Works of Charles Dickens, Philadelphia.

Dickert, D. Augustus, History of Kershaw's Brigade, Newberry, S.C., 1899.

Dictionary of American Biography, 22 vols., New York, 1946.

Dictionary of American History, Adams, James Truslow, Editor, six vols., New York, 1941.

Dix, John Adams, Memoirs of John Adams Dix, compiled by his son Morgan Dix, two vols., New York, 1883.

Dixon, Mrs. Archibald, True History of the Missouri Compromise and Its Repeal, Cincinnati.

Doubleday, Abner, From Moultrie to Sumter, Battles and Leaders of the Civil War.

Doubleday, Abner, Reminiscences of Forts Sumter and Moultrie in 1860-61, New York, 1876.

Douglas, Stephen A., The Dividing Line Between Federal and Local Authority, Popular Sovereignty in the Territories, Harper's New Monthly Magazine, September 1859.

Douglas, Stephen A., Kansas-Utah-Dred Scott Decision, Speech delivered at Springfield, Ill., June 12, 1857, Springfield, 1857.

Dowdey, Clifford, Experiment in Rebellion, New York, 1956.

Doyle, Joseph B., In Memoriam Edwin McMasters Stanton, Steubenville, Ohio, 1911.

The Case of Dred Scott in the United States Supreme Court. The Full Opinions of Chief Justice Taney and Justice Curtis, New York, 1860.

Du Bose, John Witherspoon, The Life and Times of William Lowndes Yancey, Birmingham, 1892.

Duke, Basil W., Reminiscences of General Basil W. Duke, Garden City, 1911.

Dumond, Dwight L., Antislavery Origins of the Civil War in the United States, Ann Arbor, 1939.

Dumond, Dwight Lowell, Southern Editorials on Secession, Washington, 1931.

Dumond, Dwight L., The Secession Movement 1860-1861, New York, 1931.

Dupuy, R. Ernest and Dupuy, Trevor N., Military Heritage of America, New York, 1956.

Durkin, Joseph T., S.J., Stephen R. Mallory, Confederate Navy Chief, Chapel Hill, 1954.

Dyer, Frederick H., A Compendium of the War of the Rebellion, Des Moines, 1908.

Earle, John Jewett, The Sentiment of the People of California with Respect to the Civil War, Annual Report of the American Historical Association, Washington, 1908.

Early, Lieutenant General Jubal Anderson, Autobiographical Sketch and Narrative of the War Between the States, Philadelphia, 1912.

Eaton, Clement, A History of the Southern Confederacy, New York, 1954.

Eaton, Clement, A History of the Old South, New York, 1949.

Eckenrode, H. J., Jefferson Davis President of the South, New York, 1923.

Eggleston, George Cary, A Rebel's Recollections, Bloomington, Indiana, 1959.

Eisenschiml, Otto, Why the Civil War, Indianapolis, 1958.

Eisenschiml, Otto, and Newman, Ralph, The American Iliad, Vol. I, The Civil War, New York, 1956.

Eliot, Ellsworth, Jr., West Point in the Confederacy, New York, 1941.

"Ellsworth Requiem March," sheet music, Root and Cady, Chicago.

Ely, Alfred, Journal of Alfred Ely, A Prisoner of War in Richmond, edited by Charles Lanman, New York, 1862.

Emerson, Edwin, Jr., A History of the Nineteenth Century Year by Year, three vols., New York, 1902.

Erskine, John, Leading American Novelists, New York, 1910.

Esposito, Colonel Vincent J., Atlas to Accompany Steele's American Campaigns, West Point, New York, 1953.

Evans, Clement A., Confederate Military History, twelve vols., Atlanta, 1899.

Fairbairn, Charlotte Judd, Historic Harpers Ferry, Ranson, W. Va.

Fairchild, J. H., Oberlin: Its Origin, Progress and Results, Oberlin, Ohio, 1869.

Farber, James, Texas, C.S.A., New York, 1947.

Fehrenbacher, Don G., Chicago Giant; A Biography of Long John Wentworth, Madison, Wis., 1957.

Fiske, John, The Mississippi Valley in the Civil War, Boston, 1900.

Fite, Emerson David, Social and Industrial Conditions in the North During the Civil War, New York, 1950.

Fite, Emerson David, The Presidential Campaign of 1860, New York, 1911.

Fitts, Albert N., The Confederate Convention, The Alabama Review, April 1949, and July 1949.

Fletcher, Miss A., Within Fort Sumter; or, A View of Major Anderson's Garrison Family for One Hundred and Ten Days, New York, 1861.

Flower, Frank A., Edwin McMasters Stanton, New York, 1905.

Formby, John, The American Civil War, two vols., New York, 1910.

Forrester, Izola, This One Mad Act . . . The Unknown Story of John Wilkes Booth and His Family, Boston, 1937.

Forts, Arsenals, Arms &c., Report No. 85, Feb. 18, 1861, House Reports, 36th Cong. 2nd Session, three vols., Washington, 1861.

Fox, Gustavus Vasa, Confidential Correspondence of, two vols., New York, 1920.

Fox, William F., Regimental Losses in The American Civil War, 1861-1865, Albany, N.Y., 1889.

Franklin, John Hope, From Slavery to Freedom, New York, 1952.

Freeman, Douglas Southall, A Calendar of Confederate Papers, Richmond, Va., 1908.

Freeman, Douglas Southall and Grady McWhiney, editors, Lee's Dispatches, New York, 1957.

Freeman, D. S., Lee's Lieutenants, three vols., New York, 1944.

Freeman, Douglas Southall, R. E. Lee, A Biography, four vols., New York, 1934.

Fry, James B., McDowell and Tyler in the Campaign of Bull Run, New York, 1884.

Fuess, Claude Moore, Daniel Webster, Boston, 1930.

Galbreath, C. B., John Brown, Ohio Archaeological and Historical Quarterly, July, 1921.

Gammage, W. L., The Camp, the Bivouac, and the Battlefield, Selma, Ala., 1864.

Ganoe, William Addleman, The History of the United States Army, New York, 1932.

Gihon, John H., History of Kansas, 1857.

Gilbertson, Catherine, Harriet Beecher Stowe, New York, 1937.

Gilman, J. H., With Slemmer in Pensacola Harbor, Battles and Leaders of the Civil War.

Glover, Gilbert Graffenreid, Immediate Pre-Civil War Compromise Efforts, Nashville, 1934.

Gobright, L. A., Recollection of Men and Things at Washington, During the Third of a Century, Philadelphia, 1869.

Going, Charles Buxton, David Wilmot Free-Soiler, New York, 1924.

Goldsborough, W. W., The Maryland Line in the Confederate States Army, Baltimore, 1869.

Gordon, General John B., Reminiscences of the Civil War, New York, 1904.

Gorham, George C., Life and Public Services of Edwin M. Stanton, two vols., Boston, 1899.

Govan, Gilbert E., and Livingood, James W., A Different Valor; The Story of General Joseph E. Johnston, C.S.A., Indianapolis, 1956.

Grant, U. S., Letters of Ulysses S. Grant to his Father and his Youngest Sister 1857-78, edited by his nephew, Jesse Grant Cramer, New York, 1912.

Grant, U. S., Personal Memoirs, two vols., New York, 1885.

Grant, U. S., Personal Memoirs of U. S. Grant, edited by E. B. Long, Cleveland, 1952.

Gray, John Chapman and Ropes, John Codman, War Letters 1862-1865, Boston, 1927.

Grayson, A. J., History of the Sixth Indiana Regiment in the Three Months' Campaign in Western Virginia, Madison, Ind.

Greeley, Horace, The American Conflict, two vols., Hartford, 1864.

Greeley, Horace, and Cleveland, John F. (compilers), A Political Text-Book for 1860, New York, 1860.

Greeley, Horace, Greeley's Estimate of Lincoln, Century Magazine, Vol. XX.

Grierson, Francis, The Valley of Shadows, Boston, 1948.

Gue, Benjamin F., History of Iowa, Vol. II, The Civil War, New York, 1903.

Guide to the Manuscripts in the Southern Historical Collection of the University of North Carolina, Chapel Hill, 1941.

Gurowski, Adam, Diary, 3 vols., Boston, 1862.

Hagood, Johnson, Memoirs of the War of Secession, Columbia, S.C., 1910.

Hall, Granville Davisson, The Rending of Virginia, Chicago, 1902.

Hall, Granville Davisson, Lee's Invasion of Northwest Virginia in 1861, Chicago, 1911.

Halstead, Murat, Caucuses of 1860, A History of the National Political Conventions, Columbus, 1860.

Hamersly, Lewis R., The Records of Living Officers of the U. S. Navy and Marine Corps, with a History of Naval Operations During the Rebellion of 1861-65, Philadelphia, 1870.

Hamilton, Holman, Zachary Taylor: Soldier in the White House, Indianapolis, 1951.

Hammond, M. B., The Cotton Industry; An Essay in American Economic History, New York, 1897.

Hancock, Harold, Civil War Comes to Delaware, Civil War History, Dec. 1956.

Hanson, Joseph Mills, Bull Run Remembers, Manassas, Va., 1953.

Harmon, George D., Douglas and the Compromise of 1850, Aspects of Slavery and Expansion 1848-60, Lehigh University, 1929.

Harper, Chancellor, Governor Hammond, Dr. Simms and Professor Dew, The Pro-Slavery Argument: As Maintained by the

Most Distinguished Writers of the Southern States, Containing the Several Essays, on the Subject of—, Charleston, 1852.

Harper's Encyclopaedia of United States History, 10 vols., New York, 1907.

Invasion at Harper's Ferry, Senate Report No. 278, 36th Congress, 1st Session, 1859-60, Vol. 2, Washington, 1860.

The Press Upon the Harpers Ferry Affair, pamphlet, Boston Journal, Sat., Oct. 29, 1859.

Harris, W. A., The Record of Fort Sumter, Columbia, S.C., 1862.

Hart, Albert Bushnell, American History Told by Contemporaries, Vol. III, New York, 1901.

Hart, Albert Bushnell, Slavery and Abolition 1831-1841, The American Nation: A History, Vol. 16, New York, 1906.

Harvey, Peter, Reminiscence and Anecdotes of Daniel Webster, Boston, 1878.

Harwell, Richard Barksdale, Songs of the Confederacy, New York, 1951.

Hay, John, A Young Hero, Personal Reminiscences of Colonel E. E. Ellsworth, McClure's Magazine, March 1896.

Hay, John, Lincoln and the Civil War in the Diaries and Letters of John Hay, Selected by Tyler Dennett, New York, 1939.

Haynes, Martin A., A History of the Second Regiment, New Hampshire Volunteer Infantry, Lakeport, New Hampshire, 1892.

Heitman, Francis B., Historical Register and Dictionary of the United States Army, Washington, 1903.

Helper, Hinton Rowan, The Land of Gold, Baltimore, 1855.

Helper, Hinton Rowan, The Impending Crisis of the South; How to Meet It, New York, 1857.

Helper, Hilton Rowan, Nojoque; Question for a Continent, New York, 1867.

Helper, Hinton Rowan, The Negroes in Negroland, New York, 1868.

Helper, Hinton Rowan, Noonday Exigencies in America, New York, 1871.

Henderson, Colonel G. F. R., Stonewall Jackson and the American Civil War, New York.

Hendrick, Burton J., Statesmen of the Lost Cause, New York, 1939.

Henry, H. M., The Slave Laws of Tennessee, Tennessee History Magazine, Vol. II.

Henry, Robert Selph, The Story of the Confederacy, New York, 1943.

Herndon, William H. and Weik, Jesse W., Life of Lincoln, edited by Paul M. Angle, Cleveland, 1949.

Hesseltine, W. B., The South in American History, New York, 1951.

Hesseltine, William B., Lincoln and the War Governors, New York, 1948.

Hesseltine, William B., Ulysses S. Grant Politician, New York, 1935.

Higginson, Thomas Wentworth, The First Black Regiment, Outlook, July 2, 1898.

Hinton, Richard J., John Brown and His Men, New York, 1904.

Historic Harper's Ferry, pamphlet, Baltimore.

The History of America in Documents, Part Three; The Pre-Civil War Period to the Twentieth Century, Philadelphia, 1951.

Hitchcock's Chronological Record of the American Civil War, New York, 1866.

Hodder, Frank Heywood, Genesis of the Kansas-Nebraska Act, Madison, 1912.

Hodder, Frank Heywood, Some Aspects of the English Bill for the Admission of Kansas, Washington, 1908.

Holloway, J. M., History of Kansas, Lafayette, Ind., 1868.

Holst, Dr. H. von, John C. Calhoun, Boston, 1883.

Holzman, Robert S., Stormy Ben Butler, New York, 1954.

Hopkins, Vincent C., S.J., Dred Scott's Case, New York, 1951.

Hopley, Catherine C., Life in the South; From the Commencement of the War, by Blockaded British Subject, two vols., London, 1863.

Hoppin, William W., The Peace Conference of 1861, Providence, R.I., 1903.

Hotchkiss, Jed., Virginia, Vol. III, Confederate Military History, Atlanta, 1899.

Houston, David Franklin, A Critical Study of Nullification in South Carolina, Cambridge, 1896.

Howard, McHenry, Recollections of a Maryland Confederate Soldier and Staff Officer Under Johnston, Jackson and Lee, Baltimore, 1914.

Howe, Daniel Wait, Political History of Secession, New York, 1914.

Hundley, D. R., Social Relations in Our Southern States, New York, 1860.

Hunt, Aurora, The Army of the Pacific; Its Operation in California, Texas, Arizona, New Mexico, Utah, Nevada, Oregon,

Washington, plains region, Mexico, etc., 1860-1866, Glendale, California, 1951.

Hunton, Eppa, Autobiography of, Richmond, Va., 1933.

Huse, Caleb, The Supplies for the Confederate Army, Boston, 1904.

Imboden, John D., Jackson at Harper's Ferry in 1861, Battles and Leaders of the Civil War.

Ingraham, Charles A., Ellsworth and the Zouaves of '61, Chicago, 1925.

Life of James W. Jackson, The Alexandria Hero, the Slayer of Ellsworth, the First Martyr, in the Cause of Southern Independence, Richmond, 1862.

Jackson, Mary Anna, Memoirs of Stonewall Jackson, Louisville, 1895.

James, Marquis, The Raven; A Biography of Sam Houston, Indianapolis, 1929.

Jefferson, Thomas, Notes on the State of Virginia, Newark, 1801.

Jervey, Theodore D., Charleston During the Civil War, Annual Report of the American Historical Association for the Year 1913, Vol. I, Washington, 1915.

The John Brown Invasion, Boston, 1860.

Johnson, Allen, Stephen A. Douglas; A Study in American Politics, New York, 1908.

Johnson, Charles B., The Presidential Campaign of 1860, Springfield, 1927.

Johnson, John, The Defense of Charleston Harbor, Including Fort Sumter and the Adjacent Islands, 1863-1865, Charleston, 1890.

Johnson, Ludwell H., Red River Campaign; Politics and Cotton in the Civil War, Baltimore, 1958.

Johnson, Rossiter, Campfire and Battlefield; History of the Conflict and Campaigns of the Great Civil War in the United States, New York.

Johnston, Joseph E., Narrative of Military Operations, New York, 1874.

Johnston, J. E., Responsibilities of the First Bull Run, Battles and Leaders of the Civil War.

Johnston, Richard Malcolm and Browne, William Hand, Life of Alexander H. Stephens, Philadelphia, 1878.

Johnston, R. M., Bull Run, Its Strategy and Tactics, Boston, 1913.

Johnston, William Preston, The Life of Gen. Albert Sidney Johnston, New York, 1879.

Prince de Joinville, The Army of the Potomac; Its Organization,

Its Commander, and Its Campaign, with notes by William Henry Hurlbert, New York, 1862.

Jones, John B., A Rebel War Clerk's Diary, Condensed, edited, and annotated by Earl Schenck Miers, New York, 1958.

Jones, John Beauchamp, A Rebel War Clerk's Diary, two vols., Philadelphia, 1866.

Jones, Samuel, The Siege of Charleston; and the Operations on the South Atlantic Coast in the War Among the States, New York, 1911.

Jones, Stacy V., GOP, Centenarian, New York Times Magazine, Feb. 19, 1956.

Journal of the Congress of the Confederate States of America 1861-1865, 7 vols., Washington, 1904.

Journal of the Convention of the People of South Carolina, Held in 1860-61, Charleston, 1861.

Kansas Affairs, House Report No. 200, 34th Congress, 1st Sess., Vol. II, Washington, 1856.

Kansas Constitution, House Report No. 377, 35th Congress, 1st Sess., Vol. III, Washington, 1858.

Kean, Robert Garlick Hill, Inside the Confederate Government; The Diary of Robert Garlick Hill Kean, edited by Edward Younger, New York, 1957.

Keleher, William A., Turmoil in New Mexico, 1856-1868, Santa Fe, N.M., 1952.

Keller, Allan, Thunder at Harper's Ferry, Englewood Cliffs, N.J., 1958.

Keller, Helen Rex, Dictionary of Dates, two vols., New York, 1934.

Kellogg, Sanford C., The Shenandoah Valley and Virginia, 1861 to 1865, New York, 1903.

Kelly, Alfred H. and Harbison, Winfred A., The American Constitution, Its Origins and Development, two vols., New York, 1948.

King, Horatio, James Buchanan, The Galaxy, Oct., 1870.

King, Willard, Lincoln's Manager: David Davis, Cambridge, Mass., 1960.

Kinsley, Philip, The Chicago Tribune, Its First Hundred Years, Vol. I, 1847-1865, New York, 1943.

Kirkland, Caroline, Chicago Yesterdays, A Sheaf of Reminiscences, Chicago, 1919.

Knox, Thomas W., Camp-Fire and Cotton-Field; Southern Adventure in Time of War, New York, 1865.

Korn, Bertram W., American Jewry and the Civil War, Philadelphia, 1951.

Korngold, Ralph, Thaddeus Stevens; A Being Darkly Wise and Rudely Great, New York, 1955.

Kull, Irving S. and Nell M., A Short Chronology of American History, New Brunswick, N.J., 1952.

Lamon, Ward Hill, Recollections of Abraham Lincoln 1847-1865, edited by Dorothy Lamon, Chicago, 1895.

Lang, Theodore F., Loyal West Virginia from 1861 to 1865, Baltimore, 1895.

Larned, J. N., History for Ready Reference, Springfield, Mass., 1901.

Lattimore, Ralston B., Fort Pulaski National Monument, Georgia, Washington, 1954.

Lawton, Eba Anderson, Major Robert Anderson and Fort Sumter 1861, New York, 1911.

Lay, Col. J. F., Reminiscences of the Powhatan Troop of Cavalry in 1861, Southern Historical Society Papers, Vol. VIII, 1880.

Leddy, Robert, The First Shot on Fort Sumter, The South Carolina Historical and Genealogical Magazine, July, 1911.

Lee, Fitzhugh, General Lee, New York, 1894.

Lee, R. E., Letter to Gov. John Letcher of Va., Southern Historical Society Papers, June, 1876.

Lee, Capt. Robert E., Recollections and Letters of General Robert E. Lee, New York, 1904.

Lee, Stephen D., The First Step in the War, Battles and Leaders of the Civil War.

Lee, Stephen D., Letter on Fort Sumter, Southern Historical Society Papers, November 1883.

Leech, Margaret, Reveille in Washington, New York, 1941.

Lefler, Hugh Talmadge, Southern Sketches, Number I, Hinton Rowan Helper, Advocate of a "White America," Charlottesville, Va., 1935.

Leib, Charles, Nine Months in the Quartermaster's Department; or the Chances for Making a Million, Cincinnati, 1862.

Leland, Edwin Albert, Organization and Administration of the Louisiana Army During the Civil War, Thesis, Tulane University, New Orleans, 1938.

Letcher, Governor John, Official Correspondence of, Southern Historical Society Papers, June 1876.

Levin, L. C., Speech of Mr. L. C. Levin, of Pennsylvania, On the Subject of Altering the Naturalization Laws, 1845.

Lewis, Lloyd, Captain Sam Grant, Boston, 1950.

Lincoln, Abraham, The Collected Works of, Roy Basler, Editor, 8 vols., New Brunswick, N.J., 1953.

Linder, Usher F., Reminiscences of the Early Bench and Bar of Illinois, Chicago, 1879.

Livermore, Mary A., My Story of the War, Hartford, Conn., 1888.

Livermore, Thomas L., Numbers and Losses in the Civil War in America, 1861-1865, 2nd edition, Boston, 1901.

Lloyd, Arthur Young, The Slavery Controversy, Chapel Hill, 1939.

London Times, Uncle Tom in England; The London Times on Uncle Tom's Cabin. A Review from the London Times of Friday, Sept. 3, 1852, pamphlet, New York, 1852.

Long, A. L., Memoirs of Robert E. Lee, New York, 1887.

Long, John Sherman, The Gosport Affair, 1861, The Journal of Southern History, May 1957.

Longstreet, James, From Manassas to Appomattox, Philadelphia, 1896.

Lossing, Benson J., Pictorial History of The Civil War, 3 vols., Hartford, 1868.

Lothrop, Thornton Kirkland, William Henry Seward, Boston, 1896.

Luthin, Reinhard, The First Lincoln Campaign, Cambridge, 1944.

Lyster, Henry F., Recollections of the Bull Run Campaign After Twenty-Seven Years. A Paper read before the Michigan Commandery of the Military Order of the Loyal Legion of the United States, February 1, 1887, Detroit, 1888.

McCaleb, Walter, The Conquest of the West, New York, 1947.

McCarthy, Carlton, Origin of the Confederate Battle Flag, Southern Historical Society Papers, Richmond, Jan. to Dec., 1880.

Macartney, Clarence Edward, Little Mac, Philadelphia, 1940.

McClellan, George B., McClellan's Own Story, New York, 1887.

McClellan, George B., The Mexican War Diary of General George B. McClellan, edited by William Starry Myers, Princeton, N.J., 1917.

McClellan, George B., Report on the Organization and Campaigns of the Army of the Potomac, New York, 1864.

McClure, A. K., Abraham Lincoln and Men of War Times, Philadelphia, 1892.

McCormick, R. R., The War without Grant, New York, 1950.

McCulloch, Hugh, Men and Measures of Half a Century, New York, 1888.

McDougall, Marion Gleason, Fugitive Slaves (1619-1865), Boston, 1891.

McElroy, John, The Struggle for Missouri, Washington, 1913.

McGregor, James C., The Disruption of Virginia, New York, 1922.

McKee, Thomas H., The National Conventions and Platforms of All Political Parties, 1789 to 1905, Baltimore, 1906.

McKim, Randolph H., A Soldier's Recollections: Leaves from the Diary of a Young Confederate, New York, 1910.

McMaster, John Bach, A History of the People of the United States from the Revolution to the Civil War, eight vols., New York, 1900.

McMaster, John Bach, A History of the People of the United States During Lincoln's Administration, New York, 1927.

McPherson, Edward, The Political History of the United States of America During the Great Rebellion, Washington, 1865.

Magruder, Allan B., A Piece of Secret History: President Lincoln and the Virginia Convention of 1861, Atlantic Monthly, April 1875.

Malin, James C., John Brown and the Legend of Fifty-Six, Philadelphia, 1942.

Malin, James C., The Nebraska Question, 1852-1854, Ann Arbor, Mich., 1953.

Martyn, Carlos, Wendell Phillips; The Agitator, New York, 1890.

Marx, Karl and Engels, Frederick, The Civil War in the United States, New York, 1937.

May, John Amasa and Faunt, Joan Reynolds, South Carolina Secedes.

Meade, George, The Life and Letters of George Gordon Meade, two vols., New York, 1913.

Meagher, Francis F., Last Days of the 69th in Virginia, The Irish American Historical Journal, 1861.

Mearns, David C., The Lincoln Papers, two vols., Garden City, New York, 1948.

The Medical and Surgical History of the War of the Rebellion, Prepared under direction of Surgeon General Joseph K. Barnes, six vols., Washington, 1875.

Meigs, Montgomery, The Relations of President Lincoln and Secretary Stanton to the Military Commanders in the Civil War, The American Historical Review, Jan., 1921.

Meneely, A. Howard, The War Department, 1861, New York, 1928.

Meredith, Roy, Storm Over Sumter, New York, 1957.

Miers, Earl Schenck, The Great Rebellion, Cleveland, 1958.

Miller, Francis Trevelyan, The Photographic History of The Civil War, 10 vols., New York, 1911.

Milton, George Fort, The Eve of Conflict, Boston, 1934.

Mitchell, Brig. Gen. William A., Outlines of the World's Military History, Harrisburg, 1940.

Molloy, Robert, Charleston, A Gracious Heritage, New York, 1947.

Monaghan, Jay, Civil War on the Western Border 1854-1865, Boston, 1955.

Monroe, Col. J. Albert, The Rhode Island Artillery at the First Battle of Bull Run, Personal Narratives of the Battles of the Rebellion Being Papers Read before the Rhode Island Soldiers and Sailors Historical Society, No. 1, Providence, 1878.

Mooney, Chase C., Some Institutional and Statistical Aspects of Slavery in Tennessee, Tennessee Historical Quarterly, Vol. I, Nevins' Notes.

Moore, Frank, The Rebellion Record; A Diary of American Events, 11 vols. and supplement, New York, 1861-1868.

Moore, Glover, The Missouri Controversy 1819-1820, Lexington, 1953.

Moore, John C., Missouri, Confederate Military History, Atlanta, Georgia, 1899.

Morris, R. B., Encyclopedia of American History, New York, 1953.

Morse, John T., Jr., Abraham Lincoln, two vols., Boston, 1924.

Morse, John T., Jr., John Quincy Adams, Boston, 1890.

Morse, Samuel Finley Breese, Imminent Dangers to the Institutions of the United States Through Foreign Immigration, and the Present State of the Naturalization Laws, New York, 1854.

Mosby, John S., The Memoirs of Colonel John S. Mosby, edited by Charles Wells Russell, Bloomington, Indiana, 1958.

Naser, Elias, The Life and Times of Charles Sumner, Boston, 1874.

The National Almanac and Annual Record for the Year 1863, Philadelphia, 1863.

Native American, The: A Gift for the People, Philadelphia, 1845.

Nevins, Allan and Commager, H. S., The Pocket History of the United States, New York, 1951.

Nevins, Allan, The Emergence of Lincoln, two vols., New York, 1950.

Nevins, Allan, He Did Hold Lincoln's Hat, American Heritage, Vol. X, No. 2.

Nevins, Allan, Ordeal of the Union, two vols., New York, 1947.

Nevins, Allan, The War for the Union, The Improvised War 1861-1862, New York, 1959.

Newman, Ralph and Long, E. B., The Civil War, Volume II,

The Picture Chronicle of the Events, Leaders and Battlefields of the War, New York, 1956.

Nichols, Alice, Bleeding Kansas, New York, 1954.

Nichols, Roy Franklin, The Disruption of American Democracy, New York, 1948.

Nichols, Roy Franklin, The Kansas-Nebraska Act; A Century of Historiography, Mississippi Valley Historical Review, Sept. 1956.

Nicolay, John G., The Outbreak of Rebellion, New York, 1882.

Nicolay, John G., and Hay, John, Abraham Lincoln, A History, ten vols., New York, 1886-1890-1914.

Niles Register, Baltimore, various issues.

O'Brien, J. Emmet, Telegraphing in Battle, The Century Illustrated Monthly, Sept. 1889.

Official Proceedings of the Democratic National Convention, Held in 1860, At Charleston and Baltimore, Cleveland, 1860.

Official Records of the Union and Confederate Navies in the War of the Rebellion, 30 vols., Washington, 1896.

Olmsted, Frederick Law, A Journey in the Seaboard Slave States in the Years 1853-1854 With Remarks on the Economy, New York, 1905.

Overdyke, W. Darrell, The Know-Nothing Party in the South, Baton Rouge, La., 1950.

Owen, William M., In Camp and Battle with the Washington Artillery, Boston, 1885.

Owsley, Frank Lawrence, Plain Folk of the Old South, Baton Rouge, 1949.

Owsley, Frank Lawrence, King Cotton Diplomacy, Chicago, 1931.

Paris, The Comte De Paris, History of the Civil War in America, four vols., Philadelphia, 1876.

Parkman, Francis, Letters of Francis Parkman, edited and with an introduction by Wilbur R. Jacobs, Norman, Okla., 1960.

Parsons, Brev. Maj. Gen. Lewis B., Reports to the War Department, St. Louis, 1867.

Parton, James, General Butler in New Orleans, New York, 1864.

Patterson, James, Unionism and Reconstruction in Tennessee, Chapel Hill, 1934.

Patterson, Robert, A Narrative of the Campaign in the Valley of the Shenandoah, 1861, Philadelphia, 1865.

Peckham, James, Gen. Nathaniel Lyon, and Missouri in 1861, New York, 1866.

Peissner, Elias, The American Question in its National Aspect, New York, 1861.

Perkins, Howard Cecil, Northern Editorials on Secession, New York, 1942.

Perley Poore, Ben, Perley's Reminiscences of Sixty Years in the National Metropolis, Philadelphia, 1886.

Perry, B. F., Biographical Sketches of Eminent American Statesmen, Philadelphia, 1887.

Phillips,. Isaac N., Abraham Lincoln by Some Men Who Knew Him, edited by Paul M. Angle, Chicago, 1950.

Phillips, Ulrich Bonnell, American Negro Slavery, New York, 1918.

Phillips, Ulrich Bonnell, The Course of the South to Secession, New York, 1939.

Phillips, Ulrich Bonnell, The Slavery Issue in Federal Politics, Chapt. VII, Vol. IV, The South in the Building of the Nation, Richmond, 1909.

Phillips, William, The Conquest of Kansas by Missouri and Her Allies, Boston, 1856.

Phisterer, Frederick, Statistical Record of the Armies of the United States, New York, 1883.

Piatt, Donn, Memories of the Men Who Saved the Union, New York, 1887.

Pike, J. S., First Blows of the Civil War, New York, 1879.

Political Debates Between Hon. Abraham Lincoln and Hon. Stephen A. Douglas, In the Celebrated Campaign of 1858, in Illinois, Columbus, 1860.

Polk, James K., The Diary of, edited by Milo M. Quaife, Chicago, 1910.

Polk, William, The Hated Helper, South Atlantic Quarterly, Vol. 30, 1931.

Pollard, Edward A., The First Year of the War, Richmond, 1862.

Pollard, Edward A., Jefferson Davis, Philadelphia, 1869.

Pollard, Edward A., Robert E. Lee and His Lieutenants, New York, 1867.

Porter, David D., The Naval History of the Civil War, New York, 1886.

Porter, David D., The Opening of the Lower Mississippi, Battles and Leaders of the Civil War.

Porter, General Horace, Campaigning with Grant, New York, 1897.

Porter, James D., Tennessee, Vol. VII, Conf. Military History, Atlanta, Ga., 1899.

Potter, David M., Lincoln and His Party in the Secession Crisis, New York, 1942.

Potter, E. B., editor, The United States and World Sea Power, Englewood Cliffs, N.J., 1955.

Powe, James Harrington, Reminiscences and Sketches of Confederate Times, by One Who Lived Through Them, Harriet Powe Lynch (editor), Columbia, S.C., 1909.

Powell, Edward Payson, Nullification and Secession in the United States, New York, 1897.

Pratt, Harry E., Abraham Lincoln Chronology, Springfield, 1953.

Pressly, Thomas J., Americans Interpret Their Civil War, Princeton, N.J., 1954.

Price, Dr. Henry M., Rich Mountain in 1861, Southern Historical Society Papers, Vol. XXVII, 1899.

Procter, Addison G., Lincoln and the Convention of 1860, An Address before the Chicago Historical Society, April 4, 1918, Chicago, 1918.

Pryor, Mrs. Roger A., Reminiscences of Peace and War, New York, 1904.

The Pulaski County Historical Review, Vol. V, Number 1, Little Rock, Ark., March 1957.

Putnam, Mrs. Sallie A. (Brock), Richmond During the War; Four Years of Personal Observation, New York, 1867.

Quarles, Benjamin, The Negro in the Civil War, Boston, 1953.

Ramsdell, Charles W., Behind the Lines in the Southern Confederacy, Baton Rouge, 1944.

Ramsdell, Charles W., Lincoln and Fort Sumter, Journal of Southern History, Aug. 1937.

Randall, James G., Civil War and Reconstruction, Boston, 1937.

Randall, James G., Constitutional Problems Under Lincoln, Urbana, 1951.

Randall, James G., Lincoln the President, Springfield to Gettysburg, two vols., New York, 1945.

Randall, James G., When War Came in 1861, Abraham Lincoln Quarterly, March 1940.

Rapp, William, Letter to his father, Newberry Library Bulletin, Chicago, May 1952.

Ray, N. W., Sketch of the Sixth Regiment N.C. State Troops.

Ray, P. Orman, The Convention That Nominated Lincoln, Chicago, 1916.

Ray, P. Orman, The Repeal of the Missouri Compromise, Cleveland, 1909.

Ray, P. Orman, The Genesis of the Kansas-Nebraska Act, Annual Report of the American Historical Association, Washington, 1914.

Reagan, John H., Memoirs With Special Reference to Secession and the Civil War, New York, 1906.

The Rebellion Record; A Diary of American Events, edited by Frank Moore, 11 vols. and supplement, New York, 1862.

Reconstruction, House Report No. 30, 39th Congress, 1st Sess., pt. 2, Washington, 1866.

Redpath, James, Echoes of Harper's Ferry, Boston, 1860.

Reply to the Address of the Native American Convention Assembled at Harrisburg, Pa., Feb. 1845, in a Series of Letters, Philadelphia, 1845.

Report of the Joint Committee on the Conduct of the War, 3 vols., Washington, 1863, and 3 vols., plus two supplements, Washington, 1865.

Report of the Joint Committee on Reconstruction at the First Session Thirty-Ninth Congress, Washington, 1866.

Rhett, R. Barnwell, The Confederate Government at Montgomery, Battles and Leaders of the Civil War.

Rhodes, Elisha H., The First Campaign of the Second Rhode Island Infantry, from Personal Narratives of the Battles of the Rebellion, being papers read before the Rhode Island Soldiers and Sailors Historical Society, Providence, 1887.

Rhodes, James Ford, History of the United States from the Compromise of 1850 to the Final Restoration of Home Rule in the South in 1877, 7 vols., New York, 1892-1906.

Rice, Allen Thorndike, Reminiscences of Abraham Lincoln by Distinguished Men of His Time, New York, 1888.

Richardson, James D., Messages and Papers of the Presidents, 2 vols., Nashville, 1905.

Richardson, James D., Messages and Papers of the Presidents, 20 vols., New York, 1897.

Richardson, Ralph, The Choice of Jefferson Davis as Confederate President, Journal of Mississippi History, July 1955.

Riddle, Albert Gallatin, Recollections of War Times, New York, 1895.

Riley, Gen., Speech of Gen. Riley, edited by Franklin J. Meine, Chicago, 1940.

Roberts, O. M., Texas, Vol. XI, Confederate Military History, Atlanta, Ga., 1899.

Robinson, Charles, The Kansas Conflict, Lawrence, Kan., 1898.

Robinson, William Morrison, Jr., The Confederate Privateers, New Haven, 1928.

Roman, Alfred, The Military Operations of General Beauregard, 2 vols., New York, 1884.

Rombauer, Robert J., The Union Cause in St. Louis in 1861, St. Louis, 1909.

Ropes, John Codman, The Story of the Civil War, 2 vols., New York, 1898.

Ross, Fitzgerald, A Visit to the Cities and Camps of the Confederate States, Edinburgh and London, 1865.

Rowland, Dunbar, History of Mississippi, The Heart of the South, 2 vols., Chicago, 1925.

Rowland, Dunbar, Jefferson Davis, Constitutionalist, His Letters, Papers and Speeches, 10 vols., Jackson, Miss., 1923.

Russell, Don, Lincoln Raises an Army, Lincoln Herald, June, 1948.

Russell, William Howard, My Diary North and South, New York, 1863.

Sanborn, F. B., The Life and Letters of John Brown, Liberator of Kansas and Martyr of Virginia, Boston, 1891.

Sandburg, Carl, The Prairie Years, 2 vols., New York, 1926.

Sandburg, Carl, The War Years, 4 vols., New York, 1939.

Sanger, Donald Bridgman, The Authorship of General Orders Number 29, Transactions of the Illinois State Historical Society for the Year 1933, Springfield, Ill.

Scharf, J. Thomas, History of the Confederate States Navy From Its Organization To The Surrender of Its Last Vessel, New York, 1887.

Schuckers, J. W., The Life and Public Services of Salmon Portland Chase, New York, 1874.

Schurz, Carl, The Reminiscences of Carl Schurz, 3 vols., New York, 1907.

Schurz, Carl, Henry Clay, Boston, 1899.

Schwab, John Christopher, The Confederate States of America 1861-1864; A Financial and Industrial History of the South During the Civil War, New York, 1901.

Scott, Winfield, Memoirs of Lieut.-General Scott, LL.D. Written by Himself, 2 vols., New York, 1864.

Scroggs, Jack B., Arkansas in the Secession Crisis, The Arkansas Historical Quarterly, Autumn 1953.

Sellers, James Lee, The Make-Up of the Early Republican Party, Transactions of the Illinois State Historical Society, Springfield, Ill., 1930.

Semple, Ellen Churchill, American History and its Geographic Conditions, Boston, 1903.

Seward, Frederick W., Seward At Washington, New York, 1891.

Seward, William H., Speech Delivered by William H. Seward, at St. Paul, September 18, 1860, Albany, 1860.

Seward, William H., The Irrepressible Conflict, New York, 1858.

Shanks, Henry T., The Secession Movement in Virginia 1847-1861, Richmond, 1934.

Shannon, Fred Albert, The Organization and Administration of the Union Army 1861-1865, 2 vols., Cleveland, 1928.

Sheahan, James W., The Life of Stephen A. Douglas, New York, 1860.

Sherman, John, Recollections of Forty Years in the House, Senate and Cabinet, 2 vols., Chicago, 1895.

The Sherman Letters; Correspondence Between General and Senator Sherman from 1837 to 1891, edited by Rachel Sherman Thorndike, London, 1894.

Sherman, W. T., Home Letters of General Sherman, edited by M. A. DeWolfe Howe, New York, 1909.

Sherman, William T., Memoirs, 2 vols., New York, 1875.

Shryock, R. H., Georgia and the Union in 1850, Durham, 1926.

Siebert, Wilbur H., The Underground Railroad from Slavery to Freedom, New York, 1899.

Sitterson, Joseph Carlyle, The Secession Movement in North Carolina, Chapel Hill, 1939.

Smith, Edward Conrad, The Borderland in the Civil War, New York, 1927.

Smith, Gustavus W., Generals J. E. Johnston and P. G. T. Beauregard at the Battle of Manassas, New York, 1892.

Smith, D. E. Huger, A Charlestonian's Recollections, Charleston, 1950.

Smith, Theodore Clarke, Parties and Slavery 1850-1859, The American Nation; A History, Vol. 18, New York, 1906.

Smith, William Ernest, The Francis Preston Blair Family in Politics, 2 vols., New York, 1933.

Smith, W. L. G., Life at the South; or "Uncle Tom's Cabin" As It Is, Buffalo, 1852.

Snead, Thomas L., The Fight for Missouri, New York, 1886.

Snead, Thomas L., The First Year of the War in Missouri, Battles and Leaders of the Civil War.

The Soldier in Our Civil War, 2 vols., New York, 1890.

Soley, James Russell, The Blockade and the Cruisers, New York, 1883.

Soley, J. Russell, Early Operations on the Potomac River, Battles and Leaders of the Civil War.

Southern Historical Society Papers, various issues.

Sparks, Edwin Erle, The Lincoln-Douglas Debates of 1858, Springfield, 1908.

Spaulding, Oliver Lyman, Jr., The Bombardment of Fort Sumter, 1861, Washington, 1915.

Spring, Leverett Wilson, Kansas, New York, 1894.

Stampp, Kenneth M., And the War Came, Baton Rouge, 1950.

Stampp, Kenneth M., The Peculiar Institution, New York, 1956.

Stanton, Edwin M., A Page of Political Correspondence, Unpublished Letters of Mr. Stanton to Mr. Buchanan, North American Review, Nov. 1879.

Stanwood, Edward, A History of the Presidency from 1788 to 1897, 2 vols., Boston, 1912.

Statistical Record of the Progress of the United States 1800-1906, Washington, 1906.

Stearns, Rev. E. J., Notes on Uncle Tom's Cabin; Being a Logical Answer to the Allegations and Inferences Against Slavery as an Institution, Philadelphia, 1853.

Stedman, Edmund C., The Battle of Bull Run, New York, 1861.

Steele, Matthew Forney, American Campaigns, 2 vols., Washington, 1951.

Stenberg, Richard R., The Motivation of the Wilmot Proviso, Mississippi Historical Review, March 1932.

Stephen, L., The "Times" on the American War; A Historical Study, London, 1865.

Stephens, Alexander H., A Constitutional View of the Late War between the States, 2 vols., Philadelphia, 1870.

Stevens, Charles Emery, Anthony Burns, A History, Boston, 1856.

Stewart, Rev. A. M., Camp, March and Battle-field; or Three Years and a Half with the Army of the Potomac, Philadelphia, 1865.

Stewart, Lucy Shelton, The Reward of Patriotism, New York, 1930.

Stillwell, Lucille, John Cabell Breckinridge, Caldwell, Idaho, 1936.

Stirling, James, Letters from the Slave States, London, 1857.

Stone, Charles P., Washington on the Eve of the War, Battles and Leaders of the Civil War.

Stovall, Pleasant A., Robert Toombs, New York, 1892.

Stowe, Harriet Beecher, Uncle Tom's Cabin, 2 vols., Boston, 1852.

Stowe, Harriet Beecher, A Key to Uncle Tom's Cabin, Boston, 1853.

Strode, Hudson, Jefferson Davis, American Patriot 1808-1861, New York, 1955.

Strong, George Templeton, The Diary of, 4 vols., New York, 1952.

Stroupe, Henry Smith, The Religious Press in the South Atlantic States, 1802-1865, Doctoral Dissertation, Duke University Library, 1942.

The Battle of Fort Sumter, and First Victory of the Southern Troops, Charleston, 1861.

Swanberg, W. A., First Blood; The Story of Fort Sumter, New York, 1957.

Swiggett, Howard, The Great Man, New York, 1953.

Swinton, William, Campaigns of the Army of the Potomac, New York, 1882.

Syndor, Charles S., The Development of Southern Sectionalism 1819-1848, Baton Rouge, 1948.

Taft, Robert, Review of Bleeding Kansas by Alice Nichols, Mississippi Valley Historical Review, December 1954.

Taylor, Richard, Destruction and Reconstruction, edited by Richard B. Harwell, New York, 1955.

Temple, Oliver P., East Tennessee and the Civil War, Cincinnati, 1899.

Thomas, Benjamin, Abraham Lincoln, New York, 1952.

Ticknor, George, Life, Letters and Journals of George Ticknor, 2 vols., Boston, 1876.

Tilley, John Shipley, Lincoln Takes Command, Chapel Hill, 1941.

Tilley, Nannie M. and Goodwin, Noma Lee, Guide to the Manuscript Collections in the Duke University Library, Durham, N.C., 1947.

Todd, Richard Cecil, Confederate Finance, Athens, Ga., 1954.

Toombs, Robert, Stephens, Alexander H., and Cobb, Howell, The Correspondence of Robert Toombs, Alexander H. Stephens and Howell Cobb, Washington, 1911.

Towle, G. W., Glances from the Senate Gallery, Continental Monthly, July-December, 1862.

Townsend, E. D., Anecdotes of the Civil War in the United States, New York, 1884.

Turner, Frederick Jackson, The Frontier in American History, New York, 1920.

Turner, George Edgar, Victory Rode the Rails; The Strategic Place of the Railroads in the Civil War, Indianapolis, 1953.

Tuttle, Charles R., A New Centennial History of the State of Kansas, Madison, Wis., 1867.

Twain, Mark, The Private History of a Campaign That Failed, Century Magazine, Dec. 1885.

The Union; Being a Condemnation of Mr. Helper's Scheme.

The Union Army, 8 vols., Madison, Wis., 1908.

U. S. Statutes at Large, various volumes.

Upton, Emory, The Military Policy of the United States, Washington, 1912.

Van Deusen, Glyndon G., Thurlow Weed; Wizard of the Lobby, Boston, 1947.

Vandiver, Frank, Mighty Stonewall, New York, 1957.

Vandiver, Frank, Rebel Brass; The Confederate Command System, Baton Rouge, 1956.

Villard, Henry, Lincoln on the Eve of '61, edited by Harold G. and Oswald Garrison Villard, New York, 1941.

Villard, Henry, Memoirs of Henry Villard Journalist and Financier 1835-1900, 2 vols., Boston, 1904.

Villard, Oswald Garrison, John Brown 1800-1859, Boston, 1910.

Vincent, Thomas M., The Battle of Bull Run, July 21, 1861, Military Order of the Loyal Legion of the U. S. Commandery of the District of Columbia, War Paper 58, 1905.

Visitor to Charleston, Atlantic Monthly, April 1861.

Von Abele, Rudolph, Alexander H. Stephens, New York, 1948.

Walker, George, The Wealth, Resources and Public Debt of the United States, London, 1865.

Wallace, Isabel, Life & Letters of General W. H. L. Wallace, Chicago, 1909.

Walpole, Spencer, The Life of Lord John Russell, London, 1889.

The War of the Rebellion; A Compilation of the Official Records of the Union and Confederate Armies, 70 vols. in 128 parts, Washington, 1880-1901, and atlas.

Warder, T. B. and Catlett, Jas. M., Battle of Young's Branch; or, Manassas Plain, Richmond, 1862.

Ware, E. F., The Lyon Campaign in Missouri, Being a History of the First Iowa Infantry, Topeka, Kansas, 1907.

Warren, Charles, The Supreme Court in United States History, 2 vols., 1923.

Warren, Robert Penn, John Brown, The Making of a Martyr, New York, 1929.

Welles, Gideon, Diary of Gideon Welles, 3 vols., Boston, 1909-1911.

Welles, Gideon, Fort Sumter, Galaxy, Nov. 1870.

Welles, Gideon, Lincoln and Seward, New York, 1874.

Welles, Gideon, Nomination and Election of Abraham Lincoln, Galaxy, Sept. 1876.

Wender, Herbert, Southern Commercial Conventions 1837-1859, Baltimore, 1930.

West Virginia, A Guide to the Mountain State, New York, 1941.

Westcott, Thompson, Chronicles of the Great Rebellion, Philadelphia, 1867.

Wheeler, Lieut. Gen. Joseph, Alabama, Vol. VII, Confederate Military History, Atlanta, Georgia, 1899.

White, Laura A., Robert Barnwell Rhett: Father of Secession, New York, 1931.

Whitman, Walt, The Complete Writings of Walt Whitman, 10 vols., New York, 1902.

Whitman, Walt, The Gathering of the Forces, New York, 1920.

Wightman, John T., A Discourse Delivered in the Methodist Episcopal Church, South, Yorkville, S.C., July 28, 1861, the Day of National Thanksgiving for the Victory at Manassas, Portland, Me., 1871.

Wilder, Daniel Webster, The Annals of Kansas, Topeka, 1857.

Wiley, Bell I., The Life of Billy Yank, Indianapolis, 1951, 1952.

Wiley, Bell I., The Life of Johnny Reb, Indianapolis, 1943.

Wiley, Bell Irvin, The Plain People of the Confederacy, Baton Rouge, 1944.

Wiley, Bell Irvin, Southern Negroes 1861-1865, New York, 1938.

Wilkes, George, The Great Battle, New York, 1861.

Willey, William P., An Inside View of the Formation of the State of West Virginia, Wheeling, West Virginia, 1901.

Williams, K. P., Lincoln Finds a General, 5 vols., New York, 1949.

Williams, T. Harry, Lincoln and His Generals, New York, 1952.

Williams, T. Harry, P. G. T. Beauregard, Napoleon in Gray, Baton Rouge, 1954.

Williams, T. Harry, With Beauregard in Mexico, Baton Rouge, 1950.

Wilshin, Francis F., Manassas National Battlefield Park, Washington, D.C., 1953.

Wilson, Hill Peebles, John Brown, Soldier of Fortune, A Critique, Boston, 1913.

Wilson, James Harrison, Under the Old Flag, 2 vols., New York, 1912.

Wilson, Rufus Rockwell, Intimate Memories of Lincoln, Elmira, N.Y., 1945.

Wilson, Woodrow, Division and Reunion, New York, 1912.

Wiltse, Charles M., John C. Calhoun; Nullifier, 1829-1839, Indianapolis, 1949.

Winthrop, Theodore, The New York Seventh Regiment, Our March to Washington, Atlantic Monthly, June 1861.

Wise, John S., The End of an Era, Boston, 1901.

Wolfe, Samuel M., Helper's Impending Crisis Dissected, Philadelphia, 1860.

Wood, Robert C., Confederate Hand-Book, New Orleans, 1900.

Woodburn, James A., The Historical Significance of the Missouri Compromise, Washington, 1893.

Worley, Ted R., editor, At Home in Confederate Arkansas, Letters to and from Pulaski Counties, 1861-1865, Little Rock, Ark., 1955.

Worley, Ted R., The Arkansas Peace Society of 1861; A Study in Mountain Unionism, Journal of Southern History, Nov. 1958.

Worth, Jonathan, The Correspondence of Jonathan Worth, edited by J. G. de Roulhac Hamilton, 2 vols., Raleigh, 1902.

Wright, Crafts J., Official Journal of the Conference Convention, Held at Washington City, February 1861, Washington, 1861.

Wright, Mrs. D. Giraud, A Southern Girl in '61, New York, 1905.

Wythe, John Allen, With Sabre and Scalpel, New York, 1914.

Yancey, William L., Speech of the Hon. William L. Yancey of Alabama, Delivered in the National Democratic Convention, 1860.

Acknowledgments

The co-operation and friendship of hundreds of persons and institutions has been extended to those involved in preparing this Centennial History of the Civil War.

The discussions that led to the writing of the history began at *The New York Times,* where the role of John Desmond deserves special mention.

Allan Nevins, of the Huntington Library, San Marino, California, supplied many aids and comforts, particularly in contributing his own research notes gathered from more than thirty years of work and travel. Professor Nevins read the manuscript as well.

Advance readers whose comment and correction were especially useful were Professor Avery Craven, William B. Hesseltine, Willard Webb, T. Harry Williams.

Ralph Newman brought Mr. Catton and Mr. Long together and has been a steady source of information and support.

Others who helped in *The Coming Fury*, Volume One of the history, include:

Edwin C. Bearss, Vicksburg, Miss.; Elden E. Billings, Washington, D.C.; Ray Billington, Evanston, Ill.; Robert Bruce, Reading, Mass.; Avery Craven, Chesterton, Ind.; Mrs. William Hunter de Butts, Upperville, Va., for permission to use certain papers of R. E. Lee; Mrs. Henry Clinton de Rham, Garrison on Hudson, New York, for permission to use various manuscripts; Raymond Dooley, Lincoln, Ill.; Charles Dufour, New Orleans, La.; Joseph T. Durkin, S.J., Washington, D.C.; Joseph L. Eisendrath, Jr., Highland Park, Ill.; Otto Eisenschiml, Chicago, Ill.; O. H. Felton, Lyons, Ill.; Arnold Gates, Garden City, N.Y.; C. P. Gehman, Denver, Colo.; Richard Harwell, Chicago, Ill.; Carl Haverlin, New York, N.Y.; William B. Hesseltine, Madison, Wis.; Stanley F. Horn, Nashville, Tenn.; John Hunter, Madison, Wis.; J. Ambler Johnston, Richmond, Va.; Virgil Carrington Jones, Washington, D.C.; Allen P. Julian, Atlanta, Ga.; Harnett Kane, New Orleans, La.; T. S. Kennedy, Pensacola, Fla., for use of the S. A. Mallory Papers; Frederick Klein, Lancaster, Pa.; Mrs. Katharine McCook Knox, Washington, D.C., for use of her family papers; Rabbi Bertram W. Korn, Philadelphia, Pa.; Ralston B. Lattimore, Savannah, Ga.; Charles McKnight, Fork, Md.; Franklin J. Meine, Chicago, Ill.; Earl Schenck Miers, Edison, N.J.; Mrs. Raymond Millbrook, Detroit, Mich.; Mr. and Mrs. Lewis C. Murtaugh, Winnetka, Ill., for contributing useful volumes to the research library; Harry E. Pratt, Springfield, Ill., and Mrs. Pratt; William Price, Arlington, Va.; Rep. Fred Schwengel, Washington, D.C.; J. Gay Seabourne, Washington, D.C.; Bert Sheldon, Washington, D.C.; John Y. Simon, Cambridge, Mass.; Philip Van Doren Stern, Brooklyn, N.Y.; S. K. Stevens, Harrisburg, Pa.; Samuel G. Stoney, Charleston, S. C.; Benjamin P. Thomas, Springfield, Ill.; Gilbert Twiss, Chicago, Ill.; Kenneth Urquhart, New Orleans, La.; Frank E. Vandiver, Houston, Tex.; Ezra J. Warner, La Jolla, Calif.; Bell I. Wiley, Emory, Ga.; K. P. Williams, Bloomington, Ind.

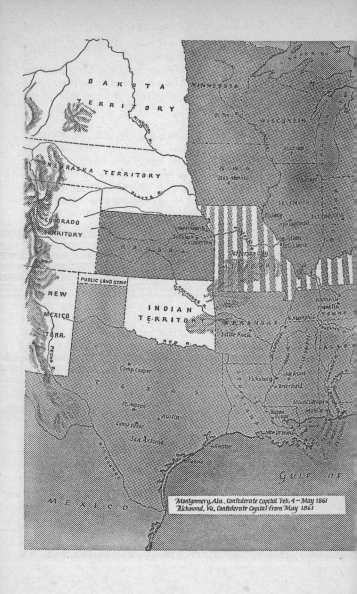

Montgomery, Ala., Confederate Capital Feb. 4 – May 1861
Richmond, Va., Confederate Capital from May 1861

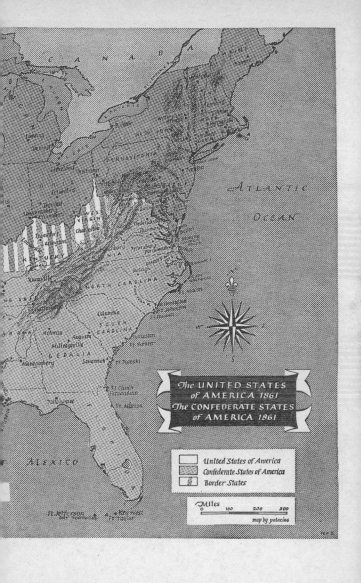

CANADA

ATLANTIC

OCEAN

The UNITED STATES
of AMERICA 1861
The CONFEDERATE STATES
of AMERICA 1861

United States of America
Confederate States of America
Border States

Miles
0   100   200   300

map by palacios

Index

Index

575